To Dad

Lots of Love

from Catriona & Dermot (Dec 1998)

A Test of Time

Volume Two

Legend
The Genesis of Civilisation

A Test of Time
Volume Two

Legend

The Genesis of Civilisation

by

David M. Rohl

C

CENTURY

1 3 5 7 9 10 8 6 4 2

David Rohl has asserted his right under the Copyright,
Designs and Patents Act, 1988, to be identified as the
author of this work.

This book is sold subject to the condition that it shall not, by way
of trade or otherwise, be lent, resold, hired out, or otherwise circu-
lated without the publisher's prior consent in any form of binding
or cover other than that in which it is published and without a
similar condition including this condition being imposed on the
subsequent purchaser.

First published in the United Kingdom in 1998 by Century,
Random House UK Ltd., 20 Vauxhall Bridge Road, London, SW1V 2SA

Random House Australia (Pty) Limited
20 Alfred Street, Milsons Point, Sydney,
New South Wales 2061, Australia

Random House New Zealand Limited
18 Poland Road, Glenfield
Auckland 10, New Zealand

Random House South Africa (Pty) Limited
Endilini, 5a Jubilee Road
Parktown 2193, South Africa

Random House UK Limited Reg. No. 954009

A CIP catalogue record for this book
is available from the British Library

Papers used by the Random House UK Ltd are natural, recyclable
products made from wood grown in sustainable forests. The
manufacturing processes conform to the environmental regulations
of the country of origin.

ISBN 0 7126 7747 X

Subject classification: 1. Archaeology. 2. Ancient History. 3. Bible Studies.

Typeset by Ditas Rohl
Printed and bound in the United Kingdom by
Butler & Tanner Ltd,
Frome and London

For my mother
Freda Kingsford Rohl
1912-1981

Contents

Part One

From the Mists of Time

Part Two

The Mighty Heroes

Part Four

Reference Section

He was superior to other kings – a warrior-lord of great stature – a
hero born in Uruk – a goring wild bull.

Gilgamesh Epic, Tablet I

1. Opposite page: A fragment of a Nakada III (late predynastic) slate palette depicting the king as a wild bull goring his enemies. Louvre Museum

2. Left: One of Hans Winkler's sketches of the high-prowed boats (this one from Site 15) discovered during his Eastern Desert survey of 1936.

PREFACE

The cold grey of the pre-dawn still enveloped the vast, sandy plain as I clambered, half asleep, from the tent. It had been a cold night and the air felt damp to the touch. The sandy dune, upon which our desert expedition base-camp had been established, sloped away to the north-east. Fifty metres below it merged imperceptibly into the floor of the Wadi el-Kash, stretching out towards the dark horizon of the surrounding mountain peaks.

I could make out the shadowy figures of other members of the Eastern Desert survey team huddled around the breakfast table clasping their mugs of steaming tea. I headed off up a narrow cleft in the rock behind the camp to reach the summit of a rocky hill which afforded a commanding panorama of the desert. By the time I had reached the highest point the dawn glow was intensifying on the eastern horizon.

Today was going to be a big day in my life. With a bit of luck and some not inconsiderable trust in my GPS satellite navigation system we would finally reach the WADI ABU MARAKAT EL-NES (formerly WADI ABU WASIL) and Winkler's long-lost 'Site 26' – the mysterious valley of the boat-people.

This was my third attempt at reaching the lost valley of the boats. The German ethnographer and explorer, Hans WINKLER, came across it in the winter of 1936-37 but had left only a few photographs and sketches of what he was able to observe. These are to be found in his preliminary report for the Robert Mond Desert Expedition, published in 1938. This is the sum total of what Winkler has to say about Site 26 in that report.

3. The Eastern Desert. One of the expedition jeeps (centre of picture) heads off to recce the route ahead.

> Site 26: Wadi Abu Wasil. Large wadi running east to west with good vegetation, bordered with sandstone cliffs, walls, and shelters. Like Site 24H it is near the edge where the sandstone touches the igneous mountains. It seems that this situation produced here and there well-watered fertile valleys, so that it attracted early men.

WADI ABU MARAKAT EL-NES: Valley of the 'Father of the Boat-People'.

WADI ABU WASIL: Valley of the 'Father of Wasil'.

WINKLER: (1900-1945).

1

BLEMYAN: Belonging to the desert dwellers from Syria who lived during the era which immediately followed the collapse of the Roman Empire.

WUSUM: The stone-carved writings of the Nabateans.

Geometrical designs. – Elephants, giraffe, asses, ibexes, ostriches, crocodile; cattle, dogs. Boats, some towed. Men with bows, man with club, men with lassoes, dancers. Ancient signs. – BLEMYAN signs, camels. – Arab WUSUM, camels, fighting men. – Some potsherds, implements of flint and quartz. Tombs?[1]

In less than one hundred words he describes one of the most magical places on earth. Here in a desert valley located 100 kilometres from human activity (in any direction) was evidence of a people who had sojourned in this place more than five thousand years ago. But these were not ordinary desert nomads or beduin pastoralists. The evidence of Winkler's photographs and drawings reveals god-like figures carried in high-prowed ships. Upon their heads stand tall plumes. They are armed with pear-shaped maces and bows. A 'goddess', hands raised above her head, seems to be performing a sacred dance. One high-prowed boat is pulled along by five figures grasping a rope tied to the prow of the vessel. It is as if the funeral barque of a dead pharaoh is being dragged through the seven gates of the underworld to reach his resurrection in the sacred Isle of Flame on the eastern horizon.

All this is to be gleaned from Winkler's brief report and accompanying plates – yet nobody has been back to re-record the inscriptions of the valley since Winkler's day. Indeed, no-one has been able to find Site 26 because no accurate location had been supplied by its discoverer. All that scholars have to guide them to the spot is an ink blob, a kilometre wide, on an out-of-date map at a scale of 1:500,000 – a map which bears little resemblance to modern cartography of the region.

As I said, I had tried twice to find Site 26 in 1997 – once from the north via Wadi Hammamat, entering Wadi el-Kash at the oasis of Lakeita, and once from the south, setting out from the rock-cut temple of Kanais in the Wadi Abbad and striking north through the mountains to Gebel es-Shalul. Neither attempt had been successful. The first ended in

4. The Wadi el-Kash just before dawn.

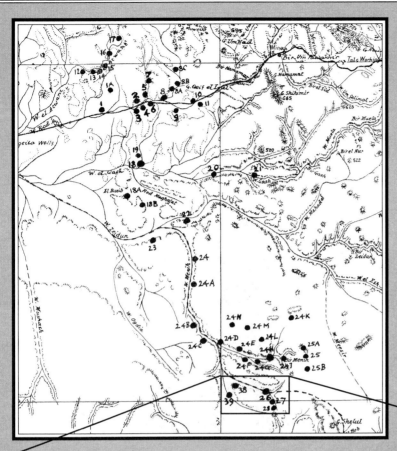

5. The left map is part of the pre-war 1:500,000 survey of the Eastern Desert used by Hans Winkler to mark his rock-art sites. Below is a tiny fragment of Winkler's map (around the location of Site 26) as it appears today in the much more accurate and detailed 1:50,000 survey maps. Seeing the two maps together gives a rather good impression of the difficulties which we encountered in trying to locate Winkler's sites using the latest maps but without the assistance of the local beduin (much less in evidence since Winkler's day). In spite of this slight handicap, we were able to pinpoint Winkler's Site 26 for the benefit of future scholarship and research. The GPS co-ordinates are:

25.31.49 north
33.35.28 east

A catalogue of the Eastern Desert sites will be published by ISIS in the year 2000.

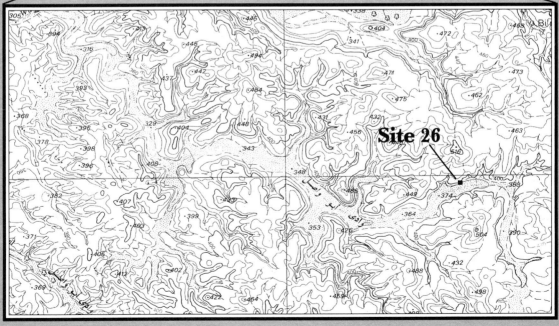

Site 26

frustration and confusion as a small team in a single vehicle got completely lost in the maze of wadi openings of the complex el-Kash drainage system. The second – a much more serious attempt with a fleet of four-wheel-drive vehicles, GPS and a collection of 1:50,000 maps – got within a few kilometres of the putative site but also came to grief. This time we were thwarted by a thirty-metre-high sand-dune which stretched across the narrow wadi leading to our target. It was far too steep to take the vehicles over and the distance beyond was simply too great on foot. A further attempt, made the following day, also led to failure as the expedition tried to reach Site 26 through the Wadi Mineh to the south-east. This time we were halted by a rock-fall which had completely blocked the canyon during a flash-flood some years earlier. Now, in this third and final effort, we were trying the northern route once again – but this time with all the necessary navigation equipment and back-up to ensure that we reached our target – subject, of course, to no new, unforeseen barriers.

As I stood on that rocky outcrop looking east towards the sunrise, all sorts of questions were running through my mind. Would I make it this time? Had I got the right location for Site 26 on my modern and much more detailed maps? The terrain was very complex. There was even a whisper going around the expedition team that Herr Winkler had made the whole thing up, having spent most of the 1936-37 season in the billiards bar of the Winter Palace Hotel in Luxor. But joking aside, could Winkler somehow have made a mistake when drawing up his map of the sites for the later publication? Had he marked Site 26 in the wrong place? Was this why nobody had been able to repeat his mission to the valley of the PREDYNASTIC boat-people? Or was it simply too hard to reach?

I stood there pondering the day's fate as the red sun-disk began to emerge from behind the black mountains. Within a couple of minutes the whole form of RE-HARAKHTY was visible in an orange sky and the grey plain turned to golden brown. I headed back down from the crag to find breakfast on the go and the camp buzzing with activity.

Half an hour later three Toyota Land Cruisers were roaring off down the dune and swinging east towards the sunrise. We soon swept past the ruins of the Roman fort of Daydamus and headed south into the mouth of the Wadi Mineh. On the previous expedition we had entered this wadi from the south and been thwarted by the rock-fall. This time the northern mouth of the wadi was wide and flat with no major obstructions. We sped along, the dust billowing up behind us.

It was not long before the survey team had its first confirmation that Hans Winkler had really been here sixty years before. A rocky spur on the west side of the wadi showed signs of human activity around its base. The sand was littered with broken potsherds. Then we spotted our first rock-drawings. This was a great moment because now we knew we were following in Winkler's camel tracks, for on his original map he had marked this place as 'Site 24B'.

6. Opposite page: Setting off for Site 26, our convoy heads into the Wadi Mineh.

GPS: Geographical Positioning Satellite.

PREDYNASTIC: The era before the unification of Egypt under the 1st Dynasty.

RE-HARAKHTY: 'The sun (Re) and the falcon (Horus) of the horizon'.

7. Waiting for sunrise.

Site 24B. Wadi Mineh. West side, opposite the entrance to the Wadi Mineh el-Her. Cave-like shelter. Full shadow all day. Ancient roads follow the Wadi Mineh as well as the Wadi Mineh el-Her. Favourite resting-place.

Giraffe, asses, ibexes. Boats. In one boat stands a woman with upraised arms. Men, archer, dancers. – Hieroglyphic inscriptions, boat, Min. – Greek, Latin, Himyaritic and Nabataean inscriptions, sailing-boat, cattle, Blemyan signs. – Some flints and late potsherds on the surface.[2]

8. The Horus falcon of Site 24B perched on the prow of a ship. The style of the vessel and the more refined cutting technique suggests a 1st Dynasty date for this graffito. However, it is cut into the same rock-face as a number of obviously predynastic boats. This association may indicate a link between the royal 'Followers of Horus' and their ancestors – the original 'Followers of Horus' who were responsible for the earlier rock-art of the high-prowed boats.

His description of the rock-art corresponded exactly to what we could see. But even more exciting was something which Winkler had failed to mention in his report. Here on the smooth face of the cliff immediately in front of us was the outline of a large high-prowed ship and on its prow stood one of the most characteristic emblems of the earliest pharaohs – the Horus falcon. No falcon totem had been previously recorded on the desert ships. At last here was a clear iconographic link between the people of the high-prowed boats and the Followers of Horus – the predynastic and protodynastic kings. We took our photos and headed on down the narrowing throat of the Wadi Mineh in search of a fork in the canyon.

Four kilometres further on and the three white Land Cruisers turned west and left the Wadi Mineh behind. Now we were in a very rocky terrain with no obvious route through. We threaded our way into the landscape searching for the entrance to the Wadi Abu Marakat el-Nes which finally revealed itself after several stops to check our position on the GPS and maps. Unfortunately this wadi bore little resemblance to Winkler's 'well-watered' valley with 'good vegetation'. This was barren and lifeless – just a rock-strewn gorge winding its way south, ever deeper into the sandstone massif. Still, we were not of a mind to turn back just yet. Perhaps the terrain would change a little further in. We pressed on.

An hour later, after tortuously slow progress, the expedition found itself at the head of a wide valley covered in green brush, its sides rising sharply upwards. There were snakes everywhere. At this point we really should have turned around and left the local wildlife to its own devices but I had a determined bunch of explorers with me and they were in no mood to retreat.

I despatched one vehicle to each side of the wadi to look for rock inscriptions as my own team of keen-eyed spotters went on ahead. Then, quite suddenly, Site 26 loomed up before us – a cliff-face smothered in wonderful rock-art. At that same instant messages were crackling through on my walkie-talkie from all sides of the valley. The teams in vehicles two and three had also discovered drawings at their locations. The boat-people were everywhere.

We spent a good two hours clambering cautiously over the cliffs, watching for movement in the scrub, taking photographs and noting the co-ordinates and orientations of the main carvings.

9. Opposite page: The main rock-face of Site 26.

This was clearly an archaeological site of major importance which I believe has a great deal to reveal about the early history of Egypt. Site 26 seems to have been a crucial watering-hole in predynastic times – a location (perhaps even with a small lake) which afforded shelter and water for desert travellers journeying to and from the Nile valley and the Red Sea coast. Who those late-fourth-millennium-BC travellers were you will eventually discover as we go in search of a much more elusive goal than Site 26.

The reason why I was so keen to rediscover the lost valley of the boats lies at the heart of the book you are about to read. It is a book which attempts to tell the historical story behind what is sometimes referred to as the 'genesis of civilisation'.

This is the story of one people and two distant lands, separated by a long sea voyage. We are going to retrace an epic journey which originally took several millennia to complete. Our voyage of discovery begins on the snow-capped peak of the Mountain of God, looking down on the Garden of Eden, and ends in the lush valley of the Nile where pharaonic civilisation came into existence. The original journey took place in truly ancient times – beyond the Pyramid Age, beyond the Unification of Egypt under King Menes. The Egyptians themselves called this legendary era the 'First Time'. It lay at the beginning of memory, when the acts of men were later to become the mythical deeds of gods. But even from this hoary age there are still historical clues for us to unearth – so long as eyes are open and hearts willing.

The high-prowed boats of the lost valley and their precious cargo are a part of this story – however, they are not from its beginning. The people of the high-prowed boats were the last generation of the prehistoric age. Just like me they had once climbed a rocky hill to watch the desert sunrise – but, unlike me, they were witnessing the dawn of history.

10. Opposite page (above): Close-up of the main rock-face at Site 26 showing, on the left, a large boat containing five figures with plumes (the two largest figures carrying bows). A smaller boat is located to the right with a large, twin-plumed figure floating above it. Higher up the rock wall is a third boat in which stands a chieftain carrying a throw-stick.

11. Opposite page (below left): 'Mace Man' in his high-prowed boat with animal's head prow. This carving is to be found on the opposite side of the wadi to the main Site 26 cliff-face.

12. Opposite page (below right): 'The Predynastic Punk', located one hundred metres east of Site 26 on the same side of the wadi.

13. Winkler's original sketch of the scene (below) from Site 26.

14. The rock beneath the main Site 26 cliff-face upon which is a scene of a boat carrying a dancing goddess with twin plumes. The boat is being dragged by five figures.

Now the earth was without form and there was darkness over the deep with a divine wind sweeping over the waters. God said, 'Let there be light' and there was light.

Genesis 1:2-3

INTRODUCTION

15. Opposite page: Gustave Doré's (1833-1883) image of the creation.

16. Above: The distant pyramids of Giza.

egend is a powerful word. It tends to conjure up images of mythological creatures and battling heroes – a world in which the supernatural predominates over the mundane. You might be tempted, therefore, to regard all legends as pure fantasy – but you would be wrong.

The word 'legend' derives from medieval Latin *legenda* meaning 'things to be read'. Its sense, within the English language, can be defined as:

> A popular story handed down from earlier times whose truth has not been ascertained.[1]

In other words, a legend is not fiction – the unfounded invention of the fertile mind – but rather a traditional oral or written history which has not *yet* been confirmed by science, historical argument or archaeology. The important thing is that, at its core, there is a basic belief, on the part of the storyteller, that the events being described were real. The quality of the narrative may often be elaborate and fantastical but the bones of the tale are understood to be genuine relics from a distant past.

The same cannot be said for legend's sister word 'myth' which comes from Greek *muthos* meaning 'fable'. The *Shorter Oxford English Dictionary* defines 'myth' as:

17. Griffin pillar capital from the royal palace of the Persian kings at Persepolis.

> A purely fictitious narrative usually involving supernatural persons, actions, or events, and embodying some popular idea concerning natural or historical phenomena.[2]

So there is a subtle but all important difference between the concepts of legend and myth. This book, bearing the former of these two words as

11

MESOPOTAMIA: The land 'between the two rivers' Tigris and Euphrates, i.e. modern Iraq.

18. A legendary hero with lion-cub. From the palace of Sargon II of Assyria at Khorsabad. Louvre Museum.

its title, sets out to demonstrate that humanity's most famous collection of legends are, in fact, far from being mere myths. Hidden beneath the poetic veil of the ancient storyteller is a great deal more genuine history than has previously been assumed.

The new millennium is a little over a year away and, justified or not, we all feel a palpable sense of the momentous – a prospect of real history in the making. Two thousand years ago there were great expectations amongst the Jews of Palestine that the Messiah was soon to appear. The coming of the saviour would usher in a new golden age and release the oppressed people of the Promised Land from the shackles of Roman rule. One thousand years later, on the eve of the second millennium, a huge crowd of Christians gathered before St. Peter's Roman basilica in the belief that their world was about to end. Over the centuries since that famous non-event various prophets of doom have predicted a similar fate for humankind as we approach the start of the third millennium since the birth of Christ. Hardly surprising, then, that the esoteric 'arts' and 'sciences' are thriving in the expectant atmosphere of the 1990s.

It is at times like these that people naturally feel a greater affinity with their past whilst, at the same time, intensifying the search for answers to the great questions of life and faith.

Many of those fundamental questions lead us back into the dark and confusing world of our primeval roots – a place inhabited by that rarest of academic species – the prehistorian. This strange, hybrid creature is part anthropologist, part mythologist, part archaeologist – a reader of epic literature and a scholar of comparative linguistics. But, above all, the prehistorian is driven by an overwhelming need to find answers to questions concerning our origins. Where and how did 'civilised Man' originate? When and why did primitive society abandon its hunter-gatherer existence for sedentary agricultural life? How did the first great cities come into being? What was the spark which ignited the flames of those most astonishing of early civilisations in MESOPOTAMIA and the Nile valley? And what was the role of 'God' in all this?

In effect, all these weighty matters prompt one basic question: After more than 2,000 years of scholarly research since HERODOTUS wrote the world's first history book, what do we *really* know about the genesis of civilisation? The short answer is 'virtually nothing'.

Of course, at one time the Judaeo-Christian world had a well-thumbed guide book with its own set of answers but, in recent years, the reputation of that primary source document as history has become somewhat tarnished by the application of science and logic. Academia has passed its judgement on the early biblical stories – the accounts of the primeval age of Man, as described in the book of Genesis, are nothing more than myths.

From Myth to History?

The fashion amongst biblical scholars of the twentieth century has been to date the composition of the Old Testament narratives as late as possible. In doing so, the texts end up so remote in time from the events they purport to describe that they take on the appearance of mythological accounts – fascinating literature in their own right but certainly not history.

My approach is somewhat different. Although I accept in principle that the final form of the biblical narratives may be late in date, this does not, in my view, mean that all the tales are the inventions of the redactor/ editor of that final composition. Much earlier historical information may still exist to be excavated from the confused remains. All that is needed is an open mind, patience, a wide interdisciplinary approach and a true sense of the epic nature of our ancient past.

In Volume One of *A Test of Time* I opened the *Introduction* with a quote from Professor Thomas L. Thompson of Copenhagen University – the great sceptic of the historical approach to biblical studies. His view that the Old Testament contains no real history – even for the United Monarchy Period of David and Solomon – is not widely supported by his academic colleagues. But if we were to ask those same scholars how far back we might go beyond the Israelite Monarchy Period in search of history, the answer would be 'not very far'. Some archaeologists would be prepared to accept that there is a skeleton of anthropological history in the Judges Period, whilst others (principally biblical historians) will even argue for an historical setting for the sojourn of the proto-Israelites in Egypt. But this would be stretching things just about as far as academic credibility could permit.

The major contribution of Volume One in the *A Test of Time* series was to demonstrate that the stories related in the second half of the book of Genesis do have a basis in historical reality. I showed that there *is* archaeological evidence for the Israelite sojourn in Egypt but in a different time period to what had previously been expected. These arguments were controversial enough, but now I am engaged in a search for historical evidence to illuminate the biblical stories of an even earlier epoch.

19. A seated statuette of a pious Sumerian official belonging to the temple of Ishtar at Mari named Ebih-il. Early Dynastic III Period. Louvre Museum.

20. The Akkadian creator-god, Ea (Sumerian Enki), with the life-giving sweet water gushing from his shoulders. Private collection of the Biblisches Institut, Fribourg University.

HERODOTUS: A Greek historian of the 5th century BC.

21. One of the many fierce lion images in decorative tiles from the palace of Darius I at Susa. Louvre Museum.

So, should we automatically assume that the stories of Eden, the Great Flood, the Tower of Babel and the dispersion of the nations, as described in the first chapters in the book of Genesis, are little more than fascinating myths?

By definition history begins with the first written records, for without records there is no [hi]story of Man's cultural and political progress. As a corollary, the era before the introduction of writing must therefore be 'prehistoric', even though what we might otherwise define as historical events will have occurred in these early times. The simple fact is that those events, however important to human development, have come down to us through snippets of oral tradition and only subsequently recorded in written sources – some of them thousands of years after the events concerned.

Most scholars would include the biblical book of Genesis in that category of documents which has evolved from a much earlier oral tradition. This second volume in the *A Test of Time* series has been given the subtitle *The Genesis of Civilisation* because it takes us all the way back to the beginning of the Bible narrative – the dawn of primeval history during which the birth of civilisation took place. It is a book about an epic journey of discovery and the story of the people who made that journey.

Genesis is a Greek word which means 'origins'. The familiar title of the first book of the Bible thus comes down to us through the SEPTUAGINT (or LXX) – the Greek translation of the Hebrew scriptures, written in third-century-BC Alexandria. However, the first book of the Hebrew (MASORETIC) Bible is headed by a quite different word – *Bereshit* – which literally means 'In the beginning'. The original title of the work thus follows the ancient Mesopotamian practice of naming a literary text by the first words of the narrative on a clay tablet.

In the beginning God created heaven and earth. [Genesis 1:1]

This in itself is an argument for a written version of the story which, in one form or another, stretches a considerable way back into antiquity.

The idea that the book of Genesis may have been edited or reworked in much later times – as is the current view – does not disprove its original authorship by an earlier Israelite patriarch – perhaps even Moses himself – who may have recovered the stories from an even older corpus of documentary sources. Moreover, some of those original sources *may* have originated in early Mesopotamia from where Moses' ancestor, Abraham, had come centuries before the Exodus. Occasional references to a great flood and the subsequent confusion of tongues do exist in ancient tablets from Assyria and Babylonia. That some ANTEDILUVIAN documents (or at least later copies dealing with this pre-flood period) also existed in ancient times is confirmed by a statement from the Assyrian king, ASHURBANIPAL,

SEPTUAGINT: The Greek translation of the Old Testament (written in 3rd-century-BC Alexandria).

MASORETIC: Belonging to the Hebrew version of the early scriptures (thought to have been compiled in the 5th century AD from earlier scrolls).

ANTEDILUVIAN: Before the flood.

ASHURBANIPAL: King of Assyria, reigned 668-626 BC.

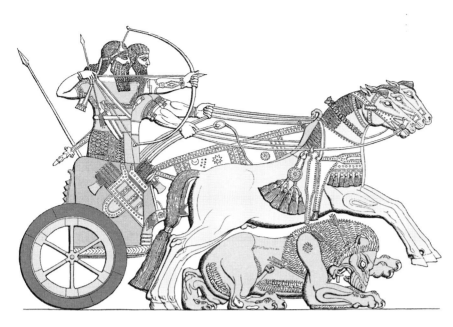

22. Line drawing of a relief from the state apartments of the royal palace at Nimrud (ancient Kalhu). King Ashurnasirpal II (883-859 BC) is depicted riding in his chariot over a fallen lion in its death throes. The slab was discovered by Layard in 1845 and is now on display in the British Museum.

CUNEIFORM: The wedge-shaped writing of Mesopotamia.

NINEVEH: The site of modern Kuyunjik by the banks of the River Tigris near Mosul.

AKKADIAN: The East-Semitic language of Mesopotamia.

SUMEROLOGISTS: Scholars who specialise in the history and culture of ancient Sumer.

who kept a great library of CUNEIFORM texts in his palace at NINEVEH. On a large tablet now in the British Museum (K-3050 & K-2964) he claims:

> I have read the artistic script of Sumer and the dark obscure AKKADIAN, which is hard to master (and I now) take pleasure in the reading of **the stone inscriptions from before the flood**.[3]

23. A temple devotee from early Mesopotamia carrying a lamb for sacrifice and wearing a long sheep's-wool coat. Louvre Museum.

So, there is absolutely no doubt that the people of Mesopotamia had a strong and persistent tradition relating to a catastrophic deluge which had swept over the land in very ancient times, and it seems that a few texts claiming to be from the period before this cataclysm still existed in the seventh century BC.

Changing Tack

In the past, it has often been the case that SUMEROLOGISTS have used archaeological and literary evidence from their own discipline in an attempt to throw new light on the early biblical tradition. But what if we try to work things the other way around? What if the book of Genesis can provide some of the answers archaeologists seek in their quest to understand the origins of civilisation? What if the Bible has, all along, carried the story of the genesis not only of the Israelite people but also of the Sumerian and even Egyptian civilisations? Perhaps we have simply misheard the message because we have been confused by all the background noise – what some might call the fantastical or miraculous elements of the Old Testament narratives. These are the all important questions which really need to be asked and answered.

The book of Genesis begins with the creation of the world and the origins of humankind in the Garden of Eden. It then takes the reader through the generations of Adam and Eve's progeny down to Noah and the biblical flood. What follows is the story of the (re)settlement in the land of Shinar, the building of the Tower of Babel, the subsequent confusion of tongues and the diaspora of Noah's descendants over the then-known world. So ends Chapter Eleven of the first book of the Bible.

Then, with Chapter Twelve (actually starting with Genesis 11:26), a new and quite distinct era begins with the birth of Abraham. This heralds in what scholars call the Patriarchal Period, extending down to Joseph and the migration of Jacob's family and followers from Canaan into Egypt.

A Test of Time Reprise

In Volume One of *A Test of Time* I attempted to demonstrate that the Old Testament narratives from the later part of Genesis (the story of Joseph) through Exodus, Joshua and Judges and on to the books of Kings and Chronicles, were based on genuine historical events.

Over the previous two centuries archaeologists had failed to recover evidence which might confirm the existence of such charismatic characters as Joseph, Moses, Joshua, Saul, David and Solomon or archaeological evidence of the events surrounding their lives. However, as I explained in Volume One, the reason why there was such singular lack of success was simply because archaeologists had been looking in the right places for the lost Israelites but in entirely the wrong time. Once the time-line of history had been adjusted, the archaeology of the Israelite Sojourn in Egypt, the Exodus and Conquest, the Judges and United Monarchy Periods, all suddenly began to make sense. A synthesis between biblical archaeology and biblical history was finally achievable

As a result, the patriarch Joseph was identified as one of Egypt's 12th-Dynasty viziers. He served the co-regent pharaohs Senuseret III and Amenemhat III and continued as the chief minister under their immediate successors, Amenemhat IV and Sobekneferu. The great famine of Joseph's time was identified with the aftermath of a series of catastrophic Nile floods which occurred during the reign of Amenemhat III.

The Exodus of Israelites from the land of Goshen in the Egyptian delta then took place towards the end of 13th Dynasty during the short reign of the obscure pharaoh, Dudimose.

We went on to discover that the cities destroyed by Joshua and the twelve tribes during their settlement of the Promised Land were indeed destroyed and burnt to the ground towards the end of the Middle Bronze Age. The city of Jericho was heavily fortified during the MB IIB and this city was subsequently devastated by an earthquake which brought its walls tumbling down. The archaeological record clearly shows that Jericho was put to the fire in this period and abandoned for several centuries, just as in the biblical story.[4]

24. Amenemhat III, sixth ruler of the 12th Dynasty, reigned 1682-1637 BC in the New Chronology (OC – 1817-1772 BC). Luxor Museum.

25. The inner burial chamber of the St. Etienne tomb in Jerusalem which is tentatively to be identified as the final resting place of Solomon's Egyptian queen and her offspring. Unusually for Israel, this chamber possesses three rock-cut sarcophagi rather than the normal stone shelves or beds for the interments. The discovery of these sarcophagi suggest coffin burials – a practice not followed by Israelite culture but certainly a requirement for Egyptian high-ranking burials. The dashed lines represent the original height of the rock-cut walls of the sarcophagi which have been subsequently smashed.

The period of Judges was contemporary with the 'Greater Hyksos' 15th Dynasty in Egypt, continuing through the first part of the New Kingdom and on down to the advent of the Amarna Period.

Much of the history recorded in the books of Samuel, dealing with the rise of the nation-state of Israel under its first kings – Saul and David – can now be further illuminated by the archive of diplomatic correspondence found in Egypt, known as the 'el-Amarna Letters'. King David was a contemporary of the heretic pharaoh Akhenaten, the latter's younger brother, Tutankhamun, and the military generals who succeeded to the throne – Ay and Haremheb.

Solomon's reign began during the second half of Haremheb's reign. The Egyptian princess who became Solomon's queen was the daughter of this pharaoh. We found evidence for her palace and tomb to the north of Jerusalem, within the high walls of St. Etienne monastery and in the grounds of the well-known 'Garden Tomb'. Much of Solomon's fame as a merchant-prince and builder-king was confirmed when it was realised that he ruled Israel during the Late Bronze Age and not in the Iron Age as in the conventional chronology. His building works, in fine ASHLAR stone, were identified at his royal city of Megiddo (Stratum VIII) which has produced clear examples of the building techniques ascribed to Solomon and his Phoenician craftsmen in Kings and Chronicles.

All these discoveries came about as a result of a reduction in the 'master chronology' of ancient Egypt.

A re-investigation of the archaeology and inscriptions of Egypt's Third Intermediate Period (conventionally dated from 1069 BC to 664 BC) showed that Egyptologists had artificially extended this period beyond

26. The antechamber of the St. Etienne tomb with steps leading up into the sarcophagus chamber.

ASHLAR: Stone which has been cut by a saw.

17

its true historical length. As a result, the so-called synchronisms between Egypt and biblical history in the conventional chronology were shown to be unreliable – more a matter of wishful thinking than true historical links. Once a clean break had been made and the chronology of Egypt reduced by more than three centuries, a whole series of new synchronisms with the Bible became possible – synchronisms which not only shed extra light in the biblical stories from the Egyptian perspective but also find strong support from astronomical evidence at key points along the time-line.

In broad outline, the New Chronology which evolved out of my Egyptological research has produced a whole set of alternative dates for Egyptian history and the history of ancient Israel. The Egyptian Third Intermediate Period now begins in the late-ninth century BC (compared to the mid-eleventh century BC of the orthodox chronology – OC); Ramesses II becomes the pharaoh who plundered the temple of Solomon in the 5th year of Rehoboam, this great pharaoh's reign beginning in 933 BC (OC – 1279 BC); Akhenaten's reign thus begins in 1022 BC (OC – 1352 BC). These key anchor points of the New Chronology give a start-date for the New Kingdom (beginning of the 18th Dynasty) in *c.* 1194 BC (OC – 1539 BC); the Great Hyksos 15th Dynasty now begins in *c.* 1290 BC (OC – 1633 BC); the 13th Dynasty commences in *c.* 1632 BC whilst the reign of Amenemhat III (Joseph's pharaoh) starts in *c.* 1682 BC (OC – 1817 BC).

That is just about where we got to in *A Test of Time* Volume One. But now we need to move even further back in time – to cover the origins of Egyptian civilisation and, before that, the beginnings of history in ancient Mesopotamia.

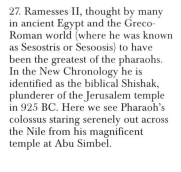

27. Ramesses II, thought by many in ancient Egypt and the Greco-Roman world (where he was known as Sesostris or Sesoosis) to have been the greatest of the pharaohs. In the New Chronology he is identified as the biblical Shishak, plunderer of the Jerusalem temple in 925 BC. Here we see Pharaoh's colossus staring serenely out across the Nile from his magnificent temple at Abu Simbel.

An Outline of the New Chronology

1682 BC		**12th Dyn (end)**	Arrival of the Israelites in Egypt
	13th Dyn	Amenemhat III	Joseph the Egyptian vizier
1632 BC	Wegaf		
	Neferhotep I	**MIDDLE BRONZE IIA**	Moses born
1529 BC	Sobekhotep IV		Moses exiled
1500 BC	Sobekhotep VIII	**MIDDLE BRONZE IIB**	
1447 BC	Dudimose		Exodus of the Israelites from Egypt
	16th Dyn		Conquest of the Promised Land
		15th Dyn	
1290 BC	**17th Dyn**	Salitis	Greater Hyksos invasion of Egypt
		Khyan	
	Tao II	Apophis	
1194 BC	**18th Dyn**		
	Ahmose	**LATE BRONZE I**	JUDGES PERIOD
	Thutmose III		
1022 BC	Akhenaten	**LATE BRONZE IIA**	Saul UNITED
	Haremheb		David MONARCHY
	19th Dyn		PERIOD
948 BC	Seti I	**LATE BRONZE IIB**	Solomon
	Ramesses II		Shishak and Rehoboam
	Merenptah	**20th Dyn**	Egyptian Civil War DIVIDED
c.850 BC		Ramesses III	MONARCHY
			PERIOD
c.823 BC	**22nd Dyn**	Ramesses XI	Egyptian Civil War
	Shoshenk I	**21st Dyn (b)**	Start of the Third Intermediate Period
		Herihor	
	Osorkon II		
	Shoshenk III	Pedubast I	Egyptian Civil War
c.712 BC		**25th Dyn**	Kushite invasion of Egypt
		Shabaka Osorkon III	
	Shoshenk V	Taharka	
664 BC	**23rd Dyn**	**26th Dyn**	Sack of Thebes by Ashurbanipal
	Pedubast II	Psamtek I	

21st Dyn (a)
Smendes
Psusennes I
Siamun
Psusennes II

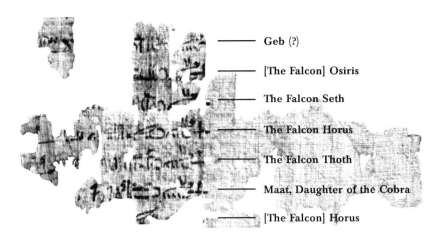

Geb (?)

[The Falcon] Osiris

The Falcon Seth

The Falcon Horus

The Falcon Thoth

Maat, Daughter of the Cobra

[The Falcon] Horus

28. Opposite page: The famous Sphinx of Giza as it appeared at the turn of the century, covered in drift-sand.

29. Left: A fragment of the Royal Canon of Turin. The right edge of the papyrus role has column I with a fragment listing the names and reign-lengths of the primeval gods.

At this point I think it would be a useful exercise to continue working backwards through the New Chronology for Egypt so as to achieve a start-date for the beginning of the 1st Dynasty. That way the whole chronological framework for pharaonic Egypt will be complete in general outline before we cross the boundary into the predynastic era. Needless to say, establishing a date for the beginning of Egyptian civilisation is a crucial first step in understanding the historical relationship between early Egypt, Mesopotamia and the book of Genesis.

Back to Menes

The Royal Canon of Turin (a pharaonic king-list drawn up in the 19th Dynasty which stretches back to earliest times) is our main documentary source for the chronology of the Early Dynastic Period, the Old Kingdom and First Intermediate Period – in other words the first eleven dynasties of pharaonic history. This badly damaged and fragmentary papyrus was acquired by Bernardino DROVETTI for the Regio Museum of Turin in 1824 from the private collection of the king of Sardinia.[5]

In its complete form the Royal Canon listed every ruler of Egypt from the end of the 18th Dynasty right back to the 1st Dynasty founder, Menes, and beyond into the fabled era of the 'Followers of Horus' – the predynastic rulers of Egypt with fantastical names and fantastically long reign-lengths. However, with the present condition of the papyrus role, not all sections are intact. Sometimes the names of the kings are preserved without their reign-lengths and sometimes the reverse is the case.

The arguments for reconstructing the earlier section in which we are interested are rather complex and so I have assigned the detailed discussion to *Appendix A* towards the end of this book. Here I will simply summarise the results by listing the New Chronology dates for the dynasties as calculated from the Royal Canon data. The orthodox chronology dates (OC), given here for comparison, are those published by Kenneth Kitchen (11th & 12th Dynasties) and John Baines & Jaromir Malek (1st to 10th Dynasties).[6]

DROVETTI: (1776-1852).

21

New Chronology Dates for Early Egyptian History

Middle Kingdom

12th Dynasty – *c.* 1800-1633 BC (OC – 1937-1759 BC)

11th Dynasty – *c.* 1943-1800 BC (OC – 2080-1937 BC)

First Intermediate Period

9th & 10th Dynasties – contemp. 7th, 8th & 11th Dynasties

8th Dynasty – *c.* 2043-1943 BC (OC – 2150-2134 BC)

Old Kingdom

7th Dynasty – *c.* 2082-2043 BC (OC – 2150-2134 BC)

6th Dynasty – *c.* 2224-2082 BC (OC – 2323-2150 BC)

5th Dynasty – *c.* 2350-2224 BC (OC – 2465-2323 BC)

4th Dynasty – *c.* 2459-2350 BC (OC – 2575-2465 BC)

3rd Dynasty – *c.* 2514-2459 BC (OC – 2630-2575 BC)

Early Dynastic Period

2nd Dynasty – *c.* 2669-2514 BC (OC – 2770-2650 BC)

1st Dynasty – *c.* 2789-2669 BC (OC – 2920-2770 BC)

So, according to my rough calculations, the beginning of pharaonic history occurred with the reign of King Menes in around 2789 BC. As you will no doubt have noted, the New Chronology date for the 1st Dynasty is not all that far from the conventional date provided by Baines and Malek in their much referenced *Atlas of Ancient Egypt*. In fact, it is only 131 years lower.

Those with a keen eye for Egyptian chronology will have observed that, at its greatest extent (during the Amarna Period), the two chronologies (orthodox and new) diverge by over three and a half centuries. However, as we move backwards in time from that point, they begin to converge once more. It should be clear, therefore, that the discrepancy between the two schemes is not fixed to a specific interval of years. That is one reason why it is important to go through the exercise of completing the New Chronology framework for the earlier dynasties. But there is another rather important reason which some may consider to be a surprising outcome of this revised chronology of Egypt.

The Great Sothic Year

In Volume One of *A Test of Time* I briefly raised the issue of Sothic dating. This is the technique of dating Egyptian history by means of the great Sothic cycle. Egyptologists have long known that the ancient Egyptian civil calendar slipped behind the natural solar calendar by one quarter of a day every year. This is because the Egyptians did not add a leap day every fourth year to allow for the fact that the solar year lasts not 365 days but 365.25 days. The Egyptian calendar consisted of twelve months of thirty days (a total of 360 days) plus five 'days upon the year' (Egy. *heryu renpet*) which were dedicated to the gods as festival days. It was thus short of the solar year by one day every four years.

The Roman grammarian, CENSORINUS, informs us that the HELIACAL RISING of the Dog Star (Sirius) coincided with the first day of the Egyptian calendar in AD 139. Given that the heliacal rising of Sirius was viewed by the Egyptians as marking the beginning of the natural year – and therefore, in an ideal world, the first day of the civil calendar – this AD 139 date signalled the start of a great Sothic cycle when the two clocks – civil and astronomical – were re-synchronised.

The Alexandrian mathematician, THEON, tells us that the preceding 'Great Sothic Year' had begun in the 'era of Menophres'. According to a simple calculation, this must have fallen in 1321 BC (1460 years earlier than AD 139). The date is arrived at by allowing one day's shift in the civil calendar every four years: thus 365 days of the Sothic cycle would have taken 1460 years to complete in order to return the heliacal rising of Sirius to the same calendar day as in AD 139.

Now the Great Sothic Year which began in 1321 BC takes us back to the Second Intermediate Period in the New Chronology. In fact, to the time shortly after the Exodus of the Israelites from Egypt and during the little-known or -understood era of the Early Hyksos Period. This is a time when foreign chieftains ruled the delta whilst the remnants of the native 13th-Dynasty line of pharaohs still held sway in Middle and Upper Egypt.

It is therefore very intriguing to note that a few scarabs survive from this period inscribed with the name of an obscure pharaoh called Men-nefer-re.[7] This is by far the closest parallel in Egyptian nomenclature to Manetho's Menophres. What is more, this Second-Intermediate-Period ruler is the *only* king of Egypt bearing this name. Have we pinpointed Manetho's 'era of Menophres'? If so, then this is further confirmation that the New Chronology is correct in its overall structure and dating.

However, another big surprise awaited me when I began to work out the dates which I have given you for the earliest Egyptian dynasties. I had already arrived at a date of 2789 BC for the start of the 1st Dynasty before it suddenly dawned on me. Was this date not close to the beginning of the next Great Sothic Year back from 1321? I quickly reached for the calculator and added another 1460 years to 1321 BC. The previous Sothic

CENSORINUS: Author of *De Die Natali* in honour of the 49th birthday of his patron, Quintus Caerellius, in *c.* AD 238.

HELIACAL RISING: The first appearance of a star or planet above the horizon just before dawn and prior to its disappearance, washed out by the sun's light.

THEON: (Late fourth century BC).

23

Breasted: (1865-1935).
Petrie: (1853-1942).

cycle had begun in 2781 BC – just eight years after the date I had calculated for the beginning of pharaonic civilisation! Given the margins of error I had been using, the two dates were in effect coincidental.

For two centuries Egyptologists had been devising chronologies for Egypt whilst at the same time suggesting that some significant political event may have been behind the inauguration of the Egyptian civil calendar at the beginning of the Great Sothic Year. James Henry Breasted remarked that the establishment of this calendar 'furnishes us with the earliest fixed date in the history of the world' but could not explain what political event instigated the new Egyptian calendar.[8] William Matthew Flinders Petrie, the 'father of Egyptian archaeology', had suggested that the foundation of the Egyptian state under King Menes may have been that event – but no chronology could be made to fit with this hypothesis. Now, without even a thought for Sothic dating, the New Chronology had achieved the impossible. Was this just another coincidence? Perhaps it was. Perhaps the ancient Egyptians had no sense of a great Sothic cycle. Maybe Sothic dating was merely an invention of Egyptology. Whatever the case, it was still comforting to know that another 'potential' cog in the great chronological wheel had locked into place.

For the sake of simplicity, and because a few years' variation make little difference when dealing with such remote time periods, I have decided to reduce the calculated start-date for the 1st Dynasty by eight years in order that the first regnal year of King Menes coincides with the beginning of a new Sothic cycle. So, for the purposes of the New Chronology, pharaonic history began in 2781 BC or thereabouts.

The Predynastic Period

The period before the 1st Dynasty is very difficult to pin down chronologically. We have no regnal dates on monuments because no stone buildings containing reliefs were constructed in this era. No highest regnal dates survive on more portable objects either and, as with the civil calendar, should probably not be expected in these early times before state bureaucracy was established. The king list known as the Royal Canon of Turin is no help because, prior to the 1st Dynasty, it descends into the chaos of gods and semi-divine beings whose reign-lengths are clearly exaggerated. Here we find extraordinary figures such as 3,420 years for the 'Followers of Horus'. None of this is usable.

All we can do is divide the archaeological artefacts into eras and assign a vague number of centuries to each of those eras based on *relative* radiocarbon dates. *Absolute* dates obtained by using the radiocarbon method (calibrated by dendrochronology) are simply not viable as a means of accurate dating and few historians are currently prepared to accept them.

Egyptologists have devised the following scheme as a general framework and I have calculated the New Chronology dates for each of the periods based on the approximate durations allotted to them.

> **1st Dynasty** (New Chronology dates) – *c.* 2781-2669 BC
> **Nakada III** (otherwise called Dynasty 0) – *c.* 2850-2781 BC
> **Nakada II** (otherwise called Gerzean) – *c.* 3050-2850 BC
> **Nakada I** (otherwise called Amratian) – *c.* 3250-3050 BC
> **Badarian** (Neolithic culture) – *c.* 4500-3250 BC

The names of these periods come from the sites where the culture was first uncovered. Thus the Neolithic culture of the Nile valley was revealed at the site of el-Badari in Upper Egypt by Guy BRUNTON and Gertrude CATON-THOMPSON between 1922 and 1931, whilst Amratian and Gerzean are named after the sites of el-Amra near Abydos (excavated by David RANDALL-MACIVER and Anthony Wilkin in 1900) and el-Gerza near Meydum (excavated by Gerald WAINWRIGHT and Ernest MACKAY in 1911). Nakada, located some twenty-six kilometres to the north of Luxor, on the other hand, was excavated by William Petrie and James QUIBELL in 1895.

BRUNTON: (1878-1948).
CATON-THOMPSON: (1888-1985).
RANDALL-MACIVER: (1873-1945).
WAINWRIGHT: (1879-1964).
MACKAY: (1880-1943).
QUIBELL: (1867-1935).

The periods we are going to focus on are Nakada I, II and III during which there is a clear transformation from stone-age culture to full-blown civilisation with kingship and centralised government.

Briefly, the distinguishing features between Nakada I and Nakada II, when the most dramatic cultural changes took place, are:

(a)   New burial practices.
(b)   New forms and decoration of pottery.
(c)   The first appearance of cylinder seals.
(d)   New types of weapons.
(e)   The use of mudbrick.
(f)   The import of lapis lazuli and obsidian.

30. The 'Two Ladies' (Nekhbet the vulture and Wadjet the cobra) have been identified amongst the earliest of the Egyptian deities. They became the titular goddesses of Upper and Lower Egypt, representing the towns of Nekheb near Edfu and Bhuto in the delta. These were two of the most important settlements in predynastic Egypt, the former being on the opposite bank of the river to Nekhen – the capital of the Followers of Horus. In pharaonic times each king was given a 'Two Ladies' name as part of his five-fold titulary. In this case we see a detail of the kingly titles of Senuseret I from his kiosk at Karnak.

With Nakada III (or Dynasty 0 as some prefer to call it) we see further developments which follow on from the new era heralded by Nakada II.

(g)   The introduction of hieroglyphs to write kings' names and titles.
(h)   Intricately carved ceremonial palettes.
(i)   Fine stone vases and bowls.
(j)   Reticulated façade mudbrick architecture.
(k)   The limited use of stone in architecture (lintels, portcullises, wall lining, etc.).

As to how long we should assign to each of the Nakada periods, this is very much a matter of interpretation. As I have hinted, even relative radiocarbon chronology is, in truth, too blunt a tool to help very much, the error ranges being too wide to provide the accurate dating needed. One could certainly argue that Nakada III was a very short period – perhaps just three or four generations – whilst the developments of Nakada II could also have been fairly rapid. I have decided to allocate just 70 years for Nakada III, 200 years for Nakada II and 200 years for Nakada I. But remember, these figures are fairly arbitrary. The crucial date to remember is *c.* 3050 BC for the appearance of the new cultural elements of Nakada II. This date will be confirmed when we determine the date for the flood and subsequent Sumerian chronology.

31. The 'Hunters Palette' from the Nakada III Period. The hunters are armed with various predynastic weapons including the composite bow, pear-shaped mace, throw-stick and spear. The fifth man from the left carries the Horus-falcon standard. Louvre Museum.

So much for Egyptian chronology. However, this book is also concerned with the origins of another very ancient civilisation – Sumer (sometimes called Sumeria) – which arose far to the north of Egypt in the region scholars and the classical authors call Mesopotamia ('[the land] between the rivers').

In *A Test of Time* Volume One I included in the *Introduction* brief outlines of Egyptian and biblical history to set the reader up for what was to follow in the main body of the book. It would obviously be a good idea to do the same here for Mesopotamian history, so that you have a framework around which to base our findings. I imagine that Mesopotamian history is even less familiar to you than the histories of Egypt or the Old Testament, and the names of the rulers are certainly going to be difficult to get your tongue around. However, the rewards will be worth the perseverance because, together, we are going to discover a story of truly epic proportions.

A Brief History of Early Mesopotamia

At the dawn of Near Eastern history we find the first cities being established in the low plain and marshes of southern Iraq. The ancient name of this region was *Shumerum* – the modern version of which is Sumer. The Bible calls the place the 'Land of Shinar' and, according to that source, this is where the descendants of Adam settled in the period immediately following the great flood. The historical epoch we are going to be studying spans the sixth to second millennia BC which corresponds to the archaeological eras known as the late Neolithic, Chalcolithic, Early Bronze and Middle Bronze Ages.

32. The archetypal long-haired Mesopotamian from the Sumerian Period. The clenched hands indicates that he is in the act of prayer. Louvre Museum.

By the way, the dates which I am employing here to give you a chronological framework are those conventionally supplied by scholars. Only when we reach the chapter dealing with the dating of the great deluge (*Chapter Five*) will I introduce you to the New Chronology dates for Sumerian and early Mesopotamian history.

Archaeologists who have excavated in the region between and around the two rivers Euphrates and Tigris have unearthed the ancient remains of great cities known to us from the Genesis text and other ancient records: cities such as ERIDU, URUK (biblical Erech) and UR. Other, less well known, population centres of ancient Sumer have also been located by the archaeologist's spade – cities such as SHURUPPAK, LAGASH, NIPPUR and KISH. All provide a picture of a thriving and inventive Sumerian civilisation. The Sumerians, whoever they were, are acknowledged to have been the creators of civilisation.

In this era humankind first begins to record his deeds and achievements by means of a new invention – the written word. At first the earliest documents (little clay tablets) consist of simple records of quantities of livestock and grain, sometimes along with the name of the owner. The earliest scribes were, in effect, book-keepers.

But within a few centuries the new invention was being put to more creative uses with complete literary works appearing for the first time. These much longer texts deal with an heroic past from which the civilised world unfolded. They are epic poems – legends (some might say myths) – with heroes pitting their wits and physical strength in protracted contests

ERIDU: Tell Abu Shahrain, 315 km south-east of Baghdad.

URUK: Warka, 250 km south-east of Baghdad.

UR: Tell al-Mukayyar, 300 km south-east of Baghdad.

SHURUPPAK: Tell al-Fara, 180 km south-east of Baghdad.

LAGASH: al-Hiba, 240 km south-east of Baghdad.

NIPPUR: Nuffar, 150 km south-east of Baghdad.

KISH: near Ingharra, 85 km south of Baghdad.

33. Opposite page (above): A typical tell or ruin mound in the Mesopotamian plain.

34. Opposite page (below): King Ashurnasirpal II of Assyria with (from left to right) the symbols of Sin, the moon-god; Ashur, the state god of Assyria; Shamash, the sun-god; and the horned crown of Enlil, Anu or Ea. Below the Shamash symbol is the lightning bolt of Adad, the storm-god; and the seven circles (one broken away) of the Pleiades. Mosul Museum.

35. Left: Austen Henry Layard (standing on the wall) supervises the removal of one of the protecting winged bull figures from the Assyrian palace at Nimrud.

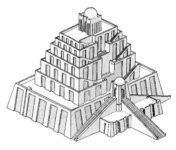

36. Reconstruction of the seven-stepped ziggurat at Ur.

37. Relief illustrating the ziggurat at Susa with the River Shaur flowing past below the city mound.

with powerful demons or, in some cases, human adversaries (i.e. brother rulers) in far-off lands. Of course, the interesting question is whether any of this material approaches what we understand as real history.

The Sumerians were also the first inspired builders of monumental architecture – principally temples to their gods – constructed out of mud-brick. Around these sacred precincts small settlements were established which eventually became enormous cities. The circumference of early Uruk, for instance, measured over nine-and-a-half kilometres and its population has been estimated at around fifty thousand.[9] The era of the 'urban revolution' has been named the 'Uruk Period' in deference to the wonders of this ancient city with its beautiful temples. Uruk is going to play an important part in our story.

All over Mesopotamia archaeologists have turned up magnificent early stone statues and reliefs from the Sumerian period. As you will soon see, at certain times in their long history, the Sumerians produced superb painted pottery. They rapidly developed the technology of smelting metals and so inaugurated what scholars call the Bronze Age. In every part of the Tigris and Euphrates river basin the Sumerians constructed canals, turning the dry plain into rich and fertile farmland. As well as transporting water to the fields, these canals also served as the main arteries for trade, permitting the movement of produce by reed boat from one city to another. The word for 'market' (Akk. *karum*) is one and the same as that for the quayside where boats, laden with goods, could tie up. It was upon these same canals that the statues of the gods and goddesses went out from their city temples aboard their sacred barges to visit each other at festival times. Their temples were huge complexes decorated with multi-coloured mosaic panels and niched-panel façades. At the heart of these sacred precincts rose the mighty platforms upon which the houses of the gods stood. These temple-towers would soon develop into the famous ziggurats of Mesopotamia – great stepped pyramids which reached up towards heaven to form stairways for the celestial deities.

38. Following page: The Early-Dynastic-Period ruler, Urnanshe, carrying a basket of earth used in the making of mudbricks for the foundation platform of a new temple at Lagash. Louvre Museum.

29

All this was the inspired invention of Sumerian civilisation.

In a few short centuries the Sumerians had succeeded in turning an uninhabited wasteland into a garden paradise in which they co-existed alongside, and in general harmony with, their gods. The legacy of that early Sumerian culture was then carried down throughout Mesopotamian history into the Babylonian, Assyrian and Persian periods, only to slip slowly back into the dust of the great plain with the arrival of Alexander and the new world order of Greece and Rome.

39. Gudea of Lagash. Louvre Museum.

40. Stone vase of Gudea showing antithetical dragons and entwined serpents. Louvre Museum.

In spite of all this cultural history, when an historian comes to writing a *political history* of this very early period of Mesopotamian culture he is soon made aware of the limited set of tools which are available to him. Because the contemporary texts are merely brief 'book-keeping' accounts (quantities of livestock and grain), he has no contemporary written sources to rely upon which can shed light on political events. As I have said, records of people and incidents surrounding them appear late in Sumerian history and then, unfortunately, they are composed in the confusing language of myth and epic saga. This leaves the historian with the difficult task of interpreting the archaeological evidence without the comforting support of a reliable political framework. So I am afraid we have to talk in terms of stratigraphy and pottery phases whilst noting technological developments such as the build-ing of irrigation canals or the invention of the potter's wheel. We are there-fore dealing for the moment with anthropological history far more than political history – though by the end of this book I hope to have given you a tangible political history full of incident and personality.

Over the last century and a half or so of endeavour scholars have been able to put together an overall picture of cultural development in the Mesopotamian plain. For the very earliest period in which we are interested the archaeological stratigraphy of Sumer has been broken down into eight basic periods. The dating given here is based on the conventional chronology for Sumerian archae-ology. Because we are dealing with a very early era, not only are the dates approximations but they can also vary by as much as several centuries, depending on which authority you happen to be reading.[10]

41. Detail from the 'Ur Standard'. This masterpiece of inlaid shell and lapis lazuli mosaic gives a good insight into warfare during the Ur III Sumerian revival. By this time the war chariot was very much in use within the Mesopotamian sphere. However, this new battle technology does not surface in Egypt until centuries later. The first evidence of the use of horses in the Nile valley comes towards the end of the 13th Dynasty, contemporary with the Old Babylonian Dynasty of Hammurabi. British Museum.

1. Eridu/Ubaid 1 (*c.* 5000-4800 BC)
2. Hajji Muhammad/Ubaid 2 (*c.* 4800-4500 BC)
3. Ubaid 3 & 4 (*c.* 4500-4000 BC)
4. Uruk (*c.* 4000-3200 BC)
5. Jemdet Nasr (*c.* 3200-2900 BC)
6. Early Dynastic I (*c.* 2900-2700 BC)
7. Early Dynastic II (*c.* 2700-2600 BC)
8. Early Dynastic III (*c.* 2600-2340 BC)

These are followed by several periods of regional dynastic control which we refer to as:

9. The Dynasty of Agade (*c.* 2340-2159 BC)
10. The Gutian Period (*c.* 2208-2117 BC)
11. The Third Dynasty of Ur (*c.* 2112-2004 BC)
12. The Elamite Conquest (*c.* 2004 BC)
13. The Isin-Larsa Period (*c.* 2025-1763 BC)
14. The Old Babylonian Dynasty (*c.* 1894-1595 BC)

With respect to the first group, most of these 'pottery periods' are named, as in Egypt, after the archaeological sites where the recognisable ceramics of the eras were first discovered. So although Ubaid pottery is found all over Mesopotamia (and therefore dates strata from the different cities to the same general time period) it gets its name from the very small and rather insignificant site of Tell al-Ubaid where it was first discovered by Henry Reginald HALL of the British Museum in 1919. The distinctive Ubaid pottery was then later SERIATED by Sir Leonard WOOLLEY in the 1920s. Ironically, the little mound of Tell al-Ubaid lies only six kilometres distant from the much larger archaeological site of Ur where the same pottery was unearthed, shortly afterwards, in huge quantities.

As is often the case with chronologies based on pottery seriation, there is much debate as to what precisely constitutes a new cultural phase and what simply reflects continuity of an existing culture. In fact, most archaeologists regard the Eridu and Hajji Muhammad phases as early developments of Ubaid (that is Ubaid 1 and 2 respectively), whilst Jemdet Nasr is thought merely to be the latest phase of the Uruk pottery period.[11] At the heart of these rather complex matters lies the issue of when scholars believe that the Sumerian civilisation first appeared in southern Meso-potamia. This rather thorny debate has become known as the 'Sumerian Problem'.

It was once generally believed that the Sumerians had migrated from some unknown original homeland and that their arrival in the Meso-

HALL: (1873-1930).

SERIATED: Put into chronological sequence based on observations of style changes and fabric.

WOOLLEY: (1880-1960).

potamian plain was marked by the new undecorated wheel-thrown pottery which appears towards the beginning of the Uruk Period (*c.* 4000 BC). Other archaeologists argued for a much earlier emergence of the Sumerians at the very beginning of the Ubaid Period (*c.* 5000 BC). The simple fact is, however, the more Mesopotamian pottery is studied the more it is realised that each ceramic phase appears to develop from its predecessor. Where there is a marked change it can usually be put down to technological innovation which, as you will realise, is not necessarily attributable to a new people arriving in the region. All this has led to a movement within Sumerology which takes the position that the Sumerians were always indigenous to the region and not invaders or immigrants from afar. We will return to this problem later when we discuss the biblical perspective which sees the descendants of Adam entering the land of Shinar (Sumer) from the east.

From a study of ancient toponyms in the region it has been argued that Sumerian was not the first language in use within southern Mesopotamia. Thus the secondary nature or appearance of the Sumerian language *does* intimate to another group of scholars the arrival of a new and distinct ethnic group which superseded or subsumed the existing population within what manifests itself as Sumerian civilisation. There is also a marked increase in population associated with the Uruk Period which might signify the incursion of newcomers at that time.[12]

But if these were the ethnic Sumerians, then who were their linguistic predecessors – the folk who had first occupied the plain once the marshy shoreline of the Gulf had begun to recede southwards sometime in the seventh millennium BC? Who founded the earliest settlement at Eridu – the first city on earth according to Sumerian tradition? Was it the Sumerian settlers or their shadowy forebears? Questions and more questions are the stuff of Sumerology. Many of those questions may ultimately be unanswerable, but it seems to me that some have the potential for resolution if we are prepared to search for clues within the stories related in the book of Genesis.

42. One of the large fragments of the Eannatum stela, known as the 'Stela of the Vultures'. The Early Dynastic III ruler of Lagash is assisted in his victory by the god Ningirsu who here grasps a net teeming with captives from Eannatum's battle against the city of Umma. Note that the god carries a pear-shaped mace as if he is about to smite his victims in a ceremonial act of divine retribution. Louvre Museum.

43. An Early Dynastic II seal from Fara depicts the 'long-haired hero' and the 'bull-man' fighting lions and bulls. These mythological characters first appear in the ED II Period and were at one time associated with Gilgamesh and Enkidu. British Museum.

33

44. A magnificent gold dagger with lapis lazuli handle from the royal burials at Ur (Early Dynastic III). Iraq Museum.

In the meantime we should return to the task in hand – familiarisation with early Mesopotamian history through its archaeology.

The Pottery Periods

Pottery is a useful though, it has to be said, somewhat ambiguous witness to the historical process. However, it is an excellent tool for relative dating because identical pottery found at different sites enables us to date the levels at those sites to the same general time period. The pottery story begins with the first settlements in the marshy plain of southern Iraq.

At Eridu a distinctive form of well-developed greenish buff ware with strong geometric decoration in dark pigments marks the arrival of the first sedentary population in the region. Associated with this fine ceramic corpus are a series of small temples or shrines built, one on top of the other, over a period of a few centuries. Eridu ware (otherwise Ubaid 1) has been found at Ur and Uruk showing that these settlements also go back to the foundation of the sacred precinct at Eridu or a little later.

A subsequent development of Eridu ware was then discovered at Kalat Hajji Muhammad near Warka (Uruk). The fabric of the pots is the same but a new shape is introduced in the form of a deep bowl with incurved sides and a sharp angle near the base. The monochrome decoration is tight and crowded on the surface of the pot leaving little of the buff base showing through. It is clear that Hajji Muhammad ware (otherwise Ubaid 2) is simply a transitional phase from Eridu ware to the fully blown classical Ubaid ware which, as I have said, was first uncovered at Tell al-Ubaid.

Classical Ubaid pottery (Ubaid 3) spans a long period of time – perhaps as much as 500 years – and covers the whole of southern Mesopotamia. Spouted vessels (like tea-pots) are common in this phase, as are a number of other new shapes. The manufacture of the pottery eventually evolves into a superb quality finish with walls of almost egg-shell thinness. However, towards the end of the Ubaid Period (Ubaid 4) the workmanship begins rapidly to degenerate, with scant attention being given to firing precision or decoration. This rather suggests that mass production has taken over from what was clearly the individual craftsmanship of earlier times. Pottery is no longer a precious commodity or status symbol but rather the stuff of everyday use. It is probably significant that it is precisely at this time (*c.* 4000 BC) that the potter's wheel is attested for the first time. From now on a rather plain pottery, bereft of painted decoration, begins to predominate. This marks the transition to the 'Uruk Period'.

It is rather ironic that the new technology of the wheel, which results in a plain ceramic in reds and greys, coincides with the introduction of both monumental architecture on a prolific scale and the first tentative steps in the formation of state administration by means of written record keeping. There is no doubt whatsoever that this new era was one of dramatic developments. In every sense, when we reach the Uruk Period we are leaving prehistory behind and entering the historical era.

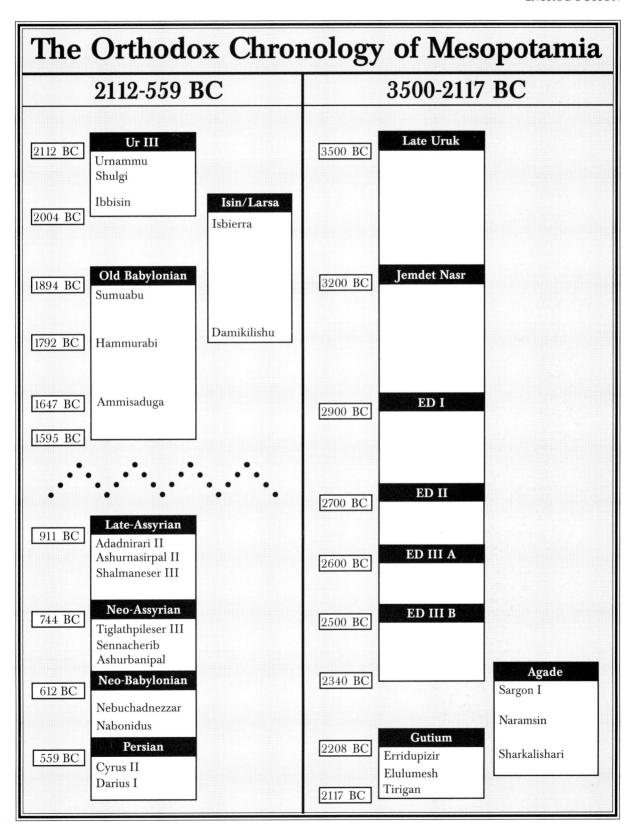

The Orthodox Chronology of Mesopotamia

2112-559 BC

2112 BC	**Ur III**	
	Urnammu	
	Shulgi	
	Ibbisin	**Isin/Larsa**
2004 BC		Isbierra
1894 BC	**Old Babylonian**	
	Sumuabu	
		Damikilishu
1792 BC	Hammurabi	
1647 BC	Ammisaduga	
1595 BC		

911 BC	**Late-Assyrian**
	Adadnirari II
	Ashurnasirpal II
	Shalmaneser III
744 BC	**Neo-Assyrian**
	Tiglathpileser III
	Sennacherib
	Ashurbanipal
	Neo-Babylonian
612 BC	
	Nebuchadnezzar
	Nabonidus
	Persian
559 BC	
	Cyrus II
	Darius I

3500-2117 BC

3500 BC	**Late Uruk**
3200 BC	**Jemdet Nasr**
2900 BC	**ED I**
2700 BC	**ED II**
2600 BC	**ED III A**
2500 BC	**ED III B**
2340 BC	

	Agade
	Sargon I
	Naramsin
	Sharkalishari

2208 BC	**Gutium**
	Erridupizir
	Elulumesh
2117 BC	Tirigan

Writing and Historical Records

45. A Sumerian tablet with the cuneiform signs impressed into the soft clay prior to hardening in the sun or baking. British Museum.

CUNEIFORM: The wedge-shaped script of Mesopotamia.

ASHURBANIPAL: King of Assyria, reigned 668-626 BC.

NINEVEH: The site of Kuyunjik, just across the Tigris from Mosul, 400 km north of Baghdad.

46. Bronze head of a ruler of Agade (possibly Sargon I or Naramsin) from the temple of Ishtar at Nineveh. Iraq Museum.

True history really begins with writing and writing appears to have been an invention of the people of Uruk and its contemporary cities in southern Mesopotamia. We can safely call the people of this era the 'Sumerians' – even if at this stage it is difficult to say just where they came from. This is not the same thing as saying they were ethnically different people from the previous Ubaid culture, but rather that we can be reasonably certain that, *by this time*, the Uruk culture is Sumerian.

The earliest written texts first appear in the Uruk IV Period when monumental architecture also has its beginnings. The Uruk documents are recorded on small clay tablets whose surfaces are scratched and indented by the application of a pointed reed stylus. The tablets concern themselves with basic accounting – for example the number of cattle being delivered to the temple for offerings. Only in the succeeding Early Dynastic Period do the documents take on what we would define as the literary form, with a full grammar and vocabulary.

The Sumerian kings of this very early period have been recorded on a later document which, for obvious reasons, has been dubbed the 'Sumerian King List'. The best copy of the CUNEIFORM text is written on a large rectangular clay cylinder now held by the Ashmolean Museum in Oxford. It was set down in this edition during the 11th year (or shortly after) of King Sinmagir of the Dynasty of Isin (OC – *c.* 1816 BC). The dynasties listed in this important document are located at different cities. Some of them we know, from later texts, to have been chronologically contemporary. However, given the paucity of documents recording kings' names found in an archaeological context, it has proved difficult to pinpoint exactly when specific rulers reigned in relationship to the archaeological stratigraphy or pottery periods. In this respect the history of Sumer is very much like the history of the Israelites whose archaeological position is equally difficult to establish with any certainty. Many of the famous rulers of Sumer – heroes such as Enmerkar, Lugalbanda, Dumuzi and Gilgamesh – have not been fixed with any real confidence into the early archaeological eras listed above.

It was towards the end of the Early Dynastic Period that the earliest Sumerian oral epics were first written down. They comprise legendary accounts of incidents in the reigns of the great hero-kings of Uruk and Kish. This epic literature became so popular that it was soon translated into Akkadian and copied for new audiences on down through the succeeding centuries until the fall of Assyria and Babylon in the seventh and sixth centuries BC. Many of the surviving versions of these texts were discovered in the ruins of the library of King ASHURBANIPAL of Assyria at NINEVEH. They include the twelve-tablet saga known as the Gilgamesh Epic, in which the famous story of the Sumerian flood is narrated, and other legendary tales dealing with Etana of Kish, and Enmerkar and Lugalbanda of the First Dynasty of Uruk.

The Early Dynastic Period in Sumer came to an end around 2340 BC with the rise of Sargon of Agade (otherwise Akkad). Sargon was an Amorite ruler who seized power in a palace *coup d'état*. Ironically his name means 'rightful king'. Presumably he chose this name to camouflage the goings-on which led to his kingship. If a ruler protests his legitimacy you can be fairly sure that there will have been one or two skeletons in the cupboard of succession.

Sargon's reign inaugurated a tremendously powerful episode in Mesopotamian history. His military conquests created the largest empire known to that date, stretching from southern Anatolia (Turkey), in the north, down to the Persian Gulf and beyond into Arabia. His dynasty went on to rule over Mesopotamia for a further two centuries until its catastrophic collapse during the reigns of Naramsin and his successor, Sharkalisharri. The mighty Agadean (or Akkadian) empire crumbled when the warlike tribes of the Gutians descended upon the Mesopotamian plain from their strongholds in the Zagros mountains. Sargon's proud legacy was brought to an ignominious end by barbaric hordes – a pattern which was to be repeated throughout history – and the Gutian invasion heralded a century-long dark age in the land of the two rivers before civilisation regained its hold under a new Sumerian dynasty based at the city of Ur. The Sumerian King List marks this period of anarchy simply by the statement 'Who was king? Who was not king?'.

47. The 'Victory Stela' of Naramsin (Dynasty of Agade) excavated from the mound of Susa by de Morgan. Louvre Museum.

48. The superb gold and lapis lazuli bull's figurehead attached to one of the lyres discovered in the royal tombs at Ur by Leonard Woolley. British Museum.

49. The complete scene carved around a steatite vase from Khafaje. The long-haired hero figure controls wild beasts and serpents. Next to his head is the six-petalled rosette symbol of the goddess Inanna of Uruk. British Museum.

50. Scene in high relief above the cuneiform text of the Hammurabi Law Code, showing King Hammurabi of Babylon I before the sun-god Shamash. One of the famous monuments excavated from the mound of Susa by de Morgan. Louvre Museum.

51. Opposite page: An Assyrian dignitary brings a sacrificial goat to the temple. From the palace of Sargon II at Khorsabad. Louvre Museum.

52. Page 40: A Sumerian high god of the mountains with bull's-horn crown and flowing beard. British Museum.

A Neo-Sumerian revival came into being with the re-emergence of Ur under its third dynastic line, inaugurated by Ur III's first king, Urnammu. In fact, he was not the one responsible for the overthrow of the Gutians. That task fell to the last ruler of Uruk, Utuhegal, whose predecessors had ruled their city-state contemporaneously with the Gutian Dynasty. Utuhegal's famous victory over Tirigan, last ruler of the Gutians, did not result in Uruk taking ascendancy because Utuhegal was without heir and the governor of Ur, Urnammu, was able to seize the reins of power.

The Ur III Dynasty came to an end with the reign of Ibbisin when Ur's hegemony passed into the hands of two contemporary dynasties – Isin and Larsa. They were later joined by a third dynastic line based at Babylon. The Babylon I Dynasty, founded by Sumuabu, was to inaugurate another great and powerful epoch – an epoch which would also become known as the Hammurabi Dynasty, after its most famous ruler.

It is with Hammurabi, writer of the famous 'Law Code', that I bring this brief history of early Mesopotamia to a close because this king and his fourth-generation successor, Ammisaduga, were established within their New Chronology setting in *A Test of Time* Volume One. When we later come to the task of determining the revised dating for the early Mesopotamian rulers mentioned here, we will be starting from the New Chronology date for Hammurabi and, using the data supplied by the Sumerian King List, we will then attempt to work our way backwards through time to the era of the great flood of Mesopotamian tradition in an effort to establish the date for the *biblical* flood.

In the meantime, I think this is the moment to begin our adventure. We might as well take a plunge into the deep end of this historical investigation to see what we can recover from the murky depths of the creation epic. Time then to go in search of the Garden of Eden.

Now the earth was without form and there was darkness over the deep with a divine wind sweeping over the waters. God said, 'Let there be light', and there was light! [Genesis 1:2-3]

God planted a garden in Eden, which is in the east, and there he put the man he had fashioned.

Genesis 2:8

Part One

From the Mists of Time

The Geography of Genesis

In the beginning ...   *Genesis 1:1*

Chapter One

IN SEARCH OF EDEN

egendary material need not necessarily be dismissed out of hand simply because it is 'fantastical' or 'miraculous'. We cannot expect ancient Man to have composed a factual history in the way we would require of a modern historian writing, for instance, about the origins of the First World War. In trying to understand events from the distant past, we should not attempt to impose our twentieth-century expectations on the ancient story-tellers. Their ancestral history was a legendary past structured around the deeds of gods and deified heroes; a world of DRAGONS and DEMONS; a time of miracles and divine intervention. Scholars refer to this material as 'epic literature' – a useful term which serves to separate these sagas from contemporary records and inscriptions which, by their very nature, ought to be more reliable historical sources.

But why should the *style* of composition prevent us from accepting the basic historicity of the personalities and events being described. If the divine hero Gilgamesh, king of Uruk, journeys from his homeland in Sumer to the 'Land of the Living' in search of immortality, and there meets the hero of the flood, granted eternal life by the gods, we may wish to reject the miraculous elements as unhistorical – but what about Gilgamesh? Should we deny his existence simply because of the story's fantastical setting? Perhaps not. Indeed, archaeology has produced documentary proof that Enmebaragesi – one of the contempories of Gilgamesh mentioned in the epics – was a genuine ruler of the city-state of Kish. This has led some historians to conclude that Gilgamesh himself was a real, flesh-and-blood character from our distant past. So, if we are to accept the view that Gilgamesh was an historical figure, should we not also acknowledge the possibility that he may have journeyed to a foreign land which had in later times been given the epithet 'Land of the Living' because of its legendary status as the earthly paradise?

55. The traditional image of Adam and Eve as visualised in Late-Medieval times.

DRAGONS: From the Greek *drakon*, meaning 'serpent'.

DEMONS: From the Greek *daimon*, meaning 'divinity'.

43

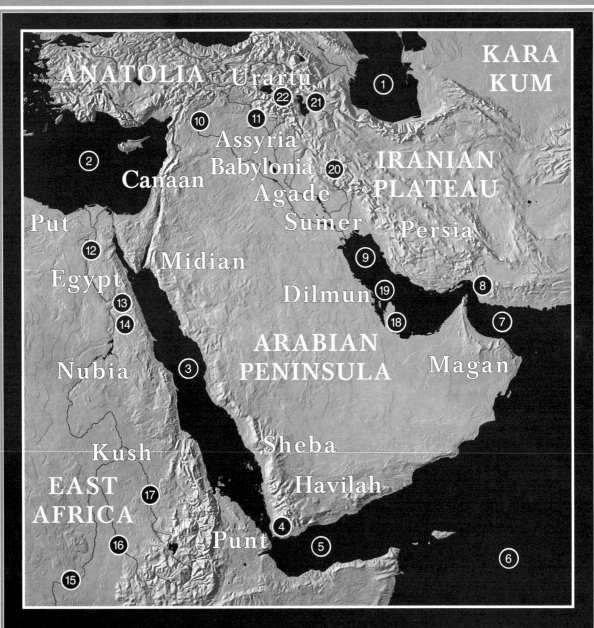

KARA KUM

ANATOLIA　Urartu

①

Put

Canaan

② ⑩ ⑪

Assyria
Babylonia ⑳
Agade
Sumer

IRANIAN PLATEAU

Persia

⑫

Egypt

⑬

⑭

Midian

Dilmun ⑨ ⑲ ⑧

Nubia ③

⑱ ⑦

ARABIAN PENINSULA

Magan

Kush

Sheba

EAST AFRICA ⑰

Havilah

⑯

Punt ④

⑤

⑥

⑮

1 – Caspian Sea	9 – Persian Gulf	17 – Atbara River
2 – Mediterranean Sea	10 – River Euphrates	18 – Katar Peninsula
3 – Red Sea	11 – River Tigris	19 – Bahrain Island
4 – Bab el-Mandeb Straits	12 – Nile Valley	20 – Zagros mountains
5 – Gulf of Aden	13 – Wadi Hammamat	21 – Lake Urmia
6 – Indian Ocean	14 – Wadi Abbad	22 – Lake Van
7 – Gulf of Oman	15 – White Nile	
8 – Straits of Hormuz	16 – Blue Nile	

We will be returning to the Sumerian epics. But what about that other major example of early epic literature – the Bible? Can we apply the same open-mindedness to the equally fantastical events described in the book of Genesis?

We all know the tale of Adam and Eve in their garden paradise; of the tree of life and the tree of knowledge of good and evil; and of the serpent which brought about humankind's fall from grace.

Most of us have vague recollections as to how the remainder of the early Genesis epic develops:

- Cain, the farmer, murders his brother Abel, the pastoralist, and is exiled from Eden into the land of Nod.

- The descendants of Cain and his other brother, Seth, become the builders of civilisation – city-founders, musicians, metal-workers, viniculturists. They live to exceptional ages.

- In these primeval times the 'sons of God' walk the earth and have sexual relations with mortal women. The offspring of these unions are the mighty heroes of legend. The Bible calls them 'giants' (Heb. *nephilim* – from the root *naphal*, to fall, i.e. the 'fallen ones').

- There is a great flood, sent by the high god of Adam's descendants, which destroys the world. One pious man, Noah, and his immediate family are saved because they build an ark in which to ride out the storm. The ark comes to rest on the mountains of Ararat.

- The descendants of Noah return to the lowlands and (re)-settle in the land of Shinar where they reconstruct the cities destroyed in the flood.

- Up until this moment the world speaks in a single language.

- The people build a great tower of mudbricks and bitumen which reaches up towards the heavens. God destroys the tower and confuses the tongues of its presumptuous builders. The population of Shinar, no longer able to communicate with each other, are scattered to the far corners of the earth where they form the numerous nations of the old world.

- These nations, descended from the three sons of Noah, are listed in genealogical order. They include numerous small tribal groupings but also the most renowned peoples of ancient times – Israelites, Elamites, Assyrians and Arameans (through Noah's eldest son, Shem); Egyptians, Cushites, Libyans, Phoenicians, Philistines, Amorites and Babylonians (through Noah's second son, Ham); and Medes, Persians, Greeks, Cypriotes, and all the peoples who dwell on the islands of the eastern Mediterranean (through Noah's youngest son, Japheth). Scholars loosely categorise these three groups by their linguistic affiliations – Semitic, Hamitic and Indo-European (Japhite) – though this is far from reflecting any actuality.

56. Opposite page: Relief map of the Middle East showing the principal civilisations of the ancient world discussed in *Legend*.

Some of the story does appear to fall within what we would understand as the human sphere – the killing of a brother, the inventing of the art of metal-working, the building of a great tower. But so much more seems to be mythological – forbidden fruit, a talking serpent, tremendous longevity and wandering giants. Surely then, with so much of the supernatural in the epic tale, there can be no hope of giving the book of Genesis any sort of historical setting.

That would undoubtedly be the 'politically correct' stance for any modern historian to take, but, as I said in the *Introduction*, the challenge of this book is to venture where others fear to tread. So, together, we will be attempting to come up with an historical explanation for one of the most difficult puzzles handed down to us from the ancient world.

We shall begin our intellectual adventure by going in search of the Garden of Eden itself. What an extraordinary idea, I hear you say! The very thought of trying to locate the earthly paradise is surely pure fantasy – isn't it?

Down the Garden Path

The location of the Garden of Eden has intrigued the inquisitive and the religious ever since the Bible was first read. Today, few scholars would be brave or reckless enough to suggest that the land of Eden actually once existed – let alone that it was from this place that civilised humankind first emerged. This approach speaks volumes for the attitudes of modern scholarship where caution and outright scepticism now seem to prevail.

In the century which preceded the Second World War, however, things were rather different. Scholars of the Victorian and Edwardian eras seem to have been rather more adventurous (some might say naive) in their thinking and, because of this, a comprehensive synthesis between the biblical text and archaeology was still a laudable aim. Intuition and reasoned speculation were acceptable tools of the ancient historian – so long as ideas were predominantly based on the available evidence. And much of that evidence came from the Bible which was still a principal source-book for ancient history.

Over that hundred-year period many Bible researchers attempted to pinpoint Eden's whereabouts on the basis of the description provided in the book of Genesis. There it states that four rivers flowed out from Eden. In Chapter Two of Genesis these rivers are named as:

(1) the Gihon – winding through the land of Cush;

(2) the Pishon – winding through the land of Havilah;

(3) the Hiddekel = Tigris – flowing east of Ashur;

(4) the Perath = Euphrates – known to everyone.

The geographical clues have always been there but, in spite of this, the various interpretations of this key passage have differed considerably.

Some scholars looked to their counterparts from the Roman world – the historians and early church fathers such as JOSEPHUS, St. AUGUSTINE and St. JEROME. Even in their time the question of the whereabouts of Eden was a subject for speculation and debate. The Jewish historian, Josephus, identified the 'land of Cush', bordering on Eden with the well-known African kingdom of Kush, south of Egypt. As a result, the first of the four rivers which flowed from Eden – the Gihon (from a root meaning 'to burst forth') – was identified as the river Nile. This seemed to be supported by the fact that both the Ethiopians and the Egyptian COPTS referred to their river as the 'Geion'. However, the great nineteenth-century biblical scholar, Friedrich GESENIUS, observed that this name may have itself derived directly from the Alexandrine exposition of the Genesis text. In other words the river was named after the Gihon precisely because of the association of African Kush with biblical Cush. The Christian communities of Africa had done exactly what the early church fathers were now doing in identifying the Nile with the Gihon.

The Hiddekel (Arab. Diglat) and Perath (Arab. Firat) were the two well-known rivers of Mesopotamia which the classical authors knew as the Tigris and Euphrates.

Thus a broad view of the primeval earthly paradise was established with the land of Eden covering a vast expanse stretching from the plain of ancient Sumer in the north to the Nile valley in the south. It then became a reasonably straightforward assumption to identify the second river of Eden – the Pishon (from a root meaning 'to spread') – with one of the other great rivers of the region – the Indus or the Ganges – which flow through modern Pakistan and India respectively. Whereas Josephus, Augustine, Jerome and other Christian fathers conjectured that the Ganges was the biblical Pishon, Gesenius opted for the Indus valley as the location of the biblical land of Havilah. His view was soon supported by the discovery of a high civilisation in this region which dated back to early biblical times.

The heart of Eden was therefore identified as the central Levant and, in particular, the Promised Land itself. This was all very convenient with the cross-roads of three faiths – Jerusalem – recognised within the theology of Judaism (and therefore Christianity) as the gateway into paradise on the final Day of Judgement.

But does this wide perspective really sit comfortably with the Genesis narrative? Many scholars did not think so. For instance, if Eden was so expansive, then the whole of biblical history must have been played out within its boundaries. Yet the descendants of Adam were removed from the Garden of Eden into the harsh world beyond. They entered the land of Shinar which scholars generally identify as the land of SUMER in southern Iraq. But Sumer falls within the boundaries of Eden in the broad perspective outlined above. The biblical narrative seems to suggest a much narrower view of the land of Eden. The setting for the post-Edenic stories – the region we today call the Levant – could not be one and the

JOSEPHUS: (AD 37-*c.* 100). Jewish historian with Roman citizenship who attended the sack of Jerusalem by Titus in AD 70. His most famous works are the *Wars of the Jews* and the *Antiquities of the Jews.*

AUGUSTINE: (354-430). Looked upon as the greatest of the early church theologians and philosophers.

JEROME: (*c.* 340-420). Reviser of the Latin translation of the Bible.

COPTS: Christian Egyptians who claim links back to pharaonic times. Their church liturgy, particularly the priestly incantations, are purported to resemble the vocalisation of ancient Egyptian.

GESENIUS: (1786-1842). German orientalist and professor of theology at Halle University. His greatest work is the monumental *Thesaurus Philologico-criticus Linguae Hebraicae et Chaldaicae Veteris Testamenti* (1858 & 1892).

SUMER: The name given to the region of southern Iraq where the so-called Sumerian civilisation developed in the third millennium BC. Also known as Sumeria.

COLCHIS: Modern Georgia on the east side of the Black Sea.

GORDON: (1833-1885).

SPADIX: Otherwise known as a catkin.

57. The large double coconut of the female palm tree, *Lodoicea Seychellarum*, known as the 'Coco de Mer'.

58. Location of the Seychelles.

same as Eden. Paradise lay beyond Sumer, beyond Canaan, beyond Egypt. It was a place that the descendants of Adam had no claim to and which remained beyond their reach.

Some scholars chose to narrow down the field of search. COLCHIS (of Jason and the Argonauts fame) was identified with the land of Havilah, 'rich in gold', partly because of the tale of the golden fleece but also on the grounds that the name of its principal river – the Phasis – bore some resemblance to the biblical Pishon. This proposal, so much dependent on Greek mythology, was just as implausible.

I remember as a teenager watching a natural world TV documentary. I can still picture the presenter clambering through the dense jungle on the tropical island of Praslin, in the Indian Ocean, telling the story of General Charles GORDON (of Khartoum) who had his own theory as to the location of the Garden of Eden. Gordon visited the Seychelles in 1881 where he came upon a lush ravine known today as *La Vallée de Mai*. This extraordinary place is still regarded as one of the botanical wonders of our planet and is a World Heritage Site.

In his book *Eden and its Two Sacramental Trees* (never published), General Gordon argued that this volcanic island was the true Eden because, within its lush canopy of vegetation, grew thirty-metre coconut palm trees (*Lodoicea Seychellarum*) bearing large, luxuriant fruit. This nine-kilogram, double coconut – known as the *Coco de Mer* – has all the appearances and size of a naked female pelvis. The male tree also posesses a two-metre-long, fleshy, pendent SPADIX. The sexual connotations are obvious. The edible part of the huge nut has long been regarded as an aphrodisiac and the fruit is also used as an antidote to certain poisons.

Putting all this together, Gordon suggested that the *Vallée de Mai* was the actual historical site of the Garden of Eden and that the remarkable *Coco de Mer* was nothing less than the 'forbidden fruit' of Eve's temptation.

Needless to say, few were to take up his idea. Yes, Praslin is indeed a paradise island. But why should the rich human tapestry of the Eden story have originated with an exotic fruit? And, yes, the *Coco de Mer* is carried by the easterly ocean currents to the shores of the Maldives near India – a distance of one thousand five hundred kilometres. But, even so, could the tradition and its people have traversed a further three thousand kilometres across the wide Indian Ocean to plant the Genesis legend into the soil of the ancient world? Clearly the Eden story is of Middle-Eastern origin.

Unfortunately there is so much nervousness about proposing new ideas within academia these days that most historians tend to be shy of using their imaginations and, as a result, the interested reader is left only with the products of the imaginations of previous generations. Those within academia who dare to venture new ideas are often ridiculed by their colleagues precisely because they are using their intuition and imagination in an attempt to answer vexing historical questions. Trained historians, armed with all the tools to make major discoveries, tend to pick at the edges of knowledge rather than attempting to penetrate to the heart of it. That much more exciting task is generally left to those who are uncumbered by academic responsibility and peer pressure. But these 'non-academic' scholars are also untrained in the methodologies of academia and have little, if any, knowledge of the tools of the trade – ancient languages, archaeological training, scholarly library source-material and access to expert colleagues for consultation. This is a great pity. On the one hand we have the academic expertise, sadly without the imagination to take ancient history anywhere, and on the other hand creative minds, with genuine enthusiasm, unfortunately without the necessary skills to exploit their intuitive ideas. Explorers are rarely scholars and scholars rarely pursue their research out into the physical landscape of the world they study.

The one field which is the exception to the rule is archaeology where there are a few specialists who still have a little of the 'explorer' left in them – but even here, in the most exotic of academic disciplines, there is a tendency to play it safe. One well-known archaeologist excavating in Egypt made this attitude very clear to me when I visited 'his site'. He knew 'his site' as he knew 'his own body'. No-one else could speculate or comment on 'his site' because only he really knew its intimate details (unfortunately as yet unpublished). Because of this attitude, he himself was unprepared to speculate or discuss other archaeologists' sites – after all only they had the right to comment on their work and findings. This extraordinary attitude exemplifies the degree of specialisation and furrow-mindedness which pervades the field of ancient world studies today. Sadly, the archaeologist concerned was unable to appreciate that his conservative approach to history – shackled by the restraints of ultra-caution and specialisation – was the very reason for the slow strangulation (both financial and intellectual) of his discipline.

Sources for Eden

So far I have introduced you to the crucial passage in the book of Genesis which locates the land of Eden at the sources of four rivers – only two of which we are able to recognise with confidence. As we have seen, there have been many attempts to identify the other rivers of Eden, but none have been particularly convincing. Soon we will be focusing on the true location of the earthly paradise by pinpointing those two rivers in the mountain region of western Iran. But first, what about the name Eden itself?

There is an ancient Mesopotamian word *edin* (Sumerian) or *edinu* (Akkadian) which first occurs in a short narrative concerning a war between the Mesopotamian city-states of Lagash and Umma. The context suggests that this *edin* is an open plain situated between the two disputing cities – a sort of wasteland or zone without cultivation. On this basis scholars have understood *edin* to mean 'open plain' or 'uncultivated land'

59. Detail from the 'Stela of the Vultures' showing Eanatum, ruler of Lagash, in his chariot leading the troops of the city into battle against the army of Umma. From Girsu, Early Dynastic III Period. Louvre Museum.

and thus some recognise in it the etymological origins of the biblical Eden.[1] The term *edin* also occurs in an important Sumerian epic tale known as 'Enmerkar and the Lord of Aratta' – but more on that later.

An alternative view is to see Eden coming from the Hebrew verbal root *adhan* meaning 'to be delighted'. Thus Eden would mean something like 'place of delight'.[2]

All this is useful to our investigations. But, even though finding early etymological origins for Eden may help to push back the biblical tradition in time, it does not *prove* that the place actually existed. We need a great deal more than that to convince a sceptical world. Most of all, we need to find the actual geographical location which lies at the heart of the ante-diluvian saga recorded in the book of Genesis.

As I have already said, my approach has always been to try and retain an open mind about all the source material we have at our disposal – even if some of that material at first seems less than reliable. This positive attitude towards the sources has always been part of my *modus operandi* when looking at an historical problem. I am simply unwilling to reject a traditional historical source out of hand without first having seen what it has to offer. This frame of mind also applies to the ideas of other scholars – especially those 'amateur' historians and chronologists who, by defini-tion, tend to be less weighed down by academic caution. It is precisely because I have a reputation for being prepared to listen, that, over the years, I have received numerous short papers and book manuscripts from these non-academic historians. All sorts of ideas flow in – some so far out that they must have been posted from another planet, but also many very interesting suggestions which deserve to be developed.

One such theory arrived on my desk in October 1987. It had been sent to me by Derek Shelley-Pearce, a member of the Institute for the Study of Interdisciplinary Sciences – a British educational charity for which, at the time, I was working as Director. Derek had seen a brief article entitled 'The Real Land of Eden' in *Still Trowelling* (the *Newsletter of the Ancient and Medieval History Book Club* in the UK[3]) and had requested a copy of a more detailed version advertised there by the author. This was what Derek had sent me.

The sky blue cover of the paper bore the title '*The Land of Eden* by R. A. Walker'. Inside were twenty-seven typed pages and a map. When I first began to study the text in 1987, I remember wondering what sort of mind had put this together. Many of the author's ideas were based on 'the name game' – identifying toponyms in eastern Anatolia with names from the pantheon of Greek gods. Walker argued that it was possible to trace the origins of Greek mythology and religion back to the area which scholars have long believed to be the original homeland of Indo-European culture – the Caucasus. In particular, he focused on the region traditionally known as Armenia. In doing so, Walker also put forward his fascinating ideas on the location of the biblical Eden, using the same 'name game' methodology.

Although I had reservations about many of the linguistic and phonetic arguments, I was still intrigued by Walker's thesis. But, at the time, I was just beginning my degree in Ancient History and Egyptology at University College London and so there was no time to follow up on Walker's work. In hindsight, I wish I had made the effort to contact this unusual scholar, for I have since learnt that Reginald Arthur Walker died in 1989.

Much of what I will be discussing in the rest of this chapter stems from Walker's original thesis, with additional findings which have come out of my own follow-up research. I am convinced that Eden has finally been located and that the prize of this modern-day discovery should be posthumously awarded to a little-known scholar named Reginald Walker.

So, what are the available written sources which we can call upon to help locate the mythical land of Eden? Primarily, of course, there is Genesis itself – the first book of the Bible. But the Sumerian myths also have much to offer, as do the published results from nearly two hundred years of archaeological endeavour in the Middle East.

I suppose, then, the obvious place to start our investigation is with the biblical text itself, just as Walker had done in the 1980s.

60. REGINALD ARTHUR WALKER: (1917-1989).

The Four Rivers of Genesis

As I have already stated, there is one key passage in the book of Genesis which is going to point us towards our goal. It gives very clear indications that Eden is a specific geographical entity – no obvious mythology here. This was a place which had boundaries and was the source of four great rivers. The geographical extract from Genesis Chapter Two is now worth quoting in full.

- God planted a garden in Eden, which is in the east, and there he put the man he had fashioned. From the soil, God caused to grow every kind of tree, enticing to look at and good to eat, with the tree of life in the middle of the garden, and the tree of knowledge of good and evil. [Genesis 2:8-9]

- A river flowed from Eden to water the garden, and from there it divided to make four heads (i.e. headwaters). [Genesis 2:10]

- The first is named the Pishon, which winds all through the land of Havilah, rich in gold. The gold of this country is pure. BDELLIUM (Heb. *bedolah*) and Shoham stone (CORNELIAN or ONYX?) are found there. [Genesis 2:11-12]

- The second river is named the Gihon, and this winds all through the land of Cush. [Genesis 2:13]

- The third river is named the Hiddekel, and this flows to the east of Ashur. [Genesis 2:14]

- The fourth river is the Perath. [Genesis 2:14]

BDELLIUM: A resin somewhat like myrrh.

CORNELIAN: A semi-transparent red quartz used in the manufacture of cylinder seals.

ONYX: A gemstone of alternating black and white parallel veins, but also a calcite marble.

Let us deal in detail with the four great rivers in reverse order.

(a) The **Perath** (Sum. *Buranun*) is the river known to the Greeks (and subsequently to the modern world) as the Euphrates. To modern Arabs it is the Firat which, of course, harks back to the biblical Perath. It is the longest river in the Middle East (excluding the African Nile). From its sources near Lake Van (not far from Erzerum), the Euphrates flows in a great arc for 2,720 kilometres before disgorging into the Persian Gulf to the south of the modern port of Basra.[4]

(b) The **Hiddekel** (Sum. *Idiglat*) is the Hebrew name of the River Tigris. It descends from the Zagros mountains to the west and south of Lake Van and Lake Urmia, journeying some 2,033 kilometres to the head of the Persian Gulf. In its upper reaches there are three major streams which flow into the main channel from the north – the Greater (or Upper) Zab, the Lesser (or Lower) Zab and the Diyala. The principal source rises in a small lake, with the modern name Hazar Golu, which is located about sixty kilometres to the west of Lake Van.[5] Much further downstream, just to the north of Basra, the Rivers Tigris and Euphrates come together at the modern town of Kurnah, to form the Shatt el-Arab, before emptying into the 'Southern Sea' as the Mesopotamians called the Gulf. The Tigris is the second great waterway of the Mesopotamian alluvial basin. Mesopotamia, of course, is Greek for the land 'between the two rivers' – the mighty Tigris and Euphrates.

(c) The identity of the **Gihon** is a little more difficult to establish but, as Walker discovered, it is to be identified with the River Araxes whose tributaries rise in the mountains to the north of Lake Van and Lake Urmia (also near Erzerum). From there they flow down to join the main channel (known as the Kur) which empties into the Caspian Sea south of Baku.

The name Araxes (more recently referred to as the Araks or Aras) and the name Gihon obviously bear no resemblance to each other. Here, then, we seem to have a clear case of a name change which has taken place at some time in the past. So how far back do we have to go to find clues to the original name of the river which is now known as the Aras? Not very far at all is the answer.

During the Islamic invasion of the Caucasus in the eighth century AD stretches of this third great river were still called the Gaihun. There was, indeed, an intermediate stage, before the Gaihun became known simply as the Aras, when the Persians of the last century referred to this major watercourse as the Jichon-Aras.[6] Interestingly enough, you will find the name Gihon-Aras in early biblical dictionaries and commentaries dating from Victorian times. Today, however, this crucial piece of information has apparently been forgotten and you would be hard pressed to find a modern work on Genesis which links the Gihon with the Aras. So much for modern scholarship!

Victorian scholars not only identified the Aras/Araxes with the Gihon but also suggested that the classical land of Cossaea, located according to the ancient geographers near Media and the Caspian Sea, was to be identified with the biblical land of Cush through which the Gihon flowed. Cush can perhaps also be identified with the land of the Kassites – the mountain people who invaded southern Mesopotamia during the second millennium BC and ruled over Kassite Babylonia for the best part of five-and-a-half centuries (OC – 1700-1160 BC).

(d) Finally, the **Pishon** is, according to Walker's arguments, the River Uizhun which rises from several springs located near Mount Sahand (an extinct volcano east of Lake Urmia) and the Zagros mountain massif around the Kurdish capital of Sanandaj. It outflows into the southern Caspian Sea not far from the modern port of Rast. The Uizhun is also known as the Kezel Uzun – 'long gold'. Here the ancient name Uizhun, of unknown meaning, has been colloquialised into the familiar Iranian word Uzun ('dark red' or 'gold'). There is no obvious connection between the names Pishon and Uizhun but the geographical overview confirms this identification.

The simple schematic diagram (below) indicates where we should look for the Pishon – having already established the identity of the three other watercourses mentioned in Genesis 2:8-14. In anti-clockwise order, we have the Gihon/Gaihun-Aras occupying the north-eastern sector; the Perath/Euphrates flowing out from the north-west; and the Hiddekel/Tigris descending from the mountains in the south-west. This leaves the south-eastern sector as the place to look for the Pishon.

The *only* great river flowing through this quarter is the Uizhun. Unfortunately, there are no modern topographical features or town-names

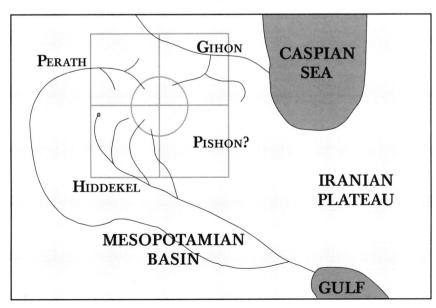

61. Three of the rivers of Eden – the Perath (Euphrates), the Hiddekel (Tigris) and the Gihon (Araxes/Gaihun) – in schematic form, giving a clear impression that the location of the fourth river (the Pishon) should be sought in the south-east sector.

which appear to retain memories of the biblical name of the river. But, as Walker argued, the name Uizhun itself may hold the key. This is our first opportunity to indulge in the 'name game'.

For a moment let us drop the initial vowel in Uizhun. This leaves us with [...]izhun which, allowing for the usual linguistic variations in vocalisation (*sh* to *s* or *z* and *o* to *u*), would be identical with biblical [...]ishon. It appears that, in the Hebrew text of Genesis, the labial vowel 'U' underwent a conversion to the labial consonant 'P'. Uizhun is thus the original name of the river, stubbornly retained by local tradition into modern times, whilst the Pishon is a biblical corruption of that original name.

At first glance this may seem a little far fetched, but an example of precisely this kind of fluidity is known. The modern name Pisdeli (ascribed to an ancient occupation mound near the southern shore of Lake Urmia) derives from the ancient Iranian toponym *Ush* or *Uash* which was in common use throughout the general region of southern Urmia. Recently discovered contemporary texts confirm that Pisdeli was ancient Uishteri (demonstrating the well-attested changes from *t* to *d* and *r* to *l* but, most importantly, also *U* to *P*).[7]

Conclusion One

The four rivers of Genesis 10:14 are the Kezel Uizhun (Pishon), the Gaihun/Aras (Gihon), the Tigris (Hiddekel) and the Euphrates (Perath).

So all four of the rivers of Genesis have their headwaters in the Lake Van and Lake Urmia region. The basins of these two large salt lakes were once the heartland of an expansive region known as Armenia. Today's political map is considerably more complex, with eastern Turkey to the west, modern Armenia to the north, Iranian Azerbaijan occupying the eastern area between Urmia and the Caspian Sea, and Kurdistan to the south. However, I will be retaining that archaeological, non-political term, 'Armenia' here for the sake of simplicity.

The name Armenia itself may derive from the first millennium BC kingdom of the Mannai (the Manneans) whose capital (modern Miyandoab), in the fertile plain to the south of Lake Urmia, would perhaps have been called Ur-Mannai ('City' or 'Foundation of the Manneans'). It is clear from several examples that *ur* is equivalent to biblical *ar*. The prefix *ur/ar* or *uru/ara* was in fairly common use throughout the ancient Near East, the two most famous instances being the Sumerian city of Ur (simply meaning 'city') and Jerusalem or Uru-Shalem ('City' or 'Foundation of Shalem'). The modern Iranian town of Urmia (with the lake named after it) also appears to be a survival from older times. Urmia (Arab. Urumiya) may represent Ur-Miya or Uru-Miya ('City of Miya' or 'City of the Water', i.e. the lake).

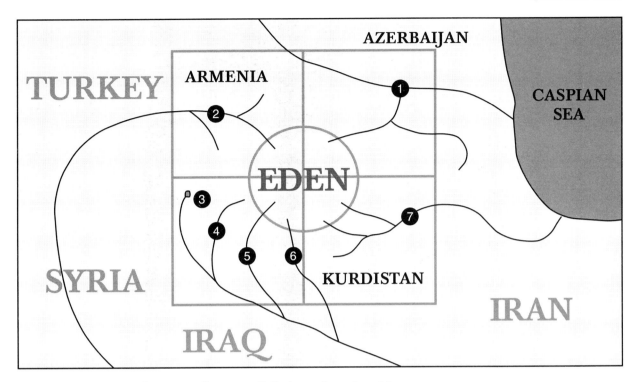

Key to Map

1. Araxes/Aras
2. Euphrates
3. Lake Hazar
4. Greater Zab
5. Lesser Zab
6. Diyala
7. Uizhun/Kezel Uzun

62. The four rivers of Eden flowing out from the four quarters of paradise. Two disgorge into the Persian Gulf whilst the other two empty into the Caspian Sea.

The Assyrians of the first millennium BC also referred to this area as 'Urartu', which is where the biblical name Ararat comes from. I think we can see in this name another ancient city-state – Ur-Ar(a)tu or Ar-Arat ('City of Arat(u)') – the capital of a kingdom which will play a major part in our search for the biblical Eden.

Having established the likely identities of the four great rivers of Genesis, and shown how they focus on the region generally referred to as Armenia, it is time to take a look at the other geographical details supplied by the same crucial biblical passage.

Cush and Havilah

Genesis 2:14 confirms what is already well established – that the River Tigris flows to the east of the heartland of Assyria (biblical Ashur). The very fact that the writer felt the need to record such an obvious geo-political detail should give us the confidence to believe that the other topographical pointers mentioned must also represent the geographical reality of his time. So what of the lands of Cush and Havilah?

Genesis 2:13 describes the River Gihon as winding 'all through the land of Cush'. Are there any classical or modern topographical clues in the general vicinity of the River Aras (formerly Gaihun) which suggest that this region may once have been called the land of Cush?

We have already mentioned Gesenius' observations concerning the land of Cossaea, but there is a much more impressive monument to ancient Cush. To the north of the modern city of Tabriz there is a high

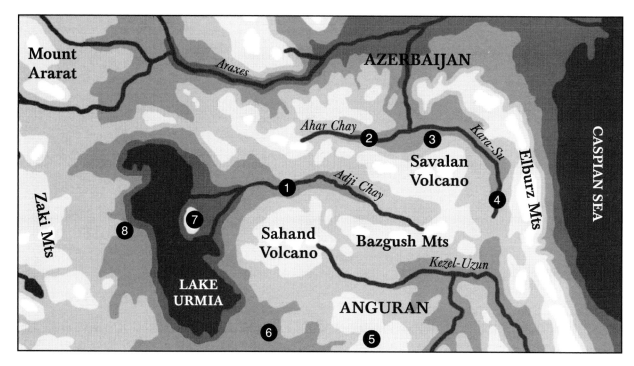

Mount Ararat

Araxes

AZERBAIJAN

Ahar Chay

2

3

Kara-Su

CASPIAN SEA

Savalan Volcano

Adji Chay

1

4

Elburz Mts

Zaki Mts

8

7

Sahand Volcano

Bazgush Mts

Kezel-Uzun

LAKE URMIA

ANGURAN

6

5

Key to Map

1. Tabriz
2. Ahar
3. Meshginshahr
4. Ardabil
5. Takht-é Suleiman
6. Miyandoab
7. Shahi Island
8. Urmia

63. Simple relief map giving an idea of the general topography of the eastern part of Eden in which the Garden of Eden was located.

AZERI: A native of Azerbaijan and the language of the region (a dialect of Turkish).

SASSANIAN: Pertaining to the era of the Sassanid Dynasty of Persia (founded by Ardashir I). The Sassanian kings succeeded the Parthian Dynasty in AD 224 but succumbed to the Islamic invasion of the Umayyad caliphs in AD 637 during the reign of Yazdigird III.

ZOROASTRIAN: Belonging to the followers of Zoroastra or Zarathustra.

TAKHT-É SULEIMAN: 'Throne of Solomon'. A sacred site set beside a volcanic spring which was fortified during the Mongol invasion.

mountain pass through which the modern road winds its way up to the towns of Ahar and Meshginshahr. Several of the Aras' tributaries have their headwaters near these AZERI towns. The modern Iranian name of the 4,000-metre mountain ridge which separates the valley of Tabriz from Ahar is *Kusheh Dagh* – the 'Mountain of Kush'.

Genesis 2:11 informs us that the River Pishon winds all through the land of Havilah and that this region is rich in gold.

Although I have been unable to find a general geological report on the river basins of the upper reaches of the Uizhun/Kezel Uzun, it is clear from the isolated information I have gathered that the mineral wealth in the entire region is significant. In recent years gold has been mined in the Ardabil region and a SASSANIAN (third to seventh centuries AD) gold mine has been identified at the village of Zarshuyan near the famous ZOROASTRIAN fire temple of TAKHT-É SULEIMAN. If the Kezel Uzun is the biblical Pishon, then this early gold mine is at the heart of ancient Havilah 'rich in gold'. Interestingly enough, the river which flows down from the extinct volcano of Takht-é Suleiman is called the Zarrineh Rud which means the 'Golden River'. The village name 'Zarshuyan' itself is formed of two Persian words: *zar* – 'gold' and *shuyan* – 'washing', strongly suggesting a link to panning for gold in the 'Golden River' (Zarrineh Rud). As we have noted, even the word *Kezel* in Kezel Uzun can have the meaning 'gold' although its more common colloquial meaning is 'dark red'.

There is no doubt then that the mountain region from which the various sources of the Uizhun/Uzun/Pishon flow could indeed be described as a land once 'rich in gold'. But, according to the author of Genesis,

Havilah is also the source of prized stones, in particular 'Shoham stone'. It is not exactly clear which stone this represents. However, recent Iranian research has shown that lapis lazuli, previously thought only to come from Badakhshan in Afganistan, is to be found in the Anguran region, at the heart of the area we have identified as biblical Havilah.

SEPTUAGINT: Meaning 'seventy' after its seventy scholarly authors.

> ## Conclusion Two
>
> The biblical land of Cush was located in Azerbaijan whilst the land of Havilah was located in the Iranian mountain region now known as Anguran.

The Garden

Having established the location of Eden, we shall now list the basic facts to be drawn from the Genesis narrative which help us to locate the Garden of Eden and which describe various aspects of its nature.

- The Garden lies east of (literally 'in') Eden [Genesis 11:8]. This appears to mean in the eastern part of Eden but still within its boundaries, because the Garden clearly belongs to the place called Eden.

- The Garden contains 'every kind of tree' [Genesis 2:9].

- The Garden is rich in all kinds of fruit and also possesses an abundance of spices such as saffron, nard, sweet calamus and cinnamon. It is the earthly paradise. Indeed, the version of the Old Testament translated into Greek by the Jews of Alexandria in the third century BC (known as the SEPTUAGINT or LXX) uses the word *paradeisos* ('parkland') for 'Garden' from which we derive the biblical paradise. This Greek word derives, in turn, from the ancient Persian *pairidaeza* which means 'enclosed parkland'. It is therefore interesting to note that the Hebrew word *gan* used for 'garden' in the Garden of Eden is derived from the verbal root *ganan* 'to hedge in' or 'protect' and thus also means 'walled garden' or 'enclosed park'. All these ideas seem to link us back to the fertile Iranian highland valleys hemmed in so completely by precipitous mountain walls.

- Two cherubim are posted at the eastern gate of Eden. These are not pretty pink babies with fluffy wings but terrifying beasts – part feline and part bird of prey. They are otherwise described as great winged creatures [I Kings 6:27] and are associated with the 'Fiery Flashing Sword' [Genesis 3:24]. They protect the Garden of Eden from intruders who might attempt to enter Eden from the east to gain access to the tree of life. The word cherub comes from Babylonian *karibu* – the word used to describe huge winged guardians which flank the gateways into temples. The Bible informs us that in later times the Ark of the Covenant was protected by two such cherubim as it rested within the holy of holies in the Jerusalem temple. The origins of these fearsome guardians of the forbidden places is difficult to establish, but, in biblical terms at least, they first appear as the protectors of Eden's eastern gateway immediately after Cain's exile from the Garden. Are they simply a demonic creation of the story-tellers or something rather more tangible, perhaps even historical? There are several examples of mythological creatures whose image and character have been created out of the mundane activities of humankind. In my view it is probable that we are dealing here with the memory of a wild, warlike tribe which once dwelt in this region and which worshipped a giant bird of prey such as the eagle or falcon. Their SHAMANS may have worn head-dresses decorated with the heads of the birds and with trailing plumage covering their long coats like giant wings. The telling of the tale through an extended process of oral tradition gradually led to this powerful shamanic image becoming itself the visualisation of the guardians of Eden – the carriers of the 'fiery flashing sword' – rather than the people who bore the creature as their emblem. A famous example of this type of interpolation of human cultic ritual into the imagery of a demonic monster can be seen in the transformation of the bull-leapers of Crete into the Minotaur of the Labyrinth – the half human and half bull figure of Greek legend. Another, more recent, example is that of the 'Ice

64. An ivory of Phoenician origin representing a winged *karibu*, half human and half vulture. British Museum.

SHAMANS: Tribal spirit priests or medicine men usually associated with wild animals or birds of prey.

65. The weather-god, carrying lightning bolts ('fiery flashing swords'?), pursues a dragon. From the temple of Ninurta at Nimrud (ancient Kalhu, biblical Calah).

Maiden' whose body, unearthed in the Altai mountains of southern Siberia, was adorned with tattoos of mythical creatures resembling deer. The archaeologists excavating the site of this PAZYRYK grave have suggested that the woman was a story-teller or shaman and that the creatures represented in the elaborate artwork of the region in later times are derived directly from the shaman imagery. In other words, the exotic animal disguises worn by the priests and priestesses of earlier times have been transformed into fantastical composite mythological creatures. A similar process seems to have taken place within native American tribal cultures.

- In TALMUDIC tradition there are seven heavens (Heb. *rakiim*) which the deceased must pass though to reach the Throne of Glory (hence the phrase 'seventh heaven', meaning ecstasy). Each heaven has a door or gate (of fire) which is reached by a ladder or stairway. The seven heavens have physical properties such as snow, hail, dew, storm and wind. The journey of the dead thus appears to be very much like crossing over mountain ranges (through passes – the ladders and doors) with alpine valleys between them (the heavens). The protecting angels represent the elements of the volcanic peaks: Michael – snow, Gabriel – fire, Jorkami – hail, Ben Nez – storm, Barakiel – lightning, Raashiel – earthquake. All this wonderful Talmudic imagery concerning the way to paradise implies the traversing of mountains.

So where is this paradisiacal garden? Well, if we begin to superimpose some geographical features onto our simple map of Eden – having established the four rivers – we will see something very interesting happening in the eastern half of the region.

> God planted a garden in Eden, which is **in the east**, and there he put the man he had fashioned. From the soil, God caused to grow **every kind of tree**, enticing to look at and good to eat ... [Genesis 2:8-9]

Immediately to the east of Lake Urmia (which we have located at the heart of Eden) is a high valley bounded on three sides (north, east and south) by snow-capped mountains. Along the valley floor runs a river (known today as the Adji Chay or 'bitter waters'). At its outflow into the lake a large salty delta, rich in wildlife, has formed over the millennia. Beyond the delta, just a few kilometres offshore, is the volcanic island of Jazireh-é Shah ('Island of the King') rising out of the water.

The valley itself is very fertile with a rich variety of fruit trees stretching up its terraced slopes. In prehistoric times, when the climate here was much warmer and wetter, this was a lush, densely forested valley with abundant water supply. Life here would have been easy compared to the less hospitable regions beyond its protecting mountains. If a prehistoric estate agent were to try to sell you a building plot here he might be forgiven for referring to this place as an 'earthly paradise'.

PAZYRYK: The name given to the culture whose graves were first found in the Pazyryk valley. Their ethnicity is apparently Mongolian but it has been suggested that they may be related to the Scythian horse-breeding tribes described by Herodotus.

TALMUDIC: From the corpus of material gathered together to form the compilation of ancient Jewish law and tradition. There are two recensions – the Palestinian Talmud (AD 375) and the Babylonian Talmud (AD 500).

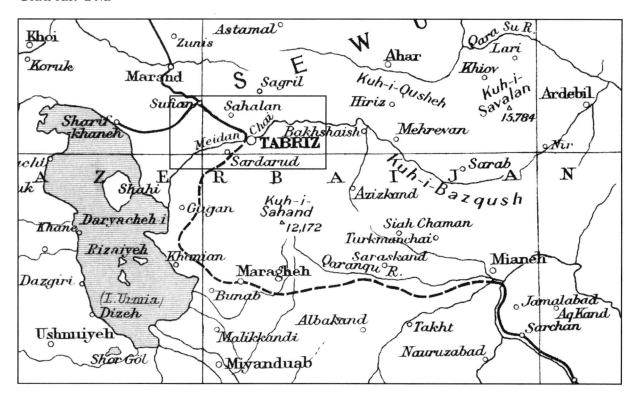

66. A nineteenth-century atlas showing the Adji Chay marked as the 'Meidan Chai' flowing through Tabriz (see inside rectangle).

Could this be the original Garden of Eden? Certain clues suggest that it just might be.

A river flowed from Eden to water the garden … [Genesis 2:10]

First, the Adji Chay flows down from the mountains of Eden (specifically the Savalan and Sahand ranges) into the valley identified as the Garden, thus explaining the strange statement that, although the Garden was 'in' the east of Eden the water source flowed out 'from' Eden into the Garden.

Second, the Adji Chay has a much older name – the Meidan. The word *meidan* is also Persian and, extraordinarily as it may seem, also has the meaning 'enclosed-court' or 'walled-garden'. We see it still in use in the names of Persian public squares such as the Meidan-é Shah ('Walled-Garden of the King') in Isfahan. We have noted that the Septuagint refers to the Garden of Eden as paradise. The word paradise was first used by Xenophon to describe the enclosed parks and gardens of the Persian kings. Thus *both* the Greek *paradeisos* and the Persian *meidan* describe an enclosed-garden or parkland. Our valley, through which the Meidan river flows and which is located in the eastern part of Eden, certainly is protected by high mountain walls on three sides and a great lake on the fourth. It is therefore nature's enclosed garden but on a gigantic scale, as befits the *Gan* Eden created by God – the '(enclosed) Garden of Eden'.

At the centre of the Meidan valley stands the sprawling city of Tabriz which covers much of the area where any early prehistoric settlements may have been located. However, there are one or two ancient ruin

67. Opposite page: The pastoral way of life, so prevalent in the Zagros mountains of today and throughout Man's history in the region. A shepherd guides his flock through a steep-sided river gorge and on up to the summer grazing grounds.

68. The great salt lake of Urmia – the heart of Eden – with the rugged volcanic peaks of Shahi island across the water.

mounds to the west of the city, rising up above the orchards which border on the delta marshlands. Only one has been excavated so far (to my knowledge) and that has revealed some intriguing finds which may have historical implications for the story of Adam and his kin. The discoveries from Yanik Tepe and related sites in the southern part of the Urmia basin will be discussed in succeeding chapters when I will be describing my own personal pilgrimage to Eden and the results of limited archaeological explorations in the region.

To the north of Tabriz rises the Mountain of Kush (Kusheh Dagh) which separates Eden from the land of Cush. To the south an even higher mountain stretches up to the sky. This is the extinct volcano known as Mount Sahand. It separates the Meidan valley from the river basin of the Uizhun/Pishon which flows through the land of Havilah. It would be hard to find a more dramatic setting for the fabled Garden of Eden.

Conclusion Three

The biblical Garden of Eden is to be identified with the Adji Chay valley (formerly known as the Meidan valley) in north-west Iran at the heart of which is the regional capital of Tabriz.

Exiled to the Land of Nod

There is a final biblical clue which confirms Walker's location for Eden. It comes from a later passage in the book of Genesis where the narrator deals with the murder by Cain of his brother Abel. When the god of Eden discovers Cain's crime he banishes him from the Garden, and so Cain settles 'in the land of Nod, which is east of Eden' [Genesis 4:16.].

If we were to follow in Cain's footsteps as he departs from Eden we would be setting off from the region around Tabriz, heading in an easterly direction towards the Caspian Sea. At first we follow the main course of the Adji Chay/Meidan river but, eventually, the road begins to rise out of the valley as it ascends through the high pass leading to modern Ardabil. Beyond a second mountain ridge, east of Ardabil, lies 1,000 kilometres of Caspian Sea. So the land of Nod, into which Cain was exiled, has to be around here somewhere.

Just to the north of Ardabil are the local districts of Upper and Lower Noqdi. Several villages in this area are called Noqdi. A small town to the east of Ardabil is called Noadi. The terminal '-i' in all these names is the Arabic word for 'of' in the sense of 'belonging to' (this letter -*i* is often replaced today with -*é* on modern maps). For example we know that an Iraqi is a person of Iraq or a Pakistani is a person belonging to Pakistan. An Arab would call an Englishman 'Inglesi'. So a number of the place-names located to the north and east of Ardabil can be read as 'belonging to Noqd' or 'Noad'. Do we have here a surviving memory of the country of Cain's exile – the biblical Land of Nod?

> ## Conclusion Four
>
> **The Land of Nod was located in the plain west of the Elburz mountains around the city of Ardabil.**

Whilst we are in this part of the world I should just take you a few kilometres to the south of Ardabil – to the town of Helabad, formerly known as Heruabad (Kheruabad). This sleepy town, located at the head of a mountain pass leading to the shore of the Caspian Sea, is strategically placed to protect the land of Eden from eastern invaders. Kheru-abad means 'settlement of the Kheru(-people)'. Is it just another coincidence that the biblical Kerubim (or Cherubs) – with their 'Fiery Flashing Sword' – were the fearsome protectors of Eden's eastern border?

A Land of Plenty

We should complete this discussion of the geography of Eden by taking a look at what tangible benefits this landscape had to offer the first 'legendary' people by way of natural resources.

69. Inside the vast crater-like ring of mountains which surrounds Takht-é Suleiman ('Throne of Solomon') – the sacred spring which is the source of the Zarrineh Rud (the 'Golden River').

NEOLITHIC AGE: The New or Late Stone Age (*c.* 10,000-5,000 BC) when Man used refined tools such as flint axes, daggers, spear and arrow-heads. This is the period when evidence for the domestication of animals and the cultivation of land first appears in the archaeological record.

MALACHITE: A hydrous carbonate of copper, green in colour, which occurs in rich veins in the northern Zagros range.

70. Opposite page: Map showing the complex river system of the Mesopotamian plain and Zagros mountain range. Also shown are the principal political regions which played a significant part in the region during the period of the Bronze and Iron Ages.

As I have already indicated, archaeological and climatological investigations have determined that the region we call Armenia was once a great deal warmer and wetter than it is today. The vegetation of Eden was considerably more lush, with hillsides cloaked in dense deciduous forests and the valley floors abundant in exotic plants. Even in today's drier climate some parts of the region remain stunningly beautiful and fertile. All this fits well with a rich-soiled Eden planted with 'every kind of tree', abundant in all wild fruit and overflowing with sweet water. As Lang notes, it is hardly surprising that 'this gives some encouragement to the view that Armenia was the site of the biblical Garden of Eden'.[8]

We have also seen that Armenia is equally blessed from the perspective of mineral wealth – minerals which played a major part in the development of early civilisation.

Primitive obsidian tools have been collected in the region by palaeo-anthropologists, demonstrating Stone Age occupation. Obsidian is a form of hard volcanic glass which can be flaked to form a sharp cutting implement. It seems that Neolithic Man was obtaining his first tools from the slopes of Eden's extinct volcanoes around Lake Van. There is evidence that several sites were occupied during the NEOLITHIC AGE, showing that human life has existed in these parts for at least ten thousand years. Recent DNA research has also shown that the earliest exploitation of einkorn (the wild form of wheat) occurred in the region. The highlands of eastern Turkey and Armenia are thus recognised by anthropologists as the most significant cradle of Neolithic culture. This is an important point which we will return to later.

Several rich deposits of MALACHITE are located in the region. Smelting this ore in charcoal furnaces produces copper – and copper, of course, is the basic ingredient of bronze. It is believed that the first exploitation of this valuable mineral took place in early-third-millennium Armenia.[9] In around 3000 BC the flourishing Early Bronze Age 'Kuro-Araxes' culture established itself in the valleys and plains of this lofty highland region

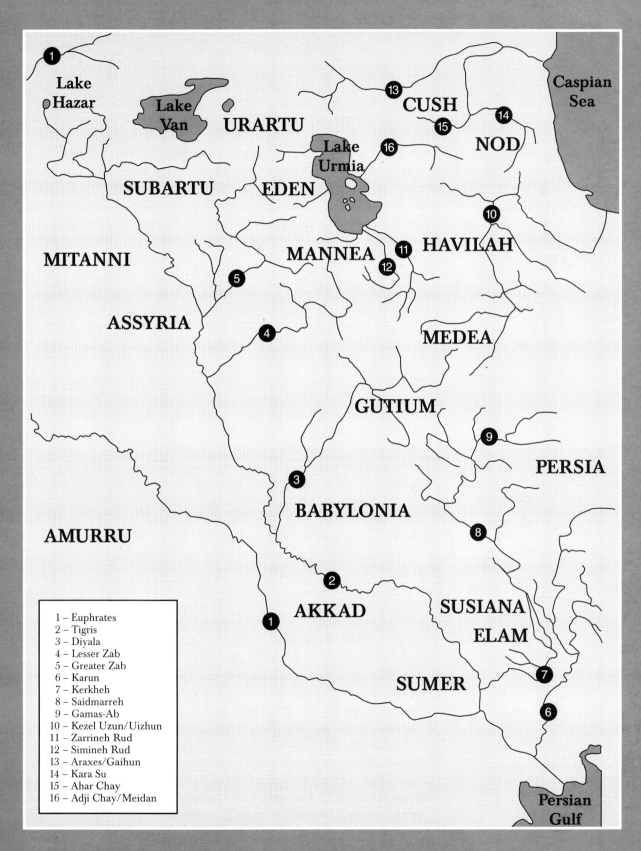

Lake
Hazar

Lake
Van

URARTU

CUSH

Caspian
Sea

NOD

Lake
Urmia

SUBARTU

EDEN

MITANNI

MANNEA

HAVILAH

ASSYRIA

MEDEA

GUTIUM

PERSIA

AMURRU

BABYLONIA

AKKAD

SUSIANA

ELAM

SUMER

1 – Euphrates
2 – Tigris
3 – Diyala
4 – Lesser Zab
5 – Greater Zab
6 – Karun
7 – Kerkheh
8 – Saidmarreh
9 – Gamas-Ab
10 – Kezel Uzun/Uizhun
11 – Zarrineh Rud
12 – Simineh Rud
13 – Araxes/Gaihun
14 – Kara Su
15 – Ahar Chay
16 – Adji Chay/Meidan

Persian
Gulf

Early Palaeolithic 600,000-250,000 BC
Middle Palaeolithic 250,000-40,000 BC
Late Palaeolithic 40,000-12,000 BC
Mesolithic 12,000-10,000 BC
Aceramic Neolithic 10,000-7,500 BC
Ceramic Neolithic 7,500-5,000 BC
Chalcolithic 5,000-3,000 BC
Early Bronze Age 3,000-2,300 BC

71. A broad chronological outline of the prehistoric and early historic archaeological eras in the Middle East.

(remember that the Araxes is the biblical Gihon). The craftsmen of these people not only created simple, exquisite black and red burnished pottery but also invented metallurgy – smelting copper and tin to make the first bronze tools and weapons. The biblical genealogy of Eden states that Cain's great-great-great-great grandson, Tubal-Cain (brother of Noah), was the ancestor of all who worked copper and iron [Genesis 4:22]. And, of course, the story of Noah and his ancestors is closely connected with Eden and Ararat. As we have seen, Tubal-Cain's people originated from the northern mountains around Lake Urmia – the heartland of Armenia. Archaeology and tradition thus agree that Armenia/Eden was the place where the art of metalworking was first developed. The Early Bronze Age began north of the Zagros mountains and migrated down into the Mesopotamian basin.

The ability to smelt metals was a powerful technological advance for any group who possessed the secret knowledge to the disadvantage of their Neolithic neighbours. Their skills would have been much in demand and almost certainly brought about a military advantage which made the carriers of copper tools and weapons invincible. There is also a spiritual ascendancy symbolised by the smelting of metals. The dark arts of the furnace have always elevated the alchemist to supernatural status. He is a controller of nature – a mixer of elements – as if divinely inspired. Such people may have been seen as in late Neolithic times as super-beings, in contact with, if not themselves, the gods of nature.

All these new discoveries, combined with the gradual transition from hunter-gatherer society to a sedentary way of life (settlement in villages, farming and the domestication of animals) were features of the Neolithic Revolution. It is now recognised that this fundamental development first came into being in the high valleys of the Zagros mountains – in the area we have identified as Eden. In effect the biblical Adam of Eden marks the change from prehistoric hunter and wanderer to spiritual Man with knowledge and technological skills. And it is knowledge which is the foundation of civilisation.

Paradise Found

Let us bring together what we have discovered so far about the mythical land of Eden and its paradisiacal garden.

First of all we can say with some confidence that Eden *does* exist – it is not a purely mythical place deprived of a real geographical setting. Eden is located in ancient Armenia with its heartland in the Lake Van and Lake Urmia basins. This is also the region the Bible calls Ararat – the Assyrian Urartu. The four rivers which flow from Eden are the Euphrates, the Tigris, the Gaihun-Aras (Gihon) and the Uizhun (Pishon).

The Garden of Eden has also been located. It lies at the western end of the Adji Chay valley, near the city of Tabriz. The Garden is 'in the east of Eden' and is protected on its north, east and south sides by the high mountain peaks of the Savalan and Sahand ranges. To the west are the treacherous marshlands of the Adji Chay delta stretching out into Lake Urmia. The Adji Chay has an older name – the Meidan – which means 'walled-garden' – this is the river, described in Genesis 2:10, which waters the Garden of Eden.

To the east of the Garden the valley gradually ascends to a mountain pass which is the eastern gateway into Eden. Beyond, in the Ardabil basin, lies the land of Nod – the destination of Cain's exile. Several villages in this area still hold a dim memory of the ancient biblical toponym in their modern names. At the outflow of the pass leading from the south and east into Nod, and therefore beyond to Eden, stands the town of Kheruabad – the 'settlement of the Kheru' – a name which may provide a link to the ferocious winged guardians of the eastern gateway into Eden. The Bible calls them the Kerubim – the Cherubs.

To the north of the valley of the Garden lies the 'Mountain of Kush' (Kusheh Dagh) and, beyond, the biblical land of Cush. Through Cush flows the Gihon river, identified with the mighty Araxes river which was called the Gaihun at the time of the Islamic invasion of Persia.

To the south of the Garden, beyond the Sahand and Bazgush mountain ranges, lies the land of Havilah 'rich in gold'. This is the Iranian province of Anguran stretching from the Talesh mountains in the east to the Miyandoab plain in the west. This mountainous region is watered by numerous fast-flowing streams which cascade down from the volcanic peaks and

72. Simplified relief map showing the locations of the Garden of Eden and the Lands of Cush and Havilah in western Iran/classical Armenia.

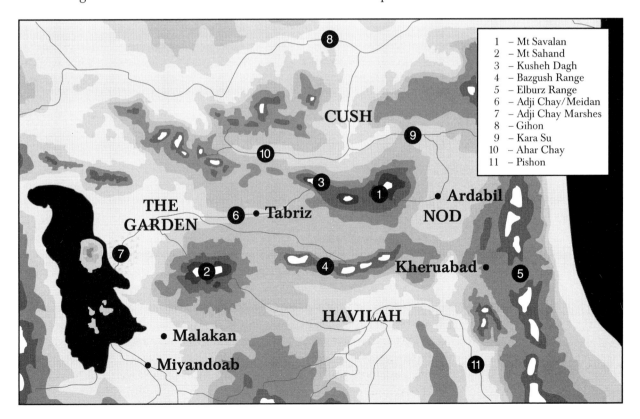

1	– Mt Savalan
2	– Mt Sahand
3	– Kusheh Dagh
4	– Bazgush Range
5	– Elburz Range
6	– Adji Chay/Meidan
7	– Adji Chay Marshes
8	– Gihon
9	– Kara Su
10	– Ahar Chay
11	– Pishon

CUSH

THE GARDEN

Tabriz

Ardabil

NOD

Kheruabad

HAVILAH

Malakan

Miyandoab

73. The upper reaches of the River Pishon (Kezel Uzun) winding down from the Anguran highlands near Takht-é Suleiman.

74. Opposite page: The Mountain of God in Eden. Below is a list of the seven heavens and seven realms of the underworld which derive from the *Midrash of the Ten Commandments* and the *Chronicle of Jerahmeel*.

gather together into the meandering Kezel Uzun river – the biblical Pishon which 'winds all through the land of Havilah'. The district of Anguran is renowned for its mineral wealth just as Havilah was renowned for its gold and semi-precious stones. And one other incredibly rare stone is found here which is going to play a part in our story – lapis lazuli (the 'blue stone' of gods and kings).

We seem to be doing pretty well in our search for the origins of the Genesis story – especially considering that any attempts to locate Eden are doomed to failure in the view of most academics. Walker's topographical discoveries have uncovered the physical geography of the Edenic legends, but is there more to unearth from sources outside the Judaeo-Christian tradition?

So far we have been concentrating predominantly on Chapter Two of Genesis and the geography of modern western Iran. I think we have probably learnt as much as we can from the biblical record. Now it is time to turn to the extra-biblical sources – in particular the epic literature of the Sumerians, the foremost of ancient world civilisations.

What we find is rather interesting. The Sumerians *do* refer to a mystical land beyond the mountains – but it is not called Eden. The Sumerian paradise is the Kingdom of Aratta, rich in gold, silver, lapis lazuli and building stone. We will learn that it is the place where the gods originated, the 'Land of the Living' and the far-off world to which the archetypal Sumerian hero journeys to seek his destiny.

Heaven and Hell

Seventh Heaven – *Araboth* – The Throne of Glory
Sixth Heaven – *Maon* – The Hosts of Angels
Fifth Heaven – *Makhon* – The Treasuries of Snow and Hail
Fourth Heaven – *Szebhul* – The Place of Sacrifice
Third Heaven – *Shekhakim* – The Clouds
Second Heaven – *Rakia* – The Twelve Windows of Day and Night
First Heaven – *Villon* – The One-Way Curtain
The Source of Life
First Netherworld – *Tebel* – The Race of Men
Second Netherworld – *Zija* – Aridity
Third Netherworld – *Neshia* – Forgetfulness
Fourth Netherworld – *Gia* – Fire
Fifth Netherworld – *Arka* – Light and Darkness
Sixth Netherworld – *Adamah* – Demons and Spirits
Seventh Netherworld – *Eretz hatachtonah* – Utter Darkness

So Yahweh expelled Adam from the Garden of Eden, to till the soil from which he had been taken. ... to the east of the garden of Eden he posted the cherubim and the fiery flashing sword, to guard the way to the tree of life.

Genesis 3:23-24

Chapter Two

THE LAND OF ARATTA

75. Opposite page: The guardians of the sacred places. The gate of Xerxes at Persepolis.

76. Above: The Mountain of God?

When I first came across the Sumerian epics of Enmerkar and Lugalbanda I was immediately struck by the similarity between the name ascribed by the Sumerians to a magical kingdom lying beyond the Zagros mountains and that given to ancient Armenia by the Assyrians of the first millennium BC. The lost kingdom of the Sumerians was called 'Aratta' whilst the Assyrian annals of the thirteenth to eighth centuries BC referred to a land of 'Urartu' which, as I have said, is identical with biblical Ararat. What also struck me was the fact that nobody (to my knowledge) had suggested that Aratta and Ararat/Urartu were the same geographical entity. The equation seemed obvious to me.

Sumerologists have searched high and low for the mysterious kingdom of Aratta.[1] I wondered if Ur-Artu or Ar-Arat might not represent the 'Foundation of 'Arat[ta]' – just as Uru-Shalem (Jerusalem) means 'Foundation of [the god] Shalem'. The Assyrian name Urartu would thus have retained a remnant of a much earlier toponym – the name of the third-millennium capital of the kingdom of Aratta. To test this idea out I needed to discover what is currently known about the general geographical location of the two kingdoms of Urartu and Aratta.

77. Part of an Agade Period cylinder seal impression showing a god seated on a mountain peak being stabbed by another god assailant whilst a female deity grasps the victim's hair from behind. Private collection of the Biblisches Institut, Fribourg University.

The Kingdom of Urartu

First it is important to locate the heartland of Urartu in its earliest recorded period.

It is in the reign of SHALMANESER I of the thirteenth century BC that we first begin to hear of the land of Urartu. In his accession year the Assyrian king undertook a military campaign into the northern mountains. There he fought against the tribal groups and petty kingdoms of

SHALMANESER I: King of Assyria, reigned OC – 1274-1245 BC.

78. Part of a scene from the 'Black Obelisk' of Shalmaneser III in which the king receives tribute from Jehu of Israel (841-813 BC). British Museum.

BARNETT: (1909-1988).

ASHURNASIRPAL II: King of Assyria, reigned OC – 883-859 BC.

79. Sargon II, from his palace at Khorsabad. Louvre Museum.

'the land of Uruatri' which, according to the author of the chapter on Urartu in the *Cambridge Ancient History*, Richard BARNETT, was 'evidently the origin of the later term Urartu'.[2] Shalmaneser's war was directed against eight city-states in the land of Uruatri.

> When Ashur, the lord, faithfully chose me (Shalmaneser) for his worshipper, gave me the sceptre, weapon, and staff to (rule) properly over the blackheaded people (i.e. the Sumerians), and granted me the true crown of lordship; at that time, in my accession year, **the land Uruatri rebelled against me**. I prayed to the god Ashur and the great gods, my lords. I mustered my troops (and) marched up to the base of their mighty mountains. I conquered the lands Himme, Uatkun, Mashgun, Salua, Halila, Luha, Nilipahri, and Zingun – eight lands and their fighting forces; fifty-one of their cities I destroyed, burnt (and) carried off their people and property. I subdued all of the land of Uruatri in three days at the feet of Ashur, my lord. [Alabaster tablet from the temple of Ashur][3]

It is clear from the campaigns of a later ninth-century Assyrian ruler, ASHURNASIRPAL II, that Urartu was regarded as a geographical region and not a single political state as such. As Barnett explains, Ashurnasirpal's wars were against the kingdoms '*in* the land' of Urartu and not directed '*against* the land' of Urartu.[4] The northern rulers who fought the Assyrians did not refer to themselves as Urartians but rather as Nairi and, indeed, the later Assyrian kings also refer to Urartu as 'Nairi Land'. They thus appear to apply both the contemporary name of Nairi and the much more ancient toponym of Urartu which was clearly retained as a traditional name for the whole region around Lake Urmia and Lake Van.

Later we find the Assyrian kings Shalmaneser III and Sargon II campaigning in the land of Urartu which now appears to be centred around Lake Van. In 1877 the British Museum inaugurated excavations in Urartu with a brief season at the site of Toprak Kale near Van where Tushpa, the capital of the ninth-century Urartian kingdom, was uncovered.

If we put all this evidence from the Assyrian war annals and archaeology together we get a picture of a geographical shift in the location of Urartu from its initial political centre south of Lake Urmia towards the north-west and the shores of Lake Van. Barnett explains why this shift took place.

> … it certainly seems to show that the original homeland of the people later generally called Urartians was well to the south-east of Lake Van, an area from which they seem to have moved to concentrate around the more easily defensible area of the lake itself. It is in the south-west of Lake Urmia that we find the most archaic portion of the Urartian kingdom or confederacy.[5]

80. The snow-capped mountains of the northern Zagros located in the region now recognised as the original land of Urartu before the shift northwards to the area around Lake Van.

In other words it was the attacks upon their lands by the Assyrians (particularly Shalmaneser I) which drove the Urartians into more remote and defensible regions. Prior to Shalmaneser I's campaign in 1274 BC (OC) the land of Urartu was located in the mountains and plains to the south of Lake Urmia – only later did it move to Lake Van.

Barnett goes on to pose an interesting question.

> Was there a single tribe, one among eight closely related tribes or 'lands', named Uruatri or Urartu, whose name the Assyrians seized on in the early thirteenth century and singled out to designate all, much as the Romans did with the Graeci, a small tribe of Illyria? It would seem possible: only one thing however is certain. The Urartians never speak of themselves as 'the people of Urartu' or use the term at all; when their inscriptions first begin some years later, they use either the term Nairi, or the name Biainili. For the Assyrians on the other hand, henceforth the 'Nairi lands' and Urartu become synonymous and interchangeable.[6]

81. The voluptuous figure of Anahita, the Persian goddess of love and the Zoroastrian equivalent of Inanna/Ishtar. This scene is part of a Sassanian relief carved into the cliff beneath the Persian royal tombs at Naqsh-é Rostam.

The answer to Barnett's question is obvious. The name Urartu did not so much belong to a tribe but rather to a much more ancient land called Aratta and that land was centred in the region immediately to the south of Lake Urmia.

The Kingdom of Aratta

We first hear of Aratta in the Sumerian epic poetry, particularly in the stories surrounding the hero-king of Uruk – Enmerkar.

Enmerkar was the son of Meskiagkasher, the first king to rule Uruk after the flood, and was a great builder-king according to tradition. He was also the first of the heroes of Sumerian legend – the one who brought the goddess Inanna down from her mountain home in Aratta to reside in the great Eanna precinct at the heart of the city of Uruk. Enmerkar will turn out to be a major player in our story and a famous, but historically lost, biblical character.

There are three epic poems detailing Enmerkar's dealings with Aratta – 'Enmerkar and the Lord of Aratta', 'Enmerkar and Ensukushsiranna' and 'Enmerkar and Lugalbanda'. The first was discovered by the great Sumerologist, Samuel Noah KRAMER, as he was sifting through the collection of cuneiform tablets housed in the Museum of the Orient in Istanbul.[7] Sadly, the original composition in Sumerian has not as yet been unearthed, but what Kramer did find in 1946 was an Akkadian copy from the Old Babylonian Period, datable to the first half of the second millennium (in the conventional chronology). Since Kramer's initial discovery, new fragments of the Enmerkar epics have been found, dating from the slightly earlier Ur III Period (close of the third millennium). It was at this time, as Roger Moorey of the Ashmolean Museum suggests, that the Sumerian epics 'were first assembled from earlier oral and written narratives into the surviving compositions'.[8]

It is readily apparent from these ancient poems that the primary political relationship between Uruk, on the Mesopotamian plain, and Aratta, beyond the mountains, was one of trade. Grain went from Uruk by ONAGER caravan to the mountain kingdom which then reciprocated by despatching the onagers on their return journey to the lowlands loaded with minerals and semi-precious stones. The road to Aratta crossed seven mountain ranges. However, in spite of the great distances involved and the very different physical nature of the two lands, there were certainly common cultural, as well as political, ties between the two 'Sumerian' states. They spoke the same language and worshipped many of the same deities – especially the powerful goddess Inanna and Dumuzi, god of the dead. They also had common administrative structures and used the same political titles. Enmerkar was the *en* of Uruk and the ruler of Aratta was also an *en* (priest-king). Assyriologist Henry Saggs wonders if these close cultural ties do not hint at the original homeland of the people of Uruk before they migrated down into the plain of Sumer.[9] In this I believe he is quite right, as we shall see in forthcoming chapters.

In spite of their close cultural and perhaps therefore ethnic ties, it is clear from the Sumerian epics that relationships between the two kindred states were often strained. But then there was nothing special in that. A number of the stories which have come down to us from ancient Sumer deal with conflicts and petty squabbles between neighbouring city-states. At this early stage in history all the tribal groupings are trying to find their political feet and mark out their dynastic territorial claims in the new lands. This was the first large-scale resettlement in history. The settlers were swapping the mineral wealth of the mountains for the arable land of the great plain.

In 'Enmerkar and the Lord of Aratta' things came to a head with the threat of a military invasion of Aratta by the king of Uruk. Enmerkar had already appropriated the goddess Inanna from her Arattan homeland and the king was busy constructing a temple for her in Uruk. This holy precinct of Uruk – the E-anna ('House of Heaven') – has been uncovered

KRAMER: (1897-1990).

ONAGER: An Iranian variety of wild donkey (*Equus hemionus*).

during excavations at Warka and therefore provides us with a tangible link to the legendary stories concerning Enmerkar.

As the story begins, we find that the king of Uruk demanding from Aratta huge quantities of gold, silver and lapis lazuli to decorate the ABZU Temple at Eridu – the 'house' of Enki ('Lord of the Earth') – and Inanna's new 'house' in Uruk. If he does not get what he wants as a gift, he will invade Aratta and take the huge wealth of the mountain kingdom by force. These threats are transmitted by envoy or royal herald – the poor man having to traverse the hard mountain road on several occasions as the conversation between the kings of Uruk and Aratta is conducted long distance. The row goes on for years but Enmerkar, as one would expect from a literary piece composed in Sumer, finally gets his way and the Eanna precinct is glorified at the expense of the natural resources of Aratta.

Aratta does at least get some much needed grain which, by implication, suggests that the mountain kingdom was incapable of sustaining its population solely from local farming resources. Sumer was the bread-basket of Aratta, and Aratta supplied all the minerals and timber which was in such short supply (actually non-existent) in the alluvial lowlands of Mesopotamia. If Saggs is right in his suggestion that Aratta was the original homeland of at least some of the people of Sumer, then one of the reasons for their migration may have been a growing population which could not sustain itself in the high mountain valleys. As the people of Aratta descended from their original homeland they found huge, virtually unoccupied, lowlands ripe for irrigation and agriculture in the plains of Sumer – the biblical land of Shinar. There they built canals and irrigation channels which turned the former swampland and flat plain into a fertile lowland dotted with cities.

No-one doubts that the Sumerians of later times viewed Aratta as a fabulously wealthy and almost magical land. One scholar has called it the 'Sumerian El-Dorado' – a mythical kingdom of half-truths, dreams, abundance and glory.[10] But few really doubt that Aratta was also a real place which gained its legendary status through the passing of the heroic age.

In *Chapter One* I demonstrated that the geography of Eden is identifiable within the topography of greater Armenia. But I also believe it may be possible to identify the historical Eden in the literature of ancient Sumer. Indeed, the evidence points to the Sumerian land of Aratta as the original prototype of the biblical Eden.

Journey to Aratta

I undertook my first expedition to Kurdistan and Iranian Azerbaijan in April 1997. On that occasion I was on a personal quest to find the route of Enmerkar's emissary – the road he had taken on his missions to the mysterious kingdom of Aratta.

ABZU: The great ocean of fresh water believed by the Sumerians to have existed beneath the earth. The realm of the high god, Enki. The Sumerian word from which derives the modern 'abyss'.

82. The enclosed court/square of the Meidan-é Imam in Isfahan.

MEIDAN-É IMAM: Formerly the Meidan-é Shah ('Garden-court of the King').

NAGSH-É ROSTAM: 'Relief of (the hero) Rostam'.

83. The court of the Royal Mosque in Isfahan.

84. Right: The Persian Gates leading down from the Iranian plateau into the Mesopotamian plain.

85. Opposite page (above): The magnificent reliefs of Persepolis.

86. Opposite page (below): The tomb of Xerxes at Nagsh-é Rostam.

After just one night in Tehran, I flew south for a few days' exploration of the Persian and Islamic sites of central Iran, staying at both Isfahan and Shiraz. The glories of the Royal Mosque and grand MEIDAN-É IMAM at Isfahan and the majestic sites of Persepolis and the royal tombs of NAGSH-É ROSTAM were truly awe-inspiring. But they only served to heighten my expectations of what was to follow in the next few days as I headed south through the Iranian oil fields of Khuzistan and down onto the low plain of ancient Susiana.

The route to Susiana from the Iranian plateau cuts through a deep ravine known as the 'Persian Gates', used by Alexander's army in its invasion of the Persian empire of Darius III. Such 'gates' are to be found all over this part of the world and have an important role in our story.

87. The ziggurat of Choga Zambil viewed from the south-east.

Choga Zambil

CHOGA ZAMBIL: 'Basket Mound'.

UNTASH GAL: King of Elam, reigned OC – *c.* 1260-1235 BC.

Early in the morning my driver, Mayis, and I traversed the River Karun, which bisects the city of Ahwaz, and headed north across a flat, feature-less plain. My first stop was to be CHOGA ZAMBIL to inspect the magnificent red-brick ziggurat built by the Elamite king, UNTASH GAL. After a walk around the perimeter of the lower step, I began to ascend the staircase which leads straight up the southern face. The air was crystal clear in the early morning light. From the top I could see the whole of the royal city of Dur-Untash-Gal spread out below me and, beyond it to the north, the meandering curves of the River Dez which forms part of the complex drainage system of the Karun.

88. The southern staircase of Choga Zambil with sacrificial altar in the foreground.

I sat down on the highest bump of red dust to absorb the panorama. Beyond the winding Dez the plain stretched on up to the mountains.

> The emissary journeying to Aratta covered his feet with the dust of the road and stirred up the pebbles of the mountains. Like a huge serpent prowling about in the plain, he was un-opposed. ['Enmerkar and the Lord of Aratta', Lines 348-51]

By lunchtime we would be beyond the outer wall of the Zagros range and heading ever deeper into the land of the Kurds. I began to imagine how Enmerkar's emissary had felt as he contemplated his long and dangerous journey towards the mountain-kingdom of Aratta.

This was my first experience of a Mesopotamian ziggurat. No-one, let alone an Egyptologist, could avoid being struck by the similarities between the platform temples of the Sumerians and the Egyptian step pyramids or, for that matter, the giant stepped temples of Meso-America. Scholars have long debated the ziggurat's religious function. The general consensus is that it was an artificial mountain upon which the house of the local god rested. In effect it was a 'stairway to heaven' by which the city deity could communicate with his worshippers. Few mortals, it seems, were privileged to climb to its summit where the god and his human concubine spent the night together in the 'Dark Chamber' (Sum. *gigunu*). The Egyptian pyramid, of course, is not a temple but rather a tomb for Pharaoh but, even so, the similarity in structure is striking.

Interestingly, a miniature ziggurat is clearly the thinking behind the strange tomb of the great Persian king, Cyrus II, at Pasargad. It has six steps rising to the burial chamber in which the king's body rested. This 'house' of the king, with cambered roof, is just like the 'house' of a god atop his artificial mountain. Thus, in this case at least, there is an obvious association between the ziggurat and the tomb of a semi-divine Persian ruler.

Susa

Having returned to the main highway, a drive of just half an hour brought us to the foot of the huge sprawling mound of ancient Susa (Shushan) and, nestling in its shadow, the bustling little town of Shush. It was here that I had my first glimpse of the watercourse which we would be following for much of the day towards its source deep in the central Zagros. At Shush the river is called the Shaur, but a few kilometres upstream it splits off from the River Kerkheh, the main arm of which disappears into the swamps of southern Iraq.

Susa is best known as the capital city of the Elamite kingdom of the third and second millennia BC and, later, the place from where Alexander the Great planned his amazing march to India. In the great palace of Darius I, ten thousand Greek soldiers and local Persian girls were married in a mass ceremony organised by Alexander to ensure a continuing interest in the eastern empire from his unsettled mercenaries.

89. View from the top of Choga Zambil looking north towards the Zagros mountains.

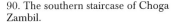

90. The southern staircase of Choga Zambil.

91. Opposite page (above): The tomb of Cyrus II at Pasargad.

92. Opposite page (below): A *karibu* demon guardian from the palace of Darius I at Susa.

93. Left: High on the tell of historic Susa stands the imposing citadel of Jacques de Morgan, built to protect his archaeological team from the various Arab brigands and nomads who roamed this desolate land towards the end of the nineteenth century when the French dig was at its height. The name de Morgan will be familiar to Egyptologists because he was Director-General of Antiquities in Egypt from 1892-97, before beginning his mission to Susa in 1897.

ISHTAR: The Babylonian high goddess of both sexuality and war known to the Sumerians as Inanna.

MARDUK: The national god of Babylon, equivalent to Canaanite Baal and Sumerian Asar, son of Enki/Ea.

The major biblical connection with Susa is to be found in the book of Esther which describes the marriage of the beautiful Jewess to the Persian emperor, Ahasuerus, who is probably to be identified with Xerxes, son of Darius the Great. It was in the palace at Susa that Queen Esther lived out her years in fifth-century-BC Persia. It has been suggested that the name Esther is derived from that of ISHTAR, the Mesopotamian goddess of love, whilst the name of her guardian, Mordecai, probably represents MARDUK, the Babylonian vegetation god.

But Susa's history goes back to much earlier times. Archaeological excavations have revealed a pre-Elamite civilisation which has no real historical identity. Archaeologists and Sumerologists simply refer to it as the 'Pre-Elamite' or 'Susiana' culture and designate the land as 'Susiana'. Unlike the Sumerians or the Akkadians or the Amorites, these people have no identity. We know virtually nothing about them. They had a primitive written language but it remains undeciphered to this day. So there are no inscriptions to tell us who they were. By the time the later texts from Sumer begin to shed light on the Sumerians' political neighbours, the land of Susiana had been taken over by the Elamites who probably originated from somewhere on the Iranian plateau.

94. Entrance to the tomb of Daniel (of local tradition) at Shush.

95. Left: The ice-cream cone of Daniel's tomb viewed from the palace of Darius I on the mound of ancient Shushan.

96. Jacques de Morgan (1857-1924) in his more familiar role as excavator of the 12th-Dynasty tombs of Egyptian queens at Dashur. Engraving from the *Illustrated London News* of the 7th of March 1896.

TEPES: Persian for ruin-mounds, like Arabic *tell* or Hebrew *tel*. *Tepe* is the scholarly spelling of local *tape*.

DARIUS I: King of Persia, reigned 521-486 BC.

NEOLITHIC: The New or Late Stone Age.

KUH-É KABIR: The 'Great Mountain'.

97. Opposite page: The journey to Aratta and Eden through the seven gates (mountain passes).

However, archaeology informs us that the people of early Susiana *also* had strong connections with the highlands of Iran. The pottery is identical to that found at the highland TEPES of Sialk, Guran and Giyan. Susa was the gateway to the mountains and, beyond, the Urmia basin. The strategic location of the city is important. As you are going to learn, its earliest citizens will play a major part in our unfolding tale.

Susa to Kermanshah

> Going to the mountain-land, Aratta: 'Emissary, by night, like the pluvious south wind – drive on! By day, like the dew – be up!' [Lines 157-59]

Given its great historical importance throughout ancient times, Susa was, to say the least, a bit of an anti-climax with little in the way of imposing architecture beyond a few scraps from the great *apadana* (audience hall) of DARIUS I. We set off northwards once more in the footsteps of Enmerkar's envoy as he carried the symbol of the great goddess Inanna before him.

> (From) Susa to the Anshan mountain-land, for her (Inanna) they humbly saluted with greetings like mice. [Lines 166-67]

For the first hour or so beyond Susa the road crosses the last one hundred kilometres of the Susiana plain, imperceptibly rising (at one centimetre per kilometre) towards the foothills in the north and, behind them, the snowcapped peaks of the first Zagros ridge. All over this plain the low bumps of ancient ruin-mounds are scattered like mole-hills on a garden lawn. Many of these settlements date back to late-NEOLITHIC times when Susa itself began its long history.

We eventually found ourselves back beside the east bank of the river which flows past Susa, but here it had become the fast-flowing River Kerkheh. Fifty kilometres upstream it cuts its way through the KUH-É KABIR ridge – the entrance into Luristan.

Beyond this first gentle pass into the Zagros I discovered a long fertile valley running northwest to southeast. As we passed down from the ridge, I pondered whether I should count this opening into the Zagros as the first 'gateway' on the herald's journey to Aratta.

At this point on the map, the Kerkheh becomes the River Saidmarreh, winding along the valley floor, where it cuts a deep scar through the soft limestone mother-rock. The modern tarmac road clings to the north side of the valley, looking down on lush pastureland dotted with thousands of grazing animals and the occasional nomadic encampment.

After about an hour the road began a steady rise out of the valley. As we made our way up onto the ridge, we were suddenly confronted by a traffic jam of sheep and their minders moving higher up into the mountains in the wake of the spring thaw. This was graphic evidence of a social pattern which had endured for thousands of years as the nomads

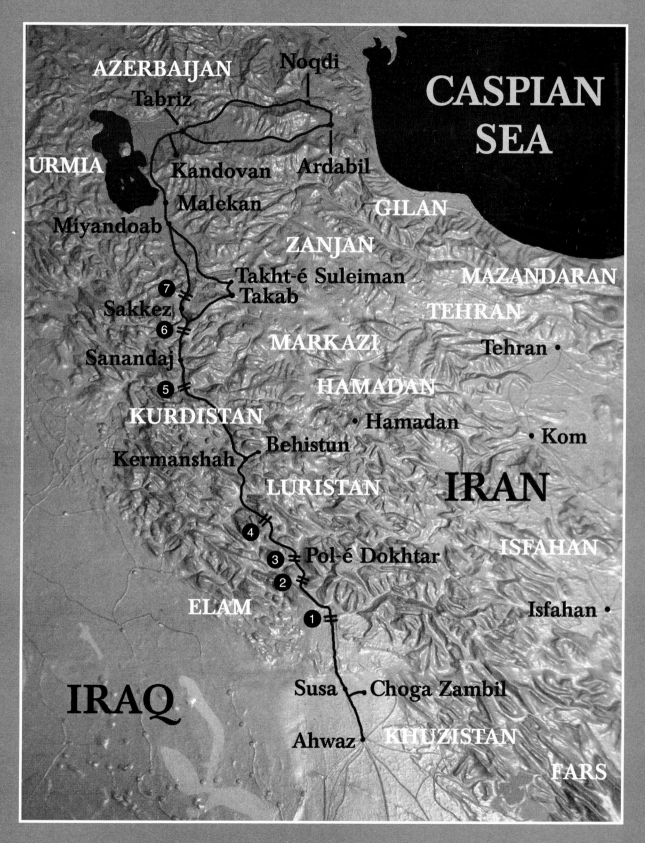

84

of the mountains found ways for their flocks to traverse the escarpments which separate the pasture grounds. The envoy from Uruk, carrying the image of the goddess, was following a well-worn path – even in his day.

> (In) the great mountain ranges, the teeming multitudes grovel-led in the dust for her (Inanna). [Lines 168-69]

Before long, we were out of the Saidmarreh valley and crossing a mountain pass into the next alluvial system. Was this the second of Enmerkar's 'gates' through the Zagros? As we reached the crest, a fabulous scene met my gaze. At the bottom of the sweeping incline was a network of crystal blue lakes surrounded by lush grazing land. Beyond, thousands of flesh-coloured hills stretched northwards until they reached the base of another gigantic blue ridge capped with the remains of the winter snows. As we stopped to stretch our legs, I spotted two parallel lines of boulders about ten metres apart, running down into the valley from the pass. It was obvious that I was looking at the remains of an ancient road which led from the Saidmarreh valley and on into the mountains. It pointed to a narrow defile cut into the ridge on the opposite side of this second valley. It looked as though we were approaching the third of the gates which had led the envoy of Uruk towards the land of Aratta.

As we reached the cleft, we found ourselves once again beside the waters of the Saidmarreh which, according to my map, had cut its way through the mountains a little further to the north. This was not the main channel of the Saidmarreh but, nevertheless, it was still a powerful river (known locally as the Kashgan Rud). As we were moving upstream it was transforming itself into a fast flowing torrent of thick brownish water. At the entrance to the gorge the shattered remains of an ancient stone bridge could be seen attached to either cliff face. This was the POL-É DOKHTAR. You can immediately see in this ancient Persian word the German 'Tochter' from which we get our 'daughter'. The modern road

98. Opposite page (above): The approaches to the Zagros mountains from Susa.

99. Opposite page (below): The Saidmarreh valley with the river cutting its way through pastureland scattered with grazing sheep and goats.

100. Above: Nomadic encampment in the Saidmarreh valley.

POL-É DOKHTAR: 'Bridge of the Daughter'.

101. The ancient road leading to Pol-é Dokhtar.

85

102. Pol-é Dokhtar.

SASSANIAN: Iranian Dynasty (AD 224-642).

TANGS: River gorges.

103. The approach to a typical tang which soon reaches hundreds of metres in depth.

heads through the last surviving arch on the eastern approach to the SASSANIAN bridge, then passes along the east side of the gorge and on into the small valley beyond.

Finally, I sensed that we had truly crossed over into the mountain kingdom – not yet Aratta but certainly no longer within the sphere of influence of the Mesopotamian city-states whose capitals lay two hundred kilometres or more downstream in the hot and humid alluvial plain.

Although the general pattern of the trade routes through the Zagros follows the major rivers, it was obvious that the deep TANGS cut by the waters often made adhering to the main riverbed a little precarious. Sometimes it was better to take a lesser stream which guided the traveller over a pass rather than trying to navigate through a 1,000-metre gorge just a hundred metres wide and lashed by violent torrents. Time and again we would find the road diverge from the river to cross a ridge, then return to the main stream as it flowed through the next valley. Only where its passage through the ridge was the *only* practical option did the road follow the main stream and then, often as not, narrow paths had to be cut into the steep sides of the gorges to keep the traveller above the thunderous rapids. In practical terms this meant that there were few safe routes through the mountains, giving me the confidence that the road we were following in 1997 was almost certainly the same as that which the envoy had trodden 5,000 years earlier.

The last few hours of sunlight on the first day of my journey to Aratta were spent driving through stunning scenery bathed in a warm evening glow. Over one more mountain pass (the fourth 'gate' so far?), we found ourselves in another wide lowland which swept majestically around a mountain spur to merge into the flat-bottomed vale of Kermanshah. Beyond the mountain ridge to our east was the valley of the Hulailan RUD in which the ruin-mound of Tepe Guran is located. This little-known archaeological site is also going to play a key part in the story of the migration of Adam's descendants down into the Mesopotamian plain. In the next chapter you will see how pottery from this tepe is traceable to major settlements on the geographical periphery of the biblical land of Shinar – but I was not aware of this on the evening of the 12th of April as we sped north.

It had taken us the best part of eight hours to make the three-hundred-kilometre journey from Susa on the plain to Kermanshah in the heart of the Zagros range. We had traversed four mountain ridges, each of the passes through which could have been one of the seven gateways leading to Aratta. Just like the envoy from Uruk, we had crossed the plain and ascended into the mountains.

> The emissary gave heed to the word of his king. By the starry night he journeyed; by day, he travelled with Utu (the sun-god) of Heaven. [Lines 159-60]

This part of the journey would probably have taken him two weeks to complete. We had taken just a day. Now it was time to rest for a few hours before the next challenge – to reach the 'Throne of Solomon' before nightfall on the second day.

Kermanshah to Behistun

It was one of my long-held ambitions to visit the famous rock inscriptions of Darius the Great at Behistun (locally known as Bisotun).

In the early morning we headed off in an easterly direction along the ancient royal highway to Hamadan – the Persian summer capital of Ecbatana and, previously, the royal city of the MEDES. At this point in our journey we had joined one of the most important highways of the ancient world – a trade route which had been in use for countless centuries. It begins at Babylon, heading north-eastwards along the Diyala river into the foothills of the northern Zagros. Then, through the Khanakin Pass, the road drops down into the Kermanshah valley, past Behistun and ever upwards, on through the Vale of Kangavar to Ecbatana and the Iranian plateau. This was the ancient highway leading to the exotic orient. Scattered along this valley are ancient mounds which have revealed some of the most ancient pottery cultures in the Middle East. Sites such as Tepe Sarab, just five kilometres outside Kermanshah, will also play a part in our story when we come to discuss the migration of early civilisation down into the Mesopotamian plain.

RUD: Persian for 'river'.

MEDES: An Iranian tribe of the first millennium BC originating from the Zagros mountains. They joined with Nabopolassar, king of Babylon, to overthrow the Assyrian empire in 607 BC. They in turn were eclipsed by Cyrus the Great in 550 BC to herald in the Persian era.

104. The rock cliff above the spring of Behistun where Darius I carved his famous decree.

105. Behistun's sacred spring with the Kermanshah valley beyond.

The Greek historian, DIODORUS SICULUS, tells us that the legendary Assyrian queen, Semiramis, passed this way with a great army.

> ... she set forth in the direction of Media with a great force. And when she had arrived at the mountain known as Bagistanus (the ancient Greek name of Behistun) she encamped near it and laid out a park, which had a circumference of twelve stades and, being situated in the plain, contained a great spring by means of which her plantings could be irrigated. The Baghistanus mountain is sacred to Zeus and on the side facing the park has sheer cliffs which rise to a height of seventeen stades. The lowest part of these she smoothed off and engraved thereon a likeness of herself with a hundred spearmen at her side. And she also put this inscription on the cliff in Syrian letters: 'Semiramis, with the pack-saddles of the beasts of burden in her army, built up a mound from the plain and thereby climbed this precipice, even to its very ridge'.[11]

DIODORUS SICULUS: Greek historian living in Sicily who wrote a partial history of Egypt in the first century BC.

Semiramis, having completed her devotions at the sacred mountain of Zeus, then went on her way to Ecbatana and the land of the Medes. Now, although this tale is certainly legendary and the reliefs are, without doubt, confused with those of Darius I, this passage from Diodorus shows how significant the cliffs of Behistun were in ancient times and that this was a well-known place of worship to the highest of the gods.

106. Opposite page: The colossus of Behistun. Clouds of steam rise, like a giant sentinel, from the boilers of a sugar factory near Behistun.

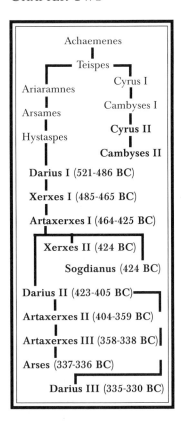

Achaemenes

Teispes

Ariaramnes — Cyrus I

Arsames — Cambyses I

Hystaspes — **Cyrus II**

Darius I (521-486 BC) — **Cambyses II**

Xerxes I (485-465 BC)

Artaxerxes I (464-425 BC)

Xerxes II (424 BC)

Sogdianus (424 BC)

Darius II (423-405 BC)

Artaxerxes II (404-359 BC)

Artaxerxes III (358-338 BC)

Arses (337-336 BC)

Darius III (335-330 BC)

107. The royal genealogy of the Achaemenid (Persian) kings.

108. Opposite page: The restoration tower of Behistun.

Mountain of the Gods

The sun was rising dead ahead through billowing clouds of industrial smog which clung to the valley floor, held down by cold mountain air. After thirty minutes weaving our way through heavy lorry traffic, we reached the foot of a rocky mountain rising sheer out of the northern side of the valley. Here, once again, we came across an old friend – the River Saidmarreh (but now called the Gamas-Ab) running down from its source towards Susiana. The Gamas-Ab/Saidmarreh/Kerkheh/Shaur had guided us all the way on our journey into the Zagros, but we were soon to leave it behind as we moved into the central massif and beyond to the land of fire and earthquakes.

Over the previous week, as we travelled through central Iran, I had been very disappointed to find many of the Persian monuments clad in acres of scaffolding and corrugated iron. For some reason best known to themselves, the antiquities authorities in Iran have developed a compulsion to 'restore' their past heritage by hiding it behind swathes of rusting iron. Behistun was no exception and, perhaps, the worst example of this practice. Under the excuse of 'restoration', workmen had erected what appeared to be a permanent tower of girders, rising up from the foot of the cliffs some seventy metres and completely masking Darius' historic relief. Alexander the Great did not have to put up with this when he came past here in 324 BC!

As we have seen, by the Macedonian's time, this was already a place of tremendous historical and religious significance. Known as Baghistanon Oros or 'Mountain of the Gods' (from which Behistun derives), the sheer rocks to the north side of the Kermanshah valley had been sacred for millennia. Archaeological investigations undertaken in the 1960s have demonstrated that caves beneath Darius' inscription had been occupied since Middle Palaeolithic times (some 35,000 years ago).[12] A reclining figure of Herakles was later carved here by Alexander's successors in 148 BC. Parthian reliefs of kings, magi (priests) and fire-altars are also scattered about the rocks along with fortification walls from the same period. Median and Sassanian ruins also abound. Beside the rock-cut steps which lead up from the ancient road to the base of the cliff there is a large fire bowl. It seems that this holy place was marked by a Zoroastrian fire-temple, probably of Sassanian date (AD 224-637).

At the top of the steps there is an ancient sanctuary in the rock niche immediately below the Darius relief. However, this open place of worship predates the Persian era because chippings from the relief above were found covering the walls of the sanctuary structure and platform. The archaeologist, Heinz Luschey, who investigated the site in 1963, believes that there is evidence here of a much more ancient fire-temple with altars for both fire and water in an open court.[13]

But, without doubt, the most impressive monument of Behistun is the great series of reliefs carved by the Persian king, Darius I, which look

CAMBYSES: King of Persia, reigned 529-522 BC.

down onto the valley below from their precarious vantage point hundreds of feet up the sheer cliff-face. The central panel shows Darius facing a row of prisoners, his foot upon the chest of the recumbent captive named Gaumata. According to the inscription accompanying the relief, a magus (Median priest) named Gaumata had seized the throne whilst the Persian king, CAMBYSES, was away ruling over the land of Egypt which he had recently conquered (in 525 BC). The king, whose reputation as a mad, tyrannical despot is legendary, had died on his way back to Persia in order to put down the challenge to his rule. So Gaumata had been accepted as his *de facto* successor by the provincial governors.

However, the usurper was soon assassinated by Darius I and six companion conspirators on the 29th of September 522 BC. The empire immediately fell into civil war. After the council of nobles had acclaimed him as the legitimate king in 521 BC, Darius set about punishing those who had supported Gaumata and who had then revolted against him when he had seized the throne. Nineteen bloody battles and a year later, the empire was secured and Darius went on to become the most powerful monarch of the Persian empire.

The new king was not in the direct line of succession from Cyrus the Great, the father of Cambyses, but claimed his right to rule through his great-great-grandfather Teispes, who was also the great-grandfather of Cyrus. The whole line was descended from King Achaemenes, which is why scholars often refer to the Persian rulers of the sixth to fourth centuries as the Achaemenid Dynasty. Its last ruler, Darius III, was murdered by his own bodyguard as he fled from Alexander the Great following the battle of Gaugamela in 331 BC. The Greeks took possession of Babylon, Susa and Ecbatana to herald in the Hellenistic Age.

The great empire of Persia, which had lasted for over one hundred and fifty years, came to a dramatic end with a warning to all those who would resist the new emperor's authority. The young Macedonian general decided to make an unforgettable example of the Achaemenid royal capital – Persepolis. His soldiers set light to the luxurious awnings of the vast palace complex. The magnificent, lofty-halled *apadana* collapsed into the ashes of revenge – only the tall trunks of its stone pillars and its beautifully decorated ceremonial staircases were left as witness to the glories of a lost empire.

The Decipherment of Cuneiform

All this was far off in the future when Darius carved his great rock inscription upon the cliff at Behistun.

If we leap forward some two-and-a-half millennia we will find a young English army officer – Henry RAWLINSON – suspended by rope from the top of the cliff as he attempts to copy the huge narrative which accompanies the conquest scene of Darius the Great. The reason why he is going to such lengths is because there are, in fact, three copies of the text

109. RAWLINSON: (1810-1895).

carved on the rock-face. Immediately beneath the relief is the Old Persian version of the narrative – the language of the Achaemenid kings. But, to the left, Darius also ordered a version of his great proclamation in Akkadian (the language of Babylonia), whilst, below that, instructions were given to cut a third copy in Elamite (the earlier language of Susiana).

With this trilingual text there was thus a golden opportunity to break the code of the ancient Mesopotamian script we call cuneiform. By Rawlinson's time Old Persian was partly deciphered, thanks to the fact that it is essentially an alphabetic script using cuneiform signs. The number of signs in use are therefore limited in comparison to Akkadian, which is not alphabetic but syllabic. In 1802 a German scholar named Georg GROTEFEND had managed to decipher a number of Old Persian words which had been copied from the walls of Persepolis. Armed with these first clues, Rawlinson was able to complete the task of translating the Darius edict which had taken him the best part of three years to copy (1835-37). Ten years later, with the help of a young Kurdish boy who was now the 'monkey on the rope' and with the Old Persian translation as his guide, Rawlinson succeeded in cracking the Babylonian version in the left panel. The first accurate translation of an Akkadian cuneiform inscription was published in 1850 and the flood-gates into the mysterious world of ancient Mesopotamia were finally thrown wide open, some thirty years after Champollion had unlocked the secrets of the Egyptian hieroglyphs by means of the bilingual Rosetta Stone.

The Thin Edge of the Wedge

Following the story of Rawlinson's shimmying down the cliffs at Behistun, perhaps this is a good time to say a little more about the cuneiform script and the languages of ancient Mesopotamia which employed it.

110. The Behistun relief of Darius I, showing the king standing on the chest of the pretender to the Persian throne. Before him a row of nine rebel governors from the far corners of the empire are shackled and tethered around their necks about to meet their fate.

GROTEFEND: (1775-1853).

111. A trilingual inscription from Persepolis.

112. The development of the sign for donkey from Sumerian (*anshu*) to Neo-Babylonian (*imeru*). The upper symbol (earliest) is scratched into the surface of the tablet. The middle symbol is how the cuneiform version would have looked if not rotated. The lower is how it actually appears rotated anticlockwise through 90 degrees in the (later) Akkadian script.

The rapid development of cuneiform and its subsequent widespread use illustrates the inherent practicality of the invention.

Writing began life in Sumer and Susiana with scratchings onto damp clay tablets using a reed with sharpened point. These were pictographs – recognisable representations of the objects being recorded. However, a realisation soon dawned that it was quicker and more practical to impress the end of a wedge-shaped reed stylus into the clay, rotating the little tablet in the left hand in order to change the direction and angle of the impressions. What previously had been easily recognisable images of objects thus became so abstract and stylised that they began to bear little resemblance to the original pictographic characters. With this *visual* abstraction came more abstract *ideas* (ideograms). Now, not only objects (nouns) and numbers (quantities) were recorded but concepts of motion and action (verbs) were introduced into the writing. The ancients had moved from basic accounting (numbers of livestock and amounts of grain) to real narrative literature with verbs and adjectives to embellish the original nouns. Eventually there were over six hundred cuneiform signs of which about half remained simple logograms (single words/ideas) with the rest being used as either logograms or syllables. Some signs were also used as determinatives to help explain or categorise a word. For

The Sounds of Ancient Tongues

113. It was the ability to read Old Persian alphabetic script, written with just thirty-six cuneiform signs, which had led Rawlinson and other scholars to the decipherment of the much more complex syllabic-with-logograms Akkadian and Elamite copies of Darius' trilingual inscription at Behistun. Elamite cuneiform, for instance, uses ninety-six syllabic signs, some sixteen logograms and five determinatives.

In the attempt to discover how the most ancient parent script (i.e. Sumerian) was pronounced, scholars have worked backwards through Greek to Old Persian to Akkadian and finally to Sumerian – a regression of three millennia through the cuneiform script. It is now somewhat difficult to see how certain Sumerian signs can be vocalised by modern scholars and thus identify where guesswork has bridged gaps in our knowledge. Over the years since the initial decipherment of the Behistun inscription a 'language of communication' has been developed between specialists so that they can all be talking ancient languages in a single tongue. This has also happened within Egyptology where a modern 'Egypto-speak' has been crafted to replace the 'unknowns' of the original Egyptian language. By dismantling this Tower of Babel, in order to ease communication with each other, scholars have inadvertently moved us so far away from the true pronunciation of some Sumerian and Egyptian words that their connection to other texts – such as the Old Testament – has been hidden deep beneath the debris of the fallen tower. A century of linguistic endeavour has undoubtedly left us with superb translations of beautiful stories from the ancient world but, at the same time, may well have moved us further away from the historical truth about our own origins.

instance, a person might have the cuneiform sign for 'man' (a single vertical stroke) placed before his name. Cities and gods had similar determinatives. These new signs would become the tools of the Sumerian poet who wrote the epic 'Enmerkar and the Lord of Aratta' and, later, the royal scribe of SARGON II of Assyria whose account is going to play an important role later in this chapter.

Over the following centuries many civilisations took up this very practical writing system, adapting it to their own languages. Akkadian, which employed cuneiform, became the *lingua franca* of the ancient world – something which Egyptian, using the more beautiful but cumbersome hieroglyphic script, was never able to achieve. It is because of the widespread use of Akkadian that we find cuneiform also being employed by the Hittites, the Urartians, the Elamites, the Persians, the Babylonians, the Assyrians, the Mitannians and the Syrians. Even the scribes of Ugarit used cuneiform to create their simple alphabetic script of twenty-three signs which was eventually to evolve into our modern alphabet through Phoenician and Greek.

Journey to Aratta (continued)

Having dipped my fingers into the cool waters of the sacred spring at the foot of the 'Mountain of the Gods' we headed off into Kurdistan.

Behistun to Takht-é Suleiman

The road began to rise once more as it penetrated the central massif of the Zagros range. It was nearing midday when we arrived at Sanandaj – the regional capital. The road down from the fifth mountain pass had taken us into another long valley at the northern end of which lay the rambling city of the Kurds.

Kurdistan is not an independent country. It is a state within a state; in fact a state within several states. The Kurdish people are of semi-nomadic stock: they are essentially mountain people – shepherds and pastoralists. The mountains of the Zagros range are their home, but these mountains cross several political boundaries. Thus the Kurds are currently ruled-over by the governments of Iran, Iraq, Syria and Turkey. Over the centuries these tough, stubbornly independent people have suffered countless oppressions at the hands of their political masters. Thousands have been killed in recent years by military bombardment and chemical warfare (Halabja was just a few kilometres to the west of us). Yet still they continue to press for an independent, autonomous state of Kurdistan.

As we slowly made our way through the bustling streets of Sanandaj, I studied the faces of its citizens. The men have a surly outward appearance with their black stubble and dark eyes. As in all parts of Iran the women are covered from head to foot in black SHADURS with only their equally dark eyes flashing at you from behind the veil. The children are unkempt – but are like kids in every part of the world in that respect.

SARGON II: King of Assyria, reigned 721-705 BC.

SHADURS: The long over-garments worn by muslim women to cover their brightly coloured clothes worn in the home.

Observing the Kurds I could not help but recall the countless ancient texts from the Mesopotamian plains referring to the wild people of the eastern mountains. It was never easy crossing the Zagros – not for Enmerkar's envoy, not for the Assyrian armies and not even today for less intrepid explorers.

We set off once more on our way to our next overnight stop in the little mountain town of Takab. Again the road began to rise. Eventually, after a good hour, we reached the very highest point of the sixth mountain pass and pulled over to look back at an incredible panorama. Thousands of feet below the blue waters of a modern reservoir filled the contours of the valley. All around green hills rose majestically out of the waters to become dark brown heathland sweeping up towards black rocks capped with glistening white snow. The air was bitterly cold.

The splendid desolation took my breath away as I stood in the ruins of what appeared to be a mountain refuge for travellers heading over the high pass. Here was further evidence that this modern tarmac road followed a much more ancient route towards Armenia.

Down from the pass we came to a junction and our road to Takab. In truth, this was a diversion from the route I had presumed for Enmerkar's envoy who would, most likely, have continued directly over the next mountain pass and down towards Lake Urmia. We, on the other hand, were heading in a north-easterly direction through Bijar and on into the western part of Anguran province (the Havilah of Genesis).

> Five gates, six gates, seven gates he traversed. He lifted up (his) eyes (as) he approached Aratta. [Lines 170-71]

114. Opposite page: A Kurdish shepherd.

115. The highest point on the road to Aratta with the ruins of a way-station, built for weary travellers, in the foreground.

TAKHT-É SULEIMAN: 'Throne of
Solomon'.

PORTER: (1777-1842).

ZENDAN-É SULAIMAN: 'Solomon's
Prison'.

From Susa to Kermanshah we had crossed four mountain passes – perhaps
the first four gates on the emissary's journey to Aratta. Since leaving
Kermanshah we had traversed two more. The seventh and final gate lay
ahead along the main road which headed into the broad valley of the
Zarrineh and Simineh rivers. We, though, were turning into Havilah.

No-one should undertake this arduous journey through the Zagros
mountains without taking the time to visit what is one of the most romantic
historical sites in the Middle East. TAKHT-É SULEIMAN is the traditional
name of a fortified temple nestling at the centre of a huge crater-like
hollow encircled by a ring of dark mountains. The place has nothing to
do with Solomon (an Islamic tradition associated with the Arab invasion
of the region in the seventh century) but very much to do with Zoroastrian-
ism. Indeed Takht-é Suleiman is claimed in one local tradition as the
birthplace of the great prophet and seer after whom the cult is named. Its
importance is underlined by the fact that, following their coronation, the
Sassanian kings each made a pilgrimage here to the ancient fire-temple
from their capital of Ctesiphon near Baghdad – a journey of over 1,000
kilometres. The Sassanians called the place Adhar Gushnasp – the
'Warrior's Fire'.

The site of Takht-é Suleiman was discovered in 1819 by the British
explorer, Sir Robert Ker PORTER. Excavations by a German team, which
began in 1959 under the direction of Professor Rudolf Naumann, have
revealed structures from Sassanian and Mongol times, but pottery from
as early as the sixth century BC has been unearthed. Signs of prehistoric
occupation are also present at other sacred sites within the 'crater' rim.

We sped along the mountain road, straight past Takab, in an attempt
to reach Takht-é Suleiman before sunset. As we approached the valley
leading up to the site, the road led us to the foot of a huge sprawling
mountain of pure red rock, rising out of the green pasture land all around.
This immediately brought to mind the passage in the 'Lugalbanda and
Mount Hurum' epic where we learn that the people of Aratta obtained
red powder from the mountain known as Kur-Hashura in order to paint
the high walls of their capital city.[14] I had a real sense that I was nearing
the magical kingdom.

We drove on around the red mountain, the road rising gradually to
the rim of the crater. It then plunged straight ahead, past a huge dark
cone of rock which the locals call ZENDAN-É SULAIMAN. Its steep sides
were apparently formed by the sediment from a calciferous spring which
once gushed from the summit. Here, beside the crater well, there was
once a prehistoric sanctuary which continued in use well into Sassanian
times. This high-place looks down upon its sister fire-temple in the eastern
part of the basin.

We arrived at the entrance to Takht-é Suleiman with just an hour of
sunlight left to explore the great Zoroastrian shrine.

The first thing which struck me was the ice-cold mountain stream
flowing out of the entrance gate of the fortress and down the slope towards

a gap in the ring of mountains. It soon became clear that the source of this babbling brook was a glistening pool of water at the very heart of the fortress. This tiny lake was almost circular, its banks sloping upwards so that the surface of the water was above the surrounding ground level. It appeared artificial but I soon realised that I was looking at a very ancient spring vent, filled to the brim with water held in by walls of solidified minerals. A narrow channel in this wall of sediment takes the water out of the pool and down towards the fortress gate. From there it flows westwards and down to Lake Urmia. A second stream gushes out from the north side of the pool and exits through the fortress wall on its east side. From there it sweeps around to join the other stream to form the Zarrineh Rud.

The intensely blue, 'bottomless' pool sparkled like an enormous gem-stone, as the light danced on its surface, before the red sun slowly disappeared behind the rim of the crater. I stood for several minutes looking down into its dark depths. At that moment it was not difficult to grasp why the ancients held this place in such high esteem. They knew that the sacred lake was a primeval *abzu* – a place where the waters of life rise up to nourish the earth. They believed that a great freshwater ocean flowed far beneath the surface of their world and that there, down in his watery abode of darkness, dwelt Enki, 'Lord of the Earth'. We will discover several more entrances to the realm of this 'Lord of the Abyss' on our journey in search of the historical Genesis, but my first encounter with a Sumerian abzu was a moment to savour.

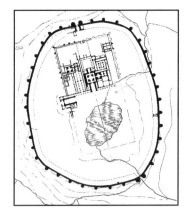

116. Plan of the fortress site of Takht-é Suleiman with the spring lake at its centre.

117. Takht-é Suleiman at sunset with the cone of Zendan-é Suleiman rising up in the background.

118. The pool of Takht-é Suleiman with the source for the Zarrineh Rud in the foreground.

119. The Sumerian sign for *edin* in its earliest form (top), classical Sumerian cuneiform (middle) and Old Babylonian (bottom). The original prototype appears to represent a water storage jar, suggesting a connection with the waters of the abzu or sacred spring.

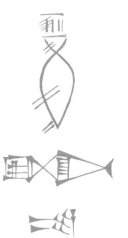

We left Takht-é Suleiman and found our way back through the darkness to Takab. I had nearly reached my target destination. Just one more morning's drive would see us through the plain of Aratta and on to Tabriz and the start of my exploration of the Garden of Eden and the lands of Nod and Cush.

By mid morning of the following day we had worked our way down off the mountain plateau to find ourselves at the southern end of a broad plain. The road had been following the Zarrineh Rud – the 'Golden River'. This was another clue to the location of biblical Havilah – the land of gold – which we were leaving behind as we continued our journey northwards. Within an hour of reaching the floor of the plain we had arrived at the town of Miyandoab – the traditional location of the capital city of the ancient Mannai or Manneans. Miyandoab means 'between the two waters' and, indeed, the town is situated between the Simineh Rud on its western side and the Zarrineh Rud to its east. Most scholars are in agreement that the plain south of Lake Urmia is where the country of Mannea should be located – this is quite clear from the annals of the Assyrian kings who fought against the Mannai once they had traversed the Zagros mountains. It is also, as we have seen, the place where the kingdom of Urartu first began.

Everything was leading me to the conclusion that I had reached the even more ancient kingdom of Aratta. However, the clincher came for me only after I had returned to England when I re-read Samuel Noah

Kramer's famous book *The Sumerians: Their History, Culture, and Character.* As I turned to page seventy-five, one sentence leapt out at me. It had been years since I had first read *The Sumerians* but that was no excuse. I asked myself how on earth I could have missed such a vital clue in my search for Aratta the first time around – but there it was:

> Enmerkar's campaign to Aratta might be compared to some extent with that of Sargon II more than two thousand years later (714 BC) to the land of the Mannai, the account of which, interestingly enough, mentions the crossing of the **river Aratta**, a name reminiscent, perhaps, of the city of Aratta.[15]

I rushed to my copy of James Pritchard's *Ancient Near Eastern Texts* but the relevant passage from the Assyrian king's war annals was not there. I rummaged through the shelves of my library and came across the much older work *Ancient Records of Assyria and Babylonia* compiled by Daniel Luckenbill in 1927. There I found the text I was looking for. It comes in the form of a 'letter' to the god Ashur recounting the events of Sargon II's recent military campaign against King Ursa of Urartu in the eighth year of the Assyrian king's reign (714 BC). The long text survives on a large clay cuneiform tablet which originally came from the city of Ashur. It is currently housed in the Louvre Museum. Two detailed studies of the campaign route were published by Francois Thureau-Dangin in 1912 and Edwin Wright in 1943.[16]

I have assigned the bare bones of the early part of the campaign to *Appendix B* so that you can see for yourself the route taken by the Assyrian king as he marched his army into Urartu. The crucial passage relating to Aratta describes the fording of a river bearing the same name as the lost kingdom we have been searching for.

120. The large (37.5 x 24.5 cms) red clay tablet of Sargon II narrating his Year 8 campaign into the lands of Mannea and Urartu. Louvre Museum.

121. Assyrian soldiers return in triumph carrying aloft the heads of their unfortunate victims in battle. British Museum.

> I crossed the Rappa and **Aratta** (Akk. *A-rat-ta-a*), streams flowing by their bases at high water, as (though they were) irrigation ditches. Against Surikash, **a district of the Mannean country** which borders on the lands of Karalla and Allabria, I descended. [Lines 30-31]

As I studied Sargon's inscription a depressing realisation began to dawn on me. Was it possible that Miyandoab was the actual site of the lost city of Aratta? Had we driven straight through the modern town, eyes closed to the possibility, in our haste to reach the comfort of our hotel in Tabriz? Perhaps … but then I recalled that Enmerkar's emissary had 'raised up his eyes' upon approaching the city of Aratta. Miyandoab was located in the plain and yet the epic poem seemed to suggest that the wondrous city was atop a hill or on a mountain slope. I reassured myself with the thought that the ruins of the Arattan capital still await discovery somewhere around here and that I would just have to return to explore the slopes surrounding the plain on some later occasion.

At this point it is probably worth a summary of the evidence which locates the mysterious land of Aratta here in the broad plain south of Lake Urmia and places it within the biblical Eden.

(a) The River Aratta, crossed by Sargon II as he entered the Miyandoab plain, locates the kingdom of Aratta in this general region.

(b) There are seven mountain passes ('gates') between Susa (the envoy's setting-off point) and the Miyandoab plain – just as described in the Enmerkar epic. Indeed, Sargon also crossed seven mountain ranges to reach Mannea. You may also recall that there are seven heavens with gates or doors leading to paradise in Talmudic tradition.

(c) In 'Enmerkar and the Lord of Aratta' the Miyandoab plain is referred to as the *edin* which, as we discussed in *Chapter One*, may explain the origins of the biblical name Eden.

(d) Scholars have determined that the later kingdom of Urartu (Ararat) was also originally located here (in the Miyandoab plain) in its early days, before shifting its heartland to the area around Lake Van.

(e) The evidence seems to suggest that the geographical entity called Urartu took its name from a more ancient forebear and that Mannea was only the latest manifestation as it appeared in the Neo-Assyrian period of the eighth century BC. In fact, Ur-Mannea may be the original source of the classical name Armenia and the heartland of classical Armenia is the Urmia basin.

(f) The mountains here are rich in mineral resources, especially gold for which Aratta was renowned. The walls of the city of Aratta were plastered in rich red-ochre mined from the mountain known as Kur-Hashura whilst we had seen just such a 'red mountain' near Takht-é Suleiman. Red ochre was also the substance used to cover the remains of the deceased in prehistoric times as attested at archaeological sites in this area. Indeed, the name Adam ('red earth') may be connected to this ritual.

(g) Archaeological surveys of the area have identified hundreds of occupation mounds and Miyandoab itself is known to have been settled in ancient times. It was here at Tash Tepe, a large mound just to the north of Miyandoab, that excavators recently unearthed an inscription of King Menua of Urartu (*c.* 800 BC) recording his conquest of the city of Meshtah – perhaps the mound of Tash Tepe itself. But Sargon II also received tribute from the Mannean 'fortresses' of Latashe and Tashtami, either of which may survive in the modern 'Mound of Tash' (i.e. Tash Tepe).

Conclusion Five

The lost kingdom of Aratta, mentioned in the earliest Sumerian epics, is to be located within the Miyandoab plain to the south of Lake Urmia in greater Armenia.

Sargon's Year 8 campaign text goes on to describe a great battle fought on Mount Uash which scholars are unanimous in identifying as the extinct volcano of Mount Sahand. This confirms that the Assyrian army had crossed the Miyandoab plain and was heading for the Adji Chay valley. Soon after, we read of the conquest of Tawri which, given its location, must be none other than the ancient town of Tawris – modern Tabriz. Sargon had marched up into the mountains from the plain to reach the *edin* of Aratta, just as Enmerkar's envoy had done 2,000 years earlier. But he had moved even deeper into God's Land. Traversing the slopes of Sahand he had fought his way into the Garden of Eden itself.

Unfortunately, this wealth of topographical and historical information was languishing, unstudied, back home in my library, as we made our journey across the Miyandoab plain on the 14th of April 1997. My mind was racing ahead of me as we sped along the highway leading to the gap between the eastern shore of Lake Urmia and the western slopes of the Mount Sahand foothills. What I was thinking about was not Sargon's campaign but the epic tale of 'Enmerkar and the Lord of Aratta'.

> The emissary journeying to Aratta covered his feet with the dust of the road, stirred up the pebbles of the mountains. Like a huge serpent prowling about in the **plain**, he was unopposed. After the emissary reached Aratta, the people of Aratta stepped up to admire the pack donkeys. [Lines 348-54]

I knew that the Sumerian word for 'plain' here was *edin* (Akk. *edin-na*) – the very word from which the biblical Eden most likely derives. Passing through Malekan – the village of the 'Guardian Angels' – I was convinced that I had finally reached Eden and was about to enter the broad valley which Walker had identified as the garden of paradise.

Over the past three days we had made our way up to the mountains along the 'highway' between Susa and the Saidmarreh valley; we had passed through the seven gates or passes; and now we had dropped down into the edin. My epic journey was nearly over. I had followed Enmerkar's envoy into the wondrous kingdom of Aratta which I believe forms the southern part of the region the author of Genesis refers to as Eden. Now I just had to travel on for another couple of hours to reach the place where, according to the Hebrew tradition, Adam and Eve lived.

The weather had been very kind to us whilst we were crossing the high Zagros. However, as soon as we dropped down into the plain, things took a sudden turn for the worse. On the far western horizon the mountains of eastern Turkey were rapidly disappearing under a canopy of dark clouds. In the cool mountain air of the last two days, I had been used to seeing for mile upon mile over ridge upon ridge. The muggy air of the Urmia basin was quite different. It seemed to suck in the sky, pulling the clouds down towards the wide lake surface and on into the valley of the Adji Chay. The snow-capped peaks surrounding Urmia merged with the white haze beneath the clouds. It began to rain.

The irony was not lost on me. Here I was arriving in the most wondrous, exotic, beneficent land of paradise – the 'Garden of Eden' – and I was being greeted by weather more befitting a dank December in England. What was even more disappointing was the fact that the great peak of Mount Sahand, although only a few kilometres to our east, was completely enveloped in cloud. We headed off the main highway on a short diversion to the shore of Lake Urmia.

This vast lake is a melancholy place. The winds whip up the surface into blustery squalls. The shoreline on the east side of the lake consists predominantly of mud flats caked in layers of salt. There seems to be no life in the waters and little along the shoreline. It reminded me of another great salt lake I had visited on my travels – the Dead Sea. This too was a 'sea of death'. Further north the road crosses mile upon mile of salty marshland into which the Adji Chay empties its bitter waters. The desolation is oppressive. Today the lake has a depth of not much more than fifteen metres but in Neolithic times it was deeper and wider.

We returned to the Tabriz road which sweeps around Mount Sahand and on into the wide valley of the Adji Chay, lying at 1,370 metres above sea level.

The main highway runs along the south side of the valley across the northern slopes of the Sahand massif. At first the plain to our left was densely packed with orchards stretching as far as the eye could see. On the slopes to our right natural terraces of rich earth were also covered in fruit trees, the branches of which cascaded with pink blossom brought on by the early spring.

122. Lake Urmia with the mountains of eastern Turkey beyond.

God planted a garden in Eden, which is in the east, and there he put the man he had fashioned. From the soil, God caused to grow every kind of tree, enticing to look at and good to eat, with the tree of life in the middle of the garden, and the tree of knowledge of good and evil. [Genesis 2:8-9]

Half an hour further on and the 'garden' had turned into a vast, grey industrial complex. Petrochemical plants, warehouses and lorry parks lined the road. We had entered the western outskirts of Iran's fourth largest city – the regional capital of AZERBAIJAN Province.

Once famous as the terminus of the Silk Road from China and, more recently, for its luxuriant carpets, Tabriz is now a sprawling industrial city with little to attract the visitor.

Tradition has it that the ancient settlement of Tawris (from which the name Tabriz derives) was founded in Sassanian times (third century AD) when it prospered as a major trade centre. But Tawris is almost certainly one and the same as the Tawri of Sargon's campaign and this pushes its foundation back another 1,000 years to the eighth century BC.

Much of the old city of Tabriz has been destroyed by a series of earthquakes which have hit this region at regular intervals (especially in AD 858, 1041, and 1721). The Arabian plate overlaps the Asian plate along the line of the Zagros range and creates a violent zone of destruction stretching across from the Black Sea to the Caspian. This fault-line is the underlying cause of the violent earth tremors and was responsible for the creation of the wide volcanic zone running through western Iran. It is because of this constant threat of disruption that Tabriz has grown outwards rather than upwards. Until recently, most of the buildings were either single or double storey and so the population spread has been extensive over the central valley, filling the floor from mountain slope to mountain slope. Through the middle of this mass of humanity passes the Adji Chay – the only river in the valley – which flows down from its

AZERBAIJAN: Derived from Atarpategan – 'Keeper of the Sacred Fire'.

three main sources in the Sahand, Bazgush and Kusheh Dagh ranges. However, there are numerous thermal springs around Tabriz which join the Adji Chay ('Bitter Waters').[17] This is what gives the water its brackish taste. Eventually the river struggles westwards into Lake Urmia where much of its flow is trapped, unable to reach the sea. Evaporation in the sultry summer heat is its only escape.

According to the evidence presented in *Chapter One*, the Tabriz valley was the location of the Garden of Eden. The sad-looking river flowing through it is therefore the primeval stream which watered paradise. Its current condition symbolises to me the untold damage humankind can do to the life-giving environment gifted to us by nature. I tried to imagine the place before the city of Tabriz had ever existed but this was not easy. Picture the prehistoric valley once the scar of Tabriz is stripped from the landscape – a place of deep, rich soil fed by mountain streams which join to form the river of the Garden; thermal springs bubbling up between wooded glades protected by high mountains – all this in magnificent isolation.

> A river flowed from Eden to water the garden, and from there it divided to make four streams (literally 'heads'). [Genesis 2:10]

This passage has always troubled scholars. How can a river divide to form four headwaters? The Hebrew word *rosh* ('head') clearly means a source and not an estuary, so we cannot be dealing with a delta. Yet a delta is the only place where a single river can divide into many streams or channels. Perhaps the author of Genesis was trying to interpret something which he did not fully comprehend. Perhaps he knew that the river of the Garden flowed into a great lake with no outlet and imagined that the river was returning to the abyss which lay deep beneath the earth. In his mind the two vast lakes of Urmia and Van were places where the abyss came to the surface – but they were also located in the heart of the mountains where the four rivers of Eden re-emerged from their 'heads'.

123. Opposite page (above): Tabrizi orchards in full bloom.

124. Opposite page (below): A panoramic view of the city of Tabriz looking north.

125. The Adji Chay/Meidan river to the west of Tabriz with the ruins of a Seljuk Period (11th century AD) bridge.

107

One might imagine the concept of a primeval river (Meidan/Adji Chay) flowing out from the Garden of Eden into the reservoir of the abyss (Urmia), then breaking forth in a sort of rebirth at the springs of the four great rivers of Eden, two of which empty into the Caspian Sea whilst the other, more famous streams flow down through the Mesopotamian plain to discharge into the Persian Gulf.

Through the Lands of Nod and Cush

The next morning we set off eastwards along the valley of the Adji Chay, skirting the northern slopes of Sahand. The weather was little better than the previous day and, in fact, it was about to get a great deal worse.

Today's adventure was to be a round-trip exploration of the lands of Nod and Cush. We would be making a wide loop in an anti-clockwise direction through the towns of Bostanabad, Sarab, Ardabil, Meshginshahr and Ahar before returning to Tabriz across the Kusheh Dagh range which bordered the Adji Chay valley on its northern side. It somehow seemed appropriate that, as we were heading eastwards out of the Garden of Eden, following in the footsteps of Adam's wayward son, we were also heading into the blackness and gloom of an awe-inspiring thunderstorm. The displeasure of Enlil, 'Lord of the Air', voiced in the roar of thunder and the howling of the wind, brought our retracing of Cain's exile into stark reality. This was the road of abandonment – the road leading to the painful birth of civilisation.

126. Mount Savalan from the pass leading into the land of Nod.

127. The volcanic lake at the summit of Savalan. This amazing place was also traditionally regarded as a sacred spring site since time immemorial.

As we reached the head of the valley and began to ascend the pass between Kuh-é Bazgush and the mighty SAVALAN volcano, the weather rapidly closed in. We were met by a wall of sleet-filled cloud which engulfed the vehicle. The winds battered our tiny refuge and the icy rain lashed at the windscreen. Every painful kilometre took us closer to the harsh and bitter landscape of Cain's exile.

Beyond the ridge which acts as a gateway into the Tabriz valley is another alpine plateau at the heart of which stands the city of Ardabil. Only two months earlier, on the 28th of February 1997, an earthquake measuring 5.5 on the Richter Scale killed over 3,000 people in this valley and made a further 40,000 homeless. In 1990 an even more violent tremor reaped a death toll of 35,000. The land of Nod is a hard place in which to survive.

According to Walker, to the south-west of Ardabil there was located a little village called Nodi which represented another distant memory of an ancient biblical toponym. Nod-i means 'of' or 'belonging to Nod'. Walker's Nodi was a village whose name retained a reference to the land in which it was located. The problem was that none of the locals knew of any village whose name sounded like Walker's Nodi. In desperation we decided to head for Ardabil and the local government headquarters to seek help.

The regional offices of the district were set in pleasant gardens. The building itself was fairly new but retained an air of a Soviet-style severity. For the Tabriz leg of my journey, Mayis and I had been joined by local guide and historian, Cyrus Rassouli. His expert knowledge of the Persian, AZERI and Arabic languages was to prove of considerable value in our search for local toponyms connected with the early Genesis narratives. Cyrus escorted me up the steps into a small office crowded with locals all

SAVALAN: The name of this mountain means 'taking of tribute'. This could suggests that there was indeed some sort of toll or brigandic levy for using the pass into Eden from the east.

AZERI: An eastern dialect of Turkish.

109

waving their little green identity cards at a harassed official pinned behind his desk. Fortunately, I stood out from the crowd and received immediate attention. That attention, however, was decidedly one of suspicion as it is not every day that these officials receive a visit from a westerner in this remote part of Iran. After a scurrying to and fro of errand boys waving pieces of white paper, we were finally allowed to pass through the sentried door and beyond into the corridors of power.

It took us a while to locate the door to the mapping department of Ardabil Province. Cyrus knocked politely and we entered, to be greeted by five young officials surrounded by walls covered in large-scale maps of the region. It took several glasses of tea to explain precisely what it was that I was searching for. Finally the atmosphere began to warm and maps started to appear on the desk before me. Hunched over the desktop we all examined segments of chart in search of villages which might be linked to Nod. The officials knew of one small town to the east of Ardabil called Noadi but this was nowhere near where Walker had located his Nodi. To the north of Ardabil were several villages called Noqdi which might plausibly be linked to the biblical Nod. Moreover, the whole region to the north of Ardabil turned out to be known as Upper and Lower Noqdi. This was an unexpected revelation, as the names of these two districts did not appear on any map I had seen.

By now I had spent long enough with my newly acquired friends and there seemed little to be gained by staying for yet another round of teas. So I bade my farewells and, armed with the new information, set off northwards into the region known as Upper Noqdi.

After an hour the road to the large settlement of Noqdi-Kandi ('Nod Village') dissolved into a narrow bumpy track which led over a barren hilltop. As I reached the crest I could see the village spread out before me. We lingered long enough to take a couple of photographs but, in that brief moment, I had noticed, beyond the village, a long mound which looked to all the world like a tepe – in other words an ancient settlement.

We drove on down to the village negotiating our way past potholes and free-roaming chickens. Our arrival was heralded by the barking of village dogs which brought curious faces to the windows of the small mudbrick houses. Eventually the minibus could go no further. The little lane was simply too narrow. So we set off on foot heading down the hill towards the heart of the sprawling village. There, outside the mosque, Cyrus and I were met by the village elders who invited us into their place of prayer for a discussion.

It was soon apparent that, in spite of the great age etched into their faces, these community leaders knew little about the long-term history of Noqdi-Kandi. Their traditions did not extend back in time much beyond five or six generations. All we could glean from them was that the village was 'very old' but that there were several other villages in the area called Noqdi and that one was even called 'Old Noqdi', indicating its seniority over the rest. As to the long, low mound which I had seen to the north of

128. The village of Noqdi with what may be a large occupation mound or *tepe* beyond.

the village, they confirmed that no excavations had been undertaken there, but that 'ruins', as they called them, had been noted on the surface of the hill. This was later confirmed during discussions with the director of the Azerbaijan Museum in Tabriz.

As we returned to the car I was feeling somewhat disappointed that we had not discovered some crucial evidence to link this region with the story of Cain's exile. But it would have been quite extraordinary if we had come up with anything more than linguistic links with the toponyms of the Ardabil region. At least I had been able to confirm Walker's premise that there were villages in this area whose names appear to have been linked to the biblical Nod. What is more, a whole region seemed to be named after the land of Nod. We made our way back to the main road and headed west into the land of Cush.

I soon found myself travelling beside the crashing torrent of the Ahar Chay which flows on down to join the Araxes-Gihon in the north. Upon approaching the mountains we entered a narrow defile carved by the river. Immediately above the gorge rose the majestic, snow-capped peak of Kusheh Dagh.

For the last two hours we had been travelling through the southern part of biblical Cush, but now the Ahar Chay gorge was funnelling us towards the northern 'gate' which led into paradise. Darkness was rapidly descending as we climbed over the mountain pass which led back to the Garden of Eden. We arrived back in Tabriz late into the night and collapsed into our beds.

129. Following page: The fast-flowing waters of the Ahar Chay – one of the tributaries of the Araxes/ Gihon – as it cuts its way through a deep gorge beneath Kusheh Dagh. The modern road from Tabriz to Ahar follows this branch of the Gihon river into the ancient land of Cush.

Mountain of the Chalice

The word of Yahweh was addressed to me as follows: Son of man, raise a lament for the king of Tyre. Say to him 'The Lord Yahweh says this: "**You were in Eden, in the Garden of God**. ... I made you a living creature with outstretched wings, as guardian, **you were upon the holy Mountain of God**, you walked in the midst of **red-hot coals**. Your manner was exemplary from the day you were created until guilt first appeared in you, because your busy trading has filled you with violence and sin. I have cast you down from the Mountain of God and destroyed you, guardian winged creature, amid the coals. ... Of the nations, all who know you are stunned at your fate. You are an object of terror gone forever.'" [Ezekiel 28:11-19]

This passage from the writings of the revelatory prophet Ezekiel is a chastisement directed at the king of Tyre. It is clear that Ezekiel believed the ancestors of the ruler of Tyre had once lived in Eden and dwelt upon God's mountain before their fall from grace. So we need to address the matter of the 'Mountain of God', located in the Garden of Eden, whose summit is covered in 'red-hot coals' – in other words volcanic ash. Clearly, if Ezekiel is referring metaphorically to the Phoenicians' earliest human ancestors and those ancestors dwelt in the Garden of Eden, then he is talking about Adam himself and his family. The book of Genesis does indeed tell us that Adam fell from grace and was exiled from the garden of God but it does not say anything about a fiery Mountain of God.

However, the idea of a sacred mountain where Yahweh resides is not a literary invention of the prophet Ezekiel. In Isaiah 14 we read of the death of the king of Babylon.

How did the tyrant end? ... Your pride has been cast down into the underworld along with the music of your lyres; under you a mattress of maggots, over you a blanket of worms. How did you come to

130. Previous page: The north face of Kusheh Dagh viewed from the land of Cush.

131. Above: The troglodyte village of Kandovan beneath the summit of the 'Mountain of the Chalice' (Azeri *Jam Daghi*).

132. Opposite page: The stream of the Garden of Eden, cascading down from the 'Mountain of God' to meet the Adji Chay/Meidan river in the valley of Tabriz.

fall from the heavens, Daystar, Son of Dawn? How did you come to be thrown to the ground, conqueror of nations? You who used to think to yourself: 'I shall scale the heavens. Higher than the stars of God I shall set my throne. I shall sit on the **Mountain of the Assembly far away to the north**. I shall climb high above the clouds; I shall rival the Most High.' Now you have been flung down into the underworld, **into the depths of the abyss!** [Isaiah 14:4-15]

The Mountain of the Assembly is the place where the gods of Mesopotamia dwelt and it is located across the Zagros mountains far to the north. Whenever we read an Old Testament passage in which human beings meet their god, we find them climbing mountains. Abraham goes to sacrifice his son atop Mount Moriah; Moses ascends Mount Sinai to meet his god for the first time within the burning bush and then later to receive the Ten Commandments; Moses is taken up Mount Nebo to be received by God as the Israelite leader's death draws near; the Israelite 'high-places' are by definition located on mountain tops; and the Temple of Yahweh is built on the highest point of Mount Moriah, looking down upon the City of David. It is clear from the biblical text that God 'the Most High' resided upon a mountain. It is then only a simple step backwards in time to understand that the original Mountain of God was located in Eden. Thus Adam visited his god on the top of a mountain looking down onto the Adji Chay/Meidan river valley.

The highest mountain near Tabriz is the 3,700-metre volcanic dome of Sahand (the 'Mount Uash' of Sargon II's campaign). At its summit the ice-cold waters of the abyss gush out through a narrow chimney. It is another Takht-é Suleiman. To the locals, scattered about the slopes of the great volcano, this is a sacred place which they call the 'Mountain of the Chalice' (Azeri: *Jam Daghi*). Every weekend and on local holidays Tabrizis can be seen ascending the mountain to collect the therapeutic waters of the Chalice spring in huge plastic containers as it flows down from its lofty source. This place has magical power.

My final morning in Iran on that first visit in April 1997 saw us heading up to the summit of Mount Sahand. My intention was simply to see if we could find a commanding location for a panoramic photograph of the

133. High-rise apartments from a bygone age.

valley of the Garden but one final surprise still lay in store for me. It took about an hour to traverse the lower foothills of the Sahand massif, passing through the town of Uski (modern Osku) which Sargon II had so violently torn asunder in 714 BC (see *Appendix B*). Eventually we left all signs of habitation behind. The agricultural terraces were gone; the animals grazing in the fields were gone, and all that was left ahead of us was the gleaming dome of the sacred volcano rising above the moorland. Still the tarmac road continued and so we pressed on – then came the surprise.

As the minibus came around a bend in the road we were suddenly confronted by an amazing rock formation. Here were jagged towers – pinnacles of rock – resembling a forest of pine trees clinging to the upper slopes of the volcano. If that were not spectacular enough, I soon realised that these natural towers had been hewn hollow and that people were living in them. We had come across a settlement of troglodytes!

The village of KANDOVAN was located above the snow-line and within just a few hundred metres of the volcanic crater at the summit of Mount Sahand. Why would people be living here? One could not imagine a harsher environment. Everything needed to sustain the occupants of the village had to be brought up from the valley below. All that was here was the mountain stream which welled up from the abyss and flowed on down to join the Adji Chay.

As we took our leave of the 'Mountain of the Assembly', I recalled another passage from 'Enmerkar and the Lord of Aratta' which describes the place where Inanna dwelt as she looked down upon Aratta.

> The great queen of heaven, who is lofty upon her awesome *me*, dwelling on the peak of the *Kur-shuba*; adorning the dais of the *Kur-shuba* … [Lines 229-31]

Kur-shuba(r) literally means 'bright mountain'.[18] The Sumerian epic poetry informs us that this mountain was the birthplace of the gods, the place of origin of Enmerkar himself, and a source of fragrant oils.

I could not help but wonder if we were descending from the very throne of the queen of heaven.

134. The fantasy world of Kandovan village, reminiscent of a scene from Walt Disney's Pinocchio.

KANDOVAN: A Persian word meaning 'honeycomb-like'.

Conclusion Six

With the Garden of Eden located in the Adji Chay valley and the kingdom of Aratta identified with the Miyandoab plain, the extinct volcano overlooking both legendary places takes on a new significance. Mount Sahand (also known as the 'Mountain of the Chalice' and Mount Uash) may once have been seen as the 'bright mountain' of the heavenly assembly of Sumerian tradition and therefore the 'Mountain of God' of the later biblical tradition.

Colour Plates

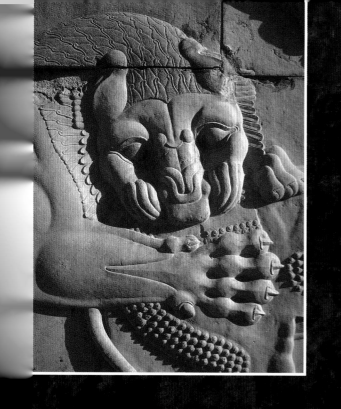

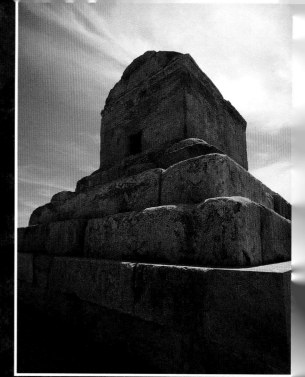

Part Two

The
Mighty Heroes

Civilisation's Rise in the
Heartland of Sumer

So God banished Adam. And before the Garden of Eden he posted
the cherubim and the fiery flashing sword to guard the way to the
Tree of Life.

Genesis 3:24

135. Opposite page: Doré's vision of the banishment from the Garden of Eden.

136. Left: The angel of Isfahan. The standard perception of an angelic being, from a lintel in the Armenian Christian cathedral in Isfahan.

Chapter Three

THE GREAT MIGRATION

So far we have determined the geographical location of Eden and its Garden, but we have hardly explored the archaeological and historical evidence. It is therefore time to ask whether the remains left by human activity in the Zagros zone confirm our topographical findings. To answer this important question we need to take a look at patterns of pottery development and spread, as well as a closer scrutiny of the textual sources of Genesis and Sumer. What were the political and historical links between the mountains and the Mesopotamian plain? In which direction did the cultural development flow? Did Sumer seed the mountains or did the mountain people seed what is recognised as the first great civilisation on earth?

By the time of Enmerkar it is difficult to determine which was the older civilisation – Uruk or Aratta. But there are clues. Directly east of Sumer (southern Iraq) is the plain of Susiana and, beyond that, the main southern route along the Kerkheh river into the Zagros range. This region holds the key because the earliest pottery to appear in Sumer seems to originate here and, immediately prior to that, in the mountain valleys which lead down to the Susiana plain. So, were the Sumerians originally mountain folk? We find a number of further indications in the Enmerkar epics which point us towards this conclusion.

First, there does appear to be a clear *cultural* relationship between the Sumerian civilisation of Mesopotamia and the mountain kingdom of Aratta. The political structures of both societies were very similar. For instance, we learn from the Enmerkar epics that the ruler of Aratta was both a religious and military leader who bore the Sumerian title *en* – 'lord'. He also had a Sumerian name – Ensukushsiranna.[1] Kramer notes

137. The ancient-world perception of an angelic being – a much less benign image altogether. Part of the scene from a Middle Bronze Age Anatolian cylinder seal impression. From the private collection of the Biblisches Institut, Fribourg University.

INANNA: Possibly derived from Nin-Anna – 'Lady of Heaven'.

E-ANNA: 'House of Heaven'.

GLYPTIC: The form of art developed for seal impressions.

138. Detail from the 'Victory Stela' of Naramsin, ruler of Agade. The king is depicted ascending a mountain peak on top of which the gods reside. He himself is portrayed as a god with horned helmet. Naramsin was one of the first Mesopotamian rulers to declare himself divine whilst still alive.

other Sumerian titles carried by the officials of the Arattan state – familiar designations such as *ensi* (local ruler), *sukkal* (vizier), *ishakku* (governor), *shatammu* (provincial administrator), *munshib* (supervisor), *ragaba* (knight) and *ugula* (officer). There was also an advisory assembly of elders just as in the Sumerian city states.

Not only was the political structure to all intents and purposes identical but the religions of the two regions were very similar, if not the same. Two of the major deities of Aratta – Inanna and Dumuzi – were also great deities of Sumer. But even more interesting is the fact that the cult of the powerful patron goddess of Aratta – INANNA – was actually exported to Uruk, the mightiest of the Sumerian cities, from the mountain kingdom. There, at the heart of the Mesopotamian plain, she became 'Queen of E-ANNA' – the sacred precinct of Uruk. It is precisely this adoption of the goddess which is the focus of the epic poem 'Enmerkar and the Lord of Aratta'.[2] It is the need to lavish her new temple at Uruk with precious stones which lies behind Enmerkar's demand that the wealth of Aratta be sent down to the plain from the mountain kingdom. The Sumerian Inanna was known as Ishtar by the later Babylonians, Astarte by the Syrians and Anahita by the Persians. To the Israelites she was Ashtaroth, whilst the Egyptians knew her as Isis – the great goddess of love.

Study of the GLYPTIC art of Mesopotamia shows the close relationship between gods and mountains. Several deities stand astride rocky peaks – they reside on mountain tops, just as with the Greek pantheon of Olympus. The shrines of the Sumerian deities were erected on top of large mudbrick platforms in the sacred precincts of the cities. These platforms later grew into huge, towering stepped structures – man-made mountains built in the lowland floodplain where no natural mountains existed – upon which the gods dwelt. These, as I have already mentioned, are the ziggurats of Mesopotamia of which the most famous is the biblical 'Tower of Babel' (usually believed to be the ziggurat of Babylon).

So it seems very likely that, like Inanna, many of the deities in the Sumerian pantheon were originally gods and goddesses of the eastern mountains. It is then logical

to assume that if the gods moved down from the mountains into the plain, the people who worshipped those gods must also have migrated in the same direction, bringing their religion and cultic rituals with them. Thus a major part of the Sumerian population came from the Zagros hinterland – the geographical region we call Armenia within which lay the ingdom of Aratta and the biblical land of Eden. This is consistent with the Genesis tradition which relates that the ancestors of the Hebrew patriarchs left Eden and eventually ended up in the 'Land of Shinar' – ancient Sumer.

139. Sir Leonard Woolley's reconstruction of the ziggurat at Ur.

140. The storm-god standing on two mountain peaks. Private collection of the Biblisches Institut, Fribourg University.

Conclusion Seven

The archaeological evidence from prehistory suggests that the 'Neolithic Revolution' originated in the Zagros mountains and gradually transferred to the Mesopotamian plain. The early Genesis narratives reflects this movement of the progenitors of civilisation down from the eastern highlands into the alluvial lowlands during the fifth millennium BC.

141. The first type of Sumerian representation – elongated with beard and long curly hair. Statuette of Nabu, god of writing. Baghdad Museum.

142. The second type of Sumerian representation – rounded face with shaven head.

TOPONYMS: The names of places or geographical regions/locations.

PUBLIC SCHOOL: In the British sense of a private fee-paying school rather than the state-run, non-fee-paying school.

It has been argued that the dynasty of Aratta was a Sumerian offshoot implying a colonisation from Sumer northwards into the mountains. The reality, however, may have been that the kingdom of Aratta was the progenitor of the Sumer civilisation and not the other way around.

At this point it is important to explain that the term 'Sumerian civilisation' does not imply ethnicity in the strict sense. Scholars have long recognised that Sumerian culture was ethnically mixed – principally consisting of people who spoke the earliest Semitic language/dialects and another group who spoke Sumerian. However, there also seems to have been a third, much earlier, group which may be identified in the earliest TOPONYMS in the region. These geographical names appear to be neither Semitic nor Sumerian in origin. For example, the names *Idiglat* (Tigris) and *Buranun* (Euphrates) are believed not to be Sumerian words. Nor, is it thought, are the city names *Eridu*, *Ur* or *Kish*. Common words such as fisherman (*shuhadak*), farmer (*engar*) and herdsman (*udul*) are also presumed to have been borrowed by the Sumerians from an earlier indigenous language.

Eventually the Semitic language – Akkadian – became predominant and Sumerian disappeared as a spoken tongue. From around the beginning of the second millennium, the latter only survived in the scribal schools where it was taught very much in the way that Latin is still part of a PUBLIC SCHOOL education today – even though the spoken language of ancient Rome has been dead for over a 1,000 years.

So when we talk of Sumerian civilisation, we see it as a multi-ethnic society. But that still leaves open the question as to the origins of the ethnic Sumerians – that is the people who introduced the Sumerian language into Mesopotamia. We have already come across the 'Sumerian Problem' which exposes the difficulties in establishing when the Sumerians arrived in the region. Now we have to address the issue of where they came from.

Conclusion Eight

The use of the term 'Sumerian', to describe the earliest written language of Mesopotamia, does not define the ethnicity of the first people to settle in the Mesopotamian plain. There is evidence in local toponyms of an earlier language which must be linked with these settlers. The fact that the Akkadian-speaking peoples referred to the 'land of Sumer' does not presuppose that the original occupiers of that land spoke Sumerian. Indeed, it is possible that the language known as Sumerian was not the spoken tongue of the people classified by both modern scholars and the ancients as 'Sumerians'.

Let me remind you where I am coming from. The whole idea behind *Legend* is to attempt a synthesis between the traditional history of the book of Genesis and the independent archaeological record for the sixth to third millennia BC. Our objective is to try to construct a narrative history based on the main thrust of the Genesis tradition. So far we have been able to locate the land of Eden in the mountainous terrain of eastern Turkey and western Iran. We have now discovered that there was a close cultural link between the Sumerian city-state of Uruk and the kingdom of Aratta which is located in the same general area as Eden. A big question is beginning to loom here. If it is possible that the ethnic Sumerians migrated from the Zagros mountains down into the plain of Sumer, then do they have any connection with the biblical tradition of a migration of Adam's descendants from Eden into the land of Shinar?

The Sons of Shem

I am now going to introduce you to an astonishing proposition put forward by Samuel Noah Kramer – who, I should perhaps remind you, is regarded as the greatest Sumerologist of the century. In his classic historical work *The Sumerians*, Kramer's final thoughts turn to the vexed question of the relationship between the biblical patriarchs and the Sumerians. He begins by comparing what is known of Sumerian civilisation with the traditional culture of the biblical Israelites.

> The achievements of the Sumerians in the areas of religion, education, and literature left a deep impression not only on their neighbours in space and time but on the culture of modern man as well, specially through their influence, indirect though it was, on the ancient Hebrews and the Bible. The extent of the Hebrew debt to Sumer becomes more apparent from day to day as a result of the gradual piecing together and translation of the Sumerian literary works; for as can now be seen, they have quite a number of features in common with the books of the Bible.[3]

So far so good. There appears to have been a cultural link between the Sumerians and the Israelites, which Kramer then goes on to elaborate upon at some length. But then this brings him to the all important question:

> If the Sumerians were people of such outstanding literary and cultural importance for the ancient Near Eastern world as a whole that they even left their indelible impression on the literary works of the Hebrew men of letters, why is it that there seems to be little trace of them in the Bible?[4]

This is a fact not often noticed by Bible readers. Nearly every other major civilisation in the ancient Near East is mentioned in the Old

Testament – Egyptians, Canaanites, Amorites, Hurrians (Horites), Hittites, Assyrians, Babylonians – they are all there. But why no Sumerians?

> In Genesis, chapters 10 and 11, for example, we find lists of quite a number of eponyms, lands, and cities. But except for the rather obscure word 'Shinar', which scholars usually identify with Sumer … there seems to be no mention of the Sumerians in the entire Bible, a fact which is hardly reconcilable with their purported pre-eminence and influence.[5]

Next we discover that Kramer is attempting to resurrect an idea first published in 1941 by his own tutor, that other great Mesopotamian scholar – Arno POEBEL.

> Interestingly enough, a solution to this rather puzzling enigma was suggested over a quarter of a century ago by my teacher and colleague, Arno Poebel, in the form of a brief comment in an article published in the *American Journal of Semitic Languages* (Vol. 58 [1941], pp. 20-26). Poebel's suggestion has found no responsive echo among Orientalists, and it seems to have been relegated to scholarly oblivion. It is my conviction, however, that it will stand the test of time and in due course be recognized as a significant contribution to Hebrew-Sumerian inter-connections.[6]

Why has this idea – I will let you know what it is in a minute – not been taken up or seriously challenged by Sumerologists or biblical scholars? Perhaps it was such a shock to the system that no-one could get their heads around it. On the other hand, the implications for biblical research are huge. I myself have first hand experience of how orthodox scholars treat revolutionary new ideas. Perhaps the Sumerologists were simply too scared to criticise the great man of their discipline and so, in spite of misgivings born of closed minds, all decided to keep silent. This tactic is often employed in academia. If something is put forward which radically diverges from orthodox thinking an effective way to kill off the idea is to 'starve it of the oxygen of publicity'. That way the minimum intellectual energy is expended and nobody puts themselves in the front line where there is a danger of embarrassing rebuttal. But enough polemic.

Kramer now introduces a grammatical point which is going to solve the problem of the absence of Sumerians in the biblical narrative and which we will find recourse to in the following chapter when we go in search of the antediluvian patriarchs.

In simple terms, the Sumerians had what scholars call 'amissable consonants' – that is to say consonants at the ends of words which were dropped or not pronounced. Thus, for example, the word for 'god' – *dingir* – was pronounced 'dingi'. The 'r' consonant, although written in the cuneiform script, was not vocalised. Kramer, having given a couple of examples, finally delivers the linguistic and intellectual *coup de grâce*.

Now to return to our problem and the quest for the word 'Sumer', or rather 'Shumer', to use the form found in the cuneiform documents. Poebel was struck by the word's resemblance to the name 'Shem', Noah's eldest son, and the distant ancestor of such eponyms as Ashur, Elam, Aram, and above all, Eber, the eponym of the Hebrews.[7]

What was that? Did he say that biblical name Shem could be the eponym for the land of Sumer itself? Yes, amazing as it may seem, that is precisely what Kramer, the Sumerologist *par excellence* is saying. He goes on to explain two important points:

(1) The Hebrew vowel 'e' is often equivalent to the cuneiform vowel 'u' – as is the case with the Hebrew word for 'name' – *shem* – which is the Akkadian word *shum*. Thus Sumerian Shumer becomes Hebrew Shemer.

(2) The letter 'r' at the end of Shumer is an amissable consonant which is not pronounced.

Thus the vocalisation of Shumer in the Hebrew tongue would be Shem! The conclusion is both inevitable and, at the same time, revelatory.

> If Poebel's hypothesis turns out to be correct, and Shem is identical with Shumer-Sumer, we must assume that the Hebrew authors of the Bible, or at least some of them, considered the Sumerians to have been the original ancestors of the Hebrew people.[8]

As Kramer recalls, no-one took Poebel's original proposal seriously and, sad to say, Kramer's attempt to resurrect the idea also fell on deaf ears. But is it really such an extraordinary proposition? Were these two eminent scholars so very wrong to pose the question? The evidence which I have presented so far indicates that they were not far from the truth in their linguistic speculations.

Conclusion Nine

The people of Sumer were designated 'Sumerians' after Shem, son of Noah, who was remembered as the eponymous ancestor of those who re-occupied biblical Shinar following the destruction of the antediluvian cities during the Mesopotamian flood. The name Shumer is therefore an eponym.

Once the original homeland of the Sumerians is located in the Zagros mountains, both Sumerian and Israelite origins and the archaeological picture converge to reveal an epic journey.

143. A superb buff-coloured vase from Susa decorated with tall-necked flamingoes (top), elongated hounds (middle) and sweeping-horned gazelle (main panel). Susa I period. Louvre Museum.

144. A large red goblet with water motif painted in black. This striking vessel comes from Shahriyar in Iran and dates from the fifth millennium BC.

Let us begin to trace that journey through the archaeological record – a journey which fits the biblical picture remarkably well once the era of the Sumerian migration into the Mesopotamian lowlands is established.

Down from the Mountains

It is now necessary to delve into regional pottery chronology, for it is only through the comparison of pottery typologies, found in different *tepes* or ruin-mounds, that contact/migration can be demonstrated between the Zagros mountain valleys and the alluvial plains of Mesopotamia.

The pattern of pottery finds shows a clear movement of culture from the highlands down into the lowlands. Archaeological investigations have shown that pottery was invented in the mountains of western Iran during the seventh millennium BC.[9] From there it spread gradually throughout the Middle East, presumably carried by the mountain people who invented the technique of ceramic firing.

According to James Mellaart of the Institute of Archaeology, London,[10] the migration seems to be in two waves – one into the northern plain, in the area which would later become Babylonia and Assyria, and the other to the south, into the region around the Persian Gulf where the civilisations of Susiana and Sumer would arise. Mellaart first deals with the northern movement.

He tells us that the Neolithic settlement at Jarmo (a hilltop village east of Kirkuk) used pottery which appears without prototypes in the region. It was probably brought from the Neolithic settlements of the Zagros mountains – places such as Tepe Guran in the Hulailan valley – where the same type of pottery has been found. The fact that this is the earliest pottery in Mesopotamia suggests that it was introduced by human migration rather than trade as might have been the case in later periods. The pottery of Guran is dated to the end of the seventh millennium BC.[11] Other sites in the valleys of the central Zagros – especially in the Kermanshah/Kangavar valley indicate that sedentary culture existed here from as early as the ninth millennium. The sacred mountain of Behistun takes on a new significance when one realises the antiquity of the ruin mounds (Ganj-é Dareh Tepe, Tepe Asyab and Tepe Sarab) located at its foot in the broad valley.[12]

In the south the pattern is similar and the source of pottery seems to be the same. At the site of Hajji Muhammad, in Sumer proper, we find the pottery which soon evolves into the famous classic Ubaid style with geometric designs painted in dark brown onto a greenish buff background. This Hajji Muhammad ware (also termed Ubaid 2 pottery) is in turn closely related to pottery from stratum Vb at Tepe Giyan in the Zagros mountains, whilst the slightly earlier Giyan Va pottery is identical to that found at sites in the Khuzistan plain (known as Susiana A). As you know from our journey following in the footsteps of Enmerkar's emissary to the kingdom of Aratta, the very ancient city of Susa lies in the Khuzistan plain to the east of the Mesopotamian lowlands and immediately to the south of the Zagros foothills. Susa is a city which is going to continue to play a major role in our story at different times. At this point it provides us with another crucial link in the pottery trail we are following. Susiana A pottery is not only identical with Giyan Va but also with the earliest pottery found at Eridu (known also as Ubaid 1 pottery). So we can say that Susiana A in the Khuzistan plain is linked to Giyan Va in the mountains and that this type of pottery also appears in the earliest levels of Eridu (traditionally the first city in Sumer) where it is classified as Ubaid 1. Ubaid pottery is the earliest form of ceramic culture in southern Mesopotamia and it continues to dominate Sumer (and its northern neighbours) for the best part of 1,000 years.

Ubaid culture is now recognised as the most likely candidate for the ethnic Sumerians of the literature and so the arrival of its pottery style in the region must signal the arrival of the Sumerians themselves. I will shortly be dealing with the issue as to the *archaeological identification* of the ethnic Sumerians in more detail. But, if the so-called Ubaid culture is indeed that of the Sumerians, then we may conclude that the Sumerians entered the lowlands from the mountains to the north-east because that is where their earliest pottery originates.

But this is only the first step in retracing their origins deeper into the Zagros range. We have worked back from Eridu and Hajji Muhammad in Sumer to Susiana on the Khuzistan plain and from there into the mountains around the site of Tepe Giyan. Now we must search for other sites in the region which will draw us northwards towards Eden.

145. A typical Ubaid bowl with buff background and black or dark-brown decoration.

146. A simplified diagram illustrating the migration pattern of the earliest pottery. Stylistic analysis suggests a two-pronged development from the central Zagros region around Behistun (a) west and north to upper Mesopotamia and Syria (Jarmo, Hassuna, Samarra, Halaf) and (b) south to lower Mesopotamia and Sumer (Susiana, Eridu).

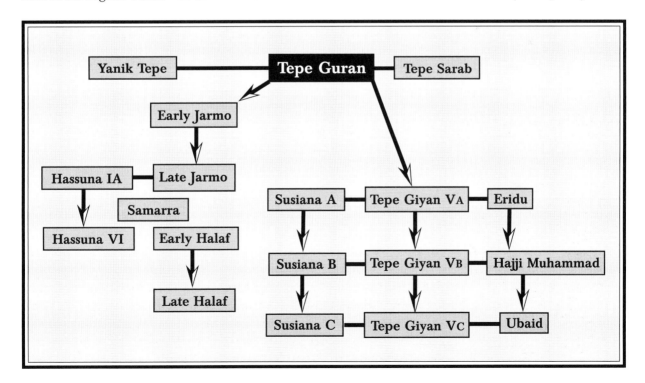

147. The Hulailan valley within which the key site of Tepe Guran is located.

148. The acropolis mound of Susa with 'de Morgan's Pillar' left by the excavator to show the numerous stratigraphic levels stretching back (downwards) into the prehistoric period (Susa I) in which the superb brown-on-buff ware was found.

Lying in the wide valley just to the east of Kermanshah, not far from Behistun, is the small, low mound of Tepe Sarab. Archaeologists have dated the occupation here to around 6300 to 6000 BC.[13] The site is less than one hundred kilometres from Tepe Giyan to the south-east and just sixty or so kilometres from Tepe Guran in the Hulailan valley to the south. The pottery chronology suggests that Tepe Sarab was earlier than Giyan Va and that Guran levels L to H contained pottery which was ancestral to that found at Tepe Sarab. Thus we have a development of Guran H to Sarab to Giyan Va to Susiana A to Eridu (Ubaid 1). However, the earliest pottery at Tepe Guran, predating any of these other sites, has no parallels in the region.[14] This makes Tepe Guran a key player in prehistory as the place where ceramic culture first appears and from where the technology of pottery-making is exported and developed throughout the ancient Near East. Of course, many sites in the region have hardly been explored, let alone excavated, so Guran may not be the only site to possess the earliest pottery. However, it is reasonable to conclude that it was in this mountainous zone around Kermanshah (known today as Luristan) where pottery was first invented.

We have traced this early pottery in a winding trail which leads down to Susiana and Sumer over a period of undetermined years. However, we can do something very similar for the northern culture of Mesopotamia. The important point is to remember that the same Tepe Guran ceramic corpus (levels L to H) has also been found at Jarmo where it appears in the first pottery levels there.

So what does all this mean? Well, bearing in mind the usual caveats about pottery links with population movements, it does suggest to me a migration of people down from the mountains into the plain via two main routes. The first leads from the Kermanshah valley along the Khanakin pass and beyond to the northern Mesopotamian sites such as Jarmo.

The second migration starts from the same valley and follows the Kerkheh river down to Susiana via Tepe Giyan. From there it continues into southern Mesopotamia and Sumer's earliest settlements – particularly Eridu, traditionally and archaeologically the first city on earth.

The Sumerian Problem

This all brings us back to the difficult problem of Sumerian origins. Kramer suggests the possibility that the name Sumer might derive from an eponymous ancestor named Shem. Yet he is, at the same time, the principal scholar to reject the idea that the Sumerians were the original settlers of the alluvial plain. He prefers to see the arrival of the Sumerians in the Uruk Period rather than in the much earlier Ubaid 1 era.

> … we seem justified in drawing the conclusion that the Sumerians were not the first settlers in Lower Mesopotamia, but that they must have been preceded by a civilized power of some magnitude, one that was culturally far more advanced than were the Sumerians.[15]

All the ingredients are there for a wide ranging synthesis between biblical tradition and archaeology, but no-one has realised it.

> … the history of Lower Mesopotamia may be divided into two major periods: the pre-Sumerian (which might be more meaningfully named the Irano-Semitic), and the Sumerian.
>
> The pre-Sumerian period began as a peasant village culture. As is now generally assumed, it was introduced into Lower Mesopotamia by immigrants from southwestern Iran noted for their specialized type of painted pottery. Not long after the establishment of the first settlements by the Iranian immigrants, the Semites probably infiltrated into Southern Mesopotamia, both as peaceful immigrants and as warlike conquerors. As a result of the fusion of these two ethnic groups – the Iranians from the East and the Semites from the West – and the cross-fertilization of their cultures, there came into being the first civilized urban state in Lower Mesopotamia.[16]

But what if these 'Iranian immigrants' were in reality the Sumerians moving down from their original homeland around Urmia; first settling in the Kermanshah-Kangovar valley at sites such as Tepe Sarab; then moving on southwards to Tepe Guran, Tepe Giyan and other sites in the

149. A typical spouted vessel from Girsu in southern Mesopotamia (second half of the fourth millennium BC). Louvre Museum.

150. A goblet from fourth-millennium Tepe Hissar in Iran. The central band is based on the meander motif (a stylised river?) winding between mountain peaks. Tehran Archaeological Museum.

151. Another fine vessel from fourth-millennium Susa with the very typical vertical zigzags representing flowing water. Tehran Archaeological Museum.

southern Zagros, before finally breaking out into the plain both in the north around Jarmo and in the south around Susa? Their last movement was then from Susiana into the swamps of southern Iraq where they established the first urban centres – centres such as Eridu, Uruk and Ur, which we associate so closely with Sumerian civilisation.

Conclusion Ten

The appearance of Ubaid pottery marks the arrival of Eden's tribal groups into the southern lowlands of Meso-potamia – a region which would only later acquire the name Sumer, following the flood and resettlement.

Sumerian or Semite?

This proposition leads us to another important topic. You may have been wondering for some time about the problem of language. Clearly, if the ancestors of Shem were Sumerian, then they must have spoken the Sumerian language and not one of the Semitic dialects.

The first point to make clear is that language does not define ethnicity. A person who speaks in a Semitic dialect is not necessarily ethnically Semitic. Indeed, there is no such term as an 'ethnic Semite'. A Semite is simply someone who speaks Semitic. The Jews of Palestine are ethnically Jewish but this is not because they speak Hebrew. A simple example will suffice to make this clear. Jesus and his followers did not speak to each other in Hebrew: they, in fact, spoke Aramaean. Does that mean that Jesus was not a Jew but a member of one of the northern Aramaean tribes? No, of course it does not. The fact is that the Jews of Jesus' time spoke the *lingua franca* of the region, which happened to be Aramaean.

Let us now transfer that historical model to Mesopotamia in the second millennium BC. Scholars acknowledge that by Abraham's time Sumerian had fallen out of use as a spoken language. The *lingua franca* of his day was East Semitic (Akkadian). If the earliest generations of Abraham's ancestral line had spoken Sumerian, then we could not know it from the language of Abraham's distant descendants (West Semitic Hebrew). In the same way that Jesus did not speak his ancestral tongue, Abraham and his descendants no longer spoke their ancestral tongue – the language of Noah and Adam.

This is not to say that intermarriage between the two linguistic groups – those who spoke Sumerian and those who spoke Semitic – did not take place over the post-diluvian generations so that 'Semitic blood' flowed through the veins of the patriarchs. However, it is dangerous to insist that the earliest traditions of Genesis lie down the Semitic linguistic ancestral line. Indeed, if the Sumerian literary traditions are anything to go by, there are clear indications to the contrary.

152. Opposite page: The geographical migration pattern of Mesopotamia's earliest pottery.

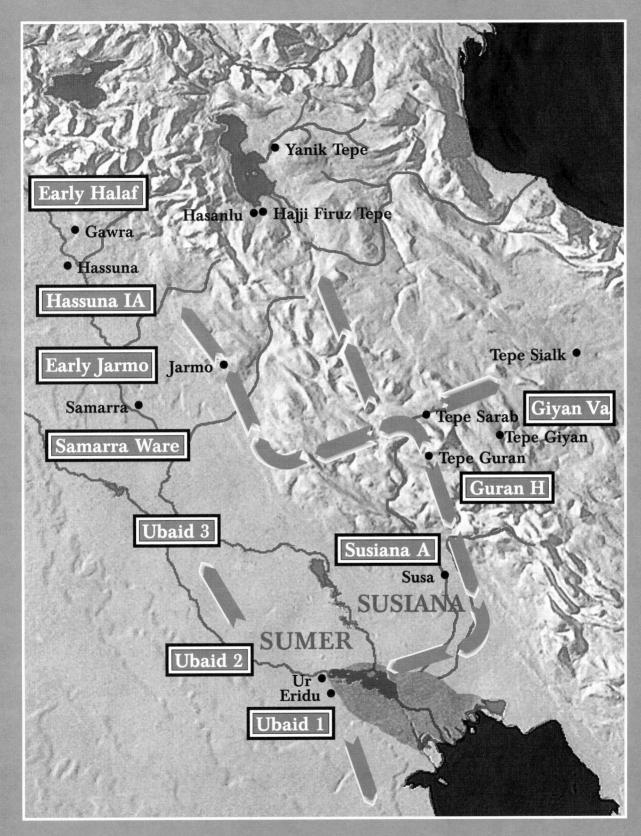

Yanik Tepe

Early Halaf

Gawra

Hasanlu Hajji Firuz Tepe

Hassuna

Hassuna IA

Tepe Sialk

Early Jarmo Jarmo

Giyan Va

Samarra

Tepe Sarab

Tepe Giyan

Samarra Ware

Tepe Guran

Guran H

Ubaid 3

Susiana A

Susa

SUSIANA

SUMER

Ubaid 2

Ur

Eridu

Ubaid 1

And all living things that stirred on earth perished; birds, cattle, wild animals, all the creatures swarming over the earth and all human beings – everything with the last breath of life in its nostrils, everything on dry land died.

Genesis 7:21-22

154. Left: Noah releases a dove from the ark. This wonderful Byzantine mosaic comes from St Mark's basilica in Venice.

Chapter Four

THE DELUGE

hrough an analysis of pottery distribution in the sixth and fifth millennia BC we have witnessed the arrival of the mountain people in the land of Sumer and we have identified their leaders with the antediluvian heroes of Genesis. By taking on board the arguments of Poebel and Kramer we have also made a possible connection between these earliest biblical patriarchs and the Sumerians. It seems that the latter may derive their collective eponym from the biblical name Shem, borne by the eldest son of Noah, with the result that Shem becomes the eponymous ancestor of Sumer (Shumer). Thus Noah's descendants – the Hebrews – may originally have been of Sumerian mountain stock.

With that important possibility in mind we find ourselves confronted by the next major event in the history of Genesis – the flood.

Noah and the Flood

We all know the story of the great flood and Noah's ark. It is one of those startling tales which is learnt young and retained as a vivid memory into old age. It is perhaps the classic Bible story – the event which brings an end to all past deeds to begin a new era with the washing clean of the sins of the earth. The flood brings an end to the primeval age and begins, in a sense, the historical age. As such it is a momentous turning point in the development of civilisation. But did it really happen? The large number of flood traditions (over one hundred and fifty) coming from all parts of the world would suggest that something like the biblical event did

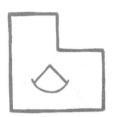

155. The Sumerian word for the deluge (Sum. *Uru*, Akk. *Abubu*) (top) and its Neo-Assyrian cuneiform counterpart (bottom) rotated through 90 degrees anticlockwise. The original Sumerian symbol suggests a throne or stepped platform with what may be a very simple depiction of a boat or ark.

143

156. A fragment of the Atrahasis Flood Epic from the Old Babylonian Period (after Lambert & Millard, 1969, pl. 1). Istanbul Museum.

157. Osiris (Egy. *Asar*), the Egyptian god of the dead, wearing the twin-plumed *atef*-crown. From the tomb of Queen Nefertari, Luxor.

occur. If these widely dispersed traditions – both geographically and culturally – are to be believed, then perhaps we should regard the flood as a 'universal phenomenon'. However, that does not in itself provide evidence of its physical scale – that is to say its depth and proportions.

It is quite possible that a catastrophic incident occurred in prehistoric times (perhaps a massive volcanic eruption or meteor strike or near miss of a comet or a combination of these), the fallout of which brought on severe climatic conditions which affected many parts of the world. In effect, each locality would have had its own 'localised flood' which was quite naturally seen by the inhabitants as the destruction of their entire world or cultural environment.

Our Judaeo-Christian-Islamic 'cultural witness' to the cataclysmic rain-storm has always been the biblical hero, Noah, but in recent years he has been joined by his Mesopotamian counterpart, thanks to the decipherment of ancient texts belonging to the land 'between the two rivers'. Scholars have unanimously agreed that the two flood-heroes – biblical and Mesopotamian – must be one and the same individual because, as we shall see, their stories are so similar. It is entirely another matter, however, as to whether there was ever a common oral or literary source for the two traditions or whether they are independent records of the same flood event.

In Mesopotamia scholars have recovered several versions of the flood epic involving no less than three different Noahs – Sumerian 'Ziusudra', Old Babylonian 'Atrahasis' and Akkadian 'Utnapishtim'. The Greeks have their own tradition in the flood story of Deucalion. The Hindus have a flood story involving a hero called Manu which probably extends back to the Bronze Age Indus Valley culture. Only the Egyptians amongst the major civilisations seem not to have had a flood story. But, again, is that actually the case?

The biblical deluge began on the seventeenth day of the second month. It is therefore interesting to note that Osiris was also cast into the waters in a sealed wooden chest or casket on the seventeenth day of the month. The Hebrew word for 'ark' (as in Noah's ark) is *tebah* which has the general meaning 'box' or 'container'. This also happens to be the word used for the basket in which the baby Moses was placed and set afloat upon the Nile waters. The English word 'ark' actually comes from the Latin *arca* which itself means 'chest'. Returning to the story of Osiris, we find that the Egyptians have a word *tjeb* which means 'sealed chest'.[1] This word, which by New Kingdom times would have been pronounced *teb* (perhaps with a final vowel), may well have the same etymological origins as the Semitic *tebah*. The words 'ark', *tebah* and *tjeb* all therefore have the meaning 'chest'. One might then legitimately translate the ancient Egyptian passage dealing with the conflict between Osiris and his brother Seth as 'Osiris was cast adrift upon the waters in an ark'.

What do we learn from Genesis about Noah himself? Well, he is clearly to be regarded as a second 'father of all mankind' (after Adam) because

158. Dionysus, god of wine and transcendent states, is sometimes depicted journeying in his ship, the mast of which is draped in vines. Black-on-red bowl in the Studio Koppermann collection.

he was the progenitor, through his sons, of the whole population which came after the flood. He can also be likened to a 'Master of Animals' because he brought the creatures of the earth, 'two by two', into the safety of the ark. A further interesting historical note is that Noah was the first to ferment wine from the grape and the first to get blind drunk on his invention.

> Noah, a tiller of the soil, was the first to plant the vine. He drank some of the wine and, while he was drunk, he lay naked in his tent. [Genesis 9:20-21]

In Greek mythology, the earliest surviving account of the flood (recorded in the ninth Olympian ode of PINDAR) names the hero as Deucalion. APOLLODORUS describes him as journeying in a 'floating chest'. The Thracian deity, Dionysus (Roman Bacchus), the god of wine and vegetation, is sometimes shown journeying over the sea in a great boat draped with grapes. In a Greek twist to the Osiris 'ark' tale, he is still in the womb of his mother when she is cast upon the sea in a sealed chest. The mother dies but Dionysus is saved and grows up to discover 'the fruit of the vine and the art of making wine from it'. The Syrian satirist, LUCIAN, records in Greek that the flood occurred in the time of 'Deucalion, called Sisythes'. This shows the influence of the Mesopotamian tradition on the Greek legend because the name Sisythes is clearly derived from Xisuthros – the name given to the flood hero by the Babylonian historian BEROSSUS which, in turn, comes from the Sumerian Ziusudra.

The parallels between the biblical story of Noah and the Classical traditions of the flood-hero and inventor of wine are certainly remarkable, especially given the quite distinct cultures and language-groups of the two regions. Again, we should note that the Egyptian Osiris is also a god of vegetation just like Dionysus. Could we then be looking at a single historical origin for this remarkable legend of the wine-making, flood hero who is transfigured into the god of nature's annual rebirth?

PINDAR: (518-*c.* 446 BC).

APOLLODORUS: (first or second century AD).

LUCIAN: (*c.* AD 125-180). Born in Samosata in Commagene in Syria but lived most of his life in Athens.

BEROSSUS: (third century BC). A Babylonian priest who wrote three books on Babylonian history utilising the archives from the temple of Bel in Babylon. His books, written in Greek, were popular in Greece and Rome. Like Manetho only excerpts survive in the writings of Josephus, Eusebius and Syncellus. His floruit was around 260 BC.

159. The young Dionysus portrayed in this Coptic relief from Egypt is surrounded by vines heavy with bunches of grapes. Louvre Museum.

145

One further point before we start our flood investigations. According to Genesis 8:4, the ark eventually landed 'on the mountains of Ararat' – not Mount Ararat, as many Christians interpret the passage. You will soon learn that the mountain of the ark is not Mount Aregats or Agri Dagh (as Ararat is locally known), located to the north-east of Lake Van, but somewhere quite different and much nearer to the Mesopotamian plain. As a result, I am afraid that all the recent impassioned expeditions in search of the ark by Christian explorers have been heading off to the wrong location.

The Place of Descent

There are a number of clues which point us back into the Zagros mountains in our search for the biblical hero of the flood.

We noted earlier that Noah was credited in the book of Genesis with the first manufacture of wine. Richard BARNETT believes that this biblical tradition has clear links with the invention of viniculture in the region of Urartu – the biblical Ararat – which we have identified with the Sumerian kingdom of Aratta.

> The fame of Urartian wine (it seems) had even reached the distant Hebrews in ancient Palestine, where its invention in Armenia was projected back to dimmest antiquity, as witnessed by their story of Noah disgraced by drunkenness on Mount Ararat (sic!). Indeed the wine grape, *vitis vinifera*, from which the cultured vine is derived, is believed to have originated nearby in the Caucasus region near the Caspian.[2]

Archaeology has made a recent contribution to the cause of establishing Armenia as the place where wine was invented. An earthenware pot discovered in the Miyandoab plain (where we place both Aratta and Eden) was found to contain a dark residue. Analysis of the remains determined that this was a primitive wine sediment. The context of the find and the pottery style places the manufacture of the container in the sixth millennium BC, which makes its contents the oldest vintage in the world – Chateau Aratta *circa* 5,500 BC.

The passage mentioning Noah's invention of wine comes immediately after the departure from the ark following the recession of the floodwaters. The resting place of the ark – if we are to believe it exists – cannot, therefore, be very far away from the place where wine was first manufactured. So we should be looking for the mountain of the descent not north of Lakes Van and Urmia, where the Christian site of the ark's landing is located (i.e. Mount Aregats), but in the Zagros mountains where the kingdom of Aratta and the biblical 'mountains of Ararat' (i.e. Urartu) are both located.

There are several other clues to the true location of the ark mountain or Place of Descent which originate from outside the Genesis narrative.

BARNETT: (1909-1988).

Berossus tells us that 'the land in which they (the occupants of the ark) found themselves was Armenia' and that:

> A portion of the ship, which came to rest in Armenia, still remains in the mountains of the Korduaians of Armenia, and some of the people, scraping off pieces of bitumen from the ship, bring them back and use them as talismans.[3]

The Korduaians are, of course, the Kurds whose homeland – Kurdistan – is located in the Zagros mountains to the *south* of Lake Van and the south-west of Lake Urmia.

The fact that the location of the Place of Descent was still known at the beginning of the first millennium AD is confirmed by the Jewish historian, JOSEPHUS, who, in his work *The Antiquities of the Jews*, states that the sacred mountain was well known from the writings of numerous scholars.[4] In the Aramaic translation of ONKELOS we find that Ararat is identified with 'the mountains of Kurdistan' (Aram. *ture kardu*). XENEPHON, in his *Anabasis*, remarks on the ferocity of the Karduchi tribesmen as the Greek army passed through the mountains of Kurdistan during the famous 'March of the Ten Thousand'.[5] There can be little doubt, then, that the ancient Aramaic toponym *bet kardu* ('House of Kardu') represents the area we know today as Kurdistan.

So if Mount Aregats is not the site of Noah's ark then where is? The answer is delivered to us through a persistent tradition which was included in the extra-biblical writings of the ancient Jewish rabbis and recorded in Louis GINZBERG's *Legends of the Jews*. The story concerns the brutal Assyrian king, SENNACHERIB, destroyer of Babylon.

JOSEPHUS: (first century AD).

ONKELOS: (fourth century AD).

XENEPHON: (*c.* 435-354 BC). A Greek historian and military commander who led a failed expedition of 10,000 Greek mercenaries back from Mesopotamia in 399 BC. The epic 'March of the Ten Thousand' is narrated in his work entitled *Anabasis*.

GINZBERG: (1873-1953).

SENNACHERIB: King of Assyria, reigned 705-681 BC. The name *Sin-ahhe-eriba* means 'Sin has compensated (for the death of) the brothers'.

160. Relief from the palace of Sennacherib at Nineveh. The king receives the submission of the citizens of Lacish following the successful siege of the city by the Assyrian army in 701 BC. King Sennacherib sits on his throne in the royal encampment as his military commanders report on their victory. British Museum.

ESARHADDON: King of Assyria, reigned 680-669 BC. The name Ashur-aha-iddin means 'Ashur has given a brother'.

161. A giant stela depicting the vanquished Baalu, king of Tyre, and Taharka of Egypt pleading for their lives before the feet of King Esarhaddon of Assyria. Discovered at Zinjirli in north-west Syria. Staatliche Museen, Berlin.

On his return to Assyria, Sennacherib found a plank, which he worshipped as an idol, because it was part of the ark which had saved Noah from the deluge. He vowed that he would sacrifice his sons to this idol if he prospered in his next ventures. But his sons heard his vows, and they killed their father, and fled to **Kardu, where they released the Jewish captives confined there in great numbers**.[6]

Another Jewish tradition confirms that the land of **Kardu**nya was 'where the ark rested'[7] – in other words Kurdistan.

History has provided a neat way of confirming at least part of this tradition. In the annals of Sennacherib's successor, ESARHADDON, we read that Sennacherib was indeed assassinated and that Esarhaddon had pursued his murderous brothers and their supporters into what the new king calls 'parts unknown'.

> A firm determination fell upon my brothers. They forsook the gods and turned to their deeds of violence, plotting evil. ... To gain the kingship they slew Sennacherib, their father.[8]

Then, soon after a brief and victorious campaign against his brothers' forces based at Nineveh, Esarhaddon entered the Assyrian capital.

> As for those villains who instigated revolt and rebellion, when they heard of the approach of my army, they abandoned their regular troops and **fled to parts unknown**. ... In the month of Adaru (Feb-Mar) – a favourable month – on the eighth day, a feast of Nabu, I entered into Nineveh, my royal city, joyfully, and took my seat upon the throne of my father in safety.[9]

Although there is no mention in the contemporary annals of the incident concerning the ark relic which led up to the murder of the king, the Assyrian texts do appear to confirm much of the traditional account. The campaigns of Sennacherib included expeditions against the 'princes of the central Zagros' and the 'city-chiefs of **Kurdistan**'.[10] The narratives also tell us that Sennacherib was 'beaten [to death] with the statues of protective deities' by his sons as the king was praying in the temple.[11] So, if Jewish tradition got all this right, then perhaps that same Jewish tradition, supplemented by Berossus, was also correct in that the retrieval of part of the ark did in some way lead to Sennacherib's death in 681 BC and the subsequent civil war. Whatever the truth behind this strange tale, we can at least be certain that the Babylonians of the third century BC (contemporary with Berossus) assumed that the remains of the ark were located in the mountains of the Kurds.

The Bible also has something to say on the subject. Not only does it confirm the royal patricide and the fact that the princes fled to Urartu (biblical Ararat) but the passage in 2 Kings 19 also supplies us with the names of Sennacherib's murderers. Following the destruction of the Assyrian army by the 'angel of Yahweh' as the troops prepared to attack Jerusalem in 701 BC:

> Sennacherib struck camp and departed. He returned home and stayed in Nineveh. One day, when he was worshipping in the temple of his god Nisroch, his sons Adrammelech and Sharezer struck him down with the sword and escaped into the territory of Ararat. His son, Esarhaddon, succeeded him.
> [2 Kings 19:36-37]

Everything we have studied so far points us to the central Zagros in our search for Noah's mountain. The Mesopotamian flood stories tell the same story but also furnish us with the ancient name of the place – Mount Nimush (formerly read Nisir). Some scholars equate Nimush with the 3,000-metre-high peak known today as Pir Omar Gudrun to the south-east of the Lesser Zab river.[12] But the Jewish and *early* Christian writers tell us otherwise. For instance, Josephus locates the Place of Descent in the 'country called Carrae'. It seems likely that Josephus' 'Carrae' is a miswriting of Cardae (for Akkadian Kardu) – the area know in classical times as Carduchi. This suggests that the sacred mountain lies in the mountains to the *north-west* of the Lesser Zab and, indeed, beyond the Greater Zab. HIPPOLYTUS designates 'Mount Kardu' as the place of the ark in 'the mountains called Ararat, which are situated in the direction of the country of the Adiabeni'. Again we find the name Kardu associated with the Place of Descent. The landing site is clearly to be located in Kurdistan, within the triangle of territory encompassed by Lake Van in the north, the Tigris in the south-west and the Greater Zab in the east.

The first recorded Christian pilgrim to go in search of the Place of Descent was Saint JACOB OF NISIBIS who made a pilgrimage to the 'district of Gartouk' (a varient spelling of Carduchi?) which Davis Young identifies with the district of Karcaik located between the Tigris and Lake Van. With all the evidence pointing away from a location for the lost ark far to the north beyond Lake Van, Young is forced to the conclusion that Mount Ararat/Aregats '... is not the same Ararat referred to in early Christian tradition ... Modern hunters of the ark appear to be looking in different places than the early Christians did'.[13]

In fact, the first we hear of Mount Ararat being associated with Noah's ark only comes with the arrival in the region of VINCENT DE BEAUVAIS

HIPPOLYTUS: (AD *c.* 155-*c.* 236).

JACOB OF NISIBIS: Bishop of Medzpin towards the end of the fourth century AD.

VINCENT DE BEAUVAIS: (*c.* 1184-1264).

who suggested that the mountain of the ark was located near the Araxes river. This was then taken up by other travellers such as Friar WILLIAM OF RUBRUCK, ODORIC and no less a figure than MARCO POLO. They all took it for granted that the high peak of Aregats was the mountain (singular) of Ararat upon which the ark came to rest. The 'Mount Ararat' location was thus a *very late* Christian tradition and seems to have been based rather more on the impressive nature of Aregats than any corpus of earlier historical writings. All those early writings pointed to a quite different region – a region where, as you are about to discover, there is a much better candidate for Noah's mountain.

The Shaitan Worshippers

We now come to an extraordinary piece of relatively recent cultural history which I (and others) believe pinpoints the precise mountain in Kurdistan upon which the ark came to rest. The story of the Yezidis was first brought to my attention when I read the book *From the Ashes of Angels* by British author, Andrew Collins, who had himself discovered the existence of these remarkable people through the writings of Kurdish historian, Professor Mehrdad Izady.[14]

Izady tells of a remote Kurdish tribe, known as the Yezidis, living in the highlands of eastern Turkey to the south of Lake Van and to the west of Lake Urmia. They are a strange sect. They worship the god, Shaitan, who is better known to us as 'Satan'. Their strongly held belief is that Shaitan is the true force of divine power in the world and that they themselves are the descendants of Seth, the third son of Adam.

The Yezidis probably get their name from the UMAYYAD CALIPH Yazid who was responsible for the massacre of the SHIITE IMAM Hussein (grandson of the Prophet Mohamed) and his followers at the battle of Kerbala in 680. Whatever the true historical connection between this strange Kurdish tribe and the despised caliph, the Yezidis keep very much to themselves in their mountain stronghold for fear of persecution from the Shiite Islamic state of Iran to their east, the Sunni Islamic state of Iraq to their south and the anti-Kurdish military forces of the Turkish government to their west. As a result, it is rather difficult these days to learn much about them. However, things were somewhat different during the early part of this century.

In 1922 two travelling scholars, the Reverend William A. Wigram and his son Edgar, wrote a splendid book entitled *The Cradle of Mankind*. It is an eye-witness account of Kurdistan's cultural history as it existed in the 1920s. The book reveals a few details of Yezidi cultic rituals, including the blood sacrifice of animals on the 14th day of September each year upon the heights of a mountain called Judi Dagh (also written Chudi Dagh). The 14th of September marks the traditional date in Kurdistan for Noah's coming out of the ark and the sacrifice to God in gratitude for saving his kin and the animals. This is in direct contradiction to the biblical

WILLIAM OF RUBRUCK: (thirteenth century).

ODORIC: (*c.* 1286-1331).

MARCO POLO: (1234-1324).

UMAYYAD CALIPH: The successor of Mohamed in the Sunni division of Islam. The Ummayads belonged to the dynasty of Muawiya of Mecca who seized the caliphate from Ali, son-in-law of Mohamed, in 656. This was the event which led to the schism between the Sunni and Shiite sects.

SHIITE IMAM: The imams were the successors of Ali who, as his lineal descendants, became the great religious leaders of the Shias ('partisans'), now predominantly based in Iran. There were twelve imams in all, the last of whom ('the mahdi') disappeared leaving no son and successor.

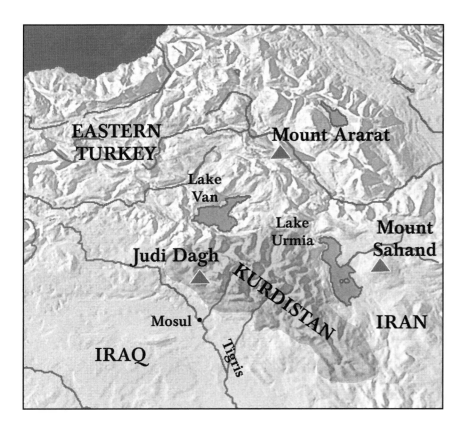

162. The location of Judi Dagh in relation to Mount Ararat and the Mesopotamian plain.

text which gives the date as the 27th of May. The Yezidis are in no doubt that Mount Judi ('the heights'), at nearly 2,000 metres above sea level, is the Place of Descent. Indeed, as Wigram himself notes, there is almost no support within the region for the candidature of Mount Ararat.

> It must be understood that no people here, save the Armenians (Christians), look on the great cone which we call Ararat, but which is locally known as Agri Dagh, as the spot where the ark rested.[15]

The fact that the Yezidis commemorate Noah's sacrifice with their own ritual near the summit of Judi Dagh, north-west of the Greater Zab and south of Lake Van, is not the only piece of evidence which we have to connect this mountain to the flood story. Josephus himself claims that 'Mount Judi near Lake Van' is the resting-place of the ark.[16] The Koran also tells us that the ark came to rest on Mount Judi.

> Then the word went forth: 'O earth, swallow up thy water! O sky, withhold (thy rain)!' The water abated and the matter was ended. The ark rested on Mount Judi, and the word went forth: 'Away with those who do wrong!' [Sura XI:44]

The tenth-century Muslim writer, IBN HAUKAL, states that 'Judi is a mountain near Nisibis. It is said that the ark of Noah (peace be upon him) rested on the summit of this mountain'. This useful statement makes

IBN HAUKAL: Arab geographer who visited Azerbaijan in AD 955.

163. The location of Judi Dagh in the mountains north of Mosul, between the Tigris and Greater Zab rivers.

164. One of the rock-carved reliefs of Sennacherib discovered on Judi Dagh in 1904 by L. W. King.

EUTYCHIUS OF ALEXANDRIA: (ninth century AD).

the important connection between Mount Judi and the pilgrim saint, Jacob. As you will remember, the venerated Bishop of Medzpin was given the title 'Jacob of Nisibis'. The mountain which he knew as the Place of Descent was Judi Dagh.

Furthermore, the early Nestorian Christians built a number of monasteries on the slopes of Judi and one on its very summit. The latter was destroyed by fire when struck by lightning in 766. Bishop EUTYCHIUS OF ALEXANDRIA informs us that 'the ark rested on the mountains of Ararat, that is Gebel Judi, near Mosul'. Mosul is one hundred and twenty kilometres due south of Judi Dagh.

In order to clinch the argument for the true location of the Place of Descent it would be useful to find some evidence which takes us back to a time before the Christian era. We must therefore return to the reign of the Assyrian king Sennacherib to reveal one final and vital detail.

Remember how tradition claims that Sennacherib brought back a 'wooden plank' from the site of the ark's resting place in the land of the Kurds but that we were unable to pinpoint the exact place from the king's contemporary war annals? Well, amazingly enough, Sennacherib himself left us spectacular proof of his visit to Judi Dagh by carving several reliefs in his own image at the foot of the mountain.[17] Moreover, reports from more recent times confirm that lumps of bitumen were still being collected by a number of travellers to the region within the last fifty years.[18] The remains of the ark of Noah may still survive to this day and could perhaps be recovered through the mounting of a well-equiped archaeological expedition.

Conclusion Eleven

Noah's ark did not come to rest in the highlands of Armenia far to the north of the alluvial plain, as in the late Christian tradition. Mount Ararat is not, therefore, to be identified as the Place of Descent. The peak of Judi Dagh, bordering upon the Mesopotamian lowlands in the region later known as Assyria is, in fact, the *original* traditional site of the ark's landing as stated by numerous early authorities.

A Mesopotamian Noah

There are three names or epithets borne by the Mesopotamian Noah. In the earliest myths he is closely connected with the Sumerian city of Shuruppak (modern Fara) and, indeed, in the Sumerian King List his traditional father, Ubartutu ('friend of (the sun-god) Tutu'), is identified as the last ruler of that ancient Sumerian city before the flood. As with the Genesis narrative, the Mesopotamian Noah's story involves the riding out of a great storm and flood in a boat – but then the two traditions diverge as the extra-biblical hero is eventually elevated by the gods to a status of immortality.

The Sumerians themselves called their hero of the flood, Ziusudra, an epithet or nickname which has been translated as 'life of long days' (presumably a reference to the hero's immortality). This name is attested in a cuneiform text from Nippur dated to around 1700 BC. In the earliest Akkadian tradition he carries the nickname, Atrahasis, meaning 'exceedingly wise'. However, as Professor Alan Millard of Liverpool University notes, this name can also be translated as 'exceedingly devout' which is one of Noah's characteristics.[19]

> Noah was a good man, an upright man among his contemporaries, and he walked with God. [Genesis 6:9]

Then, later, in the era when the great epic poems relating to Gilgamesh were copied in Akkadian, the Mesopotamian flood hero is referred to as Utnapishtim, meaning 'he found (everlasting) life'.[20]

Rather than constantly restating all the names of the Sumerian Noah I will refer to him as Utnapishtim (except, that is, when quoting directly from the different versions of the flood epic texts where the name employed by the ancient scribe will be retained).

Kramer was quite right to conclude in the 1940s that this Sumerian myth concerning the hero of the flood 'offers the closest and most striking parallel to biblical material as yet uncovered in Sumerian literature'.[21] It still remains the most famous literary link between the Bible and extra-biblical sources.

165. Statuette from Nippur, dating to the Early Dynastic II Period showing a devoted Sumerian couple much like Noah and his wife. Iraq Museum.

The Gilgamesh Epic

In 1872 Akkadian linguist George Smith began to translate part of a tablet from the seventh-century-BC archive of King Ashurbanipal of Assyria. The archive had been sent to the British Museum where scholars had been busy translating the tablets since their discovery at Nineveh by Sir Austen Henry LAYARD in 1853. Smith was the first scholar to come across the now famous Gilgamesh Epic – the tale of the adventures of a legendary hero-king of Uruk.

As he began to translate the cuneiform signs Smith was amazed to find reference to a great flood which had covered the world and destroyed

166. LAYARD: (1817-94).

mankind. In the narrative, Gilgamesh (who lived centuries after the flood) goes in search of Utnapishtim – a once mortal human being who, because of his piety, had been given eternal life by the gods. It was immediately apparent that Utnapishtim was the Akkadian name for the hero of the deluge – the Mesopotamian Noah. This was the first extra-biblical narrative to be found which made reference to the great flood of Genesis. Here was mention of an ark, of a terrible rainstorm, of a dove and a raven being sent out from the ark to find land.

Smith announced his discovery to an enthralled audience at the Society for Biblical Archaeology in London in that same year. His lecture was a sensation. The *Daily Telegraph* immediately sponsored Smith to go out to Mesopotamia with the specific brief of locating the remaining fragment of the tablet so that the narrative of the Gilgamesh Epic could be completely recovered. Amazingly Smith actually found that fragment in the dust and debris of Nineveh. The archaeological illumination of the book of Genesis had begun.[22]

The key document for the Sumerian flood tradition is Tablet XI of the Gilgamesh Epic. There Gilgamesh, king of Uruk, finds Utnapishtim living out his eternal existence in a place 'at the mouth (i.e. source) of the rivers'. The Gilgamesh asks the flood hero how he had attained his immortality. Utnapishtim explains that the assembly of gods had determined to

167. The eleventh tablet of the Gilgamesh Epic which carries the story of the Mesopotamian flood and its hero Utnapishtim. British Museum.

'Reed house, reed house! Wall, wall! Hear, O reed house! Understand, O wall!'

168. A typical reed-wall construction (this one on the island of Bahrain in the Persian Gulf).

destroy the earth by means of a great flood. However, the water-god Ea (Sumerian Enki), the friend of Man, had spoken to him through the wall of a 'reed house' (perhaps a shrine or palace) whilst Utnapishtim was living in the city of Shuruppak.

> Ea, the clever prince, was under oath with them (the gods) so he repeated their talk (of the flood) to the reed house: 'Reed house, reed house! Wall, wall! Hear, O reed house! Understand, O wall! O man of Shuruppak, son of Ubartutu, tear down the house and build a boat!

Utnapishtim was instructed by Ea to build a ship so that he might ride out the storm which the angry gods were about to cast down upon the earth. He was to keep the secret of the impending doom to himself and not tell the rest of humanity. In a somewhat earlier source which turned up after Smith's original discovery – the Atrahasis Epic – we learn that the flood hero asks his god how he should build the ship. The god then gives a detailed description of the ark so that Atrahasis can understand the design and begin his great engineering task.

When the ship was built, the tempest struck with great force, the rains continuing to fall for six days.

> [For] six days and six nights the wind blew. The downpour, the tempest and the flood overwhelmed the land …

On the seventh day the tempest began to subside and Utnapishtim took a look outside.

> I opened a window and light fell upon my face. I looked down upon the sea – all was silence and all mankind had turned to clay.

After the storm had finally subsided, Utnapishtim released first a dove, then a swallow and finally a raven to see if dry land could be reached. Eventually, the ark came to rest on Mount Nimush where he sacrificed to the gods. The gods blessed their pious servant, Utnapishtim, and his wife with the gift of eternal life, thus elevating them to godly status. They were then given a dwelling place 'at the mouth of the (two) rivers'.

> Hitherto Utnapishtim has been but a man, but now Utnapishtim and his wife shall be as the gods. In the distance, at the mouth of the rivers, Utnapishtim shall dwell.[23]

The superb literary quality of the extra-biblical flood stories is well illustrated by the earliest Sumerian version in which the hero is called Ziusudra. I suppose that if literary prose were the only factor in deciding which civilisation provided the original source for the flood story, then the Mesopotamian version would be a clear winner over the rather dry tale to be found in Genesis. The Ziusudra narrative has a wonderful originality about it.

> All the windstorms, exceedingly powerful, attacked as one. At the same time the flood swept over the cult-centers.
>
> After this, for seven days (and) seven nights the flood swept over the land (and) the huge boat was tossed about by the windstorms on the mighty waters.
>
> (Finally) Utu (the sun-god) came forth – the one who sheds light on heaven (and) earth. Ziusudra opened a window of the huge boat (and) the hero Utu brought his rays into the giant boat. Ziusudra, the king, prostrated himself before Utu.

[Lacuna in the text of around 39 lines]

Ziusudra the king prostrated himself before (the gods) Anu (and) Enlil. Anu (and) Enlil cherished Ziusudra. 'Life' like a god they gave him; 'breath eternal' like a god they brought down for him.

Then, Ziusudra the king – the preserver of the name of vegetation (and) of the seed of mankind – they caused to dwell in the land of crossing – the Land of Dilmun – the place where the sun rises.[24]

We will be returning to the Land of Dilmun – the land of the rising sun – shortly but, in the meantime, we shall attempt to date the deluge by means of a non-biblical written source – the Sumerian King List.

169. Doré's vision of the landing of Noah's ark in the mountains of Ararat.

God sent a wind across the earth and the waters began to subside. The springs of the deep and the sluices of heaven were stopped up and the heavy rain from heaven was held back. Little by little the waters ebbed from the earth. After one hundred and fifty days the waters receded and in the seventh month, on the seventeenth day of the month, the ark came to rest on the mountains of Ararat.

Genesis 8:1-4

170. Opposite page: The Sumerian King List (Weld Blundell Prism) with the antediluvian section at the top of Column I (right face, left side). Ashmolean Museum, Oxford.

171. Left: An Early Dynastic cylinder seal impression depicting the 'long-haired hero' and the 'bull-man' grappling with a lion, a deer and a bull. Private collection of the Biblisches Institut, Fribourg University.

Chapter Five

DATING THE FLOOD

As we have noted, the most important source for the chronology of early Mesopotamia is the famous Sumerian King List (SKL) which was meticulously compiled by Thorkild Jacobsen in 1939 from his study of the remains of around fifteen different fragmentary copies. The best preserved copy is now housed in Oxford's Ashmolean Museum (see opposite). It was written in the reign of Damikilishu (OC – 1816-1794 BC), last ruler of the Dynasty of Isin.

The Akkadian royal scribe who copied his version of the SKL from a then surviving tablet of an earlier date[1] begins with the Dynasty of Eridu.

> When the kingship was lowered from heaven the kingship was in Eridu. In Eridu Alulim became king and reigned for 28,800 years. Alalgar reigned 36,000 years. Two kings reigned its total of 64,800 years. [Column 1, lines 1-7][2]

172. The priest-king of Uruk pours a libation over a smaller figure who may be his son or perhaps a priest of the temple which takes up the left half of this seal impression from the Protoliterate Period (after P. Amiet, 1961, pl. 47:664).

Another document – the Babylonian Epic – also singles out this sacred centre of the god Enki ('Lord of the Earth') as the very first city created by mankind.

> A reed had not come forth. A tree had not been created. A house had not been made. A city had not been built. All the lands were sea. Then Eridu was made.

Once again it looks as if tradition and legend have been confirmed by subsequent archaeological endeavour. As French Assyriologist, Georges Roux, noted back in 1964:

173. The main cities and archaeological sites of lower Mesopotamia.

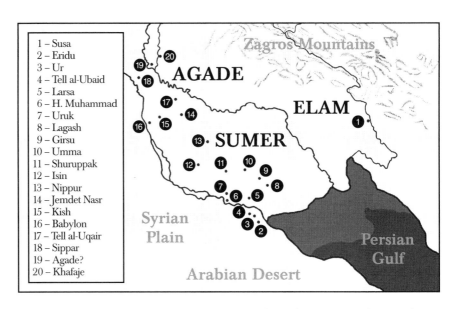

```
1 – Susa
2 – Eridu
3 – Ur
4 – Tell al-Ubaid
5 – Larsa
6 – H. Muhammad
7 – Uruk
8 – Lagash
9 – Girsu
10 – Umma
11 – Shuruppak
12 – Isin
13 – Nippur
14 – Jemdet Nasr
15 – Kish
16 – Babylon
17 – Tell al-Uqair
18 – Sippar
19 – Agade?
20 – Khafaje
```

> According to the Sumerian King List, kingship was first 'lowered from heaven' in the city of Eridu, a remarkable statement if we remember that Eridu has yielded traces of the most ancient Sumerian settlement in southern Iraq.[3]

That statement still generally applies today. At the beginning of the Ubaid Period (Ubaid 1 = Eridu) the first settlements were coming into being at Eridu, Uruk and Ur. And at Eridu itself the archaeologists discovered a primitive shrine buried deep under the later ziggurat. Again, we will be returning to this important discovery in a later chapter, but for now, it is only necessary to know that this was the first temple (to our knowledge) to be erected in Sumer.

After the dynasty of Eridu, the SKL provides us with the names of four other ruling cities and their kings before the simple but crucial line: 'The flood swept thereover'. Not only does this short sentence confirm the flood tradition from outside the Bible but it also supplies us with a temporal location for the deluge within the chronological sequence of the early Mesopotamian rulers – but, of course, this is only useful so long as we can retro-calculate its absolute date from the remainder of the King List. To do this we need to start from a fixed date in later Mesopotamian history and work backwards through the dynasties until we reach as near as we can to the time of the flood in the Sumerian King List tradition.

Ur I to Babylon I: The Great Dynasties

In *A Test of Time* Volume One it was established, through a crucial astronomical anchor point, that King Ammisaduga of the Babylon I Dynasty began his reign in 1419 BC. In the conventional chronology there are three schools of thought on the subject of this king's accession date. Using the same astronomical data, but achieving a much less convincing match than the New Chronology date, scholars of the three schools come up with a 'High' date of 1702 BC, a 'Middle' date of 1646 BC and a 'Low' date of 1582 BC.[4]

The arguments and evidence as to why the New Chronology datum point is much more likely to be correct are rather complex and I do not intend to go over them again here. Instead, as I did with the New Chronology for the early Egyptian dynasties, I have included a brief resumé in *Appendix C* (towards the end of the book) where I also incorporate the detailed synchronisms and chronological calculations for early Mesopotamian history. So that we do not get too bogged down in the chronological *minutiae* here, I will simply list the revised dates for the Mesopotamian dynasties which result from our 1419 BC starting point for the first regnal year of Ammisaduga.

As you will see, the Mesopotamian dynastic lines overlap considerably – a fact which is recognised by all authorities, conventional and revisionist. More often than not, there were several dynastic houses ruling at the same time in the early Mesopotamian historical period. The revised New-Chronology dates for these dynasties and their 'Low', 'Middle' and 'High' counterparts are as follows:

174. The New Chronology dates for the Mesopotamian dynasties compared to the three conventional dating systems.

Dynasty	NC	OC – 'Low'	OC – 'Middle'	OC – 'High'
Babylon I	1667-1361	1830-1531	1894-1595	1949-1650
Larsa	1798-1536	1961-1699	2025-1763	2080-1818
Isin	1805-1569	1953-1730	2017-1794	2072-1849
Ur III	1900-1793	2048-1940	2112-2004	2167-2059
Uruk V	1891-1885	2055-2049	2119-2113	2174-2168
Uruk IV	1922-1885	2085-2055	2149-2119	2204-2174
Gutium	1988-1889	2144-2053	2208-2117	2263-2172
Agade	2100-1920	2276-2095	2340-2159	2395-2214
Kish IV	2163-2033			
Ur II	2171-2043			
Uruk III	2112-2088			
Lagash	????-2113			
Uruk II	2221-2114			
Akshak	2238-2140			
Kish III	2173-2165			
Ur I	2348-2173			
Kish II	????-2175			
Uruk I	????-2223			
Kish I(a)	????-????			
Kish I(b)	????-????			
The Flood	????			

175. A priest-king of Uruk presents flowers to the sacred flock of the Eanna temple complex at Uruk. This seal, dating from the Protoliterate Period, carries the gatepost symbol of Inanna, thus identifying the deity of the temple. British Museum

You will note that towards the bottom of the list the start-dates for some of the earlier dynasties are not known and, eventually, as we approach the flood event, we are left with nothing but question marks. This is because the reign-lengths of the SKL in this early section are extremely high – just as with the fantastical ages of the biblical characters in the early part of Genesis. We will attempt to address this difficult problem later in the chapter but, for now, we find ourselves only capable of going back in time with any accuracy to the start of the Ur I Dynasty at 2348 BC in the New Chronology.

Jacobsen, the translator of the Sumerian King List, calculated a date of *c.* 2850 BC for the start of Ur I, so, as one might expect, the New Chronology date is considerably lower – in fact half a millennium lower! This is partly because, in Jacobsen's day, the Babylon I Period was placed much earlier than it is today. He began Babylon I in 2171 BC (NC – 1667 BC) whereas in the modern 'High' chronology this event is dated to 1949 BC. However, most scholars reject this 'High' date and plump for either the 'Middle' chronology date of 1894 BC or even the 'Low' chronology date of 1830 BC. This just goes to show that there is little in the way of a consensus about early Mesopotamian dating within academia. So, at best, if one were to adopt the 'Low' conventional start-date for Babylon I of 1830 BC and back-calculate to the beginning of Ur I, the date arrived at for the latter would be *c.* 2524 BC – still some 176 years higher than the New Chronology date of *c.* 2348 BC. However, this sort of discrepancy is hardly an issue when we find ourselves in the mystifying era preceding Ur I.

Kish I and Uruk I: The Age of Heroes

Before Ur I we are left with just two dynasties to bridge the gap back to the flood. In fact, it has been demonstrated that these two lines of rulers – Kish I and Uruk I – were, at least in part, contemporary with each other. Moreover, the Dynasty of Kish was itself perhaps composed of two contemporary lines of kings – one beginning with an obscure ruler named Ga[…]ur (Kish Ia) and the other with the famous hero of legend, Etana (Kish Ib). So, in effect, we are dealing with a period spanned by just one half of the First Dynasty of Kish (Kish 1b) which begins immediately following the flood and ends not long before the start of the First Dynasty of Ur (Ur I). The other major line – Uruk I – commences sometime after the start of Kish I and ends well into the period of Ur I. Unfortunately, as I said, the problem we are faced with here is that the earlier rulers in both the Uruk and Kish dynasties are given enormous reign-lengths in the SKL which, at this stage, makes it impossible for us to work back through the reigns to reach a date for the flood with any degree of historical confidence. This is all very frustrating and bewildering.

Nevertheless, we need to look closely at this period, not only because it holds the key to the date for the deluge but also because it contains the reigns of all the great hero-figures we have been studying. In addition it introduces us to some new characters who are going to help us bridge the gap and establish which *archaeological period* we have now reached. It is in Uruk I that we find the great heroes Enmerkar, Lugalbanda, Dumuzi and Gilgamesh, whilst Kish I is the dynasty of Etana, Enmebaragesi and Agga (also written Akka).

HARROW: A type of hoe for breaking up the soil. Similar to the sign *setep* in Egyptian hieroglyphs.

Just to remind you of the political situation leading up to the flood and immediately preceding the First Dynasty of Kish, the SKL gives the following sequence of five antediluvian cities prevailing in turn (ruled by a total of eight antediluvian kings):

(1) Eridu – ruled by Alulim and Alalgar;
(2) Badtibira – ruled by Enmenluanna, Enmengalanna and the god Dumuzi;
(3) Larak – ruled by Ensipazianna;
(4) Sippar – ruled by Enmenduranna;
(5) Suruppak – ruled by King Ubartutu.

Ubartutu's reign immediately precedes the deluge which, in turn, is followed by the hegemony of the city of Kish under King Ga[…]ur ('HARROW').

The King List then proceeds to list the dynastic rulers of Kish. In Line 35 of Column II, the twenty-second ruler of the dynasty is given as Enmebaragesi who turns out to be the first archaeologically attested human being in history. We are extremely fortunate to possess a fragment of an alabaster bowl (now in the Baghdad Museum) which bears an early form of his name written in an archaic script.[5]

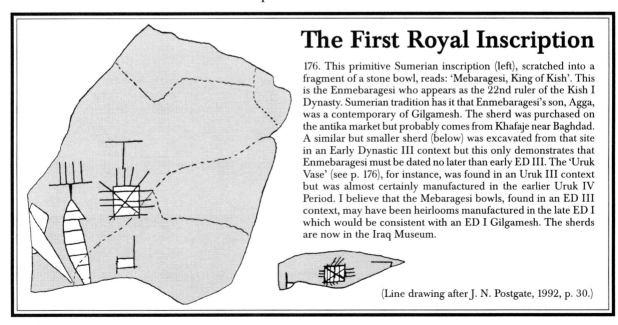

The First Royal Inscription

176. This primitive Sumerian inscription (left), scratched into a fragment of a stone bowl, reads: 'Mebaragesi, King of Kish'. This is the Enmebaragesi who appears as the 22nd ruler of the Kish I Dynasty. Sumerian tradition has it that Enmebaragesi's son, Agga, was a contemporary of Gilgamesh. The sherd was purchased on the antika market but probably comes from Khafaje near Baghdad. A similar but smaller sherd (below) was excavated from that site in an Early Dynastic III context but this only demonstrates that Enmebaragesi must be dated no later than early ED III. The 'Uruk Vase' (see p. 176), for instance, was found in an Uruk III context but was almost certainly manufactured in the earlier Uruk IV Period. I believe that the Mebaragesi bowls, found in an ED III context, may have been heirlooms manufactured in the late ED I which would be consistent with an ED I Gilgamesh. The sherds are now in the Iraq Museum.

(Line drawing after J. N. Postgate, 1992, p. 30.)

The Sumerian King List (first part)

The Antediluvian Dynasties

When the kingship was lowered from heaven, the kingship was in **Eridu**(g). (In) Eridu(g) Alulim(ak) (became) king and reigned 28,800 years; Alalgar reigned 36,000 years. Two kings reigned its 64,800 years. I drop (the topic) Eridu(g); its kingship to Badtibira(k) was carried.

(In) **Badtibira**(k) Enmenluanna(k) reigned 43,200 years; Enmengalanna(k) reigned 28,800 years; divine Dumuzi(d), a shepherd, reigned 36,000 years. Three kings reigned its 108,000 years. I drop (the topic) Badtibira(k); its kingship to Larak was carried.

(In) **Larak** Ensipa(d)zi(d)anna(k) reigned its 28,800 years. One king reigned its 28,800 years. I drop (the topic) Larak; its kingship to Sippar was carried.

(In) **Sippar** Enmenduranna(k) became king and reigned 21,000 years. One king reigned its 21,000 years. I drop (the topic) Sippar; its kingship to Shuruppak was carried.

(In) **Shuruppak** Ubartutu(k) became king and reigned 18,600 years. One king reigned its 18,600 years.

Five cities were they; eight kings reigned their 241,200 years. **(Then) the flood swept thereover**. After the flood had swept thereover (and) when kingship was lowered (again) from heaven, the kingship was (re-established) in Kish.

The First Dynasty of Kish

(1) Ga[…]ur ('harrow') – reigned 1,200 years (Sumerian name)
(2) Destroyed! Legible only to heavenly Nidaba
    (goddess of writing) – reigned 960 years
(3) Palakinatim – reigned 900 years (Akkadian name)
(4) Nangishlishma – reigned […] years (Sumerian name)
(5) Bahina – reigned […] years
(6) Bu.an.[…] – reigned 840 years (Sumerian name)
(7) Kalibum – reigned 960 years (Akkadian name)
(8) Kalumum – reigned 840 years
(9) Zukakip – reigned 900 years
(10) Atab – reigned 840 years (Akkadian name)
(11) Mashda – reigned 720 years (Sumerian name)
(12) Arwium – reigned 720 years
(13) Etana – reigned 1,560 (vari. 1,500) years (Akkadian name)

177. SKL Column I, lines 1-42, down to the start of the Dynasty of Kish.

(14) Balih – reigned 400 (vari. 410) years (Akkadian name)

(15) Enmenunna – reigned 660 years (Sumerian name)

(16) Melamkishi – reigned 900 years (Sumerian name)

(17) Barsalnunna – reigned 1,200 years (Sumerian name)

(18) Samug – reigned 140 years

(19) Tizkar – reigned 305 years

(20) Ilku – reigned 900 years (Akkadian name)

(21) Iltasadum – reigned 1,200 years

(22) Enmebaragesi – reigned 900 years (Sumerian name)

(23) Agga – reigned 629 years (Akkadian name)

178. The priest-king of Uruk. British Museum.

Twenty-three kings (thus) ruled for 24,510 years, 3 months and 3.5 days.

Kish was smitten with weapons (and) its kingship was removed to (the city of) Eanna (the temple precinct of Uruk).

The First Dynasty of Uruk

(1) Meskiagkasher, son of Utu, became high priest and king – reigned 324 years.
   Meskiagkasher went down into the sea and came out at the mountains.

(2) Enmerkar, son of Meskiagkasher, king of Uruk, the one who built Uruk – reigned 420 years

(3) Lugalbanda, a shepherd – reigned 1,200 years

(4) Dumuzi(d), the [...], his city was Kua[ra] – reigned 100 years

(5) Gilgamesh, his father was a *lillu*-demon, a high priest of Kullab – reigned 126 years

(6) Urnungal(ak), son of divine Gilgamesh – reigned 30 years

(7) Utulgalamma(k), son of Urnungal(ak) – reigned 15 years

179. SKL Column III, lines 7-10, the Enmerkar entry.

(8) Laba[...] – reigned 9 years

(9) Ennundaranna(k) – reigned 8 years

(10) Meshe, a smith – reigned 36 years

(11) Melamanna(k) – reigned 6 years

(12) Lugalkitun – reigned 36 years

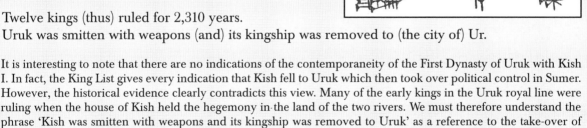

Twelve kings (thus) ruled for 2,310 years.

Uruk was smitten with weapons (and) its kingship was removed to (the city of) Ur.

It is interesting to note that there are no indications of the contemporaneity of the First Dynasty of Uruk with Kish I. In fact, the King List gives every indication that Kish fell to Uruk which then took over political control in Sumer. However, the historical evidence clearly contradicts this view. Many of the early kings in the Uruk royal line were ruling when the house of Kish held the hegemony in the land of the two rivers. We must therefore understand the phrase 'Kish was smitten with weapons and its kingship was removed to Uruk' as a reference to the take-over of Uruk at some point within the Kish dynasty and not necessarily at its end. In other words, the fall of Kish I did not take place at the beginning of Uruk I but some considerable time later. Indeed, we know from a later tradition that Kish remained in overall control of Sumer even into the reign of Gilgamesh, the fifth ruler in the dynastic line of Uruk. It is also interesting to note that the First Dynasty of Kish contains only six rulers bearing Sumerian names whilst twice that number are clearly Semitic in origin (the remaining names being difficult to classify).[6] One gets an impression of not only a complex political structure at this time, with city-states in competition for control of the land, but also a multi-ethnic mix within the royal houses themselves. This, I suppose, is to be expected at a time regarded as the dawn of history when everything we understand as political structure is in its infancy.

According to the poem 'Gilgamesh and Agga' the son of Enmebaragesi – Agga king of Kish – was a contemporary and military rival of Gilgamesh of Uruk. Thus Enmebaragesi can be placed just one generation before Gilgamesh and so it seems, at first glance, the great flood occurred twenty-two 'generations' before Gilgamesh came to the throne in Uruk.

But, as I have already indicated, there is a strong literary tradition, lying outside the King List, which informs us that King Etana was the first ruler of Kish following the flood. Now, in the SKL, Etana is positioned thirteenth in Kish I. As William Hallo and William Simpson conclude:

> These conflicting versions can be reconciled only by breaking up the King List's sequence of twenty-three rulers into two or more parallel lines, one headed by 'Harrow' (Ga[…]ur) and another by Etana.[7]

Whether we adopt Hallo and Simpson's approach or take the view that the kings of Kish who precede Etana in the list actually reigned before the flood, we must conclude that Agga – and therefore Gilgamesh – reigned in Uruk just ten 'generations' after the flood (i.e. ten reigns after Etana).

The reason why I am placing the word 'generations' in quotation marks here is because we cannot at this point regard the reigns of these rulers as normal twenty- or twenty-five-year generations. We have already noted that the kings of Uruk and Kish possess very long reigns and this we have not been able to explain – as yet.

So far the exercise we set ourselves – to date the flood – has proved to be more than a little difficult. Nevertheless, we *have* been able to narrow down the date-range to *some* degree. We know, for instance, that the deluge occurred a considerable time before 2348 BC – the date which marks the start of Ur I. In biblical terms Ur I has its floruit four centuries or more before Abraham, whilst in New-Chronology Egypt the 5TH DYNASTY is just coming into power at the same time as Ur I in Mesopotamia. At the other end of the time-scale, we also know that the flood must have occurred after the first cities were built in Mesopotamia – information

180. The ziggurat of Ur as it was (prior to restoration) at the time of the Ur excavations of Sir Leonard Woolley. Note the building in the left foreground with the niched-panel façade.

offered by both the Bible [Genesis 4:17] and the SKL. This means that we need to look in an archaeological era which post-dates the building of early Eridu, Ur and Uruk – in other words after the start of the Eridu Period (Ubaid 1) at around 5000 BC.

Even so, this still leaves us with a huge chasm of 2,650 years between these two bench marks in which to place the flood! The problem is that we have found ourselves with an absolute, *historical date* at one end of the equation (derived from the SKL) and an *archaeological date* at the other (derived from an approximate pottery chronology supplemented by a few questionable calibrated radiocarbon dates). Is there any chance that we could translate our absolute historical date into an archaeological period so that we are at least dealing with a common methodology? And is it remotely possible that we can fix either the flood itself or perhaps the reign of Gilgamesh stratigraphically? Indeed, can any of the early rulers of Mesopotamia be assigned to specific archaeological levels in the ancient city mounds? Without such links there can be little hope of accomplishing a satisfactory synthesis between the literary traditions and the cultural remains provided by archaeology.

182. **WOOLLEY**: (1880-1960). Recovering one of the lyres from the royal graves at Ur.

The Archaeology of the Flood

During his famous excavations at the ancient Sumerian city of Ur, between the years 1928 and 1934, Sir Leonard WOOLLEY unearthed a thick alluvial silt deposit deep down beneath the modern surface of the site. At first it appeared that his workmen had reached virgin soil upon which the earliest settlement at Ur had been built. But the clean zone of silt at the bottom of the excavation pit still appeared to be several metres *above* the surrounding ground level beyond the ruin mound. Woolley was not convinced by his foreman's protestations that their work was finished in the sounding and that it was pointless for him to dig deeper.

I do not like having my theories upset by anything less than proof, I told the man to get back and go on digging. Most unwillingly he did so, again turning up nothing but clean soil that yielded no sign of human activity; he dug through eight feet of it in all and then, suddenly, there appeared flint implements and fragments of painted al-Ubaid pottery vessels. I got into the pit once more, examined the sides, and by the time I had written up my notes was quite convinced of what it all meant; but I wanted to see whether others would come to the same conclusion. So I brought up two of my staff and, after pointing out the facts, asked for their explanation. They did not know what to say. My wife came along and looked and was asked the same question, and she turned away remarking casually, 'Well, of course, it's the flood'.[8]

183. Woolley's cross-section drawing of Pit F showing the four basic levels. (1) (lowest) Ubaid pottery mixed with domestic buildings which were heavily burnt; just prior to (2) a clean alluvial deposit with no sherds or signs of occupation (some graves of later date were dug into this layer during the succeeding period); above that (3) a deep level of pottery debris and a number of kilns, indicating that the abandoned area was used as a pottery factory during the Uruk period; above that (4) Early Dynastic domestic occupation consisting of the characteristic plano-convex bricks introduced at this time.

Woolley later describes his discovery as 'eleven feet of clean, water-laid silt' within which no archaeological artefacts could be found. This was in direct contrast to the levels immediately above and below the deposit which were littered with pottery sherds. Analysis of this pottery showed that the sterile layer lay on top of the high quality Ubaid 3 pottery phase and within the very last pottery phase of the Ubaid Period. In other words this 'flood layer' almost immediately preceded the Uruk Period. It was clear that the agent which brought the sedimentation was water.

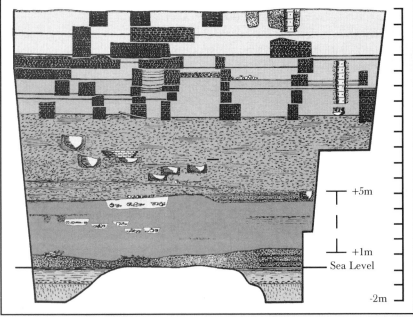

The Stratigraphy of Woolley's Flood Pit F

Early Dynastic Levels
Plano-convex mudbrick houses

+5m

+1m
Sea Level

Uruk Period
Pottery kilns, sherds and graves

Flood Deposit
Clean alluvial with the odd grave dug into it

-2m

Ubaid Period
Ubaid I & II sherds and burnt buildings

The Archaeological Phases of Prehistoric Sumer

Eridu Temple Complex	Ur Flood Pit	Uruk E-anna Complex	Archaeological Periods
Level 1	**Strata A to E houses** Plano-convex bricks	**Level 2**	**Early Dynastic I** Plano-convex bricks
Level 2	**Strata F to H houses** Flat-topped bricks	**Level 3**	**Jemdet Nasr** Polychrome ware
	Polychrome ware	Cylinder seals & Writing **Level 4** Mosaic Temple	Introduction of writing Cylinder seals
Levels 3 to 5	**Kiln Stratum**	**Level 5** Limestone Temple	**Late Uruk** Monumental building
		Level 6	
	Wheel-turned plain ware Potter's wheel	Wheel-turned plain ware **Levels 7 to 11** Uruk plain ware	**Early Uruk**
Last Ubaid ware Temple 7: a development of Temple 8 Lizard-head warrior figurine	**Level 1 (Ubaid 4)** Female lizard-head figurines	**Levels 12 to 14** Transitional	Plain red and grey ware Introduction of the potter's wheel
Levels 6 to 8 Temple 8: a formidable heavy-walled structure in early tripartite plan	**Flood Level**	**Levels 15 to 18**	**Late Ubaid** Poor firing techniques and rather perfunctory decoration of vessels
Temple 9: a development of Temple 11		Late Ubaid ware	
Levels 9 to 11 Temple 11: a large mudbrick structure with exterior buttressing	**Levels 2 to 3 (Ubaid 3)**	**Uninhabited?**	**Middle Ubaid** Superb hemispherical bowls with egg-shell walls and rosette designs
Currently little evidence of temple structures **Levels 12 to 15**	**(Ubaid 2)**		**Hajji Muhammad**
Temple 16: larger with a central altar and niche **Levels 16 to 18** Temple 17: simple square building on a sand dune	Eridu ware **(Ubaid 1)**	Hajji Muhammad ware Eridu ware	**Eridu** Highly decorated geometric designs on buff pottery
Uninhabited	**Uninhabited**	**Uninhabited**	**Uninhabited**

… microscopic analysis proved that it was water-laid, subject to the action of gentle currents, and it was composed of material brought down from the middle reaches of the Euphrates.[9]

What was equally clear was the fact that the pre-flood occupation level showed every sign of being a fairly prosperous community which was suddenly wiped out by, first of all, a terrible fire and then a great flood.

> Below it (the flood layer) came the level of human occupation – decayed mudbrick, ashes, and potsherds, in which we could distinguish three successive floor levels; here was the richly decorated al-Ubaid pottery in abundance, flints, clay figurines, and flat rectangular bricks (preserved because they had been accidentally burnt) and fragments of clay plaster, also hardened by fire …[10]

Everything seemed, at first, to fit the biblical and Sumerian flood account. Eventually though, as new discoveries were being made at other sites in southern Iraq, the picture began to change and Woolley's 'flood' was no longer the prime candidate for *the* flood. First, no other sites were producing similar flood deposits during the Ubaid pottery period. But, secondly, and more importantly, another flood candidate soon presented itself.

At the city of Shuruppak (modern Fara) – where the King List places Ubartutu, father of the Mesopotamian flood hero and the king immediately before the flood – a sterile clay deposit, mixed with sand, was revealed by the excavators. This time the archaeological horizon was datable to the beginning of the Early Dynastic Period (in fact, towards the end of ED I at around 2750 BC in the conventional chronology).[11] Evidence of a similar flood layer was found at Kish dating to the same general time period. It is now widely accepted that, if any archaeological evidence can be used to support the flood story, then it has to be the Early Dynastic flood deposit of Shuruppak and Kish rather than Woolley's much earlier Ubaid flood deposit from Ur. In Egyptian history, this would place the flood during the Old Kingdom (in conventional terms during the 2nd Dynasty).

The matter is rarely discussed these days and little further research has been devoted to either dating the flood or, for that matter, demonstrating that a major flood took place at all. Most scholars would consider that such an historical enterprise smacks rather too much of 'Biblical Archaeology' with all that implies for 'respectable' academic reputations. Small wonder, then, that whenever the flood *is* discussed in popular works on Sumerian archaeology (usually in no more than a few obligatory sentences) the ED I silt deposit is held up as the most likely archaeological counterpart for the biblical deluge. It is then argued that the events surrounding the deposition of the silt layer at Shuruppak acted as the stimulus for the Genesis flood narrative.

184. The stratigraphic sequence of Sumer, showing the relative archaeological positions of the two main flood candidates.

ED III
ED II
Shuruppak Flood ED I
Jemdet Nasr
Uruk
Ur Flood Late Ubaid
Early Ubaid

However, it seems to me that much of the historical and textual evidence in favour of Woolley's original findings in the Ur 'Flood Pit' has been overlooked and that, by accepting the ED I candidate, scholars have missed a great opportunity to achieve a more successful synthesis between archaeology and both the Genesis and Sumerian traditions.

First there is the question of Gilgamesh and his chronological relationship to the flood. We have already seen that his reign at Uruk occurred several 'generations' after the deluge in the Sumerian tradition. The conventional placement of Gilgamesh is in Early Dynastic III because of his link to Agga of Kish. The archaeological and linguistic arguments are complex but scholars have determined that Agga was a near contemporary of Mesannapada of Ur I, whose son, Aannapada, apparently built a temple at Tell al-Ubaid datable to the Early Dynastic III archaeological phase. So Gilgamesh would have lived one or two 'generations' before Aannapada – in other words during early ED III.

Other literary texts and an inscription from the reign of King Anam, a later ruler of Uruk (contemporary with the Babylon I Dynasty), tell us that Gilgamesh built the great wall surrounding the city of Uruk. In the Gilgamesh Epic specific mention of this wall, built by the hero of the tale, is made in its opening lines.

185. One of the great excavation pits dug by Woolley and his enormous team of workmen at Ur in which evidence of a great flood was discovered in the form of a deep layer of water-borne sand.

HECTARES: Equivalent to 10,000 square metres or 2,471 acres.

See if its (Uruk's) wall is not (as straight) as the (architect's) string. Inspect its […] wall, the likes of which no-one can equal. … Go up on the wall and walk around. Examine its foundations. Inspect its brickwork thoroughly. Is not its masonry of baked brick? Did not the Seven Sages themselves lay out its plans? (It encloses) one square mile of city, one square mile of palm groves, one square mile of brick pits and the Ishtar (Sum. Inanna) temple complex. (In all) three square miles and the [sacred precinct] of Uruk it encloses. [12]

The remains of the great wall of Uruk have been unearthed not within ED III where Gilgamesh is conventionally placed but in an Early Dynastic I archaeological context. [13] And they are indeed impressive. It has been calculated that the wall measures nine kilometres in circumference, enclosing an area of four hundred HECTARES – equivalent to four million square metres! Given the description above and the obvious comparison to the archaeologically attested great wall at Uruk, the question arises as to whether Gilgamesh should not be placed in the time of the ED I archaeological period rather than late ED II or early ED III.

186. A plan of the Uruk ruin-mound showing that the central area of the ancient city (including the Eanna and Anu complexes) was surrounded by a massive wall which is nine kilometres in length. Archaeological investigations of this city-wall have determined that it was constructed during the Early Dynastic I Period. (After S. Lloyd, 1984, p. 48.)

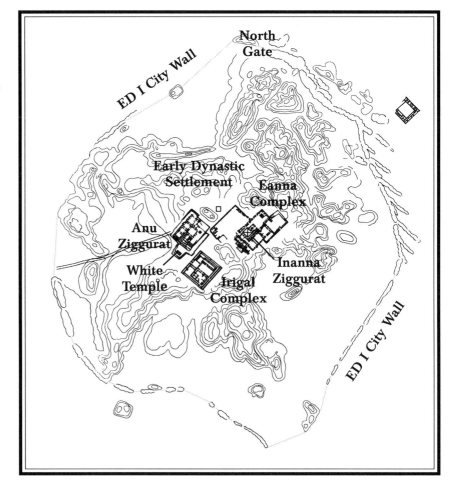

187. Left: The 'long-haired hero' and the 'bull-man' slaying a bull and lion. This Agade-Period seal has a star symbol next to the bull which suggests that the Bull of Heaven is meant. This would identify the long-haired hero as Enkidu.

This placement is supported by the fact that the GLYPTIC art of ED II and III shows heroic figures fighting wild animals and mythical beasts. This motif previously had been thought to represent Gilgamesh and his companion, Enkidu, slaying lions, the Bull of Heaven and the monster Humbaba. Now scholars shy away from this identification because the era of Gilgamesh is thought to coincide with ED III. But what if they are wrong? What if the 'Gilgamesh seals' are genuine representations of the legendary hero of Uruk? Then they cannot predate the rule of the hero-king who they celebrate but must appear some time after his reign. As a result, Gilgamesh has to be located in ED I at the latest.

Moreover, the textual evidence supports this placement. The names of Lugalbanda and Gilgamesh are found in the Tell al-Fara (Shuruppak) tablets which have been assigned on epigraphic grounds to ED III. But there the names of the two rulers of Uruk are preceded by the determinative sign for divinity, thus showing that both kings had attained deity status by the time of ED III. This strongly suggests that the human Gilgamesh and his predecessor had lived in some earlier epoch – allowing enough time for their transfiguration to take place by ED III.

188. Detail from an ED II seal impression showing the bull-man fighting a deer. In the Gilgamesh Epic the hero is referred to as the 'son of the heavenly cow' and a 'rampant wild bull'.

Conclusion Twelve

Gilgamesh, the fifth king of the First Dynasty of Uruk, is to be relocated in the Early Dynastic I archaeological period rather than the Early Dynastic III phase as is the currently held view.

But remember why we started this investigation of Gilgamesh's stratigraphic placement. It was because we were trying to fix the date of the flood in archaeological terms relative to the early rulers of Uruk and Kish. We have concluded that much of the evidence places Gilgamesh in the ED I period. So how then can the flood have taken place in that same archaeological period as implied by the late ED I Shuruppak silt

189. Detail from the same seal showing the long-haired hero fighting a bull. Enkidu is described as being 'furnished with tresses like a woman, his locks of hair growing luxuriant like grain'.

GLYPTIC: The art of seals.

deposit favoured by many Sumerologists? Surely we must look for evidence of the deluge in an earlier archaeological phase which would correspond to several (traditionally at least ten) 'generations' before an Early Dynastic I Gilgamesh?

Second there is the question of Enmerkar and his relationship to the flood. In *Chapter Two* we discovered that the epic 'Enmerkar and the Lord of Aratta' mentions the fact that Enmerkar was the first king to record his words on a clay tablet. Enmerkar's message was too complicated for his herald to remember and so the king's words were written down.

> The herald was heavy of mouth (and) could not repeat it. (And) because the herald was heavy of mouth (and) could not repeat it, the Lord of Kullab (Enmerkar) patted (a lump of) clay (and) set up the words like a tablet. **Formerly there had been noone who set words on clay**. Now, as Utu is […], it was so. The Lord of Kullab set up words like a tablet (and) it was so. ['Enmerkar and the Lord of Aratta', Lines 502-07] [14]

Archaeological investigations at Uruk have demonstrated that the first clay tablets written in the Sumerian script all came from the city known as Uruk IV which immediately preceded the Jemdet Nasr Period. The latter, in turn, coming before ED I. Moreover, the SKL places the Dynasty of Uruk I, in which Enmerkar reigned, *after* the flood. Thus, if we are to accept that the reign of Enmerkar was concurrent with the invention of writing in Uruk IV, we have to conclude that the flood occurred before the Uruk Period – in other words during the late Ubaid Period in archaeological terms.

It is also important to note that City IV at Uruk contains one of the most impressive sacred precincts ever found in Mesopotamia with its splendid temples and courts. I am, of course, referring to the Eanna complex which, according to the epic literature, was built for Inanna by

190. Plan of the excavated area of the Eanna complex at Uruk as it was during the Protoliterate Period. Note the niched-façade architecture of the temples.

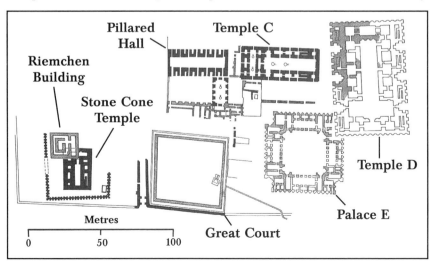

191. One of the small decorative cones used in the mosaics of the Pillared Hall at Uruk.

192. Left: Sketch of the remains of the 2.6-metre diameter engaged columns belonging to the Pillared Hall at Uruk. Below are four of the patterns composed of red, black and cream cones.

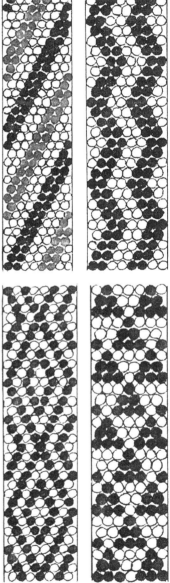

Enmerkar who brought the goddess down from her home in the mountain kingdom of Aratta. The original deity of Uruk was the sky-god, Anu, whilst Inanna was only adopted by the city some considerable time after its foundation. This is what the SKL has to say about the reign of Enmerkar.

> Enmerkar, son of Meskiagkasher, king of Uruk, **the one who built Uruk**, became king and reigned 420 years. [Column III, lines 7-11]

What does 'the one who built Uruk' mean? Of course, over the centuries many rulers added to the splendour of this fine city, but it seems that Enmerkar (like Gilgamesh) was singled out as a great glorifier of Uruk – particularly, as the epic literature recalls, the Eanna temple complex.

Turn to any popular book on Mesopotamian archaeology and you will find that the era of City IV at Uruk is singled out as the outstanding epoch of early Sumerian culture – not just because this city produced the first writing and wheel-thrown pottery but also because the building-works in the precincts of the Inanna and Anu temples are some of the finest so far unearthed. However, it is also true to say that, in general, the Uruk IV Period represents the high point of Sumerian architecture. As to why this is the case we will discover in the next chapter when we identify the shadowy biblical character who hides behind the historical figure of Enmerkar, king of Uruk.

A further pointer which identifies Enmerkar with the Uruk IV era is the appearance at this time of another glyptic art motif showing a ruler making offerings before a temple decorated with the reed-bundle-with-loop on 'gatepost' motif which is one of the iconographic symbols of the goddess Inanna. If the 'Lady of Heaven' was not worshipped in Uruk until the Early Dynastic Period (where Enmerkar is normally placed)

Enmerkar and Inanna

193. Left: The famous 'Uruk Vase', now in the Iraq Museum, datable to the Uruk IV period but surviving as an heirloom into Uruk III. The detail (right) shows Inanna (recognised by the gatepost symbol behind her) receiving offerings from a naked priest. The ruler of Uruk was originally depicted in the damaged space behind the priest.

194. Lower Right: Part of a stone vase from Uruk IV depicting a reed shrine with the more complex gatepost motif of Inanna.

195. Below: A seal impression of the Uruk Period depicting reed buildings for livestock and farming produce, so closely associated with Inanna (note her gatepost symbol).

196. Bottom left: The ruler of Uruk brings a sacrificial goat to Inanna's shrine.

197. Bottom right: A superb statue head of a goddess from Uruk, probably to be identified with Inanna – Uruk IV Period.

All these artefacts already place Inanna at Uruk in the Protoliterate Period. If we accept that Enmerkar introduced Inanna to Uruk, then this legendary ruler must be dated to the Uruk IV era and not later. He may well be represented as the long-coated ruler in much of the Uruk Period art.

then why would Inanna's symbol appear on cylinder seals of the Uruk Period? I believe that the ruler shown in the glyptic art is Enmerkar himself and that the seals were manufactured to commemorate the establishment of the cult of Inanna at Uruk.

Conclusion Thirteen

The era of Enmerkar's rule in Uruk is not to be placed in the ED I or ED II but rather in the late Uruk Period, also known as the Protoliterate Period.

---

198. The gatepost symbol of Inanna as it appears in earliest Sumerian (above) and its cuneiform counterpart (below) again rotated 90 degrees anti-clockwise.

So we may confidently identify Uruk IV as the city built by Enmerkar – a view which is wholly consistent with the tradition that this king was the first to use clay tablets to record his words and the great builder of the Eanna complex.

I have proposed that Gilgamesh was a king of the late ED I Period and that Enmerkar reigned in the earlier Uruk IV Period. As both these Sumerian rulers came to the throne after the flood, we can only conclude that the catastrophic event, remembered in both the biblical and Mesopotamian tradition, occurred in the archaeological era known as the Ubaid Period and that Woolley was right all along to identify his silt deposit at Ur with the biblical flood. The deluge struck towards the end of the Ubaid Period and was probably the catalyst for the important cultural changes which took place in the succeeding Uruk Period.

199. The portable shrine of Inanna was carried on the back of a bull. Here on this seal from the Uruk Period we see that the Inanna gatepost motif also decorated the portable shrine as well as the temple proper (after P. Amiet, 1961, pl. 46:653).

But can we assign year dates to these archaeological phases, working back from our date of 2348 BC for the start of the Ur I Dynasty? It would be nice if we could put a chronological figure to Woolley's flood level. Well, archaeologists have dated the end of the Ubaid Period at *circa* 4000 BC – but this is only based on a rough pottery chronology and a few radiocarbon dates which are likely to be too high by several centuries due to the vagaries of the dendrochronology calibration of the raw C-14 dates. We are therefore still left with trying to find alternative methods of dating a catastrophic flood which the archaeology suggests occurred some time in the fourth millennium BC.

After puzzling for weeks over the section of the Sumerian King List which predates the Ur I Dynasty, I came to the reluctant conclusion that the regnal figures given there are simply impossible to work with and that I could not retrocalculate back from the reign of Mesannapada to reach the flood with any confidence. What did come out of the exercise, however, was a strong feeling that Thorkild Jacobsen, the compiler of the modern translation of the King List, had to be wrong in his calculations for the dynasties of Kish I and Uruk I.

Although I myself am an advocate of using average reign-lengths to work out approximate dates for eras where the regnal data is missing, in the case of the earliest periods of the SKL I believe this method would produce wholly misleading results. There is something very different about the antediluvian (i.e. Ubaid) and immediate post-diluvian (i.e. Proto-literate) eras compared to the truly historical epoch which begins with Ur I (late Early Dynastic Period). As we have seen, the kings of the early legendary age are given extraordinarily long reigns. Jacobsen simply ignores these figures and assigns each king between twenty and thirty years. As a result, if we ourselves were to adopt this same approach for the New Chronology, the Dynasty of Uruk I would begin just one hundred and thirty years before the start of the Ur I Dynasty which we have determined at 2348 BC. This would place the start of Meskiagkasher's reign (the founder of Uruk I) in 2478 BC and the flood not much earlier.

Herein lies the chronological problem which prevents scholars from accepting Woolley's archaeological candidate for the flood. If the period from Meskiagkasher (Uruk I) to Mesannapada (Ur I) amounts to no more than one hundred and thirty years, then this relatively short time span has to accommodate the archaeological phases of the Uruk, Jemdet Nasr, Early Dynastic I and Early Dynastic II. This is, of course, completely unrealistic as the great depth of archaeological remains suggest a total era of around 1,000 years. This is why scholars opt for the Shuruppak silt deposit as the most likely flood candidate, because the one hundred and thirty years would then only need to span the late ED II to early ED III archaeological phases.

But is this the only solution to the problem? The evidence pointing to Woolley's flood is too strong to reject so easily. Perhaps the answer is to view the 'generations' from Meskiagkasher to Mesannapada not as Thorkild Jacobsen's twenty- to twenty-five-year generations but rather as 'eras' represented by named rulers in the King List. What I mean by this is that we should consider the possibility of treating the 'reigns' of these long-lived hero kings rather as dynasties. The heroic figures such as Enmerkar, Lugalbanda, Dumuzi and Gilgamesh were the eponymous founders of lines of kings, many of whom were not named in the King List because they made no significant contribution to the legendary history of the era.

There are plenty of precedents for omissions in the SKL. For instance, the reign of Aannapada is subsumed into the eighty-year reign of his father Mesannapada. Furthermore, the kings of Ur whose tombs were discovered by Sir Leonard Woolley do not appear at all in the SKL, in spite of their obvious wealth as illustrated by their stunning burial accoutrements. These 'missing' rulers of Ur appear in a stratigraphical context which suggests that they immediately preceded Mesannapada, yet the Ur I Dynasty only begins with the latter. Many other rulers who are called 'King of Kish' are also not attested in the SKL, so it would not be surprising to find that not all the kings of Uruk appear in the canonical version of the Sumerian King List.

200. The 'goat caught in bush' from the royal tombs at Ur. British Museum.

201. Reconstruction of the scene in the 'Death Pit' at Ur based on the archaeological remains. (Painting by A. Forestier, 1928.)

Thus the hundred-plus years of reign given in the SKL for each of the great prehistoric rulers may include the reigns of their minor successors. This permits us to assign a much longer time interval to the period than Jacobsen's one hundred and thirty years. But the question is: how long?

Unfortunately, we cannot accept the figures given in the King List literally because they are simply too fantastical. If we did, then Etana, first ruler of Kish after the flood, would begin his reign in 11,138 BC – a date some 7,000 years before the end of the Ubaid Period where Woolley's flood stratum is located. Meskiagkasher, on the other hand, would mark the foundation of the Uruk I Dynasty in 4518 BC – a much more reasonable figure given that the start of the Uruk Period in archaeological terms has been set at *circa* 4000 BC. But even this 4518 BC date for the foundation of Uruk I is probably too high – especially given that the reign-length/dynasty of Lugalbanda is recorded as an astonishing 1,200 years.

As you can see, the problems associated with accurately pinpointing the date of the flood or the start of the Uruk I Dynasty are virtually insurmountable. What we can say is that the best archaeological evidence for the flood still seems to be that found by Sir Leonard Woolley in the great Flood Pit at Ur. The archaeological date of this flood horizon is towards the end of the Ubaid Period – a point in time which is only approximately datable to somewhere between 4000 BC at the earliest and 3000 BC at the latest.

Conclusion Fourteen

What we know from the book of Genesis as Noah's flood was probably an actual historical event which took place not long before the appearance of wheel-thrown pottery and writing in the ancient Near East. This catastrophic flood brought an end to the Ubaid culture and acted as a catalyst for the rapid development of civilisation in the succeeding Uruk Period.

If we do accept the Ur flood deposit as that of the famous flood, then the general outline proposed here for the history of the heroic age fits rather well. The heroes of the Uruk I Dynasty – particularly the great builder-king Enmerkar – would be archaeologically dated to within the Uruk Period when the city of Uruk expanded and flourished. Seals of that time show a great king performing ceremonies at the temple-shrine of the goddess Inanna who was introduced to Uruk by Enmerkar according to tradition. The famous 'Uruk Vase' depicting a ruler making offerings to Inanna would become yet another representation of Enmerkar. Writing also appears for the first time in the Uruk Period and, again, tradition accords its 'invention' to Enmerkar. Some 'generations' later Gilgamesh was ruling in Uruk during the archaeological phase known as Early Dynastic I. The art of ED II and III portrays an heroic figure, very much in the mould of a Gilgamesh, on the cylinder seals of the time. The originally held view that these were 'Gilgamesh seals' could then be revived without upsetting the relative chronology.

I just want to throw in a piece of extra-biblical data from a very different cultural source which I believe may be consistent with what we have been able to achieve here.

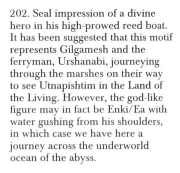

202. Seal impression of a divine hero in his high-prowed reed boat. It has been suggested that this motif represents Gilgamesh and the ferryman, Urshanabi, journeying through the marshes on their way to see Utnapishtim in the Land of the Living. However, the god-like figure may in fact be Enki/Ea with water gushing from his shoulders, in which case we have here a journey across the underworld ocean of the abyss.

Until fairly recently we knew very little about the traditions of the Meso-American civilisation of the Mayans because their written language had not been completely deciphered. We now discover that they were exceptional record keepers who had developed an historical calendar going back several thousand years. It is therefore of considerable interest to me to know that the date of *their* cataclysmic flood is given as 3113 BC.[15] This fits with the latest possible date we have come up with for the Sumerian flood based on the King List, glyptic art, literature and archaeology of early Mesopotamia. It may turn out to be the exact date we have been looking for, but the consequence of accepting this absolute date would be to reduce the length of the Uruk, Jemdet Nasr and Early Dynastic I and II periods to just seven hundred and sixty-five years. This may just be possible and would fit very well with the chronological scheme and history of predynastic Egypt which forms the third part of this book.

Perhaps then the orthodox dating of 4000 BC for the end of the Ubaid Period is too high by nearly 1,000 years. The great flood may have ended the Ubaid era and heralded in the Uruk Period, however it did not happen at the beginning of the fourth millennium but rather towards its end. The prehistoric chronology becomes a much tighter affair altogether with this New Chronology model but, as a result, the historical and biblical implications are very interesting indeed.

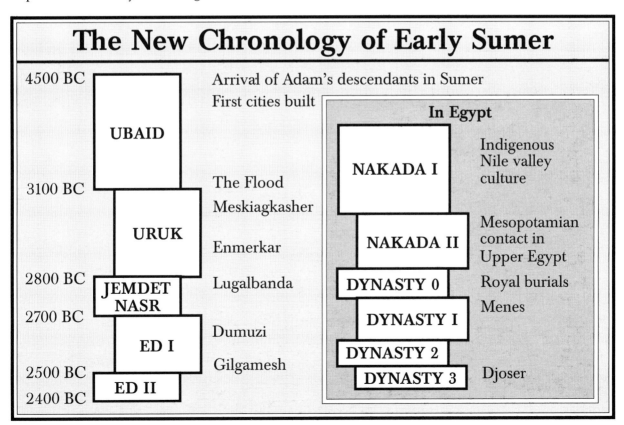

The New Chronology of Early Sumer

4500 BC		Arrival of Adam's descendants in Sumer
	UBAID	First cities built
		In Egypt
		NAKADA I — Indigenous Nile valley culture
3100 BC		The Flood
	URUK	Meskiagkasher
		NAKADA II — Mesopotamian contact in Upper Egypt
		Enmerkar
2800 BC	JEMDET NASR	Lugalbanda — DYNASTY 0 — Royal burials
2700 BC		DYNASTY I — Menes
	ED I	Dumuzi — DYNASTY 2
2500 BC		Gilgamesh — DYNASTY 3 — Djoser
2400 BC	ED II	

203. Opposite page: A large modern sculpture of the Sumerian water-god, Enki, based on a cylinder seal impression of the Early Dynastic III Period. The life-giving waters of the abyss flow from the god's shoulders as he places his foot on a mountain top. Bahrain National Museum.

204. Left: The god Ea (Sumerian Enki) is approached by three deities in this seal impression from the Agade Period. Private collection of the Biblisches Institut, Fribourg University.

Chapter Six

THE ANTEDILUVIANS

t is clear from the extrabiblical material reviewed in the last two chapters that the deluge was a real historical event – at least as far as the ancients were concerned. Even though the archaeological evidence is admittedly thin on the ground, the literary evidence remains powerful testimony to a natural disaster which befell the ancient world, causing the pre-flood cities to be destroyed and the populations of those cities to be wiped out. A common theme in the extant source material is the hero who, thanks to his piety and devotion to his god Enki/Ea, survives the flood. The hero may have been known by several, quite different names – Noah, Utnapishtim, Atrahasis, Ziusudra, Deucalion – but he was clearly regarded as a flesh-and-blood human being who only later became one with the gods in a place called the 'Land of the Living'. Only in the Hebrew version was his fate that of all humankind.

So, if Noah has been identified amongst the heroes of Sumerian and Akkadian literature, is it remotely possible that we could find other biblical characters from the book of Genesis in that same literature or in the King List which reaches back to those distant times before the great flood? Many scholars, over the last one hundred years, have searched for the antediluvian patriarchs but were unable to get very far in their quest. The conclusion which has been drawn from these protracted efforts is that very little specific or tangible can be found to link the antediluvian patriarchs of Genesis with the antediluvian heroes of the extra-biblical Mesopotamian texts.

Given that this has been the case, it seemed somewhat futile for me to tackle this intractable problem all over again when I set to the task in the last week of May 1997 – after all I am no Sumerian scholar and those

205. A bronze from Luristan with two early motifs – the 'Master of Animals' and entwined monsters. Louvre Museum.

much more qualified than me must surely have extracted all there was to learn from a comparison of the two sources. But, always ready to accept a challenge (and continuing in the spirit of this book), I saw no harm – other than perhaps a few days of wasted research – in extending the *Legend* experiment in an attempt to locate the likes of Tubal-Cain, Methuselah, Mehujael, Irad, Enoch, Cain, and even perhaps Adam himself. The experiment turned out to be surpassingly fruitful. Biblical names just seemed to leap out at me as I began to study the ancient literature of Sumer. Was I being linguistically naive or could all those eminent Sumerologists really have missed so much? Was this simply another case of scholars not being able to see the wood for the trees?

Rules of the Game

Before we begin this round of the 'name game' I should remind you of a few of the linguistic 'rules' which we need to apply if we are to break the code of the ancient writings.

Those who read Volume One of *A Test of Time* will be familiar with the arguments which led me to conclude there that Ramesses II was the historical figure behind the biblical Shishak – plunderer of the temple and palaces of Jerusalem in 925 BC. In the course of revealing that Ramesses had a hypocoristicon or short-form of his name, I demonstrated that the Egyptian 's' (*sin*) is often transcribed in the Semitic languages (sometimes in biblical Hebrew but mainly in Akkadian) as 'sh' (*shin*). Thus Ramesses II's Egyptian hypocoristicon 'Sysa' becomes the biblical 'Shisha(k)'. We find many such examples of this switch from 's' to 'sh' in the Middle East – for instance Arabic '**s**alam' for Hebrew '**sh**alom', Egyptian '**A**skelan' for Hebrew '**Ash**kelon', Egyptian Rame**ss**u to Akkadian Riama**sh**e**sh**a, Akkadian **A**starte to Hebrew **Ash**taroth, etc. But 's' is not the only consonant which suffers this fate. Thus we find 't' and 'd', 'k' and 'g', 'm' and 'n', 'b' and 'm', and 'r' and 'l' all exhibiting similar shifts in different languages and dialects. As we saw in *Chapter Two*, the same thing can happen with the vowels in syllables. So biblical '**A**rarat' becomes Assyrian '**U**rartu', '**A**rbilum' becomes '**U**rbilum' becomes '**E**rbil', '**I**shtar' becomes Canaanite '**A**starte' or Hebrew '**A**shtaroth', and Sumerian '**Du**muzi' becomes biblical '**Ta**mmuz'. The table opposite gives just a few examples of both changing consonants and shifting syllables, all of which will have some relevance to the following discussion.

Berossus and the King List

When scholars itemise the available ancient historical sources two names always appear near the top of the list – Manetho and Berossus. The former was an Egyptian priest of Heliopolis who, in the third century BC, wrote a history of the pharaohs in Greek, entitled *Aegyptiaca*. Those of you familiar with my previous research will be aware that I have had recourse

ANTIOCHUS I (opposite page): King of the Seleucid Dynasty, reigned 281-261 BC.

The Fluidity of Language

M to N
Mekdiara (Ass) = Nikdiara (Ass)

B to V
Biaina (Hur) = Van (Mod)
Erebuni (Hur) = Erivan (Mod)

B to P
bahar (Sum) = paharu (Akk)
bara.ga (Sum) = parakku (Akk)
al.hab (Sum) = alluhappu (Akk)
ab.za.mi (Sum) = apsamakku (Akk)
dub.ba (Sum) = tappi (Akk)
bur.zi (Sum) = pursitu (Akk)
Arbu (Hur) = Arpau (Hur)
Ubumu (Hur) = Pumu (Ass)

D to T to D
Dumuzi (Sum) = Tammuz (Heb)
dub.ba (Sum) = tappi (Akk)
dam.gar (Sum) = tamkaru (Akk)
Melid (Hit) = Malatya (Mod)
sa.tu (Sum) = shadu (Akk)
Mita (Akk) = Midas (Grk)

T to TH
Tushpa (Ur) = Thospitis (Grk)

Sh to S to Sh
Ushkaia (Akk) = Osku (Mod)
Ishtar (Akk) = Astarte (Can)
sa.tu (Sum) = shadu (Akk)
silim (Sum) = shulmu (Akk)
Astarte (Can) = Ashtaroth (Heb)

S to Z to S
Ishala (Hur) = Izalla (Ass)
ab.za.mi (Sum) = apsamakku (Akk)
bur.zi (Sum) = pursitu (Akk)

S to Dj
Musasir (Hur) = Mudjesir (Mod)

R to L to R
uru (Sum) = alu (Akk)
Urarti (Akk) = Alorodi (Grk)
alu (Akk) = ir (Heb)

G to K
ugula (Sum) = aklu (Akk)
gim (Sum) = kima (Akk)
bara.ga (Sum) = parakku (Akk)
dam.gar (Sum) = tamkaru (Akk)
Guti (Bab) = Kuti (Hur)
Agade (Sum) = Akkad (Akk)

hard H to K
Khulmeru (Hur) = Kullmeri (Ass)

hard H dropped
Khaldi (Hur) = Aldi (Hur)

U to A to U
uru (Sum) = alu (Akk)
ugula (Sum) = aklu (Akk)
dub.ba (Sum) = tappi (Akk)
Urme (Ass) = Arme (Ass)
Urartu (Ass) = Ararat (Heb)
Urbilum (Sum) = Arbilum (Akk)
ugula (Sum) = aklu (Akk)
aga (Sum) = agu (Akk)
bara.ga (Sum) = parakku (Akk)
an.nu.ha.ra (Sum) = alluharu (Akk)
kamamu (Akk) = kum (Heb)

A to O
kalu (Akk) = kol (Heb)
rashu (Akk) = rosh (Heb)

A to I
Khalpa (Hur) = Khalpi (Ass)
alu (Akk) = ir (Heb)
Mannai (Hur) = Minni (Heb)
Astarte (Can) = Ishtar (Ass)

U to I to U
Ushpina (Ass) = Ishpuini (Hur)
Ulluba (Ass) = Uliba (Hur)
kiri (Sum) = kiru (Akk)
silim (Sum) = shulmu (Akk)

A to E
Shamash (Akk) = shemesh (Heb)
napishtu (Akk) = nephesh (Heb)
Arbilum (Akk) = Erbil (Mod)
Sarduri (Hur) = Seduri (Ass)

I to E
ishatu (Akk) = esh (Heb)
itsu (Akk) = ets (Heb)
libbu (Akk) = leb (Heb)
napishtu (Akk) = nephesh (Heb)
Irepuni (Hur) = Erebuni (Hur)

Miscellaneous
an.nu.ha.ra (Sum) = alluharu (Akk)
Tushpa (Hur) = Turushpa (Hur)
Teisheba (Hur) = Teshub (Hur)
Argishti-una (Hur) = Erçis (Mod)
Dugdamme (Ass) = Lygdamis (Grk)
Urartu (Ass) = Urashtu (Bab)

Key	
Akk = Akkadian	Bab = Babylonian
Sum = Sumerian	Hit = Hititte
Hur = Hurrian	Grk = Greek
Heb = Hebrew	Mod = Modern
Can = Canaanite	

to this work (in its surviving redacted forms) on a number of occasions when constructing the New Chronology. However, we now need to turn to Manetho's 'rival' – the Babylonian priest named Berossus who also lived in the third century BC and composed a history of the rulers of Mesopotamia for his patron, ANTIOCHUS I.

Berossus wrote his three volumes (entitled *Babyloniaka*) on the history of his ancestors in Greek (just like Manetho) and his source (again like Manetho) was temple archives – in particular documents from the

206. A few examples of the shifts in pronunciation between the various languages of the ancient Near East. This type of fluidity is also observable chronologically within the same languages and scripts. Moreover, the views of scholarship also change so that early books on Sumerian or Akkadian have quite different vocalisations compared to more recent publications.

sanctuary of Bel (Baal) in Babylon, which was known as the Esagila. His work was highly esteemed by the later Greek and Roman historians and was much quoted. Unfortunately, no surviving manuscript is in our possession today. Again, as with Manetho, all that we possess are the quotations preserved in Josephus and Eusebius. From those secondary sources we hear that, in Book II, Berossus recorded a brief account of the deluge in which his hero – Xisuthros – appears to be one and the same as the Sumerian flood hero Ziusudra.

> After the death of Otiartes his son, Xisuthros reigned for eighteen saroi (64,800 years). Altogether there were ten kings and one hundred and twenty saroi (432,000 years). In his time the great flood occurred and the story has been recorded as follows: Cronus (Enki/Ea) appeared to Xisuthros in a dream and revealed that on the fifteenth day of the month of Daisios (Ayaru = April/May) mankind would be destroyed by a flood.[1]

The original name Ziusudra is only just recognisable in the corrupted Greek form of Berossus' day. (Berossus himself was a pretty lousy student of Greek.) Here we see shifts from Z to X and d to th as well as vowel changes. This is a good example of the kind of confusion of tongues which has prevented us from identifying the antediluvian heroes of Genesis in the Sumerian records.

At the beginning of Book II, Berossus lists ten kings who ruled before the flood, the last of whom was called Xisuthros – our Noah. Interestingly enough, it has often been noted that there were also ten biblical patriarchs from Adam to Noah listed in chapter five of Genesis. But, as Professor Samuel Külling has recently pointed out, the two traditions clearly do not derive from the same source. In Berossus we are dealing with kings possessing *exceptional reign-lengths* who are not all from the same dynasty whilst the Genesis tradition records what we understand to be a true genealogy with *exceptional lifespans*.[2]

What is more, if we compare the *names* from the two sources, we must also accept that the SKL rulers clearly do not resemble, in any way, the antediluvian patriarchs and cannot therefore represent a common tradition concerning a single family line. So scholars have been forced reluctantly to conclude that the early generations of Genesis simply do not appear amongst the ancient Mesopotamian sources. Let us now see if this really is the case.

To begin the process of uncovering the lost 'historical' identities of the antediluvian patriarchs we first ought to confirm that the pre-flood kings of Berossus are one and the same as the rulers listed in the Sumerian King List. In doing so we shall note three important phenomena:

(1) the shift of consonant and syllable which I have already mentioned;

(2) a change in the sequence or order of the ten names, and;

(3) variations in the relative positions of the syllables within each name.

This observable fluidity between the different lists is the key to deciphering the puzzle of the missing biblical patriarchs. But, before we start the exercise, I need to go into a little more detail about linguistic phenomenon (3) which goes under the name of METATHESIS.

There are many examples of metathesis which I could give but I think one from the modern world and one from the ancient world will suffice. Many ethnic Caribbeans living in the UK or USA pronounce the word 'ask' as 'aks'. This reversal of 's' and 'k' is common and widely known. The name Zaphenath which forms part of Joseph's Egyptian name in Genesis 41:45 is, according to Kenneth Kitchen, a Hebrew corruption of *zatenaf* (in Egypto-speak we would say *djedu.en.ef*) which means 'he who is called'.[3] Here we see the metathesis of the 'f' (ph) and the 't' (th) which changes the Egyptian *zatenaf* to *zafenat*.

If this were all we had to worry about it would make things difficult enough but we also find that the early Sumerian scribes wrote groups of syllables representing words randomly in boxes on their little clay tablets. In other words each word or idea (in fact usually an object plus a numerical quantity, e.g. ten sheep) was separated from its neighbour by a series of vertical and horizontal lines scratched into the soft clay to form word enclosures. The problem which then arises is that the syllables were drawn or impressed in no particular order within the boxes. Let me give you an example.

In the year 2874 BC the Sumerovision Song Contest was won by the entry from the land of Edinsu (Sum. *edin.su*), entitled 'Luwatar' (Sum. *lu.u.ad.ar*), sung by the group Bab (Sum. *ba.ab*) – at least that is what an Akkadian scribe from the late second millennium tells us in a tablet from Nippur. The trouble is that this much later scribe was not familiar with the well-known hit from the early third millennium and he read the syllables in the three Sumerian word boxes in the wrong order.

EDIN	LU	U	BA
SU	AD	AR	AB

As all pop fans from 2874 BC would have known, the original Sumerian scribe who recorded the event actually wrote 'Su-edin' (Sweden), 'U-ad-ar-lu' (Waterloo) and 'Ab-ba' (Abba).

You see the problem: if you do not know the original pronunciation of certain names in the earliest Sumerian documents you might read the elements of those names in the wrong order and thus completely garble that original version.

Perhaps I had better give you two real examples which are actually rather astonishing but, nevertheless, well attested. One of the great gods of ancient Mesopotamia is called Sin in Akkadian. He is the moon god – equivalent to the Egyptian god Thoth. The early Mesopotamians knew him as Suen. However, many of the early texts actually wrote his name

207. The two symbols (in classical Sumerian – Ur III) which spell out zu-ab (i.e. abzu/abyss). The upper symbol (zu) appears to represent a mountain or volcano with sacred spring rising up through its extinct lava chimney. The lower symbol may be an altar or perhaps a shrine built on top of a mudbrick platform. It is tempting to see in these motifs the original sacred spring on Mount Sahand (top) and the first platform temple of Eridu (bottom) dedicated to Enki, Lord of the Abzu.

as Ensu, completely reversing the true vocalisation. Or did they? How can we tell today which was the original vocalisation? A second word which is now rather familiar to us is abzu – the watery abyss. This was originally written with two signs in the order zu-ab.

You will see several examples of this kind of thing as we now turn to the search for the pre-diluvian patriarchs. As I said, we will begin by comparing the Sumerian King List (SKL) with Berossus (Ber).

The Sumerian epics tell us that Ziusudra, the flood hero, was the son of Ubartutu of Shuruppak – the last of the eight antediluvian rulers in the SKL. Thus, if we include Ziusudra, we have a tradition of nine Sumerian rulers up to and including the flood.

We have seen that Berossus calls Ziusudra 'Xisuthros' in his garbled version of the antediluvian kings of Mesopotamia. It is also not difficult to see a common identity between Ammeluanna (SKL) and Amelon (Ber) at position three in both lists, even though the reign-length of SKL 3 does not match Ber 3 but rather Ber 4. Similarly, we have Dumuzi at SKL 5 and Daonos at Ber 6, both with reign-lengths of 36,000 years. Daonos is therefore, in all likelihood, a corruption of Dumuzi. The rest

208. A typical example of early Sumerian writing in word/idea boxes. Louvre Museum.

SKL	Intermediate	Berossus
1 Alulim	Alurim -- Alorim	Aloros (1)
2 Alalgar	Alagar -- Alapar	Alaparos (2)
3 Ammeluanna	Ameluan -- Amelun	Amelon (3)
4 Ammegalanna	Ammenanna -- Ammenan	Ammenon (4)
5 Dumuzi	Dunuzi -- Daunizi	Daonos (6)
6 Enmeushumgalanna	Enmegalanna -- Megalanna	Megalaros (5)
7 Ensipazianna	Ansipizianna -- Anmempisana	Amempsinos (8)
8 Enmeduranki	Eueduranki -- Euedoraki	Euedorachos (7)
9 Ubartutu	Ubiartu -- Otiartu	Otiartes (9)
(Ziusudra)	Zisudra -- Zisuthra	Xisuthros (10)

are less obvious but the table shows how the names do indeed relate. I have added a hypothetical transitional or intermediate phase, using our observed rules of consonant and syllable shift, to help understand the processes at work between the Sumerian and Hellenised versions of the antediluvian rulers.

209. A table showing how the original names of the antediluvian Sumerian rulers can be identified with the Greek versions of Berossus from the third century BC.

Stage Two of the argument introduces us to a document known as the 'Genealogy of the Hammurabi Dynasty' (GHD), published by Assyriologist Jacob FINKELSTEIN in 1966.[4]

The twentieth to twenty-ninth rulers in this list are unequivocally identical with the rulers of the Babylon I Dynasty which independently survives in the clay tablet known as Babylonian King List B. This is a very famous line of kings which includes Hammurabi and Ammisaduga. As we have seen, the latter played a major part in *A Test of Time* Volume One – thanks to the surviving astronomical observations from his reign.

Prior to Sumuabu (the founder of the Babylon I Dynasty) the GHD has nineteen names which must be the ancestors of the kings of Babylon. It should be noted, however, that there are no specific genealogical links ('son of' or 'father of') to confirm that we have here a true genealogy or perhaps, as seems more likely, simply 'selected highlights' of the ancestral line of Babylon. We have already noted how early 'genealogies' of rulers and patriarchs sometimes miss out those individuals who did not play a significant part in the traditional history of a culture. This could be another example of such a practice.

The first eight of these early ancestors in the GHD are of particular interest to us, as will soon become clear.

In the table on the following page I have listed the Genealogy of the Hammurabi Dynasty alongside the Babylonian King List. I have also added the first seventeen rulers of the Assyrian King List who, according to that document, 'lived in tents' (i.e. were not city dwellers). I have done this so that I can demonstrate to you that the Assyrian and Baby-

FINKELSTEIN: (1922-1974).

189

The GHD and AKL Compared

Genealogy of the Hammurabi Dynasty		Assyrian King List	
1	A-ra-am-ma-da-ra	1	Tudiya
2	Tu-ub-ti-ya-mu-ta	2	Adamu
3	Ya-am-ku-uz-zu-ha-lam-ma	3	Yangi
4	He-a-na	4	Kitlamu
5	Nam-zu-u	5	Harharu
6	Di-ta-nu	6	Mandaru
7	Zu-um-ma-bu	7	Imsu
8	Nam-hu-u	8	Harsu
9	Am-na-nu	9	Didanu
10	Ya-ah-ru-rum	10	Hanu
11	Ip-ti-ya-mu-ta	11	Zuabu
12	Bu-ha-zu-um	12	Nuabu
13	Su-ma-li-ka	13	Abazu
14	As-ma-du	14	Belu
15	A-bi-ya-mu-ta	15	Azarah
16	A-bi-di-ta-an	16	Ushpiya
17	Ma-am-[...]	17	Apiashal

17 kings living in tents

		Babylonian King List B	
18	Su-?-ni-[...]		
19	Da-ad-[...]		
20	Su-m[...]	1	Sumuabu
21	Su-mu-la-[...]	2	Sumulail
22	Za-bi-um	3	Sabu
23	A-pil-Sin	4	Apilsin
24	Sin-mu-ba-li-it	5	Sinmuballit
25	Ha-am-mu-ra-bi	6	Hammurabi
26	Sa-am-su-i-lu-na	7	Samsuiluna
27	A-bi-e-su-uh	8	Ebishum
28	Am-mi-di-ta-na	9	Ammiditana
29	Am-mi-sa-du-ka	10	Ammisaduga
		11	Samsuditana

1st Dynasty of Babylon

lonian royal lines had a common ancestry – even though, at this stage, a quick glance at the two sets of names appears to show no commonality at all. But a quick glance is not what is required. Something quite extraordinary has happened which almost confuses the common ancestral lineage beyond redemption. I say 'almost' because enough clues survive to uncover what may be an astonishing biblical reality. However, at this point I must just add a brief caveat. It should be remembered that we are dealing with comparative linguistics here – a topic fraught with difficulties at the best of times. As a result, any conclusions can only be regarded as reasoned speculations and nothing more.

The Lost Patriarchs

The key to the mystery of the missing patriarchs is the simple realisation that the first *eight* names in the Genealogy of the Hammurabi Dynasty represent *eleven* of the first twelve names in the Assyrian King List (AKL). This is either because the GHD has conflated pairs of distinct names into single, longer names or, perhaps more likely, because, in some cases, the AKL has taken the combined names and *epithets* of the first three Mesopotamian rulers and split them into six distinct individuals. Thus the first name in the GHD – *Aramadara* – is represented in the AKL by its fifth and sixth names – *Harharu* and *Mandaru*. Divide the GHD name into *Ara* and *Madara* and you can see the AKL names more clearly. Now try doing the same thing with GHD *Yamkuzuhalama* (position 3) and AKL *Yangi* and *Kitlamu* (positions 3 and 4). Here we can extract the syllables *Ya-am-ku* from the GHD to get *Ya-an-gi* of the AKL and *Ku-uz-lam-ma* from the GHD to reach *Ki-it-la-ma* of the AKL. A tricky process is involved here but one which becomes clear when a little time is devoted to the study of the whole group of names in the table opposite. There you will see that the first, second and third names of the GHD are equivalent to the first six names in the AKL. The rest of the names in both lists are easily discernible as single names but appearing in a different order. Thus GHD 6 *Ditanu* is clearly AKL 9 *Didanu* and GHD 4 *Heana* is AKL 10 *Hanu*; whilst GHD 5 *Namzu* is probably AKL 7 *Imsu*.

210. The obverse of the Genealogy of the Hammurabi Dynasty tablet containing the earliest rulers in the 'Genealogy' beginning with A-ra-am-ma-da-ra (after J. J. Finkelstein, 1966, p. 96). British Museum.

211. One of the common motifs in Mesopotamian glyptic art is that of the sun-god rising up between the eastern mountains at dawn. Here in this cylinder seal impression from the Agade Period we see Shamash climbing out of the underworld, knife in hand, ready to cut his way through the mountains. Either side the guardian gods stand beside gateposts which represent the gateways to heaven. Louvre Museum.

Genesis scholar, Robert Wilson, explains the muddle of the early names from the two lists in the following way:

> This type of conflation is common at the oral level, and it is possible that the early names in the GHD and the parallel names in the tent-dwelling kings in the AKL were once part of an oral genealogy or list.[5]

He goes on to explain how the Assyrian kings and their Babylonian counterparts may have ended up claiming the same lineage for their ancestral past.

> It is worth noting that Shamshi-Adad I (of Assyria) and Hammurabi (of Babylon) were contemporaries and engaged in a struggle for political dominance. Therefore there may be political significance in the fact that both kings apparently justified their right to rule by tracing a genealogy back to the same group of nomadic kings.[6]

From this brief analysis it has become clear that the kings of Babylon and Assyria did indeed claim a common ancestry. The question which now arises is whether that common ancestry – those 'nomadic kings' – can be extended to include the ancestral line of Abraham in the biblical tradition as laid out in the book of Genesis?

At this point perhaps we should take a look at that Genesis tradition a little more closely. As already noted, what we find is that there are two versions of the genealogy of the antediluvian patriarchs. The shorter of the two is presented in chapter four where we find Adam –– Cain –– Enoch –– Irad –– Mehujael –– Methushael –– Lamech –– Tubal-Cain.

212. The obverse of the tablet containing the Assyrian King List found at Khorsabad. The seventeen kings 'who lived in tents' are located in the top left-hand corner (first two columns). Late Assyrian copy of an earlier text. Louvre Museum.

The Genesis Genealogies Compared

Genesis 4:17-22	Genesis 5:3-29
1 Adam	1 Adam
2 Cain	2 Seth
3 Enoch	3 Enosh
4 Irad	4 Kenan
5 Mehujael	5 Mahalalel
6 Methushael	6 Jared
7 Lamech	7 Enoch
8 Jabal & Jubal; Tubal-Cain	8 Methuselah
	9 Lamech
	10 Noah

213. There are two genealogies of different generation-counts for the antediluvian patriarchs in Genesis (4:17-22 & 5:3-29). Are they entirely distinct lines of descent from Adam? Or does the repetition of names suggest that they derive from a single source which has been confused by two different transmissions?

The longer by two generations is found in the following chapter where we have Adam -- Seth -- Enosh -- Kenan -- Mahalalel -- Jared -- Enoch -- Methuselah -- Lamech -- Noah. Although it is often legitimately argued that these two genealogies are *not* representative of the same line of Adam's descendants, I think the names are perhaps rather too close not to suggest garbled versions of the same basic family tree. The table above shows how the two lists might be reconciled in respect of much of their contents.

In order to move our experiment towards its conclusions I now need to assume two simple propositions.

(1) I believe that the Genealogy of the Hammurabi Dynasty should be taken as a reasonably accurate representation of the *names* of the great Mesopotamian ancestors. That is to say that there were originally three rulers at the head of the line, each of whom possessed both a name and an epithet. The Assyrian King List then mistakenly took those epithets as proper names and made six rulers out of the original three. This is made more likely by the fact that the clay tablet of the AKL, listing these rulers, presents the earliest of them in two columns so that the succession is read from left to right then down one row and left to right again. This is better understood if you refer to *Figure 210* and the table on *page 190.* The outcome of all this is that there may have been an original, much earlier document which had these rulers in a double column with their epithets immediately to the left of the actual name. The Assyrian copyist of the AKL then mistook

214. Detail of the Assyrian King List (SDAS version) showing the first ancestral rulers of the kings of northern Mesopotamia (in columns 1 and 2).

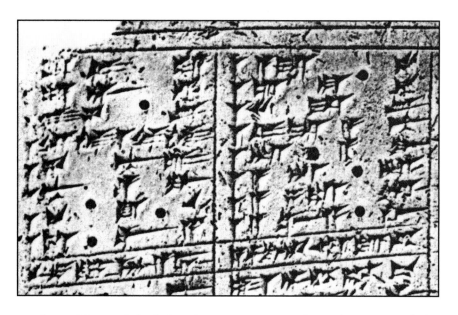

the epithets of the left column as separate kings but retained the arrangement of the names side by side as he originally found them.

Returning to the names themselves, it is necessary to remind you that in the process of copying lists of names over the centuries and the need of scribes to make sense of names perhaps not original to their tongue, the chance of metathesis taking place is quite high. In other words, *although the names have all the syllabic ingredients, they are not necessarily presented in the correct order or sequence.* The name can thus become garbled.

(2) It is also clear that there is considerable fluidity in the basic *sequence* of rulers in all three sources – the GHD, the AKL and the two genealogies of Genesis 4 and 5. Thus we cannot rely on the positions of the names in any single list. There are obvious discrepancies between the GHD and AKL in several places and this will subsequently prove also to be the case when we compare these two sources with the two biblical genealogies of Genesis which, as we have just seen, themselves disagree with each other in both the writing of the names and in respect of the order in which they appear.

With these points in mind I offer the following observations based on my brief study of the three sources.

(a) The third ruler in the GHD is called Tubtiya-Amuta. However, he appears at the head of the AKL (originally in first and second places) where he is called Tudiya-**Adam**u. This latter name may be translated as 'The Beloved of [Deity] – **Adam**'. Adam, of course, is the first antediluvian patriarch in both of the Genesis genealogies. The order of the two names suggests that Tudiya/Dudiya is an epithet. But the name Adam is also, in a sense, an epithet with the meaning 'red earth' or simply 'red'. Adam was the man created from the red earth.

> To the man (Heb. *adam*) he (God) said, 'Because you listened
> to the voice of your wife and ate from the tree of which I had
> forbidden you to eat, accursed be the earth (Heb. *adamah*)
> because of you! ... By the sweat of your face will you earn
> your food, until you return to the earth (Heb. *adamah*) from
> whence you came. For dust you are and to dust you shall return.
> [Genesis 3:17-19]

When we looked at the archaeological evidence from the Urmia basin
and elsewhere during the Neolithic Period we found that the human
remains in the burials were covered in red ochre powder. Could this
have anything to do with the biblical (and now Akkadian) tradition that
the first man in the genealogical line was related by name to the red
earth of the burial ritual? The red dust of the Hajji Firuz Tepe burials,
located at the heart of Eden, may be significant in this respect.

It is also interesting to note that metathesis has taken place in the
GHD version of the name where A-da-mu has become A-mu-ta. This,
of course, presupposes that the metathesis has not taken place the other
way around where the AKL scribe has sought to give meaning to an
unknown name and therefore switched the syllables around to produce
the common Semitic word for earth/red.

(b) The third ruler in the GHD is Yamku-Uzuhalama, corresponding to
AKL's second (originally third and fourth) name Yangi-Kitlamu. The
easiest way to see the commonality is to break the names up into
their elements. Here the common elements are Yam/Yan, ku/gi/ki
and lama/lamu.

In this case something a little different has also occurred. With the
first ruler (point (a) above) we observed that metathesis had taken
place between the AKL and GHD. It seems that a similar metathesis
is observable with the name Yamku/Yangi – but, in this case, it is
between the Mesopotamian sources and the Genesis text – so that
yam/yan and *ku/gi/ki* have been reversed. We would then have **Kiyan**
which we may equate with biblical **Kayin** – Cain, son of Adam
(Genesis 4).

(c) The first ruler in the GHD is called Ara-Madara. However, he appears
as the third (originally fifth and sixth) name in the AKL in the longer
form Harharu-Mandaru. Again let us break down these names into
their common elements: Ara/[h]aru and Madara/Ma[n]daru.

| Madara/ | MA AN | HAR A | Ara/Ha-ru |
| Ma-an-da-ru | DA RA | HA RA | |

Taking the Aramadara of the GHD, we might envisage a straight-forward biblical HYPOCORISTICON here such as **Arad**a (Ar-a-[ma]-da-[ra]) from which we would then derive the name **Irad** – that is Irad, son of Enoch, as given in Genesis 4.

(d) Equally, the AKL's Harharu could, with the inclusion of the *ma* syllable just removed from Ar-a-[ma]-da-ra, give us Maharharu. If we now apply the recognised shift from 'r' to 'l', we produce **Ma-ha-al-ha-lu** – a fair representation of the **Mahalalel** of Genesis 5 with just one simple syllable shift observed between *ha* and *lu*.

(e) Moving on to the third from last name in the AKL we see **Hanu** (GHD Heana) which appears to be the biblical **Hano**k – Enoch, son of Jared in Genesis 5.

(f) After Hanu/Enoch comes **Zuabu** who perhaps represents biblical **Tuba**l[-Cain] (Tubal[-the smith]), son of Lamech (Genesis 4).

(g) Finally, it is not difficult to see the biblical **Noa**h, also a son of Lamech (Genesis 5) in the AKL's **Nu-a**-[bu].

(h) There are further possibilities to account for the remaining patriarchs. **Lame**ch may be found in [Kit]**lamu**. Whilst the name Methuselah might just be lurking in Uz-zu-ha-lam-ma of GHD 3, where a re-ordering of the syllables might give us **Ma-zu-uz-la**(m)-**ha**.

The table opposite summarises the 'name game' experiment we have been playing which, although based on linguistic speculations, I believe produces some intriguing identification possibilities.

It is worth stressing that we are not simply dealing here with one or two linguistic coincidences but dozens of syllabic correspondences. Think about it. Just imagine an early Sumerian scribe writing the syllables of each biblical name randomly into the word boxes of a clay tablet from Uruk so that they might be read in any order. Then picture three scribes of later times independently attempting to make proper names out of the groups of sounds which they have inherited from this ancient document. Even though the Hebrew redactor (Genesis) and the two Akkadian scribes (GHD and AKL) have come up with very different sequences of syllables to make their lists of ancestral names, a later historian is still able to observe a commonality in the pre-ordered syllables. In the historical reality, what we have is three genuine documents, from widely dispersed locations and time periods, with just such a commonality of syllables. Is this simply a matter of extraordinary coincidence? What would be the chances of this being the case – unless, that is, they all really did originate from a single source document such as an early Sumerian tablet?

There thus appear to be plausible arguments for linking the common Babylonian and Assyrian ancestral traditions with the biblical tradition of the ancestors of Abraham. It should be remembered that Abraham himself is presumed to have been an Amorite and therefore of the same basic stock as the Assyrians and the Babylonian Dynasty of Hammurabi. But remember that we have also made a connection between Abraham's ancestor, Shem, and the Sumerians. Kramer believed that there was a likelihood that Abraham of Ur's ancestral line also contained Sumerian blood and that flowing through the veins of the Hebrew patriarchs was a cultural heritage from that oldest of civilisations.[7]

Conclusion Fifteen

There is linguistic evidence to suggest that the antediluvian genealogies of Genesis have common Sumerian origins along with the traditions of the early Amorite rulers.

Enoch the Builder-King

The biblical name Irad (GHD Ara[ma]da[ra]) is believed to derive from the Hebrew verb *yarad* which has the meaning 'to descend'. The Mesopotamian tradition (through the SKL and the Creation Epic) is that the first city to be founded in Sumer was Eridu (modern Tell Abu Shahrain, once by the shores of the Persian Gulf). It was first suggested by Archibald Sayce in 1885 that the city of Eridu bears the eponym of Irad – in other words that he was the eponymous founder of the city.[8] This suggestion still finds support in more recent scholarly discussions of Genesis.[9]

215. Tentative biblical identifications of the traditional ancestors of the Amorite states of Babylon I and Assyria.

GHD	AKL	Genesis
2 TU-ub-TI-YA-mu-ta ———————	1 TUDIYA ————————	ADAM – the favourite
2 tu-ub-ti-yA-MU-TA ————————	2 ADAMU	SETH
3 YA-AM-KU-uz-zu-ha-lam-ma ——	3 YANGI ————————	KAYIN/Kaynan
4 He-A-NA ————————————	10 HANU ————————	HANOK/Hanosh
1 A-RA-am-ma-da-RA ———————	5 hARhARU ————————	IRAD/Yared
1 a-ra-am-MA-DA-RA ———————	6 MAnDARU ————————	MAHALALEL/Mehujael
5 nAM-ZU-U ———————	7 IMSU	METHUSELAH/Methushael
	8 Harsu	JABAL
6 DI-TA-NU ————————————	9 DIDANU ————————	JUBAL
3 ya-am-ku-uz-ZU-HA-LAM-MA —	4 SUHLAMU ————————	LAMEH
7 ZU-um-mA-BU ————————	11 ZUABU ————————	TUBAL – the smith
8 NAm-HU-U ————————————	12 NUABU ————————	NOAH

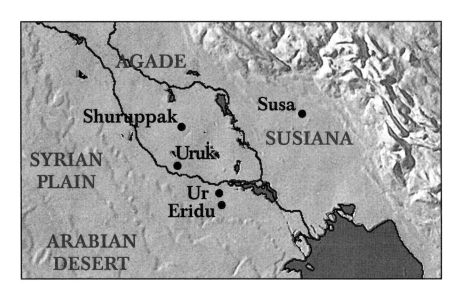

I have suggested that Adam's (Sumerian) successors moved down – 'descended' from the Zagros mountains into the plain of Susiana. Is it possible, therefore, that it was Irad, 'the one who descended', who led his people down into pre-flood Sumer and that the first city, Eridu, was named after him? There is an important clue regarding the settlement of the lowlands in Genesis 4:17.

> Cain had intercourse with his wife and she conceived and gave birth to Enoch. **He was a city builder** and gave the city the name of his son, Enoch.

At first this statement seems quite straightforward: Cain founded a city and named it Enoch. But we have come to realise that translations of the Bible can be misleading. We need to go back to the original Hebrew to recognise that there is some confusion about who founded what here. As Robert Wilson has pointed out, the subject of the phrase 'He was a city builder' is by no means clear.

> Normally one would expect the subject to be the most recently mentioned noun or pronoun, in this case the name Enoch. If this interpretation is accepted, then Enoch rather than Cain would be the city builder. [10]

The natural conclusion to draw from this reading of Genesis 4:17 is that the city built by Enoch was named after his son, Irad, and that this city was the first Sumerian city – Eridu – as originally proposed by Sayce. Indeed, the identification of the city builder as Enoch and not Cain had been suggested as long ago as 1883 by the German scholar, Karl Budde. [11] But, of course, this reading of the passage is 'undermined by the addition of the name Enoch at the end of the verse'. [12] However, Wilson tellingly points out that the standard interpretation of Cain as the builder and his son Enoch as the eponym of the city raises some serious difficulties.

(a) The clause *wayhi boneh ir* ('he was a city builder'), if it follows the normal rules of syntax displayed in the rest of the Genesis 4 genealogy, must refer to Enoch and not Cain because the name Enoch immediately precedes the clause in question. Thus we have '… she conceived and gave birth to Enoch. He was a city builder …' – the sense here is obvious.

(b) Moreover, in Genesis 4:2, Cain is described as a tiller of the earth (Heb. *obed adamah*) – in other words a farmer. It would not follow the pattern of Genesis 4 to then assign him a second occupation as a city builder. This would also deprive Enoch of a role in the genealogy.

(c) There is no known ancient city which carries the eponym of Enoch, son of Cain – according to Wilson (but see below).

Wilson concludes that 'It is therefore possible that the name Enoch at the end of 4:17 is a gloss' – that is to say an editorial addition or even a marginal note which was then, only later, placed into the main body of the text in the wrong place once the true meaning of the statement had been lost. Thus the original text would have been clear and unambiguous.

> Cain had intercourse with his wife and she conceived and gave birth to Enoch. He (Enoch) was a city builder and gave the city the name of his son (Irad).

This is all good knock-about stuff which makes a lot of sense and is supported by a number of experts including William Hallo and Donald Wiseman.[13] However, Wilson has to admit that we are dealing with linguistic conjecture here. An alternative view might be that the names of the antediluvian patriarchs have been 'invented' from ancient Sumerian documents mentioning the first cities on earth. Thus Irad is created from the early city-name Uru-du(g) where Eri and Uru are variant dialect spellings of the word for 'city'.[14]

As you know by now, I have no problem with scholars using their training, combined with imagination, to come up with new solutions to old problems. So I will offer up an extra idea which may provide us with the biblical founders for not just one but *two* great Sumerian cities. I support those who argue that Eridu was named after Irad 'the one who descended [from the mountains]' but I also believe it is possible to link the name Enoch (Irad's father) with that other important early Sumerian city which was the home of both Enmerkar and Gilgamesh – Uruk.

So far I have not given you the name of Uruk as it appears in the Sumerian language. There you will find it written Unuk or Unug – perhaps the original Sumerian name of Enoch! This may explain the biblical scribe's confusion. He added the name Enoch at the end of the city-building statement in Genesis because he knew that the mightiest city in Sumer was named after this great antediluvian patriarch. On the other hand, perhaps the marginal note 'Enoch' (proposed above) was the result of a scribe adding the name of the city which he thought was being referred to (i.e. Unuk) as a clarification. He may not have understood that Enoch had also built Eridu, naming it after his son Irad.

We could even suggest further biblical links to the eponymous founders of the Sumerian cities. The city of Ur, excavated by Leonard Woolley, is transcribed logographically as *uru.Unuki* in Sumerian. The name became shortened or hypocorised to Urum in Akkadian and then simply Uru/Ur in Semitic/Hebrew.[15] Ur means 'city' but the original Uru-Unuki might be understood as 'City of Unuki' – in other words 'City of Enoch'.

What is more, another patriarch may be identified with a Sumerian antediluvian city – Badtibira – which was the second political centre (after Eridu) to which 'kingship was handed down from heaven'.

Badtibira means 'Settlement of the Metal Worker'. If we take the Hebrew consonants which make up the name Tubal we get T-b-l. We know that the soft consonant 'l' is often representative of 'r', thus we might get an original T-b-r which could, in turn, stem from ancient Tibira.[16] Interestingly enough the Semitic epithet 'Cain' in Tubal-Cain also means 'smith' which suggests that this epithet has been added as a clarification of a little-known Sumerian word by the Hebrew author of Genesis. So there are clues which suggest that Tubal-Cain and Badtibira are connected in some way. Perhaps we have here an original eponym 'Settlement of Tubal' or, in translation, 'City of the Smith'.

217. Illustration of the fish-man, Oannes, made by Layard during the recording of the Assyrian reliefs at Nimrud.

Conclusion Sixteen

Several of the early Sumerian cities seem to have been named after their eponymous founders. They appear in Genesis 4-5 as the antediluvian ancestors of Abraham.

The Great Sages

We have closely examined the earliest ancestors of both the Genealogy of the Hammurabi Dynasty and the Assyrian King List and found a series of remarkable linguistic 'coincidences' with the names of the biblical antediluvian patriarchs. But we began this whole exercise with Berossus and the Sumerian King List. So what about the Sumerian – as opposed to Amorite – tradition regarding the pre-flood rulers? Is there anything in this source which will add to our linguistic and historical synthesis between Genesis and the extra-biblical traditions?

We now come to the question of the Sumerian *apkallu*s or wise-men. These are not the antediluvian kings themselves but the sages or advisors associated with them.

> Mesopotamian literature contains sporadic references to seven sages (apkallus), who lived before the flood and who were apparently regarded as the originators of the arts and skills of civilisation.[17]

Aalu, king	Uan, apkallu
Alalgar, king	Uanduga, apkallu
Ameluana, king	Enmeduga, apkallu
Amegalana, king	Enmegalama, apkallu
E[nm]eusumgalana, king	Enmebuluga, apkallu
Dumuzi, the shepherd king	Anenlilda, apkallu
Enmeduranki, king	Utuabzu, apkallu

218. The kings and apkallus of the antediluvian era as recorded in text W-20030,7.[18]

Who were these extraordinary beings? They are given very strange physical characteristics (fish-like bodies with human heads) and, to all intents and purposes, are mythological creatures. But, once the mythological veils are removed, there seems to be a distant memory of some of the antediluvian patriarchs of Genesis lurking in the names and deeds of these apkallus.

According to the apkallu tradition, the first and greatest of the sages was a contemporary of King Aalu (SKL – Alulim), the first ruler of Eridu. This was the 'the purification priest of Eridu', Adapa or Uan-Adapa, who 'ascended to heaven'.[19] Berossus calls him Oannes (from Uan).

In tablet W-20030, held by the British Museum, we find just the name 'Uan' given for the first sage. However, Uan also appears in other ancient texts in the double-name form of Uan-Adapa where, it has been argued, Adapa is an epithet meaning 'the wise'.[20] One possible explanation of the myth that this wise counsellor of the king was half fish and half human is to be found in the potential confusion of the word Adapa with another similar sounding Sumerian word – *utuaba* – which means 'born of the sea'. With the recognised changes from *u* to *a*, *t* to *d* and *b* to *p* we would get Aduapa. Given the apkallus' close connection with the sacred abzu in Eridu, it would hardly be surprising to find a tradition of a sea creature derived from the epithet Adapa, even though the true meaning was probably 'wise-man' and not 'one born of the sea'. According to a much later inscription of of the late SELEUCID PERIOD, Oannes-Adapa was the founder of a temple of great antiquity, perhaps the earliest sacred shrine of Eridu – the very first temple on earth.[21]

All this becomes much more significant when it is realised that many Sumerologists and biblical scholars have made the direct connection between Adapa and the biblical Adam. One simple shift from the consonantal *p* to *m* gives us the biblical name. We can then read the Sumerian Adapa Epic in a wholly new light. Let us briefly compare the broad themes of the Genesis 2-3 narrative surrounding Adam and the story of Adapa. As Bill Shea has observed, there are clear parallels to be made.[22]

- Both Adam and Adapa were tested for their obedience by their respective deities.

- The test, in both cases, involved food.

219. The lower surviving part of a door-jamb relief from the palace of Cyrus II at Pasargad, showing the figure of Oannes in his half-human and half-fish form.

SELEUCID PERIOD: 312-65 BC.

- Both forfeited immortality and became mortal human beings.

- Certain consequences were passed down upon humankind.

- Adam and Adapa belonged to the first generation of humankind.

- As we have seen, their names can be equated linguistically.[23]

Thus Adam not only appears in the Assyrian King List and the Genealogy of the Hammurabi Dynasty but may also surfaces in one of the great Sumerian epic traditions.

In this same tradition surrounding the Seven Sages of Sumer there is another potential biblical link. The last of the sages – Utuabzu – is said not to have died and been buried but instead, like Adapa, was taken up to heaven. This is a similar incident to that recorded in Genesis 5:24 where 'Enoch walked with God and was no more, for God took him'. Now there is, of course, no connection between the names Utuabzu and Enoch but there could be with the name of Utuabzu's king. The last element of the name En-me-dur-**anki** is equivalent to the biblical **Hanok**. Could the biblical tradition concerning Enoch's ascension into heaven be a confusion of the Sumerian tradition that Enmeduranki's (i.e. Enoch's) apkallu was taken up to heaven?

The Story of Adapa

Adapa was the first great sage who introduced the worship of the gods to humankind. He was the high priest of Ea's shrine at Eridu. One day he went out into the sea in his boat where he was caught in a storm. Angry with the elements, Adapa cursed the South Wind, breaking his wing. As a result, the wind did not blow for seven days. This change in the natural order of things was noticed by Anu, god of heaven, and he sent for Adapa in order to punish him. Before the priest of Eridu had reached heaven he was warned by Ea that he would be offered the bread and water of death which he must refuse. When Adapa finally arrived in heaven he explained that his curse upon the South Wind was in retaliation for the sinking of his boat by the storm. Once Anu realised what had transpired he was sympathetic to the priest of Eridu and offered him the ultimate gift – the bread and water of eternal life. But, of course, Adapa refused the priceless gift of the gods and returned to the earth to die a mortal's death. At this point the tablet breaks off and we are left without an explanation as to why Adapa's patron deity had played such a cruel trick on his devoted servant. The irony is that Adam defied God by eating the forbidden fruit, whereas Adapa refused the food of the gods. Both, however, were denied eternal life for rejecting the instructions of the high god.

> ## Conclusion Seventeen
>
> The Sumerian legends surrounding Adapa, the sage of Eridu, contain several literary elements which parallel the biblical story of Adam.

It is all very well suggesting extra-biblical counterparts for the ante-diluvian patriarchs – after all, the connections I have brought to your attention could certainly originate from a common tradition concerning real characters from the prehistoric age. However, with the biblical creation story we are surely once more back in the realms of fable. Of course, we would have to conclude that the Garden of Eden section of Genesis itself has little in the way of real history and rather more of the miraculous contained within it. But should we necessarily be looking for genuine history here? It is surely also the ancient historian's task to search for connections between the *mythological* traditions of Sumer and the Bible. If, as I have argued, the stories in Genesis lie at the heart of both cultures – because they have a common ancestry – then the creation myths in both traditions should demonstrate similar aspects or features.

It may not surprise you to learn that just such an exercise in literary synthesis has been underway since cuneiform texts first began to be translated. Sumerologists and Akkadian scholars have concentrated much of their considerable talents into finding parallels between the mythologies of Genesis and those of Mesopotamia. This is a subject of far less contention and controversy in comparison to the enterprise in which we are currently involved, because it is an exercise in comparative literature rather than historical analysis. However, there are bound to be implications for our historical research if a commonality in literary tradition were to be discovered. It is encouraging therefore to know that this aspect of Sumerology has been pursued with considerable success. Although the material is barely known outside specialist circles, there have been a number of intriguing suggestions made by leading Mesopotamian scholars which throw fascinating light on some of the more obscure aspects of the Genesis 1-11 narrative. Let us start with Adam and his creation.

Adam: Man of Clay.

The name Adam itself is not a Sumerian word but belongs to the West Semitic language group where, as we have seen, it means 'red' or 'earth'. However, it does appear as a 'Semitic loan-word' in the Sumerian vocabulary where it stands for 'people'/'humanity'.[24] Interestingly, 'Adam' occurs in a Canaanite text from the city of UGARIT in Syria where it is associated with El, the head of the Ugaritic pantheon. El, of course, is also one of the early names of God in Genesis. Such discoveries help to put the biblical narrative into an historical context and give us confidence that

UGARIT: A large and powerful trading city on the north-western coast of Syria. In the New Chronology Ugarit is a Phoenician Bronze Age city.

220. An ivory plaque known as 'Earthly Paradise' carved in ninth-century France. The uppermost panel shows Adam and Eve with the Tree of Knowledge entwined by the serpent. The rest of the panels portray the descending orders of creation known as the 'Etymologies'. Louvre Museum.

221. This seal impression from the Agade Period shows the sun-god Shamash slitting the throat of another god. We cannot be certain which myth is involved here but it may be part of the Atrahasis Epic in which a deity is slain in order to provide the life-blood for the creation of humankind.

the first book of the Bible has ancient roots. So, when we read, on a small cuneiform tablet, that the epithet for the great Canaanite god, El, was *Ab-Adam* – 'Father of Man' – it supports our contention that the Eden story extends beyond the boundaries of the biblical environment.

In 1969, Wilfred Lambert and Alan Millard, in their definitive study of the Atrahasis Epic, saw a close parallel between that elaborate myth and the biblical idea of mankind being made from the dust of the earth. [25]

> The author (of the Atrahasis Epic) used what was the generally accepted view (in Sumerian mythology) … that Man was formed from clay mixed with the blood of a slain god … 'Clay' in this context is the material substance of the human body. This can be learnt from a number of passages that speak of death as a 'returning to clay'. Exactly the same concept is shown in the Hebrew account of Man's creation … (in Genesis 3:19).

Although the additional element of the god's blood occurs in the Mesopotamian tradition, we do have this interesting parallel of the creator god crafting his human beings from clay just as a potter would throw his pots or mould clay figurines.

> Yahweh God shaped Man (Heb. *Adam*) from the dust (Heb. *aphar*) of the earth (Heb. *adamah*) and blew the breath of life into his nostrils, and Man became a living being. [Genesis 2:7]

> … return to the earth (Heb. *adamah*), as you were taken from it. For dust (Heb. *aphar*) you are and to dust (Heb. *aphar*) you shall return. [Genesis 3:19]

Here the word *aphar* is translated as 'dust' for poetical reasons, but this word also has the meaning 'clay'. So in both the biblical and Mesopotamian traditions Man was made from clay.

Returning to the Atrahasis Epic we find another parallel. Nammu, the goddess of the primeval ocean and the mother of Enki, asks her son to create human beings so that they might act as servants for the gods.

> O my son (Enki) rise from your bed … (and) work your wisdom! Fashion servants of the gods in their own likeness.

Enki gathers together all the 'good and princely craftsmen' and replies:

> O my mother, the creature whose name you uttered (shall) exist. (Instructions to the clay workers:) Attribute to it **the likeness of the gods**. Mix the heart of the **clay** which is over the abyss. (You) the good and princely craftsmen will work the clay. You shall bring the limbs into existence as Ninmah (another name for Ninhursag) supervises you. The goddess (of birth) … will stand by you as you fashion (your creations). O my mother, decree its (the new-born's) fate. Ninmah will attribute to it **the mould of the gods** – (for) it is **Man**.

222. Opposite page: The very ancient craft of pottery making. Many early civilisations conceived of the creation of mankind by a potter-deity. This potter is from the village of Áali in Bahrain.

Here we not only find Man made from clay but also that the making of humankind is in the image of the gods. The biblical parallel is clear.

> God said '**Let us make Man in our own image – in the likeness of ourselves** – and let them be masters of the fish of the sea, the birds of heaven, the cattle, all the wild animals and all the creatures that creep along the ground'. (And so) **God created Man in the image of himself. In the image of God** he created him. Male and female he created them. [Genesis 1:26-27]

Note the use of the plural in God's words: 'Let **us** make Man in **our** own image – in the likeness of **ourselves**'. Indeed, one of the words for 'God' in Genesis is *Elohim* which is itself a plural (the singular being *El*). The primeval god of Genesis has many aspects which manifest themselves, outside the biblical tradition, in the form of numerous deities, each with its own attributes – sky, earth, water, etc. You can just picture Enki speaking to the other gods (his other divine aspects), persuading them by flattery that they could do with human servants 'in their own likeness' to tend to their needs. The god of Genesis, likewise creates Eve as Adam's 'helper'.

> Yahweh God said 'It is not right that Man should be alone. I shall make him a helper'. [Genesis 2:18]

Adam himself is in effect a servant of God. He is created to 'till the soil' [Genesis 2:6] and to 'cultivate and take care of' the Garden of Eden [Genesis 2:15]. So, not only is humankind made in the image of deity but it was also invented to serve the needs of its creator(s). The parallels between the creation of Adam and Eve in the book of Genesis and the fashioning of humanity in the Sumerian Creation Epic are too close for them not to have developed from a single original concept.

The fact that Enki – the god of wisdom and the abyss – was also the Sumerian deity responsible for creating humankind, inevitably brings us to the major question of the Sumerian identity of the Hebrew/Israelite god of Moses, the traditional author of the book of Genesis.

The Name of God

> Moses then said to God, 'Look, if I go to the Israelites and say to them, "The god of your ancestors has sent me to you," and they say to me, "What is his name?", what am I to tell them?' God said to Moses, '**I am who I am**'. [Exodus 3:13-14]

As we have learnt, Enki ('Lord of the Earth') was called Ea in Akkadian (East Semitic) – that is to say in the Babylonian tradition. Scholars have determined that Ea was vocalised as 'Éya'. So, when Moses stood before the burning bush and asked the name of the god of the mountain, did he really reply 'I am who I am' (Heb. *Eyah asher eyah*)? This puzzling phrase has long perplexed theologians but now there is a simple explanation.

The voice of God simply replied '*Eyah asher Eyah*' – 'I am (the one) who is called Eyah' – the name of Ea in its West Semitic (i.e. Hebrew) form. Scholars have simply failed to recognise that this is another of those characteristic puns in which the Old Testament abounds. 'I am (*Eyah*) he who is called (*asher*) Ea (*Eyah*)' is a classic biblical play on words. It also explains God's apparently nonsensical instruction: 'This is what you are to say to the Israelites, "I am has sent me to you". God's words should really be translated as 'Eyah has sent me to you'.

'Eyah' or simply 'Ya' is the hypocoristic form of the name **Ya**hweh found as an element of so many Old Testament names. So Enki/Ea, the god who created Man and then later warned Ziusudra/Utnapishtim of the impending destruction of mankind, is one and the same as the god of Moses.

This was the great revelation given to the hero of Exodus during his long exile from Egypt in the wilderness of Sinai. It was only when Moses came into contact with the Midianite priest, Jethro, that the highly Egyptianised Israelite learnt of a much earlier history for his people – their origins in the land of Eden, their descent into Shinar and the name of their primeval God.

223. The original Sumerian symbol for 'god' (Sum. *dingir*, Akk. *ilu*) above, with its cuneiform (Old Babylonian) counterpart (below).

Like Moses, the Midianites were also descended from the patriarch, Abraham, through the sons of his lesser wife, Keturah. But they had not suffered the oppression in the land of Egypt, having split off from the Abrahamic tribe and settled in north-western Arabia [Genesis 25:1-6]. They had not lost their cultural and religious identity through slavery under the yoke of a pharaonic civilisation with different beliefs and traditions. So it is likely that the Midianites would have been culturally much closer to their origins than the Israelites. Did they have a rich oral tradition stretching back to ancestral Mesopotamia? Or perhaps they carried with them original cuneiform tablets relating the different myths and epics of their ancestors from Sumer? Was this the message which Moses brought back to his people in Egypt? It certainly seems so when we re-read Exodus 3:13-15 in this new light.

> Moses then said to God, 'Look, if I go to the Israelites and say to them **"The god of your ancestors** has sent me to you," and they say to me "What is his name?", what am I to tell them?' God said to Moses '**I am he who is called Ea**'. And he said, 'This is what you are to say to the Israelites, "**Ea has sent me to you**". You are to tell the Israelites, "**Yahweh, the god of your ancestors**, the god of Abraham, Isaac and Jacob, has sent me to you." This is my name for all time and in this way I am to be invoked for all generations to come.'

The implications are clear: the Israelites did not know the name Ea and so it follows that they had little idea of their ancestral heritage. All this had to be taught them by Moses. Hence the need for a book of 'origins' – a book which the Jewish scholars of Alexandria called 'Genesis'.

Following the plagues of Exodus, the Israelites departed from the land of the pharaohs and dwelt in the desert for forty years. So, was this the time when the book of Genesis was formulated? And did Moses employ those same ancient tablets, held by Jethro, to construct the story of the epic origins of the Israelite nation? Moses and the Midianite holy man certainly met up once again at the foot of the sacred mountain of the Ten Commandments following the Israelite Exodus from Egypt.

> Then Jethro, Moses father-in-law, with Moses' sons and wife, came to Moses in the desert where he was encamped at the Mountain of God. [Exodus 18:5]

I think it is also interesting to note that at this meeting it is Jethro – the Midianite priest – and not Moses who makes sacrifice to Yahweh.

> Jethro, Moses' father-in-law, then offered a burnt offering and other sacrifices to God, and Aaron and all the elders of Israel came and ate with Moses' father-in-law in the presence of God. [Exodus 18:12]

His officiation as the leading player in the sacrificial rites would make very much more sense if Jethro was, in fact, already a priest of Ya/Ea – the long-time god of the Midianites and the only-recently-rediscovered ancestral god of the Israelites.

With our identification of Yahweh with the Akkadian god Ea and the Sumerian god Enki we have an opportunity to compare the characters/attributes of the deities to see if they represent the same basic natural elements. The following is the authoritative view of Yahweh as presented in the Anchor Bible Dictionary.[26]

> While the date and origins of the name are debatable, the character of Yahweh is certainly clear, although multifaceted in the biblical text. He is a storm god who speaks in the thunder, who hurls or shoots lightning (Exodus 19:16-19; 20:18; Psalm 18:14; Job 37:5; Amos 1:2; Habakkuk 3:11). He is a god of the mountains (Exodus 19; 1 Kings 20:3). Fire is both a sign of Yahweh's presence and a weapon (Exodus 13:21; 1 Kings 18:38). He is a god of the desert (Judges 5:4). He has control over the waters of the earth – the sea (Exodus 14:21; Jonah), the rivers (Joshua 3:16-17), and the rain (Genesis 2:5; 1 Kings 17). He is the giver of life and one who brings death. He is a god of war and of peace.

There are some aspects here which are characteristics of Ea/Enki who is the life-giving deity of fresh water, but there are many others which reflect the more violent nature of Enlil ('Lord of the Air') who was the head of the Mesopotamian pantheon, Baal ('Lord'), the Canaanite storm god, and Seth, the Egyptian god of the desert. The god of Moses thus reflects an amalgam of deities. It would appear that 'Prince' Moses, influenced as he was by both Egyptian religious beliefs and those of the neighbouring Canaanite states, elaborated greatly upon the ancestral god of Midian and Israel. The Yahweh of Moses and Joshua was a god of his time – a god of tremendous natural destructive forces – a god who was capable of rescuing the children of Israel from bondage in Egypt and destroying all those who might prevent their march towards the Promised Land. But beneath the chaotic surface of the destructive and vengeful Yahweh of Exodus and Conquest beats the benevolent and life-giving heart of the Sumerian god of wisdom – Enki, lord of the sweet water which was so vital to survival in the arid desert.

Conclusion Eighteen

Yahweh of the Old Testament was known to the Semitic tribes of Mesopotamia as Ea and to the Sumerians as Enki.

We now turn to the question of Eve.

Eve: Mother of All the Living

The Hebrew name of the first woman is *Hawwah*. Jewish tradition links this very rare name with the prime verbal root 'to make live' – *hayah* – which is itself an Akkadian word.[27] This concept is no doubt connected with Eve's magnificent epithet or title.

> Adam named his wife Hawwah because she was the **'Mother of All the Living'** (Heb. *em kal hay*). [Genesis 3:20]

Is it pure coincidence that the 'Mother of All the Living' is precisely the title born by Ninhursag, the Sumerian 'Lady (or more strictly Mistress) of the Mountain'? I do not think so.

Earlier, in Genesis 2:21-23, we read of the creation of Eve. The first woman and great mother is not formed from clay or the earth, like her male counterpart.

224. Eve drawn from the rib of Adam. Medieval painting on display in the Condé Museum, Chantilly.

> Yahweh God made the man (Adam) fall into a deep sleep. And, while he was asleep, he took one of his ribs and closed the flesh up again forthwith. Yahweh **God fashioned the rib he had taken from the man into a woman,** and brought her to the man. And the man said: 'This one at last is bone of my bones and flesh of my flesh! She is to be called Woman (Heb. *ish-shah*), because she was taken from Man (Heb. *ish*).'

Here, again, we find a remarkable parallel with the Sumerian paradise myth but, this time, the extra-biblical text provides a fascinating explanation for the strange biblical motif of Woman being crafted from the rib of Man.

225. Opposite page: A striking symbol of the Jewish faith is the seven-branched menorah candelabrum. Above is the 'Adam and Eve Seal' or 'Temptation Seal' from the British Museum with its seven-branched Tree of Knowledge of Good and Evil.

In the Sumerian version we find that Enki (who we now identify with Yahweh) is cursed by the great mother-goddess, Ninhursag, because he has eaten forbidden plants growing in paradise. Kramer, the translator of the text, notes yet another parallel with the biblical paradise myth.

> Enki's eating of the eight plants and the curse uttered against him for his misdeed recall the eating of the fruit of the tree of knowledge by Adam and Eve and the curses pronounced against each of them for this sinful action.[28]

Enki's health begins to fail and the other gods realise that he is dying. They persuade Ninhursag to relent and she sets about the task of curing Enki's sickness, creating a goddess called Ninti to cure his failing bones.

> My brother (Enki), what hurts you? My rib hurts me. To the goddess **Nin-ti** ('Lady of the Rib') I (Ninhursag) have given birth for you.[29]

Now the word for 'rib' in Sumerian is *ti* which happens also to be the Sumerian verb 'to make live'. So the Mesopotamian author of the myth is employing a pun to equate the 'Lady of the Rib' (Ninti) with the 'Lady Who Makes Live' (Ninti) – that is the goddess who brings Enki back to life from his near-death condition.

When Kramer first translated the ancient text of the Sumerian paradise myth, he immediately saw in this passage an explanation for the biblical story of Adam's rib.[30] The author (or perhaps the later redactor) of Genesis, when he adapted this myth in order to incorporate elements of it into the biblical narrative, was clearly unaware of the fact that the Sumerian tale involved a play on words and so simply translated *ti* as 'rib'. Thus Eve is created from a rib and, because there is no similarity between the Hebrew words for 'rib' (*tsalah*) and 'to make live' (*hayah*) the pun is lost. What remains of the hidden meaning, however, is the epithet 'Mother of All the Living' which is itself the predominant attribute of the great mother-goddess, Ninhursag (also known as Nintu and Mami), who bears the epithet 'Mother of All Offspring' (Sum. *Ana-dumu-dumu-ene*). It seems, then, that Eve may have begun her existence in the literature of mankind as a goddess but, because of the monotheistic tenets of the Israelite religion she becomes humanised – made mortal – and, although retaining her status as 'Mother of All the Living' is demoted to the role of spouse to the first man to be made of clay by the god of creation. Alternatively, one might see a human Eve as the original inspiration behind the worship of the divine mother-goddess of ancient Mesopotamia.

Conclusion Nineteen

Eve is closely associated with the Sumerian high goddess Ninhursag through her epithet 'Mother of All the Living'.

Cush fathered Nimrod who was the first potentate on earth. He was
a mighty hunter in the eyes of Yahweh ...

Genesis 10:8-9

226. Opposite page: The famous Uruk Stela depicting the hunter-king of Uruk killing two lions with spear and arrow. Baghdad Museum.

227. Left: A carved stone of the Uruk Period depicting an early Sumerian ruler of Uruk offering a tall jar to the goddess Inanna. British Museum.

Chapter Seven

BEYOND THE GOLDEN AGE

We now should turn our attention to the post-diluvian period – the era of the sons and immediate descendants of Noah.

The Mighty Hunter

In June of 1995 I was invited to southern Germany to present a series of papers at the *Wort und Wissen* annual conference. Wort und Wissen ('Word and Knowledge') is a Christian evangelical group. As you can imagine, I get quite a few offers to talk to Christian organisations about my research. I have no problem with this because what I have been able to reveal about biblical history through the New Chronology is available to everyone. I see myself merely as the messenger. The message of the historical truth which forms the backbone of the Bible is there for all to study and use as they see fit and, clearly, that historical truth is of considerable interest to all devout Christians, Jews and Muslims, as well as those interested in the ancient past simply for history's sake.

The Wort und Wissen conference was held in a charming Bavarian mountain retreat just outside Stuttgart. This was the first time I had presented my discoveries to a German audience and, as had been the case in the UK, the reaction was one of amazement and great excitement. Finally, someone had been able to demonstrate that the Old Testament narratives were not merely a series of folk-tales built around a completely unhistorical framework but, as they had always felt, a true history of the Hebrew/Israelite people.

Soon after I had finished my last lecture a hailstorm of biblical proportions descended upon the mountain where we were gathered.

228. In this detail from the Khafaje bowl a divine hero, wearing a net skirt, grasps two serpents by their necks. He stands between a pair of recumbent lions, heads turned back towards this 'Master of Animals'. In front of the hero a six-petalled rosette has been carved – the earliest floral motif of the goddess Inanna of Uruk. This elaborate image represents the 'long-haired hero' so common to seals of the Early Dynastic Period and later. When such images of the long-haired Master of Animals were first discovered it was thought that they represented the hero Gilgamesh; however, I think they are more likely to be representations of Gilgamesh's companion – the long-haired wild-man, Enkidu. British Museum.

Hailstones, the size of golf-balls, came crashing down onto the terrace outside the lecture room. Within a matter of minutes they had covered the ground to a depth of ten centimetres or more. The violence of the storm was incredible, the noise deafening. I had seen nothing like this before in the harshest of winters, let alone in the middle of a long, hot Bavarian summer.

The biblical history which I had brought to light was very much constructed at the human level – explainable within a framework of known human activity. I had intentionally omitted the miraculous elements of the Old Testament narratives because I felt that I was not qualified to discuss such things on any sort of academic or philosophical level. They did not play a part in my history of the ancient world because I could not explain them without recourse to 'faith'.

Our little 'miracle', experienced in the mountains of southern Germany, served to remind me that the powers of nature are truly awe-inspiring and can be understandably unbelievable to those who have not personally witnessed them. Given nature's climatic marvels, can historians really be so confident that a terrible deluge did not take place 5,100 years ago in the heart of Mesopotamia? This most dynamic of miracles may have been real enough to those who experienced it and lived to recount the tale. In that recounting its scale may have been much exaggerated for the sake of dramatic effect in the oral tradition – but there is no doubt, as the multiple sources bear witness, that this was an event which left a deep memory in many of the cultural traditions of the ancient Near East.

We now turn to the survivors of that great flood to tell the story of what happened to them when Sumer began to pick up the pieces following the deluge catastrophe.

I have mentioned my trip to Germany as a way of introducing you to another unusual scholar who has made an important contribution to this book. As a mark of gratitude for coming to disseminate my New Chronology theory to his group, the Chairman of Wort und Wissen presented me with the gift of a book written by Werner Papke entitled *Die geheime Botschaft des Gilgamesch*.[1] This was apparently a reissue of a previous work of the author entitled *Die Sterne von Babylon*. It would not surprise me to learn that you have never heard of this German scholar. That is not difficult to understand given the somewhat esoteric nature of his research. As the two titles of his book ('The Secret Message of Gilgamesh' and 'The Stars of Babylon') imply, this highly imaginative study revolves around the identification of Sumerian hero-figures and gods with the constellations of the heavens. The epic legends of Sumer are set amongst the stars even though the original events may have been real historical incidents. The transfer of human activity to the heavenly sphere is very characteristic of ancient theology. Humans become gods and are transfigured into the undying stars. This was certainly true of both Babylonian and Egyptian religious beliefs.

In the process of putting his case Papke, like Walker, raises some very intriguing identification possibilities which have influenced my own rather more down-to-earth research. In particular, he puts forward two proposals which I find rather interesting – mainly because they fit well into the historical and archaeological framework we have been developing for the Genesis heroes.

The first of these identifications involves a figure who is by now well known to you – Enmerkar – the second ruler of Uruk after the great flood. We have already seen how this Sumerian hero was much eulogised by the minstrels and bards of later times. He and Gilgamesh stand out as the two most-written-about human heroes of the heroic age. Given what we have already discovered about the Sumerian identities of the biblical heroes of Genesis, is it really conceivable that neither of these famous Sumerian supermen appear on the biblical stage? With Gilgamesh perhaps (I have found nothing to link him directly with the Genesis narrative), but Enmerkar may well be there, hidden behind the disguise of one of the Bible's most elusive and enigmatic characters.

Let us look at the name Enmerkar. In most of the Sumerian literature Enmerkar's name is written En-me-kar. In slightly later texts we find En-me-er-kar. This is consistent with the development of the written Sumerian language where the more explicit orthography of the later texts painstakingly includes all the amissible consonants of a name which would not have been expressed in the older texts.[2] In deference to the later addition of the 'r' consonant, scholars tend to write the Sumerian hero's name as 'Enmerkar'. However, one copy of the Sumerian King List, found at Nippur and published by Arno Poebel in 1914, gives En-me-er-ru-kar.[3] We might, therefore, justifiably vocalise the name as Enmerukar.

Next we come to a crucial point. The four syllables En-me-ru-kar can be understood as a name plus an epithet – once it is realised that *kar* is the Sumerian word for 'hunter'(Akk. *habilu*). Thus we have King 'En-me-ru, the hunter'.[4]

Now put yourself into the mind of the biblical author/redactor who first wrote the book of Genesis. Whether he worked from cuneiform tablets or oral tradition can only be guessed at, although, as we have observed, there are good grounds to suggest the former. However, if we assume that he was confronted with this name 'En-me-ru the hunter', how would he have recorded

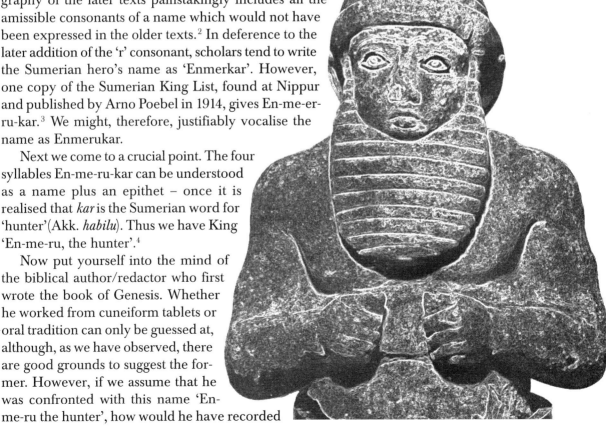

229. A statuette from Uruk representing a ruler of that city from the Uruk IV Period. Note his turban or chignon and the full beard. This is a familiar figure in early Sumerian art of the Uruk Period known as the 'priest-king'. He is often shown making offerings to the goddess Inanna before her shrine at the heart of the Eanna complex. In my view all such images represent a single individual – King Enmerkar who, according to Sumerian tradition, introduced the cult of Inanna to Uruk. Baghdad Museum.

230. A fascinating and intriguing cylinder seal impression from the Old Assyrian Period. On the left the bull-man is seen grappling with a lion. The Sumerian symbol next to the lion's thigh reads 'demon' (Sum. *dim*); the two signs to the right of the bull-man say just that – 'wild-bull-man' (Sum. *am.sag*). The divine hero Gilgamesh is constantly referred to in the Gilgamesh Epic as the 'wild-bull'. Next we see a divine being introducing a child and a ruler to the moon-god Sin. This time the label in front of the divine being (with horned helmet) reads 'hunter + mighty' (Sum. *kar.nun*, Akk. *habilu rabu*). This is precisely the epithet employed by Genesis to describe 'Nimrod the mighty hunter in the eyes of the lord'. In the view of Werner Papke this seal shows the inauguration of an early Assyrian king spiritually supported by two of the legendary heroes of Mesopotamia – Gilgamesh and Enmerkar (Nimrod) of Uruk.

it in its early Hebrew form? Remembering that the vowels of the Hebrew language were only finally indicated by the Masoretic pointing system from the fifth century AD onwards, the earlier scribe would have simply inscribed n-m-r without any written indication as to the sound of the name. As a result, over time, the true phonetic pronunciation may have been lost.

Take these three consonants and add the epithet 'the hunter' and we may easily arrive at 'Nimru the hunter'. Is this not Nimrod, the 'mighty hunter' – the great builder-king of Genesis, the son of Cush and the great-grandson of Noah?[5]

> Cush fathered Nimrod who was the first potentate on earth. He was a mighty hunter in the eyes of Yahweh, hence the saying, 'Like **Nimrod, a mighty hunter** in the eyes of Yahweh'. The main centres of his empire were Babel, Erech and Accad, all of them in the land of Shinar. [Genesis 10:8-10]

Look at what we have here. Nimrod was closely associated with Erech – the biblical name for Uruk – where Enmerkar ruled. Enmerkar built a great sacred precinct at Uruk and constructed a temple at Eridu – that much we know from the epic poem 'Enmerkar and the Lord of Aratta'. The Sumerian King List adds that Enmerkar was 'the one who built Uruk'. Nimrod was also a great builder, constructing the cities of Uruk, Akkad and Babel. Both Nimrod and Enmerkar were renowned for their huntsmanship. Nimrod, as the grandson of Ham, belongs to the second 'generation' after the flood (Noah –– Ham –– Flood –– Cush –– Nimrod) and this is also true of Enmerkar who is recorded in the Sumerian King List as the second ruler of Uruk after the flood (Ubartutu –– (Utnapishtim) –– Flood –– Meskiagkasher –– Enmerkar). Both ruled over their empires in the land of Shinar/Sumer.

Could Papke have finally found the biblical Nimrod – the first great potentate on earth? I think so. Nimrod turns out to be the Sumerian hero whose career we have been following ever since *Chapter Two* when we went in search of Aratta and the Garden of Eden. The pieces of the Genesis jigsaw puzzle continue to fall into place.

Cush and the Sea

Moving on to the second of Papke's proposals, it may have already occurred to you that another identification possibility presents itself here. If Ziusudra/Utnapishtim is Noah and Enmerkar of Uruk is Nimrod, does that not mean that Enmerkar's father and predecessor on the throne of Uruk must be the biblical Cush, son of Ham and grandson of Noah? The first ruler of Uruk following the flood is called Meskiag**kash**er [6] in the Sumerian King List. You will immediately see the name Cush or Kush here, embedded in the longer Sumerian name. It seems likely that Cush is a Semitic/Hebrew hypocoristicon of the older Sumerian name Mes-ki-ag-**ka-she**-er. We are now fairly used to the idea of hypocoristicons or short-form familiar names: Shysha for Riamashesha (Ramesses), Ameny for Amenemhat and Pul for Tiglath-pileser. This last example is very useful because it is a biblical reference to a Mesopotamian king (II Kings 15:19 & I Chronicles 5:26) and displays exactly the same shortening as we are proposing for the earlier ruler of the region. Pul is simply the single, meaningless element *pil* in [Tiglath-]**pil**[eser] just as *kash* (kush) is in the name [Meskiag]**kash**[er].

The likelihood of a second major discovery on the part of Papke becomes even more intriguing when we learn that the Sumerian King List singles out this ruler for special attention. In the list of the kings of Uruk we find the following note attached to Meskiagkasher's name.

> Meskiagkasher went down into the sea and came out to the mountains. [SKL column iii, lines 4-6]

231. One of the most famous cylinder seals from the ancient world shows a king of Uruk (with turban/chignon, beard and heavy calf-length coat) escorting the portable shrine of Inanna (carried on the back of an ox). The shrine is being transported on a high-prowed boat typically employed in the Sumerian marshlands of southern Iraq. Staatliche Museen, Berlin.

I find this cryptic line tantalising. What does it mean? Surely we cannot take the preposition 'into' to mean literally that he went for a swim or took a dip in the sea! We must understand the passage as a poetical way of saying that the king of Uruk went out *onto* the sea by ship and eventually landed in a place where there were mountains. A better translation would thus be:

> Meskiagkasher journeyed across the sea and came ashore in a mountainous land.

Conclusion Twenty

The first two legendary kings of the Uruk I Dynasty – Meskiagkasher and Enmerkar – are to be identified with the heroes of Genesis known as Cush and Nimrod.

If Meskiagkasher can be identified with the biblical Cush then we are entering new territory in both the literal and metaphorical senses. The Bible tells us that the sons of Noah were the progenitors of all the great nations of the ancient Near East. I am referring here to the famous so-called 'Table of Nations' which takes up the whole of Chapter 10 of Genesis.

The well-known event which leads us to Chapter 10 is the construction of the first great building on earth – the Tower of Babel.

A Confusion of Tongues

The earliest of the epic tales from Sumer which I introduced you to was 'Enmerkar and the Lord of Aratta'. We must now briefly return to this work to forge another link between Sumerian tradition and the Genesis narrative. The Enmerkar saga opens with a reminiscence of the peace and security which prevailed during Man's first golden age.

> Once upon a time, … there was no fear, no terror. Man had no rival. … The whole universe, the people in unison (?), to Enlil in one tongue gave praise.[7]

The phrase 'in one tongue' is a remarkable affirmation of Genesis 11:1 where we read that before the building of the Tower of Babel 'The whole world was of one language and of one speech'. In the golden age the supreme god of the Sumerians was Enlil – 'Lord of the Air' – and he was worshipped by all humanity.

Even though we may view the expression 'in one tongue' as a literary device, meaning no more than that they worshipped Enlil 'with one heart' or 'with one voice', we can still see a clear connection between the book of Genesis and the Enmerkar epic of the Sumerians.[8] The biblical text (which Jewish tradition ascribes to Moses) takes the literal view that one language prevailed in Shinar. But the more subtle understanding that I am suggesting here is very interesting from an historian's perspective. Moreover, this interpretation that there was a unity of religion rather than language is supported by the adjectival phrase 'many-tongued Sumer' which occurs just before 'the people in unison, to Enlil in one tongue gave praise'. This would clearly be a contradiction unless we understand 'to Enlil in one tongue gave praise' to mean simply that religious beliefs were common to all. We can be certain that both Sumerian *and* Semitic were spoken in Mesopotamia in this early period because many of the kings' names in the First Dynasty of Kish (contemporary with the First Dynasty of Uruk) were of Semitic origin.

I can just picture Moses, as he dwelt amongst the Midianites, either coming across this expression 'in one tongue' in Jethro's cuneiform copy of 'Enmerkar and the Lord of Aratta' or listening to his father-in-law, the Midianite priest, giving an oral rendition of the 'golden age' tradition. Remember that the earliest copy of 'Enmerkar and the Lord of Aratta' which has come into our possession is dated to the reign of Ammisaduga of the Old Babylonian Period (Babylon I Dynasty) and, in the New Chronology, this king's first year is dated to 1419 BC. The biblical date of the Exodus is 1447 BC and the period of the Sinai wanderings thus falls between 1447 and 1407 BC – precisely when Ammisaduga is on the throne in Babylon and in the very period when the great Sumerian epics

232. A typical artist's visualisation of the biblical Tower of Babel is represented by this late sixteenth century painting by Maerten van Valckenborch. However, such impressions have little to do with the reality of Man's first temple-tower which can now be revealed through archaeology. Staatliche Kunstsammlungen, Dresden.

are being written for the first time in Akkadian. If Moses was the original author of Genesis, then he was writing his history of the Israelite ancestors at the very time when the Amorite rulers of Babylon were popularising the epic stories of their Mesopotamian ancestors. Given the numerous parallels between the two sets of narratives, there must surely have been a connection by cultural transmission.

So, when Moses set to the task of composing the book of Genesis, he somehow knew of the tradition of the golden age when the people worshipped their omnipotent god in a single tongue. However, he opted for the literal meaning of a single-tongued Shinar and, in doing so, hid from us the true significance of the religious unity which prevailed before the flood. This may have been deliberate. Given his newly acquired Yahwistic theology, this literal interpretation avoided any awkward problems over his ancestors worshipping a supreme deity who was not the *sole* deity on earth and who was not actually the god of Moses – Yahweh of Sinai and the Midianites. The one-god teachings of Moses could never sit comfortably with a golden age of the ancestors when there was a father-god, Enlil (Akkadian Ellil - the biblical El?), a mother-goddess, Ninhursag, and a son-god, Enki/Ea, as well as a plethora of other minor deities. The idea of a trinity, although common to many ancient religions, did not form a part of Israelite theology and only became a Christian concept with the spread of the gospel out into a pagan world where the principle of the sacred family was a well-established theological device.

So the whole episode in Genesis of the confusion of tongues may be nothing more than a misinterpretation of an ancient Sumerian tradition. We should perhaps reinterpret the biblical story as a religious rather than linguistic development. After the great flood had swept over the land, the purity of the supreme-deity religion which had previously existed became weakened with the introduction of new gods and the raising up of the minor gods in the primeval pantheon as powerful city-state deities in their own right. Thus Inanna was brought down from Aratta and elevated by Enmerkar as an equal to Anu ('Lord of Heaven') in Uruk; the moon-god Sin ruled supreme in Ur; Enki, the god of the watery abyss, was worshipped at Eridu; Utu, the sun-god, was the lord of Shuruppak, and Inshushinak ('Lord of Susa') dominated Elamite Susiana. Enlil only remained supreme in Nippur. The oneness of early Sumerian religion evolved into a disunity of religious worship and, as a result, the world became a more dangerous place.

This was reflected in the rush, during the Uruk Period, to build huge temple complexes at the hearts of the cities. The post-Ubaid era also saw the introduction of temple platforms upon which the houses of the gods were situated. Man had begun his quest to reach up to the heavens and this brings us back to the story of the Tower of Babel. So who was the king who ordered the building of the first man-made mountain – the original stairway to heaven? You may have already determined the answer to that question.

We have now learnt so much about Enmerkar that he has naturally become our prime suspect. As we have seen, it was this king who brought the goddess of Aratta down to the Mesopotamian plain and erected for her a magnificent sacred precinct called the Eanna or 'House of Heaven'. We have noted the splendour of the architecture in Uruk City IV – the city I have ascribed to Enmerkar. We have also conjectured that Enmerkar is none other than the first great potentate on earth – the biblical Nimrod. We can now read the words of Josephus to discover that it was the biblical King Nimrod who built the first ziggurat.

> Now it was Nimrod who excited them (the people of Shinar) to such an affront and contempt of God. ... He also said he would be revenged on God, if he should have a mind to drown the world again. To that end he would build a tower too high for the waters to be able to reach and so he would avenge himself on God for destroying their forefathers![9]

Who was this god whom Nimrod despised so greatly for destroying the world in a deluge? According to the Old Babylonian flood epic, it was no less a god than the supreme deity and head of the Sumerian pantheon – Enlil (Akkadian Ellil) – who was kept awake by the clamour of the rapidly expanding human population.

> The land became wide, the people became numerous, the land bellowed like wild oxen. The god (Ellil) was disturbed by their uproar. ... [Ellil] set up his assembly, speaking to the gods, his sons: '[...] do not arrange for them. [The people] have not diminished; they are more numerous than before. [Because of] their noise I am disturbed; [because of] their uproar sleep cannot seize me.' [Atrahasis Epic, lines 2-4 Old Babylonian version & 37-41 Neo-Assyrian version]

I think we can begin to see a fascinating sequence of historical events here leading us from the antediluvian golden age of a supreme god to the realities of the post-flood era and a multiplicity of city-state deities.

- Enlil, the god of the air and the head of the pantheon, in a fit of pique over the clamour of humanity, sends the rains which bring about the destruction of mankind. Quite justifiably, the survivors of the flood are never subsequently as well disposed to him. In fact, the 'word of Enlil' was, in later times, to become the harbinger of destruction.[10] When the Gutian hordes descended upon the cities of the plain to bring about the fall of the Dynasty of Agade, the disaster was equated with the deluge and Enlil also took the blame for this *human* flood.

  > On the day that Enlil brought down the Guti from the moun-tain-land, whose coming is **the flood of Enlil** which no-one can stand ... [Lamentation Over the Destruction of Sumer and Ur, lines 75-6]

- Just as Yahweh makes Noah aware of the impending deluge, it is Ea who warns Utnapishtim that Ellil is planning to destroy mankind in a devastating flood. Ea is clearly the major challenger to Ellil's supreme authority. The former is often portrayed as going against Ellil's haughty cruelty in his desire to help and protect mankind.

So, what are the implications of all this if we recognise Ellil (the East Semitic name of Enlil) as the biblical (West Semitic) high-god El? We have already determined that Ea (the East Semitic name of Enki) may turn out to be Yahweh, the adopted (West Semitic) god of Moses. Could there be an explanation here for the confusion of the *two* names of God in the early Old Testament? Was El, the god of Abraham, eventually usurped by Yahweh because of his malevolence towards humanity?

- We should take note that Utnapishtim, upon his departure from the ark, does not make sacrifice to Ellil in gratitude for the preservation of his life but rather to Ishtar (Inanna) and the rest of the gods.

> Then I (Utnapishtim) let out (all) the four winds and offered a sacrifice. I poured out a libation on top of the mountain. … The gods smelled the sweet savour (and) the gods crowded like flies about the sacrificer. When at length the great goddess (Ishtar/Inanna) arrived she lifted up the great jewels which Anu had fashioned for her pleasure. (To Utnapishstim she said:) … Let the gods come to the offering, **but let not Ellil come to the offering**, for he, unreasoning, brought on the deluge and (caused) my people (to be) consigned to destruction. [Gilgamesh Epic, Tablet XI, lines 155-69]

- Following the flood, Enmerkar (whom we have identified as Nimrod, great-grandson of Noah) introduces a new female deity to his city of Uruk in the form of Inanna and builds a lavish temple to Enki in Eridu. According to Josephus, Nimrod also orders the construction of a great tower in defiance of the former supreme deity. This is the tower which the Bible calls the 'Tower of Babel'.

- Now, just such a tower or platform was constructed at Eridu in the period we have assigned to Enmerkar (see *Chapter Eleven*). This 'prototype' of the ziggurat is acknowledged as the first great edifice to be built by humankind. Was the massive Uruk-Period temple platform at Eridu the source for the biblical story of the Tower of Babel?

The difficulty here is that one expects the Tower of Babel to be located in Babylon. However, this may be an idea from much later times when the Jews of Jerusalem were exiled in that city. They saw for themselves the ziggurat of Babylon every day and may naturally have assumed this to be the cause of God's anger. But this ziggurat dates from the Babylon I Period (NC – 1667-1362 BC) and no evidence has come to light which shows that a temple-tower existed in Babylon as far back as the Protoliterate era. In fact, Babylon itself does not appear in contemporary texts until fairly late in Mesopotamian history, suggesting that the city was of no great importance in the immediate post-flood epoch – if it existed at all. So how could the first temple-tower have been built there? Our dilema may be put down to an error on the part of the author of Genesis.

During my research I came across the extraordinary fact that Eridu and Babylon once bore the same name. The two cities were both called *Nun.ki* ('Place of Nun') in the Sumerian language. Perhaps Moses (or whoever the Genesis writer was) simply mixed up two places with an identical Sumerian name and inadvertently located the prototype ziggurat at thecity of Babylon when, in reality, it was an achievement of the much earlier city of Eridu. This would also explain why the biblical Nimrod was responsible for great builing-works at Erech and Babel. This Babel too was derived from a misinterpretation of Nun.ki. Nimrod actually built Uruk and Eridu – just as Enmerkar, the mighty builder-king, lavished his attentions on the temples of Uruk and Eridu.

Conclusion Twenty-One

The first platform temple was that constructed at Eridu (Sum. *Nun.ki*) rather than the much later ziggurat of Babylon (Sum. *Nun.ki*). The mistaken identification of the Tower of Babel is further evidence that some of the original sources for the Genesis composition were Sumerian.

The Table of Nations

It has long been recognised that the biblical redactor saw the different civilisations and language-groups of the ancient world as originating from a single family – naturally the family of Noah – survivors of the flood which destroyed the antediluvian civilisation and its sinful multitudes. This is an obvious and rather simplistic mechanism to explain the 're-population of the earth' following the deluge. But could there be any historical reality to this list of descendant nations of the flood hero?

The rest of this book is all about investigating that intriguing possibility. The story begins, or rather continues, with Cush and his three brothers – Mizraim, Put and Canaan – whom the biblical redactor recognises as the eponymous founders of the lands of Kush (Ethiopia), Musri (Egypt), Put (Libya) and Canaan (Lebanon/Phoenicia).

In his *Chronikon*, Eusebius informs us that Cush was the ancestor from whom the Ethiopians descended.[11] Josephus has the same basic story.

> … of the four sons of Ham, time has not at all hurt the name of Chus (Cush); for the Ethiopians, over whom he reigned, are even to this day both by themselves and by all men in Asia,

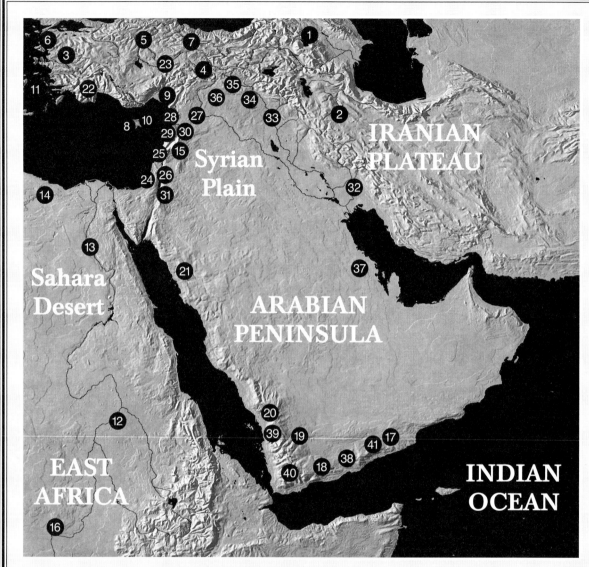

The Table of Nations

The Line of Japheth	The Line of Ham	Ham (continued)	The Line of Shem
1 – Gomer	12 – Cush (Kush)	23 – Caphtor (Kaptara)	32 – Elam
2 – Madai (Medes)	13 – Mizraim (Egypt)	24 – Philistines	33 – Ashur (Assyria)
3 – Javan	14 – Put (Libya)	25 – Sidon	34 – Aram
4 – Tubal	15 – Canaan	26 – Jebusites	35 – Eber
5 – Meshech	16 – Seba	27 – Amorites	36 – Abraham
6 – Tiras (Teresh)	17 – Havilah	28 – Arvadites	37 – Joktan
7 – Togarmah	18 – Sabtah	29 – Zemarites	38 – Hazarmaveth
8 – Elishah (Alashiya)	19 – Raamah	30 – Hamathites	39 – Sheba
9 – Tarshish (Tarsus)	20 – Sheba	31 – Sodomites	40 – Ophir
10 – Kittim	21 – Dedan		41 – Havilah
11 – Danunai (Greece)	22 – Lud (Lydia)		

called Chusites (Kushites). The memory also of the Mesraites
is preserved in their name; for all we who inhabit this country
(of Judea) call Egypt Mestre, and the Egyptians Mestreans.
Phut also was the founder of Libyia, and called the inhabitants
Phutites, from himself. [12]

The Septuagint concurs in associating Cush with the Ethiopians and the
Egyptians themselves constantly referred to their warlike southern neighbour as the land of Kush. So the Bible and the early historians all transport
Cush, grandson of Noah, to Africa. How might he have got there? By
boat perhaps? Certainly if we are looking for a route from southern Mesopotamia to the highlands of Ethiopia in north-eastern Africa we would
logically look to the sea rather than a crossing of the inhospitable Arabian
desert. Remember the perplexing gloss to the name Meskiagkasher in
the Sumerian King List – 'Meskiagkasher journeyed across the sea and
came ashore in a mountainous land'. Is this single, brief remark the key
to understanding the historical mechanism at work in the Table of
Nations? Josephus, having retold the story of Nimrod's Tower of Babel
and the subsequent confusion of tongues, goes on to explain that Cush,
his three brothers and their followers journeyed to their new homes across
the sea.

> After this they (Noah's descendants) were dispersed abroad,
> on account of their languages, and went out by colonies every-
> where … **Some also passed over the sea in ships and
> inhabited the islands** – and some of those nations still retain
> the names which were given them by their first founders.[13]

It is clear from this passage that at least part of the dispersion was across
water. It is an obvious point to make, but I will make it anyway to ensure
that no-one is in doubt about the significance of Josephus' words. The
waters which border on the land of Sumer do not form part of the Mediterranean (the 'Upper Sea') but rather the Persian Gulf (the 'Lower Sea')
and, beyond, the Indian Ocean. According to Josephus, on their way to
Africa, the followers of Cush, Mizraim, Put and Canaan occupied islands.
We will shortly discover which islands are being referred to here.

I have tentatively identified Meskiagkasher as the biblical Cush who,
according to Genesis, was the eponymous ancestor of the land of Kush
in Ethiopia/Sudan. Did Cush and his brothers really journey across the
sea to a new, virgin land on the mountainous shore of the African continent? To find out we must make our way down from the city of Uruk
through the marshes of southern Mesopotamia to Eridu and the shores
of the Lower Sea. Here in the 'harbour of the abyss', within the shadow
of the original temple-tower, our transport awaits.

Yahweh scattered them thence all over the world, and they ceased from building the city.

Genesis 11:8

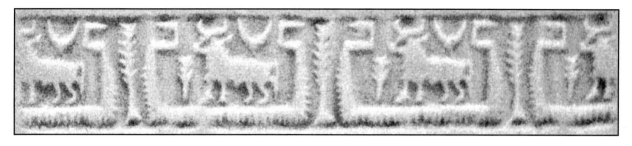

Chapter Eight

PARADISE REGAINED

So climb aboard our reed ship moored in the harbour of Eridu and head south with me through the coastal marshes and on out into the Lower Sea. The time has come to retrace the journey which Meskiagkasher and his followers made to the 'mountain land' at the dawn of the third millennium BC – a journey which will eventually take us to Egypt in search of the origins of pharaonic civilisation.

The northerly winds drive our ship quickly along the west coast of the Persian Gulf and by sunrise on the second day the peak of 'Smokey Mountain' (Arab. *Gebel ed-Dukhan*) rises above the sultry haze ahead of us. We are approaching the island of Bahrain – the ancient Abode of the Blessed.

Place of the Two Waters

Bahrain is an amazing place in many respects. Its tiny size – just forty-three by sixteen kilometres (an area of five hundred and sixty-two square kilometres) – belies its strategic importance. Located between Meso-potamia and the mouth of the PERSIAN GULF which leads to the Indian continent and the East African coast, it was perfectly positioned to act as an entrepôt or trading emporium for goods destined for Sumer and, later, Babylon and Assyria. The 'middlemen' of ancient Bahrain became the *de facto* merchants of the Lower Sea, shipping copper ore and diorite from Magan and gold, tin, ivory and semi-precious stones (such as lapis lazuli and cornelian) from Meluhha.[1]

Magan or Makan has been identified with the Musandam peninsula of Oman and adjacent coastline. This seems to be confirmed by STRABO who calls this region Macae.

233. Opposite page: Doré's Tower of Babel.

234. Above: Seal impression from Bahrain of a high-prowed boat with sacred plant, bull and Sin standard.

235. Paradise in the Persian Gulf.

PERSIAN GULF: Also called the Arabian Gulf, covering an area of 233,100 sq. km and with a maximum depth of 91 m. From the Shatt el-Arab to the Straits of Hormuz it extends for a distance of 965 km.

STRABO: (*c.* 63 BC to AD 21). Greek geographer born in Amasya, Turkey.

227

236. The sea routes from Sumer/Iraq to Dilmun/Bahrain, Magan/Oman and Meluhha/Indus Valley.

ERATOSTHENES: A mathematician, astronomer and geographer from Cyrene (276-196 BC).

CARMANIA: The ancient name of the eastern Iranian province of Kerman.

HARRAPAN CULTURE: The name given to the Early Bronze Age culture of the Indus valley which the Sumerians knew as Meluhha. Archaeologists have named the civilisation after the site of Harrapa – the ruin mound of one of its largest cities.

237. Bahrain island, showing that all the ancient sites are located in the northern plain.

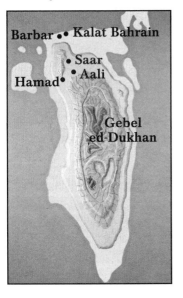

Now the Persian Gulf is also called the Persian Sea; and ERATOS-THENES describes it as follows: its mouth, he says, is so narrow that from Harmozi (Hormuz), the promontory of CARMANIA, one can see the promontory at Macae (Magan) in Arabia.[2]

So much for Magan, but what about Bahrain's other great trading partner – Meluhha? After years of discussion and debate most scholars now recognise Meluhha as the Indus valley of Pakistan and, in particular, the so-called HARRAPAN CULTURE of that region.

Evidence of occupation on Bahrain island goes back to the Neolithic Age when a small group of settlers lived on the slopes of Gebel ed-Dukhan. Then the main period of settlement began in the middle centuries of the third millennium (NC – c. 2600 BC), otherwise known as the Early Dynastic Period. However, historians acknowledge that the discovery of late-Ubaid pottery (so far in small quantities) indicates limited occupation in the fourth millennium.

The sudden decline in the archaeological remains of Bahrain which is observed around the middle of the second millennium BC is usually explained by the transfer of Mesopotamian copper ore trading links to Cyprus ('copper land') following the diminution of mining operations in Oman.[3] This marginalised the middlemen of Bahrain and left them cast adrift from their principal market. At around the same time the mineral-rich civilisation of the Indus valley was overrun by the Aryan tribes from the Iranian plateau, thus terminally disrupting Bahrain's other key supplier. The economy of Bahrain island collapsed and the once flourishing ports and villages were soon abandoned.

The main land-mass of the Bahrain archipelago is a desert island in the classical sense with several oases of palm groves scattered around its central rocky hill. The Gebel ed-Dukhan (literally 'mountain of smoke') rises only about one hundred and thirty-five metres above an otherwise flat terrain, surrounded by coral reefs and salt marshes. Close to the

shoreline in these marshy areas the Asal reed once flourished. Today the marshlands are much depleted but the Asal is still employed for the weaving of baskets and mats.

238. The central peak of Gebel ed-Dukhan ('Smokey Mountain').

The main peak is confined within what looks to all the world like a volcanic crater with a ridge forming a ring around the central cone. However, the geologists say that this was never a volcanic formation, being composed of limestone rather than igneous rocks.

The rest of the flat, lozenge-shaped island is dotted with freshwater springs which well up from a deep underground source. Sadly, the majority have been 'municipalised' and can no longer offer visitors the idyll of an earlier age. However, a typical scene of life at one of these freshwater springs has been recreated in the grounds of the island's top resort hotel which gives a good idea of the paradise that Bahrain once was. The various pools were surrounded by ruins from many periods

239. The idyll of one of Bahrain's abzu springs as it would have looked in ancient times. Re-established within the grounds of the Meridien Hotel, Manama.

240. Opposite page (above): The underwater abzu which still survives to the north of the island of Muharrak.

241. Opposite page (below): Part of the large Bronze Age (and later Assyrian) settlement exposed by the Danish excavations at Kalat Bahrain. Viewed from the walls of the Portuguese fortress.

and these sacred sites seem to have played a major role in the culture of the island in ancient times. The richness of the vegetation around the springs, with their shady date-palm groves and abundant exotic wildlife, have been acclaimed for millennia. Most of the village settlements are on the north side of the island where the modern capital Manama is located. This was also the case with the ancient sites such as Kalat Bahrain ('Fortress of Bahrain'), Barbar Temple and the settlement of Saar.

Other islands of the Bahrain archipelago include Muharrak, Sitrah, Nebbi-Saleh, Sayeh and Khaseifah. The main island, although usually referred to as Bahrain, is also known as Awal. However, we know from early geographers, such as Strabo, Pliny and Ptolemy, that Awal and Muharrak once bore the much more ancient names of Tylos and Arad.

Have you ever considered what 'Bahrain' means? If you read *A Test of Time* Volume One, you will have noted that Bahr Yussef (the name of a water channel flowing from the Nile into the Faiyum basin) is to be translated as the 'Waterway of Joseph'. *Bahr* is therefore the Arabic for 'water' or 'waters' as we would understand the waters of a lake, pool, river or sea. The Arabic word *maya*, on the other hand, is to be understood more as the physical property of water, like drinking water in a glass. Now Arabic possesses something called a 'dual-ending' which effectively converts the noun into a dual plural. Thus an *ein* or *ain* ending turns *bahr* from 'waters' to *bahrain* the 'twin waters' or 'dual seas'.

Why should Bahrain be called the 'twin waters'? The reason is that a remarkable natural occurrence takes place just off the northern shore of the island. Here, opposite the island of Muharrak (ancient Arad), you can row out into the salt sea of the Gulf, dive to the sea-bed and collect fresh drinking water. It was once possible to do the same opposite the temple site of Barbar on the north shore of the main island before land reclamation put an end to the miracle. On the floor of the sea are artesian vents or aquifers through which the water from vast underground lakes bubbles up to the surface. This remarkable phenomenon is what gives Bahrain its name. It is the place of meeting of the salt and sweet waters – the twin seas.

The Green One

The miracle of Bahrain island has been known for thousands of years. It is even featured in Sura 55 of the Koran.

> He (God) has mingled (Arab. *maraja*) the two seas (Arab. *bahrani*) which meet one another. Between them is a division which they do not overpass. From these come forth pearls (*marjan*) and coral (*marjan*). [Sura 55:19-22]

That the 'two seas' represent the salt and the sweet is confirmed by Suras 25:53 and 35:13. The Arabic word *marjan* originally meant 'pearls' but was later adopted for 'coral'. Bahrain is justifiably famous for both its

The Temple of Enki

The Sumerian water-god, Enki (Semitic Ea) (242, above left), was also one of the major deities of Dilmun. It is believed that the temple of Barbar on the northern coast of Bahrain was his local shrine. This Early Bronze Age temple has a number of interesting features which will play a part later in our story. The central section of the Barbar temple consists of a sandy core mound encased in a revetment (sloping) sleeve which is, in turn, surrounded by an outer casing of aslar (cut-stone) blocks. In places this stone wall curves around the oval mound (243, above right). On the central platform the worshippers constructed an open court within which the rituals took place. Here the archaeologists found stones with holes cut into them (244, below right) and which are believed to be tethering posts for the sacrificial animals previously coralled in the oval pen beyond the platform in the model (245, below left). But the most important element was the abzu spring (246, bottom right) which was reached down a long flight of stairs from the central platform (see model, foreground). It was within this sweet water which welled up from beneath the earth that Enki was supposed to dwell.

coral and pearls, the latter being its main source of income for centuries until the advent of petroleum oil. You will also note that the word which the Koran uses for the 'two seas' is *bahrani* – the very term from which the name Bahrain derives. Even the prophet Moses is transported to the place of 'the meeting of the two seas' in Sura 18.

> Moses was up against mysteries which he wanted to explore. He searched out a man endued with knowledge derived from the divine springs from which flow the paradoxes of life. ... [Commentary on Sura 18, Section 9]

> Behold Moses said to his servant: I will not stop until I reach the meeting of the two seas (Arab. *majma el-bahraini*), even if I travel for years. But when they reached the meeting between the two (seas), they forgot (about) their fish which made its way into the sea by a hidden passage. [Sura 18:60-61]

The mention of a 'hidden passage' which leads from the land into the sea is obscure but may be connected with the springs of the abyss which the ancients knew not only surfaced on Bahrain island but also flowed out into the salt ocean to the north of the island. It seems likely that the Koran has in mind an escape route for the fish which permits it to reach the sea by diving into an onshore pool and then swimming through the abyss to another of its outlets beneath the sea. Local tradition has an equally tall tale to tell. The inhabitants of Bahrain relate the story of a camel which once fell into one of the island's springs, its corpse to appear days later floating in the sea north of the island.

Moses journeyed to the place of the two seas to find el-Khadr ('the Green One') – a mysterious holy man who had been granted immortality by God. El-Khadr was to be found beside the 'Fountain of the Paradoxes of Life' at the place where the two seas meet. Arabian specialist, Michael Rice, explains where the Islamic scholars now believe this place to be.

> It must be said that traditionally the commentaries on the Quran have always assumed the objective of Moses' journey to have been Suez where two seas, the Red Sea and the Mediterranean, may be said to meet. However, modern scholarship has tended to suggest that the Quran means precisely what it says and that it is to 'the place of the two seas'; that is, to Bahrain in the Gulf, that Moses directs his wanderings.[4]

The episode in the Koran involving Moses' visit to Bahrain is not the only source of el-Khadr's fame. He is clearly an important figure in other Arabic and Near Eastern folklore which originates *outside* Islamic teaching. The Green One is even occasionally referred to as the 'son of Adam' – whatever we may make of that.

I must stress that el-Khadr is not simply a character from children's fables. He seems to have been regarded as a genuine figure from the past and a saint – so much so that he has a holy shrine dedicated to him on the island of Failaka, just off the coast of Kuwait. This shrine is 'of considerable antiquity' and stands upon a mound which, although it cannot be excavated because of Islamic law, may project the cult of el-Khadr much further back in time to a period well beyond the Islamic era.[5] He has always been regarded as the patron of seafarers and the resident of an island in the Gulf. So who might this immortal 'Green One' who resides by the Fountain of Life at 'the place of the mingling of the two waters' be? The Koranic references and the Arabic tradition must surely be retaining here a distant memory of the hero of the flood, Utnapishtim, who resides for eternity in the 'Land of the Living' and who was also visited by Moses' distant predecessor, Gilgamesh of Uruk.

The Two-Horned One

Right at the beginning of our adventure I argued that extraordinary human beings were often elevated to the status of deity or supernatural being by their descendants. These special humans are the very stuff of legend. All through our investigations we have seen this transfiguration mechanism at work, and there is much more to come when we turn our attention to Egypt. But, since we are at present dealing with Sura 18 of the Koran, I should just mention the most famous example of an historical character who was subsequently transformed into a legendary hero.

Sura 18 moves on from the story of Moses and el-Khadr to relate the tradition of Zul-Karnain – the 'Two-Horned One'. He was greatly favoured by God who bequeathed to him rulership over the whole world. Almost unanimously (but excluding the Iranian Shiites) the Koranic scholars recognise in Zul-Karnain the historical figure of Alexander the Great.

The Macedonian's name was known throughout the Near East – fixed for all time in the eponyms of the cities he founded, such as Alexandria, Iskenderun and Sikunder. Yet he takes on a new persona or disguise as the 'Two-Horned One' of Arabic tradition. Why? Because the instantly memorable iconographic image of Alexander during his conquest of the Persian empire and beyond into India was that of a king wearing a ram's-horn helmet. This was no doubt acquired by the young king to advertise the fact to all that he had been ordained by the Oracle of Siwa as the earthly successor of Zeus-Ammon. He was the 'son' of the Egyptian high-god, Amun, whose representative in the animal world was the ram. So it was quite natural to represent him with the horns of his deification. Many of the coins of the time show Alexander wearing his ram's-horns and these little masterpieces were undoubtedly the mechanism of transmission of the legend. The semi-divine king became the Two-Horned One – the mighty conqueror – Lord of the East and West – the nemesis of the great Persian empire. Alexander never conquered Arabia but his legend nevertheless thrives within Islamic folklore to this day, despite the fact that the individual historical events surrounding his short life have been long forgotten by the storytellers.

247. A silver coin depicting the head of Alexander the Great with ram's horns signifying his deification as the son of Zeus-Ammon. Bahrain National Museum.

Sacred Mounds of the Ghosts

So much of the ancient past is lost to us today. Sometimes, as in the case of the legendary Alexander, we can get much closer to the reality behind the legend by studying reports or commentaries about the hero's achievements, written by eyewitnesses to his campaigns. In that respect King Alexander lived in what we can safely described as the 'historical era'. Yet, in spite of this, legends are capable of attaching themselves to heroes which then mythologise the historical truth of even the best-known and attested figures of history. But in *Legend* we are dealing with much older material which was of hoary antiquity even in Alexander's time.

We now turn to one of the great enigmas of archaeology which, if we interpret it correctly, should give us more of the answers we seek in our continuing quest for the origins of civilisation. In this case we have no texts to guide us and no epic literature which deals directly with the subject now under investigation. But there are hints and whispers scattered throughout the collective wisdom of the ancient world. These tantalising clues manifest themselves in the various traditions of cultural origins, in myths of the paradisiacal islands of the dead and in the religious beliefs surrounding the journey of the soul through the underworld. All this, of course, falls beyond the realm of human experience and lies within the sphere of gods and ghosts. Yet the archaeology of the Isle of the Blest, the Isle of Avalon, Valhalla, the Abode of the Blessed, the Elysian Fields, the Field of Reeds, still exists – if only we should choose to look for it.

I introduce you to Bahrain's most amazing archaeological 'curiosity' through the words of explorer Theodore Bent who delivered a long report on his visit to the island at a meeting of the Royal Geographic Society on the 25th of November 1889. Having spent some time relating the physical and cultural aspects of nineteenth-century Bahrain, Bent eventually begins to describe the day he and his wife headed south out of Manama, the capital city, on their way to the open desert beyond the date-palm groves.

> Here we came upon what is really the greatest curiosity of Bahrain, to investigate which was our real object in visiting the island, namely the vast sea of sepulchral mounds which extends as if from a culminating point at a village called Aali, just on the borders of the date-groves; at this point the mounds reach an elevation of over forty feet, and as they extend further southwards they diminish in size, until miles away in the direction of Rufaa we found mounds elevated only a few feet above the level of the desert, and some mere circular heaps of stones. This is a vast necropolis of some unknown race, to discover which was our object in excavating.[6]

This is Bahrain's greatest and most perplexing mystery – hundreds of thousands of tumuli occupy vast swathes of the landscape. No other place on earth possesses anything like this – not even ancient Egypt. In parts

of Bahrain island the tombs once stretched as far as the eye could see, but in recent years virtually every one of these great cemeteries has been bulldozed flat for housing development. It is a sad fact to report that the modern needs of the growing Bahraini population are responsible for the destruction of what was undoubtedly one of the greatest archaeological wonders of the ancient world. A number of the largest tumuli still remain, hemmed in by the rapidly expanding village of Aali. However, even these impressive monuments to Bahrain's past have not escaped the attentions of their newly acquired neighbours. The villagers of Aali actually make use of the burial mounds as kilns for the manufacture of pottery!

When were these remarkable tombs constructed? Unfortunately for our developing thesis, archaeologists proclaim that there is no evidence to date the mounds before the Early Dynastic Period. The pottery from the burial chambers tells us that from then on the practice of burying the dead in tumuli lasted until the Hellenistic Period, but no pottery from the earlier Uruk or Jemdet Nasr periods has been found associated with these tombs. This is a very strange situation because, as we have seen, the preceding Ubaid archaeological phase is well attested all along the Arabian coast.

So the Ubaidian pre-flood culture had already exploited the Gulf as far as Bahrain and beyond, yet seemingly no serious attempt had been made to settle Bahrain island itself in this long period or during the succeeding Protoliterate Period (that is the Uruk IV and Jemdet Nasr eras) when we know that the Sumerians of southern Mesopotamia were expanding their horizons in every direction. This apparent absence of archaeological remains is even more curious when we consider the historical identity of the place we now call Bahrain.

Abode of the Blessed

It is quite clear from the archaeological investigations which have taken place over the last hundred years that Bahrain was somehow marked out as sacred or holy ground in the Sumerian era. How else could we explain the enormous number of funerary tumuli on such a tiny island? Bahrain is one vast city of the dead. Estimates of the numbers of burials have been climbing steadily and have now reached the quarter of a million mark. The figure began at 50,000 (Peter Cornwall in 1943), then doubled to 100,000 (Geoffrey Bibby in 1969) before jumping again up to 172,000 (Curtis Larsen – 1983). By the 1980s it had risen again, this time to 200,000 (Moawiyah Ibrahim in 1983) and currently stands at an incredible 250,000 to 300,000 (Serge Cleuziou).[7] All scholars now agree that the number exceeds 150,000.

The initial conclusion which many archaeologists and historians made was that the island was a Sumerian sacred burial ground – a sort of Valhalla or Isle of the Blest in the mould of the mythical abodes of the

248. Opposite page (above): The vast field of tumuli near the village of Aali. Much of the cemetery has been removed by development in recent years but, even so, the site is still very impressive.

249. Opposite page (below): Excavating one of the large mounds in the heart of Aali village.

250. Aerial view of one of the large mounds in Aali. The deep cutting is what remains of early excavations along the original entrance corridor of the tumulus to gain access into the central burial chamber.

Mounds of the Dead

The tumulus tombs of Bahrain are spectacular not just because of their enormous numbers and size but also on account of their elaborate structure – especially with respect to the so-called Royal Tombs at Aali. Typically the burial chambers are lined with stone blocks two or three deep. There are often two rooms stacked one on top of the other and separated by large slabs which act as ceiling to the lower chamber and floor to the upper chamber. The plan (251, right) and cross-section (252, below right) are based on drawings made by archaeologists and illustrate the main features of a typical Aali mound. Once the central burial complex was constructed in stone, a corridor was built to the outside edge of the proposed tumulus. Around the circumference of the tomb a low stone retainer wall was built to prevent excessive erosion and collapse of the mound. The area within this sleeve wall was then filled with rubble until the burial chambers were covered and the mound reached a height of as much as fifteen metres. The picture (253, below) shows the exposed stone retainer wall from one of the medium-sized tumuli at Aali.

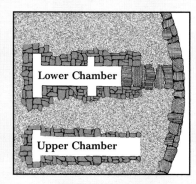

Lower Chamber

Upper Chamber

254. Opposite page (above): The ruins of one of the medium-sized tumuli at Aali, this one with a triple-chambered burial complex.

255. Opposite page (below): Excavations of the London-Bahrain Archaeological Expedition at Saar during the 1998 season.

dead in Norse and Greek tradition. It seemed that those Sumerian nobles who could afford it chose to be buried on Bahrain in order to be closer to their gods who dwelt in a place called the 'Abode of the Blessed'.

This island of the dead was a physically real place mentioned in numerous historical texts. The Sumerians called it Ni.tuk but it is better known by its Semitic name of Dilmun. The ancient literature makes it clear that Dilmun was considered to be a place which offered eternal happiness beyond death. And, as a result, burial there might be regarded as the greatest of rewards for lifelong service to the gods.

So was the island of Bahrain one and the same as sacred Dilmun – the Pure Land, the home of the gods and the resting place of the immortal soul? Before we look into this intriguing but complex question, we should just convince ourselves that a rather more mundane explanation for the huge number of mounds found on Bahrain is not justifiable.

Of course, there were and still are those who challenge the idea, originally put forward by Ernest Mackay, that Bahrain was a Sumerian island necropolis. It has been argued that the population of the main city

on the island – at Kalat Bahrain – was sufficiently large in its own right to produce the observed number of graves over the five-hundred-year period of their construction. Anthropologist Bruno Frohlich summarises this view.

> … it is *not necessary* to explain the large number of burial mounds by 'importing' the dead from surrounding geographical areas. The size of the island, the number of people it can support, is assumed to be such that it may be necessary to look for *more* burials in order to explain the known settlement patterns.[8]

However, this statement is based on an estimate of the *total* population of Bahrain, including all the women and children. Even then the figure Frohlich arrives at is a burial population of just 150,000 which is half the current highest estimate for the total number of interments on the island. Frohlich's figures simply do not add up – especially when one considers, as Peter Cornwall did, that these tumuli were not the graves of an entire population but rather the élite burials of warriors and nobility.

> … as a rule, the mounds were constructed for adult warriors of the tribe, the dead buried within the tumuli represent only a fraction of the ancient population.[9]

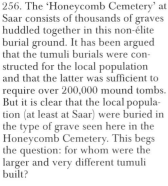

256. The 'Honeycomb Cemetery' at Saar consists of thousands of graves huddled together in this non-élite burial ground. It has been argued that the tumuli burials were constructed for the local population and that the latter was sufficient to require over 200,000 mound tombs. But it is clear that the local population (at least at Saar) were buried in the type of grave seen here in the Honeycomb Cemetery. This begs the question: for whom were the larger and very different tumuli built?

Many tumuli were never occupied. Across all types of tomb, from small to large, some seventeen per cent 'contained not a single human bone – or anything else'.[10] In the grander and more elaborate constructions the figure rises to thirty-nine per cent.[11] This suggests local construction on behalf of far-off clients living in the Sumerian homelands who felt the need to possess a tomb on the sacred isle. The idea that such effort would be expended on large tombs for the local population for them subsequently never to be used makes no sense. It seems much more likely that these empty tumuli were paid for by absentee nobles who, for whatever reason, never made it to their final resting place amongst the gods and ancestors.

257. Excavating at grave in the Honeycomb Cemetery. Two volunteers are carefully cleaning the remains of an adult male burial during the 1998 season of the Jordanian archaeological mission to Bahrain.

A well-argued case for accepting Mackay's original hypothesis has recently been voiced by Carl Lamberg-Karlovsky whose rebuttal of Frohlich's case forms the basis of my arguments here. In his article 'Death in Dilmun' he draws two main conclusions:

(1) there is an insufficient indigenous settlement pattern (i.e. population) of this date to account for the enormous number of graves in Bahrain and the adjacent eastern provinces of Saudi Arabia; and that

(2) these tumuli represent an elaborate funerary cult reflected in Sumerian literature referring to Dilmun.[12]

I believe that Lamberg-Karlovsky is absolutely right. I just cannot see how a local island population could be responsible for such a remarkable phenomenon as the Bahraini tumuli. The sheer number of tombs, crammed onto this tiny desert island, tells us that there is something very special going on here. We do not just have tumuli all over the northern part of the island but cemeteries with graves packed together in their thousands surrounding excavated villages such as Saar. These less spectacular tombs are much more likely to represent the last resting places of the local population. It is surely beholden upon those who would insist on a purely indigenous burial population to explain why the greatest cities in the ancient world, with their huge populations, have nothing remotely to compare in scale with the Bahrain cemetery.

Conclusion Twenty-Two

The island of Bahrain represents the legendary Isle of the Blessed – the idealised place of burial for the Sumerian people and their gods.

But the final word (for now) on the subject of the Bahrain burial mounds goes to Carl Lamberg-Karlovsky who appropriately reaches to the heart of the mystery.

> It is abundantly clear ... from the burgeoning literature on these Bahrain burials that the accumulation of facts alone do not provide an understanding or a meaning of their significance.[13]

The true significance of the Sumerian 'Abode of the Blessed' will be brought to light when we reach the final conclusions of this book. But now we must address the question raised a moment ago: Is the sacred land of Dilmun to be identified with the island of Bahrain?

Dilmun: The Sumerian Paradise

It was right at the beginning of Bahraini archaeological investigations that the discovery which triggered the great debate over Dilmun was made. Let me introduce you to Captain E. L. Durand – a young British officer and Her Britannic Majesty's Political Resident at the Iranian port of Bushire on the northern shore of the Persian Gulf. The Political Resident was in effect both British ambassador and military commander responsible for the Empire's interests in the region. The year is 1878 and Captain Durand has just landed on Bahrain with the intention of undertaking an archaeological survey of the islands.

He begins his investigations by looking for inscribed blocks from ancient monuments, reused in the building of the mosques which are scattered throughout the island. His efforts are finally rewarded when he comes across 'Bahrain's most celebrated artefact' – now known as the 'Durand Stone'.

> At last, having visited twenty mosques at least, which produced nothing but a cup of coffee, a KALIAN, and innumerable complaints of the tyranny of the sheikhs and their tribe, I was told of a stone that nobody could read. This, therefore, I went to see, and found it imbedded in the 'holy of holies' in the MADRASSEH-I DAOOD (mosque), in the BILAD-I KADIM. The stone is of black basalt, shaped like the prow of a boat or an animal's tongue, and is two feet two inches long. I had no difficulty in getting it, in spite of its holy situation, by telling the MOOLLAHS that it was a fire-worshipper's stone, probably an idol, and had no business (being) where it was.[14]

The inscription on the stone turned out to be Old Babylonian cuneiform and was translated by Henry Rawlinson, who we previously encountered dangling over the cliff-face at Behistun as he endeavoured to copy the great inscription of Darius I in 1835. He was now the distinguished Mesopotamian scholar Major-General Sir Henry Rawlinson – Knight Commander of the Most Honourable Order of the Bath, Baronet, Fellow of the Royal Society and President of the Royal Asiatic Society. The Durand Stone text simply reads:

KALIAN: A hookah or hubble-bubble pipe.

MADRASSEH-I DAOOD: Islamic school of David.

BILAD-I KADIM: 'Old Quarter'.

MOOLLAHS: Muslim clerics.

The palace of Rimum, servant of (the god) Inzak, (and) man of (the tribe of) Agarum.

Rawlinson was the first to recognise that this short inscription identified the island of Bahrain with Dilmun. He knew of other cuneiform texts describing the god Inzak, son of Enki, as the 'Lord of Dilmun'. If Rimum, king of ancient Bahrain, was the servant of Inzak, then this deity was, in all likelihood, a principal god of Bahrain, thus making the latter a prime candidate for sacred Dilmun.[15] But this was not the end of the matter, for strong resistance to the idea that Bahrain was Dilmun eventually surfaced from a very eminent source indeed.

259. A detail of the Durand Stone showing the palm-leaf symbol and the brief dedicatory text of King Rimum.

Kramer versus Cornwall

We have already come across the distinguished Sumerologist Samuel Noah Kramer on numerous occasions. He is the outstanding figure of the discipline of Sumerology and many of the Sumerian epics we have had recourse to quoting were translated by this most respected of scholars. Several of the texts which Kramer read (and which were not available to Rawlinson) indicated to him that Dilmun, the home of the gods, was located beyond the Zagros mountains. Bahrain simply did not fit the picture portrayed in the epic literature.

In essence Kramer felt justified in locating Dilmun somewhere in Iran because the epics suggested a faraway land across the mountains 'where the sun rises'. To him that meant the great chain of peaks which rose magnificently out of the Mesopotamian plain on its eastern horizon. Moreover, Dilmun itself was often referred to as 'Mount Dilmun' (Akk. *Kur-Dilmun*), suggesting a highland region.

Based on his translation of the Sumerian Paradise Myth, Kramer describes Dilmun as a land which is 'pure', 'clean' and 'bright'. It is a 'land of the living' which knows neither sickness nor death but which is initially lacking fresh water – the primeval element so essential to life. 'The great Sumerian water-god, Enki, therefore orders Utu, the sun-god, to fill it with fresh water brought up from the earth. Dilmun is thus turned into a divine garden, green with fruit-laden fields and meadows'.[16] This earthly paradise of Sumerian literature is surely the very same garden in which biblical Adam existed before the fall – a place of innocence, tranquillity and, above all, safety.

> In Dilmun, the raven utters no cry. The *ittidu*-bird utters not the cry of the *ittidu*-bird. The lion kills not. The wolf snatches not the lamb, …[17]

From the Old Babylonian version of the flood epic (discovered at Nippur) we learn the names of the creator gods who made this paradise.

> After Anu, Enlil, Enki and Ninhursag had fashioned the black-headed (Sumerian) people, vegetation luxuriated from the earth; animals – four-legged (creatures) of the plain (*edin*) – were brought artfully into existence.[18]

When the hero Gilgamesh makes his epic quest for the secret of eternal life he finds Utnapishtim in the 'Land of the Living' which lies across seven mountain ranges. However, according to the Old Babylonian flood story, Ziusudra – its flood hero – was transfigured to sacred Dilmun following his sacrifice to the gods.

> Ziusudra, the king, prostrated himself before An and Enlil. An and Enlil cherished Ziusudra; life like a god they give him; breath eternal like a god they bring down for him. Then Ziusudra the king, the preserver of the name of vegetation and of the seed of mankind, in the land of crossing, the land of Dilmun, the place where the sun rises, they caused to dwell.[19]

The Land of the Living and Dilmun are therefore one and the same. Kramer also makes an observation which is of considerable interest for the historical scenario we are constructing.

> … it is more than unlikely that the seven mountains crossed by Lugalbanda on his journey from Uruk to Aratta are different from the seven mountains crossed by Gilgamesh on his journey from Uruk to the 'Land of the Living'.[20]

Thus the way to the Land of the Living was also the way to Aratta and therefore to Eden. The final clue as to the location of the Land of the Living also lies buried in the text of the Gilgamesh Epic. There the abode of Utnapishtim is described as being located 'in the distance, at the mouth of the rivers' (Akk. *ina ruqi ina pi naratum*).[21] The rivers being referred to are the Tigris and Euphrates. It is clear from other Mesopotamian texts that the 'mouths' of rivers were the sources – the estuaries were referred to as the 'tails'.

As we have seen, the sources of the Tigris and Euphrates rise in the mountains of Armenia where Genesis locates the land of Eden.

260. Clay plaque representing the demon Humbaba (Huwawa) killed by Gilgamesh and Enkidu. Babylon I Period. British Museum.

Gilgamesh and the Plant of Rejuvenation

In the final episode of the Gilgamesh Epic the hero-king of Uruk goes in search of eternal life. He has just witnessed his companion, Enkidu, die a lingering death at the will of the gods because the two comrades had dared to slay the Bull of Heaven. Enkidu's death greatly affects Gilgamesh who begins to fear his own mortality. He therefore determines to seek out Utnapishtim in order to learn how the flood-hero had attained immortality. The journey to the home of Utnapishtim is long and arduous but, eventually, Gilgamesh crosses the Sea of Death to arrive in the Land of the Living. There he meets Utnapishtim and his wife who test him to decide if he is worthy of eternal life. Needless to say Gilgamesh fails the trial set for him and is denied immortality. However, Utnapishtim tells him of a plant growing beneath the sea which makes youthful those who consume it. Gilgamesh ties stone weights to his ankles and dives for the plant. As he grasps the plant of rejuvenation its sharp stems cut the king's hand. It is clear from this detail that the magic plant is a variety of coral.

Gilgamesh heads for home, content in the knowledge that, even if he cannot become one of the immortals, he can be given back his vigorous youth. However, he takes a dip in a pool and leaves his prize unguarded. A snake comes up and devours the plant thus giving all serpents the ability to shed their skins and be reborn into their youth. Gilgamesh returns to find his chance of rejuvenation gone. He departs for Uruk empty-handed to await his eventual summons into the underworld.

This colourful episode in the life of the hero-king does indeed suggest at first glance that the location of the Land of the Living was in the Persian Gulf – in other words Bahrain. Coral is indigenous to the coastline of the archipelago and the technique of tying weights to the ankle is a trick used by the pearl-divers of Bahrain even today. However, one must consider the possibility that this part of the Gilgamesh Epic is an addition made when historical Dilmun had come into existence and was a major player in the late-Sumerian trading network. Gilgamesh may have in reality visited legendary Dilmun which was then only later equated with Bahrain. It would have been at this point that the story of the plant of rejuvenation was added to the tale. It has been demonstrated by Ronald Veenker[22] that the magic plant episode is more than likely just such an addition to the original epic. There are a number of inconsistencies which lead to this conclusion, including the point that the Sea of Death is deadly to the touch just before Gilgamesh arrives at Utnapishtim's home and yet Gilgamesh does not hesitate to dive into the sea to retrieve the magic plant beside the shore of the flood-hero's domain. The two seas cannot, therefore, be the same and so the two episodes cannot have originally been connected.

Everything in the myths pointed Kramer in the direction of the eastern mountains where we have determined the biblical Garden of Eden once existed. The legendary, even mythological paradise which the Sumerians knew as Dilmun was clearly not an island located in the sultry heat of the Persian Gulf.

Kramer published his thoughts in an article entitled 'Dilmun, the Land of the Living' which appeared in the December 1944 issue of the *Bulletin of the American Schools of Oriental Research*. There he came to the conclusion that 'in all probability it is in southwestern Iran … where Dilmun is to be sought, and that it is not to be identified with the island of Bahrain'. That was the view of the great translator of Sumerian literature and there can be little argument that he was basically correct – the Dilmun of the *epic tales* does seem to be located somewhere beyond the Zagros peaks.

But sometimes it takes a 'young buck' to instigate a rethink within the well-established disciplines. Enter, stage left, the young buck of Dilmunology – American archaeologist and scholar, Peter Bruce Cornwall.

261. Terracotta plaque of the 'Bull-Man' found at Ur in strata of the Babylon I Period. I believe that these bull-man figures are very likely to be representations of the hero Gilgamesh, so often referred to as the wild-bull in the Gilgamesh Epic. Iraq Museum.

262. A chlorite vessel known as a 'hut pot' (Early Dynastic Period) because it appears to represent the façade of a reed hut. The upper register is carved with a row of triangles (usually standing for mountains) and the crescent motif found on altars used in the worship of the moon-god Sin (Sumerian Suen/Nanna). Baghdad Museum.

In 1946 Cornwall responded to Kramer's paper with a devastating series of counter arguments. His findings conclusively demonstrated that *historical* Dilmun *had* to be located on the island of Bahrain.

> … it is essential to recognise at once that the cuneiform references to Dilmun fall into two distinct categories:
>
> 1. historical, commercial, epistolary, dedicatory, and astrological inscriptions;
>
> 2. Sumerian literary compositions.
>
> In the former, Dilmun is a definite geographical locality – of that we may be certain. In the latter it is a fabulous land, a strange antechamber to the spirit world. That the two Dilmuns were thought of as being somehow identical is very likely; but I suggest that Dr. Kramer should not have decided the location of Dilmun merely on the basis of Sumerian literary compositions, especially since the evidence gleaned from the other class of source material points decidedly to the equation Dilmun = Bahrain.[23]

This extract is taken from Cornwall's short but succinct rebuttal article entitled 'On the location of Dilmun' which was published in the *Bulletin of the American Schools of Oriental Research* in October 1946. Cornwall had excavated thirty tumuli on the island of Bahrain in 1940 and knew not only the archaeology of early Bahrain like the back of his hand, but was well aware of the historical texts which linked the cultural remains on Bahrain with the Dilmunites. He had made a special study of these important texts for his doctoral thesis entitled *The History of Bahrain Before Cyrus* which, unfortunately, was never published. Michael Rice's comments on this brilliant study say it all.

> It is a remarkable and perceptive synthesis of all the historical and legendary references to Dilmun in the ancient sources, with a careful analysis of the evidence, and, in its extent and sensitivity, has hardly been bettered. It remains a mine of fascinating and significant material for the assiduous Dilmunologist.[24]

There is little doubt today that Peter Cornwall was also absolutely right to identify Bahrain with *historical* Dilmun. His arguments, summarised below, left Kramer lost for reply.[25]

(1) SARGON II of Assyria (721-705 BC) states that the king of Dilmun 'lives like a fish, thirty *beru* (double-hours) away in the midst of the sea of the rising sun'. Another Assyrian king, ASHURBANIPAL, informs us that Dilmun is situated 'in the midst of the Lower Sea' – otherwise well established as the Persian Gulf.

(2) The journey to Dilmun by sea takes sixty hours (thirty beru). A slow moving ship, sailing with the prevailing north-west wind at around eight kilometres per hour, would take about sixty hours to reach

SARGON II: King of Assyria, reigned 721-705 BC.

ASHURBANIPAL: King of Assyria, reigned 668-626 BC.

Bahrain from the mouth of the Shatt el-Arab – a journey of four hundred and eighty kilometres.

(3) The Hellenistic and classical writers knew the island of Bahrain as Tylos from which etymologists have little difficulty in extracting the more ancient name Tilmun or Dilmun.

(4) The cuneiform text, discovered on Bahrain by Captain Durand in 1879, mentions the god Inzak (Sum. *Enshag*), otherwise known to be the name given by the Dilmunites to the Babylonian god Nabu who was worshipped in Dilmun during the second half of the second millennium. Enshag was the son of Enki, Lord of the Abyss, who also dwelt in Dilmun.

These four main arguments leave little doubt that *historical* Dilmun was located, at least in part, on Bahrain. The debate as to the whereabouts of Dilmun was over. Some fifty years on nothing has happened to alter this view. But the evidence we have brought together may be leading us to a rethink. Could Kramer also have been right to place *prehistoric* or *mythological* Dilmun beyond the Zagros mountains? And could mythological or legendary Dilmun have been just as real as historical Dilmun? In other words, is it possible that there were two Dilmuns – an original primeval Dilmun, located in Eden, and a later sacred island of the dead in the 'Lower Sea' which was also the heart of a vast sea-going trading enterprise. The former was the paradise-land of the gods where life was eternal, whilst the latter was paradise regained for the souls of the deceased. In effect the primeval Dilmun of the Land of the Living had become the historical Dilmun of the land of the dead. This concept is

263. The cella (hall or chamber) of Saar temple with its square pillars which were later built up to form rounded columns. The Sin altar is attached to the right wall (partly in shadow) with the entrance beyond.

The Dilmun Seals

The Bahrain stamp seals are our most important indicators as to the cultural affiliations of the Dilmunites. Several hundred seals have been found at the archaeological sites on the main island of Bahrain, particularly at the town site of Saar. Stamp seals are impressed into the clay whilst cylinder seals are rolled across the clay to form the glyptic image.

Here we see just a few examples of familiar themes from Sumer and Susiana, including the Master of Animals motif. Two are reproduced here. On the left (264) the hero is controlling a pair of antelopes. Beneath him (to the left) is the face of a bull and (to the right) the star symbol of the sun-god. The Master of Animals in the seal impression to the right (265) is wearing a long skirt familiar from the Sumerian glyptic. He holds the antelopes by their horns.

In the next row we have on the left (266) a pair of rear-facing antithetical antelopes between which is a standard representing the crescent moon encompassing the sun. The Sin standard is also represented on the right-hand seal (267) of two men in a high-prowed boat. Either side of the figures are palm branches and beneath the boat a water ripple/wave motif.

In the third row we see on the left (268) a god and goddess drinking from straws with the Sin standard and sun-disc between them. The right seal (269) depicts two divine bull-men carrying the Sin standard and sun-disc aloft. They are surrounded by several symbols which are difficult to interpret, including rectangular objects which may be temple buildings or ritual furniture.

264

265

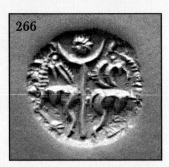

266

267

270

268

269

270. One of the most fascinating recent discoveries on Bahrain is a seal from Saar (above centre) showing what appears to be the murder of a god wearing a horned helmet. The deity is being stabbed in the chest whilst a third figure gesticulates behind the high-god. The figure of a bull has been added in the lower part of the scene. There are a few rare examples of this motif from Mesopotamia. The scene may represent the killing of the god Geshtu-e or Kingu by the primeval deities to provide the life-blood of humanity as Man is first crafted from clay. On the other hand, the scene may equally tell the story of an evil act which has not come down to us in the surviving corpus of Mesopotamian epic literature. The most famous example of the killing of a god is that from Egypt which tells the story of the murder of Osiris (Egyptian Asar) by his brother Seth.

271. Plaque of Urnanshe of Lagash from Telloh (Early Dynastic III). The king is seen carrying a reed basket associated with brick-making. He is therefore commemorating the foundation of a temple. Before him stand the queen followed by four princes. In the lower scene the king is seated upon his throne with his sons once more approaching him. The Sumerian text in front of the king states that ships of Dilmun had brought wood from foreign lands. This is the first recorded mention of Dilmun. Louvre Museum.

not so foreign to Christianity: the earthly paradise-lost of Eden is replaced by the paradise-earned of heaven where the just souls of the departed dwell for eternity.

There are other clues which suggest that we may be dealing with two Dilmuns. A Sumerian king of Lagash named URNANSHE acquired timber from Dilmun for the building of a great temple, yet Bahrain grows only date-palm trees. To obtain building woods a Sumerian king would normally look to the Zagros mountains for his supplies.[26] But then the Dilmun of Bahrain was a trading emporium and may have acted as middleman in the supplying of quality woods. This is proved to some degree by a record from the reign of GUDEA of Lagash who orders copper, diorite and wood from Magan which we know to be Oman.[27] These supplies would, no doubt, have been sent via Bahrain. However, by the time of Gudea, we are well and truly in the period of Cornwall's historic Dilmun, whereas Urnanshe ruled several centuries earlier and may well have obtained his wood from Kramer's prehistoric Dilmun beyond the Zagros mountains.

URNANSHE: King of Lagash, reigned NC – c. 2305-2281 BC.

GUDEA: King of Lagash, reigned NC – c. 1960 BC.

Conclusion Twenty-Three

There were, perhaps, two Dilmuns: an original 'prehistoric' Dilmun beyond the Zagros mountains and 'historic' Dilmun island which was later founded by the descendants of the ancestral Dilmunites originating from the mountains.

Two Lands, One Name

It occurs to me that we may be dealing here with an instance of toponym transfer. In other words, the name of a place or land has been transferred along with the people who had migrated from their original homeland to a new geographical location. As an example of this phenomenon, migrants who settled in Australia and America in the 1700s and 1800s founded settlements named after their original home towns and regions. Thus we have an American 'Manchester', 'Worcester' and 'Warwick' in New England and 'Potsdam', 'Rome' and 'Amsterdam' in New York State. Around the other side of the world, in that other colonised continent, we find Australian 'Blackburn', 'Newcastle' and the 'Liverpool Mountains' in New South Wales. The American pioneers were also fond of giving their settlements biblical toponyms. Thus we find 'Salem's (from the original Jerusalem) in Massachusetts, Ohio, Missouri, Oregon, Virginia, (etc.) and 'Goshen's in New York State and Indiana. All this is a perfectly natural thing for immigrants to do, giving them a comforting link back to their original homeland and religious upbringing. The ancients were no different. They too named their colonies after homeland cities.

The most active migrants/colonisers in the ancient world were the Phoenicians who, in the ninth to seventh centuries BC, established new settlements all around the Mediterranean seaboard and beyond the Pillars of Hercules (for example at Cadiz). Their most famous colony was Carthage on the north coast of Africa – but this was not the original Carthage (Canaanite *Karhadasht* = 'New City'). That was located on the southern shore of Cyprus at the modern port of Kition.

We can be confident that Bahrain island – the Tylos of the Greeks – was known to the Mesopotamians as Dilmun in the historic period. But is there any evidence of a much older Dilmun concealed in the landscape of biblical Eden? In our travels around the lands of early Genesis in *Chapter Two*, I revealed a number of topographical indicators which pinpointed the lands of Nod (east), Cush (north), Eden (west) and Havilah (south). These lands encircled a fertile valley which we identified as the Garden of Eden – the first earthly paradise. If the Garden of Genesis is to be equated with Enki's paradise garden of Dilmun, then we ought to be looking for clues to the latter's location in the area of our original search.

In spite of the enormous span of years between the antediluvian epoch and modern times there may just be a remnant memory of the Sumerian name of Dilmun left in the Adji Chay valley, just as we found Cush in Kusheh Dagh and Nod in Noqdi. Less than fifty kilometres to the west of Tabriz, between the salt flats of Urmia Lake and the River Meidan – the very spot we have identified as the location of the paradisiacal garden of Genesis – there stands a little village called Dilman.

272. An important archaeological artefact is this superb vase datable (according to Bahraini archaeologists) to the Jemdet Nasr Period. It was found in a grave from the Medinet Hamad cemetery on Bahrain along with other objects which date several graves to this previously unattested era. Bahrain National Museum.

The Missing Generations

One of the great mysteries of Sumerian archaeology is an apparent gap in the archaeological record throughout the region of historical Dilmun (that is the Bahrain archipelago and neighbouring coastline of Arabia). There was certainly considerable activity in this region during the Ubaid Period (especially along the western shore of the Persian Gulf) as is attested by all the sites where surface surveys have revealed large quantities of Ubaid pottery (the dispersal of Ubaid artefacts can be seen on map 273, right). But, unfortunately, few artefacts have been unearthed for the succeeding Uruk and Jemdet Nasr eras when Sumerian culture was at its height in southern Mesopotamia. Given this strange archaeological fact, it has been the general assumption that one day, sooner or later, some evidence for Protoliterate Period culture would surface in the Gulf.

In the *Legend* hypothesis I am about to suggest that Bahrain/Dilmun played a major part in the story of the dispersion of nations as described in Genesis 10. I have already proposed that this migration took place soon after the building of the Tower of Babel under Enmerkar/Nimrod during the Uruk IV Period. The importance of determining whether Bahrain was inhabited, or at least used as a staging post, during the Uruk-Jemdet Nasr epoch is thus obvious.

The local Arab scholars are convinced that archaeological material from the Protoliterate Period has now been unearthed on Bahrain island. The tumulus cemetery near Medinet Hamad has recently produced graves which they believe contain Jemdet Nasr pottery (see 272). One of these graves is shown below (274). However, there is some disagreement as to whether this pottery is really datable to the Jemdet Nasr era. The importance of the search for the protoliterate peoples of Bahrain/Dilmun will soon become apparent as we follow them across the sea towards their final destination.

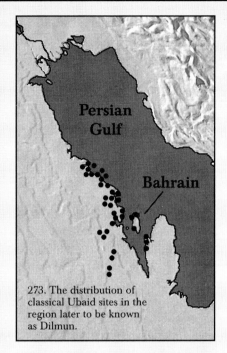

273. The distribution of classical Ubaid sites in the region later to be known as Dilmun.

Flight of the Phoenix

We have now reached a crucial point in our story. So far I have brought you down from the mountains of Eden in the footsteps of the antediluvian patriarchs and their followers. We then watched the generations of Enoch and Irad establish settlements, first in the Susiana plain and then in the marshlands of Sumer. These resourceful humans soon learnt to build reed ships so that they might journey out into the Lower Sea in search of new horizons of exploitation. Evidence of their explorations abounds in the form of Ubaid pottery found at scores of sites along the Arabian coast of the Gulf. This sea-going element of Adam's descendants have led us away from Mesopotamia and the devastating flood into the reborn world of the postdiluvian era and the migration of the sons of Ham. We are now at the threshold of a great new adventure as we board the ships of Cush, Mizraim, Put and Canaan for the long journey to Africa and the Eastern Mediterranean.

In order to trace the journey of this second generation of explorers I need to introduce you to a fascinating and tenacious legend which lies outside both the Mesopotamian and the biblical tradition, although the latter does hint at a knowledge of what we are about to discuss.

Go to visit a Lebanese school and sit in on a history class. There you will hear the teacher explain to the children that the modern Lebanese are descended from the ancient Phoenicians who, in turn, originated from the islands of the Persian Gulf. The legendary origins of the Phoenicians are not an invention of the Lebanese Christian community purely to provide a separate ethnic tradition from their Muslim neighbours. The idea that the ancestors of the Phoenicians came from far-off Bahrain to found the new cities of Canaan on the Eastern Mediterranean coast was well known to the classical writers. Justin, Pliny, Ptolemy and Strabo all regarded the original homeland of the Phoenicians in the Gulf as an historical fact. I need only quote from one to establish the point.

On sailing farther (down the Erythraean Sea), one comes to the other islands, I mean Tyre and Aradus, which have temples like those of the Phoenicians. It is asserted, at least by the inhabitants of the islands, that the islands and cities of the Phoenicians which bear the same name are their own colonies. [28]

The Tyrians (citizens of Tyre) proclaimed their original homeland as the island of Tylos in the Erythraean Sea. Now the Erythraean or 'Red' Sea was not in ancient times what we know as the Red Sea today – that is to say the long gulf which lies between the western shore of Arabia and the eastern coast of Egypt, Sudan and Ethiopia. Confusing as it may seem, the ancient name of the modern Red Sea was the Arabian Gulf! The original Red Sea was what we today call the Persian or Arabian Gulf and the Indian Ocean beyond. It was named as such after Erythraeas who, according to legend, was buried within a great mound on the island of Tylos. Of course, Erythraeas is a Greek name which has the meaning the 'Red One' (hints of Adam?).

Now it is usually accepted within scholarship that the Greek *Tylos* is a late rendition of the Akkadian Tilmun. Thus the Phoenicians of the eastern Mediterranean believed that they originated from the sacred paradise isle of Sumerian legend. Could it be that the seafaring inhabitants of the Persian Gulf in the third and second millennia BC were the ancestors of the seafaring Phoenician inhabitants of the Mediterranean? Michael Rice neatly encapsulates the historical dilemma.

We are reasonably certain that the Dilmunites were not Phoenicians; we are by no means certain now that the Phoenicians were not Dilmunites. [29]

275 & 276. Two Phoenician sea-going vessels transporting cedars of Lebanon for construction work on the palaces and temples of Assyria. Note the high (animal-headed) prow and stern and the flat-bottomed profile of the ships. Reliefs from the palace of Sargon II at Khorsabad (8th century BC). Louvre Museum.

Colour Plates

Page 255: Temple of the Moon. The altar of Sin (Sumerian Suen/Nanna) in the little temple of Saar on Bahrain island.

Page 256: Above left: Entwined Serpents. One of the characteristic motifs of Mesopotamian art is the image of entwined necks of exotic animals and snakes. This example comes from Iran and is now exhibited in the Louvre Museum.

Above right: The Bull of Barbar. This haunting bronze head of a bull was discovered in the ruins of the temple of Enki at Barbar. It is reasonable to assume that it once belonged to the sound-board of a lyre, given the examples of such bull-figureheads found in the royal tombs of Ur by Sir Leonard Woolley.

Below: Eastern Desert Dawn. Striking camp in the Wadi el-Kash in preparation for the successful attempt to reach Site 26 on Friday the 28th of February 1998.

Page 257: Heading for Site 26. Our convoy of four-wheel drive Land Cruisers enters the northern mouth of the Wadi Mineh in search of Winkler's Site 26.

Page 258: Above: The Road to Discovery. Taking a break in the vast open space of the Wadi Zeidun as the second Followers of Horus expedition attempts to reach Site 26 from the south (setting off from Kanais and heading up the Wadi Mia to Gebel es-Shalul and beyond).

Below: Stairway to Heaven. The six-stepped pyramid of Djoser at Sakkara with the *heb-sed* complex surrounding this man-made mountain of the god-pharaoh.

Page 259: The Tower of Babel. A reconstruction (after F. Safar, *et al.*, 1981, p. 51) of the platform Temple 2 of Eridu. The huge platform behind Temple 2 may have supported an even larger and higher building which was destroyed during the construction of the later Ur III Period ziggurat. Nothing remains of this upper Temple 1 today but the platform must have been erected as a base for a holy shrine. It is this now lost giant structure which was remembered as the biblical 'Tower of Babel' simply because the Sumerian name of Eridu (Nun.ki) was the same as that for Babylon and so the location of the first great temple-tower was confused with the impressive (but much later) ziggurat at Babylon.

Page 260: Above left: Steps to Eternity. The shrine of Senuseret I at Karnak once stood at the heart of Amun's temple in Thebes. The temple shrines of Egypt were raised up in order to signify that the gods resided on a sacred mound or mountain.

Above right: A God of Old. The *serdab* statue of King Djoser shows him wearing a huge, heavy wig and beard. Given that the climate of Egypt is not conducive to such fashions, why did the pharaohs portray themselves like this? Perhaps they had an image of their ancestral gods which they were trying to emulate?

Below: Horizon of Eternity. The spectacular view from the top of Meretseger (above the Valley of the Kings) looking across the Nile valley to the Eastern Desert and the land of sunrise.

Page 261: The King's Barque Awaits. The great funerary boat is moored at the quay ready to transport the deceased pharaoh across the waters of the abyss to the Isle of Flame where he will be reborn as the morning sun on the eastern horizon.

Page 262: Sunrise Over the Red Sea.

Part Three

The
Followers of Horus

The Origins of Egyptian Civilisation

Meskiagkasher journeyed upon the sea and came ashore at the mountains.

Sumerian King List

Chapter Nine

SHIPS OF THE DESERT

The origins of pharaonic civilisation have always been shrouded in mystery. What caused dynastic culture to burst forth in the Nile valley within such a relatively short period of time? It has long been recognised that 'the emergence of pharaonic rule coincided with an entirely unprecedented series of phenomena' which formed the recognisable foundation of what we identify as pharaonic Egypt.[1] There is little evidence of kingship and its rituals very much before the beginning of the 1st Dynasty; no signs of the gradual development of metal working, art, monumental architecture and writing – the defining criteria of early civilisation. Much of what we know about the pharaohs and their complex culture seems to come into existence in a flash of inspiration.

The next five chapters are devoted to a question occasionally raised within Egyptological circles but rarely spoken of outside the discipline. The academic debate, instigated nearly a century ago, centres on a single controversial question: what were the origins of the first pharaohs? It seems clear that there was a major civilising stimulus from outside Egypt in the late predynastic era – but in what form did that stimulus manifest itself? Put simply, were the 'FOLLOWERS OF HORUS' (Egy. *Shemsu-Hor*) – the immediate ancestors of the first pharaohs – native to the Nile valley or a foreign élite who had conquered the land of Egypt by superior military force?

In *Chapter Ten* we will take a look at this 'Dynastic Race Theory' advocated by the likes of Petrie, Derry, Baumgartel, Murray and Emery – all Egyptologists and most from the university department where I completed my own degree. Their views are very unfashionable today

277. Opposite page: One of the most important rock drawings in the Eastern Desert is the chieftain in a high-prowed boat with animal's figurehead, from Site 26. The solitary figure in the boat wears two plumes and is carrying a pear-shaped mace.

278. Above: The desert survey team at Site 26 in the Wadi Abu Maraket el-Nes.

279. A high-prowed boat, from Winkler's site 26, with large rectangular sail and twin steering oars.

FOLLOWERS OF HORUS: The name the Egyptians gave to the legendary predynastic rulers of Egypt and the entourage of the king during the *heb-sed* jubilee rites.

because ideas of 'master race' are irrevocably linked to the ideology of Aryanism which tore Europe apart in the 1930s. But can we deny the actuality of distant historical events simply because of the traumas suffered in our own era?

Throughout Part Three of *Legend* I will be looking in detail at the art and iconography of the pharaohs, demonstrating that many pharaonic motifs are in fact Mesopotamian in origin. This has been known for many decades but not widely disseminated. We will explore the desolate wadis of the Eastern Desert with Arthur Weigall in 1908 and Hans Winkler in 1936; dig with Flinders Petrie at Nakada; and discover evidence for the first battle in Egyptian history. All this will lead to the Step Pyramid at Sakkara where, with a little imagination, we will witness the secret rituals of spiritual rejuvenation performed by Pharaoh Djoser and his priests. Finally, we shall accompany the king on his epic journey through the underworld – a journey along the river of darkness which carries the dead to the mystical Isle of Flame.

Let us begin our new adventure by following in the footsteps of two explorers of the early twentieth century – Arthur Weigall and Hans Winkler. They were to reveal to the archaeological world tantalising evidence of an epic journey across the parched Eastern Desert of Egypt made by a people who appeared not to be native to the Nile valley. These folk were from much further afield. Their journey over the sands from the Red Sea to the River Nile was remarkable because they appear to have brought their boats with them!

We begin with Weigall's visit to the desert wadis east of the town of Edfu, famous for its wonderfully preserved Greco-Roman temple dedicated to the falcon-god, Horus.

280. Arthur and Hortense Weigall.

Weigall and the Wadi Abbad

Arthur WEIGALL was a remarkable man – a hands-on archaeologist who spent a number of years in Egypt employed as Inspector General of Antiquities for the Egyptian government (1905-14). We come across him out in the Eastern Desert, bivouacked amongst the ruins of a Roman military outpost in the company of his American wife, Hortense.

Weigall had a burning passion for the desert. In reviewing his popular book *Travels in the Upper Egyptian Deserts* the *Manchester Guardian* wrote of him:

> Mr Weigall carries the reader with him; in his company the dead past lives again. Yet we suspect that the desert itself means more to the author than all its departed glories. … He has felt its spell. He has rejoiced in its burning days and starry nights … He loves it for itself, not less than for its human monuments.[2]

281. Arthur Weigall on his favourite camel during the couple's visit to Kanais temple. This rather blurred and faded photograph was taken by Hortense and is now in the possession of the Weigalls' grand-daughter, Julie Hankey.

Arthur and Hortense spent a couple of days in March of 1908 on this private expedition by camel into the Wadi Abbad which leads from the Nile at the town of Edfu towards the Red Sea near the port of Mersa Alam. About half way along its course there is a south-eastern route which heads down to the ancient port of BERENIKE.

Hortense was recently arrived from England and so her husband had offered to take her on the adventure she had always dreamed of – a trip into the desert. Weigall was a meticulous recorder of isolated archaeo-logical sites and their related inscriptions, so, for him, this was to be a working break from his regular Antiquities Service duties.

Some fifty kilometres up the Wadi Abbad stands the small, rock-cut Temple of Kanais (also known as the 'Temple of Redesiya') built by Seti I, the father of Ramesses the Great. The temple, dedicated to Amun-Re, was established here to mark Seti's successful reopening of an ancient route to the Red Sea and Eastern Desert gold mines. The desert road had been virtually impassable for centuries. The wadis were far more inhospitable in the 19th Dynasty than they had been in predynastic times when north-east Africa had enjoyed a much less arid climate. A reliable water supply was desperately needed. As a result, Seti's soldiers were instructed to dig a deep well two days' journey out into the desert so as to ensure the survival of traders travelling from the Red Sea to the Nile valley and, perhaps more importantly for Seti, to improve the route to and from the gold mines of the Wadi Barramiya (Gebel Zebara). One of the dedicatory inscriptions decorating the temple walls proclaims the importance of the enterprise:

BERENIKE: The Ptolemaic and Roman port built on the coast of the Red Sea to facilitate trade with the Indian sub-continent.

282. The speos (rock-cut) temple of Seti I at Kanais in the Wadi Abbad.

ENNEAD: The pantheon of nine gods.

283. Seti I presents an offering (spelling out his prenomen) to the god Amun with tall plumes rising from his crown. From the portico of Kanais temple.

The Horus – Mighty-Bull-Appearing-in-Thebes; Vivifier-of-the-Two-Lands; the Dual King, Menmaatre (Seti I). He made (this place) as his monument for his father, Amun-Re, and his divine ENNEAD, making for them a new temple, pleasing to the gods, before which he dug a well. Never had the like been made by any king – except by this king, the maker of glorious things, the Son of Re, Seti-Merenptah. He is the good shepherd who keeps his soldiers alive – the father and mother of all.

They proclaim amongst them: "O Amun, give him eternity! Double for him everlastingness! You gods dwelling in the well, give to him your endurance; for he has opened for us the route of march which had previously been closed. We set out saved! We arrive alive! The difficult way of past recollection has become an easy way."

He (the king) has caused the mining of gold to be like the sight of the Horus-falcon. All future generations request for him eternity, so that he may celebrate jubilees like Atum and flourish like Horus of Edfu. For he has made monuments within the desert hills for all the gods. He has dug for water in the mountains far from civilisation.

For every messenger that traverses the highlands it is a gift of life, stability and satisfaction from the Dual King, Menmaatre (Seti I), beloved of Amun-Re, king of gods.[3]

Close to the desolate spot where the Temple of Kanais is located, and where a later Roman military governor established a guard post, are rock drawings from the predynastic era. Travellers throughout history – especially those undertaking difficult journeys through wild country – like to leave their mark for posterity. Whether modern beduin tribesmen or soldiers from Kitchener's expeditionary force to relieve Khartoum or, much further back in time, Greek mercenaries fighting for the Egyptian pharaohs along the upper reaches of the Nile – all find time to etch their presence in the shadow of a rocky outcrop. The dry desert climate ensures that their handiwork remains so fresh to the eye that it is sometimes difficult to believe that these scribblings were not carved yesterday.

The Weigalls were in the Wadi Abbad on a mission to record as many graffiti as they could find. This was part of Arthur's ongoing research into rock inscriptions which had already taken him to other locations out in the Eastern Desert on earlier expeditions.

In Weigall's popular book on his desert wanderings, published in 1909,[4] we see for the first time in the Egyptological literature several ink facsimiles of these rock drawings – drawings which were to become a thorny topic of debate over subsequent decades.

On Weigall's Trail

In January 1997, having been a regular visitor to Egypt for more than thirty years, I finally decided it was about time I took a first-hand look at Weigall's discoveries in the Wadi Abbad. This was to become the first of several expeditions into the desert in search of prehistoric rock drawings.

It all began at dawn on the 14th of January amidst the fury of another tremendous hail storm. It appeared that Seth was not very keen to accept newcomers into his desert domain. At that moment, stuck in the security convoy queue just outside Luxor town, I almost decided to cancel the trip. It is never wise to venture into the desert when thunder storms are in the air. My thoughts turned to the young students who had recently been killed in Oman, their vehicles having been caught in a desert wadi flash flood.

These sudden torrents are Seth's most devastating weapon against intruders. Without warning a tidal wave of muddy water and boulders hurls itself down the narrow passes sweeping all away before it. This can happen even when there is no rain falling immediately in the vicinity. The flood is caused by the build-up of rainwater on the desert plateau above the wadis which then merges in gullies, channelling the previously placid water into a fast-flowing torrent, all the time picking up extra rocks and debris. Even though this may be occurring several kilometres away from your location, you are not safe if you happen to be between the angry waters and its destination – the Nile valley – especially if you are in a narrow defile. The only warning is the distant rumble of crashing boulders moving westwards.

GALABEYAS: Long cotton robes.

It is one of those ironies of nature, so keenly observed by the ancient Egyptians, that water is at one time the life-saving gift of Pharaoh Seti I's Wadi Abbad well, but at others the bringer of death and destruction as the weapon of the Lord of Chaos after whom Seti ('The One who Belongs to Seth') was named. Incidentally, again we can observe the '-i' suffix denoting 'belonging to' or 'of' just as in 'Noqdi' – 'belonging to (the land of) Nod'. This linguistic trait is common to both ancient Egyptian and Persian. Arabic also displays the same rule: a 'Masri' is a man 'of Masr', that is the Arabic for Egypt which in turn comes from the same source as Assyrian Musri and Hebrew Mizraim. We will return to the etymology of Masr in the last chapter when we reveal the Sumerian identity of the biblical Mizraim and his deity.

As I sat in the car waiting for the hail storm to subside, I watched men in GALABEYAS frantically dashing to and fro in search of cover. Through the windscreen I could see a young bull-calf, in a state of complete panic, dragging his young master all over the road. The hailstones were the size of marbles and I was just glad to be safely cocooned inside the car. I could not help feeling that Seth was giving me a gentle warning to stay away. But then, as quickly as it had struck, the storm abated and the sun was back. The angry cloud crossed the Nile and headed for the Valley of the Kings. I decided to go on.

After a further ten minutes the convoy set off southwards towards its destination – Aswan. These ramshackle convoys are more of an irritation than a reassurance against terrorist attack. One jeep leading the convoy with four armed men is hardly going to deter an attack upon the last tourist bus in the line which may be as much as five kilometres from the head of the convoy. As we struggled along the east-bank road, the constant hold-ups at security check-points were frustrating and completely negated the early start. Needless to say, time was of the essence if I was to accomplish my mission. I had the added problem that it was not my intention to go to Aswan – the destination of everyone else joining the convoy. My driver, Mohsen, had been specially picked to get me to where I wanted to go by hook or by crook. His plan was rather clever. Everybody knows how crazy Egyptian taxi drivers are. Put them in a convoy and each will try desperately to leapfrog the vehicle in front of him. My driver simply refused to retaliate and soon we found ourselves bringing up the rear. We stayed there all the way to the outskirts of Edfu. Just before the river bridge to the west bank the road takes a sharp left and then right turn. The convoy followed the main road south, but we simply went straight on at the junction on the second bend, heading down the narrow road which leads eastwards into the desert and towards the Red Sea coast at Mersa Alam. We were free at last and, even though it was now eleven o'clock in the morning, I felt we had a good chance of reaching my goal with a few hours left to complete my investigations.

After a fifteen-minute drive through farming villages and green fields we finally left the Nile valley behind. The cultivation soon became a distant line on the western horizon as the great mouth of the Wadi Abbad swallowed us up. Nothing but sand now, as we headed east along the well-made tarmac road. We had the place to ourselves.

The kilometres flashed by as Mohsen's car sped along the solitary black thread. Above us the sky was clear and blue, but on the distant horizon more ominous black clouds were gathering. Still, this was no time to turn back, having successfully made our break for freedom. An hour passed and the darkness grew nearer. Finally, the wide, flat wadi bed began to narrow and, immediately before us, rose the craggy peaks of the Eastern Desert mountains. I had arrived at my destination.

At the bottom of a dark rock-face stood the dilapidated Temple of Kanais and, beside it, a small guard-post attended by three beduin employees of the Antiquities Service. They greeted us with the usual hospitality – even though our arrival had taken them somewhat by surprise. A glass of hot mint tea soon followed. As Mohsen and I sipped beneath the palm-leaf canopy, a clap of thunder bounced around the walls of the wadi and, before the final echo had rumbled away, rain-drops began to spatter the sandstone rocks around us. The desert was turning from pallid gold to a melancholy grey-brown as the sun retreated behind a veil of clouds. There was no time to waste. I decided I had to get my exploration of the rocks on the southern side of the wadi underway without delay.

Leaving Mohsen with his second glass of tea, I headed east along the base of the cliff. Everywhere there were signs of inscriptions – nearly all of great antiquity. What is more, the vast majority were clearly of predynastic date. Only occasionally did I spot the odd hieroglyph. After about one hundred metres I reached a recess in the sandstone where two small stelae had been carved by Seti's men. Here was a record of the cutting of the artesian well which I could see, still in use, just fifty metres

284. The wide, flat-bottomed Wadi Abbad as it approaches the desert mountains and the temple of Kanais, 60 km east from the Nile.

285. The modern guardians of King Seti I's well at Kanais. In the foreground is a trough for watering animals and, beyond, the temple can just be seen nestling beneath the cliffs. The boat graffiti are all over the rocks and cliff-face behind the well.

286. Three of Weigall's drawings of the remarkable high-prowed ship carvings found near the temple of Kanais in 1908.

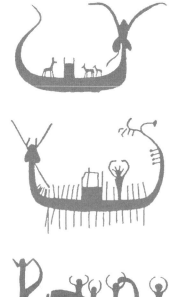

away. It was amazing to think that it had been cut into the floor of the valley some 3,000 years ago and yet the beduin GAFFIRS were still drawing water from it to make their tea.

Suddenly there was an almighty sizzling flash as the desert god reached down from heaven to his earthly domain. The blue lightning fork crashed into a rocky crag just across the wadi. Seth's great roar of displeasure at my intrusion thundered all around. Believe me, you have never felt the awesome power of nature until you have experienced a full-blown Eastern Desert storm. The naked sandstone mountains act as giant deflectors bouncing a single crash of thunder from side to side until it peals like a thousand Big Bens. In between these bursts of sudden violence the rain falls in a steady, monotonous patter. I felt quite alone as I stood in the shelter of an overhanging cliff-face.

The sandstone rocks were soon soaked and to my dismay the previously clear shallow carvings began to fade back into the dark surface. The light was so bad that I was taking photographs at one-thirtieth of a second with 200 ASA film. In spite of these difficult circumstances, during a brief respite in the downpour, I began to record the predynastic rock art on two huge boulders lying just to the east of the temple. I then discovered a smooth section of cliff behind the boulders with dozens more drawings. In my years of travelling through Egypt I had seen nothing like this.

The Square-Boat People

Here, near Seti's temple, were numerous graffiti – some crude, others well illustrated – of strange boats. Yes, for some reason, people in very early times – before the foundation of the Egyptian state – were drawing pictures of boats out in the desert! What is more, these boats were highly unusual. They were not typical NILOTIC boats, familiar to us from the

GAFFIRS: Supervisors or guardians.

NILOTIC: Characteristic of the Nile.

272

Egyptian art; instead they resembled the SUN BARQUES illustrated in the tombs of the pharaohs – the ships which carried the gods on their westward celestial journey by day, to be followed by the nightly passage through the darkness of the underworld to the eastern horizon of a new dawn.

The Wadi Abbad boats had high prows and sterns. Many had flat-bottomed hulls which gave a square profile to the vessels. As a result, some Egyptologists refer to these ships of the desert as 'square boats' and the little human figures carved in association with them as the 'Square-Boat People'.

The various interesting details of the boats and their passengers will be dealt with after I introduce you to the second major discovery of these extraordinary rock carvings – a little later in time and a little farther north in the desert massif to the east of Luxor. For now just take a look at Weigall's drawings and my more recent photographs of the boats and try to imagine the surprise felt by the Weigalls upon finding such nautical illustrations so far out in the desiccated desert.

287. An enormous carving of a sixty-nine-crew battleship can be seen at site WB-4, some 20 km beyond Kanais on the road to Mersa Alam (near the site of the Wadi Barramiya gold mines). A close inspection reveals that the ship is being towed or dragged by members of the crew. All around are animals and huntsmen. There is a second, smaller craft located immediately above the larger vessel.

SUN BARQUES: The ships which transport the sun across the day sky and night ocean of the underworld.

288. Another large high-prowed ship with fifty crew and central cabin, located at site DR-1 just to the east of WB-4. A much larger figure than the rest of the crew, with twin plumes, points west towards the Nile valley.

289. Entrance to the schist mountains of the Wadi Hammamat, some 80 km east of the Nile valley. The gold mines of the Wadi Hammamat are just a few kilometres beyond the quarries where the pharaohs acquired their prized black stone.

Winkler and Wadi Hammamat

290. An impressively carved ship with two major figures and a crew of twenty-two. Copied by Hans Winkler in the Wadi el-Atwani, to the north of the Wadi Hammamat. The craft appears to have a small rectangular sail at the stern, topped with antlers, whilst the prow has a streamer and two pendent palm fronds attached to it.

In spring of 1936 Swiss art historian, Hans Winkler, spent several weeks exploring the rock cliffs of the Wadi Hammamat, through which the main desert route to the Red Sea winds its way. Like Weigall, nearly thirty years before him, Winkler had come in search of rock drawings. In his investigations he too found numerous illustrations of the square boats. The results of this initial survey were so impressive that Sir Robert Mond, a wealthy English chemist and generous benefactor of Egyptological projects, decided to sponsor a more detailed exploration of the Eastern Desert in the Wadi Hammamat region. The 'Sir Robert Mond Expedition', headed by Winkler, spent the following winter of 1936-37 recording the graffiti in several isolated wadis, the tangible result being the publication of an initial report on the inscriptions entitled *Rock Drawings of Southern Upper Egypt*[5] which included over one hundred facsimiles of newly discovered desert boats.

Most of the boat graffiti were located at three main sites. Two are in the great wadi system which runs south-eastward from a point one third of the way along the Wadi Hammamat down to the Red Sea at Berenike. This is the route I mentioned earlier which eventually intersects the Wadi Barramiya and continues on down to the Greco-Roman trading port. The Berenike track also leads to the gold mines at Barramiya which were of such interest to Seti I. The first of these graffiti locations – Site A – is to be found in the Wadi el-Kash whilst the more important – Site B – is just to the west of Gebel es-Shalul between the Wadi Mineh and Wadi Abu Wasil. The third site – Site C – is to the north of the Wadi Hammamat road in a narrow side valley known as the Wadi el-Atwani. A short distance eastwards from here along the Wadi Hammamat are the gold mines of

Umm el-Fawahir. The focus is pretty clear. The locations of all the boat carvings have three things in common: (1) they are to be found on or near major trans-desert routes between the Nile valley and Red Sea; (2) these routes also happen to lead to the Eastern Desert gold mines; and (3) the wadis with the most abundant rock-drawings are quite rich in vegetation and may once have been camp sites beside open water.

It is time, then, to take a look at these drawings in more detail and to see if we can explain their appearance in what are now such wild and inhospitable places.

On Winkler's Trail

During the course of 1997 I made two attempts to investigate Winkler's graffiti sites, both of which were unsuccessful in that specific aim. The first (in February) demonstrated to me that the Eastern Desert needed to be treated with great respect. Its vastness and complexity is really brought home when you are stuck in the middle of it with no idea as to exactly where you are. Without highly detailed maps and modern electronic navigation systems the explorer has no chance of success and could end up in severe difficulties. Looking for rock inscriptions a metre or so across

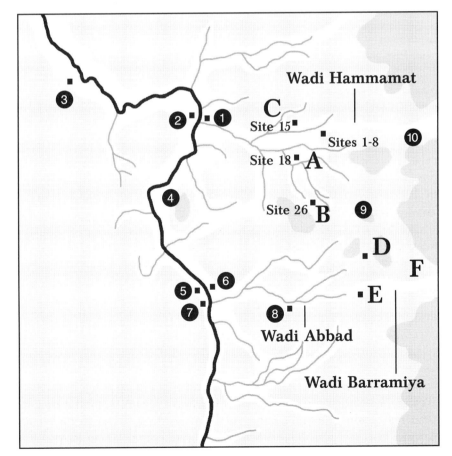

291. Distribution of the currently known graffiti sites of the Square-Boat People.

Key to Map

1 – Kuft/Gebtu
2 – Nakada/Nubt
3 – Abydos/Tjenu
4 – Thebes
5 – Kom el-Ahmar/Nekhen
6 – el-Kab/Nekheb
7 – Edfu
8 – Kanais Temple
9 – Gebel es-Shalul
10 – Bir Hammamat gold mines

A – Wadi el-Kash sites
B – Wadi Abu Marakat el-Nes
    (formerly Wadi Abu Wasil
    west-east branch) sites
C – Wadi el-Atwani sites
D – Wadi Umm Sallam sites
E – Wadi Barramiya sites
F – Barramiya gold mines

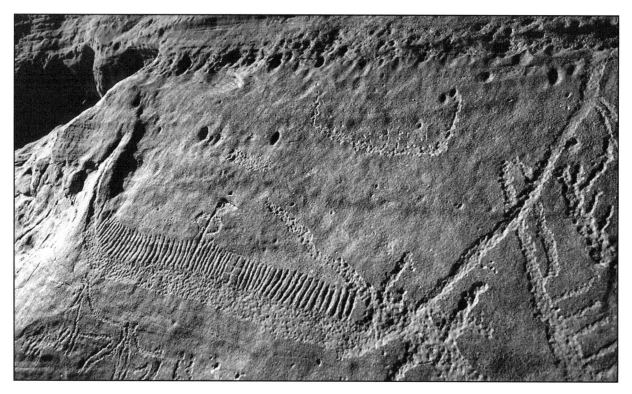

292. A huge vessel with a crew of seventy-five and one chieftain figure at the centre. This battleship is also located at Site DR-1 in the Wadi Barramiya.

293. Opposite page (above): The fleet of high-prowed boats at Site DR-1 in the Wadi Barramiya.

294. Opposite page (centre): Two of the many vessels in the canyon of Wadi Umm Sallam – an extension of the Wadi Abu Muawwad (Site MAM-2).

295. Opposite page (below): More square boats and animals from Site MAM-2.

hidden in winding canyons is nigh impossible unless you can pinpoint your location to within fifty metres or so – then you have a fighting chance. Unfortunately, on that first attempt I had no GPS and only Winkler's outdated map to guide me. The mission was aborted after two days, having reached Daydamus fort in the heart of the Wadi el-Kash.

The next attempt was in November 1997 and this time I was armed with GPS, 1:50,000 maps and four desert vehicles crammed with tents, rations and a large team of helpers. I was not going to fail through lack of resources this time! The plan of campaign had also been changed. On this occasion we were to come at Winkler's sites from the south via the Wadi Abbad and Weigall's Temple of Kanais.

As I explained in the *Preface*, this mission also failed to reach Winkler's main site due to the fact that two major routes northwards had become blocked by a sand-dune and a rock-fall. But it was a major success in other respects. During that trip my survey team discovered a brand new, previously undiscovered graffiti site which was overflowing with rock-drawings of high-prowed boats (area D). This was located in a narrow gorge in the mountains beyond the Wadi Mia extension to the Wadi Abbad. Neither Weigall nor Winkler had reached here and it is highly likely that other important sites in this region will be discovered in subsequent years.

The November 1997 mission also located a site previously found by Gerald Fuchs in the Wadi Barramiya where a 1.8-metre carving of a high-prowed boat contains a crew of seventy oarsmen (area E).[6] Not only is

296. A chieftain figure with raised arms standing in a multi-crewed boat. Detail from Wadi Hammamat site WD-2 (Winkler's Site 5).

297. Detail of a chieftain with plumes and throw-stick, from Winkler's Site 26.

the boat clearly a large vessel but it is shown being pulled along by members of its crew. This is a feature which occurs in several of the representations of the Square-Boat People.

As you now know, my third attempt to reach Winkler's main site (his 'Site 26') got underway in February 1998 and was finally successful in locating the lost valley of the boats. Much of what we are now going to discuss comes from that site and the two sites located in November 1997. I have no doubt at all that the Eastern Desert is going to reveal a great deal more as the ongoing survey progresses through the uncharted region between Wadi Abbad and Wadi Hammamat. Many surprises have already been thrown up and more are sure to come out of this important research. But, for now, we will concentrate on what we *already* know about the Square-Boat People and their amazing flotilla of ships.

The Shape of Things to Come

As I have already noted, the basic shape of the desert boats is flat-bottomed with high prow and stern. But there are other variations of this general profile. Many have curved hulls but retain the high prow and stern. Others have high in-curved prow and stern. Even so, there is a clear overall character to the entire corpus which distinguishes them from typical Nilotic vessels. In my own research on the subject I have never come across this observation from other scholars, but these boats are, without question, the forerunners of the solar boats found all over the walls of the temples and tombs of New Kingdom Egypt. The big question for me was how these desert drawings could be connected with the great solar mythology and religion of the pharaohs.

I have put together a sample set of the high-prowed boats to illustrate some of the common features and associations.

(a) Many vessels have what appear to be animal heads on the prow. These heads have either long horns or antlers and/or plumed pendant feathers or palm fronds.

(b) There is often a central cabin or shrine on the deck of the boat.

(c) Some have a large figure of a woman represented with arms raised aloft as if dancing or performing an act of prayer. Others show rows of dancing figures.

(d) A number of scenes show a man carrying a composite bow or a throw-stick or, in one case, a mace with round head. This male figure is regularly illustrated with two tall feathers rising from his head. From now on we will refer to him as 'the chieftain'. In some cases he is accompanied by two other figures, smaller than himself. As Michael Rice notes in his book *Egypt's Making* 'this constant repetition of the boat with three occupants is too frequent not to be especially significant'.[7]

298. Some of the copies made by Weigall and Winkler of the rock drawings seen by them on their expeditions into the Eastern Desert.

299. Two important figures with plumes from site MAM-2.

(e) The more complex drawings show several oarsmen/oars (sometimes as many as sixty or seventy), indicating that at least one of the ships (perhaps frequently represented) was a very large vessel.

(f) Several show an object hanging down from the prow which appears to represent a stone anchor (familiar to marine archaeologists from all parts of the Near East).

(g) A few illustrations represent a ship with a single, large, rectangular sail.

(h) Perhaps the most extraordinary feature is that, in an ever-increasing number of drawings, the boats are being pulled or towed by their crews with the chieftain occasionally shown directing operations from the deck of the boat.

300. Above:A smaller vessel with animal's head and a chieftain holding a throw-stick and what may be a pear-shaped mace. Site MAM-2.

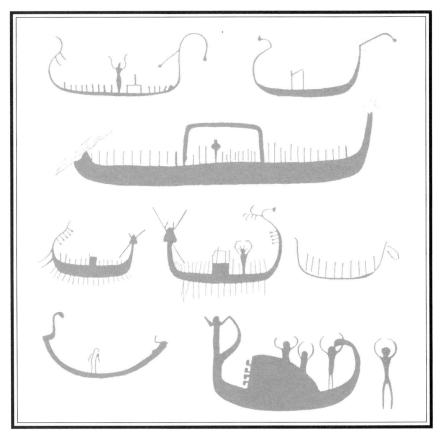

301. Right: Further sketches of the various types of high-prowed ship seen by Weigall and Winkler. There are examples here of the 'dancing goddess', horned prow and central cabin. The extraordinary vessel from Kanais (bottom right) has been dubbed the 'Golfer's Boat' for obvious reasons.

302. A large figure with tall twin plumes, carrying a bow. From Site MAM-2.

303. Right: A typical high-prowed boat with raised-arm chieftain or goddess, central cabin and twenty-eight crew. Site WB-4.

So what sort of conclusions were initially drawn from the study of this fascinating desert art? Well, Winkler was convinced that the rock drawings represented an expedition of foreign seafarers who had landed on the west coast of the Red Sea and then journeyed across the desert to the Nile valley. Given their military character, they appeared to be invaders who had come to occupy Egypt. This interpretation became widely accepted in the early days because it fitted in well with other evidence found during archaeological excavations in the Nile valley itself – evidence which indicated that a new group of people had been buried in the

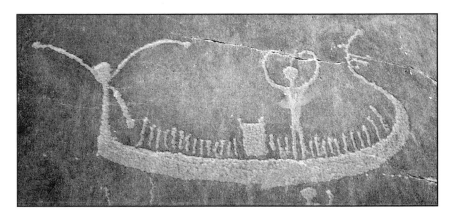

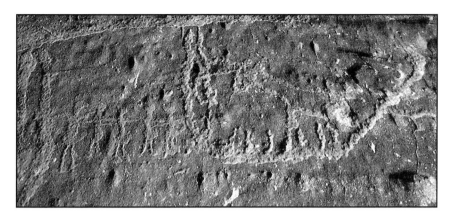

304. One of the high-prowed boats is being pulled by five of its crew. The actual numbers of draggers and size of crew illustrated in the rock drawings may well be unrepresentative of the reality – shorthand versions of larger numbers which were impractical to illustrate by means of these primitive 'cartoons'. Where large numbers are shown each of the crew is represented by a single stroke. But where there is an attempt to flesh out the figures with arms, legs and heads (as here) the number of crew is reduced because of the added complexity.

FELLAH: An Egyptian who lives off the land.

305. The obverse of the Gebel el-Arak knife handle. Louvre Museum.

cemeteries of the original indigenous population. The dragging of boats seemed to suggest that these 'invaders' had succeeded in transporting their sea-going craft across the desert – a journey of two hundred and thirty kilometres – in order to re-deploy them in the River Nile itself. This, at first, rather implausible scenario appeared to be confirmed by a remarkable artefact which had come to light some time earlier.

History's First Battle

In 1916 the Louvre Museum in Paris acquired an exquisite flint dagger which was reported as having been purchased from a local FELLAH of Gebel el-Arak village near the western end of the Wadi Hammamat. Many similar blades had been discovered previously in known pre-dynastic contexts, so the dating was not really an issue, nor was the quality of the workmanship of the knife's ivory handle – it was immediately acknowledged as a true masterpiece. No, what really got the art historians excited were the scenes carved on either side of the handle.

This single artefact has so many details of interest that it is probably best if I describe and discuss each element in turn rather than starting with a general description. Beginning at the top of one side of the handle, I shall work my way down and then around to the other side. The implications will come thick and fast as each scene tells its own story.

The first cameo is one of the most remarkable. In the centre stands a male figure with full beard. His body is wrapped in a long coat which extends down to his knees. The coat is tied with a belt or cloth band. On his head he wears what can only be described either as a turban or his long hair is wound around his head and tied up in a bun. His arms are extended outwards, hands grasping the throats of two enormous lions with long flowing manes. Our 'chignoned' hero is literally lifting the front halves of the lions off the ground so that they stand, bi-pedal, on their haunches. The hero is completely in control of these huge feline beasts, posed in what art historians call 'antithetical composition' – that is to say they are a reflection or mirror image of each other. This is heraldic imagery, akin to a coat of arms.

306. Right: Detail from the Gebel el-Arak knife handle showing the Master of Animals.

307. Below: Button stamp seal from Susa depicting a Master of Animals controlling lions. Note that he wears two tall plumes on his head (after P. Amiet, 1961, pl. 6, 119A).

308. The Master of Animals (this time the 'bull-man') from the facia of the Ur lyre sound-board. Part of the treasure found in the royal tombs of Ur by Sir Leonard Woolley. British Museum.

The Gebel el-Arak knife handle scene is not the only such representation of a hero figure 'controlling' wild animals. Many such scenes exist – but not in predynastic Egyptian art. This motif is recognised as originating in the lands of Sumer and Susiana. The first archaeologically attested illustration of this kind appears on a button seal from Susa – the city which we have identified as the gateway to Eden – datable to the immediate post Susa I level. Here again the semi-divine, hero figure is controlling two antithetical lions; he wears a long garment down to his knees and what appear to be two tall feathers rising from the top of his head.[8] Other more famous examples can be seen in the British Museum – in particular the 'Khafaje Bowl' and a similar scene on the facia of the beautiful lyre found by Sir Leonard Woolley in the 'Queen's Tomb' at Ur.

309. Right: The Master of Animals from the Khafaje bowl. Note the six-petalled rosette of Inanna in front of the head of the hero. This suggests the possibility that the Master of Animals being represented is a hero from Uruk – perhaps the long-haired wild-man, Enkidu.

310. Left: Upper scene of the Uruk Stela showing the bearded hero with turban or chignon and long coat spearing a lion. Baghdad Museum.

311. Above: Lower scene of the Uruk Stela showing the same figure hunting a lion with bow and arrow. Although just off the picture to the right, the arrowhead is chisel shaped – a characteristic of the arrowheads illustrated on the Hunters' Palette from predynastic Egypt.

It has been long recognised that the type of coat worn by the man on the Gebel el-Arak knife handle is otherwise found on human figures in the art of ancient Susa and Uruk.[9] The chignon worn by our hero is typical of Mesopotamian rulers. An extraordinarily close parallel to the Gebel el-Arak figure is to be found on the 'Lion Hunt Stela' from Uruk, now in the Baghdad Museum. Here we see the chieftain hero in two scenes, one slaying a lion with a spear, the other downing his feline prey with bow and arrow. This ruler of Uruk also has a long beard and chignon. He wears a heavy coat down to his knees. In every respect he is the spitting image of the Gebel el-Arak chieftain from Egypt.

The iconography of our first scene is therefore foreign – there is no doubt about it – the hero on the Gebel el-Arak knife handle found in Egypt is Sumerian. This is what seal specialist, Dominique Collon, has to say about the archetypal Sumerian hero figure.

312. The miniature head of King Hammurabi of Babylon I with similar headgear to that worn by the hero on the much earlier Uruk Stela. Louvre Museum.

> One recurrent figure is a bearded man who wears his hair in a bun and a thick, rolled band around his head; he is dressed in a kilt or skirt which is diagonally cross-hatched. This figure appears in a variety of roles which have led to his being called the priest-king since he seems to fulfil both functions: he plays an important part in ritual, he feeds stylised plants to flocks, he takes part in hunting and he is shown in battle and with prisoners.[10]

Scholars have a term for this controller of nature – they call him the 'Master of Animals'. In biblical imagery, there is one early hero who had power over the wild beasts of the earth.

> Of the clean animals and the animals that are not clean, of the birds and all that creeps along the ground, one pair boarded

313. An Early Dynastic II Period seal impression depicting the motif of the Master of Animals. On the left we see the long-haired, naked hero fending off a lion. In the middle the Master of Animals controls two lions by their tails. To the right the bull-man grapples with a lion and a bull. Louvre Museum.

EDWARDS: (1909-1996).

314. The lower part of the obverse of the Gebel el-Arak knife handle. The top motif depicts two antithetical hunting hounds. Below the handle boss are various animals including a lion leaping onto the haunches of a gazelle.

the ark with Noah, one male and one female, as God had commanded Noah. [Genesis 7:8-9]

We have also identified Enmerkar of Uruk with Nimrod who, in biblical tradition, is remembered as a great hunter. He too then is a Master of Animals. Both Noah and Enmerkar/Nimrod are of the same heroic age – the late-Ubaid, Uruk and Jemdet Nasr Periods. Gilgamesh too is probably portrayed in Early Dynastic glyptic art as the victor in human-animal contests. The former Keeper of Egyptian Antiquities at the British Museum, Eiddon EDWARDS, is in no doubt about the origins of the Arak Master of Animals motif.

> … so closely does the composition of the scene resemble the so-called Gilgamesh motif, frequently represented on Meso-potamian seals, that the source of its inspiration can hardly be questioned. [11]

It is only in later times that the Egyptians themselves adopt the icon-ography of the Master of Animals in representations of two of their gods – Bes and Horus the Child – both of whom are protector-deities from the chaotic forces of nature – the wild animals of the marshes and deserts.

I will call upon perhaps the most renowned comparative art historian in ancient world studies, Henri Frankfort, to testify to the un-Egyptian character of our Gebel el-Arak hero.

> The most striking example of the copying of an alien, Meso-potamian, motif is the group of the man dominating two lions on the Gebel el-Arak knife-handle. Such groups are common at all times in Mesopotamia but exceedingly rare in Egypt. And in the present case the derivation cannot be doubted: the hero between the lions copies in every detail of his appearance – his garment, his beard, his hair, wound round his head and bound up in a chignon at the back – the often recurring figure of the 'leader' or king depicted on a granite stela from Erech

(Uruk) and on numerous seals. Even the style of the figure, the way in which the muscles in the legs are rendered, for instance, is entirely un-Egyptian … [12]

The next vignette on the Gebel el-Arak knife handle, below the Master of Animals, is of two dogs, also antithetically posed. One paw of each dog surmounts the central boss of the knife handle. These are not wild dogs for they have collars and chest straps. They are trained hunting hounds. But they are not the typical Egyptian dogs resembling jackals with long snouts and tall pointed ears. These are stocky, muscle-bound dogs with short snouts typical of those found in Mesopotamian art.

315. The reverse side of the Gebel el-Arak knife handle showing the two battle scenes (land and water).

Below them are various animals such as gazelles or oryx and a female lion attacking a gazelle from the rear. Scenes such as this are also typical of early Mesopotamian art.

Turning the knife over we can now study the earliest battle scene to survive from the ancient world. It is divided into two fields: the upper scene is a land battle whilst the lower shows a naval conflict between two very different types of vessels. In the upper scene we see almost naked men (wearing only phallus sheaths) – some in hand-to-hand combat, others slugging it out with wooden clubs. At the top left, one man – brandishing a round-headed mace – escorts a prisoner whose hands are tied behind his back. If you look closely at the heads of the victor and the vanquished you will see that the former has short cropped hair or perhaps a shaven head whereas his prisoner appears to have long flowing locks down to his shoulders. Now look at the rest of the combatants and you will observe that it is the short-haired fighters (nearly always on the left, facing to the right) who are getting the better of their long-haired enemy (on the right, facing to the left).

We should now focus on the naval battle. This is a very confusing melée but if you look hard enough you will see two square boats (one behind the other) underneath which men are floundering or dead in the water. Below them is another row of three boats – but these are the typical crescent-shaped boats of the Nile. The standard interpretation of this scene is that the people of the square boats are the victors: their ships appear above the Nilotic boats, indicating supremacy, whilst the drowning men resemble the long-haired types who are getting the worst of it in the land battle above. This ceremonial knife, found in the vicinity of the Wadi Hammamat, appears to show a successful invasion of the Nile valley by the Square-Boat People whose ships we first encountered out in Egypt's Eastern Desert.

A Great Black Ship

316. Detail of the high-prowed boats on the Gebel el-Arak knife handle showing the stone weights in the prow, crescent-moon-with-solar-disc standard, central cabin and rear struts.

Much of the evidence so far presented points to the arrival in the Nile valley of a group of foreign seafarers who had close ties to the civilisation of the Sumerians. Not only does their ancestral, semi-divine ruler on the Arak knife handle look like a Sumerian hero but, as I will now demonstrate, his square boat was also of Mesopotamian design.

Below I have extracted one of the foreign boats from the other side of the knife handle and flipped it on its vertical axis so that the prow faces to the left. I have also stretched the hull a little so that it corresponds better to the length of a second vessel which I have positioned immediately below the first in order for us to make a detailed comparison.

As you can see, the similarities are immediately obvious. The straight hull and the high prow and stern of the second vessel conform to the typical square shape with which you are now familiar. The stern is supported by lashings or struts in both vessels. This is typical of a Mesopotamian reed boat which requires this re-enforcement to prevent the spine of the boat from breaking as a consequence of the outward stresses created by the high stern.

Papyrus does not grow along the banks of the Euphrates and Tigris rivers, so the Sumerians instead built their first boats from a tall, freshwater reed which is called *berdi* by the modern Marsh Arabs of southern Iraq.[13] The berdi reed is similar to the papyrus plant in that it has a pithy core, but it is more absorbent than its Egyptian cousin and is therefore

317. A comparison between the high-prowed boat design of the Gebel el-Arak knife handle of Nakada II or III (317a, top) and that on a cylinder seal from Uruk datable to the Uruk Period (317b, bottom). Note, in particular, the rear struts on both craft and the horned prows. The figure of the priest-king on the Uruk seal is very similar to the Master of Animals on the obverse of the knife handle.

318. Berdi reeds growing in their natural habitat within the marshes of southern Iraq.

less suited, in its natural state, to the craft of boat making. The Sumerians were able to counter this disadvantage by giving their vessels a special coating to protect the vulnerable reed core. Their boats were daubed with bitumen to repel the water and therefore increase buoyancy. Mesopotamian reed vessels were therefore distinctive black ships!

Bitumen was readily available from open springs near the city of Ur, around Kara Dagh in northern Mesopotamia and also on the islands of Bahrain – ancient Dilmun. We have several references in the ancient literature to this practice of asphalting both riverine and sea-going vessels.

The building of Gilgamesh's ship:

> When Gilgamesh [heard] this, he raised the axe in his hand, drew [the dagger from his belt], went down to the woods and cut [twice-sixty poles] of sixty cubits each. **He applied the bitumen** and attached the *ferrules*; and he brought [(them) to him]. Gilgamesh and Urshanabi boarded [the boat]. They launched the boat on the waves and they [sailed away].[14]

319. The underside of a reed basket coated in bitumen. Bahrain National Museum.

The building of Utnapishtim's ship:

> With the first glow of dawn, the land was gathered [about me]. **The little ones [carr]ied bitumen**, while the grown ones brought [all else] that was needful. On the fifth day I laid her framework. One (whole) acre was her floor space, … **Six *sar* (measures) of bitumen I poured into the furnace, three *sar* of asphalt [I also] poured inside.** Three *sar* of oil the basket-bearers carried, aside from the one *sar* of oil which the *calking* consumed, and the two *sar* of oil [which] the boatman stowed away.[15]

The building of Noah's ark:

> God said to Noah … 'Make yourself an ark out of resinous wood. Make it out of reeds and **caulk it with pitch inside and out**.' [Genesis 6:13-14]

The making of Moses' basket:

> There was a man descended from Levi who had taken a woman of Levi as his wife. She conceived and gave birth to a son and, seeing what a fine child he was, she kept him hidden for three months. When she could hide him no longer, she got a papyrus basket for him; **coating it in bitumen and pitch**, she put the child inside and laid it among the reeds at the river's edge. [Exodus 2:1-3]

Even the modern Marsh Arab canoe, known locally as the *mashhuf,* though now made of wood, is still coated in bitumen, more in respect for tradition than for practical purposes. As the world-famous Norwegian explorer, Thor Heyerdahl, notes, the profile of the *mashhuf* still retains the original shape of its earlier reed counterpart.

> This was their usual *mashhuf,* the slender, flat-bottomed long-boat built to standard lines by all Marsh Arabs today. While formerly built of their own reeds, they are now pegged together from imported wood and covered, like their reed prototypes, with a smooth coating of black asphalt. Prow and stern soar in a high curve like the Viking ships, following the five-thousand-year lines of their Sumerian forerunners. [16]

You may be thinking to yourself that such comparisons between today's small marsh-water canoes and large, prehistoric, sea-going ships hardly amounts to proof that the latter were, or even could be, built and successfully sailed by the ancient Sumerians. Surely the huge bulk and weight of such vessels would have made them unseaworthy? Apparently not. In the 1970s, Thor Heyerdahl personally inspected thirty-seven-metre-long by five-metre-wide rafts made of berdi reeds. [17] These gargantuan river craft were moored in the Shatt el-Arab next to a local insulation factory, their hulls – some three metres in thickness – waiting to be dismantled so that the reeds from which they had been made could be employed in the manufacture of cardboard. The total mass must have represented a huge tonnage and yet they floated, without any visible signs of deterioration for several months, whilst awaiting dismantling.

As Richard Barnett, Keeper of Western Asiatic Antiquities in the British Museum, noted back in 1958, the black high-prowed reed boat had a very long history in southern Mesopotamia.

> Assyrian sculptures show us the Babylonian marsh-dwellers and Elamites using elongated boats of reeds, in which they try to make their escape from the Assyrians. Such boats are mere

mastless canoes; they are still made of reeds, basketry and bitumen (today) at Hit on the Euphrates. A barge derived from such a boat, called *maqurru* in Assyrian, was used for the ritual processions of the Gods by water; it appears to be mastless, but has each end raised high above the water line and tied back, and it was no doubt in use from the very earliest Sumerian times, since from it is derived the cuneiform sign for ship. Illustrations on cylinder seals carry it back at least to the Jemdet Nasr period ...[18]

Also common to both the Egyptian predynastic square boat on the Gebel el-Arak knife handle and its Mesopotamian counterpart is a prow mounting of animal horn or antler configuration in which a large boulder has been placed in the Gebel el-Arak craft. One can only imagine that the extra weighting at the front of this vessel indicates that the ship was required to cut through waves. It is not merely a riverine craft but a sea-going vessel. One might also imagine that the weighted prow would improve the ramming qualities of a square boat, preventing an attacking ship from being lifted out of the water upon impact with a lower-lying target vessel. The horned mounting may also be the housing for a stone anchor. Although the image of the Figure 317b boat does not show a boulder, it does have the same design feature of the horned mounting which, by the simple and rapid installation of a rock, could then permit the vessel to journey on the seas. Seals from Failaka Island at the head of the Persian Gulf show exactly this feature – apparently the horns of a gazelle, sometimes the actual animal skull but on other occasions a wooden carving of the animal. The triple-point prow shown on the knife handle boats may therefore, in fact, be the head (snout) and two horns of the gazelle in stylised form. What we do know is that this symbol represents the Sumerian writing sign for ship and, remarkably, at the same time the earliest Egyptian hieroglyphic sign for 'marine' or 'fighting sailor'. It is also interesting to note that the Sumerian word for the 'bow' of a ship is the same word as that used for 'animal horn'.

Both boats have cabins, but on the lower version we have, in addition, two crew members and an ox carrying what appears to be the portable shrine of the goddess Inanna bearing her sacred standard. A male figure stands before the shrine suggesting that he is a priest-king in the act of transporting the goddess to her temple. I am sure you will have noticed that, exactly as with the master of animals on the Gebel el-Arak knife handle and the hero on the Lion Hunt Stela from Uruk, this Meso-potamian king is clad in a long coat, has a heavy beard and wears a turban or hair-bun on his head. One is tempted to see in this scene the transportation of Inanna from Aratta to Uruk by Enmerkar, whom we have identified with the biblical Nimrod, 'the first potentate on earth'.

All you need to know now is in what form the second illustration (figure 317b) appears and precisely when and where it derives. Well, it is the glyptic design on a large (4.3 x 3.5 cm) lapis lazuli cylinder seal

320. Impression from the lapis lazuli cylinder seal datable to the Uruk IV Period.

found in the temple precinct of Inanna at Uruk. It dates from Collon's Period 1A which coincides with the Sumerian Protoliterate Period (Uruk IV and Jemdet Nasr).[19] So yet another motif points us back to the ancient city of Uruk whose founding we have linked to Enoch and his followers when they entered the land of Shinar from the east. Not long after, it was Enmerkar/Nimrod who built the great temple precincts of Inanna and Anu in his royal city. I have identified the Mosaic and White Temples of Uruk IV as his work which scholars have determined predates the 1st Dynasty of Egypt by a century at most.

Perhaps, then, we can assume for now that the arrival of the square boats in Egypt, carrying their passengers and crew, took place around the time of Enmerkar or at least within a couple of generations either side of his time – the era scholars call the Mesopotamian Protoliterate Period because it was at this time that writing was invented. In the New Chronology this would be *circa* 2900 BC.

Conclusion Twenty-Four

The high-prowed boats, so typical of the predynastic rock-art of the Eastern Desert, seem to have derived from Sumerian prototypes of the Protoliterate Period (Uruk IV & Jemdet Nasr). Their design is not Nilotic. The ships would appear to have been intended for both river and sea usage, their fabric being almost certainly reed bundles coated in bitumen.

There are numerous other examples of these high-prowed, bitumen-ised reed boats in the glyptic art of protoliterate Sumer and Susiana, a number having direct connections with the transportation of kings or gods.

It is therefore of some considerable significance to our developing theory that just such a large black ship is an important feature within the first painted scene of Egyptian prehistoric art. I am, of course, referring to the famous Hierakonpolis Tomb 100 painting which we will be studying in more detail in the next chapter. But, for now, the illustration of the Hierakonpolis ship (Figure 321) will suffice.

Could this mighty black ship, which plays such an important role in the art-history of predynastic Egypt, have carried a member of a royal house of Sumer and his family? As we saw in the previous chapter, the Sumerian King List could hold the answer. In a rather cryptic verse dealing with the kingship of Uruk – a passage which has been admittedly difficult to interpret historically – we learn that Meskiagkasher was remembered for a spectacular seafaring exploit.

> Meskiagkasher, son of the sun god (Utu), became high priest and king (of Uruk) and reigned for 324 years. Meskiagkasher journeyed upon the sea and came ashore at the mountains.[20]

In *Chapter Seven* we identified Meskiagkasher, predecessor of Enmerkar, as the biblical Cush, father of Nimrod. We noted that the eponymous ancestor, Cush, son of Ham and grandson of Noah, is also the traditional founder of the land of Kush – the great expanse of north-east Africa to the south of Egypt. If we treat the biblical land of Cush in this wider geographic sense (in the same way that the classical geographers refer to pharaonic Kush's descendant, Ethiopia, as everything south of Egypt), then Cush would cover not only Sudan but also the mountainous region of Ethiopia along the west coast of the Red Sea. Are these the mountains to which Meskiagkasher journeyed? If so, then the traditions of Sumer and the Bible may hold, between them, a vague memory of a great seafaring adventure which brought Meskiagkasher/Cush and his family to Africa.

Cush, in turn, was regarded as the elder brother of the biblical Mizraim, the traditional eponymous ancestor of Egyptian civilisation. The

321. The large black ship from the Hierakonpolis Tomb 100 wall painting.

extraordinary possibility therefore arises that the leader of the foreign expedition which journeyed up the Red Sea and through the Eastern Desert wadis into the Nile valley was the historical figure behind the biblical tradition. This was no insignificant event in the history of the Middle East.

Again, we will be returning to this intriguing doorway to further discovery later, but first we need to learn a great deal more about the Square-Boat People and their astonishing seafaring adventure.

Journey from Paradise

Given that the first illustrations of the high-prowed, black, reed vessel are Sumerian and not Egyptian, there can hardly be any doubt that the design is of Mesopotamian origin. It is simply not an Egyptian vessel and to suggest so, as some Egyptologists have done in recent times, is surely to present a case for special pleading not merited by the evidence.

But is it likely, or even remotely possible, that ships of Sumer travelled to distant Egypt and ended up participating in a naval battle on the River Nile? How would they have reached there? As I have already intimated, given the pictographic evidence of the square boats found by Weigall and Winkler in the wadis of the Eastern Desert, it would appear that they did not enter Egypt from the north – via the Mediterranean – but instead came around the Arabian peninsula, setting off from the Persian Gulf, past Magan (Oman), beyond the Straits of Hormuz, and then on out into the Indian Ocean – always hugging the coastline in case of storms. Modern seafarers know that for half the year the winds and currents of the Indian Ocean drive sailing ships south-westwards towards the Horn of Africa.[21] The fleet simply went with the flow of nature. Eventually the black flotilla would have slipped through the straits of Bab el-Mandeb ('Gate of Mourning') and into the Red Sea.

From there the final stage of the sea journey took them northwards along the western (African) coast, carefully weaving their way through the dangerous coral reefs, until they reached a suitable landing place opposite the entrance to the transverse wadi system leading to the Nile valley. Again the wind would have come to their aid because in the summer months it changes its normal north to south direction and begins to blow from south to north up the Red Sea. Of course, the 4,000-nautical-mile sea journey from the Gulf to the shores of the Red Sea must have taken several months[22] – but the evidence from Sumer and Dilmun shows that long journeys were never a real disincentive for ancient traders and travellers. It seems perfectly feasible to me that reed ships could have hopped from anchorage to anchorage, making running repairs to any potentially unseaworthy vessels to ensure the safe passage of its crew and cargo to the next 'service station' along the route. Amazingly, this type of 'primitive' transport is still employed in one part of the Middle East in modern times.

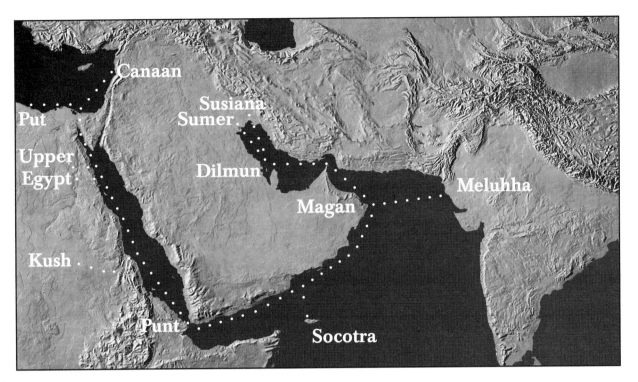

The labels on the map read: Canaan, Put, Susiana, Sumer, Upper Egypt, Dilmun, Magan, Meluhha, Kush, Punt, Socotra.

322. The sea journey of the Square-Boat People from Sumer or Susiana to Dilmin/Bahrain and then on to Magan/Oman, Punt and eventually the western shores of the Red Sea opposite Upper Egypt.

… even today reed craft are in use along 670 kilometres of Arabian coast and the *shashah*, an apparently frail wicker fishing-boat of Oman, makes voyages of 85 to 170 kilometres.[23]

It is well known that much longer journeys than these were being made by the sailors of ancient Dilmun (Bahrain), for, as we have seen, they brought the produce of Meluhha (the Indus valley) and Magan (Oman) to Sumer. And it seems highly likely that these trading missions were made in large reed and bitumen seagoing vessels. If the Roman historian and geographer, PLINY THE ELDER, is anything to go by, long voyages undertaken by reed or papyrus vessels were not only feasible but entirely practical. In his book *Natural History* he even discusses the differences in journey time between the older reed craft and the modern vessels of the Roman empire.[24]

You may remember that Thor Heyerdahl himself built a reed ship – which he named 'Tigris' – in order to prove precisely the point that Mesopotamian sailors could have made the long journey to the Indus Valley and around the Arabian peninsula to Egypt. He constructed his over-eighteen-metre-long vessel from berdi reeds (which he did not coat in bitumen) on the banks of the River Tigris in Iraq during the summer months of 1977. On the 11th of November Heyerdahl and his crew sailed down the Shatt el-Arab and out into the Persian Gulf.

They sailed past the island of Failaka and on to Bahrain/Dilmun which they reached within a couple of days. A week later they were on their way to Oman/Magan and then beyond, across the Indian Ocean, to the

PLINY THE ELDER: (AD 23-79).

Indus Valley/Meluhha reaching the coast of Pakistan near Karachi by the 30th of January 1978. They had been at sea for fifty days and their reed ship was still riding high in the water.

Having spent a couple of weeks exploring the ancient ruins of ancient Meluhha, including Mohenjo Daro, Heyerdahl's Square-Boat People set off once more – this time heading south into the vast expanse of the Indian Ocean.

> All night the storm raged. The wind howled and whistled in the empty rigging ... Like Noah we waited inside cover for the weather to abate. ... It was an incredible comfort to all of us to know that we were on a compact bundle-boat and not inside a fragile plank hull. No worry about the vessel springing a leak; no need for bailing. ... with breaking seas tumbling on board by the tens of tons ... next moment all the frothing water ... was gone, dropping straight down through the sieve-like bottom. And the bundle-boat rose from the sea like a surfacing submarine, ... No wonder that this simple kind of self-bailing craft was the first to give primitive boat-builders the security to venture upon the waves ...[25]

After another voyage of several weeks' duration, through these heavy storms and then days of complete becalmment, they reached the Gulf of Aden off the Horn of Africa. The 'Tigris' was still in perfect working order after twenty weeks afloat in the seas around Arabia and after having made a journey of some 6,800 kilometres!

Unfortunately, our modern Square-Boat People's onward journey to Egypt through the straits of Bab el-Mandeb was thwarted by the government of North Yemen (then at war with communist South Yemen) who refused to permit their passage northwards into the Red Sea 'for security reasons'. Even so, 'Tigris' and its crew had made their point – the reed ships of Sumer, Susiana and Dilmun could certainly have reached Egypt without any difficulty. The berdi-reed ship 'Tigris' met her sad but triumphant end off the coast of Djibouti on the 3rd of April 1978. She was torched by her crew and went to the bottom of the Gulf of Aden in a blaze of glory.

So the long sea journey around the Arabian peninsula was certainly possible and, very likely, a well-tried trade route supplying the produce of Africa to Sumerian Mesopotamia. As I have suggested, no doubt there were numerous expeditions ashore for repairs, resupply and recoupment during the epic adventures of these expert seafarers – although Heyerdahl had proved that it could have been done in giant leaps. A whole system of temporary anchorages may have been established which, by their very nature, would now be extremely difficult to detect. It seems logical to me that these trading contacts with Africa – and no doubt therefore with predynastic Egypt – may have been the catalyst for a later military adventure – a campaign of conquest which is evidenced by the Eastern Desert rock drawings, the Gebel el-Arak knife handle and the Hierakonpolis painted tomb.

I am not the first, nor likely to be the last, to suggest this route for Mesopotamian contacts with Egypt: Flinders Petrie, way back in 1939, was proposing just such a journey.

> Sailing south from Sumer the prevailing winds would carry the craft, which were quite substantial and capable of bearing, for example, twenty tons of merchandise, down to Bahrain (Dilmun), on to the northern Oman coast (Magan), skirting the copper port of Umm an-Nar, round the towering headland of Ras Musandam, down the Omani coast, and out into the Arabian Sea. The currents prevailing in the northern Indian Ocean would now take over and carry the craft along the southern Arabian coast to the Bab el-Mandeb, at the entrance to the Red Sea.[26]

PALERMO STONE: The earliest Egyptian king list.

323. One of the Square-Boat People dragging teams.

Conclusion Twenty-Five

The appearance of Mesopotamian culture in Egypt was instigated by sea trading activities between the Persian Gulf and north-east Africa.

As we have seen, from their final landing point on the west coast of the Red Sea, the Square-Boat People had one amazing last trick up their sleeve. They planned physically to drag their great sea-going vessels along the flat-bottomed, sandy wadis until they were able to re-launch them, at last, into their new environment – the River Nile.

If they had chosen the season of the Nile inundation for their cunning stratagem, they may have been able to launch their vessels a considerable distance east of the Nile's true course because there is some evidence that in predynastic times the flood levels in Egypt were much higher than in the later pharaonic era. It may well be that the wider, flatter wadis were flooded during part of the year for some distance out into the Eastern Desert. The PALERMO STONE records annual Nile flood levels several metres higher than those of the early Middle Kingdom (kiosk of Senuseret I at Karnak) and Third Intermediate Period (Karnak west quay). This raises the distinct possibility that the Wadis Hammamat and Abbad were partially navigable during the summer months during the Predynastic Period. In modern times the Wadi Kena (also near Kuft) has been flooded to a considerable depth well out into the desert, whilst an ancient dam has been discovered in the Wadi Garawi just south of Cairo.[27]

Whatever help the inundation-god, Hapy, may have given to our intrepid Mesopotamian heroes, they somehow appear to have successfully negotiated the desert crossing. This gargantuan feat of endurance and

324. Detail from the Palermo Stone listing the predynastic rulers of Egypt (top row) known as the Followers of Horus.

325. The Kiosk of Senuseret I at Karnak records the heights of the floods at different points along the length of the River Nile.

326. The large battleship from site WB-4 with a smaller vessel carrying a chieftain with raised arms carved immediately above it (after G. Fuchs, 1989, p. 138).

determination could then begin to pay its dividend as the vastly superior Sumerian berdi-reed ships, led by the great black flagship, wreaked havoc amongst the less substantial Nilotic papyrus craft of the indigenous defenders of the valley. This would not have been much of a contest. The foreign élite ensured victory and their domination of Upper Egypt by a daring stratagem which would not be witnessed again for many centuries to come – and, even then, never on such a scale.

Such adventures are the stuff of legend which, by their very nature, are difficult to pin down historically or archaeologically. Few sea journeys can be proven to have taken place, for obvious reasons. The only signs we have of such voyages – either undertaken as trading *ventures* or as colonisation *adventures* – are the discovery of recognisable artefacts of those cultures at their final destinations (and, of course, along their way to those destinations). But we also possess memories and stories carried through into ancient literature which tell of such epic journeys – some closely paralleling the saga of the Sumerian invaders of Egypt. Every child knows of the Argonauts' quest for the Golden Fleece of Colchis on the far shores of the Black Sea and the adventures of Odysseus in the Mediterranean. Scholars of Greek and Roman history have long accepted the Phoenician colonisation of the western Mediterranean and their journeys beyond the Pillars of Hercules to found cities such as Cadiz. It has been suggested that tin from Cornwall reached the Near East by sea as well as by land across the European continent. From Egyptian history we hear of the resourceful transportation of boats by the army of THUTMOSE III from the Mediterranean coast of Syria across hundreds of kilometres of open plain to the Euphrates river so that they could raid, commando-style, the kingdom of MITANNI on the opposite bank.

This 'epic' saga of the Square-Boat People, which took place at the dawn of history and as yet – so far as our discussion is concerned – only attested through desert graffiti, raises a number of interesting issues for ancient historians which we now need to address.

A Mysterious Land Called Punt

Throughout their history, the ancient Egyptians referred to a far-off land called Pwenet or Punt. It was the place to which expeditions were sent,

THUTMOSE III: King of the 18th Dynasty, reigned 1514-1493 BC.

MITANNI: Also known as Naharin in the Egyptian texts – the land between the two rivers of the Euphrates and Khabur in modern Syria/Iraq.

charged with the task of bringing back the produce of the gods – that is to say the exotic natural products needed for temple rituals and the ceremonials intimately connected with Egyptian kingship. The land of Punt was no ordinary place. The Egyptians often referred to it by the epithet 'God's Land' (Egy. *Ta-Netjer*). Reliefs from the reigns of several pharaohs illustrate Punt's produce, so we should be able to get a fair idea where God's Land was located simply by finding the geographical region which possesses all the natural resources displayed in the reliefs and mentioned in the texts.

We need, therefore, to find a location where frankincense (Egy. *senetjer?*), myrrh (Egy. *antyu?*), ebony (Egy. *hebny*), gum resin (Egy. *kemy*), elephant ivory (Egy. *abu*), monkeys, baboons and panther and cheetah skins can be found. It does not require a geography degree to work out what part of the world fits the picture. We are clearly talking about Africa and, in particular, given its proximity to Egypt, the Horn of Africa at the southern end of the Red Sea. It should not be surprising, then, to learn that the Egyptian expeditions to Punt involved either a journey by river and then land or a journey by sea. One method was to set off from Aswan, heading up the Nile through Wawat (Nubia) and Kush (Sudan) and then beyond into the lands of Irem and Nemay (locations unknown). Only then was Punt reached. Alternatively (and more often), the expeditionary forces made the trek to the Red Sea coast through the Eastern Desert before boarding sea-going ships for a journey of several weeks' duration southwards along the African coast of the Red Sea. All this confirms that Punt lay south of Egypt.[28]

The most famous expedition to the land of Punt was that undertaken during the reign of the female pharaoh, Hatshepsut. The scenes illustrating this journey to God's Land are to be found at the mortuary temple of Deir el-Bahri in Thebes. There you will find several interesting, though sometimes puzzling, clues which may help to locate Punt more precisely.

327. The temples of Deir el-Bahri.

328. Right: The characteristically *African* beehive huts of Punt built on stilts. From the reliefs of Hatshepsut's mortuary temple at Deir el-Bahri.

329. Above: The characteristically *Asiatic* features of 'Parehu, the Great One of Punt' – short-cropped hair and pointed beard. The determinative of the chieftain's name is a throwstick which is equally characteristic of Asiatics in Egyptian reliefs from all periods. Detail from the Punt reliefs at Deir el-Bahri.

330. Ati, wife of Parehu of Punt. Her large buttocks are rather characteristic of Hottentot women from southern Africa.

First, it is clear that the type of dwellings used by the Puntites in the scene are African. You can see beehive-like round huts, raised above the marshy ground on stilts, with ladders leading up to the entrances. The Puntites who bring the produce to the Egyptian ships for loading are clearly of two ethnically distinct types. We see 'Africans' bringing ivory tusks, but there are also 'Asiatics' in evidence. For example, the chieftain who greets the commander of Hatshepsut's expedition is clearly Asiatic, with the typical pointed beard. His name is Parehu and he bears the title 'Ruler of Punt'. His wife, Ati, on the other hand, looks for all the world like a HOTTENTOT from southern Africa!

In the text accompanying the reliefs, Punt is referred to as being located 'on the two sides' and it is this clue, above all others, which has led some scholars to suggest that Punt was centred on both coastal regions of the southernmost part of the Red Sea, where Africa and Arabia almost come together. This suggestion has much to commend it. First, it would explain the representations of both African and Asian ethnic types in the Deir el-Bahri reliefs. And, second, it would fit with other written sources which proclaim ancient Sheba (modern North Yemen) – famed for its travelling queen – as the great incense centre of the ancient world. Egyptian texts refer to 'the *antyu* (myrrh?) terraces of Punt' and Yemen has ancient mountain terraces upon which both myrrh and frankincense trees once grew. Indeed, the frankincense tree still grows today in the region of Dhofar in southern Arabia.

Equally, on the African side of the Red Sea we find all the exotic animals (and animal skins) shown in the Egyptian reliefs as well as myrrh trees in Somaliland. North-east Africa is also the ivory land *par excellence*. It can be reached by journeying up the River Nile and, in that context, it becomes fairly obvious why the large rocky island wallowing in the Nile opposite modern Aswan (the setting-off point for expeditions into Africa) was called 'Elephantine' by the Greeks and 'Abu' by the Egyptians. 'Abu' is the Egyptian word for ivory.

331. Left: Punt is described as being 'on the two sides' which suggests both coasts of the southern part of the Red Sea near the Bab el-Mandeb – in other words Eritrea and Yemen.

332. A Puntite of Asiatic appearance from the Old Kingdom reliefs of the mortuary temple and causeway of Sahure's pyramid at Abusir (after L. Borchardt, 1913, plate 7). He wears a chevron arm-band of a type still worn today by the Masai of Kenya.

Some illustrations of the Asiatic Puntites show them wearing chevron arm-bands. Interestingly, the Masia warriors of Kenya – famous for their tall, regal stature – still wear just this sort of chevron arm-bracelet today. Could their ancient ancestors have adopted this body jewellery from their Puntite neighbours when they delivered elephant ivory to the Red Sea coast from the plains of the Masai Mara? If so, then the African figures in the Egyptian scenes are not themselves Puntites but merely porters from the hinterland (perhaps the land the Egyptians called Nemyw) – casting the Asiatics of the Punt reliefs in the role of 'middlemen' – the true Puntites – residing on the coast at a place where produce could not only be delivered overland from the continental interior but also where the Egyptian ships could find safe anchorage.

It may well be that Punt was the Egyptian designation for the whole region south of Egypt, beyond the territory of Kush. In different periods its exact geographical centre (that is the trading port from where business was done) may have shifted – sometimes on the African side around Eritrea and Djibouti (but perhaps as far north as Port Sudan) and at other times on the Arabian side in Yemen. But there is also the possibility, raised by Flinders Petrie, that Punt originally included a large island not

HOTTENTOT (previous page): The Khoikhoi culture of southern Africa whose women are often distinguished by their protruding breasts and buttocks.

333. A ship of King Sahure returns from Punt laden with the produce of God's Land. The vessel's crew includes Puntites of clear Asiatic appearance. From the Sahure reliefs at Abusir (after L. Borchardt, 1913, plate 12).

CUBIT: The standard measure in Egypt and much of the Levant approximately equivalent to the length of a forearm from elbow to fingertips (52.5 cm).

far to the south-east of the entrance to the Red Sea known today as Ha-Fun. This would at least be consistent with the narrative of a well-known Egyptian tale known as 'The Shipwrecked Sailor' (Papyrus Leningrad 1115 – much translated by students of hieroglyphcs).

This well-crafted tale, composed in the Middle Kingdom when Egyptian literature was at its peak, relates the adventures of an Egyptian sailor who, following the sinking of his ship, is cast onto the beach of a tropical island laden with exotic produce.

> A storm came up whilst we were at sea and before we were able to reach land. As we sailed it made a swell within which was a wave eight CUBITS tall. It struck the mast. Then the ship sank and, of those in it, not one survived. I was cast upon an island by a wave of the sea. I spent three days alone, my heart as my only companion. Lying in the shelter of trees I embraced the shade. [Lines 33-45]

On this mysterious island resides a great serpent who identifies himself as the 'Lord of Punt' (line 151).

> Then I heard a thunderous noise and thought that it must be a wave of the sea. The trees began to splinter and the ground shook. Uncovering my face, I saw that a serpent was coming. He was thirty cubits long; his beard was over two cubits in length. His body was sheathed in gold; his eyebrows were of pure lapis lazuli. He reared up before me. [Lines 57-67]

After explaining his great misfortune and successfully pleading for his life to be spared, the sailor is permitted to remain on the island in the company of his serpent-lord. Eventually he is rescued by another Egyptian vessel which takes two months to return to Egypt (lines 170-75). The shipwrecked sailor brings with him huge quantities of exotic produce given to him by the Lord of Punt.

> Then he (the serpent) gave me huge amounts of myrrh, hekenu-oil, laudanam, hesyt-spice, tishpeses-spice, perfume, eye-paint, giraffes' tails, great lumps of antyu, elephants' tusks, greyhounds, long-tailed monkeys, baboons, and every kind of precious thing. [Lines 160-66]

The tale is certainly allegorical and therefore it could be argued that the island of the Lord of Punt is purely mythological. But it is just as likely that a real island located a couple of months' journey from Egypt lies behind this fantastical story. Two such islands – Socotra in the Gulf of Aden (visited by Heyerdahl's 'Tigris') and Ha-Fun (Petrie's candidate) may be good candidates for the mythical home of the serpentine Lord of Punt. But, were we to consider this strange tale as a didactic religious text, heavily laden with allegory concerning the journey through the underworld, then another magical island appears on the horizon – the

Isle of Flame where the gods of Egypt reside amongst the blessed dead. Its identity in the modern world will be revealed to you in due course, but for now we may conclude that the exotic and mystical land of Punt – God's Land – was probably all places beyond the known and mundane to the ordinary Egyptians. There was certainly an historical Punt, located in the southern regions of the Red Sea and the Horn of Africa, but as for the mysterious island of the Serpent-Lord of Punt – that lay somewhere beyond the reach of the Egyptian seafarers of the New Kingdom. By their time it had become a place which existed within the realm of the spirit world of the 'First Time' (Egy. *sep tepi*) – the age of the gods.

But what about Punt's history? Well, to be frank, there is no archaeological history of the land of Punt as such. No artefacts, to my knowledge, have ever been found in the coastal regions of Sudan and Ethiopia to prove the existence of the historical Puntites. No other civilisation in the ancient Near East mentions Punt or the Puntites in their own texts. It is as if the place was a mirage after all. Yet the Egyptians definitely journeyed there and returned, laden with exotic produce, to tell their tale.

All the way through this discussion of God's Land I have been liberally spreading clues as to what I believe may be the lost history of Punt and the Puntites. Their dealings with the Egyptians go back to earliest times; they are Asiatic traders with both Arabian and African contacts; their base of operations is on the route which we have suggested for the passage of the Sumerian venturers who came to settle in Egypt. Could it be, then, that the Puntites of dynastic times were descendants of that group of Sumerian traders who first established contact with Africa in prehistoric times? In would be logical to assume that some of those who went on the series of epic sea journeys to Africa may have stayed behind at crucial locations to provide staging posts for the traffic from Sumer to Egypt and back again. If the first journeys of the Sumerians were essentially trading missions, then Punt would have been not only a vital port-of-call on the way to Egypt but also the ideal entrepôt for African produce – the very produce later prized by the Egyptians themselves.

The People of Poen

The name Punt or Pwenet is a feminine word. This is indicated by the letter 't' which is the standard feminine ending in the Egyptian language. But we know from a study of the vocalisation of ancient Egyptian that these 't' endings were left unpronounced unless followed by a vowel. Thus Punt of Pwenet would have been vocalised something like 'Pun' or 'Poen'. With this important linguistic point in mind, we now return to an amazing tradition from the ancient world which brings all the different threads of our story together into a single unifying saga.

The Phoenicians of the eastern Mediterranean coast were first brought to the western world's attention through the Bible and the writings of the Greeks and Romans. One of their most famous kings, Hiram of Tyre, was a political ally of King Solomon and it was this Hiram who despatched expert craftsmen to advise in the building of Solomon's great temple in Jerusalem and who provided fine Lebanese cedar-wood for the interior decoration of that temple and the palace of the Israelite king.

> Hiram king of Tyre sent an embassy to Solomon, having learnt that he had been anointed king in succession to his father (David) and because Hiram had always been a friend of David. … And Hiram sent word to Solomon, 'I have received your message. For my part, I shall supply you with all that you require in the way of cedar wood and juniper. Your servants will bring these down from Lebanon to the sea, and I shall have them towed by sea to any place you name. … King Solomon raised a levy throughout Israel for forced labour: the levy numbered thirty thousand men. He sent these to Lebanon in relays, ten thousand a month; they spent one month in Lebanon and two months at home. … Solomon also had seventy thousand porters and eighty thousand quarrymen in the mountains, as well as the administrators and officials who supervised the work. At the king's orders they quarried huge stones, special stones for the laying of the temple foundations, dressed stones. Solomon's workmen and Hiram's workmen and the Giblites (men of Byblos) cut and assembled the wood and stone for the building of the Temple. [I Kings 5:15-32]

We learn that the Phoenicians possessed a number of major Mediterranean coastal cities, the majority of which remain thriving centres even today. We have all heard of Tyre (Tsur), Sidon, Arvad (Aradus), Beirut (Berytus), Byblos (Gubla, Egy. *Kebnet*) and Tripoli. These 'Phoenician' cities have long archaeological histories – some extending back to the Early Bronze Age – but historians only associate their *Iron Age* levels with ancient Phoenicia. This is partly because Solomon, until recently, has always been perceived as an Iron Age king of Israel – but now we know better. The New Chronology, laid out in *A Test of Time* Volume One, places this wealthiest of Israelite kings in his true archaeological setting – the prosperous Late Bronze Age.[29] In moving Solomon into this earlier era, we have also shifted his ally Hiram – and therefore the high point of Phoenician culture – back into the Late Bronze Age when the Egyptian texts simply refer to the people of coastal Lebanon/Syria as 'Asiatics' (Egy. *Amu*) or 'Canaanites' (Egy. *Kananu*). The term 'Canaanite' actually means 'trader' – a fitting appellation for a Phoenician merchant seafarer. The book of Genesis, on the other hand, attributes the founding of the country of the Canaanites to Cush's youngest brother Canaan.

> **Canaan** fathered **Sidon**, his first-born, then Heth, and the Jebusites, the Amorites, Girgashites, Hivites, Arkites, Sinites, **Arvadites**, Zemarites and Hamathites. Later, the Canaanite clans spread out. The Canaanite frontier stretched from Sidon

334. The principal cities of ancient Phoenicia.

to Gerar near Gaza, and all the way to Sodom, Gomorrah, Admah and Zeboiim near Lesha. [Genesis 10:15-19]

A major question which arises from all this is whether the Bronze-Age peoples of the land later referred to as Phoenicia were nevertheless ethnically or culturally Phoenician throughout the history of these great cities – even as far back as their original foundation? To find an answer we should turn to what the Phoenicians themselves had to say on the matter.

Unfortunately, we have no direct texts from Phoenicia itself. Rather we possess the report of 'the father of history' – Herodotus. He tells us that the Phoenicians themselves believed that they had originated in the Erythraean Sea ('Red Sea') and that in some distant era they had made an epic journey to the eastern Mediterranean coast where they then founded new cities. These cities had endured through the centuries to become the great metropoli of the Phoenician nation.

> The Persian learned men say the Phoenicians were the cause of the feud (between the Greeks and Persians). These (they say) came to our seas (i.e. the Eastern Mediterranean) from the Erythraean Sea, and having settled in the country which they still occupy (i.e. Phoenicia/Lebanon), at once began to make long voyages.[30]

It is clear that many civilisations of the ancient world acknowledged the supremacy of Phoenician seamanship. It is also readily apparent from the biblical text and other extra-biblical sources that the Phoenicians were not only recognised as superb craftsmen but also as the greatest traders of the old world. Most of this trade was carried out by sea. The archaeological evidence indicates that this sea trade even extended back to the Egyptian Old Kingdom when excavations have demonstrated a close trading and political relationship between Egypt and the Lebanese sea port of Byblos. The Egyptians even referred to a certain type of sea-going vessel as the 'Byblos Ship' (Egy. *kebny*) and we have already noted that Hiram's fleet towed logs of Lebanese cedar to Israel for the construction of the Jerusalem temple.

Knowing the Phoenicians believed that they heralded from the Erythrean Sea, it now becomes of considerable interest to recall another aspect of King Solomon's reign. Chapter Nine of the first book of Kings tells us that the Israelite ruler of Jerusalem commissioned the building of a large sea-going fleet at the port of Ezion-Geber on the Gulf of Akaba. The fleet was crewed by Israelite trainee sailors and experienced Phoenicians sent by Hiram of Tyre. It was the latter's task to navigate to and from the distant land of Ophir (probably India) bringing the luxurious produce of that place to Solomon's court.

> King Solomon equipped a fleet at Ezion-Geber, which is near Elath on the shores of the Red Sea, in Edom. For this fleet Hiram sent men of his, experienced sailors, to serve with those

335. One of the most famous ivories from Ugarit is this Late Bronze Age cosmetic box cover depicting the Mistress of Animals (usually identified as Astarte – the Canaanite equivalent of Ishtar/Inanna). Louvre Museum.

336. Pharaoh's Island, probably Solomon's port of Ezion Geber – the setting-off point for the Israelite king's expeditions to Ophir. The navigators for these expeditions down the Red Sea were Phoenician sailors. This tiny island is located at the northern end of the Gulf of Akaba.

TALE OF SINUHE: A Middle Kingdom story of a courtier who flees Egypt upon the assassination of Pharaoh Amenemhat I. Sinuhe wanders for many years through the land of Canaan in the region later to be known as Phoenicia (i.e. Lebanon) before returning to Egypt to tell his tale.

in Solomon's service. They went to Ophir and took on four hundred and twenty talents of gold, which they brought back to Solomon. [1 Kings 9:26-28]

Could it be that Solomon chose Phoenicians not only because they were practised sailors but also because they were familiar with the currents and treacherous coral reefs of the Red Sea? It seems clear that the Phoenicians were not just the best seafarers in the Mediterranean but also the right men to navigate the seas around Arabia. They knew these waters because they had sailed them for centuries prior to Solomon's reign.

Although the term 'Phoenicia' does not appear until later periods, we do find one Middle Kingdom Egyptian source – the 'TALE OF SINUHE' – referring to the land of 'Fenku' which may be an early vocalisation of the familiar Greek appellation 'Phoinike' from which we derive Phoenicia. The 'Punic' wars between Phoenician Carthage and Rome also demonstrates that the Phoenician people were referred to as the 'Pun' or 'Poen'. I have previously offered examples of this switch from 'p' to 'f' ('ph'), the most obvious of which is Arabic 'Faiyum' for ancient Egyptian 'Pa-Yam' ('the sea'). It is through the appellation 'Pun' or 'Poen' that we are able to uncover the true origins of not only the Phoenicians of the classical world but also our seafaring invaders of the predynastic Nile valley.

Again, I am not by any means the first to suggest this. Back in 1939 Flinders Petrie was convinced that the invaders (which he called the 'Falcon Tribe') who arrived in Egypt just prior to the founding of the 1st Dynasty were the same people as the Pun (the Puntites) who were, in turn, the founders of Phoenicia. His definitive statement on the matter includes some interesting further suggestions worthy of exploration.

This Falcon tribe had certainly originated in **Elam** (Susiana), as indicated by the hero and lions on the **Araq knife handle**. They went down the Persian Gulf and settled in '**the horn of Africa**'. There they named the 'Land of Punt', sacred to later Egyptians as the source of the race. The **Pun** people founded the island fortress of **Ha-fun** which commands the whole of that coast, and hence came the **Punic** or Phenic peoples of classical antiquity. ... Those who went up the Red Sea formed the **dynastic invaders** of Egypt entering by the Kuseir-Koptos road. **Others went on to Syria and founded Tyre, Sidon and Aradus, named after their home islands in the Persian Gulf.** [31]

Could Petrie have been on the right track all along in accepting Herodotus' explanation of the origins of the Phoenician people? There are indeed a number of remarkable coincidences which require explanation. First we have the Egyptian term *fnkw* (possibly pronounced Foenke), which may refer to Phoenicians of early times, and the island of Ha-Fun – perhaps, as Petrie suggested, the original island of Pun(t) which is the focus of the story of 'The Shipwrecked Sailor'. But then there is the amazing fact that two of the islands of Bahrain were originally called Aradus and Tylos (Tyros) – precisely the names of two greatest Phoenician island cities. In this context it is also intriguing that the Persian Gulf was once called the Erythrean Sea (that is the 'Red Sea'). The name seems to have transferred to the modern Red Sea along with the seafarers of Sumer when they relocated to Africa. And quite independently of these 'coincidences', there is the strong continuing belief amongst the Christian Lebanese that their Phoenician ancestors came from the Persian Gulf. This historical tradition is still taught in the schools of modern-day Lebanon.

Finally, we call upon the witness of archaeology. At the site of later 'Phoenician' Byblos excavations undertaken in the 1920s revealed the arrival of a new people who had brought with them the technology of metal-working and the potter's wheel. These people buried their dead in large storage jars with the bodies tightly flexed in the foetal position. They arrived at Byblos at the end of the Fourth Millennium BC – precisely the time when the foreign élite appear in the archaeological record of Egypt. In the context of the story we are developing here we may tentatively identify these new peoples, appearing on the coast of Canaan, as the followers of Ham's youngest son, Canaan, who were also known to the ancients as the people of Poen (Egyptian Punt) and to us as the Phoenicians.

Conclusion Twenty-Six

There is considerable evidence to suggest that the people known as the Phoenicians once inhabited the Islands of Bahrain. In effect, they were one and the same as the ancient Dilmunites. However, the Egyptians knew them as the Poen – the people of God's Land, the mysterious land of Punt.

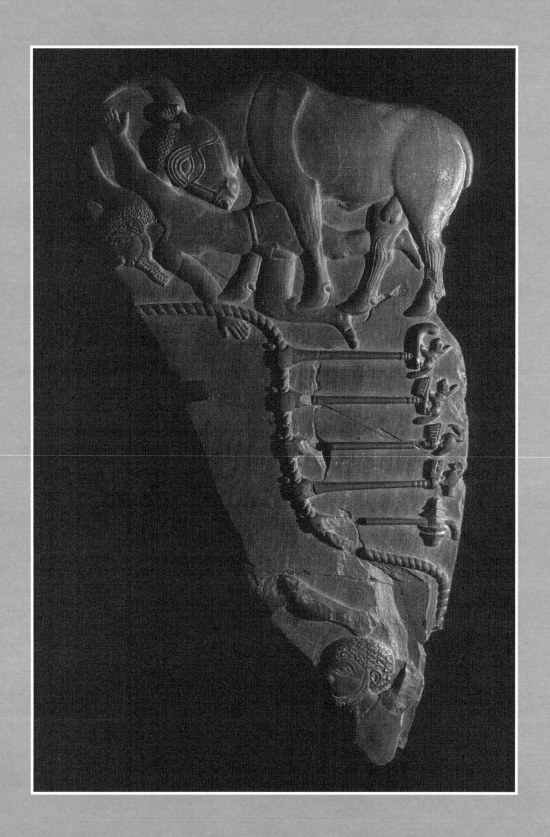

338. Left: (a) Two important motifs from the predynastic era – the Horus falcon perched on the crescent moon and the scorpion. (b) Some of the armed figures from the 'Hunters' Palette' dated to the late Predynastic Period. Note the leader carrying a Horus standard and, behind him, the chisel-shaped arrowhead similar to that used by the hunter on the Uruk Stela.

Chapter Ten

THE DYNASTIC RACE

So far as any one individual can be the dominant figure in a particular scholarly discipline, when it comes to Egyptology it has to be William Matthew Flinders PETRIE. He is regarded by his successors as the father of Egyptian archaeology, his excavation techniques having established Egyptology as a true science rather than merely an organised plundering of pharaonic monuments. However, Petrie is also known for his radical and often controversial ideas, perhaps the most contentious being his 'Dynastic Race' theory which he advocated as an historical explanation for the origins of Egyptian civilisation.

Petrie was the first holder of the Edwards Chair of Egyptology at University College London (1892-1933) – the place where I undertook my own undergraduate degree. The UCL Department of Egyptology was also the first of its kind in the United Kingdom and, in the hands of Petrie's distinguished successors – GLANVILLE, CERNY, EMERY, Smith and Martin – it has enjoyed a fine reputation within the field. The Egyptology department has recently celebrated the centenary of its foundation by Amelia Edwards in 1892. Perhaps not surprisingly – due to the great first professor's Horus-like influence over the department – many of the strongest advocates of the Dynastic Race theory have hailed from UCL or had connections with the Egyptology department there. These 'Followers of Horus' (also known as 'Petrie's Pups') were not insignificant scholars by any means – as their abbreviated 'list of credentials' (on the following page) testifies.

339. PETRIE: (1853-1942).

GLANVILLE: (1900-1956).

CERNY: (1898-1970).

EMERY: (1903-1971).

Petrie's Pups

Margaret MURRAY: one of Petrie's first students (referred to as 'Petrie's Pups'), later UCL Assistant Professor (1924-35); author of over eighty books and articles, especially her popular book *The Splendour that was Egypt*.

Henri FRANKFORT: another of Petrie's Pups, who became the Research Professor at the Oriental Institute in Chicago (1932-49) and later Director of the Warburg Institute and Professor of the History of Pre-Classical Antiquity at the University of London (1949-54); author of fifteen books and over seventy articles, his most important works being *Kingship and the Gods, Studies in Early Pottery of the Near East, Cylinder Seals* and *The Art and Architecture of the Ancient Orient*.

Rex (Reginald) ENGELBACH: yet another of Petrie's Pups, later Chief Keeper of the Cairo Museum (1931-41); author of numerous articles and archaeological reports including *Harageh, Gurob,* and *Ancient Egyptian Masonry*. He also prepared the vast index of artefacts known as the Cairo Museum Register – one of the most important research tools of the discipline.

Elise BAUMGARTEL: UCL tutor in Egyptology (1936-41); author of *The Cultures of Prehistoric Egypt*.

Douglas DERRY: UCL tutor in Anthropology (1910) and great mummy specialist; author of 'The Dynastic Race in Egypt' in *JEA* 42 (1956), pp. 80-5.

Bryan Emery: Edwards Professor of Egyptology at UCL (1951-70) and excavator of the 1st Dynasty mastaba tombs at Sakkara; author of *Archaic Egypt*.

I myself was first introduced to the Dynastic Race and their square boats by Dr David Dixon who has only recently retired from his teaching post in the department (1967-96). In effect then, UCL Egyptology became the home of the Dynastic Race theory.

On the other hand, there are very few Egyptologists teaching or working in the field today who would go out of their way to promote the Dynastic Race scenario. As to why this is the case I have my own ideas – which I will put forward later in this chapter. However, at this stage, I think it would be more useful to gather together the remaining evidence, not so far touched upon, which points to the arrival of a foreign élite in Egypt – the newcomers who did so much to influence the character of the later pharaonic state. In the course of our discussion we will draw upon the evidence and views of many of the scholars mentioned above.

All have a contribution to make. But first we need to learn what precisely it was that Petrie himself unearthed during his single momentous season of excavations seven kilometres north of the small village of Nakada in the winter of 1894-95.

Petrie and the Cemetery at Nakada

Petrie's most important work in Egypt began on the 3rd of December when, along with his colleague, James QUIBELL, he arrived at Nakada, located just twenty-six kilometres north of Luxor on the west bank of the River Nile.[1] During the previous season's excavations across the river at Kuft, Petrie had uncovered the sacred precinct of the primeval fertility-god Min, the foundation of which, he realised, stretched back to the earliest historical periods. Inscriptions identified the ancient settlement as Gebtu (Grk. *Koptos*, hence Arabic *Kuft*).

During that 1893-94 season Petrie and Quibell had taken the opportunity to survey the surrounding area, including the low desert plateau near the village of Nakada, across the river on the west bank. Here they quickly discovered what appeared to be a huge archaeological site stretching from el-Ballas in the north to Tukh in the south. The ground all around them was covered in smashed pottery – the tell-tale sign of ancient occupation. The place was a lunar landscape of low burial mounds – literally thousands of graves seemed to have been dug in this three-kilometre stretch of desert north of Nakada. Close by they also found limestone blocks which Petrie correctly guessed marked the site of another sacred precinct. This turned out to be the location of the temple of Seth, god of chaos and lord of the Red Land (Egy. *deshret* = the desert). Again, as at Kuft, the recovered inscriptions told Petrie that he had found the ancient town of Nubt (Grk. *Ombos*) which simply translates as 'Gold Town'.

340. A stela from Nakada depicting Seth, Lord of Nubt.

QUIBELL: (1867-1935).

341. Part of the vast necropolis of Nakada on the west bank of the Nile just north of Luxor.

AMRATIAN: The archaeological era equivalent to Nakada I, named after the site of el-Amra near Meidum.

GERZEAN: The archaeological era equivalent to Nakada II, named after the site of el-Gerza near Abydos.

In an elaborate operation involving scores of workmen from his previous year's excavations, Petrie and Quibell, in a single season, uncovered over 2,000 graves of previously unknown type. They turned out to be from a time before the 1st Dynasty – the era scholars call the 'Predynastic Period'. It soon became apparent from the pottery and artefacts unearthed that there were two distinct groups of burials.

The earlier, which Petrie designated 'Nakada I' (otherwise known as 'AMRATIAN'), were simple interments of the deceased in shallow oval pits cut directly into the sand, the body laid out on its left side in the contracted semi-foetal position on a plaited mat of rushes with the head at the southern end of the grave. The pit was then roofed with a lattice of palm branches before being covered in sand and gravel forming a low mound. The pottery associated with these interments included highly polished red ware and the easily recognisable black-on-red ware, so characteristic of the early predynastic era. Numerous small objects were common to the burials such as flint knives, ivory combs, pins and stone mace heads. Also found in several pits were small mudstone palettes for grinding eye-paint, with the small bag of green malachite powder lying nearby. No writing was discovered with any of these interments.

The later group of burials, which Petrie named 'Nakada II' (otherwise known as 'GERZEAN'), were dramatically different in several respects. The most important group of these Nakada II burials was located in a special area which the excavator designated 'Cemetery T'. Petrie believed that in Cemetery T he had found the burial ground of an élite family – possibly the actual rulers of Nubt. Many new features were introduced within this Nakada II phase of the cemetery, not least being the lining of the graves with mudbricks to form a rectangular pit. These pits were then covered

342. The remains of one of the brick-lined élite graves in Cemetery T at Nakada.

with a roof of palm logs before the sand was replaced over the burial site. Inside the tombs – for that is what these more elaborate structures are – the bodies were surrounded by a new type of pottery. As Michael Rice notes:

> The earliest Nakada II pottery seems to be influenced by foreign forms: vessels supplied with filter spouts and triangular lug handles look like imitations of wares produced by the Ubaid potters of Mesopotamia. [2]

This is in stark contrast to the earlier periods of Nile valley culture when, as Helene Kantor observes, '… objects indisputably foreign in manufacture or type are almost non-existent …'.[3] So it appears that at least two styles of pottery found in the Nakada II graves were derived from Mesopotamia and that this was a new phenomenon. The first type – the lug-handled pottery – is well attested in the Uruk and Jemdet Nasr periods.

> Among the decorated pot shapes are relatively large jars with three or four triangular lug handles on the shoulder. These lugs are reminiscent of those which were already in use on Mesopotamian pottery in the Ubaid Period and which became particularly typical and frequent on protoliterate pottery (Uruk/ Jemdet Nasr periods).[4]

Although this lug feature might be considered part of a functional change in the pottery vessels (enabling them to be suspended by cord from carrying poles) and therefore part of a natural evolution, the fact is that again the 'invention' is of Mesopotamian origin. But the second type – the spouted vessel – seems much more a matter of fashion and therefore stronger evidence for the presence of Sumerian potters in the Nile valley.

> More convincing are the vessels with tilted spouts … Although made in the old, indigenous polished red ware, the spouts are completely un-Egyptian; as a whole these jugs resemble Mesopotamian ones of the earlier part of the Protoliterate Period. [5]

However, the most obvious change in pottery style manifests itself in the famous Nakada II buff-ware – also known as 'Decorated Ware'. Margaret Murray is quite justified in extolling the quality of these superb vessels.

> Gerzean (Nakada II) pottery is perhaps the finest of all prehistoric Egyptian pottery in material, texture, form, manufacture and colour. The clay is well levigated, the firing is perfect, there is not a trace of black in the substance of the clay, the colour being buff right through.[6]

These large and elaborate wheel-made vessels with pale yellow slip (coating) had been decorated in painted designs of red manganese before firing. Here were images of boats, chieftains with plumed feathers and throw-sticks, females with raised arms, flamingoes, mountains and other

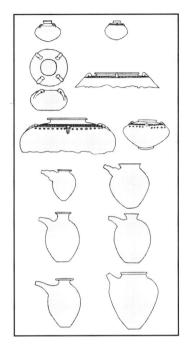

343. Comparing the profiles and decoration of predynastic pots from Upper Egypt on the left and Mesopotamian/Iranian pottery vessels on the right (after E. Baumgartel, 1955).

344. Lug-handle jars from Sumer (above) and predynastic Egypt (below).

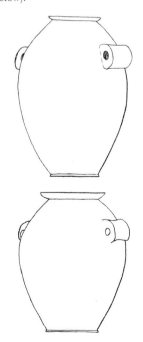

345. Right: Decoration from one of the buff-ware vases so characteristic of Nakada II. A line of mountain peaks runs across the top, below which are two boats, a sacred palm motif (centre), ostriches or flamingoes and a pair of dancing goddesses.

346. Below: A Nakada II buff-ware jar decorated with a boat carrying two cabins and tall standard.

347. A clay figurine of a dancing goddess from one of the Nakada II tombs.

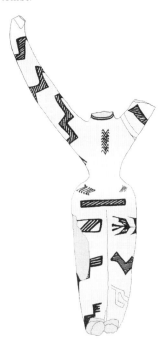

strange iconographic details including spirals and 'snooze' motifs (lines of 's's). Many of these designs are, of course, reminiscent of the Eastern Desert rock-art of our Square-Boat People which we studied in the previous chapter. Amongst the burial goods were also clay models of boats, whilst the make-up palettes were now of high quality slate. In the earliest Nakada II graves a number of clay figurines were found representing the female with raised arms which were common to the desert rock-art and the slightly later buff painted ware. This female was obviously an important element in the iconography of the time.

Let us look at one particular tomb, designated T5 by Petrie, to get a better impression of a typical Nakada II warrior-élite burial.[7]

The tomb showed no sign of being plundered, so what Petrie found was exactly as it was laid out some 5,000 years ago. At the northern end of a rectangular pit, about four metres by two metres, stood eight large jars filled with grey ash from the burning of wood and vegetable matter (plants, vegetables and fruit). There were no human remains (i.e. bones) in the jars. It was clear from this that burnt offerings were despatched up to the gods at the burial of the deceased. Petrie was even able to determine that thick beer had been poured over the fire as a libation.

A set of wavy-handled vessels containing strongly scented vegetable fat were also positioned at the southern end of the pit.

Lying between these two sets of pots were the human remains. Five detached skulls lay at the centre and one more next to the jars at the southern end of the tomb. The latter was standing on a mudbrick. Around the five central skulls were three fine porphyry or syenite stone vases with lug handles. These contained beads and brown pebbles. One skull was stuffed full of more beads. Next to another skull was a slate palette with birds' heads carved at the top.

The rest of the bones were gathered in a neat pile towards the northern part of the tomb with the exception of the long bones which were scattered in different locations. All the larger bones had been broken at one end and there was clear evidence here (and in other burials) that the marrow had been extracted by means of a sharp implement which had left grooves on the inner surfaces of the bones. Teeth marks were also found on some bones.

Given that the burial had not been disturbed, Petrie concluded that the bodies had been dismembered before being placed in the tomb, the heads having been severed or detached from the spinal vertebrae. This was common to many of the Nakada II graves in Cemetery T. It appears that the flesh of the dead person (and especially the bone marrow) was partly devoured by his offspring, probably 'to secure the transmission of the qualities of the dead to his descendants' (as Petrie puts it) or to imbibe the spirit and power of the honoured ancestor who had just passed into the netherworld.[8] Petrie considered the possibility that the heads (and perhaps the hands) of the deceased were kept at the family home for several years in some kind of ancestor worship. Finally, the skulls were interred with the rest of the remains which had been buried soon after death. What made tomb T5 so interesting was that a whole group of deceased family members had been buried simultaneously, with the skull of the most important individual placed on a brick at one end of the tomb.

Here, then, was clear evidence not only of dismemberment but also of cannibalism. Petrie's 'New Race', which he had unearthed at Nakada, were proving to be culturally very different to the 'civilised' Egyptians of later times. This was all a bit of a shock and Egyptologists of today prefer not to talk very much about this aspect of predynastic culture.

Two other important classes of object dramatically point to a major change in the culture of the cemetery at the archaeological horizon between Nakada I and Nakada II.

First, Petrie found that the exotic blue stone known as lapis lazuli suddenly begins to appear in the early Nakada II tombs, whereas it is completely absent in the earlier Nakada I graves. Amazing as it may

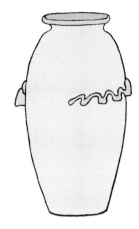

348. A wavy-handled vase from Nakada. Changes in the development of this type of pottery enabled Petrie to chronologically sequence the graves at Nakada and therefore the artefacts of the Predynastic Period found in them.

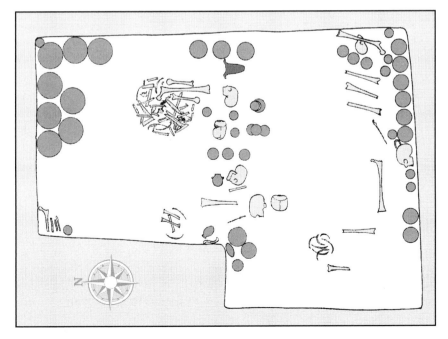

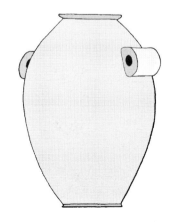

349. (a) Plan of grave T5 containing the disarticulated skeletons of several members of a single family and attendant pottery. The marrow from the long-bones had been removed with a sharp implement. (b) One of the lug-handle pots from T5.

313

seem, this stone is presumed by scholars to have come from the only known source location in the region – the mountains of Badakshan in Afghanistan, over 3,700 kilometres from Egypt as the crow flies! As we have already noted, lapis lazuli was highly prized in Sumer and was imported all the way from Meluhha (Indus valley) via Dilmun (Bahrain).

As we saw in *Chapter Six*, lapis was a prized stone in protoliterate Mesopotamia. So the pattern of distribution is again the same: a product or material first appears in Sumer and Susiana before it arrives in Egypt. Petrie noted that the occurrence of lapis in the Nile valley is restricted to the late Predynastic Period. It then disappears from the archaeological record before resurfacing in the late Old Kingdom, some six centuries later.[9] This suggests a relatively short period of contact between Mesopotamia and Egypt which is consistent with the scenario of migrating Sumerians followed by a period of settlement and then a gradual break in contact with the homeland as the newcomers become 'Niloticised'.

Second, the warrior graves of the Nakada II folk contained a new weapon, previously unknown in the Nile valley. Here for the first time we find the 'pear-shaped mace' – the ceremonial weapon *par excellence* of the later pharaohs. The mace head is rounded at its top whilst narrowing towards the shaft handle, giving its characteristic pear shape. In the previous Nakada II warrior graves the maces are disc-shaped, like a miniature discus. This change in ceremonial weapon is dramatic.

I would like you to think back to the Wadi Hammamat drawings for a moment. You may remember that I mentioned the carrying of just such a rounded, pear-shaped, mace by the chieftain figure standing in the boat. Exactly this type of weapon is also shown in the hands of the victorious warrior in the battle scene on the Gebel el-Arak knife handle. There can be little doubt about it – the Square-Boat People were the introducers of the pear-shaped mace into Egypt. Margaret Murray, one of the strongest advocates of the Dynastic Race theory, sees in this new technology a crucial military advantage for the newcomers.

> In all warfare there is but one main idea, so to strike your enemy as to prevent his striking you. In primitive hand-to-hand fighting the man who has the heavier weapon, who could kill or at least stun his enemy with one blow, would be the victor over a more lightly armed man. This was certainly the case with the Gerzean (Nakada II folk). The Amratian (Nakada I) mace was quite effective if the blow fell exactly in the right place, breaking the skull or cutting an artery, but the Gerzean warrior was armed with a greatly superior weapon. Instead of being disc-shaped with a cutting edge, it was a solid pear-shaped object, hafted like the Amratian on horn or hippopotamus hide, and by one blow could kill the enemy or stun him or break his arm and so render him helpless. The Gerzean mace head is a truly formidable weapon.[10]

350. Profiles of a Nakada I disc-shaped mace (top) and Nakada II pear-shaped mace (bottom).

351. Pharaoh's ceremonial weapon *par excellence* – the pear-shaped mace – here held in the left hand of Senuseret I at Karnak.

So, had Petrie uncovered the tombs of these powerful foreign invaders at Nakada? Indeed, were the Nakada I graves those of native Nile valley dwellers (i.e. the indigenous Egyptians) whilst the Nakada II folk were the elusive foreign élite from Sumer who had subjugated their predecessors of the Nakada I cemetery? Anthropologist Douglas Derry seemed to think so – based on his analysis of cranial dimensions from the cemetery.

> The predynastic people are seen to have had narrow skulls with a height measurement exceeding the breadth, a condition common also in negroes. The reverse is the case in the Dynastic Race, who not only had broader skulls but the height of these skulls, while exceeding that in the Predynastic Race, is still less than the breadth. This implies a greater cranial capacity and of course a larger brain in the invading people. [11]

352. The chieftain with pear-shaped mace from Site 26 in the Wadi Abu Marakat el-Nes.

Derry goes on to draw some startling – what might be considered racist – conclusions from his anthropological analysis.

> It is also very suggestive of the presence of a dominant race, perhaps relatively few in numbers but greatly exceeding the original inhabitants in intelligence; a race which brought into Egypt the knowledge of building in stone, of sculpture, painting, reliefs, and above all writing; hence the enormous jump from the primitive predynastic Egyptian to the advanced civilization of the Old Empire (i.e. Old Kingdom). [12]

353. The warrior with pear-shaped mace from the Gebel el-Arak knife handle.

Such views were still being held in the 1950s and 60s by certain academics – particularly in the traditional Victorian disciplines such as Egyptology and Mesopotamian studies. There is considerable evidence to suggest that British Egyptology was one of the last bastions of such academic colonialism.

In two public speeches (published in the *Yale Review* in 1918 and 1922) Petrie made *his* colonial attitude very clear.[13] Both lectures came soon after the end of the First World War when 'Western Civilisation' was in the throes of self-examination after the bloodiest battles in history. Petrie's views would certainly upset late-twentieth-century sensibilities but, as our modern history was soon to demonstrate, such ideas were surfacing all over Europe in the 1920s. In a sense, Petrie was very much a man of his time. However, although the Dynastic Race theory was undoubtedly *influenced* by the colonial world in which Petrie and his colleagues had worked all their archaeological lives, it does not follow that we must instantly dismiss the archaeological evidence produced by them simply because their historical conclusions were tainted.

The past is the past and lessons learnt from the present cannot change that bloody past one iota. It is quite feasible for an influx of new people to stimulate an explosion of civilisation in an undeveloped region – and just such a region was predynastic Egypt where Petrie's Dynastic Race first appeared in the early third millennium BC. The archaeological evidence for them is clear. Their 'foreign' presence, along with all that they brought which was new, is historically undeniable.

A generation after Petrie's death Bryan Emery took up the Dynastic Race theory and compounded the problem by renaming the newcomers to the Nile valley as a 'super race'. This was hardly a sensitive move given that the holocaust had run its course just fifteen years earlier. The effect was to assign the Dynastic Race skeleton to the academic closet where it has remained ever since.

We, of course, would do well to abandon Petrie and Emery's unfortunate terminologies for something more appropriate to our own day and age, as I have attempted to do in my tackling of the subject.

We can start by discarding the term 'Dynastic Race' itself, replacing it with a less emotive expression such as 'foreign élite'. By doing so we would be conforming to the language of modern scholarship. This should enable us to review the archaeological remains without prejudice and prevent some politically correct scholars from rejecting the evidence for an invasion of Egypt in predynastic times simply on the basis of the embarrassing terminology of its original discoverers. The dramatic appearance of foreign cultural influences in the predynastic Nile valley is clearly visible in numerous other ways which deserve to be highlighted.

> ## Conclusion Twenty-Seven
>
> **There is clear archaeological evidence for an influx of foreigners into the Nile valley in the Nakada II Period. These people introduced new technologies – particularly in warfare – and buried their deceased in a different way to the Nile valley folk of Nakada I. Anthropological examinations of the two burial populations show marked differences, with the newcomers of Nakada II exhibiting Armenoid characteristics indicating Zagros mountain origins. The artefacts and art of the Nakada II élite graves confirm that these foreigners were culturally connected and contemporary with the Square-Boat People.**

Innovations of Invasion

The introduction of lapis lazuli and the pear-shaped mace, combined with the anthropological evidence, were not the only clear indications that a new culture had arrived in Egypt. During Nakada II and the next archaeological phase – Nakada III – we witness the appearance of (a) the cylinder seal, (b) the first hieroglyphic writing and (c) remarkable brick architecture. All three 'inventions' are known to have originated in Sumer.

(a) Cylinder Seals

Cylinder seals were often used as funerary amulets but also as a means of registering possessions in daily life. The earliest of these little seals were carved with motifs and patterns which, when rolled over the wet clay stoppers of storage vessels, left the mark or insignia of the owner for all to see. Later, throughout the Old Kingdom, they were carved with short hieroglyphic inscriptions denoting the name and titles of the owner. But by the Middle Kingdom (NC – 1800-1633 BC) they had been entirely replaced by the more familiar stamp seal in the shape of a scarab.

354. An early Egyptian cylinder seal (left) with its impression (right).

It is no coincidence that the cylinder seal first appears in Egypt at the same time as the pear-shaped mace and lapis lazuli. The cylinder seal was not an invention of the Nile valley people for, as we have seen, these remarkable little objects were already being employed for the same purpose in the city of Uruk during the late Ubaid Period.[14] The cylinder seal was therefore another Sumerian invention.

The great Dutch Egyptologist and orientalist, Henri Frankfort (who studied under Petrie at UCL), sees the appearance of the cylinder seal as 'the strongest evidence of contact between Mesopotamia and Egypt'. Three seals in particular showed 'by their very material and by their designs to have been made in Mesopotamia during the second half of the Protoliterate Period'.[15] One of these was specifically found by Petrie in a Nakada II grave.

The iconography of these early cylinder seals includes 'heraldic animal motifs typical of early Mesopotamian culture' and also 'the griffin with horizontal wings which Amiet has shown comes specifically from Susa'.[16] These same motifs recur throughout early pharaonic art, especially on the great cosmetic palettes which we will be looking at in *Chapter Eleven*.

(b) Writing and Language

One of the most amazing aspects of late predynastic civilisation is the virtually instantaneous introduction of writing into the Nile valley. It suddenly appears in full flow, without any signs of gradual development from primitive pictographic art. Henri Frankfort sums up the position in his book *The Birth of Civilisation in the Near East*.

355. The extraordinary image of the 'griffin with horizontal wings' was a creation of Mesopotamian culture. Here the top two images are taken from cylinder seals excavated at Susa whilst the bottom griffin comes from the late-predynastic 'Dog Palette' found at Hierakonpolis. It seems hardly credible that the Egyptian version could have been an entirely independent invention from the Mesopotamian original.

It has been customary to postulate prehistoric antecedents for the Egyptian script, but this hypothesis has nothing in its favour. … the writing which appeared without antecedents at the beginning of the First Dynasty was by no means primitive. It has, in fact, a complex structure. It includes three different classes of signs: ideograms, phonetic signs, and determinatives. This is precisely the same state of complexity which had been reached in Mesopotamia at an advanced stage of the Proto-literate Period. There, however, a more primitive stage is known in the earliest tablets, which used only ideograms. To deny, therefore, that Egyptian and Mesopotamian systems of

356. The well-known ivory label of King Den of the 1st Dynasty bearing some of Egypt's earliest hieroglyphs. The name of the pharaoh is written within a *serekh* surmounted by a falcon. To its left we read the name of the chief minister – Hemaaka. The right half of the panel shows the king seated on his jubilee throne and performing the heb sed run between two groups of D-shaped markers.

writing are related amounts to maintaining that Egypt invented independently a complex and not very consistent system at the very moment of being influenced in its art and architecture by Mesopotamia where a precisely similar system had just been developed from a more primitive stage. [17]

Here, then, is yet another Mesopotamian import. But this time there is a clear 'native Egyptian' element which must be added to the equation – for it has to be recognised that the hieroglyphs of Egypt bear no resemblance to Sumerian signs and the later Akkadian cuneiform script. This, though, has a great deal to do with the method of writing – that is the medium and tools used for recording the scripts. Both systems originated with signs representing objects and animals – what we call pictographs.

(b1) Writing

357. The archetypal image of an Egyptian scribe with papyrus roll spread across his lap. Louvre Museum.

The Sumerian scribe used a selection of pointed and wedge-shaped reed styli to scratch and imprint his signs into a damp clay tablet. The little tablet was then either dried in the sun or oven fired. The pointed stylus was soon dropped as the scribe's skill in using the wedge-shaped tools became more sophisticated. Scholars have dubbed this developed form of the Mesopotamian script 'cuneiform' – a term which derives from the Latin *cuneus* meaning 'wedge'.

By pressing the end of his reed stylus into the clay in different ways and combinations the Mesopotamian scribe was able to approximate the shapes of the objects which he was trying to portray. But, as we have seen, the objects naturally took on the somewhat abstract form dictated by the limited application of the wedge-shaped tip of the writing tool. Thus, for example, you may be able to identify the bull's head in figure 357 which is turned on its side in the cuneiform script. It then becomes somewhat more difficult to recognise the original animal's head in our modern capital 'A' which derives indirectly from the Sumerian sign –

having gone through several metamorphoses – Proto-Canaanite to Phoenician to Greek and through yet another ninety degree rotation. With some signs it is relatively easy to identify the original pictographs but these are few and far between. The majority are unrecognisable to the untrained eye. For example, it is much more difficult to spot the donkey's head (Figure 358) which lies behind its later cuneiform sign or the cuneiform symbol for the human head in its metamorphosis.

The Egyptian medium for writing was predominantly the papyrus roll or sheet. Here the scribe also used a reed – but this time to apply ink onto the dry papyrus surface. This technique permitted a much more flowing style of writing which could more faithfully represent the object which lay behind the hieroglyphic sign. Thus abstraction was not a natural development of the Egyptian script in the same way as it was in Mesopotamia. The late predynastic and early dynastic Egyptians could apply their painted signs to the surfaces of pots and other ornamented surfaces. The hieroglyphs would therefore become more than simple writing – they also rapidly evolved into graphic art or decoration – a very important aspect of the Egyptian sacred script. It was then a natural step to move from primitive symbols on painted pots to the beautiful monumental hieroglyphs which are so characteristic of the later pharaonic civilisation. The intermediate stage between the ink or painted glyphs of the predynastic era and the stone-cut formal hieroglyphs of the Old Kingdom are the small ivory plaques and wooden labels, into the surface of which the first true hieroglyphics were incised along with scenes of early royal rituals. Two other major classes of object which carry examples of the first hieroglyphs are the ceremonial mace heads and slate palettes.

It would thus appear that, although the two writing systems – Mesopotamian and Egyptian – both began as an attempt to portray objects graphically, the two forms rapidly diverged as a direct result of the major differences in writing materials. The Egyptians maintained accurate representations of their objects by the use of the flowing pen whilst the Sumerians developed an abstract angular script because they employed a wedge stylus. The argument that the élite Nile dwellers of the late Predynastic Period were not of Mesopotamian origin because they did not employ cuneiform writing does not hold so much weight when the adaptation of different writing materials is considered. It is very likely that the 'idea' of writing was introduced from Mesopotamia by the invading élite but then the newcomers rapidly adapted their original invention to suit the environment of Egypt – both for the medium of writing and the type of objects being portrayed.

(b2) Language

We have looked at the writing script, but we need also to consider the Egyptian language itself. Here there are clear indications, based on detailed comparative linguistic studies, that ancient Egyptian was influenced by the Semitic languages of Mesopotamia. Indeed, it seems that

358. The development of our letter 'A' from its Sumerian bull's-head original, through Akkadian cuneiform, via the Proto-Canaanite bull's head to Phoenician to Greek.

359. From recognisable donkey to abstract cuneiform in a single leap. At a point in time the cuneiform script was rotated through ninety degrees (anticlockwise) making the comparison even more difficult.

the two languages stem from a single original mother tongue. The point at which the two separated from each other is hard to pinpoint but there is no doubt that it was way back in the distant past. As the great Semiticist, William Foxwell ALBRIGHT, wrote in 1970:

> If a language community splits into two or more groups which are subsequently and immediately isolated from one another, the language of each group will continue to evolve. But because there is no fixed direction for linguistic change, these languages will gradually diverge from one another in both form and content, until, after a suitable time, they will have become quite distinct. [18]

It is easy to see the sorts of change which take place when we consider the similarities and differences between two modern Indo-European languages – English and German. There are many common words such as 'brother'/'Bruder', 'bread'/'Brot', 'water'/'Wasser' and 'grave'/'Grab', but many more which are completely at variants. It is hard to see any connection between 'woman'/'Frau', 'flour'/'Mehl', 'tree'/'Baum' and 'bone'/'Knochen'. An English speaker who has not learnt the German language at school, listening to an animated discussion between two Germans on the London Underground, might be forgiven for believing that the two tongues were born of quite different mothers. This, however, as we know, would not be true. Most of the languages of Europe can be traced back to a common ancestor spoken around 2000 BC.

We do not only have the vocabulary of Mesopotamia and Egypt to consider but also the basic structure of the two language groups. Although less obvious to a non specialist, the *rules* of language are a better indicator of a common linguistic origins. Words for objects and ideas may be changed or loaned from other languages, but an understanding of the way a language functions – the grammatical rules by which it is structured – is the key to identifying the original 'gene pool' of the mother tongue.

> Although Egyptian is not to be placed within the Semitic family, there are few grammatical features which can be considered alien to that group. A close genetic relationship is thus indicated and accepted; only on details is there a divergence of scholarly opinion. [19]

So the grammar of the two language forms have common roots and a good number of Egyptian words can be traced back to Semitic originals. However, one crucial little word is very important to our discussion of the origins of the pharaonic state. The concept of *maat*, 'divine truth' or 'cosmic order' is fundamental to Egyptian royal theology. The pharaoh is the protector of cosmic order; he is the sentinel against the encroachment of chaotic forces into Kemet, the 'Black (Land)', i.e. the Nile valley. The word maat is again a feminine word which carries an unpronounced 't' ending and we would therefore expect it to be pronounced something like 'ma' or 'mua'. It is interesting to note that the Sumerian word for the elements (plural) of cosmic order is *me*.

This linguistic clue aside, the greater part of the Egyptian vocabulary appears to be native to the Nile valley and may be of African – what we call Hamitic – origins. This would be consistent with the idea that the Nakada II newcomers had initially spent an intermediate period in a third geographical location where they adopted new terms from the local inhabitants which better described their more exotic environment. One such African location may have been Punt. Some of the migrators could then have moved on up into the Nile valley where again they would have quickly adapted to their new home by readily incorporating elements of vocabulary from the local population. Indeed, as a minority group, they would undoubtedly have been forced to adopt the local tongue in order to comunicate with the majority. This whole process may have spanned several generations, by which time the original mother-tongue of the migrating clan would have become submerged, only surfacing as a small percentage of the total pharaonic vocabulary.

This would be rather like the Roman military occupying northern Europe in the first to fifth centuries AD and, through the Latin- speaking Normans, bequeathing a number of Latin words to our modern English vocabulary. In spite of this Roman élite's obvious influence on European culture and the retention of Latin in both church and government for centuries after, the language of modern Britain retains much of its Anglo-Saxon roots. The English language of today is clearly a hotchpotch of Celtic, Anglo-Saxon, Latin, Norse and French.

Ancient Egyptian is classified within the Hamito-Semitic group of languages which include Berber, Tuareg and Cushitic. The latter is spoken by the indigenous folk who live in the geographical territory of modern Sudan and Ethiopia. You will no doubt recognise a biblical connection with such linguistic terms. When these language groups were first being classified, the scholars of the day, raised on the biblical stories, chose to name them after the 'Table of Nations' listed in the book of Genesis. Thus 'Cushitic' was spoken by the descendants of Cush and the broader term 'Hamitic', used for the languages of north-east Africa, is derived from Ham – the father of Cush and son of Noah. Shem – the brother of Ham – needless to say, gives his name to the Semitic family of languages. In adopting these biblical terms for the linguistics of the ancient world, nineteenth-century scholars were actually conforming to the historical picture which is beginning to imerge from our own investigations. Their use of biblical terminology may not have been so far from the actual reality.

(c) Niched Façade Architecture

The most visually dramatic of the new cultural elements is monumental architecture. Suddenly, and without any signs of prior development, large rectangular tombs built of mudbrick begin to appear towards the end of the Predynastic Period. The earliest of these tombs were discovered at the site of Umm el-Gaab ('Mother of Pots') in the desert behind the sacred precinct of Abydos where Osiris, god of the dead, was believed to have been buried.

In ancient times the settlement of *Tjenu* (Grk. *Thinis* or *This*) was located somewhere nearby (perhaps at modern Girga) and the burial ground at Abydos seems to have been its cemetery. Tradition – in the form of Manetho's *Aegyptiaca* – informs us that Thinis was the seat of power of the 1st Dynasty – the founding line of the pharaohs. Virtually all of the superstructures of the tombs (if they had any) were removed over the intervening millennia. However, the substructures, including the burial chambers, remain preserved under the sand. These monuments are clearly 'royal' in both their dimensions and attendant funerary trappings – including scores of 'servant burials' surrounding the main burial complex. Many of these subsidiary graves were found to have been roofed in a single operation (palm logs and matting covering adjacent pits in a single span), indicating that the deceased were victims of ritual sacrifice at the time of the main 'royal' burial.[20]

Petrie excavated here from 1899 to 1903, following the disastrous plundering of the site by Émile AMÉLINEAU in the previous four seasons. With his customary precision and diligence Petrie managed to recover several ivory and wood labels, fragments of fine alabaster vases and seal impressions bearing royal names. These inscriptions represent the first known occurrence of hieroglyphs in Egypt. Scholars have been able to determine that several of the names – Djer, Den, Anedjib, Semerkhet and Kaa – belonged to kings of the 1st Dynasty. Others, such as Peribsen and Khasekhemwy were borne by kings of the 2nd Dynasty. But a number of the earliest tombs, grouped together in 'Cemetery B' were clearly attributable to rulers who must have immediately preceded the 1st Dynasty.

360. The footprint of one of the royal tombs at Umm el-Gaab, nearly a century after their discovery by Amélineau and Petrie and just before the site's re-excavation by the German archaeological mission to Abydos.

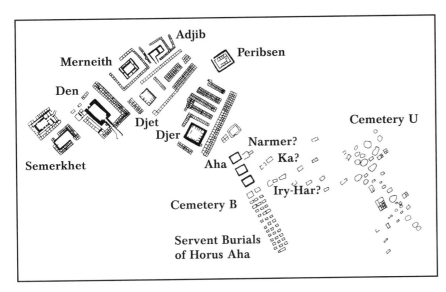

361. The royal cemetery at Umm el-Gaab behind the temples of Abydos. Note the mass burials of servants and officials surrounding each king's burial complex. In the case of Aha the sevant burials extend away from the king's tomb in a triple row.

Here in Cemetery B were the tombs of Iry-Har, Ka, Narmer and Aha. From an assessment of the recovered artefacts, there is little doubt that many of the trappings of pharaonic iconography were already in place at this time which in itself suggests that Upper Egypt was, by the close of the predynastic era, a true unified kingdom. Because the Cemetery B rulers (with the exception of Aha – see below) could not be identified with any of the names on the official, monumental king lists (which generally start with Menes, the founder of the 1st Dynasty) scholars have resorted to placing these earlier kings of Upper Egypt in 'Dynasty 0', designating their archaeological phase as the 'Protodynastic Period' (roughly equivalent to Nakada III).

There is still a question over the archaeological/historical identity of Menes, the traditional unifier of Upper and Lower Egypt and founder of Memphis. Some Egyptologists favour Narmer (his name written with the signs for 'catfish' and 'chisel') whilst others – perhaps now the majority – prefer to identify Menes with Aha ('the fighter'). The arguments are complex and have been well rehearsed elsewhere. So, rather than re-opening that debate, which although interesting has little relevance to our topic, I will follow the majority view and make Aha the conqueror of Lower Egypt and founder of the 1st Dynasty, whilst identifying Narmer as his father. I do this primarily because Aha is clearly attested at Memphis whereas, to date, there is no evidence for Narmer in the royal capital which tradition says was founded by Menes. However, there is little doubt that Narmer had much to do with the conquest of the north and the unification process.

By the start of the 1st Dynasty the superstructures of monumental buildings become elaborately decorated with niched façades. Recent investigations at Umm el-Gaab suggest that the royal tombs there did not, in fact, possess this feature but other large tombs of the period demonstrate that the introduction of these faceted walls was a major architectural

362. One of the 1st Dynasty 'royal' mastabas at Sakkara in the foreground with the pyramids of Userkaf (left) and Djoser (right) on the horizon. The deep recesses of the niched façade design can still be seen in spite of the ruined condition of the mastaba's superstructure.

363. This photograph was taken at the time of Emery's excavations of the 1st Dynasty mastaba field at Sakkara and shows the excellent state of preservation of the niched-façade belonging to a tomb constructed during the reign of King Kaa of the 1st Dynasty. Not only is the plaster still attached to the brickwork but clear traces of the elaborate painted patterns can still be seen on the pilasters. These patterns are identical to the designs found on the pillars of the cone mosaic temple at Uruk.

DE MORGAN: (1857-1924).

development. The most spectacular examples of the new niched façade feature were uncovered by Bryan Emery at Sakkara in the 1950s, where the excavator located a row of enormous mudbrick tombs extending along the eastern scarp of the desert plateau. These tombs were so much larger and more impressive than the 1st Dynasty tombs at Abydos that Emery became convinced that they were the true royal tombs of the first pharaonic kings. In this he still has his supporters but again the majority of today's Egyptologists have returned to the former view that Abydos is the true royal cemetery and that the Sakkara tombs belonged to the high court officials.

Another superb example of monumental niched-façade architecture was excavated much earlier by Jacques DE MORGAN at Nakada in 1897. This turned out to be the tomb of Queen Neithhotep, believed to be Aha's Great Royal Wife. Her name suggests that she was the daughter of a Delta ruler based at Buto, where the sanctuary of the goddess Neith was located. This in turn implies that the marriage between Aha and Neithhotep sealed the political unification of Upper and Lower Egypt following a military victory by Aha of Thinis over the delta region.

364. Remains of the niched-façade of mastaba 3507 at Sakkara.

As I have already indicated, Aha means 'the fighter' – his name being written with the hieroglyph of a falcon clutching a pear-shaped mace and shield in its talons. The falcon stands above a tall rectangle with the mace and shield framed in the upper half of the rectangle. The lower section is made up of a series of parallel vertical lines representing the niches of the mudbrick façades found in 1st Dynasty tomb architecture. Egyptologists call this the 'palace façade' or *serekh* motif because it also occurs in representations of royal buildings for the living monarch. All the kings of the 1st Dynasty are known by their 'Horus names' or serekh names which completely differ from the cartouche names recorded for them in the later king lists. This, of course, makes it rather difficult for Egyptologists to identify precisely who is who and in which order the Horus kings reigned.

I would remind you that their appears to have been no gradual development of this form of architecture in Egypt – but we already know where earlier prototypes *have* been found.

> In the second half of the fourth millennium, post-3500 BC, a very distinctive form of building design began to appear in the Sumerian cities, notably in Uruk. It is evident … in the platforms on which the temples were built – temples which eventually evolved into the ziggurats, so typical of Sumerian cities in their full flowering. A distinctive feature of these buildings is the recessed and alternating buttresses which mark the faces of the walls. … Several seal impressions from the Jemdet Nasr Period, roughly contemporary with the end of Naqada II, show high-walled, fortified palace buildings with recessed buttresses and other details which are repeated on Egyptian buildings of a time only shortly later. [21]

365. An example of the serekh-name of Horus Aha. The Horus falcon is perched on top of an enclosure with niched façade. The hawk grasps a shield and pear-shaped mace in its talons, spelling out Aha – 'the fighter'.

366. Reconstruction of the mastaba of Queen Neithhotep, wife of Aha, at Nakada showing the complex decoration of the niched façade which was later filled in with a plain outer skin.

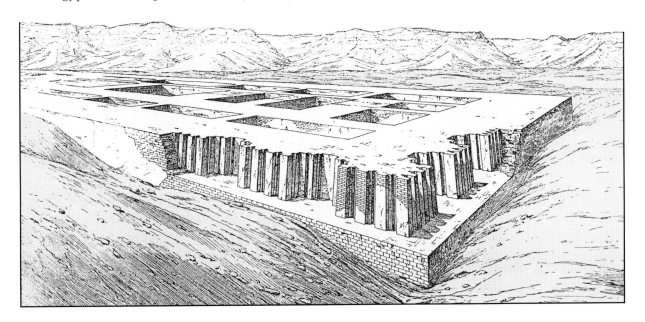

367. Plan of the mastaba of
Neithhotep at Nakada with its
elaborate niched façade.

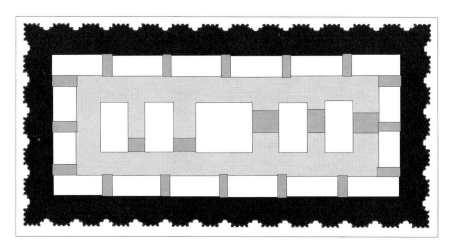

368. Temple VII at Eridu with its
niched façade – one of many
ceremonial buildings in the land of
Sumer decorated with this very
Mesopotamian artistic invention.

Yes, yet again there is a Mesopotamian precursor to the Egyptian version
– and this time, as Henri Frankfort observes, the technique is identical.

> Under the (Egyptian) First Dynasty, when brick architecture
> came into its own, this new and more permanent architecture
> was used, at first, for the royal tombs which were decorated
> with buttresses and recesses on all four sides. This ornamen-
> tation was achieved, in some cases, by the use of two kinds of
> bricks – large ones for the core of the building and smaller
> ones for the recessing. These small bricks are of a size and
> shape peculiar, in Mesopotamia, to the latter half of the Proto-
> literate Period and were used in an identical fashion, three rows
> of stretchers alternating as a rule with one row of headers. The
> recesses and buttresses duplicate exactly the recessing of (Meso-
> potamian) protoliterate temples. Other technical details – the
> manner in which a plinth or platform is constructed, the use of
> short timbers inserted horizontally as the strengthening in the
> niches – likewise reflect Mesopotamian usages of the Proto-
> literate Period. … In view of this great variety of detailed
> resemblances there can be no reasonable doubt that the earliest
> monumental brick architecture of Egypt was inspired by that
> of Mesopotamia where it had a long previous history.[22]

369. The first section of the Abydos
King List beginning with nomen
cartouche of Meni (left), followed
by Teti, Iti, Ita, Zemti(?), Merbiap,
(figure in long cloak, name not
readable), and Kebekh. These
nomens are thought to belong to
the Horus Kings Aha, [...], Djer,
Djet (Wadj), Den, Anedjib,
Semerkhet and Kaa.

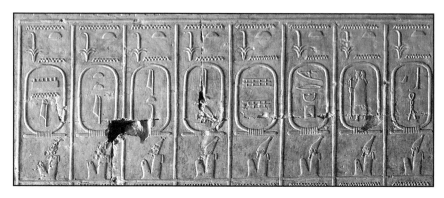

I could quote a dozen similar statements from various authorities in the field but will simply employ the words of Emery, excavator of the Sakkara 1st Dynasty tombs, to summarise the position.

> ... with the advent of the Dynastic Race, this form of monumental architecture makes its first appearance, and it is in this form of building that the Mesopotamian connection is most apparent. The striking similarities of the recessed brick buildings of both areas is too obvious to be ignored, particularly when we consider that in Egypt there is apparently no background or evidence of development for these immense and intricate structures.[23]

370. The simple niched façade of the Choga Zambil ziggurat in Susiana/Elam.

Conclusion Twenty-Eight

The most dramatic evidence of Sumerian technological, artistic and religious influence in the Nile valley was the introduction of niched-façade architecture. It is highly improbable that such specialised building techniques were independently invented in two widely separated regions at the same historical period without cultural transmission.

The Modern Sceptical View

When we look at all this evidence of Mesopotamian influence upon the culture of early pharaonic Egypt it is difficult not to conclude that the Sumerians played a major role in the formation of the Egyptian state. Few ancient historians would contest this 'influence' but there remains a major question as to the degree of that influence and in precisely which form it was manifest. There are two basic points of view.

(1) The archaeological and art-historical evidence indicates that a migration of foreigners into the Nile valley took place at around the Nakada II archaeological horizon. These people initially came as traders but,

1st Dynasty
Aha (Meni)
[...] (Teti)
Djer (Iti)
Djet (Ita)
Den (Zemti)
Anedjib (Merbiap)
Semerkhet (Semsem)
Kaa (Kebekh)

2nd Dynasty
Hetepsekhemwy
Reneb
Ninetjer
Peribsen
Khasekhemwy

3rd Dynasty
Zanakht
Netjerykhet (Djoser)
Sekhemkhet
Khaba
Huni

371. Foundations of the niched façade of the treasury at Persepolis built in the Mesopotamian tradition.

372. A large Nakada II buff-ware vessel decorated with several of the now familiar motifs: mountain range, dancing goddess, crescent standard with Horus falcon (replacing the sun-disc), palm fronds, godlike figures on the boat, central cabins or shrines, and flamingoes.

realising the potential for exploitation of Egypt's natural resources, they soon returned as invaders, conquering the local inhabitants and establishing ruling houses over the subjugated native population. In the course of several generations the petty kingdoms set up by groups of these élites fought internecine wars with each other for control of the Nile valley before the Upper Egyptian kingdom of Thinis/This became dominant. Under their Horus kings, Narmer and Aha, the élite warriors of Upper Egypt eventually conquered the Lower Egyptian kingdom of the Delta and established a new capital at Memphis. Thus began Manetho's 1st Dynasty which heralded in pharaonic Egypt. In reality, then, the first pharaohs were the descendants of a foreign élite from Mesopotamia. This hypothesis was later encapsulated by Derry.[24]

Or:

(2) The archaeological evidence does indeed point to close trading contacts between Mesopotamia and Egypt, but with the former merely introducing new technologies and artistic motifs to the native Egyptians. There was no invasion. The influence of these visiting foreigners was such that many of their cultural traits were adopted by the local chieftains in the Nile valley. These chieftains subsequently battled each other for control of Upper Egypt before the rulers of Thinis (Egy. *Tjenu*) were finally victorious. The unification of Upper and Lower Egypt was then accomplished by Menes who was of the Thinite royal bloodline. In effect, the pharaohs of the 1st Dynasty were the

descendants of native Nile valley rulers who had readily adopted aspects of the culture of foreign traders – they themselves were not of this foreign stock. [25]

Subtle variations based on these opposing views aside, here we have two quite distinct historical scenarios which I will call (1) the 'élite dominance theory' and (2) the 'indigenous development theory'.

Rex Engelbach in his article 'Essay on the Advent of the Dynastic Race in Egypt and its Consequences', published in *Annales du Service* volume 42, sums up the arguments for the élite dominance model.

> Though gradual infiltration by an alien people might well profoundly modify the culture of Egypt, it could hardly produce that terrific wave of national energy which followed close on the advent of the Dynastic Race. Such a result, however, might well follow the invasion and conquest by a race superior in fighting strength, though perhaps far inferior numerically to the old Egyptian stock, the one having discipline, unity and a set purpose, and, above all, the art of writing, and the other having trading enterprise and a good knowledge of the arts and crafts. I consider that the balance of probability is that the Dynastic Race arrived in Egypt as a horde, perhaps after a considerable amount of peaceful penetration had already taken place … [26]

Interestingly enough, you would be hard pressed to find a single general history book on Egypt, published in the last thirty years, which favours this view of early pharaonic origins. Whilst many of the archaeologists and art-historians who originally dealt with the predynastic archaeological material were advocates of the élite dominance model for the foundation of the Egyptian state, few modern scholars would express such a view. I have looked at why this is so and have come to the conclusion that it has much to do with the types of historical models which are acceptable to today's historians. No-one likes to be seen as advocating 'super race' history when such histories were at the heart of the politics of Nazism. Moreover, anthropological history is now the current fashion within academic circles. Such anthropological models generally require slow evolutionary changes in the development of civilisation. Rapid and violent events are no longer to be regarded as satisfactory mechanisms for cultural change in ancient-world history. But, I come back to the question I raised at the beginning of this story of Egypt's foundation: can we really distance ourselves from historical reality simply because of modern attitudes towards the opinions of earlier scholars raised in a very different world to our own? Few of us today would think like Petrie, Derry and Emery. But terms like 'Dynastic Race' or 'super race' are just that. They are terminologies of language and political view – they do not, by their use, deny the historical reality of past events. The evidence these archaeologists discovered is not devalued by their politics. One of the objectives

373. Another Nakada II buff-ware vessel with lug handles.

HYKSOS CONQUEST: The foreign take over of the delta and (later) the Nile valley down to Middle Egypt at the end of the 13th Dynasty (Middle Bronze Age).

DORIAN INVASION: The conquest of Bronze Age Greece by the Dorian tribes.

SEA PEOPLES: A confederacy of Indo-European nations which migrated into the coastal regions of the Levant and attempted to enter Egyptian territory during the late 19th Dynasty and, in particular, in Year 5 of Ramesses III of the 20th Dynasty.

RAMESSES III: King of the 20th Dynasty, reigned OC – 1184-1153 BC.

of this book is to redress the imbalance brought about by the modern sceptical view and review the evidence afresh. If done with an open mind, I personally believe it is hard to resist the conclusion that a foreign élite did indeed migrate to the Nile valley and that it was the descendants of these seafaring adventurers who initiated the pharaonic state.

It is fairly obvious why the writings of some Egyptologists were so unpalatable to the next generation of scholars, raised in the aftermath of the Second World War. But unfortunately, as is often the case in scholarship, rather than modifying the language whilst retaining the model indicated by the evidence, the pendulum began its inevitable swing in the opposite direction. By the 1970s the trend was to dismiss or downgrade conquests and invasions of the dim and distant past. Many of the best known ancient historical 'events' were either watered down or completely denied. The HYKSOS CONQUEST of Egypt, described by Manetho as a traumatic episode in his country's history, became a gradual and peaceful infiltration of foreigners into the eastern Delta; the DORIAN INVASION of Greece was never as dramatic and far-reaching as we had been led to believe by the ancient writings; the attempted invasion of Egypt by the SEA PEOPLES in the reign of RAMESSES III was nothing more than a minor skirmish; and, as I highlighted in Volume One of *A Test of Time*, the Conquest of the Promised Land by the Israelites – as narrated in the book of Joshua – never really happened.

So, the modern approach is to downplay unpalatable conflicts – especially victories by 'barbarians' over 'civilised' nations – and to reject what might be called the traditional histories of such events in favour of archaeological evidence – or rather the absence of such evidence. But archaeology rarely reveals direct evidence of conflict and invasion. The burning of cities may perhaps indicate warfare (though often has alternative explanations) but what of bloody battles? Many historically accepted conflicts of more recent times have gone unattested in the archaeological record. By their very nature battles are ephemeral. They occur suddenly with great violence, but the scar of the conflict is soon healed by nature, leaving only human memory to carry the wounds. The poppy fields of Flanders attest to this. In the absence of written records, what archaeological evidence will remain for the Great War of 1915-19 in 4,000 years' time?

Historians accept the invasions of civilised Europe by the barbarian Huns and Mongols, so why do they no longer accept the reports of ancient writers on similar conquests from earlier history? This cannot in any way erase the memory of twentieth-century fascism, nor does it deny the reality of barbarism in modern warfare. Again, Bosnia attests to that. In reality the opposite is true. Our recent history, extending as far back as historians wish to take it, is all the evidence we need to demonstrate that humankind is a territorial animal, always in search of new pastures, mineral wealth and natural resources. These are often gained by military conflict or the application of superior military technology.

374. This extraordinary seal from
Susiana, in spite of its damaged
state, holds a vital clue as to the
origins of at least one group of the
foreign élite who came to Egypt.
Look closely at the figure standing
before the crescent moon standard
(top left). If this example of glyptic
art had been found in Egypt you
would not hesitate to identify the
figure as a pharaoh wearing the tall
white crown (illustrated below) of
Upper Egypt (after P. Amiet, 1961,
pl. 17:282).

If this is an inescapable truth about our modern world, then we ought
to have little difficulty in accepting the reality of the violent nature of
ancient times. In the old world children were indeed sacrificed to the
gods; kings were interred in tombs surrounded by sacrificial victims;
pharaohs did crush in the skulls of captives in ceremonial re-enactments
of battles for their domestic audiences; whole cities were wiped out, their
populations slaughtered in the name of one god or another; and civilisations often fell victim to less 'civilised' neighbours who had been fortunate
enough to discover a superior military technology. Common sense tells
you that there is nothing inherently unhistorical in the proposition that
Egypt was invaded by a technologically superior foreign élite just before
the dawn of pharaonic civilisation and the archaeological evidence
genuinely supports such an invasion hypothesis.

Within the pages of the last two chapters I have demonstrated that the
archaeological and artistic evidence for the arrival of foreign migrants
into the Nile valley is considerable – I would say almost overwhelming.
But did the Egyptians themselves believe that their primeval ancestors
came from abroad? The immediate response from the Egyptological
experts to such a question would undoubtedly be no – nothing in Egyptian
literature indicates such a tradition. This has been the consistent understanding within the discipline for the best part of 150 years. However, I
believe that a rethink is now needed. Given the strength of the archaeological evidence for the arrival of newcomers in Nakada II, we should
perhaps look again at the legends surrounding Egypt's earliest gods. In
my view, it is here that we may find a hint of Egypt's pharaonic origins –
origins which reach back to far distant lands across the wide ocean. It is
time, then, to return, in the company of the Followers of Horus, to their
island home, so that we may be witnesses to the building of the primeval
temple of the creator-god of the 'First Time'.

This is the gate of the netherworld. It is the door through which my father Atum
passed when he proceeded to the eastern horizon of heaven.

Book of the Dead, Spell 17

375. Opposite page: The huge pylon façade of Edfu temple. The two great towers may represent mountains between which the sun rises at dawn. In effect the gateway is akin to the gates of the eastern mountains of Mesopotamia through which the land of sunrise is reached.

376. Left: The Carnarvon ivory knife handle, datable to the Egyptian late-Predynastic Period, depicting wild animals surrounding the central boss carved into a six-petalled flower. This rosette was one of the early symbols of Inanna, patron goddess of Uruk.

Chapter Eleven

THE FOUNDERS

377. The golden head of Horus of Nekhen found buried along with other redundant masterpieces in the temple mound of Hierakonpolis.

Egyptologists have always naturally thought that the creation myths of Egypt were set in the Nile valley environment. However, I think they may be wrong in this long-held belief. The place of the primeval mound which rose out of the waters of Nun was not located in Egypt but in the *original* homeland of the gods.

Horus of Edfu

Many readers of this book will have stood before the towering pylons of Edfu Temple and marvelled at the achievement of Egypt's HELLENISTIC rulers. Edfu is the best preserved of all ancient Egyptian temples. The structure visible today was begun by Ptolemy III (Euergetes I) in 237 BC and took one hundred and thirty-two years to complete, the opening ceremony being held on the 10th of September 105 BC.

The Ptolemaic temple of Horus at Edfu was a truly spectacular endeavour, but it was only the last of a number of temples built on this spot. In recent years stone blocks forming the pavement of the great open court were lifted to make the surface more even for the heavy tourist traffic. To everybody's surprise the paving slabs turned out to be reused blocks from a much earlier structure. The undersides were finely carved with reliefs dating from the Second Intermediate Period (NC – 1632-1194 BC). Remains of a pylon gateway built by Ramesses III have been unearthed showing that the temple was once orientated towards the east rather than the current south-to-north alignment.

Horus, the sky-god, was closely associated at Edfu with the winged sun-disc, Harakhty ('Horus of the (Eastern) Horizon') emphasising his solar nature (hence the Greeks renaming of the place as Apollinopolis

HELLENISTIC: The epoch of Greek cultural influence over the ancient Near East from Alexander (332 BC) to the death of Cleopatra (30 BC).

378. A typical Hathor pillar capital showing the human head of the goddess with cows ears and the characteristic omega-shaped hairstyle. This latter feature is also characteristic of Ishtar and Astarte.

PRONAOS: The area of a temple which precedes the holy of holies.

379. Plan of Edfu temple with the two locations of the Shebtiu scenes: (A) inner face of enclosure wall (B) exterior of pronaos, west side.

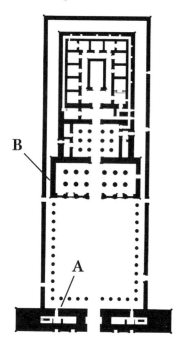

after their own sun-god, Apollo). The consort of Horus was the cow-goddess, Hathor, whose temple was at Dendera, to the north of Thebes. The most important festival in the Edfu calendar was the annual re-enactment of the sacred marriage between Horus and Hathor when the statue of the goddess made its journey upriver from Dendera to Edfu to perform the sacred marriage rites. This is just like the religious ceremonies of Sumer in which the gods journeyed to each other's temples by boat along the intricate canal and river system.

The relationship between Horus and Hathor is very interesting because the name Hathor means the 'House of Horus' – the implication of which is that she represents the womb from which Horus emerged. So how do we explain the apparent contradiction of Hathor as both wife *and* mother of Horus? We do this by invoking a second Horus – Horus the Younger – who is the offspring of Hathor and Horus the Elder and therefore the heir to his father's throne. This concept lies at the heart of pharaonic kingship – the legitimacy of succession of the Horus kings – those who 'followed' in the footsteps of the original Horus king. The reigning monarch is the human manifestation of Horus the Elder; his queen (and mother to the heir apparent) is Hathor; and the heir himself is Horus the Younger before his succession. The Egyptians themselves believed that the original Horus kings of the 1st Dynasty were a line of rulers descended from an original god-king known as Horus.

Inside the hallowed halls of Edfu's great temple the walls are covered in reliefs typical of the Ptolemaic Period – pharaohs embracing gods, performing rituals before the sacred shrine in the holy of holies, burning incense and making offerings of fruit, vegetables and meat. But there are other images here which appear to go back to a much more distant tradition – the era of the 'First Time' or 'Primeval Age' (Egy. *sep tepi*).

The Coming of the Shebtiu

On the inner west face of the enclosure wall of the temple (third register) there is a scene relating to the foundation of the first sacred precinct on earth.[1] Here we see an assembly of primeval deities labelled 'Thoth and the Seven Sages' attending the foundation rituals of a mythical temple called the 'Great Throne' (Egy. *set weret*). The Seven Sages are accompanied by two otherwise unknown deities named Wa (the 'Distant One') and Aa (the 'Great One').

In another scene forming part of the outer west wall of the PRONAOS we find six different gods in the company of Wa and Aa. They are seated behind the Horus falcon which is perched on the 'Djeba' (a stand made of reeds) in a place called the 'Exalted Throne of Horus' (Egy. *wetjeset-Har*). The sacred enclosure of the Djeba marks the primeval resting place of the gods. Before the falcon stands the figure of the king, his arms raised in an attitude of adoration. In this instance the pharaoh wears the blue crown of war. The text accompanying this second scene refers to

these six gods variously as the 'Senior Ones', the 'Children of Tjenen (the 'Risen One')', 'Offspring of the Creator', the 'Glorious Spirits of the Early Primeval Age', 'Brethren of the Sages', the 'Builder Gods' and the 'August Shebtiu'. The inscription then goes on to mention Wa and Aa.

> Two among them are leader(s) for them, (namely) Wa and Aa, the Lord(s) of the Island of Aggression. They are the two gods who founded this place and who were first to exist therein in the company of Re.[2]

Wa and Aa are elsewhere designated the 'Two Companions of the Divine of Heart' (Egy. *teswy netjery-ib*). This suggests a supreme being worshipped by Wa, Aa and the other Primeval Ones which must be the god referred to here as Re. But remember that the Edfu texts are very late. All the early religious inscriptions make it clear that the primeval creator-god of the Egyptians was originally known as Atum, then Re-Atum and only finally Re. In effect, the sun-god Re was identical with the creator-god Atum who was also called the 'First Primaeval One' (Egy. *pauty tepy*) and was known as:

> ... he who caused the earth to be when he had come into existence in the past, the Sole Unique One without peer, who was first to fashion the earth upon his (potter's) wheel, who created men, gave birth to the gods, Lord of the Universe, Ruler of the Primeval Ones, the First Primeval One who came into being before the Primeval Ones.[3]

Here we find another link with the Sumerian creation myths which seems to point us back to Enki and the moulding of humankind from clay. As Eve Reymond notes:

380. The location of the main Shebtiu scene on the outer west wall of the pronaos can best be seen from the exterior of the temple.

381. A Hathor capital from the Chapel of Births in Hatshepsut's mortuary temple at Deir el-Bahri.

382. Horus of Edfu.

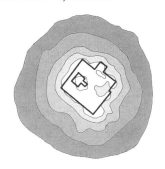

383. The original circular island of Eridu with its Temple of the Abyss, surrounded by marshes.

> The idea of fashioning the earth on the potter's wheel is foreign to the ideological background of the main Edfu records.[4]

Is this a surviving remnant of Mesopotamian theology in Egypt? Perhaps, but I think we will find a great deal more if we delve a little deeper.

The names Wa and Aa are clearly titles or epithets and we will probably never know their true identity. They were understood to be semi-divine beings with super-human attributes. They were also members of a divine family known from our only Egyptian source as the Shebtiu or 'Senior Ones'.[5] These Senior Ones were greatly venerated at Edfu. Their worship, as the ancestral founders of the original sacred precinct of Horus at Djeba, played a major part in the later Ptolemaic temple festivals and rituals.[6] But where was this original temple? Where was Djeba? Was it in Egypt? Or, given what we *now* know about the origins of pharaonic civilisation, should we not be looking for that first holy sanctuary in Mesopotamia? Also in the light of our discoveries, could the Egyptian phrase *sep tepi* – the 'First Time' – be referring to the golden age before the flood?

I have always been uneasy about the conventional explanation of Egyptian creation mythology. Although it would seem quite natural to set the story of the primeval mound rising from the waters of Nun in the Nile valley, it somehow feels wrong to me. Yes, the valley is flooded annually by the inundation and, as the flood dissipates, small islands form. But that is precisely the point: this is a cyclical event, witnessed year in year out, whereas Nun represents the eternal waters of chaos. The emergence of the sacred primeval mound was a singular event. The Nile valley setting just seems inappropriate. But set the story in the marsh-lands of ancient Sumer and the mythological concept fits much better. Think of the sand island of Eridu surrounded by the freshwater lake of the abzu – the home of the Lord of the Abyss. Think of the first temple being erected on this island by primeval beings who have arrived there from the sea. These are the first humans to discover the island and the very first settlers of antediluvian Sumer. Think of that original holy shrine being constructed from the reeds which surround the island. All this fits the Egyptian creation myth perfectly.

The Edfu texts are very difficult to interpret. They seem to hint at more than one sacred island and at least two eras of foundation. As Czech Egyptologist and Edfu specialist Eve Reymond (formerly Jelinkova) suggests, the overall text of the foundation inscription 'hints at the view that the Shebtiu were not the first generation of creators'.[7] They were the offspring of the gods – the descendants of the original supreme beings.

As I understand the Edfu foundation myth, there are two locations being referred to: (a) an original temple foundation of the great gods and (b) a second, later, foundation on an island where the dead gods were buried and where their spirits resided. The former was the realm of the 'Ancestors' – the original Primeval Ones; and the second the place which the Shebtiu founded as the Djeba of the falcon.

What I am about to propose is that the foundation texts at Edfu form part of a distant memory concerning the ancestors of the Followers of Horus. These short texts represent a record of the establishment of the sacred island of the first temple on earth which was founded in the golden age, long before the Shebtiu came to Egypt. Centuries later, the descendants of the primeval ones briefly sojourned on a second island which, in the Edfu tradition, is called the 'Blessed Isle'.[8] This lay somewhere on the route taken by the Followers of Horus as they made their long journey across the sea to the Nile valley.

The Edfu foundation texts make it clear that they are extracts from a very ancient book of wisdom called 'Specifications of the Mounds of the Primaeval Age' (Egy. *sesher iaut en paut tepet*).[9] The book is said to record 'the words of the sages'.[10] But this mythological tradition was not simply the creation of the Edfu priests. As Reymond observes, it is hinted at in a number of Egyptian temple inscriptions.

> The fact that the land in which the creation was to be effected was at the same time a territory of the Ancestors can be illustrated by a passage in the 'Karnak Myth of Creation'. The 'place of the origin' is the *satau*, the 'ground of the Ancestors'. The same tradition is known from the texts of the Temple at Philae. The 'Sanctified Territory' which Ptah founded, and which men call the 'Beginning of the Earth', was at the same time a burial place in which Osiris was believed to rest.[11]

Let me piece together a theoretical sequence of events which I believe could fit the Edfu myth of the primeval temple of the First Time and the later temple of the falcon.

Temple of the Golden Age

The Primeval Ones (Egy. *pautyu-tepyu*) came from a place called the 'Exalted Throne of God'. This, I believe, was the great temple platform (or early ziggurat) of Eridu. The great deities were the 'Ancestors (Egy. *tepyu-a*) who Created the Primeval Ones' and the 'First Among the Ancestors' was the earth creator-god himself.[12] Remember that the name of the Sumerian creator-god, Enki, means 'Lord of the Earth'.

At the beginning of the myth we witness the Ancestors colonising an island which is surrounded by the waters of Nun. Here they establish the first temple. We already know where that temple was located. Once it is realised that the original homeland of the Followers of Horus was ancient Mesopotamia, we are immediately drawn to the sandy dune of Eridu situated in the reed marshland of southern Sumer. The Edfu texts then refer to the *pay*-lands – outlying islands upon which settlements are created. In our model these are the numerous sand-banks of the southern marshes on which the first cities of Sumer were established – in particular Ur and Uruk. It turns out that the Egyptian creation myth may be the

384. A decorated pot from the Isin-Larsa era found in southern Mesopotamia. Note the high-prowed ship and the row of crescent-moon standards. Louvre Museum.

385. The crescent-and-rising-sun standard carved in the rock at Kanais alongside the predynastic high-prowed boats.

337

386. The symbol for the sacred shrine of the sun-god Utu/Shamash at Larsa, taken from Sumerian seals is the crescent-with-sun-disc on top of an altar or tower-temple.

387. The Sumerian symbol for the sun-god, Utu (Akk. *Shamash*) is the crescent-with-sun-disc – precisely the symbol which appears on the desert rocks and on Nakada II pottery. The lower sign is its cuneiform version (rotated through ninety degrees anticlockwise).

388. The location of Eridu adjacent to the ancient coastline of the Gulf.

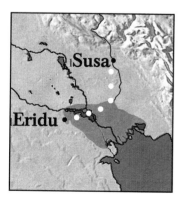

only literary source to record this momentous event in Man's early history. The surviving Mesopotamian sources remain silent, leaving us only the dumb archaeology of the first temple of Eridu stratum 17 and the broken sherds of Ubaid pottery left by the Founders.

I say that the Edfu texts are our only source but we, of course, also possess the book of Genesis which provides us with the biblical names of those Founders. We have noted that this earliest settlement – the first city – was probably named after Irad, son of Enoch, and that his name means 'the one who descended (from the mountains)'.

A consistent story is beginning to emerge here from the combined mythologies: a gradual descent by the 'sons' of God(s) from an ancestral homeland in the mountains down into a marshlands where a small island becomes the new home of antediluvian ('First Time') Man. This forms part of the mythology of both Sumer and Genesis but it is only with the arrival of the Primeval Ones at Eridu that the Egyptian creation myth begins – there appears to have been no memory of the earlier Edenic epoch within the mountains of heaven.

I have chosen to describe the primeval temple of Eridu here, rather than in an earlier chapter, because this magical place needs to be viewed within an Egyptian mythological perspective. I want you to imagine the Iraqi excavators uncovering the very structures erected by the Builder-Gods of pharaonic legend.

According to Fuad Safar, who revealed the archaeology of Tell Abu Shahrain, primeval Eridu was a small, roughly circular, sandy island surrounded by a freshwater swamp which led out into the salt-water Gulf.

> At some time, perhaps towards the close of the sixth millennium BC, the first human settlement was established at the site now called Tell Abu Shahrain. The location chosen for the settlement was a high dune of wind-drifted sand, probably forming a convenient island in a wide area of marshland, once a tidal lake at the head of the Arabian Gulf. [13]

The Primeval Ones reached this place by boat. The Egyptian texts refer to the 'Ancestors' arriving on the island from out of the primeval waters of Nun. The newcomers to the marshes of Sumer brought with them the distinctive pottery which marks the beginning of the Ubaid Period.

> The settlers themselves, on arrival, were already possessed of a well-developed and distinctive culture of their own, characterised notably by a class of painted pottery not previously discovered in south Iraq. [14]

At the very beginning the site of the sacred Eridu foundation was marked by the dedication of a simple shrine which Sumerologists have attributed to the god Enki/Ea. This makes perfect sense in a biblical context if Ea is to be identified with Ya[wheh], later re-introduced to the Israelites by Moses through his contacts with the Midianites.

In its first manifestation the simple shrine was probably made of reeds surrounded by a reed enclosure wall, but soon low, parallel brick walls (perhaps foundations) were being built within the enclosure. Immediately on top of these walls the builders erected a brick temple measuring just under three metres square.

> The earliest traces of building were separated from the virgin sand only by a few centimetres of occupational debris. These were fragmentary walls, constructed of well-made, rectangular liben bricks. It is therefore safe to assume that our settlers brought with them from elsewhere a fairly advanced knowledge of building. In any case, after a sojourn at the site corresponding in length to three distinct occupation-levels, we find them erecting a building, again in rectangular liben, whose function is recognisable as that of a religious shrine.[15]

This more solid structure, known as Temple 17, was the first recognisable religious building – complete with central offering stand – to be built in Sumer. Just above Temple 17 the Iraqi archaeologists found a more elaborate structure which they called Temple 16. This had a recess in the rear wall within which the symbol or statue of the god stood. Immediately in front of this recess was another low offering table for sacrificial offerings.

Eventually, over the long period defined by the Ubaid pottery phase, the Eridu temple grew into a large, complex structure, the walls of which were fashioned in the well-known niched-façade architectural style which we have witnessed in both Sumer and Egypt. The last great phase of the prehistoric temple was raised upon a massive platform which dominated the surrounding landscape. Temple 1 at Eridu must have been a spectacular monument by any standards. By the Uruk Period the Eridu temple had become the holiest site in Mesopotamia.

Then, quite suddenly, the island of Eridu suffered some unknown but cataclysmic fate.

> … the Uruk Period … appears to have been brought to a conclusion by no less an event than the total abandonment of the site. … In what appears to have been an almost incredibly short time, drifting sand had filled the deserted buildings of the temple-complex and obliterated all traces of the once prosperous little community. … At this point, there is a considerable hiatus in the history of the site, as it is known to us from the results of our excavations. … the Jemdet Nasr epoch … is not represented at Eridu. During the Early Dynastic period also, there is reason to suppose that the fortunes of Enki's shrine at Eridu had reached an extremely low ebb. In fact, the only meager remains of this period, were indications on the slopes of the mound which now represented the ruins of the prehistoric shrine, that some kind of impoverished sanctuary still survived at its summit.[16]

389. The earliest temple-shrine in Sumer. Temple 17 at Eridu was a simple square structure with central offering table and two grain silos outside. Beneath the mudbrick walls of the building the excavators found four low parallel brick walls which may have served as some sort of foundation.

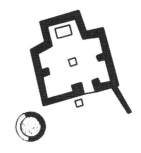

390. Eridu Temple 16 was built immediately on top of the first temple. It has a slightly more complex structure with a deep rear niche for an altar or statue podium. Fish bones were found on the floor of the temple, suggesting offerings dedicated to Enki, god of the freshwater.

Only with the Ur III revival was the great shrine at Eridu restored to anything like its former glory.[17]

What happened? No-one really knows. Nothing about the holy shrine's demise is mentioned in Mesopotamian literature – but perhaps the legend from Egypt relating to the fate of the Primeval Ones can fill in this missing piece of the historical jigsaw puzzle which has been revealed by the archaeological record.

The names given to the Egyptian sacred island of the First Time include the 'Island of Aggression' (Egy. *iu titi*) and the 'Island of Combat' (Egy. *iu aha*), both of which suggest that a great battle was fought there.[18] Was the island of the Primeval Ones invaded and sacked in a devastating conflict between the existing inhabitants and foreign invaders?

Needless to say, given the remote era we are dealing with, it is unlikely that we will ever get a clear picture of this first legendary battle, but it is entirely possible that Eridu, located as it was near to the shore of the Persian Gulf, suffered an invasion from the sea. This was the first city of Mesopotamia in more senses than one. Not only was it the first to which 'kingship descended from heaven' but it was also the first settlement to be reached from the sea. It was, in effect, the gateway into the Land of the Two Rivers.

We have already noted that there has been an ongoing debate as to precisely when the Sumerian-speaking people entered southern Mesopotamia. Here, then, is one option to resolve the 'Sumerian Problem'. Perhaps the ethnic Sumerians arrived as an invading horde in sea-going ships from the east, taking over from the 'indigenous' Primeval Ones who had arrived in the land of Shinar centuries earlier when they migrated down into the marshes from the plain of Susiana. The indications we have that there was once a primeval (pre-Sumerian) language in the region – exemplified by the names of the great rivers of the alluvial plain – bring us as close as we can get to the original language of the first descendants of Adam.

Was a protracted conflict with migrating ethnic Sumerians the signal for a group of the Primeval Ones to depart for horizons new? Was Meskiagkasher – the biblical Cush – who 'went down into the sea' the leader of the seafaring pioneers? Indeed, can he and his companions be identified with the Shebtiu? There is so little to go on, but an historical mechanism for the Mesopotamian migration could be constructed by combining the legends of Genesis, Sumer and Egypt. So, let us first see what else we can learn from the rest of the Edfu foundation texts.

Following the abandonment of the original sacred temple site in Eridu, we rejoin the Edfu story with the foundation of a second holy sanctuary in a place called Djeba. We know from the archaeological excavations at Tell Abu Shahrain that the temple of Eridu was not rebuilt until well into the historical period – far too late to fit the Egyptian legend. The site effectively lay in ruins for several centuries. We must therefore look to a quite different location for the new foundation of the Shebtiu. So, what do we know about the place of the second mythological temple?

This sacred site was also on an island – but this time the place is called the 'Blessed Isle'. The temple itself is named the 'Exalted Throne of Horus', established on the 'Foundation Ground of the Ruler of the Wing'. It has another name – the 'Place of Uniting of the Company' (Egy. *bu sema djasu*) which suggest a gathering together of forces or an alliance of some sort. It is almost as though the island becomes a staging post for something much bigger.

Now let us incorporate elements of the story from the traditional history of Sumer. Meskiagkasher was, according to the Sumerian King List, the 'son of the sun-god (Utu)'. Was Meskiagkasher therefore a sun worshipper? Remember that in the Mesopotamian flood story it is Utu who brings light and warmth into the world following the terror of darkness brought on by the deluge and it is before this god that Ziusudra prostrates. The proposition emerges that Meskiagkasher (the biblical Cush, son of Ham) was the first Horus-king – a celebrant of the sun cult of the falcon sky-god.

We have an extraordinary parallel from the Indo-European world which drives the point home. Noah's third son, Japheth, was the eponymous ancestor of the Indo-European races – in other words the Greeks, Hittites and Vedic culture of India. Japheth surfaces in the mythology of Greece as Iapetos, the son of heaven and earth, and in Sanskrit where his divine father Pra-Japati ('Father of Japheth') is the sun and lord of creation. [19] So Japheth was also regarded as being closely related to the sun-god. Much of the extra-biblical evidence suggests that the generation which followed the flood were sun worshippers.

The Names of the Shebtiu

1. The Distant One (*wa*).
2. The Great One (*aa*).
3. The Sailor (*nay*).
4. The Sacred Head (*djeser tep*).
5. The Serpent-Creator of the Earth (*kema sa ta*).
6. Lord of the Twin Hearts (*neb haty*).
7. Lord of Life and Divine Power (*neb ankh was*).
8. The Mighty-chested Lord who made slaughter; the Spirit who lives on blood (*neb sekhem haut iry adjy ba ankh em senef*).

Abode of the Blessed

392. The great sky-god of Egypt and the principal deity of kingship is the Horus falcon (the 'Distant One') epitomised by the great granite statue of Horus at Edfu.

Upon the Blessed Isle the Shebtiu built the 'Great Primeval Mound' which was also known as the 'Mound of the Radiant One' (i.e. the sun-god). Around this great primeval mound they constructed more tumuli which were called the 'First of the Mounds'. This in itself presupposes that other tumuli were built at a later date.

Why do I say that these primeval mounds were the work of the Builder-Gods and not sandbanks rising from the water of the primeval ocean (the usual interpretation Egyptologists place on the creation myth)? The reason is because we have mention of a sacred book belonging to these Builder-Gods which is entitled 'Specifications of the Sacred Mounds of the Primeval Age'. If there were plans and specifications detailing how to build these mounds, then they must have been constructions and not natural formations. Why do I call them tumuli – in other words burial mounds? Because the area of the primeval mounds was called the 'Place of the Ghosts' – that is to say the realm of the dead. This is reinforced by the fact that the 'Underworld of the Soul' was also located in the vicinity.[20] The Blessed Isle was therefore not only the location of the first temple of Horus (not to be confused with the temple of Enki at Eridu) but also a sacred burial ground for the dead gods, near which an entrance to or exit from the underworld was to be found. It was also the burial site of the sun-god in his Mound of the Radiant One – hence why the Blessed Isle also bore the name 'Island of Re'.

Were the gods of Egypt buried on a sacred island within their great tumuli – just as the human nobility of Sumer had been buried in mounds on Bahrain island?

> It would follow that the concrete shape of the original creators may have been believed to have been concealed in the earth, in the actual land of the island which they created first. We learn from our sources that the Egyptians believed in the divinization of the physical form of the original creators, and that their embodiment became divine in the *iaut en tau* – the Sacred Mounds of the Earth.[21]

Furthermore, the heart of the divine necropolis was the tomb of the great sun-god himself.

> … closely connected with the island of creation there was a place that had obvious funerary associations, a place which was conceived as the burial place of a deity who died, whose soul had flown to the sky and whose material form remained in the same place: this KA who dwelt among the reeds of the island.[22]

393. The Horus falcon as represented in Egyptian art.

Was the Egyptian Blessed Isle one and the same as the Sumerian Abode of the Blessed which scholars have identified with Bahrain? As we have seen, on that island necropolis which the Mesopotamians knew as sacred Dilmun, home of the gods, there are great funerary mounds surrounded by thousands upon thousands of lesser mounds. Did the Egyptians of later times believe that the largest of these mounds were the actual tombs of their primeval gods?

This seems like an appropriate place to mention another interesting link between pharaonic civilisation and the Persian Gulf. The sky-god Horus who played such an important role in Egyptian religion also had close connections with the Arabian peninsula. The word Har or Heru (which scholars translate as 'The Distant One') was the name the Egyptians gave to their falcon-god; Horus is simply the Greek form of the god's name. A number of scholars have recognised that Heru is identical with the Arabic name of the falcon – *huru*.[23]

It is well known that falconry is of significant cultural importance amongst the people of the Gulf states. The hawk is held in high esteem today throughout the Arabian peninsula and one can hardly doubt that this reverence towards Huru goes back to earliest antiquity. The abiding imagery of the falcon is that of a majestic bird soaring skyward just as the soul of the great deceased god of the Edfu texts flies up to heaven. We now also discover that one of the two leaders of the Shebtiu was named Wa – another Egyptian word which means 'The Distant One'.

394. An Arabian falcon from the island of Bahrain.

This, in turn, begs the question as to who we might identify as the 'sun-god' buried on the sacred isle of Dilmun. We have learnt from the Sumerian flood epic that Ziusudra resided for eternity in the place of sunrise which is otherwise identified as Dilmun. The final element of the floods hero's name – *sudra* – means 'the far-distant'. That other early name of Noah – Atrahasis – is usually followed by the epithet *ruku* which in Akkadian also has the meaning 'far-distant'.

KA: The creative life force of a person or god.

Conclusion Twenty-Nine

The early Mesopotamian flood hero, known as Ziusudra or Atrahasis, may be mythologically connected in some way with the Egyptian solar sky-god known as Har (Horus) – 'the far-distant'.

TEMENOS: A Greek word meaning temple compound.

395. A masterful relief of Seti I wearing the *atef*-crown, from his temple at Abydos. Note the pair of tall plumes attached to the even taller reed crown.

Here, then, we have a group of beings – a divine family – called the Shebtiu who were long dead by the time of the Egyptian sacred books' composition. They had been great builders; indeed they were responsible for founding the original sacred TEMENOS of Djeba. The temples of Djeba (for there seems to have been more than one shrine in the holy precinct) are not simply temples of the imagination. The Egyptians believed that they were real, physical buildings from the remote past. The sacred books possess dimensions for the structures so that future temple foundations may conform to the ideals of their primeval forerunner.

> These temples, though they are described as the work of the gods themselves, appear to be conceived as actual, physical entities. The descriptions are so precise and detailed that it is reasonable to suspect that they embody an attempt to describe the history of the growth of such early temples, which are now lost. … There is every reason for assuming that this narrative reflects a genuine tradition of a remote date. [24]

The Shebtiu were closely connected to the Seven Sages – a reminder of the seven *apkallu* or sages of Sumerian tradition. Indeed, immediately beneath the Edfu register depicting Wa and Aa and the six Shebtiu is a scene showing Thoth and seven ram-headed deities who are thought to be one and the same as the Seven Sages listed in the foundation inscription. Here the king standing before the deities is wearing the *atef*-crown with its ram's horns and tall feathers. These iconographic associations with the ram once again point us to the great creator-god and solar-deity, Atum, who appears as the ram when he descends into the western horizon at the close of day. The tall feathers which are such a predominant feature of the crowns of the primeval deities in the Egyptian temple and tomb reliefs instantly recall the figures depicted in the Eastern Desert rock art with their tall twin plumes.

Lord of the Earth

Our reconstruction of the First Time now brings us to the reason for the gathering of the Shebtiu on the Blessed Isle – the great migration.

396. A cylinder seal impression dated to the Early Dynastic II Period from Fara (Shuruppak). It depicts (on the left) a Master of Animals with long hair (Enkidu?) controlling lions; (centre) a hero with horned helmet (Gilgamesh?); and (right) a high-prowed boat containing two seated figures in conversation (Utnapishtim and Gilgamesh?), plus a standing figure (the ferryman Urshanabi). Note the falcon above the prow of the boat (after P. Amiet, 1961, pl. 104: 1374).

The Ancestors had settled on the Island of Aggression or Combat upon which the temple of Eridu was founded. But, having established the first temple there, the descendants of the Ancestors were driven away by newcomers. We then witnessed the coming together of the Shebtiu confederacy on a new island which we have identified with the island of Bahrain/Dilmun in the Lower Sea. Now, according to Dr Reymond's reading of the Edfu texts, the Shebtiu, having established their new temple of Horus on the Blessed Isle, set sail once more, heading for a new destination.

> The Shebtiu appear to have arrived at Wa and Aa's island where, together, they formed a confederacy. The crew of the Falcon having arrived, the Shebtiu seem to have sailed away. The crew seems to exercise protection over this land. [25]

Note that the Shebtiu are associated with sailing – one of their number is called Nay ('Sailor'); they are a 'crew' and they sail away, leaving the sacred island under the protection of those of their kin who are left behind. Yet they remain the spirit guardians of the Island of Ghosts with its holy temples and primeval mounds. Where were they going? Given that most of the material we have been looking at in this chapter comes from Egypt, I think we can reasonably assume that their destination was the Nile valley and, more specifically, the regions of Edfu and Hierakonpolis in the south and Kuft and Nakada, opposite the Wadi Hammamat, in the northern part of Upper Egypt.

In another section of the Edfu foundation texts we discover the Egyptian names for the gods who resided with Wa and Aa on the Blessed Isle. These are not the Shebtiu who arrive at the island from their own homeland (perhaps Susiana and Sumer) but rather the resident gods of the Isle of Ghosts. They are: a god called Pen (the value of the vowel given here as 'e' is not known), the Ka, the Heter-her, the sacred *Djerty*-Falcon, the Falcon-Lord of the Djeba, the Protector-God, and the God of the Temple. [26] These must be the great gods – perhaps the original Ancestors – whose temples and tombs/cenotaphs were established on the Blessed Isle.

There can be little hope of making much sense out of this list of obscure divinities – except, that is, for the first and apparently most important of them. Pen could simply be translated as 'This One', but that seems rather unsatisfactory. If the Blessed Isle is the Sumerian Abode of the Blessed and is therefore to be identified with Bahrain, then where is the Egyptian version of the Lord of the Earth, the 'friend of Man', the Lord of the Abyss – Enki? The answer may lie in a brief analysis of Enki's character. It is clear from the numerous incidents in the myths associated with Enki that he is a clever, even cunning, deity; he is mischievous and non-conformist; in his aspect of the creator of humanity he is a fertility-god; he liaises with humans by whispering through reed walls so that he may circumvent the ban, placed on him by his fellow deities, which prevents

397. Amun of Karnak is depicted here on the fallen obelisk of Hatshepsut. He wears the two tall plumes which are so familiar in scenes of Egyptian gods and now in the rock drawings of the Eastern Desert.

398. This small tablet (now in the Louvre) shows an early Mesopotamian ruler wearing two tall plumes and supporting what appears to be a staff with pear-shaped mace-head.

345

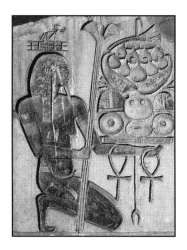

399. The Nile-god Hapy presents the produce of the Nile valley to the temple foundation of Ramesses II at Abydos.

400. The ram-headed god Khnum crafting humanity on his potter's wheel.

401. The great primeval god Ptah of Memphis.

direct communication with humans. One could look upon him as a bit of a wily prankster. He is sometimes shown with the legs of a goat complete with cloven hooves, whilst his upper body is clothed in the scales of a fish. Enki is also, as we have seen, very much the protector of his creation – humankind – and the provider of the life-sustaining sweet water. Much of this points us in the direction of the Greek god Pan (the Peter Pan of Never-Never-Land).

But is there a primeval Egyptian god who might, at least in part, fit this profile? Let us start by finding out what we can about the god Pen of the Edfu texts. Perhaps the most interesting of the few things we learn about Pen is his abode within the sacred precinct of the first temple. We have identified that place as early Eridu, the settlement which was later to be associated with Enki. Even though the sun-god, the Radiant One, seems to predominate on the Island of Aggression, he is not the sole occupant of the holy landscape according to the Egyptian text. At the heart of the island is a sacred pool within which another great god dwelt upon his Exalted Throne of the God (Egy. *wetjeset-netjer*).

> The god of the pool is not the sun-god. The Egyptians called him simply Pen – 'This One'.[27]

Pen is therefore a god of the primeval spring-water just as Enki is the Lord of the Abyss.

But who was Pen in the Egyptian pantheon? Surely he must have another name with which we are more familiar? The obvious candidate would be the god of the freshwater, the ram-headed Khnum of Aswan. But remember that the great creator-god, Atum, was also ram-headed when he descended into the underworld. Is there some link between these two deities both of which are associated with the watery abyss and are represented by the same animal form?

Khnum was also the Lord of the Inundation which itself was manifest in the form of the fecunditity figure of Hapu or Hapy. Is there some garbled link here with the Sumerian abzu or apsu? Indeed, it has long been recognised that the Memphite sacred bull, Hapu or Apis, was closely connected with the annual Nile flood. Tradition has it that the bull was not permitted to drink Nile water because it would be, in effect, a form of self-mutilation or cannibalism. Only when Apis met his end was he to be reunited with Hapy. According to Pliny the Elder and other classical authors, if the sacred bull did not die of natural causes before his allotted time – that is to say the life-span of Osiris – he was taken to a pool of Nile water near Memphis known as the *kebehet* and drowned.[28]

However, Apis in life was also the manifestation of Ptah, the great god of Memphis who was himself a major player in Egyptian creation mythology. In the Memphite Theology (inscribed on a block now in the British Museum) Ptah is the one who occupies the Exalted Throne; he is the personification of the primeval waters of Nun and the one who fathered (and mothered) Atum, the sun-god.

Ptah who is upon the Great Throne (*set weret*);
Ptah-Nun, the father who [begot] Atum;
Ptah-Nunet, the mother who bore Atum;
Ptah the Great, that is, the heart and tongue of the Ennead;
[Ptah] ... who gave birth to the gods;[29]

Ptah was Tatjenen (the 'Risen Land') – the primeval mound which rose
from the waters of Nun (conventional translated as 'waters of chaos').
Ptah, in his anthropomorphic form, was the great artificer, the creator of
humans. If we now put on our Sumerian spectacles, I think we can begin
to see a reflection of the Sumerian creation mythology behind all this
Egyptianised imagery. Ptah-Tatjenen was the sacred mound which existed
in the primeval waters of chaos (the Sumerian abzu) – in other words the
city of Eridu itself; the Exalted Throne of God in the Edfu texts is thus
the towering E-abzu (the 'Temple of the Abzu') at Eridu; the Apis bull is
both the manifestation of Ptah, the artificer of Man (identified with Enki
in Sumerian mythology) and, at the same time, the embodiment of Hapy,
the life-giving waters which surround the sacred isle of the abyss. In the
Egyptian texts the waters of the abyss are called Nun. Given what we
have surmised, it is tempting to link this Egyptian word of unknown
origin with the original Sumerian writing of Enki's city. Eridu was not
only known as *Eridu(g)* but also as *Nun.ki* – the 'Land of Nun'.

402. The life-size statue of an Apis bull calf found by Auguste Mariette at the Serapeum. Louvre Museum.

Conclusion Thirty

Ptah, the great creator-god of the Egyptians, may be identified with the Sumerian creator-god, Enki, whose primeval temple was built by the waters of the abzu at Eridu. This sacred place was known to the Egyptians by its ancient Sumerian name of Nun.

Swapping our Sumerian specs for the pinch-nose bifocals of the Egyptologist once more, we can now read the opening lines of the Sumerian Epic of Creation in a new 'pharaonic' light.

A reed had not come forth. A tree had not been created.
A house had not been made. A city had not been built.
All the lands were sea.

Then, we move effortlessly to the Egyptian myth of the Creation of Atum where the sun-god makes his first appearance.

'I am Atum when I was alone in Nun; I am Re in his (first)
appearances, when he began to rule that which he had made.
... I am the great god who came into being by himself.' Who
is he, this great god who came into being by himself? He is
water – he is Nun, the father of the gods.

403. The two Sumerian symbols (top) which spell out *Nun.ki* and (bottom) their cuneiform counterparts (again rotated). It has been remarked that the left symbol resembles the Egyptian djed-pillar (below) – one of the most important motifs of the god of the dead, Osiris. The right-hand symbol could be a boat viewed from above.

404. A statuette in green faience of Queen Tiye (wife of Amenhotep III) depicting her wearing the high twin plumes of a goddess. Louvre Museum.

So Atum is also Nun who is, in turn, the father from which all the other gods derive. Thus we now have two Egyptian manifestations of Nun – the Memphite Ptah and the Heliopolitan Atum.

This brings me to a very important theological point. The Egyptians were both polytheists and monotheists (or rather SYNCRETISTS) at the same time. There is no doubt that they worshipped many gods – some very exotic in form and nature. But they also believed in the one great creator-god who was both male and female.

> The bisexual nature of Atum is asserted, not only by calling him 'that great He/She' but by saying that he 'gave birth' to Shu (the air-god). [30]

This bisexual monoplicity may seem rather confusing but is quite simple really. The single, all-encompassing creator-god(dess) had many manifestations, each of which served to represent a different aspect of his/her character. These 'characteristics' included kingship (Horus), chaos (Seth), agricultural fertility (Min), death (Osiris), mummification (Anubis), resurrection (Khepri), motherhood (Hathor), love and fertility (Isis), etc. But remember that the Egyptians themselves constantly refer to 'God' in the singular. As Carol Andrews of the British Museum notes:

> The Egyptians saw no inconsistency in such a situation. In Egyptian religion old beliefs were rarely discarded, new ideas and concepts were merely tacked on, even when in direct contradiction to existing views. [31]

The attributes of one god may be transferred to another precisely because of this collective oneness. It is not surprising therefore to find both Ptah and Atum associated with the waters of Nun. Each city or religious foundation in Egypt naturally wished to elevate their 'aspect' of the one-god to the supremacy of the divine family of 'aspects'. As John Wilson, translator of the Egyptian creation myths for James Pritchard's influential source-book *Ancient Near Eastern Texts Relating to the Old Testament* states:

> Every important cult-centre of Egypt asserted its primacy by the dogma that it was the site of creation. [32]

So, at different times in Egypt's history there were claims from different city priesthoods that their 'god' was the great creator and, indeed, they were all correct because the primeval god was all things to all men. Atum of Heliopolis was the sun-god creator; Ptah of 1st-Dynasty Memphis was equally the primeval-mound creator (Tatjenen); Re of the later Pyramid Age was both Atum and the creator, Harakhty ('Horus of the Horizon') was the reborn sun-god who rose into the eastern sky above the primeval mound at dawn. Thus one prayer refers to a supreme being called Amun-Re-Atum-Harakhty. [33] All this may be confusing to the modern mind but was never a conceptual problem to the ancients. As Anthony Spencer notes in his book *Death in Ancient Egypt*:

The lack of a consistent view-point did not trouble the Egyptians, whose theology was well able to accept the identification of king or god with several entities at the same time.[34]

The lesser gods were simply the elements of a single, all powerful divinity. Where all these theologies were inaccurate was in their claims that the *place* of creation was located at their city. They could not all be right and, in reality, none were. What each city did was to recreate the setting of the First Time within its temple compound. Each built a primeval mound as the foundation of the god's holy shrine – but these were only replicas. The true place from which the original creation story of the Egyptians derived was far away to the east in the marshes of Sumer.

The Sumerian Epic of Creation continues with the establishment of the first settlement on the primeval mound: 'Then Eridu was made.' So begins the story of the Ancestors who built the first temple on earth.

We now recognise how the traditions concerning the First Time may have reached Egypt. They were probably transmitted as an integral part of the culture of the Followers of Horus and, as one might expect, the imagery and ritual of the Ancestors took root in the major political centres of the Shebtiu colonies. The most important of these centres was Nekhen ('Falcon City'), which archaeologists refer to as Hierakonpolis ('City of the Hawk') after its Greek name. This first Egyptian city of the Horus kings was located just a few kilometres to the north of Edfu, at the site known today as Kom el-Ahmar (the 'Red Mound').

Nekhen was a holy place even before the period of the unification of Upper and Lower Egypt under Menes and remained so throughout pharaonic history. Its primitive reed temple, set on a mound of clean desert sand (enclosed in a sloping revetment wall of bricks), was the first foundation of the Shebtiu in the Nile valley. Here is a striking architectural feature which links us with both Bahrain and Mesopotamia. As Petrie noted in 1939, the temple of Barbar on Bahrain was constructed on top

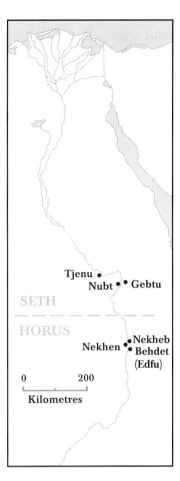

405. Locations of the main predynastic sites in Upper Egypt showing the Horus of Nekhen (Hierakonpolis) and Seth of Nubt (Nakada) groupings.

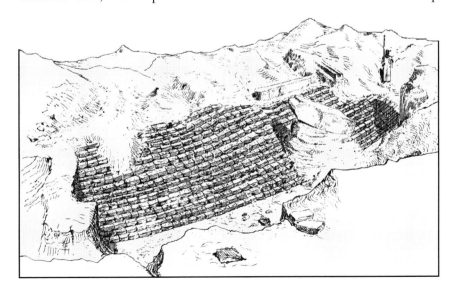

406. The sloping revetment wall which the archaeologists discovered at ancient Nekhen and which encased a mound of pure sand upon which the predynastic reed-shrine temple was erected. This construction closely matches the earliest temple foundation at Eridu and the later temple at Barbar on Bahrain.

407. A comparison between the Master of Animals of the Gebel el-Arak knife handle (top) and that of the Tomb 100 painting at Hierakonpolis (bottom).

QUIBELL: (1867-1935).

GREEN: (1869-1949).

408. The only surviving excavation picture of the now lost Tomb 100 at Hierakonpolis. Traces of the famous painting (the crescents of two ships) can just be made out on the right-hand wall.

of a hill or platform of clean sand as were many of the holy sites in Sumer. Such sandy mounds represent the primeval hill upon which the first temple of creation at Eridu was constructed.[35] The Egyptian religious texts mention another sacred mound of sand at Heliopolis upon which the Benben was erected. The Benben was the sacred stone onto which the mythological Benu-bird (the fabulous Phoenix) alighted to establish the temple of Atum at the city of the sun (which the Egyptians knew as Iunu and the Greeks as Heliopolis). This was the most important centre of Atum/Re worship in Egypt and its roots go back to the legendary era of the predynastic Horus kings.

So the earliest temples in Egypt would not have been out of place if they had been found in Sumer or Dilmun. The *indirect* link to the Ancestors of Eridu is there to be made and the *direct* link to the eastern invaders was discovered just a year after the excavation of the temple of Nekhen in 1897 by James QUIBELL and Frederick GREEN.

In the winter season of 1898-99 Green led a second archaeological mission to Hierakonpolis – this time to the cemetery behind and to the south of the temple site. There he found the famous Painted Tomb 100 – a rectangular, brick-lined chamber whose walls were plastered smooth and painted with primitive scenes similar to the rock art of the invaders found in the Eastern Desert.

Here we find the Master of Animals, the high-prowed black ship and the smiting of captives. All motifs which we have associated with the Square-Boat People. It may well be that Tomb 100 was the burial place of one of the leaders of the invading élite – perhaps the first ruler of Nekhen himself and therefore one of the original Followers (i.e. descendants) of the primeval Horus. If we are right in this assessment, then the anonymous ruler of the city of the hawk who was buried in Tomb 100 may actually have been the first Horus king of Egypt. Whatever the case, Hierakonpolis was certainly the seat of the Followers of Horus and the spring-board for the eventual domination of the whole Nile valley.

409. A scene from the contest of Horus and Seth at Edfu temple. Horus, astride his papyrus boat, harpoons the figure of Seth in the form of a tiny hippopotamus (beneath the prow). In effect this is an act of suppression by the legitimate heir to the Egyptian throne (i.e. the pharaoh as Horus) of nature's chaotic forces (epitomised by the lumbering hippo).

However, before the momentous event of the Unification of the Two Lands, a conflict took place in Upper Egypt which was to form a new, purely Nilotic, element in the religious tradition of the formative Egyptian state.

The Contest of Horus and Seth

The Followers of Horus of Nekhen were not the only tribe to establish roots in the Nile valley during the period of Nakada II. Indeed, the period itself acquires its name from the site where we have observed Petrie unearthing the first archaeological evidence for the 'Dynastic Race'. It is clear that within the century or so following the first arrivals of the Shebtiu confederacy, a second group of foreign invaders had entered the Nile valley further north in the vicinity of Thebes. They had crossed the Eastern Desert through the Wadi Hammamat and had established their capital at Nubt (near modern Nakada). There and at Kuft they built their own sacred precincts to their primary gods – Seth and Min.

The relationship between the Followers of Horus at Nekhen and the Followers of Seth at Nubt is unknown, but it is possible that they both belonged to the original Company of the Shebtiu with blood ties between them. However, the legends of the contest between Horus and Seth hint at a breakdown or quarrel which soon led to a war between the two élite tribes. This was later personified in the one-to-one contest for power between the gods Horus and Seth which resulted in a unification of the lands (of Upper Egypt) under the rule of the victorious Horus. The story is depicted on the inner west enclosure wall of Edfu Temple where Horus, astride his reed boat and armed with a spear, is seen vanquishing Seth in the form of a hippopotamus.

If we translate this allegorical scene into a putative historical event we might presume an original battle between the Followers of Horus and the Followers of Seth which led to a major expansion northwards of the kingdom of the hawk. This 'victory' of the Horus clan may have been sealed by a political marriage between the Horus-king of Nekhen and a princess of the Seth tribe. She was later to be personified in the figure of Hathor, the mother of Horus the Younger who was the first ruler of the unified state of the upper Nile valley. The sacred marriage rite performed annually at Edfu temple was a celebration of that fundamentally important political event. What we understand as the later kingdom of Upper Egypt was thus formed and a new capital established at This (Thinis) with its royal cemetery at Abydos. The unification of Upper Egypt heralded in what Egyptologists have dubbed 'Dynasty 0', the rulers of which were soon to conquer the rest of the Nile valley and delta, establishing the pharaonic state under Menes – first ruler of the 1st Dynasty and founder of Memphis.

Descendants of the Shebtiu

There is a collective noun in the ancient Egyptian texts used to describe a very special group of people who existed in early pharaonic times. The word is *Patu* (plural of *Pat*) and those who belonged to the clan were called *iry-pat* (literally 'one of Pat descent'). These iry-pat were an élite nobility which surrounded the pharaoh – they were effectively the courtiers of the royal palace. They also had ancestral links back to the Followers of Horus. The ancient texts make a clear distinction between the Patu and the two other population groups of the Nile valley – the *Henemmet* and the *Rekhyt*. As Pierre Montet notes:

> As early as the Pyramid Texts, the *Pat* were associated with Horus whose earthly representative was the king. On the day of his coronation the king received the *Pat* as if they were his own flesh and blood. When the king died, he was mourned by the *Pat*, while the *Henemmet* and the *Rekhyt* appeared to be unmoved by the event.

The most famous iry-pat was none other than the great architect, magician and sage, Imhotep – the genius who built the magnificent Step Pyramid complex at Sakkara for his king, Djoser. But this remarkable servant of the pharaoh was just one of many iry-pat recorded in Old Kingdom times. Indeed, the great queens of the early kings carried the title iret-pat (the feminine form of iry-pat) showing that the royal line was itself a part of the élite Pat clan. Many high-ranking officials of the Old Kingdom (royal sons, provincial governors and magistrates) bore the title iry-pat – but not all. The occasional biographical funerary text notes that the deceased reached his exalted position within the pharaonic government *despite* the fact that he was not iry-pat. This is important point because it

410. The rekhyt bird or lapwing is seen here with arm raised in salutation before the cartouche of the king. The bird is positioned above the basket symbol which means 'lord' with a star completing the sign-grouping. The whole composition spells out 'Lord of the Egyptian People'. The rekhyt bird originally represented the Lower Egyptian delta enemy of the Upper Egyptian kings but later became the symbol of the population of Egypt as a whole.

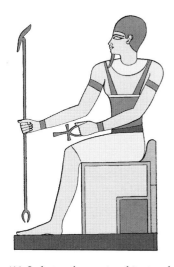

411. Imhotep the great architect and adviser to King Djoser of the 3rd Dynasty was the most renowned of the *iry-pat* nobility. He is seen here in his later deified form as the god of medicine.

shows that we are dealing with a bloodline or aristocracy rather than merely an administrative or honorific position. So not all high officials were iry-pat but, at the same time, it is clear that many iry-pat were chosen to rule precisely because they could demonstrate their descent from the original entourage of the first Horus kings – in other words the Followers of Horus themselves. We have learnt that these Followers of Horus were one and the same as the foreign invaders of the Nile valley who arrived in their high-prowed boats. They appear in the archaeological horizon known as Nakada II. Thus the iry-pat were descendants of the migrants from Dilmun and Sumer whose ancestral leaders, as we have seen, came from the direct line leading back to Adam.

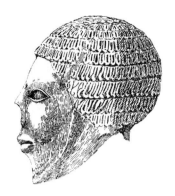

The other two population groups – the Henemmet and Rekhyt – appear to have been indigenous to the Nile valley. The Henemmet were probably the indigenous Upper Egyptians conquered by the eastern invaders. They too are described as sun-worshippers. The Rekhyt, on the other hand, seem to have occupied the Nile delta having entered Egypt from the west (i.e. the Libyan coastal lands). They are depicted as lapwings and are shown as the vanquished enemy of the Upper Egyptian kings who conquered the north in the campaign of reunification which took place during Dynasty 0 and was complete by the reign of Menes.

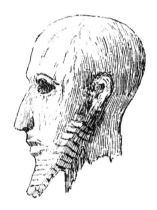

The Horus Kings of Abydos

There is more to learn about the early Horus kings of Upper Egypt and their immediate successors of the 1st and 2nd Dynasties from their burial ground at Abydos. As I have said, the anonymous Horus-king of Nekhen, having conquered the territory of the Followers of Seth around Nubt, established a new capital of Upper Egypt at Thinis (Egy. *Tjenu*). A site for the royal cemetery was chosen nearby at a place which the Egyptians referred to as Abdju (Grk. *Abydos*).

Behind the temples of Seti I and Ramesses II at Abydos is a vast desert necropolis pitted with thousands of tombs dating from all periods of Egyptian history. They are here because of Abydos' association with Osiris – it is the place where the Egyptians believed the head of the great god of the dead was buried.

Right at the back of the cemetery, immediately before a narrow cleft in the cliff which defines the western boundary of the lower desert shelf, a series of low mounds marks the necropolis of the kings of Thinis. Here at the Umm el-Gaab ('Mother of Pots') are the tombs of the Horus kings Iry-Har, Ka and Narmer from Dynasty 0; Aha, Djer, Djet, Den, Anedjib, Semerkhet and Kaa from Dynasty 1; and Peribsen and Khasekhemwy from Dynasty 2. The archaeological history of Umm el-Gaab has been patchy. The site was first plundered by treasure-hunter Émile AMÉLINEAU in 1895-6 but then carefully re-excavated by Petrie in 1900-1. It is currently being re-examined and restored by a German team under the direction of Gunter Dreyer and new discoveries are being made every season.

412. Examples of predynastic heads which may represent a North African Kushite type (top) and a Mesopotamian with Asiatic Puntite appearance (below, profile and full-face).

AMÉLINEAU: (1850-1915).

413. The Den ivory label from Umm el-Gaab depicting the king in the act of smiting his enemy with a pear-shaped mace. In front of the pharaoh's head is his serekh-name and, to the right, the standard of Wepwaut – 'Opener of the Ways'.

414. The finest of the 1st Dynasty funerary stelae is that of Djet discovered in the sand outside his Abydos tomb. Louvre Museum.

An early pharaonic tomb consisted of a series of underground mud-brick chambers surrounding a central burial chamber. This complex was then covered by a mound of clean sand supported by a retainer wall. This 'primeval mound' not only recalls the sand platforms of Hierakonpolis, Heliopolis, Barbar and Eridu but also the funerary mounds of Bahrain.

All around the royal sepulchres are hundreds of small, rectangular grave pits laid out in neat rows. These are the servant burials of their Dynasty 0 and Dynasty 1 masters. Careful examination of these subsidiary tombs by both Petrie and Dreyer has shown that the servants and officials of the royal household were all buried at the same time which strongly suggests that these are sacrificial burials. Just as was the case with the early kings of Ur, whose famous tombs were excavated by Woolley in the 1920s, the early Egyptian rulers went to the afterlife replete with their palace entourage.

Scores of ivory labels from the site of Umm el-Gaab show the kings celebrating religious rights, including what may be the first depictions of the *sed*-festival or royal jubilee (see next chapter), as well as a scene of Pharaoh Den smiting his enemies with a pear-shaped mace. The German team has recently recovered approximately one hundred and fifty new labels which appear to have once been attached to storage jars. These tiny dockets contain early hieroglyphs representing the grave goods and their numerical quantities. These are the first examples of hieroglyphics in Egypt and yet they appear for the first time in their fully developed form with some signs actually representing phonetic symbols rather than objects. Scholars have often observed how remarkable this sudden appearance of writing is in Upper Egypt, without any precedence in earlier periods. This has led many to suggest that an outside influence must have been at work – an influence which could only have come from Mesopotamia.

A large funerary stela of King Djet was found by Amélineau at Umm el-Gaab, erected before the 1st Dynasty tomb. It shows the Horus falcon perched on top of a palace façade (Egy. *serekh*) within which the name of Djet is simply spelt out by the sign of the snake. Below the snake is an intricate carving of the niched-panelling with which we are now familiar.

So many of these royal iconographic elements which surround the pharaohs throughout later Egyptian civilisation are to be found here at Abydos already in their fully developed forms. And so many of these elements can be traced to Mesopotamia in the centuries immediately preceding the 1st Dynasty in Egypt. But perhaps the most astonishing discovery to have been made at Abydos in recent years was made by David O'Connor and his American team from Yale and Pennsylvania Universities.

Between the cultivation zone and the 1st Dynasty tombs, stands the mudbrick enclosure of the Shunet el-Zebib ('Fortress of Dates'). These ruins, still standing to a height of eleven metres, represent what remains

415. The Shunet el-Zebib enclosure of Khasekhemwy, last ruler of the 2nd Dynasty and father of Djoser.

of the fortified funerary temple of King Khasekhemwy of the 2nd Dynasty. The Shunet el-Zebib is, in effect, the forerunner of the pyramid complex of the Old Kingdom and the immediate predecessor of the Step Pyramid complex of Pharaoh Djoser. The hieroglyphs of Netjerykhet (the Horus name of Djoser) have been found in the tomb of Khasekhemwy by the German expedition, confirming for the first time that the last king of the 2nd Dynasty was buried by his son, the first ruler of the 3rd Dynasty.

O'Connor's careful re-excavations of the great enclosure of Shunet el-Zebib have revealed two new and startling discoveries. First, within the wall of the court he uncovered a surface of mudbricks gradually sloping up towards the centre of the open space. It would appear that the giant niched-façade enclosure wall surrounded an artificial mound which represented the 'mound of creation'. When I heard about this new discovery I immediately thought of the great mound of Eridu sheathed in its sloping mudbrick sleeve. This was even more starkly reinforced by O'Connor's second discovery – a row of twelve enormous boat pits containing the remains of wooden boats which measure twenty-two metres in length. It was as if the Egyptians were attempting to recreate the island of the Ancestors itself, with the temple platform resting upon the primeval mound and the harbour of the abzu adjoining it, replete with a fleet of ships ready to carry the king and his entourage upon their hazardous journey through the underworld.

416. Looking along the niched façade of the Shunet el-Zebib.

417. The great Lebanese-cedar funerary barque of Khufu with its high prow and stern, central cabin and long oars. This is the archetypal square boat – transport of the gods.

As yet the boats have not been excavated but it is very likely that they will turn out to be vessels similar to the ships of the Eastern Desert rock drawings. I say this with some confidence because of the sensational discovery made by Kamal el-Malakh in 1954 of the Khufu solar-boats dismantled and buried in two boat pits upon the death of the king. These pits were located beneath the south face of the Great Pyramid. You only need to take a look at the photograph above to see that the great funerary boats of Khufu (which may well have been used to transport the funeral cortege from Memphis to the pyramid) a high-prowed ship is identical to the solar-barques of Re-Atum and the Company of gods which would transport the deceased pharaoh to the Isle of Flame on the eastern edge of the world.

But more on that shortly, after we have investigated the immediate successor to the Shunet el-Zebib – the funerary complex of King Djoser surrounding his great primeval mound – the first pyramid on earth.

The Narmer Palette

The most famous artefact of the predynastic era is the Narmer Palette, now held in the Cairo Museum. Both sides of this extraordinary work of art contain fascinating historical details and several elements which can only be described as Mesopotamian iconographic features or Eastern Desert rock-art motifs. The obverse (418a, top) depicts the king smiting an enemy with his pear-shaped mace. He wears a bull's tail attached to his waistband. Behind him stands a smaller male figure carrying a pair of sandals and a small pot. To his left there is a tiny hieroglyphic label (a six-pointed rosette above a *hem*-vessel). Together they read 'sandal-bearer of the god-king'. Narmer's name (centre-top) is written within the niched-façade motif. Either side of the king's name are Hathor cowheads. The Horus falcon controls a bearded enemy representing the delta marshes. Beneath the king's feet two of the defeated enemy flee in terror.

418a

The reverse side of the palette (418b, bottom) has two antithetical long-necked beasts as its main motif. The necks of the animals are entwined in typical Mesopotamian fashion. The lowest register represents the king as a wild bull overturning the walls of a town and crushing an enemy underhoof. However, the most interesting scene is that in the uppermost panel. Here the king parades at his victory celebrations, carrying his pear-shaped mace and followed by his faithful sandal-bearer. Before the king marches a female labelled 'Tjet' (perhaps his queen) and four standard-bearers carrying the totems of two falcon tribes, Wepwaut and the symbol of what is thought to be the royal placenta. Beyond lie rows of beheaded corpses belonging to the vanquished enemy above which we see a high-prowed ship identical to the reed craft illustrated in the Eastern Desert rock-art.

Could all these foreign elements really have been adopted wholesale by native chieftains of the Nile valley? Or is it not much more likely that Narmer himself was a descendant of those who came to Egypt in their high-prowed boats several generations before the founding of the pharaonic state?

418b

Chapter Twelve

STAIRWAY TO HEAVEN

419. Opposite page: Guardian of the 14th gate.

420. Above: The Step Pyramid with its cobra protectors.

have argued that many of the Mesopotamian influences in the late predynastic era appear to have their focus in the iconography and symbolism of Egyptian kingship. This suggests to me that Petrie and his followers were indeed right to propose that the early pharaohs themselves were foreign to the Nile valley. It seems far less likely that all this 'royal' iconography can be explained away by the mechanism of trade alone. The idea that visiting Sumerian merchants were somehow responsible for 'educating' native Egyptian chieftains in the art of kingship and kingship ritual is surely stretching credulity to its limits. There seems little doubt that the first Horus kings were descendants of an élite family whose origins lay buried in a far-away place many months' journey from the Black Land.

To see how persistently this foreign iconography adhered to the pharaonic state we have to move forward in time from the birth of pharaonic civilisation by a few centuries – to the beginning of the Old Kingdom and the construction of one of Egypt's most spectacular and famous monuments.

A Mansion of Millions of Years

Forty minutes' drive southwards out of the sprawling metropolis which is modern Cairo lies the vast desert necropolis of Sakkara – the burial ground of ancient MEMPHIS. Today the visitor approaches this city of the dead through lush date-palm groves, past the country estates and weekend villas of wealthy CAIREANS. Occasionally along the road a break in the palms reveals the desert escarpment and, looming majestically above it like a stairway to heaven, the Step Pyramid of King DJOSER.

421. Djoser's *serdab* statue. Cairo Museum.

MEMPHIS: Located at the modern village of Mit Rahina. Memphis was ancient Egypt's capital and principal residence of the pharaohs through-out most of the pharaonic era.

CAIREANS: Citizens of Cairo.

DJOSER: Alternatively Djeser or Zoser, meaning 'sacred (ruler)'. The Step Pyramid complex records only the king's Horus name, Netjerikhet, meaning 'god-like in body'. The name Djoser is linked to Netjerikhet by graffiti left at the Step Pyramid naming it as the work of Djoser.

MANETHO: A man of Sebennytus who became a high priest at Heliopolis. He was commissioned by the early Ptolemies (third century BC) to write a history of Egypt. His original narrative no longer exists, but excerpts are given in Josephus: *Contra Apionem*, whilst redactions, in the form of king lists, have been preserved in the works of the early Christian chronographers Africanus and Eusebius.

HORIZON OF ETERNITY: One of the ancient Egyptian names for a tomb used, in particular, to describe the pharaoh's last resting place.

ASHLAR: Sawn blocks of stone.

Djoser's tomb is a momentous landmark in the faltering progress of civilisation. Not only was it the first pyramid but it was also the very first monumental building to be constructed in stone. It is recognised as a work 'unique in Egyptian architecture'[1] which, in its innovative design, 'represents a bold challenge to the imagination'.[2] The Egyptian priest-historian, MANETHO, described Djoser's architect, Imhotep, as 'the inventor of the art of building in hewn stone'.[3] The titles of Imhotep have been found on a statue base in the great court of Djoser's funerary complex. They are:

> The chancellor of the King of Lower Egypt; the first after the King of Upper Egypt; administrator of the great palace, hereditary lord, the high priest of Heliopolis, Imhotep – the builder, the sculpture, the maker of stone vases.

In identifying Imhotep as the inventor of stone architecture Manetho was not strictly correct, since blocks of stone have been found in the mastaba tombs of the 1st and 2nd Dynasties. However, before Imhotep conceived his great plan, the tombs of the kings had been built of mudbrick with only the odd portcullis or chamber-lining made of cut stone.[4] Under the guidance and inspiration of Djoser's royal architect, the enterprise of building the king's 'HORIZON OF ETERNITY' was radically different. No gradual evolution in Egyptian stone architecture here, rather a quantum leap in both concept and technology. This was intended to be a royal tomb which would truly endure for eternity, constructed from imperishable ASHLAR limestone blocks, meticulously smoothed to a gleaming white finish to reflect the rays of the sun. Even today the pyramid's six giant steps reach to a height of sixty metres above the desert ridge.

It is difficult to avoid the conclusion that, just as in ancient Sumer, this is truly a mountain of the god. Egyptologists have sometimes postulated that the theology behind the Step Pyramid is a stairway which enables the spirit of the dead king to ascend to the stars. However, you would not be the first to observe that the Step Pyramid closely resembles the ziggurats of Mesopotamia and, as we have seen, they had a quite different, though theologically related, function. A staircase is clearly a two-way mechanism which, in the case of the Step Pyramid, not only gives the dead ruler access to the gods but also provides a means by which the gods can make their presence felt within the human sphere of their creation. By building his Step Pyramid on the Sakkara ridge – the physical boundary between the fertile valley and the inhospitable desert – Djoser may have had this additional motive in mind. Perhaps he believed that he was providing a means by which the gods of heaven could descend to his earthly resting place, thus establishing an alliance between his own spirit and those of his fellow deities. This would certainly have been a power capable of holding back the chaotic forces of the Red Land (Deshret = desert) – the kingdom of Seth – from encroaching upon the ordered existence of the Black Land (Kemet = Egypt) – the kingdom of Horus.

422. The six giant steps (the lowest much eroded) of Djoser's stairway to heaven.

In a sense, the Step Pyramid and all its successors were, at least in part, potent machines built to defend Egypt from the chaos of the outside world. This idea might best be understood by employing a well-tried metaphor from modern 'Chaos Theory'.

Imagine standing in the desert with a handful of sand. Now, take a black felt-tipped pen and mark a single grain of that sand. Chaos Theory observes that, if you were to pour the sand onto the desert floor, you could not predict precisely where your black grain would come to rest. Of course, having poured the sand, you can once again determine where the black grain has come to rest simply by observing its position with your own eyes. If you were now to pour more sand onto the same spot, the millions of collisions between the particles would again set up a chaotic event which prevents any precise prediction as to where your black grain is going to end up. But pour the sand anyway and keep pouring more sand whilst trying to imagine what is happening to your black grain within the desert mountain you are creating. Although it is no longer visible, you can readily understand that your grain is no longer in a state of turbulence. Its position has become stable and ordered whilst the chaotic world on the surface of the mound remains completely unpredictable. Substitute the body of the deceased king for the black grain of sand and you will begin to appreciate the way Maat (divine/cosmic order) and Seth (chaos) interact within the theology of ancient Egypt. The king rests in his burial chamber at the heart of his desert mountain. There, in that stillness of air and stone, nothing moves; nothing disturbs the order of the inner universe surrounding the deceased pharaoh. Outside, the surface of the pyramid is assaulted day after day by the chaotic elements – wind and sandstorms; the heat of day and the cold of night; rain and hail; stone robbers and clambering tourists – all take their toll. Yet the god-king sleeps on within his sacred mountain, existing in the twilight world of Osiris. There, his other-worldly task is to continue his earthly role as protector of the people of Kemet – sustainer of Maat and defender of the Black Land from chaos.

But the Egyptian pyramid is much more than a single theological concept and the Step Pyramid complex of Djoser is very much more than a typical pyramid. It has many extra elements for us to study which its later counterparts – the true or straight pyramids (as exemplified by the pyramids of Khufu, Khafre and Menkaure at Giza) – do not possess. I can best explain what I mean by taking you for a stroll around and through Djoser's great tomb to see if we can learn some of its secrets and recover the code of pharaonic theology which exudes from every stone in the place.

As we pass up to the desert plateau, leaving the verdant Nile valley behind us, we are entering the world of the spirits. This is the place of the westerners – those who accompany the setting sun into the nether-world of night – the spirits of the dead. Our destination lies ahead, about half a kilometre along a dusty desert track.

Immediately before us the pile of rubble which is the 5th-Dynasty pyramid of Userkaf punctuates the horizon and, to its left, our first close-up view of the majestic steps of Djoser's pyramid. To gain access we will have to head for the south-east corner of the pyramid's giant enclosure protected by its high limestone wall. This is no ordinary wall. It is twenty cubits high (10.5 metres) and over one-and-a-half kilometres in circumference, encompassing an area of some 150,000 square metres. Along its length there are fourteen bastions containing gateways to the complex. But, amazingly, thirteen of these are false doors, their entrances sealed with solid, impenetrable stone. Only one is a true gateway designed for human access. The others are for the spirits of the dead who can pass effortlessly into the netherworld beyond. We of mortal flesh will have to gain our entry to that other world by more conventional means. Fifteen Egyptian pounds secures the ticket which allows the visitor to venture beyond the modern guardian of the fourteenth gate and into the Step Pyramid complex.

Before we enter we should first examine the enclosure wall itself. Here there is an architectural feature with which we are now quite familiar. The entire length of the wall is made up of projecting buttresses separated by deep bays. The actual surface of the wall is also decorated in shallow recessed panelling – the cut stones measuring the same dimensions as mudbricks of earlier royal monuments. So again the striking building technique of the Sumerians, previously observed in mudbrick architecture in the tombs and mortuary buildings of the first two pharaonic dynasties,

423. The deep and intricate niched-façade architecture of the Djoser complex enclosure wall.

is here elevated to new heights as mudbrick gives way to majestic lime-stone. The effect is dazzling. Recessed or niched panelling, invented in the land of Sumer, reaches its zenith in the hands of Imhotep the Egyptian architect who was a member of the *iry-pat* aristocracy.

But now it is time to venture inside the Step Pyramid complex to see what else we can discover.

A narrow corridor leads from the entrance door into a tiny court. As we pass beneath the portal, take a look up and you will see that the roof lintels of the corridor are carved to represent palm logs. This is the first clue that something extraordinary is going on here. Ask yourself why the stone masons went to all that effort – rounding the stone beams when flat slabs would have been much more practical? The small court has another puzzling feature: the great cedar door which, when closed, would have prevented access from the corridor into the complex beyond is standing ajar. How did such a door survive for over 4,000 years? The answer is simple: the door is not made of perishable wood but of eternal stone. It is a dummy door, just like the thirteen sealed doorways of the enclosure wall, and just like the stone beams imitating palm logs.

Everything here is fake. All the moving parts are rigidly cast in stone. Nothing in the Step Pyramid complex functions within the human world – the whole structure is a petrified facsimile of an original building complex located near the city of Memphis in which Djoser performed his kingly rituals. But this place we are now entering is not for the living. It is rather for the deceased king (transformed into Osiris 'Lord of the Westerners') and his followers – a place where the dead could perform the kingship rituals, year in year out, for all time – thus perpetuating the divine order of things. Here there was no need for moving doors or real log ceilings. Solid stone is no barrier to the spirits of the dead. What was required was a structure made of imperishable stone, to guarantee the continuance of the rituals for eternity. The only concession to the living was the single south-east entrance to the complex with its great stone door left ajar, thus permitting mortal flesh to pass through to the interior. In practical terms this meant the mortuary priests who were responsible for the maintenance of the cult of the dead king and, in more recent times, any admiring pilgrims – like you and me – who might wish to come and wonder at the magnificent achievement of King Djoser and his architect, Imhotep. We, of course, are not the first tourists to visit the Step Pyramid. Graffiti from the 18th and 19th Dynasties extol the virtue of this foremost of royal tombs. One visitor, named Ahmose, compares the Step Pyramid complex to the glow of a dawn sky, remarking that 'it is as if heaven were within it'.

Beyond the small court is a magnificent columned passageway leading westwards. Twenty 6.6-metre-high engaged columns stand on either side of the long passage. Each is attached to a wall at the rear which 'engages' the pillar to the side walls of the building, forming niches or bays between pairs of columns. In all, there are as many bays as Egyptologists believe

424. The imitation palm-log roof of the only entrance to the Djoser funerary complex.

425. An artist's restoration of the colonnaded entrance corridor of the Djoser complex. Note the palm-log roof and the convex-fluted imitation reed columns with imitation leather capping (after J.-P. Lauer, 1936, pl. XLV).

NOMES: The name given by the Greeks to the provinces (Egy. *hebti* or *hesep*) of the Nile valley and delta, established in pharaonic or perhaps even predynastic times. The chieftains or governors of the nomes were called nomarchs.

there were NOMES or districts of Egypt at the time of the Old Kingdom. Each alcove may once have contained statues of the local gods of the nomes or double statues of king and nome-god, thus transforming our walk along the corridor into a journey through the whole land of Egypt.[5]

The columns themselves are very interesting. Each is carved with convex-fluted shafts standing on low circular bases. At the base the columns are one metre in diameter. Surviving pigment shows that they were originally painted a reddish brown. At the top there is no 'capital' – as we understand the term. Instead the last, uppermost metre is carved smooth with two arched projections pointing downwards. What seems to be the intent here on the part of the architect is a representation in stone of reed-bundle columns identical in appearance to what must have been used in perishable domestic and ritual buildings of earliest times. A bunch of tall reeds were tied together to form the shaft of the column, the smooth top being an animal skin wrapped around the bundle to prevent splaying. By Djoser's time these reed-bundle columns had been replaced in major public buildings and royal architecture by wooden copies – hence the red paint to mimic wood. It was therefore a logical step on the part of Imhotep to replicate these early-dynastic, wooden facsimiles of predynastic reed columns in the latest technology – limestone. As leading pyramid expert Eiddon Edwards notes:

> The architect of the Step Pyramid was ... chiefly concerned with reproducing in stone forms which were already well established in less durable materials rather than inventing new designs in which the special properties of stone could be exploited to greater advantage.[6]

At the far end of the corridor is a transverse vestibule supported by four double-columns joined by engaging walls. These too were copies of reed-bundle columns.

As we walk out into the bright sunlight of the great open court it is perhaps worth pondering the significance of what we have seen so far: a Mesopotamian recessed panelling façade and numerous stone replications of plant-life, such as wood and reeds, which had been used as building materials in the earliest ritual and domestic architecture. So this 3rd-Dynasty building complex of King Djoser can be used as a unique guide book to help us understand and appreciate the art and architecture of a much earlier period – the period we are particularly interested in – the time when the Followers of Horus ruled the Black Land.

Standing at the southern end of the great court reveals the full extent of the huge six-stepped pyramid of Djoser, rising up on the northern side. The inner enclosure wall, which marks out the other three sides of the court, is also panelled like the exterior façade of the whole complex – but it has an extra feature. All around the top of the wall the Egyptian craftsmen sculpted a frieze of giant cobras, their hoods puffed out ready to strike. This is potent magic at work. We learn from ancient texts that the cobra-goddess, Wadjet, was a deadly personal protectress of the king. Egyptologists call her the 'URAEUS-serpent' whenever she is represented on the brow of the pharaoh's head. Her special role is to spit deadly poison and flame in the direction of any transgressor who dares to threaten the person of the king.

> I place your terror in all lands. I rear up between your eyebrows. My flames are fire against your enemies.[7]

The frieze of hundreds of uraei surrounding the Djoser court thus forms a powerful ring of protection within which the king can safely perform the most important rituals of his enduring reign in the afterlife – rituals designed to maintain the divine order of the universe.

Situated at the centre of both northern and southern ends of the court is a peculiar feature. Here are low double D-shaped structures intimately

426. Convex-fluted columns at the western end of the entrance corridor.

URAEUS: Latin, from Greek *Ouraios*. The cobra which rises up to protect the king, worn on the brow of Pharaoh and the gods.

427. Statue of Amenhotep III with the Uraeus-serpent on his crown. Luxor Museum.

428. Two of the three D-shaped markers in the Great Court of the Djoser complex around which the king performs his heb-sed runs.

429. The rounded corner leading out from the inner heb-sed court.

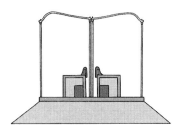

430. The double throne dais of Upper and Lower Egypt upon which the king is recrowned at the heb-sed. This motif is one of the hieroglyphic signs for the royal jubilee.

related to the rituals performed by the king. But an explanation of these elaborate ceremonies will have to wait until we have reached the festival court to where we will now head.

Halfway along the eastern wall of the great open court there is an opening which leads around a specially rounded corner into the much smaller court of the *heb-sed*. The ancient Egyptian term heb-sed means the 'festival of the tail'. The reason for this peculiar name for the most important ceremony in the king's reign will shortly become apparent. Suffice it to say that the tail concerned is that of a bull.

As we turn the corner we find ourselves in the most beautiful part of the whole Step Pyramid complex. Before us is a long oblong court lined on east and west sides by stone chapels or shrines. At the centre of the southern end of the court stands a throne dais with two staircases ascending on the north-east and south-east corners. We know from surviving scenes (both reliefs and smaller ivory carvings) that this was the setting for a re-crowning of the king at his thirty-year jubilee and then subsequently every third year thereafter until his death.[8] This moment of re-establishing the red and white crowns of Lower and Upper Egypt upon the head of Pharaoh was the culmination of a mysterious rite of rejuvenation which appears to have involved an enactment of regicide – the ritual slaying of the king. We do not know all the details or even properly understand those aspects of the ceremony for which we do have documentation. However, as the rituals of the heb-sed go back to predynastic times, and involve the Followers of Horus, we should have a brief summary of the main elements and try to explain them as best we can.

Murder and Rebirth

I want you to imagine that we have travelled back in time to witness the heb-sed rights of Pharaoh Djoser in the year 2484 BC. We arrive in Memphis on the last day of the civil year to find the capital bursting at the seams with visitors from every part of the Black Land. They have all come from their towns and villages to attend the festivities of the king's royal jubilee. Every major town in Egypt has sent an official delegation. They have brought with them statues of their local gods, complete with retinues of priests and priestesses. The papyrus barges of the regional temples are moored six abreast at the dock. Banners and flags decorate the broad thoroughfares and temple façades. Music and chatter issues from every nook and cranny. King Djoser is ensconced in his royal palace preparing for the most important moment in his long reign. The excitement is palpable.

Just outside the white walls of Memphis craftsmen have been busy building a great festival enclosure by the Nile. They have been at it for months, erecting reed shrines, throne daises, and open courts. Everything is now ready for the intricate series of ceremonies which make up the

431. The western row of imitation reed shrines in the inner heb-sed court where the most secret rituals take place.

Sed Festival. Time to bed down for the night and try to get some sleep. The next five days are going to be very full.

Early the next morning – the first day of the first month of PERET – a large and noisy crowd has already gathered along the processional route to the festival site by the time we arrive. Market traders are doing a roaring trade selling their snacks and trinkets. The impatient mob begins to chant the name of Pharaoh as we squeeze through to our cramped vantage point.

Finally, the king, his Great Royal Wife, the statues of the gods, the court officials and temple priests are on their way. A deafening roar rises from the crowd as the gleaming standards of the procession are spotted in the distance, streamers fluttering in the pleasant morning breeze. A team of court officials runs before the king shouting 'to the ground!'. The people prostrate themselves before the god-king as he passes by.

Djoser reaches the entrance to the heb-sed complex and enters a long passage bounded on either side by niches containing statues of the lesser nome gods and goddesses which had arrived ahead of the king. He is introduced to these minor deities by a priestess dressed as **the cow-headed-goddess** Sekhat-Hor ('She who remembers Horus'). Before each the pharaoh makes an offering in the form of an allocation of cattle to the deity's temple. In return he receives a blessing of 'all life and dominion'. These offerings to the forty or so nomes, punctuated by presentations of Pharaoh to the populace to receive homage and loyalty oaths, take up the best part of the first day.

The second day is devoted to a circumnavigation of the great enclosure wall of the festival complex by the ruler. The reed wall has been plastered and painted a brilliant white. Between the fourteen gateways the wall is **elaborately niched**. It is the king's duty to inspect the wall checking its security. In effect he is demonstrating his diligence towards the task of protecting Egypt's borders, symbolically represented by the wall.

PERET: The season of 'going forth' – that is to say the winter season when the fields emerge from the receding flood waters and the people can go out to prepare the fields for planting.

432. Part of an ivory label depicting what may be early heb-sed rituals. Narmer of Dynasty 0 sits on his throne wearing the red crown and long robe, protected by the vulture goddess, Nekhbet. In the middle right a figure which may be either the king or a captive runs between the D-shaped markers. The Wepwaut standard (above the runner) is being carried by a Follower of Horus. To the left of the runner and before the enthroned ruler there is a palanquin in which sits the queen or crown prince or perhaps a substitute king who is about to be sacrificed. Below is a bull which may well be Apis.

367

On the third day the king enters the smaller festival court (measuring 100 by 25 metres) known as the 'Court of the Great Ones'. Surrounding the court are large reed shrines housing the great deities of Egypt. There Djoser proceeds up the steps of the 'Throne of the Crowns of Horus' where he greets his 'mother', the vulture goddess Nekhbet, offering her a CLEPSYDRA (Egy. *sheb* = water clock) perhaps to signify the passage of time since his original coronation.

After a royal wardrobe change, the proceedings transfer to the great open court – the crowd having relocated around its four sides. In the middle stands a large platform with staircases leading up from each of the cardinal points of the compass. All sides of the platform are protected by **a frieze of cobras**. At the centre of this royal dais a low throne, ornamented with twelve lion heads, is shaded by a billowing canopy of white linen.

The royal procession **enters from the eastern side** of the court. The parade is led by a prince representing the *iry-pat* ('Descendant of the Pat') carrying a curved wand or **throw stick**. Behind him are two fan-bearers with their great **ostrich-feather fans** carried aloft on long poles. Then come the vizier, a priest with **an oar** and *hepu* **steering mechanism**, and a prophet of the temple who carries a large shrouded **image of a scorpion**. They are followed by two priests, bearing royal sceptres; and behind them another priest holding aloft **two large feathers**.[9] Two more priests bring up the rear with rolls of embalming linen.

The next group are led in by two fan-bearers. There is a hush as all eyes fall upon the portable golden shrine of the wolf-god, Wepwaut – the **'Opener of the Ways'** – as it is borne into the court by six priests clad in wolf pelts, the heads of the animals covering their shaven heads. The intoxicating smell of **myrrh and frankincense** wafts from a dozen incense burners – the sacred breath of **God's Land** (Punt) fills the air. Wepwawet is followed by a prophet carrying **an enormous composite bow** which is to be used by the king later in the festival. Behind him come the standard-bearers representing the **'Followers of Horus'** (Egy. *Shemsu-Hor*). Bringing up the rear we see the lector-priest (Egy. *hery-heb*) who holds the all important papyrus scroll known as the *imyt-per* ('House Document') – Pharaoh's deed of ownership of the Black Land. Finally, after a short gap, the monarch himself appears, wearing the double crown of Upper and Lower Egypt. Djoser is now dressed in the long heb-sed robe with a bull's tail attached to it. In his hands he holds the crook and flail crossed upon his chest.

Once seated upon his throne beneath the awning, Djoser begins to perform the ceremony of proclamation. The king faces towards each of the four cardinal points in turn. To the south he is blessed and proclaimed by priests wearing masks of the gods **Seth** and **Tjenen**; to the west by two more representing **Geb** and **Khepri**; to the north by a pair identified as **Atum** and **Horus**; and, finally, to the east by priestesses representing the goddesses **Isis** and **Nephthys**.

433. Osiris (Egy. *Asar*), god of the dead and vegetation. Depicted as a mummiform king wearing the Atef crown with twin plumes. Similar to Mesopotamian Marduk.

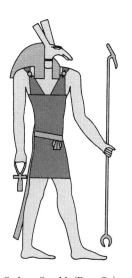

434. Seth or Sutekh (Egy. *Set*), god of the desert and storm/chaos. Depicted as a strange animal with long, curved snout and tall square-topped ears. Similar to Baal or Hadad.

CLEPSYDRA: A water clock used for marking time during the night hours when the sun does not cast shadows on a sundial.

All around the platform the royal ladies and the children of the ruler are gathered in their palanquins, along with the 'Great Ones of Upper and Lower Egypt' and the mysterious '**Spirits of Nekhen and Pe**'. A forest of nineteen standards on long poles represents the '**Gods Who Follow Horus**'. The massed ranks pledge their loyalty the king in a great shout of proclamation. The public ceremony now complete, Djoser and his entourage return to the smaller festival court where temporary quarters have been prepared for the royal family during the five-day jubilee. The third day of the heb-sed is over.

The fourth day centres around the enactment of a series of important secret ceremonies. As we, along with the rest of the ordinary population of Egypt, are not privy to such inner sanctum rites, we will have to rely on the well-informed gossip of our neighbours in today's crowd to learn what is going to happen during the next few hours.

Apparently, the king will be offering incense up to the greatest gods of Egypt whose statues are housed in the **huge reed shrines** which enclose the festival court. There he will communicate, on a one-to-one basis, with the most powerful deities in the universe. These personal rituals will take up much of the morning. Then the royal household will partake of a great banquet in the pavilion known as the 'Hall of Eating'. We, on the other hand, will have to make do with some bread, dates, onions and beer for our lunch as we await the afternoon's public ceremonies.

The ritual splendour is relaunched with a procession to the temple of Ptah within the city walls. The king is now carried aloft on his portable throne so that all may see him in his resplendent glory. Djoser is on his way to make offerings in the sacred temple of Memphis before escorting the mighty god Ptah, 'Lord of Memphis', to the Sed-Festival court. By evening the procession returns. The king and queen lead the portable shrine of Ptah which shimmers with gold in the flickering torchlight.

Everything is building up to the supreme climax of the Sed-Festival – the ceremony of 'Resting Inside the Tomb' – which is going to take place during the hours of night. This magical rite will be performed in the utmost secrecy. But the crowd is well aware that the king is about to die – but hopefully to undergo a miraculously rebirth with the sunrise which heralds the fifth and final day. There is real concern that the king may not survive the ordeal. Will he successfully negotiate his passage through the underworld to be resurrected at dawn? Or will the demons and serpents of darkness vanquish the god-king?

Again, we will have to rely on local knowledge to fill in the details of what we are unable to witness ourselves. We may not understand precisely what each element of the ritual signifies, but the basics of the ceremony are well known to all Egyptians – after all, the funeral rites performed by the son for his deceased father are not significantly at odds with those for the god-pharaoh – the differences are more a matter of scale! Of course, there is that extra element of the divine mystery of kingly rebirth which

435. The fertility-god Min with tall plumes, erect phallus and raised arm. He stands before his symbolic plant – the lettuce.

436. Isis (Egy. *Aset*), goddess of love, wife of Osiris and mother of Horus. She wears a throne symbol on her head. Similar to Inanna, Ishtar or Astarte.

437. Nephthys (Egy. *Nebet-hut*), funerary goddess, sister of Isis and partner of Seth.

369

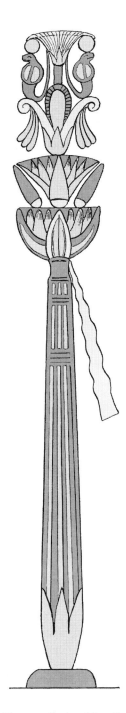

438. The complex heraldic pillar with four superimposed capitals. The lower pair are two varieties of lotus; the upper pair represent the papyrus plant of Lower Egypt (top) and the mysterious plant of Upper Egypt (bottom).

only the gods may grant to Djoser. Resurrection of the pharaoh was as pivotal to Egyptian beliefs as the resurrection of Christ is to the Christian world.

Now that darkness encompasses the land from horizon to horizon, King Djoser and his closest officials are gathered together within the confines of the small heb-sed court. They are alone under the canopy of stars, with only the celestial gods looking down upon the scene. All around the great enclosure wall of the festival palace a thousand fires are burning, the Egyptians huddled around them for warmth and comfort during these uncertain hours. Prayers for the ruler are heard in every quarter.

The great gods now encircle the king to witness his ritual murder. Seth, 'Lord of Chaos', steps forward with the long knife which had previously been carried by a prophet in the procession of the first day. The deed is swiftly done. The dead pharaoh is proclaimed by the gods for his brave end. The rolls of white linen are wound around his body. His face is painted green – the colour of fertility and Osiris. He is laid on a bed protected by golden lions, reclining on his stomach like a sphinx. During the death ritual there is a ceremony involving the head of the sacrificed king. It is completely shrouded in mystery but may hark back to what Petrie found in the Nakada II graves where the skulls of the deceased had been severed from their bodies.

The body of Djoser is carried to a small reed shrine designated 'the tomb' where he will pass the long night struggling with the malevolent forces of the netherworld. Through the hours of darkness Djoser's spirit will make a journey along the river which flows beneath the earth towards the eastern horizon. His destination will be revealed in the next chapter. For now we must wait, along with the crowd, to discover if the king is able to rejoin the world of the living when the sun-god Harakhty ('**Horus who is upon the Eastern Horizon**') returns to the skies over Egypt.

The night is long and cold, but eventually the dawn glow begins to appear over the eastern desert hills. The people make their way back to the great court. This time the mood is solemn. The vendors are nowhere to be seen: they too have mingled with the crowd to make the pilgrimage to the Sed-Festival site.

The huge sandy rectangle of the court is empty. Gone is the platform with its throne and canopy; gone are the palanquins for the princes and princesses of the blood-royal; gone are the priests, officials and soldiers. All is silent as the crowd waits patiently for the return of their earthly protector.

Suddenly, without warning, a fanfare echoes to the four corners. All heads turn towards the eastern entrance which leads from the heb-sed court. King Djoser reappears, running like the wind around the **curved corner** into the great open space before him. He is wearing nothing but a short white kilt and a crown surmounted by two tall ostrich feathers. Somehow he looks stronger, fitter, younger. Djoser has been reborn as the shining sun – he is the living Horus. The crowd roar with delight and, at the same time, sigh with relief. The women cry out in unison: 'Horus appears, he has received **the two plumes**, King Djoser, given all life'. They know that the 'Great Ones of Upper and Lower Egypt' have witnessed the fixing of the primeval crown upon Pharaoh's head by the **'Keeper of the Great Feather'**. [10] The king has been re-crowned upon the '**Throne of Atum**'. [11]

Pharaoh has the great COMPOSITE BOW in his left hand and four arrows in his right. When he reaches the centre of the court he plants three of the arrows into the sand at his feet. The fourth is brought to the bow and loosed to the south-east corner of the court. The crowds cheer. The king fires the second arrow towards the south-west corner. Another cheer. The remaining arrows are despatched with equal expertise to the north-east and north-west corners. Thus the king has re-established the boundaries of Egypt. He is once more the invincible defender of the Black Land who protects his subjects from the forces of chaos beyond Egypt's borders. Djoser, as the living Horus, has been victorious over his perennial rival – his malevolent uncle Seth.

During the remaining hours of the fifth day the king performs numerous tasks and feats of strength to demonstrate his successful rejuvenation. There are several running ceremonies around the great court. In one he canters with the sacred Apis bull. Djoser himself now carries **an oar** (Egy. *user*) and wooden implement (Egy. *hep*) which appears to be part of **the steering mechanism of a ship**. He wears **a bull's tail** attached to his kilt. The hieroglyphic signs *user* and *hep* when put together form a sportive writing of the name Osiris-Apis (Egy. *User-Hepu*). In this ceremony the king is as one with the sacred bull of Memphis. The king and Apis circumnavigate three **D-shaped markers** set around the court. Pharaoh is performing the ritual of dedicating the field – touring the land of Egypt to announce his miraculous rebirth.

COMPOSITE BOW: Made from sections of wood mitred together rather than a single tree stem.

439. Amenhotep II performs one of the heb-sed runs holding the oar and steering mechanism which spell out *user-hep* – Osiris-Apis.

440. Ramesses II performs one of the heb-sed runs holding two jars. The Apis bull runs along beside him. Karnak hypostyle hall.

441. King Djoser performs his heb-sed run carrying the flail and *imyt per* scroll. Relief from a recess in the subterranean chambers of the southern tomb of the Step Pyramid complex.

Returning to the heb-sed court for the last time Djoser undergoes another re-coronation. Two thrones have been set up, one facing south and the other facing north. The crowns of Upper and Lower Egypt are now placed on the king's head by the gods Horus and Seth as he sits on each throne. He receives the crook and flail and is then presented to the people for the final time.

Before the last great procession, which returns the monarch and the royal entourage to the palace in Memphis, there is one outstanding task for the king to perform. The god Geb, 'Lord of the Earth', presents Djoser with the *imyt per* scroll. On it is written the 'Secret of the Two Partners' – the legal contract which records Seth's recognition of Horus as the true and undisputed ruler of Egypt. Djoser clutches this 'will of inheritance' in his left hand and the flail in his right as he performs the final run around the great court to a tumultuous reception. He is led by **the standard of Wepwaut** which 'opens the way' for the king. The god Thoth and the goddess Meret, pleased with their brother deity's performance, begin to clap rhythmically to the pharaoh's long, prancing stride. The huge audience takes up the rhythm as the king's run is transformed into a joyous dance of victory. They all shout, beckoning Djoser to 'Come! Bring it!' (i.e. the scroll) to each side of the court which has now become a spiritual model for the whole land of Egypt. Every part of the Black Land is thus informed that Djoser has re-inherited the kingship.

> I have run holding the Secret of the Two Partners – the will which my father (Osiris) has given me before Geb. I have passed through the land and touched its four sides. I run through it as I desire.

With this happy event the jubilee festival comes to an end. But, in another three years, Djoser must undergo his trial of strength all over again, continuing to demonstrate his fitness to rule the people of the Black Land.

Houses of the Gods

Having taken you through the basics of the jubilee festival, we should now return to our exploration of the Step Pyramid complex where I want to highlight two more plant motifs which are going to lead us back to Mesopotamia, Susiana and even, perhaps, to Eden.

We had just entered the heb-sed court when we took our diversion back in time to attend Djoser's mystical resurrection. On the third day of the festival we learnt that the king had made offerings to the great gods of Egypt in their huge reed shrines surrounding the heb-sed court. It is time then to study the stone versions of these shrines set up by Imhotep in Djoser's dummy Sed-Festival court.

Many of the shrines stand out because of their unusual shape. They have great arched roofs – a tricky structure for early stone-working technology and therefore demonstrably faithful copies, constructed at con-

442. Above: A shrine of the inner heb-sed court at Sakkara.

443. Left: A Marsh Arab *mudhif* from southern Iraq.

siderable effort, of earlier shrines which had been made of more flexible materials. It is clear from the hieroglyphic sign for the archetypal shrine of Upper Egypt that this structure was originally made of reeds[12] and it has long been recognised that the design is identical to the reed-built *mudhif* of southern Iraq – the traditional dwelling of the Marsh Arabs. The marshes of southern Iraq are, of course, the wetlands of Sumer and these extraordinary buildings are clearly of very ancient origin. For example, there are a number of seal impressions from Sumer depicting the god Enki ('Lord of the Earth') sitting in his reed shrine.[13] Inanna's earliest shrine was also constructed of reeds. The modern Marsh Arab versions of this ancient structure are built on top of reed platforms – islands floating on a freshwater swamp. In spite of this somewhat precarious foundation, the *mudhif* (Arabic for 'guest-house') is a large structure. As Thor Heyerdahl notes, some of the taller examples 'are big enough almost to resemble (aircraft) hangars'.[14]

444. The glyptic art of the Uruk Period shows a reed shrine or animal fold with the symbol of Inanna rising from its roof. Inanna was closely associated with animal husbandry (after P. Amiet, 1961, pl. 42:623).

A typical *mudhif* consists of a great arched tunnel made of bundles of reeds, tied together to form the ribs of the roof. Each rib is formed from two bundles which are set in the ground some ten metres apart. The tops are then pulled downwards towards each other and secured at the centre of the roof to form the arch. Sitting inside, it is not difficult to imagine how Jonah felt in his floating hotel. The front and rear open sides of the *mudhif* are closed off with reed matting which is attached to the bottom half of tall, vertical poles, also made of reed bundles, which divide the façade into panels. Above these reed panels cloth hangings are usually suspended to keep out the bright sunlight but also to allow air to circulate. A small doorway is left in the reed wall next to one of the reed poles.

All this is to be seen in Djoser's stylised stone versions of the Upper Egyptian reed shrine. Again, therefore, a Mesopotamian architectural design is employed in early Egypt. But here, in the heb-sed court, we can observe some interesting details which are not featured in the modern Marsh Arab *mudhif*.

445. One of the concave-fluted columns attached to a shrine of the inner heb-sed court, showing the petiole capital and socket hole which once received a wooden standard of the district represented by the shrine.

446. The archaeological drawing of a pendent petiole column found in the heb-sed court (after J-P. Lauer, 1936, pl. LX).

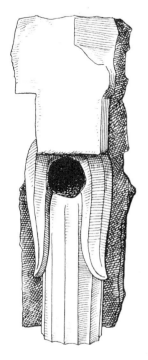

The Egyptian shrines have representations of the three slender support columns attached to their façades as decoration but they are not facsimiles of reed bundles. Instead we appear to have here the stem of a plant enlarged a hundredfold. The archaeologists who first uncovered the shrines noticed that, unlike the columns of the entrance corridor to the complex which had convex fluting (indicating bunches of reeds), the shafts of these much thinner columns were deeply fluted. These *concave* vertical grooves represent the very first example in art history of the much later 'Doric' column so well known to the western world through classical Greek architecture. The ancient Greeks are lauded for their beautifully proportioned Doric columns with their elegant fluting – but it was actually Imhotep who had invented this architectural form some 2,000 years earlier!

Given the Egyptian desire to mimic the natural world in stone, we now have to ask ourselves what plant this pillar motif represents. This is quite a difficult matter, and was a subject of debate throughout the middle decades of this century, but there are a number of clues. First we have to look for a plant which exhibits concave fluting along its tall, thin stem. This single feature radically redefines the boundaries of our search. But a second element narrows down our options even further.

At the top of the stone shafts of the Djoser shrines the masons carved an amazing capital which has never since reappeared in any other architectural structure. Here in the heb-sed court we see a capital of two pendent petioles draped down the left and right sides of the attached columns. Between the petioles is a hole which was once presumably a socket to hold the wooden standard of the god who resided in the shrine.[15] To find our mysterious plant we are going to have to journey far from the Nile valley, but first we need to eliminate the indigenous flora of Egypt as the source of the stone-carved motif.

A Giant Among Plants

As I indicated, these particular columns were discussed at length in the 1940s and 50s in order to try to identify the original plant source for the design. Herbert Ricke attempted to maintain that the fluting represented coniferous timber pillars on which 'stylised traces of the incisions made by the rounded cutting-edge of the tools used by the early Egyptians in dressing the surface of the trunk' had created a scouring effect in parallel lines.[16] This seemed a rather tenuous hypothesis. Jean-Philippe Lauer, the architect-turned-Egyptologist whose name is synonymous with the Step Pyramid (thanks to the years he has spent in reconstructing the complex), also viewed the columns as representing tree trunks. But he regarded the concave fluting rather as a deliberate additional decorative device.[17] This also appeared to be unlikely, since tree trunks do not form part of the corpus of Egyptian column designs which are, in nearly every instance, giant versions of plants – not trees. The single exception to this rule is the palm tree column which does not possess, or cannot be carved to form, a fluted shaft. On the other hand, we have noted that wood was certainly in use in Memphis for palace and temple architecture at the time of the Step Pyramid's construction. This timber most likely came from Lebanon (in particular Byblos) which supplied most of Egypt's constructional woods – especially cedar – throughout pharaonic history. But this cut timber was used as a building material – not as an artistic motif representing its natural tree state. So, although we can be reasonably confident that the stone attached columns of the heb-sed court were copies of wooden precursors and contemporaries down in Memphis, we are still no nearer finding out what plant the carved timber versions, with their pendent capitals and fluted decoration, represent in the natural world.

So we come to the third hypothesis proposed by botanist and Egyptologist, Percy Newberry.[18] He suggested that, like the giant papyrus and lotus columns, these engaged columns represented the single stem of a plant. The plant he at first offered for comparison with the shrine motif of Djoser's jubilee court was known in ancient times as *Silphium* – a species which itself has engendered much debate amongst botanists. The Silphium motif was engraved on Greek coins from CYRENAICA on the north African coast and was initially thought to be *Thapsia Garganica*, which grows today around CYRENE. Thapsia, however, has none of the medicinal properties ascribed to Silphium by the classical writers. The fact that it grows to a height of only one metre and does not possess a straight stem section seems also to rule Thapsia out as the model for the Sakkara motif.[19] In selecting Silphium as the initial model for the mysterious long-stemmed plant Newberry had simply substituted one problem of identification with another. He realised that there had to be another solution.

Sticking with his idea that we had here an enlarged representation of a single plant, he therefore searched for an alternative UMBELLIFER. Eventually he came up with *Heracleum Giganteum* which grows to around five metres in height and has a stem diameter of ten centimetres at the base.[20] This was more like it. Here was a plant which had all the typical attributes of the other plants used in column architecture by the Egyptians – tall, straight species with thick shafts. He found that 'The stems (of Heracleum) are hollow and when in the green state are ribbed, but when dry are beautifully fluted.'[21] Just as in the stone column capitals of the heb-sed court, Heracleum also had broad pendent petioles spaced at intervals along the stem.

Thus a botanical specimen had been found to match the design characteristics of the unusual 'Doric' pillars of the heb-sed court shrines. The only snag was that, as Newberry observed, Heracleum Giganteum is a native plant of eastern Anatolia and the Caucasus and no similar species are to be found in Egypt or north Africa. Pyramid expert Iaddon Edwards succinctly summarises the Egyptologists' dilemma:

447. A concave-fluted column from the Step Pyramid complex.

CYRENAICA: The coastal region of ancient Libya.

CYRENE: The Greek colonial foundation on the north African coast and capital of Cyrenaica.

UMBELLIFER: A plant with a bell-like flower.

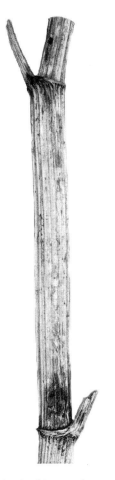

448. The dried hogweed stem with concave-fluted trunk and petiole branches formed at regular intervals along the stem.

Newberry's interpretation of the columns would probably have received more general acceptance than has yet been accorded to it if he could have shown that the Heracleum Giganteum grew in Egypt, but, although this plant is widely distributed in its occurrence, there is no evidence that it has ever flourished in the Nile valley.[22]

This is not only because the Heracleum family, a genus of seventy species, thrives in cool, wet climates but also because this type of plant requires a turf-like soil which enables its shallow roots to support the weight of the tall stem. None of these conditions were prevalent in the dry Egypt of pharaonic times or were in existence during the more tropical times of the prehistoric fourth millennium BC. In either case Egypt possessed a climate too hot to sustain Heracleum and a soil which could not support the growth of thick turf grasses. Only in the temperate zone which spreads around the globe far to the north of African Egypt do you get the correct conditions for Heracleum Giganteum.

Heracleum Giganteum is another name for *Heracleum Mantegazzianum* – otherwise known as the 'Giant Hogweed'. This plant is, of course, a very common weed in many parts of Europe and America today. It is rather dangerous to handle in its growing state as the stem can cause a nasty rash if inadvertently grasped.[23] However, when the Hogweed dies, towards the end of autumn, its fleshy exterior dries and the stem becomes extremely hard and rigid. It can then be handled with impunity. A few years ago I managed to cut a section from a dead plant which had grown to a height of two metres in woods near my home. I have photographed it to show you not only the pronounced fluting but also the horizontal ridge from which the pendent petioles grew. The stem still retains its rigidity, even after five years languishing in my study.

As I have said, the Giant Hogweed grows best in a temperate climate where the grasses are thick and tufty. Botanists have noted that it especially thrives in the lush valleys of the mountainous terrain which stretches from the coast of western Turkey eastwards, through ancient Armenia, to the shores of the Caspian Sea. When I travelled to Iranian Azerbaijan in my search for Eden I discovered that the Hogweed is to be found in abundance on the hill-slopes surrounding the flood plains of the rivers which have their head-waters in the region – that is around Van and Urmia. Here it grows to a staggering height of five metres – nearly as tall as a two-storeyed house! There is no doubt about it, Heracleum Giganteum is a native plant of the kingdom of Aratta (Urartu) and Eden.

Another giant weed belonging to the same family as Heracleum Giganteum and Heracleum Mantegazzianum is *Heracleum Persicum* which is native to western Iran – in particular, as you may have guessed, the region of ancient Susiana. It too grows to a height of five to six metres. It is this latter species which I believe to be the direct model for the fluted columns of the Djoser festival court. It has been stated that Heracleum Persicum is an extremely rigid plant when dry and has the characteristic strength of the bamboo.[24] It would therefore have been an excellent choice as a load-bearing material and may well have been used in the construction of reed buildings in Susiana at an early date.

A few examples of miniature fluted pillars have been found in the tombs of the 1st Dynasty. In particular, a fine ivory 'Doric' column from the Abydos tomb of King Djer was discovered by Petrie and is thought to be part of a piece of furniture.[25] This miniature copy of Heracleum Persicum provides the link to the Djoser fluted pillars and extends the archaeological evidence for the use of the hogweed design back to the period of Egyptian history immediately following the arrival of the foreign élite. Did our immigrants from Susiana bring with them yet another artistic motif from the natural landscape of their original homeland – a motif which, in turn, had its precursor in Adam's Garden of Eden?

The White Lily

The first concerted excavations of the Step Pyramid complex began in January 1924 under the direction of the British Egyptologist and Inspector of Antiquities for Sakkara, Cecil FIRTH. In that first season his team elected to begin their work in the north-east corner of the enclosure where Firth had observed two large mounds. These turned out to be the remains of the great jubilee shrines of Upper and Lower Egypt, which must have played an important, though undetermined, part in the Sed-Festival. I have held back from mentioning this part of the heb-sed complex until now because it holds within its high walls one of the most important talismans of the foreign élite.

The Houses of the North and South are situated immediately to the north of the oblong heb-sed court where the ritual death, rebirth and coronation continue to be re-enacted by the spirits of the dead assigned to perform Djoser's everlasting jubilee rites. The House of the South stands immediately opposite the east side of the Step Pyramid itself, with its Lower Egyptian counterpart slightly further north, opposite the mortuary temple located within the northern shadow of the pyramid.

Let us first deal with this House of the North (that is the main shrine of LOWER EGYPT). Firth was greatly surprised to discover here three 'Doric' columns on the façade of the structure because, at this early stage of the excavations, the Giant Hogweed columns attached to the heb-sed court shrines had not yet been unearthed. These slender fluted pillars were attached directly to the façade of a huge chapel, measuring eleven metres in height, which faced onto its own private courtyard. The House of the North was shaped like a giant Marsh Arab *mudhif.* The inner east wall of its open court was interrupted by a broad niche containing three pillars. These columns served no structural purpose but were attached to the rear wall of the shallow recess at approximately one-and-a-half-metre intervals. Again, the pillars were acting as symbolic decoration – but they were not fluted like those on the façade of the main chapel. Instead,

449. The giant hogweed of the Caucasus, Alburz and Zagros mountains can grow up to five metres in height and five centimetres in diameter.

FIRTH: (1878-1931).

LOWER EGYPT: The Egyptian delta and Nile valley upstream as far as the Faiyum.

450. Right: The House of the South of the Step Pyramid complex (after J-P. Lauer, 1936, pl. LXXIII).

451. Above: The triple papyrus column motif in the court of the House of the North.

452. The living papyrus plant growing in its natural marshland environment.

453. The single column motif of the court of the House of the South.

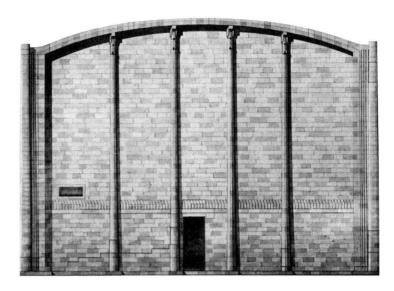

their shafts had a smooth surface which reached up to capitals formed in the shape of stylised open umbels resembling an inverted bell. These were clearly papyrus columns – the earliest so far discovered. Although virtually extinct in Egypt today, this perennial sedge with stout, triangular, leafless stems,[26] can still be found in the upper reaches of the White Nile in the Sudan and in parts of central Africa. It is suggested that this species, known as *Cyperus Papyrus,* which grows to a height of up to five metres, may well be descended from the original ancient Egyptian variety.[27] With these beautifully crafted papyrus columns, Djoser's artisans had demonstrated, once again, a real desire to mimic the natural plant. They had shaped the stone shafts into the characteristic triangular cross-section of the papyrus stem and slightly tapered them from bottom to top with a pronounced swelling at the base, also just as in the natural plant. The Egyptian sculptors of later times abandoned this practice of accurate mimicry for the expediency of the simpler rounded shaft.

By the time of the Step Pyramid excavations, Egyptologists had known for decades that the papyrus plant, with its unusual green triangular stem, was the heraldic plant of the kingdom of Lower Egypt. This important emblem was attested from at least the Middle Kingdom onwards and Firth's new discovery neatly demonstrated its existence at least as far back as the 3rd Dynasty. As a result of this surprise find, the archaeologists working at the Step Pyramid complex keenly anticipated finding a similar niche in the court of the House of the South which should contain the early heraldic pillar motif of Upper Egypt.

When they came to clearing the southern of the two mounds they did indeed find the House of the South and its associated courtyard. And, as expected, they located the recess containing the heraldic plant emblem of Upper Egypt – but this time there was just one pillar at the centre of the niche. Egyptologists have reasonably assumed that the single plant represents the Nile valley, whereas the three papyrus plants represent three separate kingdoms which once made up the political structure of the delta in predynastic times, prior to the unification.

The single column in the niche of the southern court was not triangular in cross-section as was the case with the northern pillars. Its shaft was rounded and therefore represented a quite different species of plant. Unfortunately the column capital was missing and has never been found. But we have numerous later representations of the heraldic plant of Upper Egypt to indicate just how it looked. The best three-dimensional example is to be found at Karnak – which is where we must now head.

On this visit to Karnak we are going to head down the main axis of the temple to the small court which stands before the holy of holies. But, as we pass through the great hypostyle hall built by Seti I and his son Ramesses II, just take a quick glance at a few of the one hundred and thirty-four columns. At the bottom of the shafts each has a plant motif for its decoration. To the left side of the hall (that is the northern half) you will find the papyrus plant representing Lower Egypt. To the right side (that is the southern half) all the columns are decorated with the plant emblem of Upper Egypt. I have often sat here, resting in the shade of one of these mighty pillars, listening to the guides giving their description of the unification of Egypt. They will tell their audiences that the heraldic plant of the south is the lotus. This they have learnt from their teachers, text books and from the majority of general books on ancient Egypt. But they have been misled, just as they now mislead their groups. If only people were to use their eyes they would immediately see that the plant of Upper Egypt is not a lotus at all but something very different. The lotus is a water lily with a broad cup-like flower whereas the plant of the south possesses a slender trumpet-like flower. The Egyptians had no difficulty representing a true lotus plant, with its spiky leaves, as numerous reliefs and paintings demonstrate. There is absolutely no doubt that the Egyptian artists represented the lotus and the heraldic emblem of Upper Egypt as two very distinct forms – for they are two quite distinct species.

A wall painting from a Theban tomb, shows King Amenhotep III sitting beneath a canopy which has two supporting pillars at the front and one at the rear. The single column at the back is represented as a papyrus plant and therefore indicates the direction of Lower Egypt. To the front, and therefore facing Upper Egypt, one of the two capitals is a lotus; the other is the traditional heraldic plant of the south. The two are shown side by side – which should remove from our minds any thoughts of ambiguity. It seems that towards the end of the late 18th Dynasty the lotus was gradually being adopted as a substitute flower of the south. The reason for this will become clear in a moment. We may regard the Amarna Period as a transitional period as it is clear from the Amenhotep III canopy that both the original plant and the lotus are sharing the role at this time. This, however, was not the case just a few reigns earlier when Thutmose III was on the throne of the Two Lands.

454. The 'plant of the south' carved on the columns of the southern half of the hypostyle hall at Karnak. Clearly this plant is not a lotus.

455. An Egyptian lotus as depicted on the 11th Dynasty sarcophagus of Princess Kawit. Cairo Museum.

456. The highly stylised twin plant motifs of Upper Egypt during the late-18th Dynasty (reign of Amenhotep III) – the lotus and mystery flower. Luxor Museum.

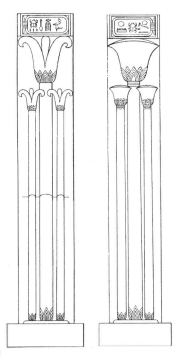

Having continued with our walk down the west-east axis of the Karnak temple we have arrived at the open court which is the object of our visit. Here, two free-standing columns, built by Thutmose III, guard either side of the entrance to the innermost part of the holy precinct. These pillars are symbolic – they do not support a roof. They are here purely as totems of the two kingdoms. The pillar on the north side of the axis shows three papyrus plants in pronounced raised relief. The pillar on the south side has three tall stems ending in an elaborate stylised flower with partly pendent petioles. If one were to trace its outline and transfer the design to the coat of arms of the French monarchy you would immediately

457. Above: The heraldic pillars of Thutmose III from Karnak.

458. Right: View of the Karnak heraldic columns.

459. Below: A triple capital column – (bottom to top) lotus, papyrus and the mystery plant. Cairo Museum.

460. Left: Lily gatherers from the Late Period. A scene showing the cultivation of the Madonna Lily for royal perfume. Louvre Museum.

461. Above: The striking Madonna Lily with its long pendent petals.

recognise the 'Fleur-de-Lys'. Your eyes are telling you that the heraldic plant of Upper Egypt – the plant of the kingdom of Menes, the founder of Pharaonic Egypt – has to be a lily.

But any botanist will tell you that lilies do not grow naturally in Egypt and never have done. Just like the Giant Hogweed, the lily requires a much cooler environment than that available in the Nile valley. The plant likes to grow in scrub and on cliffs and rocky slopes as high as six hundred metres above sea-level. It flourishes in 'a well-drained chalky soil with good fertility' and, given the right conditions, can reach to a height of nearly two metres.[28] This is not a particularly tolerant species and is rather 'difficult to establish' as a cultivated plant[29] – especially in hot, dry conditions. Paul Schauenberg makes it clear that the climatic conditions in Egypt make it impossible for long-stemmed lilies to have ever been indigenous to the region.

462. The living lotus plant with its distinctive pointed petals.

> (Lilies) are not tolerant as regards soil and flourish under certain definite physical and hydrological conditions only. ... Prolonged dryness is anathema to them. At the same time, too great heat can destroy them if the base of the plant is not protected by a layer of organic debris or thick turf-like vegetation.[30]

463. Caerulea Lotus, the blue waterlily indigenous to the Nile valley.

Clearly the very conditions that weigh against the successful natural growth of the lily are those that are characteristic of Upper Egypt. The only way a species of long-stemmed lily could have grown in Egypt during the pharaonic era was if it had been introduced from outside and then carefully nurtured before harvesting the flowers for perfume. In such specialised cultivation of the lily is attested on a relief from the 26th

464. This Phoenician ivory depicts a Kushite boy being attacked by a lion. The background consists of alternating papyrus and lily flowers. British Museum.

465. (a) The papyrus plant carved into the northern door-jamb of the entrance to the tomb of Ramesses III in the Valley of the Kings. Note the marshy terrain at the base of the plant. (b) The lily plant on the southern door-jamb of Ramesses III's tomb. Note that the lilies grow out of the Egyptian symbol for garden or plantation, demonstrating that this is a cultivated and not indigenous plant.

Dynasty. Such an activity is, by its very nature, a royal or ruling class prerogative – especially when considered in terms of very early civilisation. The lily was never indigenous to the Nile valley and can only have been introduced by the rulers of Upper Egypt from abroad.

So, where is the natural habitat of the long-stemmed lily? A number of species of these elegant flowers are to be found in a fairly broad zone stretching from the Alps of south-eastern France (hence the Fleur-de-Lys motif) and northern Italy, through Albania and Macedonian Greece, across Turkey to the Caucasus and down through the valleys of the Zagros mountains. However, the majority of the thirty-two wild varieties grow only in the Far East, especially in south-east Asia, China and Japan.[31] These oriental varieties need not concern us here, as it is fairly obvious that we need to search for our Upper Egyptian heraldic emblem rather nearer to home. For some considerable time now, it has been recognised that one species of lily, in particular, was famous in the ancient world of the eastern Mediterranean where it had been cultivated for its perfume for at least three millennia.

This most beautiful lily of them all is *Lilium Candidum* – the 'Madonna Lily' – with a flower of six large white petals forming a flared trumpet to protect the golden stamen. The green of its long, elegant stem extends up the outside of the petals where it gradually merges into the milk white of the perianth segments. The crushed petals give off an exotic perfume which was much sought after by the ancients. It was a royal flower of the ancient world without equal.

The modern distribution of the uncultivated or wild Madonna Lily spans an area from the hill slopes of Macedonia, across Anatolia to the mountains of the Balkan peninsula and southward to the hills of Lebanon and Mount Carmel in Israel.[32] Schauenberg has made a study of the Madonna Lily and has come to the conclusion that it could only survive naturally in temperate zones such as that across southern Europe and Western Asia and further notes that the Mount Carmel ridge is the southernmost point where Lilium Candidum could grow in a wild state – and then only on high ground. As I have already mentioned, the Madonna Lily has a white flower, but there is a similar variety – *Lilium Monodelphum* – which is bright yellow. This equally striking lily is native to the Crimea, the Caucasus from the Black Sea to the Caspian Sea, and parts of northern Turkey. This, of course, includes the region in which we have located Aratta and Eden.

Unfortunately no lilies grow today in the southern Zagros mountains – the region which forms our link to predynastic Egypt. But, having noted that the Madonna Lily is now reluctant to seed (which indicates cultivation over a lengthy period), F. Ferns goes on to suggest that it may have been cultivated in ancient Iran before deforestation and over-cultivation changed the character of the landscape in that area.[33] Given its requisite growth conditions, one would expect the ideal environment for the long-stemmed lily to have been not too dissimilar to that pertaining on the southern slopes of the Zagros mountains in ancient times. Today we will simply have to imagine our two lilies – the white and the yellow – growing up to four feet tall and looking stunningly spectacular as they cluster in their thousands on the mountain meadows of the southern Zagros range, just to the north of ancient Susa. As we have noted throughout the Mesopotamian chapters of this book, the six-petalled lily flower was one of the main symbols of the goddess Inanna.

By the time of the 6th Dynasty pyramid texts, the Egyptian scribes were referring to the heraldic plant of Upper Egypt as the *seshen* or *sesheshen* (Pyramid Text Utterance 395), clearly terminating the hieroglyphic writing with the determinative of a long-petalled flower.[34] Egyptologists have constantly referred to this plant as a lotus but, in my view, quite erroneously. There is another word in the Egyptian language for 'lotus' and that is *nekhebet* (Pyramid Text Utterance 439) which has a squatter, cup-like determinative. It seems improbable that both seshen and nekhebet refer to the same species of plant and so I have come to the conclusion that seshen originally meant 'lily' whilst nekhebet was the true nilotic lotus. It then becomes extremely interesting when one considers the remarkable 'coincidence' that the west-semitic word for the white lily is *shoshan*. If you happen to be a 'Susan' then you may already be aware that your name comes from the Hebrew word for lily. The whole of the ancient Near East knew the lily as *shoshan* and so it therefore seems highly probable that the Upper Egyptian lily emblem is what is being represented by the hieroglyphic symbols which spell out *s-sh-n or s-sh-sh-n*. This adds new significance to the phrase *seshen-wab* which would now translate as the 'sacred lily' – an epithet for the sun-god, otherwise Atum-Re or Re-Harakhty.

466. The two hieroglyphic determinatives for nekhebet (left) and seshen (right). Note that the seshen plant is much taller and resembles the form of a lily whilst the cup-like shape of the nekhebet resembles the true lotus.

467. We can confirm that the lily was known as the 'sesh' in Late Period times by the hieroglyphs above this scene of essence extraction from the lily flower. Louvre Museum.

Conclusion Thirty-One

The heraldic plant motif of Upper Egypt is a lily which grows only in temperate mountain zones. This royal symbol is clear evidence of the foreign origins of the first pharaohs.

---

468. The funerary stela of Taperet (Third Intermediate Period) showing the deceased receiving the rays of the sun-god. Note that these rays take the form of lily flowers making a clear connection between this heraldic plant of Upper Egypt and the realm of the dead where the sun rises (i.e. the Isle of Flame on the eastern horizon). Louvre Museum.

Having taken you through all the evidence linking southern Mesopotamia with the predynastic kings of Upper Egypt, it should not come as too great a surprise to learn that the capital of Susiana and one of the oldest cities in the world was called Shushan (modern Susa). There is but one conclusion which can be drawn from all this: the heraldic emblem of the first pharaohs was a direct symbolic link to the great pre-Elamite city of Susa. The kingdom of Upper Egypt must have been founded by predynastic rulers who had brought their royal symbol with them from an original homeland in the region where the lily once grew in abundance.

Chapter Thirteen

THE ISLE OF FLAME

I̸n a number of traditions there are magical places – usually located across the seas – to where the heroic dead journey in search of eternal rest. These mysterious kingdoms of the afterlife are usually islands. In British tradition we have Arthurian 'Avalon'; the Vikings had 'Valhalla'; the Sumerians the 'Land of the Living' (associated with Dilmun); and the Egyptians conceived of a place called the 'Blessed Isle', the 'Place of the Ghosts' or the 'Isle of Flame'[1] where the deceased king would be resurrected as the morning sun. Intriguingly enough, as we have seen, mythological Punt – 'God's Land' – was also sometimes identified as an island, reached after a sea-voyage from Egypt of two months.[2]

Have you ever wondered where Never Never Land is? Think, for a moment, back to your childhood. Never Never Land is a magical island where mortals never grow old – it is a mysterious isle of eternal life. The leader of the eternal ones is called Peter Pan. The story, although a Victorian creation, is as old as time itself.

There are a number of interesting parallels between these different cultural paradises. For instance, Avalon carries the epithet 'Isle of the Blessed' whilst Dilmun is also referred to as the 'Isle of the Blessed'.[3] It should not be surprising to discover that the Greeks too had their 'Isles of the Blessed' where the immortals dwelt. And the Egyptian Book of

469. Opposite page: View from the rock cleft in which the tomb of Thutmose III is concealed.

470. Above: The view across the Nile valley from Meretseger towards the eastern mountains of the sunrise.

471. Scene from the tomb of Haremheb depicting the ram-headed sun-god Atum-Re journeying to the eastern horizon in his barque of the underworld.

472. Mourners at the funeral of the deceased. Relief from the Sakkara tomb of Haremheb. Louvre Museum.

the Dead refers to the 'Field of Reeds of the Blessed' and, as we have seen, the Edfu texts associate the 'Blessed Isle' with the deceased ancestor-gods. There is usually a ferryman waiting to take the deceased hero to the island: in the case of Mesopotamian tradition his name is Urshanabi (who ferried Gilgamesh to meet Utnapishtim residing in the Land of the Living) and the deceased Egyptian pharaoh was taken to 'Middle Island' – another name for the Isle of Flame – by the boatman Anty, also called Mahaf ('Backwards-looker').[4]

The Egyptian island of resurrection was seen as a sandy hill surrounded by reed marshes and other scattered islands. As we have noted, the Book of the Dead calls the abode of the afterlife the 'Field of Reeds' and locates it on the very eastern edge of the world.[5] The oldest recorded religious incantations in the land of the pharaohs – the Pyramid Texts – constantly refer to the birth-place of the gods which is far to the east where the sun rises.

> I go up this eastern side of the sky where the gods were born. (Utterance 265).[6]

Petrie notes that the primeval mound of the Egyptian creation myths is synonymous with the 'Pure Land' of the same texts. The parallels continue, because this is also one of the most frequently employed epithets for Dilmun in the Mesopotamian literature.[7]

A Visit to the Netherworld

My first visit to the Valley of the Kings was at the age of ten. The year was 1960 and the Suez Crisis of 1956 was not the distant memory it is today and, needless to say, English and French visitors were few and far between. But here was this young English Egyptophile climbing the steps leading up to the rock gully which hides the narrow entrance to KV 39 – the royal tomb of Thutmose III.

I remember everything as if it was yesterday. It was late afternoon and the Valley was empty but for the Antiquities Inspectorate guardians. My mother, who had brought me to Egypt, had endured enough climbing in and out of tombs for one day but I was still full of energy and determined to explore the earliest accessible sepulchre in the Valley of the Kings. So Hathor/Isis decided to wait outside in the shade of the cliff overhang whilst her little Horus ('the Younger') prepared to head down into the darkness.

Before the completion of the High Dam at Aswan, Egypt was prone to periods of electrical black-out. We had arrived at the tomb just as the power went down and so the gaffir thrust an oil-lamp into my hand with a broad grin on his face, gesticulating in the direction of the stairwell.

The steps plunged down at a steep angle before reaching a rickety wooden bridge which spanned the deep well-shaft. As I paused to look down into the dark depths I could hear the footsteps of the tomb guardian

473. The steps leading up to the well-hidden tomb of Thutmose III in the Valley of the Kings.

474. The southern branch of the Valley of the Kings leading up to the tomb of Thutmose III.

forty paces behind me. He was willing to let me have my moment of adventure, but wanted to be sure that help was at hand, just in case the self-imposed solitude got the better of me.

Beyond the bridge I found a room with two pillars supporting the roof and, immediately to the left, another staircase heading down to a lower level. This opened out into a magnificent oval-shaped burial chamber, also with two pillars, which housed the red-granite sarcophagus of the 18th-Dynasty pharaoh. I had entered one of the most magical places on our planet.

Everyone who visits the burial chamber of Thutmose III is affected by the experience, even when the place is thronging with tourists. But to be alone there at such an impressionable age was simply unforgettable. Within the few moments it took to catch my breath after the steep descent I began to distinguish strange, surreal images by the flickering lamplight as it gradually penetrated the gloom. The walls of the CARTOUCHE-shaped chamber were covered in mysterious figures painted in black and red on a plain papyrus-coloured background.

The scenes represented 'That Which is in the Underworld' – the *Amduat* – a book detailing the rites of passage of the deceased king as he made his way beneath the earth to the eastern horizon and his rebirth as the morning sun. I followed the progress of the king and accompanying gods as the story swept around the walls in a continuous visual narrative. At one point the black dado just above the floor and beneath the Amduat scenes had a rectangular area of pigment missing. It was clear that the painting of the dado had been interrupted by a box or chest which had already been positioned against the wall. The decorator had simply painted around the obstruction in his haste to finish the job! At the time I wondered why this servant of Pharaoh had been so careless but I failed to consider the implications of this minor personal discovery. Knowing a great deal more now than I did then, it is obvious that this little clue

CARTOUCHE: The French word for rifle cartridge used by Egyptologists to refer to the rope or cord oval within which the pharaoh's two most important names are written.

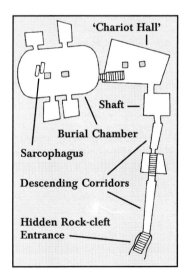

475. Plan of the tomb (KV 34) of Thutmose III.

was proof that the burial chamber of the tomb had already been crammed full of its funerary trappings when the walls were being decorated. The body of the king was resting in his sarcophagus as the Amduat was being composed on the walls of his House of Eternity.

This was the potent magic of KV 34. The king had been laid to rest and only then were the magical spells of protection set down by the mortuary priests in the burial chamber. Amazingly, the priests not only recited the incantations but actually painted them onto the walls and illustrated the journey through the underworld at the same time as and immediately after the funeral rites. The king was being sealed in a great circle of magic which prevented the incursion of malevolent forces intent on reaching the holy remains of Pharaoh. What a concept! What an astonishing ritual!

Just picture the extraordinary scene – a room glinting with treasure; the royal mummy being lowered into its granite coffin; a priest wearing the mask of Anubis reciting the incantations from a long papyrus roll; other priests frantically trying to keep up with him as they scribble the sacred spells on the walls. After the burial rites are complete the priestly scribes continue to copy the text from the holy papyrus roll (already of some antiquity) onto the walls. In the rush to complete their task one of them makes a mistake. He has copied the same line twice. He simply runs his papyrus brush through the duplicated line of text and continues. At another place the papyrus roll is damaged and the incantation lost. The scribe tacitly records the words 'found defective' (Egy. *gem ush*) and picks up the text after the break. All must be complete by sunset so that the tomb chamber can be sealed. Everything has to be in place for the king to begin his journey to the Isle of Flame – a journey which begins with the descent of the sun-god Atum beneath the western horizon at the end of day.

476. The burial chamber of Thutmose III with his red-granite sarcophagus in the foreground and the extraordinary paintings of the Amduat on the cartouche-shaped wall of the chamber.

Amduat

To tell the story of the dead king's journey to the Isle of Flame I will be combining the spells and incantations from several sacred books which survive from different periods. The four main sources are:

(a) The Pyramid Texts (Old Kingdom), which cover the walls of the 6th-Dynasty pyramids (beginning with that of Unas, last ruler of the 5th Dynasty). The individual incantations are called 'utterances' to distinguish them from the later 'spells' of the Book of the Dead.

(b) The Coffin Texts (Middle Kingdom) which show a direct development from the Pyramid Texts. These were painted onto the coffins of the deceased. The most important series of incantations comes from a work known as the 'Book of the Two Ways' which was a guide-book for the journey through the netherworld.[8]

(c) The sacred books inscribed on the walls of the tombs in the Valley of the Kings (New Kingdom). These include: 'That Which is in the Under-world' (Egy. *Amduat*), which was also known as the 'Book of the Secret Chamber'; the 'Book of Gates'; the 'Litany of Re'; and the 'Book of Caverns'.

(d) The Book of the Dead (New Kingdom onwards), which consists of a series of spells written on papyrus rolls and deposited with the deceased at burial. Like the Coffin Texts, these spells are designed to aid the deceased on his journey through the underworld. The term 'Book of the Dead' was coined by Egyptologists; the ancient Egyptians called this collection of incantations the 'Chapters of Coming Forth by Day'.[9]

So let us climb on board the night-barque of Re (Atum) so that we may escort the deceased pharaoh Thutmose III on his journey through the

477. Detail from the Pyramid Texts inscribed onto the walls of the antechamber of Teti's pyramid at Sakkara. Note the nine flags or pendants grouped together to represent the divine ennead.

hours of darkness to his new dawn on the eastern horizon. This was the great desire of every Egyptian when he died – to join their dead king on the great celestial boat of Re-Atum.

> … may a place be made for me in the solar barque on the day when the god ferries across, and may I be received into the presence of Osiris in the Land of Vindication. [10]

First it is important to understand that, although there are clear references to a celestial passage across the night-sky in the Pyramid Texts and the later Book of the Dead, the journey still takes the king beneath the earth. The Egyptians conceived of a great subterranean freshwater ocean just like the Sumerian abyss. The sacred barque which carries the dead god is called the ferry-boat of the abyss [Spell 99]. [11] The night-sky with its Milky Way and twinkling stars was merely a reflection of what was below. Hence the Egyptians refer to the netherworld as the 'Lower Sky' [Spell 15]. [12] The journey of the night-barque along the river of the Milky Way was at the same time the way of the dark waters of the underworld. The body of the king is placed beneath the earth in his 'hidden chamber' just as the dying sun descends below the western horizon. Both sun and royal spirit are reborn on the eastern horizon at dawn. The journey must therefore take place beneath the living world even though the texts have this clear celestial character.

The Amduat in Thutmose III's burial chamber begins with one of literature's most spine-tingling introductions.

> [These are] the writings of the hidden chamber. The places where the souls, gods and spirits dwell and what they do [there]. [This is] the beginning in the **Horn of the West** – the gate of the western horizon. It is the knowledge of the power of those [who dwell] in the netherworld; … the knowledge of the **gates** and the way upon which the god passes. [13]

478. The nine deities journey together on their barque of the underworld – four at the rear, Horus in front of them, the ram-headed Atum-Re in his shrine, Hathor with the bull's horns and solar disc, and two gods at the prow including Wepwaut, the Opener of the Ways. The vessel has a high prow and stern and twin steering oars. It passes through a door or gate represented by the rectangular panel at the prow. Leading the way are goddesses with plumes attached to their head-bands.

479. The impressive peak of el-Gurn ('the horn') which the Egyptians identified with Meretseger, the cobra-goddess and guardian of the royal necropolis.

The 'Horn of the West' is the sacred mountain of Meretseger, sentinel guardian of the Valley of the Kings. The modern Egyptians still refer to this holy mountain as 'el-Gurn' – 'the horn' – 3,000 years after the last pharaonic remains were placed within its protection. At the heart of the king's tomb lies the portal leading to the afterlife.

> It is the **gate of the netherworld**. It is the **door** through which my father Atum passed when he proceeded to the eastern horizon of the sky. [Spell 17] [14]

Note that the journey of the dead king to his heavenly domain involves the passage through 'gates' and 'doors' – in fact there are seven, just as in the Sumerian and Jewish tradition.

> The doors of the (Lower) Sky are opened for you, the **doors** of the firmament are thrown open to you, that you may **travel by boat** to the **Field of Reeds**, that you may cultivate barley, that you may reap EMMER and prepare your sustenance therefrom like **Horus the son of Atum**. [15]

> ... the **ferry-boats** are made ready for the **son of Atum**, for the son of Atum is not boatless. [16]

> O Re commend me to **Mahaf** ('He who Looks Backwards'), the ferryman of the **winding waterway**, so that he may bring me his **ferry-boat** which belongs to the winding waterway, in which he ferries the gods to yonder side of the winding waterway to the **eastern side of the sky** ... [17]

EMMER: An early variety of wheat cultivated in the ancient Near East.

480. A funerary papyrus illustrating the same magical scenes as the royal tombs. The lower part depicts the barque of Atum-Re carrying the gods who are being pulled or dragged through the underworld to the eastern horizon. We now know where this motif originates – the Eastern Desert. Cairo Museum.

So we begin our journey to the 'Field of Reeds' on the 'eastern side of the sky' in the company of the gods of the night-barque who protect the Horus king, son of Atum, as he undertakes his dangerous passage along the 'winding waterway'.

An extraordinary image reveals itself to us from out of the 'utter darkness' of the caverns beneath the earth. The high-prowed ship slips silently through the black waters. It is so completely black that there is no visible horizon to aim for. Then the cobra-goddess, Wadjet, 'Lady of the Devouring Flame' [Spell 17],[18] entwines herself around the prow of the boat and spits out her protective flame to light the way forward.

> The flames coming out of the mouths of the barque guide him (Pharaoh) towards the mysterious ways. He does not see their forms. [Instead] he calls to them (the spirits of the netherworld) and it is his words that they hear.[19]

Behind the flaming goddess Wepwaut, the wolf-god and 'Opener of the Ways', pilots his precious cargo towards the east. Perhaps Wepwaut is Mahaf the ferry-man himself and Nay (the 'Sailor') of the Edfu texts. All the great primeval gods are on board – Shu, Tefnut, Geb, Nut, Osiris, Isis, Horus, Hathor and, of course, the spirit of the king as Atum.

Over the twelve hours of night the 'crew' journey ever on towards the east, passing through the seven portals guarded by demon spirits. At each the king is interrogated and must answer the questions correctly if he is to be allowed to pass.

An interesting detail now comes to light. Mahaf the ferryman and navigator is given the epithet 'Lord of the Red Cloth' [Spell 99].[20] How intriguing then to discover that the Sumerian kings were buried wrapped in a red shroud. The Mesopotamian deity of the underworld, Dumuzi (Akk. Tammuz), was prepared for burial in just this fashion.

For Dumuzi, the lover of her (Inanna's) youth, wash (him) with pure water and anoint him with sweet oil. **Wrap him in a red robe**. Let the lapis lazuli piper play and let the girls raise a loud lament.[21]

Even the primeval Followers of Horus are described as being 'clad in red linen'.

To the god's nobles, the god's friends who lean on their staffs. (They are the) guardians of Upper Egypt, **clad in red linen**, living on figs, drinking wine, anointed with unguent, that they may speak for Pharaoh to the great god and let Pharaoh ascend to the great god! [Utterance 440][22]

The 'red linen' surely refers to that most famous of fabrics – the deep red cloth dyed by the Phoenicians from the fluids of the murex fish. This only becomes understandable within the context of our story in which the ancestral Phoenicians are one and the same as the earliest navigators of the Erythraean Sea – the Red Sea – which encompassed the Arabian peninsula. But this association between the colour red and death must also hark back to the practice of covering Neolithic bones in red-ochre powder – a ritual from which first 'historical Man' – Adam ('red earth') – gained his name.

More connections with the early Phoenicians surface in a number of spells from the Book of the Dead which mention the mysterious benu-bird or phoenix.

The **battleship of the gods** was made according to what I (Re-Atum) said. Now I know the name of the great god who was therein. I was **the great phoenix** (Egy. *benu*) who is in Heliopolis who looks after the decision of all that is.

I come from the **Isle of Flame**, having filled my body with *Hike*-oil, like 'that [phoenix] bird' who filled the world with that which it had not known.[23]

Here the phoenix, which dwelt on the Isle of Flame beyond the limits of the world, is associated with the sun-god himself. The sacred heron appears in Egypt having travelled 'over oceans, seas and rivers'[24] to bring to the Black Land 'that which it had not known'. The phoenix was the bringer of knowledge, just as the 'Dynastic Race' had journeyed across the seas to bring the crafts and mysteries of Sumer to the Nile valley in Nakada II times. The sacred bird from the Isle of Flame is also a guide for the gods of the Blessed Isle when they journey from their homeland.

I am the phoenix, the soul of Re, who guides the gods to the netherworld when they go forth. [Spell 29B][25]

But also notice that the sacred barque of the gods is described as a 'battleship'. This reminds us of the black ship of war from the Hierakonpolis

481. The sacred benben stone of Heliopolis (Iunu) with the standard of Wepwaut erected before it. From the kiosk of Senuseret I at Karnak.

482. The fabulous phoenix (Egy. *benu*) from the 19th-Dynasty tomb of Irynefer. Note that the heron is travelling in a high-prowed boat with the symbol of the *Shemsu-Hor* ('Followers of Horus') before it.

Tomb 100 wall-painting and the high-prowed ships of the Gebel el-Arak knife handle. Henri Frankfort, the much-respected scholar of Mesopotamian and Egyptian iconographic art, observes that the Egyptians played out naval battles re-enacting the great events of the primeval age.

> The manoeuvres of the boats took place on the lake at Abydos which represented the waters separating the world of the living from the world of the dead, and the dead king on his journey was assisted in overcoming the danger which the waters symbolised by means of mock battles. [26]

The name Abydos in Egypto-speak is Abdju but, just as the Egyptologist's Djoser was probably pronounced Zoser by the ancients, we might ligitimately render the lake of the water battle as abzu – the Egyptian abyss.

Abydos was another of those 'gates' leading into the underworld but, of course, the place also had major associations with Osiris, god of the dead, and the Horus kings of Dynasties 0 and 1 whose burials were located here.

> … the Island of the Just, it is Abydos (Abzu). … It is the road on which my father Atum went when he proceeded to the Field of Reeds. [Spell 17] [27]

Many battles take place with the enemies of Pharaoh as the night-barque draws closer to dawn. Great serpents lash out at the ship but the power of the gods is with the spirit of Thutmose. All his enemies are finally vanquished. In triumph Atum's high-prowed bark is pulled towards the eastern horizon. Now we witness the lesser gods dragging the ship containing the great gods and the soul of the king in his form as Atum. The gods of the underworld are pulling as one, their hands clasping the rope which is tethered to the prow of the night-barque.

O you **gods who are dragged in the bark** of the Lord of Millions of Years, who bring the Upper Sky to the netherworld and who raise up the Lower Sky, who let souls draw near to

483. On the side of the sarcophagus of Ramesses III we see the lesser gods dragging the barque of Atum-Re with its high prow and stern. Louvre Museum.

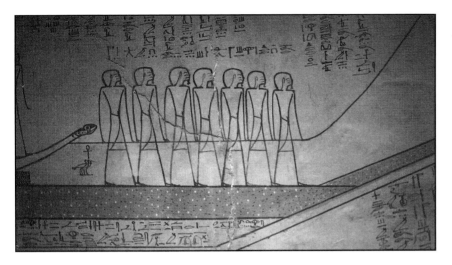

484. At the culmination of the journey through the underworld the lesser gods drag the barque of Atum-Re up towards the horizon where the deceased king's spirit can be reborn as the rising sun. Tomb of Thutmose III.

the noble dead, **may your hands be filled with your ropes**, may your grip be on your harpoons, may you drive off the enemy. [Spell 89]²⁸

Suddenly the ancient images on the wadi walls of the Eastern Desert are given meaning. The figures in the high-prowed boats are the gods of Egypt. The men dragging those boats are the lesser gods, otherwise known as the Followers of Horus. The 5,000-year-old prehistoric desert carvings lie at the very heart of Egyptian religion. The archaeologically attested arrival of the gods in Nakada II was the outward journey from Mesopotamia to Egypt. The sacred books of the underworld describe the return journey to the original homeland of the gods – the place to where the dead must retrace their steps. The Followers of Horus came westwards from the east. Their deceased ancestors must journey eastwards from the west to complete the cycle – just as the sun does for every day of existence.

Down in the dark tomb I stood before the very last scene of the Amduat – the culmination of the long journey through the twelve hours of night. Here the empty shell of the king (his mummy) is discarded, propped up against the curving wall of the underground cavern.

Rise up, O Pharaoh! Take your head. Collect your bones. Gather your limbs. Shake the earth from your flesh! [Utterance 373]²⁹

485. The empty body of the dead king is left in the underworld as his spirit soars into the sky above the Isle of Flame on the eastern horizon. Tomb of Thutmose III.

Here, again, we see very ancient connections with the burials at Nakada. Remember that Petrie found the élite graves contained disarticulated skeletal remains with the detached skulls placed together in the multiple burials. Here also lies a possible explanation for the mysterious heb-sed rite of the severing of the head just prior to the rebirth of the king.

The final moment of the Amduat sees Pharaoh transformed into Re-Harakhty – the rising sun. The red disc is being pushed above the eastern horizon in a blaze of glory by Khepri, the sacred scarab beetle. The

486. The falcon sky-god wearing the crescent-with-sun-disc emblem.

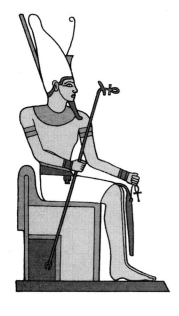

487. The primeval creator-god, Atum, represented in his human form as great ruler of the world.

Blessed Isle is lit by the glow of dawn as if on fire. The king has reached his final destination and boards the day-barque of the sun-god, his transfiguration and rebirth complete.

> I [Pharaoh] arrive at the Island of the Horizon-dwellers. **I go out from the holy gate**. [Spell 17][30]

> Ferried is this pharaoh to the eastern side of lightland. Ferried is this pharaoh to the eastern side of sky. His sister is Sothis, his offspring the dawn. [Utterance 263][31]

> I [Pharaoh] have gone in as a falcon-bird, I have come out as a phoenix-bird, the god who worships Re. [Spell 13][32]

> Pharaoh will take his pure seat in the bow of Re's barque. The sailors who row Re, they shall row Pharaoh! The sailors who convey Re about lightland, they shall convey Pharaoh about lightland! [Utterance 407][33]

Atum: The Lord of All

It is clear from the most ancient Egyptian literature – in other words the Pyramid Texts of the Old Kingdom – that Atum (later Re-Atum) was the original supreme deity of the pharaonic pantheon. Egyptologists have proposed that the name Atum means 'the all' as in all that exists.[34] His principal temple was at Heliopolis (Egy. *Iunu*), now located within the north-east suburbs of modern Cairo.

Atum was both man and god. He was the first being on earth who brought himself into the world – the self-created one. He was closely connected with the primeval mound, upon which the phoenix landed at the dawn of time. He is often envisaged as a great serpent in his watery abode. The allegorical Tale of the Shipwrecked Sailor which we came across in *Chapter Nine* casts our unfortunate seafarer onto the shore of a lush desert island upon which a fabulous serpent dwells. He is the Lord of Punt, the great Pen-god himself. It seems fairly obvious to me that this marvellous tale is all about death and rebirth. It is the story of a journey to and from the primeval island of the gods in which the sailor miraculously returns from certain death. The serpent Lord of Punt is none other than Atum himself, the Lord of the Abyss which surrounds the Isle of the Blessed – which we have identified with Dilmun/Bahrain.

> I am Atum at the head of the abyss, my protection is from the gods, the lords of eternity. [Spell 7][35]

But at the same time Atum is more than the serpent of the abyss; he is also the great sun-god in the form of Atum-Harakhty ('Atum the distant one of the eastern horizon') and, later, Re-Atum.

> [I am the] great illuminator (i.e. the sun) who shines forth from the abyss ... [Spell 15][36]

The Sacred Barques of Karnak

488a

We have seen how the dragging of high-prowed boats plays an important part in the journey through the underworld, as illustrated on the walls of the tombs of the kings. But this is not the only place where you can see such scenes. These high-prowed vessels and their associated iconography are to be found everywhere. As Rundle Clark notes 'The paraphernalia of the solar barque are the most sacred things in Egyptian religion.'[37] We can see a good example of what he means at Karnak.

Just walk through the second pylon gateway of the Temple of Amun and turn immediately to your right. There, on the interior façade of the pylon you will find a huge scene of two boats. The leading vessel has the familiar high prow and stern (488a). It carries a group of gods. At the prow (488b) is Wepwaut (the navigator); then comes the deified Ramesses II and Horus; behind them is the ram-headed Khnum who crafted Man on his

488b

potter's wheel. They are all grasping a thick rope which is attached to the prow of the second vessel. This boat is sickle-shaped and contains the shrines of the Theban triad – Amun, Mut and Khonsu. Here again we have imagery reminiscent of the eastern invaders: boats being towed by the gods, the gods' ship with high prow and stern, the central cabin and the totem or standard.

When the Shipwrecked Sailor asks the Lord of Punt why he is alone on the magical island he hears that the great serpent's offspring were all destroyed in a cataclysmic fire. Could this cryptic passage be an allusion to the incident which gave its name to the Isle of Flame? And, if so, were the serpent's offspring one and the same as the Ancestors of the First Time? There seems to be a reference to the Serpent Lord of Punt in one of the spells from the Book of the Dead which again links the tale of the Shipwrecked Sailor to the mythology of the First Time.

489. The jewellery of Tutankhamun from his tomb in the Valley of the Kings displays many of the motifs we have been studying. Here the *khepri* beetle pushes the sun-disc (resting in the crescent) above the eastern horizon. Not only is this the motif or rebirth but the central figures spell out the king's coronation name – *Neb* (the basket beneath the beetle) – *Kheperu* (the scarab beetle with three plural strokes beneath it) – *Re* (the sun-disc). But also remember that the crescent surmounted by sun-disc is a Mesopotamian symbol for Utu/Shamash, the sun-god.

490. Here with this pendant from Tutankhamun's burial we see an even more dramatic link to the predynastic Followers of Horus. The sun-disc resting in the crescent moon is being carried in a high-prowed boat. All three elements are to be found in the Eastern Desert rock-art and in ancient Sumer.

As for the mountain of Bakhu on which the sky rests, it is in the east of the sky; it is three hundred rods long and one hundred and fifty rods broad. … A serpent is on the top of that mountain; it is thirty cubits long, eight cubits of its forepart are of flint, and its teeth gleam. I know the name of this serpent which is on the mountain; its name is 'He who is in his burning'. [Spell 108][38]

Finally, the Shipwrecked Sailor is rescued by a passing ship and the magical island of the Lord of Punt disappears beneath the sea, never to be seen again. Perhaps we can see an allegory here for the Blessed Isle which is usually beyond the reach of the living and only visible to the spirits of the deceased. So, the awe-inspiring serpent, the Lord of Punt of the Tale of the Shipwrecked Sailor, is the primeval sun-god who dwells on the island of the dead. But the great sun-god of Egyptian religion is much more than this.

Atum as the first being – and therefore the first ruler on earth – was regarded as the patron deity of royalty – the personal protector of the pharaoh and all kingship rituals. In this aspect he acted as guardian of the dead king on his hazardous journey through the underworld and, in his form of the *khepri* (scarab) beetle, the elevator of the king into the heavens at dawn as the reborn sun.

Is it remotely possible that the Egyptian high god can also be identified with a character from the Bible? We have made the link between the Egyptian gods and the first settlers in the marshlands of Sumer. But I also suggested a connection between those Founders and the settlement of Shinar by the antediluvian patriarchs.

We then discovered a number of biblical heroes from the book of Genesis in the king lists, myths and epic tales of Sumer. Enoch was identified as the eponymous ancestor of Uruk (Unuk); Cush, son of Ham, turned out to be Meskiagkasher; and Nimrod, his son, was recognised as the famous Enmerkar, mighty builder of Uruk and Eridu.

A further fascinating possibility arises when we discover that Eridu's great god, Enki, had a first-born son called Asar-luhi who was the local god of agricultural fertility. The Babylonians adopted him as their supreme national deity in the guise of Marduk son of Ea. To the Assyrians he was the eponymous ancestor-god of their capital city, Ashur.

If Asar-luhi of of the Sumerians can be equated with Assyrian god Ashur, then the Bible identifies him as Ashur, son of Shem and grandson of Noah who, according to Jewish tradition, was the eponymous founder of the Asyrian empire. However, he may also have an Egyptian identity. We know the great pharaonic god of agricultural fertility as Osiris after his Greek name, wheras the Egyptians simply knew him as Asar.

But what about Atum – the first god and living being in Egyptian theology? You may be ahead of me but, just in case you need a little encouragement, we shall return to the vagaries of comparative language to complete the picture.

The name Atum is written as A-t-m with the loaf-of-bread sign for the letter 't'. However, it is recognised by linguists that the letters 't' and 'd' are often interchangeable within the different language groups of the ancient Near East. For example, Kenneth Kitchen has shown that Egyptian *Twtw* is Semitic Dadu – 'the beloved' (i.e. the name David).[39] As we saw in *Chapter Six*, the Sumerian Adama becomes Atamu in Akkadian. So I believe we are equally justified in substituting the Egyptian 't' in A-t-m with a 'd' – giving us Adam!

Of course, both of these changes, although quite justifiable linguistically, are no more than speculations. But, as I stated in the *Introduction* to *Legend*, this whole exercise is based on intuitive and reasoned interpretation of the archaeological and textual evidence – in my view the defining criteria of a 'history'. If the name Adam appears at the head of one of the earliest king lists in Mesopotamia and, as we have demonstrated, the pharaonic state was born from the arrival of Mesopotamians into the Nile valley, then why should we be so reticent to entertain the possibility that the first being in Egyptian mythology was a legendary ruler from the prehistory of the Sumerians? A number of Sumeriologists take precisely this view with regard to the origins of the Genesis tradition.[40] It is argued that, as the Patriarchs heralded from Sumer, the mythological source for Genesis probably belongs to a common prehistory shared by all the Mesopotamian ethnic groupings. So, if it can be demonstrated that Egypt's first pharaohs also belonged to this same milieu of cultures, I do not believe it is beyond reasonable speculation to propose that the legends of Atum, Adam and Adapa had a common origin. The fact that the stories surrounding the three creation myths are culturally distinct may confuse the issue but does not rule out the possibility of a single historical source for the first being in ancient Middle Eastern mythology.

A Funeral Fit for a God

When a pharaoh of the New Kingdom died he was buried in the Valley of the Kings. It is very likely that the body of the king was mummified

491. The hieroglyphs which spell out Atum. The upper version is the full writing with the loaf symbol for 't' (above the sledge). However, the god's name was also rarely written with the hand symbol which Egyptologists recognise as the letter 'd', giving us A-d-m.

492. A Mesopotamian cylinder-seal impression of the sun-god Shamash riding in his high-prowed reed barque. Both the Mesopotamians and Egyptians thus had the concept of the sun-god journeying in a solar boat.

493. The dragging team at Tutankhamun's funeral. Are the nobles of the court re-enacting an event which occurred back in predynastic times when the original Followers of Horus came to the Nile valley?

up in Memphis, where the royal household was in residence for most of the year, before it was brought upstream by boat to the holy city of Thebes. Having arrived, the great flotilla entered the canal which led from the River Nile up to the mortuary temple of the king where final preparations for the burial were to be made. Finally the day of interment arrived and Pharaoh's body was transported to the royal wadi and his sepulchral resting place from where he would begin his journey to Lightland and the Isle of Flame. But how was the mummy taken to the Valley of the Kings? The most famous funeral scene is that to be found in the tomb of Tutankhamun on the north wall of his tiny burial chamber. There we see the coffin of the king inside a golden shrine which is itself mounted on a sledge. The king's coffin is being pulled by courtiers and priests as if they were dragging a boat across the desert sands. The shrine containing the royal corpse is equivalent to the cabin/shrine shown at the centre of the high-prowed vessel's deck and which can be seen on the solar-barque of Khufu. Frankfort makes the point when discussing the rituals of Osiris, the archetypal dead ruler.

We are once more reminded of funerary usages when we read that toward the end of the Great Procession Osiris embarked

494. A seal from the Agade Period depicting the sun-god Shamash/Utu rising between two mountains, with Ea/Enki on the right (water flowing from his shoulders) and Ishtar/Inanna (with wings) standing on one of the mountains. The symbol of the sunrise between two peaks is also a major element of Egyptian iconography in the form of the *akhet* hieroglyph (below). British Museum.

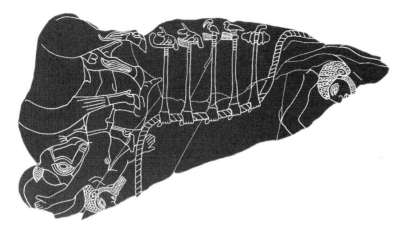

495. I have turned this illustration of a late predynastic bull palette (from the Louvre) on its side to show you that the standards we recognise as representing the Followers of Horus have hands at the base of the shafts. These hands are grasping a thick rope which the standards of Wepwaut, Anubis (?), Thoth, Horus and Min are pulling as one. Once again we see the iconography of dragging which was clearly of major significance in early Egyptian culture.

on a 'ship'. The word used is *wrt*. This 'ship' was used in the funerals of the Old Kingdom and depicted in some tombs. It was, in reality, a ship-shaped sledge upon which the coffin was placed so that it might be dragged to the necropolis in the desert. [41]

In effect, Tutankhamun is beginning his journey to Lightland by retracing the steps of the original Followers of Horus. The dragging of the 'boat' carrying the person of his majesty is a journey across the desert and through the narrow wadi which leads to the entrance of the underworld at 'the horn' (the holy mountain). Once the king is buried he will board the ferryman's high-prowed boat waiting at the shore of the dark sea to begin his journey along the long winding waterway of the underworld which rises to the surface at the far-distant horizon. We now know where that place is. The ancient Egyptians conceived a theology which returned their deceased ruler to the island from which the Shebtiu had originated. We now know that place to have been Bahrain (the 'twin waters') where the sweet waters of the netherworld – Enki's abyss [42] – burst forth from beneath the salt waters of the Lower Sea. There Pharaoh was reborn as Horus of the Eastern Horizon – the one who came from the place where the 'holy gate' of the underworld was to be found [Book of the Dead, Spell 17] and where the primeval mounds of the gods were located.

Conclusion Thirty-Two

The journey to the Isle of Flame, so crucial to the resurrection cycle of Egyptian mythology, is a return voyage to the Persian Gulf. The pharaoh must return along the dark river of the underworld to the island of Bahrain where the predynastic ancestral gods originated. There he joins the great ancestor, Utnapishtim 'the far distant' – the first of the Horus rulers and descendant of the high-god Atum.

496. Opposite page: A winged-bull guardian from the palace of Sargon II at Khorsabad. Louvre Museum.

497. Left: The Mesopotamian perception of paradise. The high-god (or goddess) is escorted into the Dilmunic garden by two griffins. The god Enki/Ea, with water gushing from his shoulders, kneels before the central figure. Either side stand the trees of paradise with exotic birds perched in their branches and filling the air. The whole garden is enclosed by a wall of mountains, just like those found on the decorated pottery from predynastic Egypt. This seal was found at Nippur and is dated to the reign of Nazimaruttash, 23rd ruler of the Kassite Dynasty.

Chapter Fourteen

GENESIS

The time has come to bring all our discoveries together to see what we have achieved in the way of a cohesive historical picture. In the *Introduction* I promised to turn the current anthropological history of the birth of civilisation into a political history overflowing with incident and personality. What follows is a new and much more detailed version of the Genesis story.

This is a full-blooded, colourful version of history. It is not a dusty 'academic' history full of caveats and diversions into the minutiae of scholarship. I am going to tell this story in the way a Sumerian orator might entertain his audience with the Epic of Gilgamesh or how a Hebrew patriarch might recall to his grandchildren the heroic tales of their great ancestors before the flood. In the telling there will be a liberal use of poetic licence – but that is all part of the art of storytelling.

498. A lion leaps onto the back of a bull. A timeless motif from the apadana staircase at Persepolis.

The Garden of Eden – *c.* 6000 BC

Once upon a time (as the Enmerkar Epic puts it) – a very long time ago – high up in the alpine valleys of the Zagros mountains, Stone Age Man was beginning to stir. Humankind was gradually realising a greater potential than the simple subsistence of its hunter-gathering ancestors. The tribal system, based on the extended family, was already institutionalised around a ruler-chieftain who was both king and high priest of his clan. Simple tools were being manufactured from volcanic glass (obsidian) and animals such as the goat, sheep, dog and onager were beginning to be domesticated.

All around, the black volcanic mountains pierced the heavens. In the mind of primitive Man these were the pedestals from which the gods viewed the handiwork of their creation. Occasionally the lords of heaven and earth (the biblical Elohim) would descend from their lofty thrones to communicate with their human creations. These communications manifested themselves in various forms. This was a land of fire and earthquake; of thunder and lightning; of wind and storm. The gods spoke with thunderous voices which shook the earth. Their will was manifest both in the beneficence of nature and in its destructive forces. The gods were the essence of nature – Egyptian *netjer* – the name the later Nile valley civilisation would give to the very concept of godhood. One can only wonder if our word 'nature' does not find its origins in the ancient land of Egypt.

In the beginning ... one particular valley in the Zagros range, lush with a canopy of 'every kind of tree', became the setting-off point on the long march to civilisation. This was the place where humankind turned away from the Neolithic (late Stone Age) and headed first east then south through the mountain passes towards the Chalcolithic (Copper Age) and on into the Early Bronze Age. We cannot be sure what triggered that momentous event but the usual mechanism for such migrations is detrimental climate change.

Before we accompany our migrants on their journey to Mesopotamia we should first get to know them and their original habitat a little better.

The small group, perhaps numbering a couple of hundred or so, were based at the western end of a primeval valley extending from the eastern shore of a great salt lake. Today we call that lake 'Urmia'. The sun rose due east along the valley. This was the mythical land of sunrise – a paradisiacal garden which was the home of the gods. From here, atop their lofty throne known as the 'bright mountain', the heavenly assembly observed the fate of primeval mankind in the valley below.

Immediately to the west of their tiny settlement spread the marshy delta of a river which ran through the valley and emptied into the lake. The Bible does not name this river but we have come to know it as the River of the Garden of Eden. Over time, tradition accorded it the name Meidan – the 'royal garden' – perhaps because of its paradise-like setting and its connection to the first ruler in history. The Jews of Alexandria, when composing the Greek version of the Hebrew Bible, called the place 'paradise' after the ancient Persian word for 'walled park'. We will call the valley of the Meidan – the Garden – in deference to the Israelite oral traditions about this place around which the first chapters of Genesis are focused.

The primeval ones did not call their valley 'Eden' for this is a later name given to a much larger region, of which the Garden forms only the eastern part. The most ancient name of the valley of the primeval ones was Tilmun – the *original* 'Land of the Living' of the epic poetry. It was the place whence the Sumerians of later times believed their gods had

499. The world of Eden – sky, mountains and sweet water.

originated – the mountainous home of Enki (Ea/Ya/Yahweh), Ninhursag ('Mistress of the Mountain' and the 'Mother of All the Living' – Eve), Inanna (Ishtar/Astarte/Isis) and, later, Dumuzi (Asar/Marduk/Ashur/Osiris).

To the east of the Garden the valley rose up towards a mountain pass which led on into another high and fertile basin. The author of Genesis knew this eastern plateau as the land of Nod.

The northern boundary of our Garden valley was marked by precipitous snow-capped mountains rising up to 3,000 metres. The highest of these guarded a second pass through which the Primeval Ones of our settlement had contact with the people of the land of Cush. The mountain sentinel which looks down upon the valley of the River Gihon (Gaihun-Aras) is still called the 'Mountain of Kush' (Kusheh Dagh) today.

To the south, our Garden is also hemmed in by high mountain ranges, dominated by the huge extinct volcanic dome of the 'Mountain of the Chalice', known to the Assyrians as Mount Uash and today as Mount Sahand. At the very summit of the peak the narrow funnel of its crater overflows with the ice-cool waters of life rising up from the underworld. This was the original abyss (abzu) of Sumerian mythology – the exalted throne of the gods – the 'bright mountain' of Sumerian tradition. Its waters cascaded down the northern slopes of the mountain and joined the river of the Garden as it flowed east into the marshes and salt-flats of the great lake. The abyss was the sacred water source of the Garden of Eden.

500. One of the legendary creatures of Eden – the griffin. From the palace of Persepolis.

501. The god of Eden.

The author of Genesis tells us that the river of Eden parted into four streams, which he calls the 'heads' (i.e. sources). These headwaters became the four great rivers which flowed down from Eden to water the rest of the then-known primeval world. The author knew these rivers as the Gihon (Araxes), the Pishon (Uizhun), the Euphrates (Perath) and the Tigris (Hiddekel). The two great lakes – today known as Urmia and Van – were the catchment reservoirs of the world's fresh water supply which flowed into them from all the abzus (sacred springs) of the high volcanic peaks within Eden.

Back in our beautiful valley the primeval ones at first lived a pleasant enough life surrounded by all that was needed to sustain them. Natural orchards heavy with fruit extended up the slopes of the surrounding mountains. The people had unlimited supplies of the strong, tall reeds and giant hogweed used to build their primitive dwellings. Everywhere was the perfume of alpine flowers and the scent of the beautiful white lily.

The people of the Garden believed in an afterlife. They had developed the concept of eternal life beyond death. They buried the bones of their dead in shallow graves along with personal objects which the deceased might need on his journey into the netherworld. These included little statuettes painted red. Before filling in the tomb the relatives of the deceased covered the mortal remains in red ochre which they had obtained from the 'Red Mountain' (Kur-Hashura) located to the south of the holy mountain of the abyss. You can almost hear the priest-king utter the immortal words over the grave:

> Return to the ground as you were taken from it, for dust you
> are and to dust you shall return. [Genesis 3:19]

In death, so in life. The folk of Eden decorated their living bodies in red-ochre dye for some religious purpose or ritual, the significance of which is now lost to us. The use of red colouring permits us to call this tribe of primeval ones the 'people of the red earth' – the 'Adamites'.

God of Eden

The Adamites of the Garden, above all, valued the most important of life-giving elements – the fresh water which flowed down through the Garden and nourished all the plants and beasts of the earth. As we have learnt, they called their god of the sweet water, Enki – 'Lord of the Earth'. His main role was his lordship over the abzu – the dark, limitless ocean which existed beneath the ground and bubbled to the surface from the peaks of the high mountains. The people of Eden especially sanctified the places where the life-giving waters of the abyss burst forth upon the dry earth. This practice would continue in the Zagros mountains for thousands of years, right down to Persian times when it was clearly still manifest in the fire-temple rites of the Zoroastrians.

The holiest site of all for our red-earth people was the sacred well at the summit of the Mountain of the Chalice, for this was the source of the waters of the Garden and the high throne of the 'Lord of the Earth' and the other gods. The people of the Bible called the high-god 'Ya' (Akk. *Ea*, pronounced Eya) – the hypocoristicon of Yahweh. The Old Testament prophets knew the 'Mountain of God' was far off to the north, out of reach of mere mortals. It dominated the garden of creation whose gates were protected by a fearsome tribe of the cherubim (Akk. *karibu*) with their fiery flashing sword – the volcanoes of Azerbaijan (the land of fire).

The First Ruler in History

The first great chieftain of the Garden tribe whose name survived down the ages was *the* red man – the biblical Adam. He was later known to the Amorite genealogists of Mesopotamia as Dudiya-Adamu – the 'Beloved of [God] – the Red One'. The Bible tells us that he was brought into the Garden by his god.

> God Yahweh took the man and settled him in the Garden of Eden to cultivate and take care of it. [Genesis 2:15]

The implication is that Adamu led his people into the valley from elsewhere. That original home may well have been the valley to the south of Lake Urmia – the place the Sumerians of later times would call Aratta. This was the heart of the land of Eden – the 'Land of the Living'.

As Adamu's people moved east into the Meidan valley they made an alliance with an indigenous tribe of the Garden – an alliance which was sealed by the marriage of the Adamites' chieftain to the daughter of the chieftain of the Hawwah tribe. In our story the first political marriage in history was between Adamu (Adam) and Hawwah (Eve) and that marriage bore fruit in the shape of three sons (or dynasties) – Cain, Abel and Seth.

502. The good shepherd. Sumerian statuette from the Louvre Museum.

A Tiller of Soil and a Good Shepherd

The story of Cain and Abel personifies the natural tensions between the two forms of subsistence which developed out of hunter-gatherer society. Whether this was a genuine incident – the first recorded murder in history – or simply a literary mechanism to explain future conflicts over land resources between city-dweller agriculturalists and nomadic pasturalists, it becomes a crucial turning point in the accelerating progress towards civilisation. It is interesting that, of the two documentary sources which make up the final Genesis narrative, it is the J or Yahwistic source which contains the story of Cain and Abel. Given my own view that J is the work of Moses, I find it illuminating that the god of Exodus, projected back into primeval Eden by the author, rejects the offerings of the farmer as unworthy but praises the shepherd for his blood sacrifice. This clearly

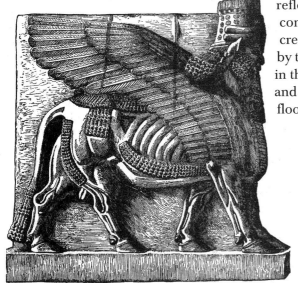

503. Eden's most fearsome guardian – the *karibu* or winged demon, protector of the holy places.

reflects the very different nature of the god of Moses compared to the sympathetic nature of the Sumerian creator god, Enki/Ea. The murder of the blood-sacrificer by the jealous baker of bread seems somehow out of place in the pre-flood story where Man is forbidden to take life and is only permitted to kill animals for food after the flood. Adam and his people were apparently vegetarians.

> God blessed Noah and his sons and said to them, 'Breed, multiply and fill the earth. Be the terror and the dread of all animals on land and all the birds of heaven, of everything that moves on land and all the fish of the sea; they are placed in your hands. Every living thing that moves will be yours to eat, no less than the foliage of the plants'. [Genesis 9:1-3.]

The tiller of the soil, rejecting his ungrateful god, departed from the scene of his crime in search of lands where he could eke out a new existence within the gaze of more sympathetic deities. He found a new home in the land of Nod which lay over the mountain ridge to the east of the Meidan valley. From there the descendants of this son of Adam would journey southwards towards the mountain valleys of the central Zagros and finally on into the plain of Susiana.

The Start of the Great Migration – *c.* 5500 BC

So Cain (Kiyan son of Adamu), was banished to the land of Nod. There he settled to establish a new tribe of agriculturalists in the open plain around what is now the provincial capital of eastern Azerbaijan – Ardabil.

It was Cain's descendants who eventually migrated southwards through the pass which leads over the northern slopes of Mount Alwand into the Kangavar valley. There they dwelt within the shadow of the high cliffs of Behistun (Baghistanon – the 'Mountain of God') before moving on to the next valley south, along the upper reaches of the Said-marreh river.

At the site of Tepe Guran, Cain's descendants discovered the new technology of the kiln. The startling new product of this invention – pottery – began to spread over the whole region. This dispersion of pottery enables us to trace the continuing movement southwards into the Tigris-Euphrates valley of Adam's descendants. Their pottery began to appear in the plain of Susiana to the south. Once more the tribe had followed the course of the Saidmarreh/Kerkheh river as it flowed towards the swamps of southern Iraq. Tracing the pottery development from generation to generation indicates a further population movement into the marshy plain at the head of the 'Lower Sea' (Persian Gulf) where the civilisation of Sumer was born. The Tepe Guran pottery also points us directly eastwards along the pass from Kangavar to the rolling plains of what will later become the empire of Agade (Akkad).

Enoch the Builder-King – *c.* 5000 BC

Our story has now moved to the generations of Enoch (Hanu) – the new ruler of Adam's much expanded tribe. Enoch was the renowned leader of the migrants who finally reached their new homeland in the land of Shinar. They entered into the marshlands from the east, via the plain of Susiana, having broken out of the highlands through the Saidmarreh valley just to the north of Susa.

> Now, as the people moved from the east, they found a valley in the land of Shinar where they settled. They said to one another, 'Come, let us make bricks and bake them in the fire.' For stone they used bricks and for mortar they used bitumen. [Genesis 11:2-3] [1]

It was impossible for Enoch and his son Irad to lead their people directly across the swamps which were impassable on foot. They instead chose to build reed boats on the north-east boundary of the marsh and then sailed along the shore of the Gulf to reach the southern boundary of the Mesopotamian wetlands. There at the site which would later be known as Eridu (named after Irad) they established their first settlement on a low-lying turtleback (sand island). Their first duty was to construct a primitive reed shrine to their principal god, Enki. Soon, though, they had turned their energies to the new invention of mudbrick. The fertile river-borne silt was in abundant supply all around them whereas the hard stones of the mountains were virtually inaccessible. One of the hallmarks of Sumerian civilisation is the use of mudbrick combined with bitumen mortar – the materials used to build the monumental stepped temple-towers which we know as the ziggurats.

Eridu lay on a low circular island amidst the reed swamps of the Gulf marshlands with open access to the 'Lower Sea'. The Sumerian King List informs us that divine kingship first 'descended from heaven' here. That first king was the biblical Enoch, founder of Eridu. The earliest reed shrine at Eridu was soon replaced by a simple mudbrick structure which, in turn, over the years developed into a major religious complex built on a raised mudbrick platform. After the flood at least two deities were worshipped here – the old creator-god Enki/Ea, seated on his 'Exalted Throne' of the abyss, and the sun-god, Utu. The latter's temple is now completely lost to archaeology but the massive

504. The bull-man, perhaps a legendary metaphor for the hero Gilgamesh. 'He was superior to other kings, a warrior lord of great stature, a hero of Uruk – a goring wild bull.' [Gilgamesh Epic, Tablet I, column 1]

505. A Persian seal depicting a hero-king killing a ferocious lion with his dagger. This motif is extremely common throughout Mesopotamian history and goes back to the legendary hero-king of Uruk, Gilgamesh. Private collection of the Biblisches Institut, Fribourg University.

platform upon which it was built still remains to attest to its former grandeur. This first temple complex on earth was remembered in Egyptian tradition as the place of the Founders of the First Time – the home of the 'Pen-god' (Ptah-Tatjenen). So the Egyptian concept of creation did not begin in the mountains of heaven – in Eden – but with the establishment of the first temple of the creator in the marshy world of the waters of Nun – the swamps of southern Sumer – at the eastern limit of the world.

Out of necessity, the people of Eridu, located as they were by the sea, rapidly became conversant with the maritime crafts. They had abundant supplies of reeds in the marshes surrounding them and so they turned these to good use, not only to make their houses but also to construct bigger and stronger reed boats capable of sailing to the islands of the Persian Gulf. The archaeological evidence of their seafaring adventures is represented by the enormous number of sites on the eastern littoral of the Arabian peninsula which have produced Ubaid pottery – the invention of the antediluvian peoples of Genesis.

Enoch also established other settlements in southern Mesopotamia which were later named after him. Thus Uruk (Sum. *Unuk*) and Ur (Sum. *Unuki*) were founded shortly after Eridu. The tell-tale archaeological evidence of their early foundation is the appearance of 'Eridu Ware' at all three sites. Archaeologists have shown that Eridu Ware was a direct descendant of the pottery from Tepe Guran and other Neolithic sites in the Zagros mountains.

City of the Metal-Workers – *c.* 4500 BC

The smelting of copper was another invention of the mountain folk to the north of Sumer but the ascendancy of the copper-smiths only came about with the passing of the kingship, once again handed down from heaven, to the city of Badtibira ('City of the Metal Worker'). The eponymous ancestor of this city of the smiths was the biblical Tubal-Cain (both elements of whose name mean 'metal-worker').

Copper smelting was another great leap on the road towards civilisation because it immediately stimulated a search for new mineral resources. The original ore supplies from the northern mountains were not only limited in extent but also difficult to access and transport down into the lowlands. So, with the explosion in demand for metal tools and weapons came the first concentrated effort towards maritime trade – especially with copper-rich Magan (Oman).

The Island of the Two Waters – *c.* 4000 BC

The folk of Eridu had migrated along the eastern shore of Arabia, establishing harbours for their reed ships as they went. The Ubaid pottery of the era is found all along the coast stretching down as far as the islands of Bahrain and beyond to the Oman peninsula. The pottery trail tells us that the sailors of Eridu and other cities of Sumer had settled in these locations in order to handle the burgeoning trade of copper from Magan (Oman) and, a little later, the produce of far-off Meluhha (the Indus Valley). Their principal trading emporium was established at the northern tip of the main island of Bahrain which the ancients called Dilmun/Tilmun after their original homeland in the mountains. At first the settlements were very temporary affairs. Only by Early Dynastic times did they become truly established. The sacred temples of the hawk-god of the island were simple reed shrines during the Uruk and Jemdet Nasr eras.

There, on the island of the 'two waters' (*Bahr* = 'water', plus *ein* = dual ending), the seafarers of Sumer and Susiana saw a reflection of their original homeland setting. Just as in the now semi-mythical Garden of Paradise of the Primeval Ones beyond the mountains of sunrise, here there was an outflowing of the abyss at the Isle of Dilmun – in this case a powerful fresh-water spring which burst up from the depths of the salt-water sea. Naturally this was taken as a sign that Enki had established a new home in the south – a place where his worshippers would eventually come to be buried in the new realm of the guardian of the abyss. The Sumerians of later centuries came to know this place as the 'Isle of the Blessed' and the 'Pure Land'. Paradise – the 'Land of the Living' – was thus transferred from its original mountain location down onto a desert island within the steamy waters of the Gulf.

The Great Flood – *c.* 3100 BC

Meanwhile, back in the land of Sumer, kingship had passed on to the city of Larak, then to Sippar, before finally ending up in the hands of the lords of Shuruppak. Then came the terrible flood which was to wipe out all that had been achieved. The thick waterborne silt deposit found by Woolley in the latest Ubaid strata of Ur marks this cataclysmic event.

The biblical flood hero is known to us as Noah. The Amorite tribal groups (Assyrian and Babylonian) listed him in their ancient genealogies as Nuabu. The Sumerians called him Ziusudra. The Akkadians of Agade referred to him as Atrahasis – 'Exceedingly Devout'. The later Babylonians knew him from the Gilgamesh Epic where he was called Utnapishtim the Far Distant.

In some traditions he was connected with the city of Shuruppak where the last king before the flood – Ubartutu – ruled. The Bible does not tell us where the events leading up to the flood (i.e. the building of the ark) took place. What we do learn is that the ark came to rest on the 'mountains of Ararat' – that is to say the Zagros mountains in the region later known as Urartu but which was earlier known as the kingdom of Aratta. Ancient historians state that the ark came to rest on the mountains of Kurdistan.

I have shown that the heartland of Aratta was located in the wide plain to the south of Lake Urmia. In the mountains to the west of this plain was the peak known today as Judi Dagh. It was from the slopes of Mount Judi that, for millennia, the remnants of the ark had been collected by pre-Christian pilgrims – including the powerful Assyrian ruler, SENNACHERIB.

The site of the ark's landing is still a place of pilgrimage and sacrifice today. Every year on the first day of the month of Ilul (14th September) the Shaitan-worshipping Yezidis – the descendants of Adamu's third son, Seth – ascend Judi Dagh to commemorate the day when Noah sacrificed to Yahweh. In gratitude for the survival of humankind, and on behalf of all the species which inhabited the earth, 'the smoke of a hundred offerings goes up once more on the ancient altar'. [2]

Cush and the Sea – *c.* 3050 BC

After the great flood had subsided, the survivors returned to the lowlands and began to rebuild the ravaged world. The story given in the Bible and in the Sumerian literature is centred on Noah/Utnapishtim. It is a tale about the saving of a pious man by his god whilst all around perished. The historical reality was more likely that many thousands did indeed die – perhaps millions – but many of the tribes living in the high mountain passes of the Zagros would have survived. They, along with Noah's family, descended into the plain in a second migration and rebuilt the devastated cities. The flood had brought an end to the 'First Time' (Egy. *sep tepi*) and we now enter the antediluvian age of the 'Builder Gods'.

The descendants of Noah rebuilt the cities of Uruk and Eridu, founded by their great ancestor Enoch. Two of Uruk's rulers are particularly remembered by the Sumerians as great kings. We will deal with Enmerkar in a moment, but first I should relate the strange tale of King Meskiag-kasher – the biblical Cush, son of Ham and grandson of Noah.

The Sumerian King List tells us that Meskiagkasher journeyed over the southern sea and came ashore in a mountainous land. We can trace his journey from Eridu to the sacred island of Dilmun (Bahrain) which had been used as a resting place by Sumerian sea traders with Magan for many centuries. His fleet of ships had then journeyed on into the open ocean and along the southern shore of the Arabian peninsula to reach the coast of Africa near the mouth of the Red Sea. There they came ashore in the mountainous land we today call Ethiopia but which was anciently known as Kush. Throughout their history, the later Egyptians would call the people of the Upper Nile 'Kushites', after their eponymous ancestor.

At first the immigrants settled along the Red Sea coast where they could obtain luxury produce used in religious ritual, such as myrrh and incense from the mountain slopes. They also made contact with the Negroid population from the African hinterland who brought them ivory, ebony and animal skins. The same objective was at work here as was the case with both Magan and Meluhha – the simple quest for exotic produce

506. The great black ship, with high prow and stern, which appears on Nakada II pottery in Egypt at around 2900 BC. Note what appears to be a falcon perched on the stern.

507. Kushite captives of the later pharaonic epoch (clearly of African origin) continued to wear the single feather as a symbol of their distant connection to their high-plumed founder of primeval times. This was also true of the Libyans whose traditional founder was Put, the younger 'brother' of Cush. Relief from Abu Simbel (19th Dynasty).

for despatch to their homeland back in the valley 'between the two rivers'. During the centuries which followed the initial arrival of Cush and his fleet, many return journeys would be made by individual ships laden with the produce of Africa. Eventually, after trade with the Indus Valley had ceased (probably due to the invasion of Meluhha by the Aryan tribes) and supplies for copper ore in Magan had begun to diminish, the new resources of Africa became much more important to the later Meso-potamian civilisations. As a result, the new regions which supplied the produce of the more ancient overseas lands were named after the original toponyms. Thus Ethiopia became known as Meluhha whilst Egypt was named Magan. However, the pharaohs continued to regard their southern neighbour as the kingdom of Kush.

In the company of Cush (or perhaps following on later) came Ham's younger 'sons', Mizraim, Put and Canaan. They were not to stay with their Cushite brethren but went in search of new lands of their own to conquer. But, at this point, we will briefly leave Meskiagkasher, Mizraim, Phut, Canaan and their followers and return to Mesopotamia in order to complete the story of the descent of Adamu's line down to Abram.

Nimrod the Mighty Hunter – *c.* 2900 BC

By the time Meskiagkasher had arrived in Africa the kingship of Uruk lay in the capable hands of his 'successor', Enmerkar. Again, I should remind you that we need not take this legendary succession literally. Enmerkar may indeed have been the son and direct heir of Meskiag-kasher, but he might equally have been a later descendant of the first king of Uruk after the flood. This would explain why Meskiagkasher is given 324 years of rule – over three centuries of time which represents the entire dynasty of the eponymous founder of the line.

The late-Uruk Period was the golden age of Sumerian prehistory – the era of the great hero-figures Enmerkar, Lugalbanda, Dumuzi and (later in Early Dynastic times) Gilgamesh. We have discovered that Enmerkar was none other than the legendary builder-king of Genesis – Nimrod – the first potentate on earth. He is traditionally regarded as the builder of Uruk, Ur and Babylon and, according to Jewish legend, the ruler who ordered the construction of the infamous Tower of Babel. The first great temple-towers were not built at Babylon but rather in the sacred precincts of Eridu and Uruk. The remains of the former are represented by the ruins of a massive platform dating to the Uruk Period which was then suddenly abandoned to the wind-blown sands. This legendary temple at Eridu, so famous in Mesopotamian lore, was built over the first tiny mudbrick shrine dedicated to the god of the abyss. It was the primeval temple of the great Builder-Gods of Egypt before they perma-nently settled in the Nile valley.

One Sumerian epic informs us that Enmerkar came down from the mountains to rule over Uruk. This is, of course, consistent with the biblical

508. Another, rather grander representation of the hero-king in hunting tradition. Here, in this relief from Persepolis, the king slays a bull (perhaps the bull of heaven).

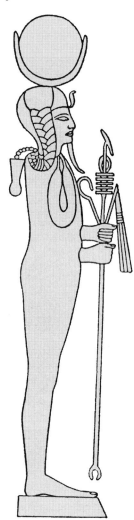

509. One of the Egyptian moon-gods, Khonsu, with his crescent-with-sun-disc crown. This is the motif of both Nanna/Sin and Utu/Shamash but may originally have represented the symbol for 'heaven'. The Egyptians often transformed the crescent into bull's horns – as in the case of the crowns of Hathor, the cow-goddess, and the Apis bull.

tradition which relates that the descendants of Noah came down from the mountains of Ararat to repopulate the Mesopotamian plain following the destruction of the pre-flood civilisation. At Uruk Enmerkar constructed a magnificent sacred precinct for his patron deity, the goddess Inanna. The epics tell us that Enmerkar introduced the worship of the goddess at Uruk. Inanna was the daughter of Ninhursag ('Mistress of the Mountain'), whose epithet was 'Mother of All the Living'. The divine mother and daughter's original home was Aratta at the heart of Eden, and Eden was the place where Hawwah (Eve) was queen over the Adamites. The book of Genesis retains a clue to Eve's true identity in the epithet which it accords to Adam's spouse:

> The man named his wife 'Hawwah' because she was **the mother of all the living**. [Genesis 3:20]

Eve was the great Sumerian fertility-goddess, Ninhursag, mother of Inanna.

Noah had three sons in all and we learn that they were the ancestors of many nations. We have been following the line of the eldest brother Ham, but it is important to remember that the Israelite line descended through Shem down ten generations to Abram of Ur who became the great biblical patriarch. According to the Septuagint and Samaritan versions of Genesis these 'ten generations' down to Abraham's adulthood lasted for around 1,000 years, bringing the wanderer Abraham and his followers down into the archaeological phase known as the MB I – that is the time when the Early Bronze Age came to a catastrophic end with the destruction by earthquake and fire of virtually all the great cities in the Levant. For a period of some years the cities lay abandoned, the people having returned to sedentary life out in the hills and valleys. Even Egypt succumbed and the Old Kingdom collapsed into anarchy. The Early Bronze Age kingdoms had come and gone but the story of Genesis continued on into the Middle Bronze Age and the arrival of Joseph in Egypt.

God's Land

Meanwhile, back on the Indian Ocean 1,000 years earlier, Meskiagkasher, his younger brothers and their followers had passed through the narrow straits which lead into, what we call today, the 'Red Sea'. In ancient times, however, the whole of the western side of the Indian Ocean and, in particular, the Persian Gulf was known as the Red Sea (the Erythraean Sea of the Greeks). Its waters were named after the mariners who first sailed upon them – the descendants of the red-ones from Tilman/the Garden of Eden. The desert island home from which they had embarked on their ocean journeys to Magan and Meluhha, and then later to Ethiopia and the Nile valley, was also named Tilmun/Dilmun as a direct link to the mythical kingdom of their primeval ancestor, Adamu.

In their own language these skilled mariner-traders were known as the Poen or Pun. At the entrance to the southern end of the Red Sea they established a port which would act as an emporium for the exotic produce of Africa and Arabia for centuries to come. The later pharaonic Egyptians called the place Poene or Pun(t) after its people. Here is where Meskiagkasher had come out of the sea by the shores of a mountainous land.

The Poen people have a long history which sees them colonising the eastern Mediterranean littoral where they founded new city-ports, two of which – the islands of Tyre and Arad – are named after their homeland islands of Tylos (from Tilmun) and Arad on Bahrain. The Greeks knew the Poen as the Poenike – the Phoenicians of classical times.

Several thousand years after their original migration from the Persian Gulf into the Mediterranean via the Red Sea they began to colonise the western Mediterranean and beyond along the Atlantic seaboard. In doing so they eventually found themselves up against the new power in the region – Rome. Thus began the 'Punic' wars between the Roman empire and Carthage. In this name we see the remnant of the ancient name of the Phoenician seafarers – the Pun or Poen. But again we must cast ourselves back to the beginning of the third millennium BC to find one of the elements of the Poen deciding to make their new home in the region of East Africa which was soon to become the Land of the Pharaohs.

Horus the Ruler

Amongst the followers of Meskiagkasher was his younger 'brother' – in his own right a strong and charismatic leader of men. He is the head of the falcon tribe – the descendants of Horus 'The Far Distant'. The Bible calls this new Horus-king 'Mizraim' but this name is, in reality, no more than an epithet. It means 'follower of Asra' or 'Asar' (Arabic *m-asr* with the Egyptian preposition *m* 'from'). Mizraim is merely m-Izra with the majestic plural ending 'im'. Likewise, that other great Semitic-speaking people – the Assyrians – called the country of the pharaohs 'Musri' (m-Usri). We thus learn that the Semitic name for Egypt – Masr (Arabic)/ Mizr (Hebrew)/Musri (Akkadian) – derives from an epithet for the leader of the Mesopotamian conquerors of the Nile valley.

510. A rock-drawing from the wadi behind Hierakonpolis (after M. A. Berger, 1992, p. 108). The bull above this predynastic boat may represent the ruler of ancient Nekhen. Later palettes show the king as wild bull destroying his enemies whilst the title 'wild bull of Thebes' (Egy. *Khaemwaset*) was much employed in the titulary of the New Kingdom pharaohs. Remember that 'wild bull' was also the major epithet of the archetypal hero-king of Mesopotamia – Gilgamesh.

511. You might be forgiven for thinking that this is an Egyptian relief of the winged sun-disc, however you would be wrong. It comes from the palace of Darius I at Susa. The Persians, Urartians, Hittites and Mesopotamians all employed this striking motif to represent their high sky-gods. The winged sun-disc was not an original invention of the Egyptians. Louvre Museum.

So this worshipper of Asra or Asar is a follower of one of Mesopotamia's most important deities – the god of fertility, magic and wisdom, Asar. In Mesopotamian mythology Asar was the son of Enki. Over the centuries he was to become the greatest deity of the Babylonian pantheon. I am referring to Marduk, the son of Ea. He was also, in all likelihood, one and the same as Ashur – the mighty eponymous god of the Assyrians whose holiest city was named after him. The symbol of Ashur was the winged sun-disc which had been appropriated from the sun-god Shamash (Sumerian Utu). It is also representative of the Persian god of the mountains – Ahurumazda – later worshipped by the Zoroastrians. Likewise, in Egypt the winged sun-disc is both the symbol of Horus and the sun-god in the form of Re-Harakhty ('Re-Horus of the Eastern Horizon').

Our Mesopotamian chieftain, Horus, is a worshipper of Asar and 'Asar' is how the ancient Egyptians wrote the name of their great god of the dead whom we know through the Greek form of his name – Osiris. Moreover, in Egyptian mythological tradition, Horus, the inheritor of the Egyptian throne, was the son of Osiris. He was thus 'the one who came from Asar' – that is m-Asr, the biblical Mizraim. Every modern Egyptian still calls himself 'el-Masri' – which we may thus translate as 'the one who is descended from Osiris'.

512. The chieftain with high plumes.

Land of Gold – *c.* 2900 BC

I want you to imagine yourself as an eye witness to a momentous event which took place sometime around 2900 BC.

You are a young, nomadic goatherd tending his flock on the eastern slopes of the mountains which hug the western shore of the Red Sea. One day, in the clear early-morning light of late spring, you spot the sails of boats on the distant southern horizon. A great fleet of around a dozen ships is approaching. Soon the black-hulled vessels have swung towards the beach below you. Foreign boats have come to these parts before to trade with your tribe for the mineral produce of the mountains where you live, but nothing on this scale has ever been seen before. Your anxiety grows as warriors carrying pear-shaped maces and bows leap into the

513. The Eastern Desert – a land of gold.

water and wade ashore. You spy their leader – a tall, powerful man whose stature is enhanced by two majestic plumes attached to a band of gold around his head. The grey heron feathers swirl in the breeze as he gesticulates to his men to drag the reed ships onto the beach. You run back to your encampment to tell your aged father what you have seen.

Having brought their fleet ashore, the Horus-king and his followers prepare a camp by the sea at a place which today is marked by the small fishing port of Mersa Alam. They had left their nearest kith and kin behind in Punt – the setting-off point for exploratory trading missions into Africa. But 'Horus' and his people were concerned with far greater things than establishing new trading links. Their mission was nothing less than the conquest and settlement of the Nile valley so as to seize control of its abundant natural wealth.

Over a one-hundred-year period the Dilmunites had been trading with the indigenous people of north-eastern Africa. The produce of this region, just like that of Meluhha, was much prized back in Sumer. Here were spices, incense, rare woods, ivory and exotic animal skins. But the greatest prize of all was the gold of Egypt's Eastern Desert. Expeditions had been sent before to mine this precious and prestigious metal. The sea route from Dilmun, via Punt, to Egypt was already well travelled.

The conditions in the eastern mountains which bordered the Red Sea were hard but not as inhospitable as they are today. The climate in the fourth millennium was wetter and the Eastern Desert plateau was then more like a dry savannah with its wadis, some with permanent water, capable of sustaining life. During the inundation season, the flood waters of the Nile, far to the west, penetrated deep into the desert along the main flat, wide-bodied wadis. In some years they may even have reached almost as far as the mountains – just a hundred kilometres or so from the shore of the Red Sea.

The Horus expedition had not set out, like its predecessors, simply to mine the gold of Wadi Barramiya. What you had witnessed arriving on the beach was something new. What you do not as yet realise is that the intent of the men in black ships is to establish a centre for mining operations in the Nile valley itself. King Horus is not merely looking to exploit Egypt's mineral wealth for the benefit of the folk back home. His plan is to establish a second flourishing kingdom – this time in the Nile valley. In the end Horus and his followers would succeed beyond their greatest expectations, for within a few generations his successors – the 'Followers of Horus' – ruled over a civilisation to rival anything the world had seen.

514. The high creator-god Atum, wearing the tall white crown of Upper Egypt from which grow ram's horns.

The Bold Strategy

The next day you return to your high vantage point with some of the elders of your tribe. Together you watch a strange ceremony in the camp of these people from the sea. You now see that there are females and children amongst the followers of the chieftain with the plumed headdress.

417

515. The Square-Boat People were to become the gods of ancient Egypt, remembered for their astonishing feat of dragging high-prowed ships across the desert from the Red Sea to the Nile valley. It was then quite natural for the Egyptians to invent a complex mythology of death which involved a return journey to the original island home of the primeval gods.

One woman in particular stands out. She is garlanded in necklaces and bracelets strung with bright blue stones, the likes of which you have never seen before. It is as if the very jewels of heaven had been gifted to her by the gods. Upon her head she wears a great golden disc supported between the horns of a bull. The warriors are all kneeling with arms raised towards the rising sun on the eastern horizon. The woman is performing a slow, graceful dance, weaving her way between them. Her arms are raised to mirror the curving upward thrust of the bull's horns of her crown. She spins slowly as if in a trance. Is she a priestess or a queen – perhaps both? You are terrified but, at the same time, fascinated by what you see. These people are similar in some respects to those who came to this land by ship before, but this time their leaders are more like gods than mere mortals.

The rituals complete, you watch the people of the sea break camp. You try to count them but with all the activity going on it proves impossible to get an accurate number. However, there are at least four hundred warriors plus all their camp followers.

Strange things are now happening down on the beach. The men are unfurling long lengths of thick reed-fibre rope. They attach two of these to each of the high prows of the black boats and trail them out in front of the vessels. Twenty men are assigned to each rope. They grasp them over their shoulders and begin to pull. A foreman claps out a slow rhythm to concentrate the pulling-power of the teams. The pilot of each vessel yells encouragement from his position at the prow of his ship. After an initial struggle the boats slowly begin to move. Within a short time the momentum is with the pullers as the great black boats begin to pick up speed on the soft sand. You can now see that, during the night, palm-logs had been attached to the undersides of the vessels to act as sledge runners and to prevent the bitumen-covered reed hulls from being torn on the stony desert ground.

The column of twelve high-prowed ships is heading for the open mouth of the wadi which heads west towards the Nile valley. You watch in awe as the column snakes its way into the mountain pass.

516. Dragging a huge battleship through the desert.

With every day that passes the 'square-boat people' progress further into the mountains. Ahead of the column a scout leads the way. He wears a wolf's pelt across his shoulders which appears to accord him special status. This wolfman seems to know his way through the labyrinth of wadis and canyons which make up the schist and sandstone hills. Perhaps he has been here before on an earlier mining expedition? His knowledge of the Eastern Desert truly makes him the 'Opener of the Ways' (Egy. *Wepwaut*) for the charismatic expedition leader and his followers.

At the centre of the column of ships is the biggest of all the foreign vessels. This is the flagship of the fleet and the boat which carries both the chieftain and his priestess-queen. In the middle of the deck stands a reed cabin and, behind it, a tall totem at the top of which is attached the symbol of the golden sun-disc resting on the crescent moon. The recumbent moon is just like a ship carrying the sun across the sky. You have been told by previous visitors from afar that this is the totem of a special god, known to his followers as Re-Harakhty.

A whole month passes by before the mountains have been cleared. The invaders have reached the western side just as the high flood of the Nile stretches out towards them across the flat terrain. Within a few days the inundation has reached the beached ships. Gently the high-prowed vessels are dragged into the shallow water. The crews and their families climb aboard and begin to punt their reed ships towards the deepest channel. Soon they are moving freely and slipping away into the distance. You never see them again but the memory of the giant ships and their human cargo remains with you all your life. Perhaps it was you and your young friends (or perhaps several generations of your tribe) who carved the images of the square-boat people upon the rocks where you rested in the shade whilst tending your flocks. I think you might be pleased to hear that your humble efforts at recording what you saw still remain today – a 5,000-year-old testimony to the most astonishing epic of ancient times.

517. The Opener of the Ways. One of the rock drawings from Site 26 shows a man with pointed beard and twin plumes standing at the prow of the boat as if navigating. He wears what appears to be a wolf's pelt with bushy tail. Could this be the original Wepwaut?

518. The new Followers of Horus.

Part Four

Reference Section

Appendices A to C
Acknowledgements
Abbreviations
Picture Sources
Bibliography
Notes & References
Index

Appendix A

THE NEW CHRONOLOGY FOR EARLY EGYPT

To complete the New Chronology for ancient Egypt we need to consider the four eras known as the Early Dynastic Period, the Old Kingdom, the First Intermediate Period and the Middle Kingdom up to the reign of Amenemhat III – the point which we reached in Volume One of *A Test of Time*. This total period covers Dynasties 1 through to 12.

So let us work our way backwards through those dynasties in order to try to establish their duration from the fragmentary information contained in the Royal Canon of Turin. I will be using the orthodox chronology (OC) dates as published by John Baines and Jaromir Malek in their *Atlas of Ancient Egypt* for comparison throughout this exercise.

(a) Completing the 12th Dynasty

Before the reign of Amenemhat III we find his father, Senuseret III, on the throne. As I argued in Chapter Fifteen of *A Test of Time*, there is strong evidence to suggest a lengthy co-regency of 20 years between Senuseret III and Amenemhat III. I therefore proposed that the two pharaohs were ruling together when the young Joseph arrived in Egypt and that Senuseret was still alive when his son (now playing the leading role in the co-regency) appointed Joseph as vizier. Senuseret III's reign thus began in 1700 BC, some 67 years before the end of the dynasty. The Royal Canon is reasonably well preserved at this point (Col. V, Lines 20 to 25) and the 12th Dynasty reign-lengths are pretty much intact. The following data is thus obtainable from the papyrus and the monuments:

	Royal Canon	Highest Regnal Date
Amenemhat I	29 (?) years	Year 30
Senuseret I	45 years	Year 44
Amenemhat II	10 + x years	Year 35
Senuseret II	19 years	Year 6
Senuseret III	30 + x years	Year 39
Amenemhat III	40 + x years	Year 45
Amenemhat IV	9 years	Year 6
Sobekneferu	3 years	Year 3

I think we can therefore establish, with reasonable certainty, the following reign-lengths giving us a total of 222 years for the dynasty.

Amenemhat I	29 full years
Senuseret I	45 years
Amenemhat II	34 full years
Senuseret II	19 years
Senuseret III	38 full years
Amenemhat III	45 full years
Amenemhat IV	9 years
Sobekneferu	3 years
Total	222 years

Interestingly enough, the Royal Canon has a summation line for the 12th Dynasty which gives a total of 'eight kings for 213 years'. How this figure is arrived at we cannot be absolutely certain but it is close to the figure calculated from the highest regnal dates of the monuments. This suggests something very interesting.

It seems clear from this total that the scribe of the Royal Canon was simply adding up the reign-lengths given in the original document from which he was copying or assembling his king list. He was not taking into account any overlaps brought about by co-regencies. Yet we know for certain that in the 12th Dynasty the co-regency mechanism was very much in practice. So the actual duration of the 12th Dynasty was considerably less than a simple summation of its parts. The totals 222 years (our calculation) or 213 years (the Royal Canon total) are overestimates by several decades. In reality, the latest best guesstimates for the lengths of the various known co-regencies reduce the total duration of the dynasty down to around 137 years. If we add this figure to our end-date of 1633 BC, we arrive at the neat round number of c. 1800 BC for the first regnal year of Amenemhat I and the start of the 12th Dynasty (OC – 1937 BC).

(b) The 11th Dynasty

Fortunately the Canon also gives us a total for the 11th Dynasty of 'six kings for 143 years' (Col. V, Line 18) – a datum which we can be more confident in using because we are now in the era prior to the invention of the co-regency. It was only with the assassination of Amenemhat I that the practice of co-regency was first established to ensure the royal succession from father to son. There is every reason to believe that Crown-Prince Senuseret had to suppress a palace *coup d'état* to secure his throne (as Senuseret I) following the murder of his father. The lesson was well learnt by the second ruler of the 12th Dynasty and, from then on, the crown-princes of his line were appointed co-regents whilst their fathers were still alive.

Accepting the 143-year total for the 11th Dynasty as recorded in the Royal Canon, the New-Chronology dates for that dynasty would therefore be 1943 to 1800 BC (OC – 2080-1937 BC).

The 11th Dynasty was based at Thebes and for the first part of its existence was contemporary with a rival line of kings ruling from the city of Herakleopolis in the Faiyum.

(c) The 9th and 10th Dynasties

We learn from Manetho that these two dynasties (the one following on from the other) had their dynastic seat at Herakleopolis. The Royal Canon lists eighteen (perhaps nineteen) rulers of the 10th Dynasty (Manetho gives nineteen). As Egyptologists understand it, this entire line was roughly contemporary with the 11th Dynasty in Thebes. The earlier Herakleopolitan 9th Dynasty was then contemporary with the plethora of minor rulers who set up petty kingdoms along the Nile valley following the collapse of the Old Kingdom – perhaps actually towards the end of the incredibly long reign of Pepy II (94 years). These minor kings belong to Manetho's 7th and 8th Dynasties. In terms of our calculations, the 9th and 10th Dynasty add nothing to our total because they were entirely contemporary in one way or another.

(d) The 8th Dynasty

This dynasty represents the era of political confusion just referred to when the unified Egyptian state collapsed towards the end of the 6th Dynasty. It is because of this collapse that the era from the start of Dynasty 8 to the middle of Dynasty 11 (when Egypt was reunified under Mentuhotep II) is referred to as the First Intermediate Period.

The Royal Canon appears to give a total of 100 years for the 8th Dynasty in a summary line which is unfortunately badly damaged and therefore difficult to interpret. Manetho (Eusebius version) does, in fact, attribute 100 years to Dynasty 8. However, Egyptologists tend to assign just a couple of decades to Dynasties 7 and 8 together which I believe may be rather too radical a revision and contradicts the evidence outlined above. I would prefer to make use of the total at Column IV, Line 15 in the Royal Canon and assign a total of 100 years to this dynasty. We thus arrive at a start-date for the 8th Dynasty of *c.* 2043 (OC – 2150-2134 BC).

(e) The 6th and 7th Dynasties

On our journey back through time we have now reached the Old Kingdom and the 'Pyramid Age' proper. This is the era of Khufu of the Great Pyramid and Djoser of the Step Pyramid – the age of huge monumental undertakings but sadly almost entirely bereft of history. We have all the monuments to demonstrate the power and conviction of the pharaonic state but very little documentation to fill in the political history of this astonishing time.

It came to a close with the six ineffectual rulers of the 7th Dynasty who succeeded the female pharaoh, Nitokerty (Manetho's Queen Nitocris), the last ruler of the 6th Dynasty. According to the Royal Canon, the two dynasties lasted a total of 181 years (Col. IV, Line 14). This takes us back to *c.* 2224 BC for the first regnal year of Teti I, founder of the 6th Dynasty (the OC assigns the 6th Dynasty dates of 2323-2150 BC).

(f) The 5th Dynasty

The Royal Canon lists nine kings for the 5th Dynasty with the reign-lengths of seven still preserved. The sum of these seven is 96 years ($7+12+x+7+x+11+8+28+30=96$). This leaves us with two reign-lengths which we must estimate before we can arrive at an approximate date for the start of the dynasty. So, what should we establish as an average reign-length for this period? The best way to obtain this working figure is to add together all the extant regnal figures in the Royal Canon from the 5th Dynasty back to the 1st Dynasty. The grand total can then be divided by the number of kings represented by this figure to achieve an average reign-length.

The total number of regnal years which are preserved amounts to 302 from twenty-one reigns. Thus 302 divided by 21 gives us an average of 14.4 years for each ruler. If we then round this up to 15 years we can assign that average reign-length to our two 5th-Dynasty rulers who are lacking extant dates and arrive at a total duration for the dynasty. Thus 30 years must be added to our original 96 years for the other seven pharaohs to give us a total of 126 years. The 5th Dynasty therefore began in *c.* 2350 BC (OC – 2465-2323 BC).

(g) The 4th Dynasty

Again the Royal Canon supplies us with useful data. This time there are six extant reign-lengths out of eight which together total 79 years ($24+23+8+x+x+18+4+2=79$). If we allow another 30 years for the two missing regnal figures, we arrive at a total for the dynasty of 109 years. Thus the 4th Dynasty – the era of the Giza Pyramids – began in *c.* 2459 BC (OC – 2575-2465 BC).

(h) The 3rd Dynasty

The Royal Canon has four kings of the 3rd Dynasty ruling for 19, 6, 6 and 24 years respectively, adding up to a total of 55 years. Thus, Djoser – the builder of the Step Pyramid and the first king of the line according to the Canon – began his reign in 2514 BC (OC – 2630 BC).

(i) The 2nd Dynasty

Just two dynasties to go and we will have secured our New-Chronology date for the start of pharaonic history. We have now passed from the Old Kingdom (Dynasties 3 to 7) and moved back into the Early Dynastic or Thinite Period (Dynasties 1 and 2), sometimes also called the Archaic Period. Unfortunately the Royal Canon of Turin is badly damaged at this point and we will need to rely more on our average reign-length of 15 years to fill in the missing details.

The Canon gives the names of ten kings of the 2nd Dynasty but only four reign-lengths are preserved. They add up to 65 years $(x+x+x+x+x+x+8+11+27+19=65)$. If we allow a further 90 years (six reigns x 15 years) we arrive at an approximate start-date for this dynasty of *c.* 2669 BC (OC – 2770-2650 BC).

(j) The 1st Dynasty

The regnal data for the very first dynasty is non-existent – the section where the reign-lengths were recorded having been lost. Only the names of the eight kings survive. So we are entirely reliant on our average reign-length to determine the duration of the dynasty. A total of eight kings for 15 years each gives us a dynasty duration of 120 years and therefore a start date for pharaonic civilisation of 2789 BC (OC – 2920-2770 BC).

However, there is still one year-total from the Royal Canon which I have not employed. Line 17 of Column IV informs us that 955 years had elapsed between the reign of Menes, founder of the 1st Dynasty, and the start of the 10th Dynasty. We have worked out that the 10th Dynasty began in *c.* 1943 BC (roughly at the same time as the contemporary 11th Dynasty). If we add 955 years to 1943 BC we arrive at a date of 2898 BC for Year 1 of Menes. This, of course, is some 109 years earlier than the date we have calculated working back through the dynasties. At this time I have no real answer to this discrepancy other than to suggest that, if the scribe who drew up the Canon was adding together regnal figures as if they were all sequential (as is obviously the case with the 12th Dynasty), there is a chance that he might have done the same for the confused period of the 8th and 9th Dynasties which we know to have been contemporary.

Appendix B

SARGON II'S YEAR 8 CAMPAIGN

Sargon II campaigned against Urartu in his 8th year and, in doing so, crossed the River Aratta as he entered the land of the Mannai. It is logical to assume that the Aratta river flowed through the kingdom of Aratta and so it is important to determine the route-of-march of the Assyrian army if we are to confirm the location of Aratta in the Miyandoab plain.

Sargon set off eastwards from his capital, Kalhu (modern Nimrud), with a great army and crossed the two fast-flowing streams of the Tigris – the Greater and Lesser Zabs – flowing down from Eden. He then entered the foothills of the Zagros (near modern Kirkuk) and, just to the north of Suleimaniya, passed around Mount Kullar (Kollara Dagh) into the land of Zamua and then up through the Babite mountain pass.

> In the month of Duzu ... I departed from Kalhu, my royal city, and had a rough passage across the Greater Zab at its flood. On the third day ... I caused the armies of Shamash and Marduk to jump across

> the Lesser Zab, whose crossing was (also) difficult … I entered into the passes of Mount Kullar, a high mountain range in the land of the Lullumi which they call the land of Zamua. [Lines 6-11]

The Assyrian invasion force slashed its way through the dense forests of the Zagros and crossed over seven named mountains (none of which can really be identified today). However, it seems clear from their setting-off point that they were using the now well-worn caravan route which crosses the mountains through the Bana Pass.

> I marched between Mount Nikippa and Mount Upa, high mountains, covered with all kinds of trees, whose surface was a jungle, whose passes were frightful, over whose area shadows stretch as in a cedar forest, the traveller of whose paths never sees the light of the sun. The Buia river, which (flows) between them, I crossed … Mount Simirria, a large mountain peak, which stands out like the blade of a lance, … Sinahulzi and Biruatti, mighty mountains … Turtani, Sinabir, Ahshura and Suia – these seven mountains I crossed with much difficulty. [Lines 15-29]

Finally, Sargon and his army descended from the mountains and poured into the plain of the Manneans. But just before the Assyrian king reached the kingdom of the Mannean ruler, Ullusunu, his army crossed two rivers.

> I crossed the Rappa and **Aratta** (Akk. *A-rat-ta-a*), streams flowing by their bases at high water, as (though they were) irrigation ditches. Against Surikash, a district of the Mannean country which borders on the lands of Karalla and Allabria, I descended. [Lines 30-31]

As Sargon's army descended from the mountain pass, its route of march intersected the south-to-north road along which Enmerkar's envoy had travelled. The two caravan routes converge into a single road at the town of Sakkez, just to the south of the Miyandoab plain. Izirtu, an important Mannean city, is generally recognised as being located in the area of Sakkez. This major ancient highway then heads north towards Lake Urmia. So the Rappa and Aratta rivers appear to have been to the north of the road junction at Sakkez. Indeed, cutting through the modern town is a major tributary of the Zarrineh Rud ('Golden River') which heads eastwards to join the main stream flowing down from Takht-é Suleiman. During the spring thaw this fast-flowing watercourse is a clear barrier to anyone travelling north into the Miyandoab plain.

A few kilometres further on the plain – what the Enmerkar poem calls the 'edin' – is finally reached. However, the traveller is immediately confronted by another wide river – the modern Simineh Rud ('Silver River') – whose crossing is at the small town of Bukan.

Are these the two rivers mentioned by Sargon as he descended into Mannean territory? This seems very likely because they are the *only* major rivers in the region. The first river crossed by Sargon was the Rappa which must therefore be the western stream of the Zarrineh Rud. This leaves the Simineh Rud as the River Aratta. The two watercourses then sweep northwards to become the main arteries of the Miyandoab plain.

Down at the heart of that plain is the modern city of Miyandoab, the ancient capital of the Mannean kingdom. As its name implies, the city 'between the two waters' is located with the Simineh Rud immediately to the west and the Zarrineh Rud to the east. Miyandoab was therefore located at the heart of the kingdom of Aratta, the river of like-name flowing to its west and the 'Golden River' to its east.

We need briefly to return to Sargon's Year 8 military campaign in order to confirm that the Assyrian king was definitely ravaging and plundering his way through the plain of Miyandoab. His report to the god Ashur goes on to explain in gory detail how he met the armies of Ursa of Urartu and Metatti of Zikirtu on the southern slopes of Mount Uash. Scholars are generally agreed in identifying Uash with the impressive volcanic peak of Mount Sahand, lying to the north-east of Miyandoab. The battle took place near the village of Malekan ('Guardian-Angels'). The slaughter of the combined Urartian and Zikurtan forces was terrible to behold as the Assyrian victors pursued their defeated foe into the high valleys of the Sahand massif and eastwards into the heartland of Zikirtu (which we have identified as biblical Havilah).

> On Mount Uash, a great mountain, which (lifts) its summit into the region of the clouds, in the midst of heaven,… [Ursa] assembled his fighters, strong in battle … I, Sargon, king of the four regions, ruler of Assyria, … plunged into his midst like a swift javelin. I defeated him and turned back his advance. I killed large numbers of his troops; the bodies of his warriors I cut down like millet, filling the mountain valleys (with them). I made their blood run down the ravines and precipices like a river, dyeing the plain, countryside and highlands red like a royal robe. … in the midst of Uash mountain … I filled the gullies and gorges with their horses while they, like ants in distress, made their way over most difficult trails. In the heat of my terrible weapons I went up after them, filling the ascents and descents with the corpses of (their) warriors. Over twelve hours of ground, from Mount Uash to Mount Zimur, the jasper mountain, I pursued him at the point of the lance. … Adad, the violent (storm god), the powerful son of Anu (god of the heavens), let loose his fierce tempest against them and, with bursting cloud and thunderbolt, he annihilated them. [Lines 96-147]

Ursa, lord of Urartu, fled towards his strongholds around Van leaving the door wide open for Sargon to march into eastern Urartu unopposed. His defeat of Zikirtu complete, Sargon descended from the heights of Sahand/Uash and regrouped at the city of Uishdish (modern Maragheh). He then marched his army through the Sahand massif and entered the Adji Chay valley. There he immediately took the town of Ushkaia which Sargon calls 'the outer frontier of Urartu', rasing its strong walls to the ground. Scholars have suggested that Ushkaia is none other than the modern town of Uski (sometimes written Osku) which nestles on the northern slopes of Sahand.

The Assyrian army then crossed the wide plain of Dalaia. There, in the middle of the plain, Sargon's men destroyed the walled cities of Tawri (Tabriz, previously Tawris) and Tarmakisa before moving on around the northern shore of Lake Urmia and into the heartland of Ursa's kingdom.

> From Uishdish I departed … I drew near to the city of Ushkaia, the great fortress on the outer frontier of Urartu, which bars the pass into the Zaranda district like a door … and stands out on Mount Mallu, the cypress mountain, like a boundary-(stone) and robed in radiance, over the plain of the land of Subi. … With the advance of my mighty arms, I went up into that fortress, carried off its over-flowing wealth, and brought it into my camp. Its great wall, whose foundation platform was founded on the bedrock of the mountain and whose thickness measured eight cubits, … I destroyed it com-pletely, … From Ushkaia I departed, … Tawri and Tarmakisa, strong walled cities, situated in the plain of the land of the Dalaia, where he

(Ursa) had great supplies of grain, whose walls were very strong, whose outer walls were well built, whose moats were very deep and completely surrounded them; … the people who live in that district saw the deeds of my royal (valor) which I accomplished against the cities of their neighbours, and were terrified. They left their cities and fled into an arid region, a place of thirst, like the desert, and (so) sought to save their lives. [Lines 167-193]

Between this fertile plain and Lake Urmia lay Sargon's 'arid region, a place of thirst' – surely the vast expanse of salt flats which make up the Adji Chay delta. Sargon's 'land of the Dalaia' is probably the flat plain around Yanik Tepe adjacent to those salt marshes.

Appendix C

THE NEW CHRONOLOGY OF EARLY MESOPOTAMIA

The easiest way to understand the New Chronology time-line for early Mesopotamia is to constantly refer to the charts (on pages 431 and 432) as we progress backwards through time. These charts provide the key synchronisms and astronomical anchor points which tie reigns and dynasties to each other. As you will see very little is actually 'floating' and the margins (at least in the period back to Ur I) are fairly tight.

Let us begin by establishing our starting point – the first regnal year of king Ammisaduga of the Babylon I Dynasty.

The period from Sargon I to the end of Babylon I

In *A Test of Time* Volume One I explained the 'Venus Solution' – how Ammisaduga can be fixed in time by means of astronomical retrocalculation. Rather than go through all that again, I will simply summarise the conclusions here.

(a) A series of documents – astronomical observations of the rising and setting of Venus and a collection of twenty-five contracts made on the thirtieth day of the lunar month during particular years in Ammisaduga's reign – give astronomers an opportunity to compare these ancient observations/calendar dates with actual astronomical events as calculated by computer astronomy programs.

(b) The alternative dates on offer from the various historical chronologies are called 'Venus Solutions' (VS). The 'High' conventional date for Year 1 of Ammisaduga is 1702 BC. The 'Middle' conventional date is 1646 BC. And the 'Low' date is 1582 BC. The New Chronology date, on the other hand, is even lower at 1419 BC.

(c) There is a test we can do to decide which is the correct date on astronomical grounds. The thirty-day lunar months recorded in the twenty-five contracts fall in a sequence. If a contract which dates to Day 30 is found – through retrocalculation – to fall on a twenty-nine-day lunar month, then it must be regarded as a 'miss' and go against a particular Venus Solution. To get an exact match the Venus Solution must produce twenty-five correspondences ('hits') between the recorded observations and the retrocalculations. The higher the number of hits, the stronger the case for a Venus Solution being chronologically correct.

(d) The 'High' VS has twenty out of twenty-five hits (5 misses). The 'Middle' VS scores just fourteen hits (11 misses). The 'Low' VS fares little better with eighteen hits (7 misses). But the New Chronology gets an amazing twenty-three hits (2 misses) – a ninety per cent accuracy rate. The remaining two misses may have been caused by cloud cover which prevented an accurate observation by the ancient astronomers who, having failed to observe the new crescent moon, ascribed thirty days to the previous month by mistake.

(e) This makes Venus Solution 1419 BC by far the most likely historical date for the first year of King Ammisaduga of Babylon.

Having demonstrated the strength of the New Chronology date for Year 1 of Ammisaduga, we can now retrocalculate the start of the Babylon I Dynasty to 1667 BC, using the regnal dates supplied in the Babylonian King List A.

Contemporary records from the reign of Hammurabi (four reigns before Ammisaduga) inform us that the king of Babylon defeated Rimsin of Larsa and brought an end to the Larsa Dynasty. This secures the end-date for Larsa at 1536 BC. Using the Sumerian King List we can then arrive at a date for the beginning of the Larsa royal line at 1798 BC.

Contemporary with the dynasty of Larsa was a line of kings based at their capital of Isin. The Isin Dynasty came to an end with the capture of their city by Sinmuballit, the predecessor of Hammurabi in Babylon. Because the dates for Babylon I are fixed by the 1419 BC Venus Solution and the Babylonian King List, it is a simple matter to determine that Isin fell in 1569 BC. Again, using the Sumerian King List, we arrive at a start-date for the Isin Dynasty of 1805 BC.

The first king of Isin was Ishbierra and ancient documents record that he was a contemporary of the last ruler of the Third Dynasty of Ur – Ibbisin. An omen tablet mentions a lunar eclipse on the 14th day of Addaru (mid-March to mid-April). The omen heralds the end of the Ur III Dynasty.

> The prediction is given for the king of the world. The destruction of Ur; the destruction of the city walls will occur; the heaping up of barley; the devastation of the city and its environs.

Astronomical retrocalculation, using computer programmes specifically designed for the purpose, reveal that a lunar eclipse did take place above the city of Ur on the 19th of April in 1793 BC. This astronomical date is entirely consistent with the date we have determined for Ibbisin through his contemporaneity with Ishbierra of Isin. So we may fix the last year of Ibbisin and therefore the end of Ur III to 1793 BC.

I should just briefly explain that the omen tablets are based on real observations and historical events. They are later texts which the soothsayer-priests compiled from original data held in their temple archives. This enabled them to predict a political event if the astronomical event which originally preceded its first occurrence should recur sometime in the future. In other words, if astronomical event X were to happen again, then political event Y attached to that celestial event was bound to occur again just as it had done the first time around. You can understand why the *baru*-priests – the specialists in omen interpretation and so knowledgeable about past events – were such an important influence on political decisions in Mesopotamia.[1] They held the secret knowledge of the cycles of history which were attached, they believed, to the cycles of the heavenly bodies.

The Sumerian King List gives a total dynasty length for Ur III of 108 years. Thus Ur III began in 1900 BC. The end of the reign of King Shulgi, another king of Ur III, is presaged by another lunar eclipse omen.

> If an eclipse occurs on the 14th day of Simanu (mid-May to mid-June) ... The prediction is given for Ur and the king of Ur. The King of Ur will experience famine; there will be many deaths; the king of Ur, his son will wrong his father ... he will die in the place of mourning of his father; the son of the king will seize the throne.

Scholars have understood this omen as referring to the end of Shulgi when just such events are recorded. We can confirm we are correct in our chronology because the lunar eclipse of the omen text did indeed happen on the 31st of July 1835 BC. This is exactly the last year of Shulgi retrocalculated from our end date for Ur III of 1793 BC.

We can now link the beginning of Ur III with the end of a line of rulers from Uruk. Utuhegal, the sole ruler of Uruk V according to the Sumerian King List, records that Urnammu was governor of Ur (i.e. city ruler) during his short reign at Uruk. This makes the two rulers contemporary. Utuhegal's reign must have fallen in the period from 1900 to 1883 BC when we have determined Urnamu was ruling in Ur. But we can be much more accurate than that because we have another lunar eclipse omen to call upon.

> If an eclipse (of the moon) occurs on the 14th day of Duzu (mid-June to mid-July) ... The prediction is given for the king of the Gutians; there will be a downfall of Guti in battle; the land will be totally laid waste.

This text enables us to kill two birds with one stone. Not only does it pin down the reign of Utuhegal, the vanquisher of Tirigan, the last ruler of the dynasty of Gutium, but it also gives us the end-date of the Gutium royal line. Amazingly, an ancient text survives which suggests that a strange celestial portent did occur on the night before the great battle between Utuhegal's army and the forces of Tirgan. The astronomical retrocalculation gives us the very lunar eclipse we are looking for. It occurred on the 28th of June 1889 BC – the date when the hegemony of the Guti was overthrown by the last king of Uruk.

According to the SKL the Gutium Dynasty endured for ninety-one years and so we can place its start in 1982 BC. Likewise the Uruk IV Dynasty, which preceded Utuhegal, is accorded thirty years by the SKL and its beginning can therefore be established at around 1922 BC.

There are two synchronisms between the Gutium Dynasty and the famous dynasty of Sargon I, which is variously referred to as the Dynasty of Agade, the Sargonic Dynasty or the Agadean Dynasty. I will refer to it as the Dynasty of Agade (the name of Sargon's capital city in Sumerian). The first synchronism falls in the period following the death of King Sharkalisharri of Agade when there was a power struggle for the throne of Agade. At this point in the SKL we find the cryptic remark:

> Who was king? Who was not king? Was Igigi king? Was Nanum king? Was Imi king? Was Elulu king? Their tetrad was king and reigned for three years! [Col. vii, Lines 1-7]

Only one of these political combatants for the throne is known to us. He is Elulu, the king of the Guti, listed in the Gutium Dynasty as Elulumesh. The three-year interregnum when several rulers vied for control of Agade can be placed in the years 1958 to 1956 BC. This New Chronology date for the period of chaos following the death of Sharkalisharri is confirmed by yet another astronomical omen text.

> If an eclipse occurs on the 14th day of Nisannu (mid-April to mid-May) ... [The prediction is given] for Agade; [the king] of Agade will

The New Chronology
from Agade to Babylon I

Agade
2100 BC

Sargon

Rimush

Naramsin

Sharkalisharri

1959 BC

Interregnum

Shudurul

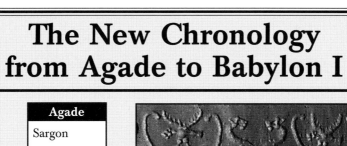

Gutium

Imta

Sarlagab

Elulumesh

Tirigan

519. Entwined long-necked leopards from the Uruk Period and characteristic of Nakada III art. British Museum.

Sarlagab temp. Sharkalisharri.

Lunar eclipse (Mar. 27) of 1959 BC. Elulu[mesh] in Agade.

Uruk IV
Umigin
Urutu

Uruk V
Utuhegal

Ur III
1900 BC
1889 BC
Urnammu

Shulgi

1835 BC
Bursin

Ibbisin

1793 BC

Lunar eclipse (Jun. 28) of 1889 BC.

Lunar eclipse (July 31) of 1835 BC – end of Shulgi.

Larsa

Naplanum

Gungunum

Sumuel

Rimsin

Isin

Ishbiirra

Urninurta

Damiklishu

Ishbiirra temp. Ibbisin.
Lunar eclipse (Apr. 19) of 1793 BC.

Joseph in Egypt from 1683 BC.

Babylon I
1667 BC
Sumuabu

Sinmuballit
1569 BC
Hammurabi
1536 BC
Ammiditana
1419 BC
Ammisaduga
1362 BC
Samsuditana

Sinmuballit captures Isin in 1569 BC.

Hammurabi defeats Rimsin in 1536 BC.

Israelite Exodus from Egypt in 1447 BC.
Venus Solution Year 1 Ammisaduga = 1419 BC.

Double solar (Feb. 25) and lunar (Mar. 12) eclipse of 1362 BC.

The New Chronology from Ur I to Uruk III

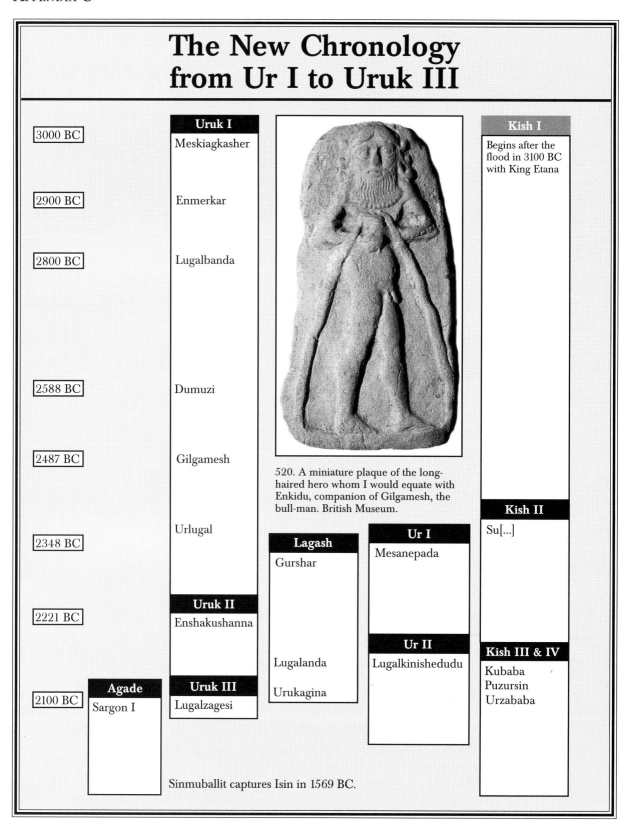

3000 BC	
2900 BC	
2800 BC	
2588 BC	
2487 BC	
2348 BC	
2221 BC	
2100 BC	

Uruk I
Meskiagkasher

Enmerkar

Lugalbanda

Dumuzi

Gilgamesh

Urlugal

Uruk II
Enshakushanna

Uruk III
Lugalzagesi

520. A miniature plaque of the long-haired hero whom I would equate with Enkidu, companion of Gilgamesh, the bull-man. British Museum.

Lagash
Gurshar

Lugalanda

Urukagina

Ur I
Mesanepada

Ur II
Lugalkinishedudu

Kish I
Begins after the flood in 3100 BC with King Etana

Kish II
Su[...]

Kish III & IV
Kubaba
Puzursin
Urzababa

Agade
Sargon I

Sinmuballit captures Isin in 1569 BC.

432

die, but his people will be well; the reign of Agade will fall into anarchy, (but) its future will be good.

After the anarchy, immediately following the death of Sharkalisharri, the Dynasty of Agade did indeed recover with the accession of King Dudu who reigned for twenty-one years. The lunar eclipse which presaged the death of Sharkalisharri was that which occurred on the 27th of March 1959 BC – precisely the year which we have determined preceded the first year of anarchy in 1958 BC.

The SKL informs us that the Dynasty of Agade lasted for 181 years. Thus, with the data from the astronomical retrocalculations we can work out that it came to an end in 1920 BC and began in 2100 BC – again a nice round number which is easy to remember.

So the pivotal reign of Sargon I, which marked the end of the Sumerian era and heralded in the new age of the Agadean Period, can be set at 2100 BC. The conventional dates for the start of the Dynasty of Agade are High – 2370 BC, Middle – 2334 BC and Low – 2300 BC. The New Chronology date is therefore two centuries lower than the lowest conventional date at this point.

The Early Dynastic Period

Prior to his accession Sargon was the cup-bearer to King Urzababa of Kish in the latter's 37th year. The last five rulers of the Kish IV Dynasty were thus contemporary with the reigns of Sargon, Rimush and Manishtushu in Agade. With Urzababa's Year 37 falling just prior to the Sargon's accession we can place Year 1 of Urzababa in about 2138 BC and the start of Kish IV (beginning of the 25-year reign of Puzursin) in 2163 BC.

Another dynasty – Uruk III – can also be tied to the reign of Sargon I. In Sargon's 13th year he defeats Lugalzagesi of Uruk III bringing an end to the latter's 25-year reign. Lugalzagesi was the only ruler of the dynasty, so Uruk III began in 2112 BC and Uruk II ended in 2113 BC.

The last ruler of Uruk II was Lugalkisalsi who was also the second king of the Ur II dynasty. His reign in Uruk and Ur was probably contemporary, thus we can estimate the start of Ur II in around 2171 BC.

We have now reached the era when dating is much more difficult because we have no astronomical checks which we can call upon and the king-list regnal data is often damaged. Dates from now on therefore become approximations.

Lugalzagesi's rise to kingship in Uruk is as a direct result of his defeat of Urukagina, the last ruler of Lagash. During the latter part of Urukagina's reign Lugalzagesi was actually the En ('lord') of Umma when Lugalkisalsi was ruling in Uruk and Ur. The end of the Lagash dynasty coincided with the defeat of Urukagina in 2112 BC and began (very approximately) in 2341 BC.

The end of Uruk II falls in the year before the accession of Lugalzagesi which we have determined as 2112 BC. Uruk II thus began in around 2221 BC. This takes us back to the end of Uruk I – the dynasty of Meskiagkasher, Enmerkar and Gilgamesh – but here we also reach the era of the fantastical reign-lengths. The reigns of the last seven rulers of the dynasty are all normal (30, 15, 9, 8, 36, 6 and 36 years from Urlugal to Lugalkitun) but, then, before Urlugal we find Gilgamesh with 128 years, Dumuzi with 100 years, Lugalbanda with 1200 years, Enmerkar with 420 years and Meskiagkasher with 324 years. All this makes the chronology of Uruk I very difficult to determine. Ur I, on the other hand, ends in 2172 BC and begins in around 2348 BC which becomes the earliest historical date in the New Chronology of Mesopotamia when it marks the start of the Early Dynastic III Period.

ACKNOWLEDGEMENTS

A number of colleagues and associates have greatly helped in the preparation of this second volume in the *A Test of Time* series, all of which deserve my gratitude. Their talents range widely across the academic disciplines as well as technical and creative skills. I can say, without exaggeration, that their support and encouragement has made a difficult and challenging adventure a great deal more doable than it first appeared in 1995 when the *Legend* project got under way.

It is the standard practice with works of a controversial nature to make it clear to the reader that the ideas expressed here are not necessarily to be regarded as the views of those who have helped me in the making of this book.

My first thanks must go to Peter van der Veen for his constant assistance on matters of Old Testament research, as well as to one of scholarship's recognised specialists in languages and their contextualisation, Dr Penelope Hall, for her encouragement and advice. I am also grateful to Dr John Milsom of University College London Geophysics Department for his help in gathering information on the physical geography and mineral resources of the Zagros mountains and Armenian plateau.

My researcher, Alda Watson, has been busy gathering material on the widest range of subjects, from the natural habitat of the Madonna Lily to the births and deaths of numerous scholars. Thank you Alda for all your time and energy.

During the last twenty-four months I have undertaken several expeditions into the geographical regions discussed in *Legend*. The logistics of such adventures are extremely complex but I was fortunate enough to have brilliant support teams to ensure safe passage through the mountains and deserts. The person who found himself in charge of all these adventures was Michael Ackroyd, Operations Director of Ancient World Tours, who put together all the transport and accommodation, as well as organising the ground support teams and travelling with me on several of the journeys. It is true to say that without Michael's unstinting efforts it would not have been possible to transport you to the wondrous landscapes of *Legend* through its many photographs and descriptive narratives. Michael, thank you so much for everything you did to make those spectacular journeys happen.

I should also thank my longtime friend Peter Allingham, Managing Director of AWT, for allowing Michael to devote so much of his time to the *Legend* project. Peter and I have also put together a number of tours for the coming year to Iran and the Eastern Desert of Egypt so that readers of this book have the opportunity to examine the evidence for themselves first hand. So, if you are interested in joining one of the journeys to Eden or participating in an Eastern Desert survey in search of the Followers of Horus, you can write to Ancient World Tours at PO Box 12950, London W6 8GY, UK, for details.

In Iran we were extremely fortunate to have the support of Pasargad Tours as ground agents. In Egypt we were in the expert hands of Pan Arab Tours who

521. The Pan Arab support team for the February 1998 Followers of Horus expedition, lined up in front of Kanais temple.

provided a marvellous team of four-wheel-drive desert vehicles and drivers. A very special thank-you is due to Ahmed Mousa, head of Pan Arab, who went with us on the first two expeditions organised through his company in order to ensure our every need and, above all, safety.

Next follows a long list of names which represents the volunteer members of the Eastern Desert Survey, sponsored by AWT and ISIS: Jane Williams, Jane Ford, Malcolm Gay, Ian Matthews, Doug Flower, Keith Scarterfield, Julie Colburn, Stephen Holmes, Simon Cox, Ditas Rohl, Michael Ackroyd, Tony Judd, Richard Morrow, William Dixon, Peter Dixon, Corran Crawford, Francis Lankester, Peter Cherry, Colin Thomas, Valerie Felton and Shirley Greenfield. Their important work in recording the rock-art of the Square-Boat People will undoubtedly prove to be of considerable importance to Egyptological studies in years to come. The work of the Eastern Desert Survey will be published in the year 2000 by the Institute for the Study of Interdisciplinary Sciences (ISIS). Copies will be made available through the ISIS Treasurer, Mike Rowland, 127 Porter Road, Basingstoke, Hants, RG22 4JT, UK. If you would like to follow up on the New Chronology debate or other aspects of my research you may wish to enrol as a member of ISIS by writing to Mike at the same address.

In Bahrain we had the assistance of Bahrain International Travel who arranged our accommodation and transport. Thank you Chandra Warnakul-asuriya and Jude Halahackone. I am also very grateful to Ali Hassan Follad and Mirza al-Nasheet from the Ministry of Cabinet Affairs & Information and the Director of the Bahrain National Museum, Abdulrahman Saud Musameh, for all their help and courtesy during our stay. The management of the Royal Meridien in Manama were also kind enough to permit me to take photographs of their beautiful recreation of paradisiacal Dilmun in the grounds of the hotel.

Many friends (too many to mention) have encouraged and supported me over the three years spent researching and writing this book. Four deserve special mention.

I have been fortunate to retain the computing and communications expertise of Edward Rogers who has regularly been over to sort out my overworked computer groaning under the weight of gigabytes of text, pictures and graphics. Time to get a new system I think.

Aegean pottery specialist and archaeologist, Vronwy Hankey, sadly passed away whilst I was away on my last trip to Iran. She had always been enthusiastically supportive of an interdisciplinary approach to Near Eastern studies and was a great personal friend. Those who were privileged to know this remarkable scholar will sadly miss her.

Vronwy's daughter-in-law, Julie Hankey, has been preparing a fascinating biography of her grandfather, Arthur Weigall, which she was kind enough to allow me to read in manuscript form. Julie also gave me permission to reproduce the snap taken by Hortense Weigall of Arthur on his favourite camel during their trip to the Wadi Abbad. I trust that Weigall's biography will be published in due course as it gives a marvellous insight into one of Egyptology's most intuitive archaeologists.

I must also thank Heather Walker for sending me a photograph of her late husband, Reginald Walker, so that I could include it in the book.

David Ellis of the Genesis Laboratory has been a strong supporter of my work since he became acquainted with the New Chronology through *A Test of Time* Volume One. I look forward to working more closely with Genesis in the coming years as we put together an international lecture-tour programme. If you belong to a group, church or society which would like to hear first hand about the New Chronology and its implications for our understanding of the Old Testament, you can write to David at Genesis Laboratory, C.A.C. – Waterloo, Secker Street, London, SE1 8UF, UK.

I have been very fortunate to have retained the services of copy editor Kate Truman and my *A Test of Time* editor, Mark Booth. Mark possesses a great talent for clarifying the complex and gently persuading his authors to explain what may seem obvious to an ancient historian but might not be so straightforward to the lay-reader. His personal assistant, Liz Rawlinson, has also been a valuable co-ordinator on this very complex publication project, whilst Barry Featherstone continues to be the foundation of professionalism and quality control which is so important to a book of this nature. Indeed, thanks must go out to all the staff and directors at my publishers in the UK, Century, for their faith in me and their patience during the extended gestation period of this book.

Jonathan Harris of Associated Publicity Holdings has been my literary agent ever since I first conceived of the idea of the *A Test of Time* series of books. Over those years he has paid for more lunches than he has earned in agency commission. Thank you Jonathan for all your support and encouragement – especially during those times of self-doubt and frustration when a quiet word dished out along with several plates of *dim sun* did so much to revive my spirits.

Finally, once again I have to thank my wife Ditas for all her work in typesetting this volume and for putting up with an absentee husband for such long periods. Without her love and support I doubt whether it would have been possible to tackle such huge projects as the New Chronology and the Genesis story. And there is more to come!

It has been a busy time since the publication of the first volume of *A Test of Time*. Over the last three years I have undertaken a huge amount of travelling around the world, giving lectures and interviews on the New Chronology. This has meant that the *Legend* project has taken much longer than at first envisaged. I hope you feel that the wait has been worthwhile and that you will be prepared to endure a similar interval before Volume Three in the series is available to add to your collection.

Thank you for taking the time to read this book. I trust that it has given some food for thought about the way we interpret the archaeological evidence from our distant past as we stand at the threshold of this important new era in human history.

Abbreviations

AASOR = Annual of the American School of Oriental Research

AJA = American Journal of Archeology

AJSL = American Journal of Semitic Languages and Literature

ANET = Ancient Near Eastern Texts

An. Or. = Analecta Orientalia

ASAE = Annales du Services des Antiquités de l'Égypte

AUSS = Andrews University Seminary Studies

AWT = Ancient World Tours

BA = Biblical Archaeologist

BASOR = Bulletin of the American Schools of Oriental Research

BES = Bulletin of the Egyptological Seminar

BBVO = Berliner Beitrage zum Vorderen Orient

CAH = Cambridge Ancient History

DE = Discussions in Egyptology

Dilmun = Journal of the Bahrain Historical and Archaeological Society

HML? = High Middle or Low?

ISIS = Institute for the Study of Interdisciplinary Sciences

JACF = Journal of the Ancient Chronology Forum

JAOS = Journal of the American Oriental Society

JARCE = Journal of the American Research Center in Egypt

JBL = Journal of Biblical Literature

JCS = Journal of Cuneiform Studies

JEA = Journal of Egyptian Archaeology

JNES = Journal of Near Eastern Studies

JRAS = Journal of the Royal Asiatic Society

JSSEA = Journal of the Society for the Study of Egyptian Antiquities

MDAIK = Mitteilungen des Deutschen Archäologischen Instituts Abteilung Kairo

Or. = Orientalia

VA = Vorderasiatische Abteilung, Thontafelsammlung

VT = Vetus Testamentum

ZA = Zeitschrift für Assyriologie

ZÄS = Zeitschrift für Ägyptische Sprache und Altertumskunde

ZAW = Zeitschrift für die Alttestamentlische Wüssenschaft

Sources for Illustrations

All photographs and illustrations are by the author except for the following:

Some images have been taken from works published before 1945 which are out of copyright.

The author thanks the following for permission to reproduce their photographs and illustrations (all rights reserved):

Courtesy of the Ashmolean Museum, Oxford – 170; courtesy of the Bahrain National Museum – 250, 256, 272; S. Cox – 469; Egyptian government survey – 5b; A. Forestier – 201; courtesy of J. Hankey – 281; Hierakonpolis 1898 Excavations – 408; L. W. King – 164; E. V. Rohl – 7, 80, inside rear cover; J. C. G. Röhl – 336; P. van der Veen – 77, 112, 155, 198, 207, 223, 358, 359, 387, 403; A. Watson for the photographs taken by her father S. W. Marlow – 16, 28; J. Wilton – 462; R. Wiskin – 20, 137, 140, 171, 188, 189, 204, 505; Ur 1928-34 Excavations – 181, 182, 185; courtesy of H. Walker – 60; M. Warmels – 225; courtesy of V. Wilkins – 127.

Special thanks must go to: the Biblisches Institut, Fribourg University, for permission to use so many of their glyptic masterpieces and to Richard Wiskin for his excellent photographs of this world-renowned private collection; the Bahrain International Museum for permission to photograph its exhibits and the management of the Meridien resort, Manama, for permission to photograph the hotel's recreation of an abzu spring.

Bibliography

A

Al-Khalifa, H. A. and **Rice**, M. (eds.) – 1986: *Bahrain Through the Ages: The Archaeology* (Proceedings of the Bahrain Historical Conference 1983, London).

Albright, W. F. – 1919: 'The Mount of the Rivers' in *AJSL* 35, pp. 161-95.

Albright, W. F. – 1921: 'Magan, Meluha, and the Synchronism Between Menes and Naram-Sin' in *JEA* 7, pp. 80-6.

Albright, W. F. – 1922: 'The Location of the Garden of Eden' in *AJSL* 39, pp. 15-31.

Albright, W. F. & **Lambdin**, T. O. – 1970: 'The Evidence of Language' in *CAH* I:1, pp. 122-55.

Almoayed, T. A. R. – 1984: *The Temple Complex at Barbar, Bahrain* (Bahrain).

Alster, B. – 1983: 'Dilmun, Bahrain, and the alleged Paradise in Sumerian myth and literature' in D. Potts (ed.) *Dilmun: New Studies in the Archaeology and Early History of Bahrein, BBVO* 2, pp. 39-74.

Alster, B. – 1995: 'Epic Tales from Ancient Sumer: Enmerkar, Lugalbanda, and Other Cunning Heroes' in J. M. Sasson (ed.): *Civilisations of the Ancient Near East*, Vol. IV, pp. 2315-26.

Amiet, P. – 1957: 'Glyptique susienne archaique' in *Revue d'assyriologie* 51, pp. 121-29.

Amiet, P. – 1961: *La glyptique mésopotamienne archaique* (Paris).

Amiet, P. – 1986: 'Susa and the Dilmun culture' in H. A. Al-Khalifa and M. Rice (eds.): *Bahrain Through the Ages: The Archaeology* (Proceedings of the Bahrain Historical Conference 1983, London), pp. 262-68.

Amiet, P. – 1993: 'The Period of Irano-Mesopotamian Contacts 3500-1600 BC' in J. Curtis (ed.): *Early Mesopotamia and Iran: Contact and Conflict 3500-1600 BC* (London), pp. 23-30.

Andersen, H. H. – 1986: 'The Barbar Temple: stratigraphy, architecture and interpretation' in H. A. Al-Khalifa and M. Rice (eds.): *Bahrain Through the Ages: The Archaeology* (Proceedings of the Bahrain Historical Conference 1983, London), pp. 165-77.

Andrews, C. A. R. – 1972: 'Introduction' in R. O. Faulkner: *Book of the Dead*, pp. 11-16.

Arkel, A. J. & **Ucko**, P. J. – 1965: 'Review of Predynastic Development in the Nile Valley' in *Current Anthropology* 6, pp. 145-66.

Aström, P. – 1987: *HML?* (Gothenburg).

Aubet, M. E. – 1987: *The Phoenicians and the West: Politics, Colonies and Trade* (Cambridge).

B

Baines, J. R. – 1970: '*Bnbn*: mythological and linguistic notes' in *An. Or.* 39, pp. 389-404.

Baines, J. R. & **Malek**, J. – 1980: *Atlas of Ancient Egypt* (Oxford).

Barnett, R. D. – 1958: 'Early Shipping in the Near East' in *Antiquity* 32, pp. 220-30.

Barnett, R. D. – 1982: 'Urartu' in *CAH* III:1, 2nd ed., pp. 314-71.

Bartholomew, J. – 1952: *The Citizen's Atlas of the World* (Edinburgh).

Baumgartel, E. J. – 1947: *The Cultures of Prehistoric Egypt*, Vol. 1 (London).

Baumgartel, E. J. – 1960: *The Cultures of Prehistoric Egypt*, Vol. 2 (Oxford).

Baumgartel, E. J. – 1966: 'Scorpion and Rosette and the Fragment of the Large Hierakonpolis Mace Head' in *ZÄS* 92, pp. 9-14.

Baumgartel, E. J. – 1970: 'Predynastic Egypt' in *CAH*, 3rd edn, Vol. 1, pt. 1 (Cambridge), pp. 463-97.

Bénédite, G. A. – 1916: 'Le Couteau de Gebel el-Arak' in *Fondation Eugene Piot, Monuments et Mémoires* 22, pp. 1-34.

Bénédite, G. – 1918: 'The Carnarvon Ivory' in *JEA* 5, pp. 1-15.

Bent, J. T. – 1889: 'The Bahrein Islands, in the Persian Gulf' in M. Rice (ed.): *Dilmun Discovered* (London, 1983), pp. 67-102.

Berger, M. A. – 1992: 'Predynastic Animal-headed Boats from Hierakonpolis and Southern Egypt' in R. Friedman and B. Adams (eds.): *The Followers of Horus: Studies Dedicated to Michael Allen Hoffman*, pp. 107-20.

Berlin, A. – 1979: *Enmerkar and Ensuhkesdanna: A Sumerian Narrative* (Philadelphia).

Berry, A. C. *et al.* – 1967: 'Genetical change in ancient Egypt' in *Man* n.s. 2, pp. 551-68.

Berry, A. C. & **Berry**, R. J. – 1973: 'Origins and relations of the ancient Egyptians' in D. R. Brothwell (ed.): *Population biology of the ancient Egyptians*, pp. 200-8.

Bibby, T. G. – 1972: *Looking for Dilmun* (Harmondsworth).

Bibby, T. G. – 1984/85: 'The Land of Dilmun is Holy ...' in *Dilmun* 12, pp. 3-4.

Bibby, T. G. – 1986a: 'The land of Dilmun is holy...' in H. A. Al-Khalifa and M. Rice (eds.): *Bahrain Through the Ages: The Archaeology* (Proceedings of the Bahrain Historical Conference 1983, London), pp. 192-94.

Bibby, T. G. – 1986b: 'The Origins of the Dilmun Civilization' in H. A. Al-Khalifa and M. Rice (eds.): *Bahrain Through the Ages: The Archaeology* (Proceedings of the Bahrain Historical Conference 1983, London), pp. 108-15.

Bimson, J. – 1978: *Redating the Exodus and Conquest* (Sheffield).

von Bissing, W. F. & **Kees**, H. – 1923: *Das Re-Heiligtum des Königs Newoser-re (Rathures)*, Vol. III (Leipzig).

Black, J. & **Green**, A. – 1992: *Gods, Demons and Symbols of Ancient Mesopotamia: An Illustrated Dictionary* (London).

Blackman, A. M. – 1915: *The Rock Tombs of Meir* (London).

Borchardt, L. – 1913: *Das Grabdenkmal des Königs SAHU-RE, Band II: Die Wandbilder* (Leipzig).

Borger, R. – 1994: 'The Incantation Series *Bit Meseri* and Enoch's Ascension to Heaven' in R. S. Hess & D. T. Tsumura (eds.): *"I Studied Inscriptions from before the Flood": Ancient Near Eastern, Literary, and Linguistic Approaches to Genesis 1-11*, pp. 224-33.

Bradley, J. T. – 1936: *History of the Seychelles Islands* (Port Victoria).

Breasted, J. H. – 1905: *A History of Egypt* (Chicago).

Breasted, J. H. – 1988: *Ancient Records of Egypt: Historical Documents from the Earliest Times to the Persian Conquest*, Part 1 (London).

Brickell, C. (ed.) –1989: *The Royal Horticultural Society Gardeners' Encyclopedia of Plants & Flowers* (London).

van der Broek, R. – 1972: *The myth of phoenix according to classical and early christian tradition* (Leiden).

Budde, K. – 1883: *Die Biblische Urgeschichte* (Giessen).

van Buren, E. D. – 1945: *Symbols of the Gods in Mesopotamian Art* (Rome).

Burney, C. A. – 1964: 'The Excavations at Yanik Tepe, Azerbaijan, 1962: Third Preliminary Report' in *Iraq* 26, pp. 54-62.

Burney, C. – 1977: *From Village to Empire: An introduction to Near Eastern archaeology* (Oxford).

Burrows, Fr. E. – 1928: 'Scriptura Sacra et Monumental Orientis Antiqui: Heft 2, Tilmun, Bahrain, Paradise' in M. Rice: *Dilmun Discovered: The early years of archaeology in Bahrain* (1983), pp. 168-91.

Burstein, S. M. – 1978: *The Babyloniaca of Berossus* (Malibu).

C

Cameron, G. G. – 1936: *History of Early Iran* (Chicago).

Caplice, R. – 1988: *Introduction to Akkadian* (Rome).

Carter, H. – 1916: 'Report on the Tomb of Zeser-ka-ra Amenhetep I, Discovered by the Earl of Carnarvon in 1914' in *JEA* 3, pp. 147-54.

Case, H. & **Payne**, J. C. – 1962: 'Tomb 100: The Decorated Tomb at Hierakonpolis' in *JEA* 48, pp. 5-18.

Castellino, G. – 1994: 'The Origins of Civilization According to Biblical and Cuneiform Texts' in R. S. Hess & D. T. Tsumura (eds.): *"I Studied Inscriptions from before the Flood": Ancient Near Eastern, Literary, and Linguistic Approaches to Genesis 1-11*, pp. 75-95.

Cervicek, P. – 1992: 'Chorology and Chronology of Upper Egyptian and Nubian Rock Art up to 1400 B.C.' in *Sahara* 5, pp. 41-7.

Chahin, M. – 1987: *The Kingdom of Armenia* (London).

Childe, V. G. – 1928: *New Light on the Most Ancient East: The Oriental Prelude to European Prehistory* (New York).

Civil, M. – 1969: 'The Sumerian Flood Story' in W. G. Lambert & A. R. Millard: *Atra-hasis*, pp. 138-45.

Civil, M. – 1995: 'Ancient Mesopotamian Lexicography' in J. M. Sasson (ed.): *Civilisations of the Ancient Near East*, Vol. IV, pp. 2305-14.

Cohen, S. – 1973: *Enmerkar and the Lord of Aratta* (Dissertation in Oriental Studies, Pennsylvania).

Collins, A. – 1996: *From the Ashes of Angels: The Forbidden Legacy of a Fallen Race* (London).

Collon, D. – 1987: *First Impressions: Cylinder Seals in the Ancient Near East* (London).

Comfort, A. – 1964: *The Biology of Senescence* (London).

Cooper, B. – 1995: *After the Flood: The early post-flood history of Europe traced back to Noah* (West Sussex).

Cooper, J. S. & **Heimpel**, W. – 1983: 'The Sumerian Sargon Legend' in *JAOS* 103, pp. 67-82.

Cornwall, P. B. – 1943: *Dilmun: The History of Bahrain Island Before Cyrus* (unpublished PhD. dissertation, Harvard University).

Cornwall, P. B. – 1946: 'On the Location of Dilmun' in *BASOR* 103 (October), pp. 3-11.

Cornwall, P. B. – 1983: 'On the Location of Dilmun' in M. Rice (ed.): *Dilmun Discovered*, pp. 193-200.

Cotterell, A. (ed.) – 1980: *The Penguin Encyclopedia of Ancient Civilizations* (London).

Crawford, H. –1991: *Sumer and the Sumerians* (Cambridge).

Crawford, H. – 1991/92: 'Patterns of Trade in Mesopotamia 3,500-2,500 BC' in *Dilmun* 15, pp. 17-21.

Crawford, H. *et al.* (eds.) – 1997: *The Dilmun Temple At Saar: Bahrain and its Archaeological Inheritance* (London).

Curtis, J. – 1993: *Early Mesopotamia and Iran: Contact and Conflict 3500-1600 BC* (London).

D

Dalley, S. (trans.) – 1989: *Myths from Mesopotamia: Creation, The Flood, Gilgamesh and Others* (Oxford).

Dawson, W. R. & **Uphill**, E. P. – 1972: *Who Was Who in Egyptology*, 2nd ed., (London).

Derry, D. E. – 1956: 'The Dynastic Race in Egypt' in *JEA* 42, pp. 80-5.

Dever, W. G. – 1984: 'Asherah, Consort of Yahweh? New Evidence from Kuntillet Ajrud'n in *BASOR* 255, pp. 21-37.

Doe, D. B. – 1984: 'The Barbar Temple site in Bahrain: conservation and presentation' in H. A. Al-Khalifa and M. Rice (eds.): *Bahrain Through the Ages: The Archaeology* (Proceedings of the Bahrain Historical Conference 1983, London), pp. 480-84.

Doe, D. B. – 1986: 'The Barbar Temple: the masonry' in H. A. Al-Khalifa and M. Rice (eds.): *Bahrain Through the Ages: The Archaeology* (Proceedings of the Bahrain Historical Conference 1983, London), pp. 186-91.

Dreyer, G. – 1993: 'Umm el-Qa'ab: Nachuntersuchungen in Frühzeitlichen Königsfriedhof 5./6. Vorbericht' in *MDAIK* 49, pp. 23-62.

Drioton, É. & **Lauer**, J.-P. – 1939: *Sakkarah: The Monuments of Zoser* (Cairo).

Drower, M. S. – 1985: *Flinders Petrie: A Life in Archaeology* (London).

Durand, E. L. – 1880: 'Extracts From A Report On The Islands And Antiquities of Bahrain' in *JRAS* 12, pp. 189-227.

Dyson, R. H & **Cuyler Young**, T. – 1960: 'The Solduz Valley, Iran: Pisdeli Tape' in *Antiquity* 34, pp. 19-28.

E

Eaton-Krauss, M. – 1987: 'The earliest representation of Osiris' in *VA* 3, pp. 233-36.

Edzard, D. O. – 1995: 'The Sumerian Language' in J. M. Sasson (ed.): *Civilisations of the Ancient Near East*, Vol. IV, pp. 2107-16.

Edwards, I. E. S. – 1949: 'Some Early Dynastic Contributions to Egyptian Architecture' in *JEA* 35, pp. 125-26.

Edwards, I. E. S. – 1985: *The Pyramids of Egypt* (Harmondsworth).

Edwards, I. E. S. – 1980: 'The Early Dynastic Period in Egypt' in *CAH* 1:2, pp. 1-70.

Edwards, M. – 1986: '"Urmia Ware" and Its Distribution in North-Western Iran' in *Iran* 24, pp. 57-78.

Emery, W. B. – 1952: *Saqqara and the Dynastic Race: An Inaugural Lecture delivered at University College London* (London).

Emery, W. B. – 1961: *Archaic Egypt: Culture and Civilization in Egypt Five Thousand Years Ago* (London).

Empson, R. H. W. – 1928: *The Cult of the Peacock Angel: A Short Account of the Yezidi Tribes of Kurdistan* (London).

Engelbach, R. – 1943: 'An Essay on the Advent of the Dynastic Race in Egypt and Its Consequences' in *ASAE* 42, pp. 193-221.

F

Faulkner, R. O. – 1969: *The Ancient Egyptian Pyramid Texts* , 2 vols. (Oxford).

Faulkner, R. O. – 1972: *The Ancient Egyptian Book of the Dead* (New York).

Faulkner, R. O. – 1981: *A Concise Dictionary of Middle Egyptian* (Oxford).

Ferns, F. E. B. – 1978: *Quarterly Bulletin of the Alpine Garden Society* 146:1 (March), pp. 24-27.

Finch, C. E. & **Hayflick**, L. (eds.) – 1977: *The Biology of Aging* (New York).

Finch, C. E. & **Johnson**, T. E. (eds.) – 1990: *Molecular Biology of Aging* (New York).

Finkelstein, J. J. – 1963: 'The Antediluvian Kings: A University of California Tablet' in *JCS* 17, pp. 39-51.

Finkelstein, J. J. – 1966: 'The Genealogy of the Hammurapi Dynasty' in *JCS* 20, pp. 95-118.

Firth, C. M. & **Quibell**, J. E. – 1935: *The Step Pyramid*, Vol. II, (Cairo).

Fisher, W. B. (ed.) – 1968: *The Cambridge History of Iran Volume 1: The Land of Iran* (Cambridge).

Foster, B. R. – 1995: *From Distant Days: Myths, Tales, and Poetry of Ancient Mesopotamia* (Bethesda, Maryland).

Frankfort, H. – 1936: *Oriental Institute Communications* no. 20 (Chicago).

Frankfort, H. – 1944: 'A Note on the Lady of Birth' in *JNES* 3, pp. 198-200.

Frankfort, H. – 1948: *Kingship and the Gods: A Study of Ancient Near*

BIBLIOGRAPHY

Eastern Religion as the Integration of Society and Nature (Chicago).

Frankfort, H. – 1951: *The Birth of Civilization in the Near East* (London).

Freedman, D. N. – 1992: *Anchor Bible Dictionary* (New York).

Friedman, R. & **Adams**, B. (eds.) – 1992: *The Followers of Horus: Studies dedicated to Michael Allen Hoffman 1944-1990* (Oxford).

Frifelt, K. – 1984: 'Burial Mounds near Ali Excavated by the Danish Expedition' in *Dilmun* 12, pp. 11-14.

Frolich, B. – 1983: 'The Bahrain Burial Mounds' in *Dilmun* 11, pp. 5-9.

Fuchs, G. – 1989: 'Rock engravings in the Wadi el-Barramiya, Eastern Desert of Egypt' in *The African Archaeological Review* 7, pp. 127-53.

Fuchs, G. – 1991: 'Petroglyphs in the Eastern Desert of Egypt: new finds in the Wadi el-Barramiya' in *Sahara* 4, pp. 59-70.

G

Gadd, C. J. – 1937: 'The Infancy of Man in a Sumerian Legend: An Assyrian Parallel to an Incident in the Story of Semiramis' in *Iraq* 4, p. 33-4.

Gardiner, A. H. – 1944: 'Horus the Behdetite' in *JEA* 30, pp. 23-60.

Gauthier, H. – 1912: *Le Livre des Rois d'Égypt*, Vol. II (Cairo).

Gelb, I. J. – 1957: *Glossary of Old Akkadian* (Chicago).

Gelb, I. J. – 1994: 'The Name of Babylon' in R. S. Hess & D. T. Tsumura (eds.): *"I Studied Inscriptions from before the Flood": Ancient Near Eastern, Literary, and Linguistic Approaches to Genesis 1-11*, pp. 266-69.

Gilbert, A. G. – 1996: *Magi: The Quest for a Secret Tradition* (London).

Ginzberg, L. – 1919: *Legends of the Jews* (Philadelphia).

Godley, A. D. (trans.) – 1920: *Herodotus* (London).

Goff, B. L. – 1963: *Symbols of Prehistoric Mesopotamia* (New Haven).

Gordon, C. H. – 1968: *Forgotten Scripts: The Story of their Decipherment* (London).

Gordon, C. H. – 1988: 'Notes on Proper Names in the Ebla Tablets' in *Eblaite Personal Names and Semitic Name-Giving: Papers of a Symposium Held in Rome, July 15-17, 1985*, pp. 153-58.

Graves, R. & **Patai**, R. – 1989: *Hebrew Myths: The Book of Genesis* (London, 1st ed. 1964).

Grayson, A. K. – 1972: *Assyrian Royal Inscriptions, Volume 1: From the Beginning to Ashur-resha-ishi I* (Wiesbaden).

Grayson, A. K. – 1976: *Assyrian Royal Inscriptions, Volume 2: From Tiglath-pileser I to Ashur-nasir-apli II* (Wiesbaden).

Greenfield, J. C. – 1984: 'A Touch of Eden' in *Orientalia J. Duchesne-Guillemin Emerito Oblata* (Hommages et Opera Minora 9, Leiden), pp. 219-24.

Griffiths, J. G. – 1980: *The origins of Osiris and his cult* (Leiden).

H

Hassan, F. A. – 1980: 'Radiocarbon chronology of Archaic Egypt' in *JNES* 39, pp. 203-07.

Hall, H. R. – 1922: 'The Discoveries At Tell el-Obeid In Southern Babylonia, And Some Egyptian Comparisons' in *JEA* 8, pp. 241-57.

Hall, H. R. – 1923: 'Ur and Eridu: The British Museum Excavations of 1919' in *JEA* 9, pp. 177-95.

Hallo, W. H. – 1968: *Essays in Memory of E. A. Speiser* (New Haven).

Hallo, W. H. – 1971: *Encyclopaedia Judaica* (New York).

Hallo, W. W. & **Simpson**, W. K. – 1971: *The Ancient Near East: A History* (San Diego).

Harer, W. B. – 1985: 'Pharmacological and biological properties of the Egyptian lotus' in *JARCE* 22, pp. 49-54.

Harpur, J. (ed.) – 1987: *Great Events of Bible Times* (London).

Hawkins, J. D. – 1979: 'The Origin and Dissemination of Writing in Western Asia' in P. R. S. Moorey: *The Origins of Civilization*, pp. 128-66.

Hay, R. (ed.) – 1985: *Reader's Digest Encyclopaedia of Garden Plants and Flowers* (London).

Hayes, W. C. – 1970: 'Chronology: I, Egypt – To The End Of The Twentieth Dynasty' in *CAH* I:1, pp. 173-193.

Healey, J. F. (trans.) – 1991: *Pliny The Elder: Natural History: A Selection* (London).

Heidel, A. – 1942: *The Babylonian Genesis: The Story of Creation* (Chicago, 2nd edition 1951).

Heidel, A. – 1946: *The Gilgamesh Epic and Old Testament Parallels* (Chicago).

Heller, J. – 1958: 'Der Name Eva' in *An. Or.* 26, pp. 636-56.

Henrickson, E. F. – 1985: 'An Updated Chronology of the Early and Middle Chalcolithic of the Central Zagros Highlands, Western Iran' in *Iran* XXIII, pp. 63-108.

Hepper, N. – 1969: 'Arabian and African frankincense trees' in *JEA* 55, pp. 66-72.

Herrman, G. – 1968: 'Lapis lazuli: the early phases of its trade' in *Iraq* 30, pp. 21-57.

Hess, R. S. – 1994: 'One Hundred Fifty Years of Comparative Studies on Genesis 1-11: An Overview' in R. S. Hess & D. T. Tsumura (eds.): *"I Studied Inscriptions from before the Flood": Ancient Near Eastern, Literary, and Linguistic Approaches to Genesis 1-11*, pp. 3-26.

Hess, R. S. – 1994: 'The Genealogies of Genesis 1-11 and Comparative Literature' in R. S. Hess & D. T. Tsumura (eds.): *"I Studied Inscriptions from before the Flood": Ancient Near Eastern, Literary, and Linguistic Approaches to Genesis 1-11*, pp. 58-72.

Heyerdahl, T. – 1980: *The Tigris Expedition: In Search of Our Beginnings* (London).

Hincks, E. – 1969: 'On the Language and Mode of Writing of the Ancient Assyrians' in T. B. Jones (ed.): *The Sumerian Problem*, pp. 9-10.

Hoffman, M. A. – 1984: *Egypt Before the Pharaohs* (New York).

Hooker, J. T. (ed.) – 1990: *Reading the Past: Ancient Writing from Cuneiform to the Alphabet* (London).

Huehnergard, J. – 1995: 'Semitic Languages' in J. M. Sasson (ed.): *Civilisations of the Ancient Near East*, Vol. IV, pp. 2117-34.

Hughes, D. R. & **Brothwell**, D. R. – 1970: 'The Earliest Populations of Man in Europe, Western Asia and Northern Africa' in *CAH* I:1, pp. 156-172.

I

Ibrahim, M. – 1982: *Excavations of the Arab Expedition at Sar el-Jisr, Bahrain* (Bahrain).

Irving, C. – 1979: *Crossroads of Civilization: 3000 Years of Persian History* (London).

Izady, M. R. – 1992: *The Kurds – A Concise Handbook* (London).

J

Jacobs, L. – 1995: *The Jewish Religion: A Companion* (Oxford).

Jacobsen, T. – 1939: *The Sumerian King List* (Chicago).

Jacobsen, T. – 1976: *The Treasures of Darkness* (New Haven).

Jacobsen, T. – 1980: 'Sumer' in A. Cotterell (ed.): *The Penguin Encyclopedia of Ancient Civilizations*, pp. 72-108.

Jacobsen, T. – 1994: 'The Eridu Genesis' in R. S. Hess & D. T. Tsumura (eds.): *"I Studied Inscriptions from before the Flood": Ancient Near Eastern, Literary, and Linguistic Approaches to Genesis 1-11*, pp. 129-42.

Janssen, R. M. – 1992: *The First Hundred Years: Egyptology at University College London 1892-1992* (London).

Jelinkova, E. A. E. – 1962: 'The Shebtiw in the temple at Edfu' in *ZÄS* 87, pp. 41-54.

Johnston, P. – 1980: *The Seacraft of Prehistory* (London).

Jones, D. A. – 1988: *A glossary of ancient Egyptian nautical titles and terms* (London).

Jones, D. A. – 1995: *Boats* (London).

Jones, H. L. (trans.) – 1930: *The Geography of Strabo*, Vol. 7 (New York).

Jones, T. B. (ed.) – 1969: *The Sumerian Problem* (New York).

Jones, W. H. S. (trans.) – 1980: *Pliny, The Elder: Natural History* Book VI (Cambridge, Massachusetts).

K

Kantor, H. J. – 1944: 'The Final Phase of Predynastic Culture' in *JNES* 3, pp. 110-48.

Kantor, H. J. – 1949: Review of Baumgartel (1947) in *AJA* 53, pp. 76-79.

Kantor, H. J. – 1952: 'Further Evidence for Early Mesopotamian Relations with Egypt' in *JNES* 11, pp. 239-50.

Kantor, H. J. – 1954: 'The Relative Chronology of Egypt and its Foreign Correlations Before the Late Bronze Age' in *Chronologies in Old World Archaeology*, pp. 1-46.

Keel, O. – 1978: *The Symbolism of the Biblical World: Ancient Near Eastern Iconography and the Book of Psalms* (London).

Kelley, A. L. – 1974: 'The evidence of Mesopotamian influence in Pre-dynastic Egypt' in *Newsl. Soc. Study Egypt. Ant.* 4, pp. 2-22.

Kelley, A. L. – 1983: 'A review of the evidence concerning early Egyptian ivory knife handles' in *The Ancient World* 6, pp. 95-102.

Kemp, B. J. – 1976: A review of Hellstrom's The Rock Drawings in *JEA* 62, p. 926.

Kemp, B. J. – 1967: 'The Egyptian 1st Dynasty royal cemetery' in *Antiquity* 41, pp. 22-32.

Kemp, B. J. – 1973: 'Photographs of the decorated tomb at Hierakonpolis' in *JEA* 59, pp. 36-43.

King, L. W. – 1969: 'History of Sumer and Akkad' in T. B. Jones (ed.): *The Sumerian Problem*, pp. 50-62.

Kitchen, K. A. – 1971: 'Punt and how to get there' in *Orientalia* 40, pp. 184-207.

Kitchen, K. A. – 1987: 'The Basics of Egyptian Chronology in Relation to the Bronze Age' in P. Aström (ed.): *HML?*, pp. 35-55.

Kitchen, K. A. & de Conceicao, M. (eds.) – 1990: *Catalogue of the Ancient Egyptian Monuments in the National Museum, Rio de Janeiro* (Warminster).

Kitchen, K. A. – 1993a: 'The Land of Punt' in T. Shaw *et al.* (eds): *The Archaeology of Africa*, pp. 587-608.

Kitchen, K. A. – 1993b: 'Genesis 12 to 50 in the Near Eastern World' in R. S. Hess *et al.* (eds.): *He Swore an Oath: Biblical Themes from Genesis 12 to 50*, pp. 67-92.

Kovacs, M. G. (trans.) –1985: *The Epic of Gilgamesh* (California).

Kramer, S. N. – 1944: 'Dilmun, The Land of the Living' in *BASOR* 96, pp. 18-28.

Kramer, S. N. – 1952: *Enmerkar and the Lord of Aratta* (Philadelphia).

Kramer, S. N. – 1956: *From the Tablets of Sumer (History Begins at Sumer)* (Indian Hills, new enlarged ed.: Philadelphia, 1981).

Kramer, S. N. – 1959: *Studia Biblica et Orientalia* III (*Analecta Biblica* 12), pp. 203ff.

Kramer, S. N. – 1963: *The Sumerians: Their History, Culture, and Character* (Chicago).

Kramer, S. N. – 1963: 'Dilmun: Quest for Paradise' in *Antiquity* 37, pp. 111-15.

Kramer, S. N. – 1968: 'The "Babel of Tongues": A Sumerian Version' in *JAOS* 88, pp. 108-11.

Kramer, S. N. – 1969a: 'Sumerian Myths and Epic Tales' in J. B. Pritchard (ed.): *ANET*, 3rd ed., pp. 37-59.

Kramer, S. N. – 1969b: 'Sumerian Miscellaneous Text' in J. B. Pritchard (ed.): *ANET*, 3rd ed., pp. 646-52.

Kramer, S. N. & Maier, J. – 1989: *Myths of Enki, the Crafty God* (New York).

Kramer, S. N. – 1948: 'New Light on the Early History of the Ancient Near East' in *AJA* 52, pp. 156-64.

Kramer, S. N. – 1994: 'Dilmun, The Land of the Living' in *BASOR* 96 (December), pp. 18-28.

Kuhrt, A. – 1995: *The Ancient Near East* c. *3000-330 BC*, Vol. 1 (London).

Külling, S. R. – 1996: *Are the genealogies in Genesis 5 and 11 historical and complete, that is, without gaps?* (Riehen).

L

Lamberg-Karlovsky, C. C. – 1982: 'Dilmun: Gateway to Immortality' in *JNES*, Vol. 41, No. 1, pp. 45-50.

Lamberg-Karlovsky, C. C. – 1984: 'Death in Dilmun' in *Dilmun* 12, pp. 15-24.

Lambert, W. G. & Millard, A. R. – 1969: *Atra-hasis: The Babylonian Story of the Flood* (Oxford).

Landstrom, B. – 1970: *Ships of the Pharaohs* (London).

Lang, D. M. – 1980: 'Urartu and Armenia' in A. Cotterell (ed.): *The Penguin Encyclopedia of Ancient Civilizations*, pp. 117-22.

Langdon, S. H. – 1921: 'The Early Chronology of Sumer and Egypt and the Similarities in Their Culture' in *JEA* 7, pp. 133-53.

Langdon, S. H. – 1923: *Historical Inscriptions, Containing Principally the Chronological Prism, W-B. 444* (Oxford Editions of Cuneiform Texts, II, London).

Larsen, C. E. – 1983: 'The early environment and hydrology of ancient Bahrain' in Potts (ed.): *Dilmun, BBVO* 2, pp. 3-34.

Lauer, J.-P. – 1936: *La Pyramide a dégres*, Vol. II: *Compléments* (Cairo).

Lauer, J.-P. – 1939: *La Pyramide a dégres*, Vol. III: *Compléments* (Cairo).

Lauer, J.-P. – 1948: *Etudes complementaires sur les monuments du roi Zoser a Saqqarah* (*Suppl. aux Annales du Service*, No. 9).

Lauer, J.-P. – 1962: *Histoire Monumentale des Pyramides D'Egypte, Volume I - Les Pyramides a Déegres* (Cairo).

Lauer, J-P. – 1976: *Saqqara: The Royal Cemetery of Memphis* (London).

Lenzen, H. J. – 1968: *Uruk-Warka*, Vol. XXIV (Berlin).

Lesko, L. H. (ed.) – 1984: *A Dictionary of Late Egyptian* (Providence).

Levine, L. D. – 1969: *Contributions to the Historical Geography of the Zagros in the Neo-Assyrian Period* (Dissertation in Oriental Studies, Pennsylvania).

Lichtheim, M. –1973: *Ancient Egyptian Literature, Volume I: The Old and Middle Kingdoms* (Berkeley).

Lichtheim, M. –1976: *Ancient Egyptian Literature, Volume II: The New Kingdom* (Berkeley).

Lionnet, G. – 1972: *The Seychelles* (Newton Abbot).

Lloyd, S. – 1984: *The Archaeology of Mesopotamia: From the Old Stone Age to the Persian Conquest* (Revised edition, London).

Lucas, A. & Harris, J. R. – 1962: *Ancient Egyptian Materials and Industries* (London).

Luckenbill, D. D. – 1927: *Ancient Records of Assyria and Babylon*, Vol. II (Chicago).

Luschey, H. – 1968: 'Studien zu dem Darius-Relief von Bisutun' in *Archäologische Mitteilungen Aus Iran* I, pp. 63-94.

M

Mackay, E. – 1931: *Report on Excavations at Jemdet Nasr, Iraq* (Chicago).

Mackenzie, D. A. – 1915: *Mythology of the Babylonian People* (London).

Magnusson, M. – 1977: *BC: The Archaeology of the Bible Lands* (London).

Majer, J. – 1992: 'The Eastern Desert and Egyptian Prehistory' in R. Friedman & B. Adams (eds.): *The Followers of Horus: Studies dedicated to Michael Allen Hoffman 1944-1990*, pp. 227-34.

Malamat, A. – 1994: 'King Lists of the Old Babylonian Period and Biblical Genealogies' in R. S. Hess & D. T. Tsumura (eds.): *"I Studied Inscriptions from before the Flood": Ancient Near Eastern, Literary, and Linguistic Approaches to Genesis 1-11*, pp. 183-200.

Mallowan, M. E. L. – 1964: 'Noah's Flood Reconsidered' in *Iraq* 26, pp. 62-82.

Mallowan, M. E. L. – 1970: 'The Development of Cities From Al-Ubaid to the End of Uruk 5' in *CAH* I:1, pp. 327-462.

Masry, A. H. – 1977: *Prehistory in Northeastern Arabia* (London).

Matheson, S. A. – 1972: *Persia: An Archaeological Guide* (London).

BIBLIOGRAPHY

Mathews, B. (ed.) – 1981: *Bulbs* (London).

McCall, H. – 1990: *Mesopotamian Myths* (London).

Medawar, P. B. & **Medawar**, J. – 1977: *The Life Science* (London).

Mellaart, J. – 1970: 'The Earliest Settlements in Western Asia from the Ninth to the End of the Fifth Millennium B.C.' in *CAH* I:1, pp. 248-303.

Mellaart, J. – 1979: 'Early Urban Communities in the Near East, *c.* 9000-3400 BC' in P. R. S. Moorey (ed.): *The Origins of Civilization*, pp. 22-33.

Michalowski, P. – 1995: 'Sumerian Literature: An Overview' in J. M. Sasson (ed.): *Civilisations of the Ancient Near East*, Vol. IV, pp. 2279-91.

Millard, A. R. – 1984: 'The Etymology of Eden' in *VT* 34, pp. 103-6.

Millard, A. R. – 1994: 'A New Babylonian "Genesis" Story' in R. S. Hess & D. T. Tsumura (eds.): *"I Studied Inscriptions from before the Flood": Ancient Near Eastern, Literary, and Linguistic Approaches to Genesis 1-11*, pp. 114-28.

Miller Jr., P. D. – 1994: 'Eridu, Dunnu, and Babel: A Study in Comparative Mythology' in R. S. Hess & D. T. Tsumura (eds.): *"I Studied Inscriptions from before the Flood": Ancient Near Eastern, Literary, and Linguistic Approaches to Genesis 1-11*, pp. 143-68.

Millet, N. – 1990: 'The Narmer Macehead and Related Objects' in *JARCE* 27, pp. 53-9.

Montet, P. – 1965: *Eternal Egypt* (London).

Moorey, P. R. S. – 1985: *Materials and Manufacture in Ancient Mesopotamia* (Oxford).

Moorey, P. R. S. – 1993: 'Iran: A Sumerian El-Dorado?' in J. Curtis (ed.): *Early Mesopotamia and Iran: Contact and Conflict 3500-1600 BC*, pp. 31-43.

Moran, W. – 1995: 'The Gilgamesh Epic: A Masterpiece from Ancient Mesopotamia' in J. M. Sasson (ed.): *Civilisations of the Ancient Near East*, Vol. IV, pp. 2327-36.

Mortensen, P. – 1980: 'On the Date of the Temple at Barbar in Bahrain' in *Dilmun* 9, pp. 15-20.

Mortensen, P. – 1984: 'The Bahrain Temple: its chronology and foreign relations reconsidered' in H. A. Al-Khalifa and M. Rice (eds.): *Bahrain Through the Ages: The Archaeology* (Proceedings of the Bahrain Historical Conference 1983, London), pp. 178-85.

Mullen Jr., E. T. – 1980: *The Divine Council in Canaanite and Early Hebrew Literature* (HSM 24; Chico, Cal.).

Murnane, W. J. – 1981: 'The sed festival: a problem in historical method' in *MDAIK* 37, pp. 369-76.

Murnane, W. J. – 1983: *The Penguin Guide to Ancient Egypt* (London).

Murray, G. W. – 1945-6: 'A note on the Sad el-Kafara: the Ancient Dam in the Wadi Garawi' in *Bulletin de l'Institut d'Égypte* 28, pp. 33ff.

Murray, M. A. – 1949: *The Splendour that was Egypt* (London).

N

Nashef, K. – 1986: 'The Deities of Dilmun' in H. A. Al-Khalifa and M. Rice (eds.): *Bahrain Through the Ages: The Archaeology* (Proceedings of the Bahrain Historical Conference 1983, London), pp. 340-66.

Naville, E. – 1894-1908: *Temple of Deir el Bahari* III (London).

Newberry, P. E. – 1922: 'The Set rebellion of the second dynasty' in *Ancient Egypt*, pp. 40-6.

Nibbi, A. – 1991: 'The So-called Plant of Upper Egypt' in *DE* 19, pp. 53-68.

Nissen, H. J. – 1986: 'The occurrence of Dilmun in the oldest texts of Mesopotamia' in H. A. Al-Khalifa and M. Rice (eds.): *Bahrain Through the Ages: The Archaeology* (Proceedings of the Bahrain Historical Conference 1983, London), pp. 335-39.

Nissen, H. J. – 1987: 'The chronology of the proto- and early historic periods in Mesopotamia and Susiana' in O. Aurenche *et al.* (eds.): *Chronologies du Proche-Orient*, pp. 607-14.

Nissen, H. J. – 1993: 'The Context of the Emergence of Writing in Mesopotamia and Iran' in J. Curtis (ed.): *Early Mesopotamia and Iran: Contact and Conflict 3500-1600 BC*, pp. 54-71.

O

Oates, J. – 1960: 'Ur and Eridu, the Prehistory' in *Iraq* 22, pp. 32-50.

Oates, J. – 1969: 'Ur and Eridu; the Prehistory' in T. B. Jones (ed.): *The Sumerian Problem*, pp. 126-34.

Oates, J. – 1986: 'The Gulf in prehistory' in H. A. Al-Khalifa and M. Rice (eds.): *Bahrain Through the Ages: The Archaeology* (Proceedings of the Bahrain Historical Conference 1983, London), pp. 79-86.

Ogdon, J. R. – 1985-6: 'Some notes on the iconography of Min' in *BES* 7, pp. 29-41.

Oldfather, C. H. (trans.) – 1933: *Diodorus Siculus* (London).

Oppenheim, A. L. – 1969: 'Texts from the Beginnings to the First Dynasty of Babylon' in J. B. Pritchard (ed): *ANET*, pp. 263-317.

P

Papke, W. – 1993: *Die geheime Botschaft des Gilgamesh: 4000 Jahre alte astronomische Aufzeichnungen entschlüsselt* (Augsburg).

Parker, R. A. – 1950: *Calendars of Ancient Egypt* (Chicago).

Parrot, A. – 1960: *Sumer* (France).

Payne, J. C. – 1968: 'Lapis lazuli in early Egypt' in *Iraq* 30, pp. 58-61.

Peet, T. E. – 1915: 'The Art of the Predynastic Period' in *JEA* 2, pp. 88-94.

Petrie, W. M. F. – 1896: *Koptos* (London).

Petrie, W. M. F. – 1900: *The royal tombs of the first dynasty*, Vol. 1 (London).

Petrie, W. M. F. – 1901: *The royal tombs of the first dynasty*, Vol. II (London).

Petrie, W. M. F. – 1906: *Researches in Sinai* (London).

Petrie, W. M. F. – 1918: 'The Tutelage of the East' in *The Yale Review*, pp. 335-49.

Petrie, W. M. F. – 1922: 'The Outlook for Civilization' in *The Yale Review*, pp. 1-17.

Petrie, W. M. F. – 1939: *The Making of Egypt* (London).

Petrie, W. M. F. & **Quibell**, J. E. – 1896: *Naqada and Ballas* (London).

Phillips, R. & **Rix**, M. – 1981: *Bulbs* (London).

Phillips, R. & **Rix**, M. – 1991: *Perennials, Volume 2: Late Perennials* (London).

Piankoff, A. – 1968: *The Pyramid of Unas* (Princeton).

Pinches, T. G. – 1969: 'Sumerian or Crytography' in T. B. Jones (ed.): *The Sumerian Problem*, pp. 40-6.

Piotrovsky, B. B. – 1969: *The Ancient Civilization of Urartu* (London).

Poebel, A. – 1914: *Historical and Grammatical Texts*, Vol. IV:1 (Philadelphia).

Poebel, A. – 1942: 'The Assyrian King List from Khorsabad' in *JNES* 1:3, pp. 247-306.

Porada, E. – 1993: 'Seals and Related Objects from Early Mesopotamia and Iran' in J. Curtis (ed.): *Early Mesopotamia and Iran: Contact and Conflict 3500-1600 BC*, pp. 44-53.

Postgate, J. N. – 1992: *Early Mesopotamia: Society and Economy at the Dawn of History* (London).

Potts, D. T. (ed) – 1983: *Dilmun: New Studies in the Archaeology and Early History of Bahrein* (Berlin).

Potts, T. – 1994: *Mesopotamia and the East* (Oxford).

Powell, M. A. Jr. – 1972: 'The Origin of the Sexagesimal System: The Interaction of Language and Writing' in *Visible Language* 6, pp. 5-18.

Prideaux, F. B. – 1983: 'The Sepulchral Tumuli of Bahrain' in M. Rice (ed.): *Dilmun Discovered*, pp. 103-28.

Pritchard, J. B. (ed.) – 1969: *ANET: Relating to the Old Testament* (Princeton).

Q

Quibell, J. E. and **Green**, F. W. – 1902: *Hierakonpolis*, 2 vols. (London).

R

Raikes, R. L. – 1966: 'The Physical Evidence for Noah's Flood' in *Iraq* 28, pp. 52-63.

Rawlinson, G. – 1889: *History of Phoenicia* (London).

Rawlinson, H. – 1880: 'Notes on Capt. Durand's Report upon the Islands of Bahrain' in *JRAS* 12, pp. 201-27.

Reade, J. – 1986: 'Commerce or Conquest: variations in the Mesopotamia-Dilmun relationship' in H. A. Al-Khalifa and M. Rice (eds.): *Bahrain Through the Ages: The Archaeology* (Proceedings of the Bahrain Historical Conference 1983, London), pp. 325-39.

Redman, C. L. – 1978: *The Rise of Civilization: From Early Farmers to Urban Society in the Ancient Near East* (San Francisco).

Reiner, E. – 1961: 'The Etiological Myth of the "Seven Sages"' in *Or* 30, pp. 1-11.

Renfrew, C. – 1987: *Archaeology and Language: The Puzzle of Indo-European Origins* (London).

Reymond, E. A. E. – 1969: *The Mythical Origin of the Egyptian Temple* (New York).

Rice, M. – 1983a: *The Barbar Temple Site, Bahrain* (Manama).

Rice, M. – 1983b: 'Cornwall, Bahrain and Dilmun Identified' in *Dilmun Discovered*, p. 192.

Rice, M. – 1984a: *Dilmun Discovered: The early years of archaeology in Bahrain* (London)

Rice, M. – 1984b: 'The island on the edge of the world' in H. A. Al-Khalifa and M. Rice (eds.): *Bahrain Through the Ages: The Archaeology* (Proceedings of the Bahrain Historical Conference 1983, London), pp. 116-24.

Rice, M. – 1985: *The Search for the Paradise Land* (London).

Rice, M. – 1990: *Egypt's Making: The Origins of Ancient Egypt 5000-2000 BC* (London).

Rice, M. – 1994: *The Archaeology of the Arabian Gulf c. 5000-323* BC (London).

Ricke, H. – 1944: *Beitrage zür agyptischen Bauforschung und Altertumskunde*, Vol. 4, (Zurich).

Roaf, M. – 1990: *Cultural Atlas of Mesopotamia and the Ancient Near East* (New York).

Roberts, A. – 1995: *Hathor Rising: The Serpent Power of Ancient Egypt* (Totnes).

Rohl, D. M. – 1995: *A Test of Time, Volume One: The Bible – From Myth to History* (London).

Rose, M. R. – 1991: *Evolutionary Biology of Aging* (Oxford).

Roux, G. – 1964: *Ancient Iraq* (Middlesex).

Roux, G. – 1969: *Ancient Iraq* in T. B. Jones (ed.): *The Sumerian Problem*, pp. 134-38.

Rowton, M. B. – 1970: 'Ancient Western Asia' in *CAH* I:1, pp. 193-239.

Rundle Clark, R. T. – 1959: *Myth and Symbol in Ancient Egypt* (London).

S

Sabar, Y. – 1982: *The Folk Literature of the Kurdistani Jews: An Anthology* (New Haven).

Safar, F. *et al.* – 1981: *Eridu* (Baghdad).

Saggs, H. W. F. – 1984: *The Might That Was Assyria* (London).

Saggs, H. W. F. – 1989: *Civilization Before Greece and Rome* (London).

Saggs, H. W. F. – 1995: *Babylonians* (London).

Saleh, A. A. – 1969: 'The So-called "Primeval Hill" and other Related Elevations in Ancient Egyptian Mythology' in *MDAIK* 25, pp. 110-20.

Sasson, J. M.(ed.) – 1995: *Civilisations of the Ancient Near East*, Vol. IV (New York).

Sassoon, J. – 1993: *From Sumer to Jerusalem: The Forbidden Hypothesis* (Oxford).

Sayce, A. H. – 1885: 'Miscellaneous Notes' in *Zeitschrift für Keilschriftforschung* 2, p. 404.

Schauenberg, P. – 1965: *The Bulb Book* (London).

Schmandt-Besserat, D. – 1983: 'Tokens and Counting' in *Biblical Archaeologist* 46, pp. 117-20.

Schmandt-Besserat, D. – 1992: *Before Writing*, Vol. 1 (Austin).

Schmidt, B. B. – 1995: 'Flood Narratives of Ancient Western Asia' in J. M. Sasson (ed.): *Civilisations of the Ancient Near East*, Vol. IV, pp. 2337-51.

Schoene, A. (ed.) – 1875: *Eusebi Chronicorum Libri Duo* (Berolini: APVD Weidmannos).

Sethe, K. – 1908-1922: *Die altägyptischen Pyramidentexte*, 4 vols. (Leipzig).

Sethe, K. – 1935-1962: *Übersetzung und Kommentar zu den altägyptischen Pyramidentexten*, 6 vols. (Glückstadt).

Seton-Williams, M. V. – 1988: *Egyptian Legends and Stories* (London).

Seton-Williams, M. V. & **Stocks**, P. – 1983: *Blue Guide: Egypt* (London).

Shaw, I. & **Nicholson**, P. – 1995: *British Museum Dictionary of Ancient Egypt* (London).

Shea, W. H. – 1977: 'Adam in Ancient Mesopotamian Traditions' in *AUSS* 15, p. 39.

Sidebotham, S. E. & **Wendrich**, W. Z. (eds.) – 1996: *Berenike 1995: Preliminary Report of the 1995 Excavations at Berenike (Egyptian Red Sea Coast) and the Survey of the Eastern Desert* (Netherlands).

Simons, J. – 1994: 'The "Table of Nations" (Genesis 10): Its General Structure and Meaning' in R. S. Hess & D. T. Tsumura (eds.): *"I Studied Inscriptions from before the Flood": Ancient Near Eastern, Literary, and Linguistic Approaches to Genesis 1-11*, pp. 234-53.

Simpson, W. K. – 1957: 'A Running of the Apis in the Reign of `Aha and Passages in Manetho and Aelian' in *Orientalia* 26, pp. 139-42.

Smith, G. – 1873-74: 'The Chaldean Account of the Deluge' in *Transactions of the Society of Biblical Archaeology* 2, pp. 213-34.

Smith, H. S. – 1992: 'The Making of Egypt: A Review of the Influence of Susa and Sumer on Upper Egypt and Lower Nubia in the 4th Millennium B.C.' in R. Friedman and B. Adams (eds.): *The Followers of Horus. Studies Dedicated to Michael Allen Hoffman* (Oxford), pp. 235-46.

Smith, P. E. L. – 1967: 'Ganj Dareh Tepe' in *Iran* 5, pp. 158-60.

Smith, R. M. & **Porcher**, E. A. – 1864: *History of the Recent Discoveries at Cyrene* (London).

Smith, S. – 1922: 'The Relation of Marduk, Ashur, and Osiris' in *JEA* 8, pp. 41-4.

Speiser, E. A. – 1928: 'Southern Kurdistan in the Annals of Ashurnasirpal and Today' in *AASOR* 8, pp. 18-31.

Speiser, E. A. – 1930: *Mesopotamian Origins* (Philadelphia).

Speiser, E. A. – 1950-1: 'The Sumerian Problem Reviewed' in *Hebrew Union College Annual* 23, pp. 339-55.

Speiser, E. A. (trans.)– 1969a: 'Akkadian Myths and Epics' in J. B. Pritchard (ed.): *Ancient Near Eastern Texts: Relating to Old Testament*, pp. 60-119.

Speiser, E. A. – 1969b: 'The Beginnings of Civilization in Mesopotamia' in T. Jones (ed.): *The Sumerian Problems*, pp. 76-92.

Speiser, E. A. – 1969c: 'The Sumerian Problem Reviewed' in T. Jones: *The Sumerian Problem*, pp. 93-124.

Speiser, E. A. – 1994: 'The Rivers of Paradise' in R. S. Hess & D. T. Tsumura (eds.): *"I Studied Inscriptions from before the Flood": Ancient Near Eastern, Literary, and Linguistic Approaches to Genesis 1-11*, pp. 175-82.

Speiser, E. A. – 1994: 'In Search of Nimrod' in R. S. Hess & D. T. Tsumura (eds.): *"I Studied Inscriptions from before the Flood": Ancient Near Eastern, Literary, and Linguistic Approaches to Genesis 1-11*, pp. 270-77.

Spencer, A. J. – 1982: *Death in Ancient Egypt* (London).

Spencer, A. J. – 1993: *Early Egypt: The Rise of Civilisation in the Nile Valley* (London).

Stevenson Smith, W. – 1962: 'The land of Punt' in *JARCE* 1, pp. 59-60.

T

Tackholm, V. – 1954: *Flora of Egypt*, Vol. III (Cairo).

Teissier, B. – 1987: 'Glyptic Evidence for a Connection Between Iran, Syro-Palestine and Egypt in the Fourth and Third Millennia' in *Iran* 25, pp. 27-54.

Thompson, R. C. – 1936: *A Dictionary of Assyrian Chemistry and Geology* (Oxford).

Thompson, T. L. – 1992: *Early History of the Israelite People: From the Written and Archaeological Sources* (Leiden).

Thureau-Dangin, F. – *Une Relation de la Huitieme Campagne de Sargon* (Paris).

Trigger, B. G. *et al.* – 1983: *Ancient Egypt: A Social History* (Cambridge).

Tsumura, D. T. – 1994: 'Genesis and Ancient Near Eastern Stories of Creation and Flood: An Introduction' in R. S. Hess & D. T. Tsumura (eds.): *"I Studied Inscriptions from before the Flood": Ancient Near Eastern, Literary, and Linguistic Approaches to Genesis 1-11*, pp. 27-57.

Tsumura, D. T. – 1994: 'The Earth in Genesis 1' in R. S. Hess & D. T. Tsumura (eds.): *"I Studied Inscriptions from before the Flood": Ancient Near Eastern, Literary, and Linguistic Approaches to Genesis 1-11*, pp. 310-28.

U

Uphill, E. – 1965: 'The Egyptian Sed-Festival Rites' in *JNES* 24, pp. 365-83.

V

Vandier, J. – 1952: *Manuel d'archeologie Égyptiéne,* Vol. 1 (Paris).

Veenker, R. A. – 1981: 'Gilgamesh and the Magic Plant' in *BA* 44.4, pp. 199-205.

Velikovsky, I. – 1976: *Ages in Chaos* (London).

Vinson, S. – 1994: *Egyptian boats and ships* (Princes Risborough).

Voigt, M. M. – 1983: *Hajji Firuz Tepe, Iran: The Neolithic Settlement* (Pennsylvania).

W

Waddell, W. G. – 1971: *Manetho*, Loeb Classical Library (London).

Walker, C. B. F. – 1987: *Reading the Past: Cuneiform* (London).

Walker, R. A. – 1987: *The Garden of Eden* (Rhyl).

Wallis Budge, E. A. – 1907: *The Sculptures and Inscription of Darius The Great on the Rock of Behistun in Persia: A new collation of the Persian, Susian and Babylonian Texts with English translation, etc.* (London).

Walton, J. – 1981: 'The Antediluvian Section of the Sumerian King List and Genesis 5' in *BA* 44.4, pp. 207-08.

Ward, P. – 1993: *Bahrain: A Travel Guide* (Cambridge).

Weigall, A. E. P. – 1909: *Travels in the Upper Egyptian Desert* (London).

Weir, J. D. – 1972: *The Venus Tablets of Ammizaduga* (Istanbul).

Weisgerber, G. – 1984: 'Dilmun – A trading entrepôt: evidence from historical and archaeological sources' in *Dilmun* 12, pp. 5-10; republished in H. A. Al-Khalifa and M. Rice (eds.): *Bahrain Through the Ages: The Archaeology* (Proceedings of the Bahrain Historical Conference 1983, London), pp. 135-42.

Wenham, G. J. – 1994: 'Sanctuary Symbolism in the Garden of Eden Story' in R. S. Hess & D. T. Tsumura (eds.): *"I Studied Inscriptions from Before the Flood": Ancient Near Eastern, Literary, and Linguistic Approaches to Genesis 1-11*, pp. 399-404.

Whitcomb, J. C. & **Morris**, H. M. – 1961: *The Genesis Flood: The Biblical Record and its Scientific Implications* (Michigan).

Wigram, W. A. & **Wigram**, E. T. A. – 1922: *The Cradle of Mankind: Life in Eastern Kurdistan* (London).

Wilcke, C. – 1969: *Das Lugalbandaepos* (Wiesbaden).

Willcocks, Sir W. – 1904: *The Nile in 1904* (London).

Willcocks, Sir W. – 1919: *From the Garden of Eden to the Crossing of the Jordan* (London).

Williams, B. – 1988: 'Narmer and the Coptos Colossi' in *JARCE* 25, pp. 35-59.

Wilkinson, R. H. – 1985: 'The Horus name and the form and significance of the *serekh* in the royal Egyptian titulary' in *JSSEA* 15, pp.

98-104.

Wilson, E. – 1986: *Ancient Egyptian Design* (London).

Wilson, J. A. – 1969a: 'Egyptian Myths, Tales, and Mortuary Texts' in J. B. Pritchard: *ANET*, 3rd ed., pp. 3-36.

Wilson, J. A. – 1969b: 'Egyptian Hymns and Prayers' in J. B. Pritchard: *ANET*, 3rd ed., pp. 365-81.

Wilson, J. V. K. – 1985: *The Legend of Etana* (Warminster).

Wilson, R. R. – 1975: 'The Old Testament Genealogies in Recent Research' in *JBL* 94, pp. 169-89.

Wilson, R. R. – 1977: *Genealogy and History in the Biblical World* (New Haven).

Winkler, H. A. – 1938-39: *Rock Drawings of Southern Upper Egypt*, 2 vols. (London).

Wiseman, D. J. – 1994: 'Genesis 10: Some Archaeological Considerations' in R. S. Hess & D. T. Tsumura (eds.): *"I Studied Inscriptions from before the Flood": Ancient Near Eastern, Literary, and Linguistic Approaches to Genesis 1-11*, pp. 254-65.

Wolkstein, D. & **Kramer**, S. N. – 1983: *Inanna: Queen of Heaven and Earth* (New York).

Wood, M. L. – 1982: 'Kramer's Contribution to Sumerology' in *Dilmun* 10, pp. 15-19.

Wood, M. – 1992: *Legacy: A Search for the Origins of Civilization* (London).

Woodburn, M. – 1995: *Ancient Saar* (London).

Woolley, C. L. – 1954: *Excavations at Ur* (London).

Woolley, C. L. – 1982: *Ur 'of the Chaldees'*, new revised edition by P. R. S. Moorey (London).

Woolley, C. L. – 1969: 'The Sumerians' in T. B. Jones (ed.): *The Sumerian Problem*, pp. 66-73.

Wright, E. M. – 1943: 'The Eighth Campaign of Sargon II of Assyria (714 B.C.)' in *JNES* 2, pp. 173-86.

Wyatt, N. – 1981: 'Interpreting the Creation and Fall Story in Genesis 2-3' in *ZAW* 93, p. 19.

Y

Young, D. A. – 1995: *The Biblical Flood: A Case Study of the Church's Response to Extrabiblical Evidence* (Michigan).

Young, T. C. & **Smith**, P. E. L. – 1966: 'Research in the Prehistory of Central Western Iran' in *Science* 153, pp. 386-91.

Yusuf Ali, A. (transl.) – 1975: *The Holy Qur'an* (London).

Z

Zadok, R. – 1984: 'The Origin of the Name Shinar' in *ZA* 74, pp. 240-44.

NOTES AND REFERENCES

Preface

1. H. A. Winkler, 1938, p. 8.
2. H. A. Winkler, *op. cit.*, p. 7.

Introduction

1. *Collins English Dictionary,* 1979, p. 839.
2. *The Shorter Oxford English Dictionary*, 1973, p. 1381.
3. Based on a translation by D. Luckenbill, Vol. II, 1927, p. 379.
4. The theory that Middle Bronze Age Jericho was the city destroyed by the Israelites was first proposed by John Bimson in his book *Redating the Exodus and Conquest* (Sheffield, 1978).
5. W. C. Hayes, 1970, p. 174, n. 2.
6. K. A. Kitchen 1987, pp. 49; J. Baines & J. Malek, 1980, p. 36. The reason I use the latter for the earlier dynasties is because, to my knowledge, Kitchen has not published his dates for the era before the Middle Kingdom.
7. H. Gauthier, 1912, p. 167.
8. J. H. Breasted, 1905, p. 32.
9. H. J. Nissen, 1993, p. 56.
10. J. N. Postgate, 1992, p. 22.
11. H. W. F. Saggs, 1984, p. 15.
12. H. W. F. Saggs, *op. cit.* [11], p. 16.

Chapter One

1. For a summary see A. Millard, 1984, pp. 103-04.
2. A. Millard, *op. cit.* [1], pp. 104-05.
3. No. 11, 1986.
4. S. Lloyd, 1978, p. 16.
5. S. Lloyd, *op. cit.* [4], p. 16.
6. R. A. Walker, 1987, p. 8.
7. *Ibid.*
8. D. M. Lang, 1980, p. 118.
9. G. Roux, 1964, p. 30.

Chapter Two

1. The capital of Aratta has been tentatively located in just about every part of Iran – but only Samuel Noah Kramer, to my knowledge, proposed to focus the search in the north-western mountains of Azerbaijan.
2. R. D. Barnett, 1982, p. 329.
3. A. K. Grayson, Vol. I, 1972, p. 81.
4. R. D. Barnett, *op. cit.* [2], p. 333.
5. R. D. Barnett, *op. cit.* [2], p. 332.
6. *Ibid.*
7. S. N. Kramer, 1968, pp. 108-11.

8. P. R. S. Moorey, 1993, p. 35.
9. H. W. F. Saggs, 1995, p. 32.
10. S. Cohen, 1973, p. 55 & P. R. S. Moorey, *op. cit.* [8], pp. 35-37.
11. C. H. Oldfather, 1933, p. 391-93.
12. P. E. L. Smith, 1965, pp. 158-60; T. C. Young & P. E. L. Smith, 1966, p. 387.
13. H. Luschey, 1968, pp. 63-94.
14. See C. Wilcke, 1969, p. 38.
15. S. N. Kramer, 1963, pp. 275-76.
16. F. Thureau-Dangin, 1912; E. M. Wright, 1943, pp. 173-86.
17. W. B. Fisher (ed.), 1968, p. 13.
18. S. Cohen, 1973, pp. 50-51.

Chapter Three

1. As given in the the epic 'Enmerkar and Ensukushsiranna'.
2. S. N. Kramer, 1963, p. 274.
3. S. N. Kramer, *op. cit.* [2], p. 290.
4. S. N. Kramer, *op. cit.* [2], p. 297.
5. *Ibid.*
6. *Ibid.*
7. S. N. Kramer, *op. cit.* [2], p. 298.
8. *Ibid.*
9. J. Mellaart, 1970, p. 290.
10. Retired from his teaching post in June, 1991.
11. J. Mellaart, *op. cit.* [9], p. 259.
12. J. Mellaart, *op. cit.* [9], p. 262.
13. *Ibid.*
14. J. Mellaart, *op. cit.* [9], p. 263.
15. S. N. Kramer, 1956, p. 237.
16. S. N. Kramer, *op. cit.* [15], pp. 237-39.

Chapter Four

1. R. O. Faulkner, 1981, p. 304; A. M. Blackman, 1915, p. 21, note 5.
2. R. D. Barnett, 1982, pp. 326-27.
3. S. M. Burstein, 1978, pp. 20-21.
4. Josephus, *Antiquities*, Book I, Ch. 3, 5-6.
5. Xenophon, *Anabasis*, Books III-IV.
6. L. Ginzberg, 1919, Book 5, p. 186; and Book 4, p. 269.
7. L. Ginzberg, *op. cit.* [6], Book 6, p. 479.
8. D. D. Luckenbill, 1927, pp. 200-01.
9. D. D. Luckenbill, *op. cit.* [8], p. 202.
10. G. Roux, 1964, p. 294.
11. G. Roux, *op. cit.* [10], p. 298.
12. For example, E. A. Speiser, 1928, pp. 18-31.
13. D. A. Young, 1992, p. 22.
14. A. Collins, 1996, Chapters 13-14; M. R. Izady, 1992.
15. W. A. Wigram & E. T. A. Wigram, 1922, p. 335.
16. R. Graves and R. Patai, 1989, p. 117, n. 5.

17. G. Roux, *op. cit.* [10], p. 299.
18. Y. Sabar, 1982, p. xiii, n. 4, citing Benjamin II, p. 94: 'I myself obtained several fragments of the ark (from the base of Al Judi) which appeared to be covered with a kind of substance resembling tar.'
19. A. R. Millard, 1994, p. 124.
20. W. W. Hallo & W. K. Simpson, 1971, p. 35; G. Roux, *op. cit.* [10], p. 112.
21. S. N. Kramer, 1946, p. 42.
22. H. W. F. Saggs, 1995, p. 17.
23. G. Roux, *op. cit.* [10], p. 112.
24. Based on the translation of a tablet (found at Nippur) by S. N. Kramer, 1969, p. 44.

Chapter Five

1. T. Jacobsen has demonstrated that the original King List was compiled during the reign of Utu-hegal of Uruk who in the New Chronology is dated by a lunar eclipse which took place on the 28th of June 1889 BC.
2. T. Jacobsen, 1939, p. 71.
3. G. Roux, 1964, pp. 109-10.
4. D. Rohl, 1995, pp. 243-46.
5. The jar was found at ancient Tutub (modern Khafaje) in the Diyala region. There his name is written Mebaragesi, strongly suggesting that the 'En' which forms the first element in many of the antediluvian rulers' names in the King List simply means 'Lord'.
6. G. Roux, *op. cit.* [3], p. 115.
7. W. W. Hallo & W. K. Simpson, 1971, p. 40.
8. L. Woolley, 1982, p. 25.
9. L. Woolley, *op. cit.* [8], p. 29.
10. *Ibid.*
11. L. Woolley, *op. cit.* [8], p. 35.
12. Translation based on J. N. Postgate, 1992, p. 74.
13. M. Roaf, 1990, p. 60.
14. S. N. Kramer, 1952, pp. 37-38.
15. B. Cooper, 1995, p. 128.

Chapter Six

1. Translation from S. M. Burstein, 1978, pp. 19-20.
2. S. R. Külling, 1996, pp. 6-7.
3. K. A. Kitchen, 1993b, pp. 80-84.
4. J. J. Finkelstein, 1966, pp. 95-118.
5. R. Wilson, 1975, p. 185.
6. R. Wilson, *op. cit.* [5], pp. 185-86.
7. S. N. Kramer, 1963, p. 299.
8. A. H. Sayce, 1885, p. 404.
9. R. Wilson, 1977, p. 139 & p. 154; D. J. Wiseman, 1994, p. 260; P. D. Miller, 1994, p. 157.
10. R. Wilson, *op. cit.* [9], p. 139.
11. K. Budde, 1883, pp. 120-23.
12. R. Wilson, *op. cit.* [9], p. 139-40.
13. W. H. Hallo, 1971, 16:1483; D. J. Wiseman, *op. cit.* [9], p. 260.
14. See W. F. Albright & T. O. Lambtin, 1970, p. 149 where they state: 'The name of the ancient sacred city of Eridu in the extreme south of Babylonia was written two ways: (1) URU.DU(G), probably the direct source of Eridu, since URU also had the value eri, perhaps in one of the dialects; …'.
15. W. F. Albright & T. O. Lambtin, *op. cit.* [14], p. 149.
16. See S. H. Langdon, 1923, p. 8, n. 2.
17. R. Wilson, *op. cit.* [9], p. 149.
18. R. Wilson, *op. cit.* [9], p. 150.
19. *Ibid.*
20. R. Wilson, *op. cit.* [9], pp. 150-51.
21. R. Wilson, *op. cit.* [9], p. 151.
22. W. H Shea, 1977, p. 39.
23. I have slightly modified Bill Shea's words here but the points are almost direct quotations from his 1977 paper.
24. D. T. Tsumura, 1994, p. 36.
25. W. Lambert and A. Millard, 1969, p. 21.
26. D. N. Freedman (ed.), 1992, Vol. VI, p. 1012.
27. S. N. Kramer, 1956, p. 144.
28. S. N. Kramer, *op. cit.* [7], pp. 148-49.
29. S. N. Kramer, *op. cit.* [27], p. 147.
30. S. N. Kramer, *op. cit.* [7], p. 148-49.

Chapter Seven

1. W. Papke, 1993.
2. See T. Jacobsen, 1939, pp. 86-87, n. 115.
3. A. Poebel, 1914, pp. 73-78.
4. *Kar* is a Sumerian logogram which is the equivalent of Akkadian *habilu* with the meaning 'trapper' or 'hunter'. Habilu is actually the word used in the Gilgamesh Epic for the hunter who finds the wild-man, Enkidu, in the forest.
5. The final 'd' in Nimrod can be explained by assuming that the biblical redactor has attempted to turn the Sumerian name Enmeru into an appropriate Hebrew name for the builder of the Tower of Babel. He therefore chooses to add a 'd' to turn the last part of Enmeru's name into the Hebrew word *marad* – 'to rebel' – thus giving us 'Lord of Rebellion'.
6. The name of this first ruler of Uruk I is usually written Meskisg**g**asher but the observed fluidity of vocalisation between 'g' and 'k' in Sumerian/Akkadian permits the alternative vocalisation Meskiag**k**asher used here and by Papke.
7. S. N. Kramer, 1956, p. 255.
8. S. N. Kramer, *op. cit.* [7], p. 256.
9. Josephus, Book I, Chapter IV:1-2.
10. S. N. Kramer, 1969b, pp. 646-47.
11. A. Schoene, 1875.
12. Josephus, Book I, Chapter VI.
13. Josephus, Book I, Chapter V.

Chapter Eight

1. P. Ward, 1993, p. 67.
2. Strabo, Book XVI, Chapter 3:2.
3. P. Ward, *op. cit.* [1], pp. 67-68.
4. M. Rice, 1994, pp. 316-17.
5. M. Rice, *op. cit.* [4], p. 315.
6. J. T. Bent, 1889, republished in M. Rice, 1983a, pp. 80-81.
7. C. C. Lamberg-Karlovsky, 1984, p. 15.
8. B. Frohlich, 1983, pp. 5-11.
9. P. B. Cornwall, 1946, p. 11.
10. P. B. Cornwall, 1944, p. 122.
11. C. C. Lamberg-Karlovsky, *op. cit.* [7], p. 18.
12. C. C. Lamberg-Karlovsky, *op. cit.* [7], p. 15.
13. C. C. Lamberg-Karlovsky, *op. cit.* [7], p. 19.
14. See the comments of M. Rice, *op. cit.* [6], pp. 9-11 and the republication there of E. L. Durand: 'Extracts from a Report on the Islands and Antiquities of Bahrain' in *JRAS* 12 (1880), pp. 189-227.
15. H. Rawlinson, 1880, pp. 14-40.
16. S. N. Kramer, 1963, pp. 147-48.
17. S. N. Kramer, 1956, p. 144.
18. S. N. Kramer, *op. cit.* [17], p. 149.

19. S. N. Kramer, *op. cit.* [17], pp. 152-53.
20. S. N. Kramer, 1944, p. 26.
21. S. N. Kramer, *op. cit.* [17], p. 27.
22. R. A. Veenker, 1981, pp. 199-205.
23. P. B. Cornwall, *op. cit.* [9], p. 4.
24. M. Rice, 1983b, p. 192.
25. P. B. Cornwall, 1983, pp. 192-200.
26. H. Crawford, 1991, p. 20; G. Weisgerber, 1984, p. 7.
27. G. Weisgerber, 1984, p. 7.
28. Strabo, Book XVI, 3,4.
29. M. Rice, *op. cit.* [4], p. 32.

Chapter Nine

1. H. Frankfort, 1948, p. 15.
2. I am very grateful to Julie Hankey for drawing my attention to this review.
3. Adapted from J. H. Breasted, 1988, Vol. 3, pp. 86-7.
4. A. E. P. Weigall, 1909.
5. H. Winkler, 1938.
6. G. Fuchs, 1989, pp. 127-153 and 1991, pp. 59-70.
7. M. Rice, 1990, p. 47.
8. P. Amiet, 1961, pl. 6.119A.
9. M. Rice, *op. cit.* [7], p. 113.
10. D. Collon, 1987, p. 15.
11. I. E. S. Edwards, 1980, p. 42.
12. H. Frankfort, 1951, p. 102.
13. T. Heyerdahl, 1980, p. 18.
14. E. A. Speiser, 1969, p. 92.
15. E. A. Speiser, *op. cit.* [14], p. 93.
16. T. Heyerdahl, *op. cit.* [13], p. 21.
17. T. Heyerdahl, *op. cit.* [13], p. 25.
18. R. D. Barnett, 1958, pp. 220-21.
19. D. Collon, *op. cit.* [10], pp. 174-75.
20. Sumerian King List column III, lines 1-5.
21. M. Rice, *op. cit.* [7], p. 45.
22. *Ibid.*
23. P. Johnston, 1980, p. 175.
24. W. H. Jones, 1980, p. 82, see J. F. Healey, 1991, p. 67.
25. T. Heyerdahl, *op. cit.* [13], pp. 318-19.
26. W. M. F. Petrie, 1939, p. 255.
27. M. A. Murray, 1945-6, pp. 33 ff.
28. I. Velikovsky, 1976, pp. 103-42.
29. See D. Rohl, 1995, pp. 173-94.
30. Herodotus, Book I:1, see A. D. Godley, 1975, p. 3.
31. W. M. F. Petrie, *op. cit.* [26], p. 246-47.

Chapter Ten

1. See their report in W. M. Flinders Petrie, 1896.
2. M. Rice, 1990, p. 33.
3. H. Kantor, 1954, p. 6.
4. H. Kantor, *op. cit.* [3], p. 8.
5. *Ibid.*
6. M. A. Murray, 1979, p. 6.
7. The tomb is described in W. M. F. Petrie, *op. cit.* [1], pp. 19-20.
8. W. F. M. Petrie, 1896, pp. 30-33.
9. W. M. F. Petrie, 1939, p. 259.
10. M. A. Murray, 1949, pp. 5-6.
11. D. E. Derry, 1956, pp. 83-4.
12. D. E. Derry, *op. cit.* [11], p. 85.
13. W. M. F. Petrie, 1918, pp. 338-39; 1922, pp. 1-17.
14. C. Burney, 1977, p. 62.
15. H. Frankfort, 1951, p. 101 where he states: 'The strongest evidence of this contact between Mesopotamia and Egypt is supplied by three cylinder seals shown by their very material and by their designs to have been made in Mesopotamia during the second half of the Protoliterate period, but found in Egypt. One was excavated at Naqada, in a Gerzean (Nakada II) grave; and the same origin is probable for the other two. These importations were not without consequence: from the beginning of the 1st Dynasty the cylinder seal was adopted in Egypt and made at once in considerable quantities. Since it is an odd form for a seal, used only in countries in contact with Mesopotamia, and since one of the Mesopotamian cylinders was found in Egypt in a context just ante-dating the earliest native seals, it would be perverse to deny that the Egyptians followed the Mesopotamian example.'
16. P. Amiet, 1957, p. 126.
17. For a full summary of Frankfort's views on Mesopotamian influences over early Egyptian civilisation see H. Frankfort, *op. cit.* [15], pp. 100-11 (including the quotation).
18. W. F. Albright & T. O. Lambdin, 1970, p. 124.
19. W. F. Albright & T. O. Lambdin, *op. cit.* [18], p. 133.
20. See I. E. S. Edwards, 1980, pp. 58-59.
21. M. Rice, *op. cit.* [2], pp. 59-60.
22. H. Frankfort, *op. cit.* [15], pp. 104-05.
23. W. B. Emery, 1961, p. 177.
24. See especially W. M. F. Petrie, *op. cit.* [9], p. 77; Vandier, 1952, pp. 330-32.
25. See especially Arkel & Ucko, 1965, pp. 145-66.
26. R. Engelbach, 1943, p. 199.

Chapter Eleven

1. For a full discussion see E. A. E. Jelinkova, 1962, and E. A. E. Reymond, 1969.
2. E. A. E. Jelinkova, *op. cit.* [1], p. 41.
3. E. A. E. Reymond, *op. cit.* [1], p. 61.
4. *Ibid.*
5. E. A. E. Reymond, *op. cit.* [1], p. 119.
6. E. A. E. Jelinkova, *op. cit.* [1], p. 53.
7. E. A. E. Jelinkova, *op. cit.* [1], p. 43.
8. E. A. E. Reymond, *op. cit.* [1], p. 17.
9. E. A. E. Reymond, *op. cit.* [1], p. 8.
10. E. A. E. Reymond, *op. cit.* [1], p. 9.
11. E. A. E. Reymond, *op. cit.* [1], p. 117.
12. E. A. E. Reymond, *op. cit.* [1], p. 118.
13. F. Safar *et al.*, 1981, p. 44.
14. *Ibid.*
15. F. Safar *et al.*, *op. cit.* [13], p. 45.
16. F. Safar *et al.*, *op. cit.* [13], p. 46.
17. *Ibid.*
18. E. A. E. Reymond, *op. cit.* [1], pp. 12-13 & 107, where she states: 'Theoretically titi can be interpreted as trampling or aggression. It may, therefore, be surmised that there was a fight in the island. The exact nature of this fight is difficult to explain. That a time of combat was, indeed, connected with the early history of this island, is quite clear when we refer to the subsidiary names of the island: Island of the Combat and Island of the Peace appear to reflect the same situation.'
19. B. Cooper, 1995, p. 40.
20. E. A. E. Reymond, *op. cit.* [1], p. 110.
21. E. A. E. Reymond, *op. cit.* [1], p. 90.
22. E. A. E. Reymond, *op. cit.* [1], p. 111.
23. P. Montet, 1965, p. 20.
24. E. A. E. Reymond, *op. cit.* [1], pp. 45 & 46.
25. E. A. E. Reymond, *op. cit.* [1], p. 27.
26. E. A. E. Jelinkova, *op. cit.* [1], p. 51; *Edfu* VI:181,14;

182,2,4,17,18.

27. E. A. E. Reymond, *op. cit.* [1], p. 88.
28. See for example Pliny: *Natural History*, Book VIII, 46; Ammianus Marcellinus, Book XXII, xiv, 7; Solinus, 32. See also a discussion of the cult of Apis in M. Ibrahim & D. Rohl: 'Apis and the Serapeum' in *JACF* 2 (1988), pp. 6-26.
29. J. A. Wilson, 1950, p. 5.
30. R. T. Rundle Clark, 1959, p. 80.
31. C. A. R. Andrews in R. O. Faulkner, 1972, p. 12.
32. J. A. Wilson, *op. cit.* [29], p. 8.
33. J. A. Wilson, *op. cit.* [29], p. 371.
34. A. J. Spencer, 1982, p. 141.
35. W. M. F. Petrie, 1939, p. 262.

Chapter Twelve

1. V. Seton-Williams & P. Stocks, 1983, p. 421.
2. W. Murnane, 1983, p. 163.
3. W. G. Waddell, 1971, p. 43.
4. See the chapter entitled 'Architecture' in Emery, 1961, pp. 175-91 for a discussion on the materials and methods of production employed in the construction of the early royal mastabas of the Archaic Period.
5. I. E. S. Edwards, 1986, p. 49.
6. I. E. S. Edwards, *op. cit.* [5], p. 123.
7. Urk. 4, 286, lines 14-16.
8. The heb sed ritual was often first performed in the thirtieth year of a reign – but not always. It remains unclear as to what the precise circumstances were to require the performance of the king's rejuvenation rites.
9. H. Frankfort, 1948, pp. 129-30.
10. H. Frankfort, *op. cit.* [9], p. 130.
11. H. Frankfort, *op. cit.* [9], p. 149.
12. C. M. Firth *et al.*, 1935, plate 17.
13. M. Rice, 1990, p. 61.
14. T. Heyerdahl, 1980, pp. 22-23.
15. For the method of attachment of these proposed standards see J-P. Lauer, 1962, pp. 156-57.
16. H. Ricke, 1944, pp. 78-79.
17. J-P. Lauer, 1948, p. 36.
18. I. E. S. Edwards, 1949, pp. 125-26.
19. R. M. Smith & E. A. Porcher, 1864, pp. 87-89.
20. R. Phillips & M. Rix, 1991, p. 72 & R. Hay, 1985, p. 337.
21. I. E. S. Edwards, *op. cit.* [18], p. 126.
22. I. E. S. Edwards, 1985, p. 57.
23. R. Phillips & M. Rix, *op. cit.* [20], p. 72 where they state 'The plant contains a poison which can cause the skin to burn when exposed to sunlight. The witch hunts directed at this plant, as a "triffid", are quite unjustified. It is less dangerous than wild hemlock or the common rue.'
24. I. E. S. Edwards, *op. cit.* [18], p. 127.
25. W. M. F. Petrie, 1901, plate XXXIV, no. 73.
26. C. Brickell, 1989, p. 181.
27. E. Wilson, 1986, pp. 18-19.
28. R. Phillips & M. Rix, 1981, p. 209.
29. R. Hay, 1985, p. 405.
30. P. Schauenberg, 1965, pp. 197-98.
31. R. Hay, *op. cit.* [29], pp. 403-07.
32. V. Tackholm, 1954, p. 274.
33. F. E. B. Ferns, 1978, pp. 24-27.
34. A. H. Gardiner, 1979, p. 480.

Chapter Thirteen

1. W. M. F. Petrie, 1939, p. 248.

2. W. M. F. Petrie, *op. cit.* [1], p. 252-53.
3. W. M. F. Petrie, *op. cit.* [1], p. 247.
4. W. M. F. Petrie, *op. cit.* [1], p. 249.
5. *Ibid*; Frankfort, 1948, p. 120.
6. W. M. F. Petrie, *op. cit.* [1], p. 248.
7. W. M. F. Petrie, *op. cit.* [1], p. 251.
8. A. J. Spencer, 1982, p. 142.
9. A. J. Spencer, *op. cit.* [9], p. 144.
10. R. O. Faulkner, 1972, p. 27.
11. R. O. Faulkner, *op. cit.* [11], p. 95.
12. R. O. Faulkner, *op. cit.* [11], p. 40.
13. J. Romer, 1981, p. 166.
14. R. O. Faulkner, *op. cit.* [11], p. 45.
15. R. O. Faulkner, 1969, p. 12.
16. R. O. Faulkner, *op. cit.* [16], p. 13.
17. *Ibid.*
18. R. O. Faulkner, *op. cit.* [11], p. 49.
19. J. Romer, *op. cit.* [14], p. 166.
20. R. O. Faulkner, *op. cit.* [11], p. 95.
21. S. Dalley, 1989, p. 77.
22. M. Lichtheim, 1973, pp. 44-5.
23. R. T. Rundle Clark, 1959, p. 247.
24. *Ibid.*
25. R. O. Faulkner, *op. cit.* [11], p. 55.
26. H. Frankfort, *op. cit.* [6], p. 206.
27. R. O. Faulkner, *op. cit.* [11], p. 45.
28. R. O. Faulkner, *op. cit.* [11], pp. 84-5.
29. M. Lichtheim, *op. cit.* [23], p. 41.
30. R. O. Faulkner, *op. cit.* [11], p. 45.
31. M. Lichtheim, *op. cit.* [23], p. 34.
32. R. O. Faulkner, *op. cit.* [11], p. 37.
33. M. Lichtheim, *op. cit.* [23], p. 43.
34. I. Shaw & P. Nicholson, 1995, p. 45.
35. R. O. Faulkner, *op. cit.* [11], p. 36.
36. R. O. Faulkner, *op. cit.* [11], p. 43.
37. R. T. Rundle Clark, *op. cit.* [24], p. 211.
38. R. O. Faulkner, *op. cit.* [11], p. 101.
39. K. A. Kitchen & M. da Conceicao, 1990, pp. 64-7.
40. See the views of contributors to R. S. Hess & D. T. Tsumura (eds.), 1994.
41. H. Frankfort, *op. cit.* [6], p. 206.
42. R. T. Rundle Clark, *op. cit.* [24], p. 230.

Chapter Fourteen

1. I have taken this passage from a much later Genesis story which takes place immediately after the flood. But it is clear, from both the archaeological record, the Genesis narrative (Enoch was a city-builder) and the Sumerian tradition, that the original migration into Shinar preceded the deluge. Bricks were also being made during this earlier antediluvian epoch. Enoch's city was one of the antediluvian cities of Sumer.
2. W. A. Wigram & E. T. A. Wigram, 1922, p. 335.

Appendix C

1. S. Lloyd, 1978, p. 44.

INDEX

449